Life Sciences Foundation

PEARSON CUSTOM PUBLISHING

Life Sciences Foundation

Compiled from:

Study Skills for Science, Engineering and Technology Students

by Pat Maier, Anna Barney and Geraldine Price

Campbell Biology

Ninth Edition
by Jane B. Reece, Lisa A. Urry, Michael L. Cain, Steven A. Wasserman,
Peter V. Minorsky and Robert B. Jackson

Get Ready for Physics

by Edward Adelson

ALWAYS LEARNING

PEARSON

Harlow, England • London • New York • Boston • San Francisco • Toronto • Sydney • Auckland • Singapore • Hong Kong
Tokyo • Seoul • Taipei • New Delhi • Cape Town • Sao Paulo • Mexico City • Madrid • Amsterdam • Munich • Paris • Milan

Pearson Education Limited
Edinburgh Gate
Harlow
Essex CM20 2JE

And associated companies throughout the world

Visit us on the World Wide Web at:
www.pearsoned.co.uk

Compiled from:

Study Skills for Science, Engineering and Technology Students
by Pat Maier, Anna Barney and Geraldine Price
ISBN 978 0 273 72073 7
Copyright © Pat Maier, Anna Barney and Geraldine Price 2009

Campbell Biology
Ninth Edition
by Jane B. Reece, Lisa A. Urry, Michael L. Cain, Steven A. Wasserman,
Peter V. Minorsky and Robert B. Jackson
ISBN 978 0 321 558 23 7
Copyright © 2011, 2008, 2005 Pearson Education, Inc., publishing as Pearson
Benjamin Cummings, 1301 Sansome St., San Francisco, CA 94111

Get Ready for Physics
by Edward Adelson
ISBN 978 0 321 55625 7
Copyright ©2011 Pearson Education, Inc., publishing as Addison-Wesley,
1301 Sansome St., San Francisco, CA 94111

ISBN 978 1 78086 415 0

Printed and bound in Italy

Contents

1 Managing your stress

Most of your time at university will be a happy and enjoyable one. There may be times, however, when you feel things are getting out of control and you feel uncomfortably stressed. This can be related to your studies, your personal life, or both. Knowing what stress does to our bodies, our own tendencies towards being stressed, and the approaches we use to handle stressful events is an important life skill.

In this chapter you will learn how to:

1. identify signs of stress in yourself and others
2. develop proactive strategies to dealing with stress
3. recognise a personal tendency to be more stressed
4. recognise what your stressors are and how to manage them.

USING THIS CHAPTER

Estimate your current levels of confidence. At the end of the chapter you will have the chance to reassess these levels and incorporate this into your personal development planner (PDP). Mark between 1 (poor) and 5 (good) for the following:

I can recognise my own signs of stress.	I can recognise what stresses me.	I can apply proactive strategies to combat stress.

Date: _____

1 Introduction

Of students surveyed for the Student Experience Report in 2006, 98% said that university life is a happy one. You may well be one of those and may look at the title of this chapter and feel that you are not particularly stressed and that, if you were, you could cope with it. However, 56% of those students also said that since being at university they were under a lot more stress than before.

If you are thinking of not reading this chapter because you currently don't feel stressed, **stop now** and consider the following: I know what happens to my body when I am stressed; I can recognise the symptoms and I fully understand what stresses me. I have also reflected on my attitude to things in my life and realise this plays a role in how stressed I feel and I have enough belief in myself to solve any issues that cause anxiety. If you are happy with all these statements, move on. If not, and you wish to develop or hone this life skill, read on.

2 What happens to our bodies under stress?

Richard Lazarus, an eminent psychologist who won the prestigious award of 'American Psychologist' in 2002, claimed that stress and anxiety mainly occur when we believe we can't cope with the problem we perceive as stressful (Lazarus and Folkman, 1984). When we see this problem as overwhelming and feel we have no way of escaping or solving it, we experience anxiety or stress. However, we don't all see the same events as stressful. We have different perceptions of what is stressful, we have different levels of confidence in dealing with it and different ways of coping with it. There is therefore no one solution, but in general it is the feeling of being out of control that makes us anxious and stressed.

How do our bodies respond to stress?

When we perceive an event as stressful, our bodies react physiologically to it. The Harvard physiologist Walter Cannon coined the term 'fight or flight' in the 1920s and it refers to our body's physiological response to a threatening situation, be this physical or emotional. When we feel threatened our heart rate speeds up, our blood pressure rises and our muscles tighten. At the same time our body releases the hormone cortisol that increases the flow of energy to our muscles. This makes us ready for action; we either stay and fight or run. Once we have dealt with the threat our body returns to normal. However, if our perceived threat doesn't result in action, then cortisol takes longer to disappear. If we 'run away' from a piece of coursework, for example, it isn't going to help very much. We may find ourselves even more stressed. 'Running away' from many of our stressors often means making excuses, and this can make things worse in the long run, making us feel even more stressed. If this continues over a long period of time, it attacks our immune system, our cardiovascular system, digestive system and musculoskeletal system until we are exhausted and eventually become ill.

Excess cortisol also affects the part of the brain that is central to learning and memory by interfering with how our brain cells communicate with one another. In a crisis, we often don't remember what went on exactly; it is as if our 'lines are down' and we only react to that which is vital. So, not handling stress well, or being under constant stress, will affect our ability to learn.

Being alert to what creates stress in our lives, and developing techniques that can enable us to cope with this, and reduce excess flow of cortisol, is therefore an essential life skill.

NOTE Although stressors increase the amount of cortisol in our bloodstream, we also have 'daily shots' of cortisol throughout our daily cycle (circadian rhythm). This helps to keep us alert, by maintaining our blood pressure and enabling us to react to our environment.

3 What are the symptoms of stress?

When we feel stressed we notice changes in our emotions and our behaviour. Activities 1 and 2 help you to identify stress in yourself and others.

ACTIVITY 1 Identifying signs of stress

Look at the scenarios below and complete the table.

Carlos is a very outgoing and confident person and has decided to study abroad. He is now reaching the end of his first semester. He is very gregarious and has a good friendship group. However, his friends are noticing that he is becoming increasingly withdrawn, is not eating properly and appears 'on edge' a lot of the time. When they try to talk to him he becomes irritable and no one feels they should pry any further.

Lucy is a third-year student and has always had a very full social life. Her tutors have spoken to her many times for handing work in late and missing classes. However, she always seemed to pull things together at the last minute. Just recently, however, you have noticed that she has started drinking more and when you pointed this out to her she said she wasn't sleeping well and needed some alcohol to help. You have also noticed that your fun-loving friend has little interest in the things you used to do together. She is also getting into difficulties with her third-year project group who are complaining of her forgetfulness and lack of interest in the project.

	Signs of stress	What he/she might be feeling	What he/she should do
Carlos			
Lucy			

Check the feedback section for more information.

ACTIVITY 2 Recognising your own symptoms of stress

When **you** feel stressed what symptoms do you have? List them under how you **feel** – including physical characteristics (e.g. heart pounding, feeling sick, tired) and how you **act** (e.g. irritable, lack of interest, get emotional).

How do you feel? (Include physical and emotional characteristics)	How do you act and behave?

Check the feedback section for more information.

Let's keep things in proportion. We all get stressed at times. Most of the time symptoms are uncomfortable but short-lived and manageable. Sometimes we aren't even aware of feeling stressed until someone points out how irritable we are. However, we can get chronic stress symptoms and this needs to be dealt with.

Is all stress bad?

Stress can be both positive and negative. Positive stress is having just about enough stress to motivate and challenge us. It can give us a buzz. However, generally, when we hear the word 'stress' we associate it as a negative state, as our symptoms above show. So, for some, a group project, an essay or a presentation may be seen as positive and challenging while for others it could be seen as negative and worrying.

Also, we need some stress in our lives to keep us alert and ready for that challenge. We have probably all experienced a rise in our heart rate just as we are about to do something we feel challenging or stressful, but often that is what we need to get us up and running – a healthy dose of cortisol that dissipates quite soon afterwards. How many of us have put off a task because the deadline is just too far away? As the deadline approaches, we get the 'rush' and this stimulates us into activity. The trick is knowing when this can flip over from being the kick-start you need to being stressful.

Reflect on how you deal with deadlines: are you generally operating too close for comfort or just about right? You will probably find you have a particular tendency (see Chapter 2, 'Managing your time'). You need to identify this so you can tackle it, if you need to.

Some symptoms of positive stress are:

- I feel excited
- I get motivated
- it gives me a buzz
- it stretches me intellectually or physically
- it enables me to learn.

4 Personal development in handling stress

Broadly speaking, our attitudes will affect how we relate to others, how we cast blame when things don't work out, how we go about our tasks and the degree of control we feel over our lives. We need to develop our self-awareness in identifying stress and stressful events as well as confidence (self-belief) in being able to regain control over our lives.

Making personal changes – developing emotional intelligence

Daniel Goleman, author of the popular book *Emotional Intelligence* (1995), claims that intellectual IQ alone does not give us all the skills needed to be successful in everyday life. We need to develop self-awareness and recognise what others are feeling (empathy), know how to handle our emotions and to have self-discipline. This, Goleman claims, is emotional intelligence or emotional quotient (EQ). Group work projects, for example, if taken seriously, develop our interpersonal skills (emotional literacy). Similarly, effective use of the personal development planner (PDP) enables us to reflect on our progress and personal development. These aspects of the curriculum therefore have good reasons for being there.

Activities 1 and 2 have been included so that you can see the importance of being aware of your own and your friends' behaviour as an initial step in dealing with stress.

Emotional intelligence comprises, in essence, three areas: know yourself, choose yourself, give yourself. These are summarised in the next table.

By developing your emotional intelligence, you have the grounding to develop your self-belief and self-confidence, which gives you confidence to become more in control of your life. You also become aware of your own behaviour and how this can limit you as well as increasing your empathy towards your friends' troubles.

Emotional intelligence categories	Questions	Application to your studies
Know yourself	• What makes you think and feel the way you do? • What parts of your reactions are habitual or consciously thought through? • What are you afraid/ anxious of?	Being honest with yourself enables you to reflect on your qualities and faults. You learn from your experiences. Reflect on this through your studies, part-time work, etc., and make notes in your PDP. This reflection should alert you to habitual actions – possibly fear of exams, particular course work, etc. When you become aware of this you can then try to prevent yourself being a hostage to previously learned negative reactions.
Choose yourself	• How do you know what's right for you? • If you were not afraid or anxious what would you do? • Can you increase your awareness of your actions?	Manage your feelings. If something starts to stress you, identify exactly what it is and objectively assess why this is a stressor for you. Can you manage it yourself or do you need help?
Give yourself	• Am I helping or hurting people? • Am I working interdependently with others? • Have I developed empathy? • Do I work by a set of personal standards?	Be aware of your fellow students. When working together be alert to their needs as well as yours (be empathic).

Adapted from the Emotional Intelligence Network, **http://6seconds.org/index.php**.

Making personal changes – developing self-belief

As we have mentioned, an important aspect of dealing with stress is this ability to feel you can control your life. The modern-day reaction to 'flight or fight' is our ability to change things that stress us, and to do that we need to have confidence in ourselves (see Activity 3).

Albert Bandura, a famous Canadian professor of Psychology, began to see personality as an interaction between psychological processes, the environment and our behaviour. He noticed that those who felt more in control of their lives (had high self-efficacy) behaved differently and personally achieved more (Bandura, 1997).

ACTIVITY 3 Is it all down to fate?

Look at the following statements – do you agree with them or not?

	Agree	Disagree
When things go wrong for me, it is just bad luck.		
It doesn't matter how well I plan, what's going to be, will be.		
Friendships are a result of chemistry – they work or they don't.		
Some people have all the luck.		
When things go wrong, I can usually find out who is to blame.		

As you probably realised, these are statements that reflect someone who has little self-belief in their own ability to make changes. Make a note of where your tendency lies. Check the feedback section for comments on these statements.

Write a new list of statements below that reflects someone who has self-belief.

	Generally me	Generally not me

Check the feedback section for some more examples once you have written your own.

Strategies for improving self-belief

1. Select a specific task/activity you want to improve and feel confident about. Think of a specific task.

2. This activity needs to be important to you as this will give you the motivation to work on it.

3. Has your previous experience of doing this activity been negative? If so, identify the specific negative aspects so you can work on them (don't generalise because you can't work with generalisations).

4. Develop a picture of yourself, or someone, doing this activity well. What makes it good? Make sure you 'see' this performed well. Keep that picture in mind.

5. Set yourself specific and short-term goals to deal with aspects of the activity you have identified. See the section below on approaches to dealing with stressful events.

6. Seek feedback and work with it positively. If you feel you 'can't do something' always say 'I can't do that *yet*.' It has a powerfully confident feel about it.

7. Verbalise (write out) your strategy for achieving your short-term goals. This way you have articulated your success and you can 'hear' it, and it primes you for action.

8. Small successes breed overall success.

NOTE Being 'in control' of events in your life is not about being a 'control freak'. It is about feeling that you can *do* something to help. The higher your emotional intelligence, the better you will be at trusting others in order to give and receive help. Recognise when you need support and be proactive in seeking it out.

Checklist for signs of stress

Take the list of symptoms here as a warning signal. If these symptoms become chronic you must seek help.

Physical

Headaches, backache, exhaustion, insomnia, pounding heart, diarrhoea or constipation, stiff neck and shoulders, rashes, nausea.

Emotional

Feeling useless, worthless, not confident of abilities, not recognising your strengths, talking yourself down, feeling lonely, feeling 'out of control', feeling irritable and angry.

Intellectual

Feeling you can't learn another thing, you can't remember things, you don't process information very well in class, you have to keep going over something to make it 'stick'.

As a result of some of these symptoms you may find that you have negative reactions, such as: withdrawal from friends, mood swings, angry outbursts, inability to make decisions, weepy, not hungry or eating too much, feeling sick when you open 'that' book or go past the library, possibly excessive drinking, drug abuse or self-harming.

NOTE If things have gone on too long or have become worse you may start to show more serious symptoms such as obsessive behaviour, suicidal feelings or depression. If you feel your symptoms are getting worse and you are worried, you must get professional help from either your doctor or the counselling service at your institution. If you do this, make sure you tell your personal tutor so that he or she can make allowances for late work or postpone certain assignments.

5 Do I have a personality that stresses me out?

We are all aware that some of our friends get more stressed than others and we may envy them if we are the one that gets stressed out while they remain calm. We should be aware by now that there are: (a) individual differences in how stressful or challenging we see particular events, and (b) individual differences in how we think we can deal with these events, once we see them as stressful. One of the factors for these individual differences is our different personality styles.

How does your personality affect your stress levels?

In the 1950s, two cardiologists, Meyer Friedman and Ray Rosenman, observed that there was more heart disease in their male patients with high-pressured jobs. This may seem obvious to us now but it wasn't at the time. They also noted that particular personality types were also more prone to heart disease. The personality type they felt was more 'at risk' was their so-called 'Personality A' person. Incidentally, Friedman regarded himself as a 'recovering type A'. The type A personality has now become synonymous with 'driven' people, obsessed with time and perfection. The counter to that is the type B personality that is laid-back and easy going.

Are you a type A or a type B?

Type A and type B are essentially a continuum of personality traits from being uptight to laid-back. They are not an intricate measure of your personality but serve to give you a guideline of where your tendencies are.

Type A personalities tend to:

- be very goal driven (in the extreme, often at all costs)
- be competitive
- need recognition and advancement
- multi-task when under time pressure

- be keen to get things finished
- be mentally and physically alert (above average).

NOTE There is continuing debate as to whether type A personality people are more at risk from heart disease. But the potential anger and hostility aspect of this personality type does seem to be a factor.

Type B personalities tend to:

- be more relaxed
- be more easy-going
- socialise a lot
- be less competitive
- set realistic goals that don't overstretch them.

If you are not sure which personality type you are, the Science Museum has a short online fun quiz that allows you to find out. This can be found at: **www.sciencemuseum.org.uk**. Search on 'stress' from the museum's search engine.

Help! I'm a type A personality and I'm already stressed out about it

Not all characteristics of type A people are bad. You will know yourself if you feel too driven or uptight. If you feel you are a type A person you may feel stressed out: for example, if you can't achieve what you set out to do, or if you see coursework deadlines looming and you think you are going to be late. You may need to re-adjust your personal standards and become a little more relaxed, if you feel you are overdoing things. Some of your friends may hint at your behaviour and you may want to consider if you are being too 'driven'.

Think about yourself and develop your emotional intelligence. Are there ways you can tone down your type A characteristics? Identify some of your characteristics you think you can work on. Also, check out the stress-busting techniques to help you when you need them.

Why bother – I'm a type B personality?

Not all the characteristics of extreme type B personalities are good. You may find yourself too laid-back where nothing stresses you until things get out of hand. You need to submit work tomorrow and suddenly you have got to get into action and you may not have the time to give your best. But, if you are an extreme type B, this may not worry you either! However, try to balance your relaxed style and ensure you are keeping to the goals you have set.

We need to get a balance

As with everything, we need a balance of drive and relaxation. Ideally you should be halfway between a type A and type B person. This way, you can deal with unexpected deadlines and other stressors by calm planning. You feel in control and not stressed out.

So once you have become self-aware, emotionally literate and believe in yourself, how do you approach stressful events?

6 Proactive strategies for dealing with stress

Stress-busting techniques are one way of coping with stress (see Section 8), but they are just that, 'techniques', and they are good to have. However, a more fundamental way of dealing with stress is to be **proactive** in your management of it. Psychologists have identified two broad types of coping strategy:

- problem-focused strategy
- emotion-focused strategy.

Problem-focused strategy	<ul><li>Know your stressors.</li><li>Analyse what stresses you about an event.</li><li>Break down the various components of the situation into manageable chunks.</li><li>Identify which part is the problem.</li><li>Look at the options.</li><li>Develop an action plan.</li><li>Check your resources – do you need help?</li></ul>
Emotion-focused strategy	<ul><li>Know your stressors.</li><li>Reflect on how you *feel* when confronted with this stressor.</li><li>Resist your feeling to avoid thinking about this.</li><li>Reflect on how you can start to change this emotion.</li><li>Trust in others and discuss with a friend or counsellor.</li></ul>

Source: Based on coping strategies from Lazarus and Folkman (1984)

If you are already a proactive stress-buster, you may find you have a preference for one or other of the strategies above. Ideally, you should be using both strategies as they tap into your self-belief and your emotional intelligence. Activity 4 asks you to think about how you solve problems.

ACTIVITY 4 Problem solving as a way of dealing with stress

Now think of an example that is pertinent to you. How would you use this problem-solving strategy?

1. Identify a stressful problem.
2. What makes it stressful?
3. How do I feel about it?
4. What can I do now to manage it?

Checklist for proactive coping strategies	
	Need to work on this ✓
Personal development: • Self-belief (I am a 'can do' person) • Emotional intelligence (I know myself and trust others)	
Personality type: • Type A (perfectionist, driven, high standards) • Type B (relaxed)	
Strategies: • Problem-focused (analyse, action plan) • Emotion-focused (realign emotions)	

7 What makes studying stressful?

Learning can cause stress and your ability to handle some degree of stress will help you. You may well find you are in your comfort zone at the beginning of a course where you feel in control of your learning and you can predict what is going on. However, you may find that as the difficulty increases, you feel less in control of what you know and don't know and very soon fall outside your comfort zone. At this stage you are learning! It is important to recognise that you must go through this stage in order for your new knowledge to find its place and become your new comfort zone. It is important to fit into your new comfort zone, although for some students this takes until the exams before everything starts to fall into place. Look at the graph in Figure 1.1.[1] Where do you feel you are now? Are you happy to be outside your comfort zone while you learn?

Becoming a student can be seen as a 'rite of passage'. It is something you probably feel you want to do; it does mature you. You leave home, make a new home for yourself, make new friends and learn about something you are interested in. These are all exciting challenges and can give you such a buzz **or** completely stress you out. Which is it for you? Activity 5 asks you to identify stressors in academic life.

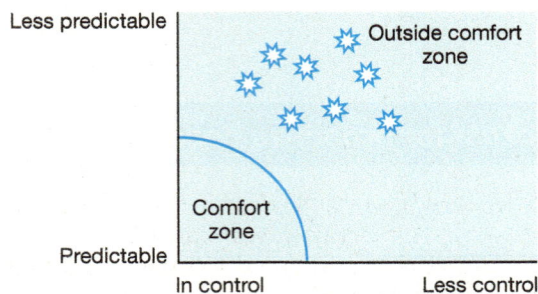

Figure 1.1   Are you in your comfort zone?

ACTIVITY 5   Stressors in academic life

Identify some of the stressors in academic life from this typical scenario. What do you think Joanne should do? Then identify academic stressors that particularly affect you.

Joanne was the first of her family to go on to further study and she was very excited at studying engineering. She made friends quickly through her studies and the clubs she joined. However, now in her third year, money, or lack of it, is an increasing worry. She has taken out several loans but has now decided to take a part-time job to make ends meet and has found herself a job in a local restaurant. She works two evenings a week on four-hour shifts finishing at midnight. She has also taken on another small job in the local supermarket working a busy afternoon shift. While her bank balance is now looking healthier, she feels that the late nights and the extra supermarket job are beginning to affect her work. Her studies are increasingly complex and she has several projects to complete. As this is her third year she needs good grades to get the degree she wants. She is beginning to feel there are too many demands on her life and doesn't know how to cope, especially since her boss at the restaurant is pressurising her to work more shifts.

---

[1] Thanks to Professor Mark Lutman from the University of Southampton who discussed these ideas. He feels that a good learner is one who can cope with being outside their comfort zone – as long as it is not for too long.

	Academic stressors	Coping strategies
Joanne		
You		

Will I/do I fit in?

When you leave home to study you leave behind something you have grown familiar with: your friends, your town, your boyfriend/girlfriend and your family. This familiar environment has helped make you and support you. Although you are excited by leaving all this behind, you may find that once you are away things do not feel as comfortable or safe as they did at home. You are basically homesick. Many of your fellow students will also be feeling the same and you know you have to make an effort to fit in, find new friends and belong. The best time to do this is right at the beginning of your studies when everyone is looking out for new friends. You may find that you don't mix with the right group in the first instance, but by the second semester you will be feeling confident enough to know who you'd like to be with and how to go about it. Being shy may make this process slower, but try and join clubs you are interested in and that should automatically link you with like-minded people.

I never seem to have enough money

The Student Experience Report 2006, carried out by MORI (Unite, 2006), with over 1000 face-to-face interviews with undergraduate and post-graduate students, found that of those sampled, over half reported difficulties managing their finances and one-third had already asked their families to help them out in a crisis. Postgraduate and mature students, however, were least likely to turn to their families for financial support.

Finances are an increasing source of stress for students and finding part-time work is an obvious solution. The trend towards part-time work when in full-time education is growing. The Student Experience Report 2006 reported that four in ten of those interviewed had done part-time work during their studies, and this is set to increase. In a *Guardian Unlimited* article in 2002 it was reported that the National Union of Students in the UK estimated that approximately 42% of students worked part time, whereas the Trades Union Congress's survey in 2000 claimed that 60% of students needed to work to meet basic living costs (Henessey, 2002). Although working gives you that added work experience and responsibility, too much can damage your studies. The UK Government recommends that you spend no more than 10 hours/week in part-time employment.

Lack of money is the route cause of other stressors, e.g. poor accommodation, cheap food and lack of course materials. So getting your finances right is crucial (see Activity 6).

ACTIVITY 6 Budgeting

Budgeting is something we have to do all our lives. However, if finance is a particular stressor for you then you must get to grips with budgeting. This is rarely anyone's favourite activity, but to prevent debts building up you need to know what comes in and what goes out and work within that budget as much as you can.

How do your finances look? Work on a weekly or monthly basis, whichever suits you best.

	Amount incoming weekly/monthly	Amount outgoing weekly/monthly
INCOME:		
Loan		
Part-time work		
Family		
Savings		
Other		
ACCOMMODATION:		
Rent		
Electricity		
Gas		
Water		
Telephone		
Council Tax		
Other		

	Amount incoming weekly/monthly	**Amount outgoing weekly/monthly**
STUDIES:		
Tuition fees		
Field trips		
Stationery		
Project costs		
Other		
LIVING COSTS:		
Food		
Eating out (evening and day)		
Toiletries		
Mobile phone		
Travel: car		
Travel: bus fares – daily		
Travel: long-distance trips (home?)		
Clothes		
Other (dentist, doctor, prescription, etc.)		
SOCIAL LIFE:		
The pub		
Cinema, clubs		
Sporting activities		
Other		
TOTAL		

Do the incoming and outgoing columns balance?

What should you do if you find yourself in need of financial support? Your institution will have a student support centre where you can find out information on the student hardship fund that it operates. The centre may have other schemes to help you budget more effectively. There are people in your institution whose job it is to help you; you should be proactive and seek them out.

I don't know what my tutors expect of me

A problem for first-year students is the move into Higher Education. You may have come from an 'A'-level course in the UK, be an international student or a mature student returning to full-time education.

Always check your programme and course documentation (see 'Learning in Higher Education') as this describes the aims of your courses and the learning outcomes. Always make sure you know exactly what is needed in an assignment, never assume. Remember: you will be expected to develop an independent style of learning (see 'Learning in Higher Education'). If you are in doubt regarding what is expected, ask either your tutor or a student in the second or third year.

If you have a study buddy or peer mentoring scheme in your institution, take full advantage of it. If not, you may want to ask if one can be set up. See the Peer Assisted Learning website at Bournemouth University in the UK.

I just can't learn everything I am expected to

The academic load and demands of coursework are another area that has been identified as a cause of stress. You may find that your assignments are bunched towards the end of the semester and you struggle to hand in by the deadlines.

Assignment deadline bunching is a problem. But, if you are given the task way ahead of time, you will be expected to time-manage all your assignments (see Chapter 2, 'Managing your time'). Plan when you can fit each assignment in, given the amount of knowledge you know at the time. Sometimes you may have to get started before you have had the lecture, seminar or laboratory class. You can make an outline plan and fit in as much as you can as you go along.

Academic load in terms of sheer quantity of what you are expected to learn will mean that you need to develop some effective academic skills. The chapters in this book are designed to do just that. Actively take what you need from each chapter and **act on it** and this will start to reduce your stress as you begin to feel in control. Activity 7 asks you to identify your stressful events.

The complexity of the material you have to learn will also increase with the years and this has been shown to be another stressor. Don't suffer in silence over something you are struggling with. Ask your tutor and possibly a postgraduate teaching assistant who may be helping on the course. Don't forget that you can ask your friends or student mentors, if you have this set up in your programme.

In 'Learning in Higher Education' we discussed the characteristics of a novice and an expert; you may want to check this out again later.

ACTIVITY 7 Identifying your stressful events

Which of the following, if any, do you find stressful:

■ bunched assignment deadlines
■ the sheer quantity of work to get through
■ complexity of the work
■ lack of understanding of what is expected of you
■ anything else?

How can you be proactive in managing these potential stressors for you?

Complete the concept map below with the different types of study stressors and list ways of dealing with them. Place each study stressor on the first branch and the ways of dealing with it on the lower branches.

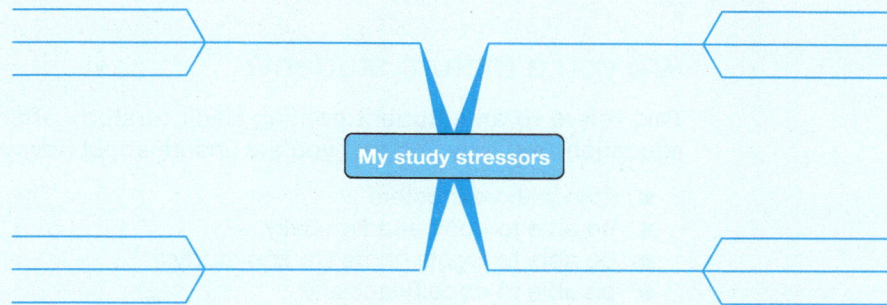

My study stressors

See feedback section for a map of the result of stress on study.

Dropping out: a response to stress?

Dropping out from your studies can be a response to stress, but not necessarily. If you feel that you really have chosen the wrong subject, the wrong place to study and you now know exactly what you want to do and it is not studying, then leave. You will become even more stressed if you stay and will only be staying because you want to 'save face' or not offend someone. According to a BBC article (BBC News, 2004) one in seven students in the UK drop out. However, this varies greatly across institutions. Learning how to keep stress under control and not letting it ruin your life is vital.

If you want to leave because you feel you can't cope or you are generally unhappy, **think again**. With the help of your personal tutor, a student adviser, a friend or a religious leader, discuss why you are unhappy and what your options really are. You will find there are various options and one could be just right for you, enabling you to go on and graduate. **Don't let wanting to leave be a flight reaction to stress**.

Who gets more stressed out?

As we should know by now, being stressed out varies between individuals. However, some groups of students are more likely to feel the pressures than others. Stressors can be external or internal. External stressors refer to things outside of us that we have to deal with, e.g. exams, coursework, finances, etc. Internal stress refers to our own personality characteristics, or if we are dealing with some incapacity or illness. So, all stress is an interplay between what we bring to the event and the event itself. The imbalance between internal and external stressors can affect our psychological and physiological well-being and cause stress (Lazarus and Cohen, 1977).

Since external factors play a role in stress, certain students may find themselves under additional pressures.

Are you a mature student?

This refers to any student coming back to study after some time out of education. You may find that you are unsure about how you will:

- fit in with youngsters
- be able to cope academically
- be able to juggle home life and study
- be able to cope financially.

Are you an international student?

As an international student you also have additional things that add pressure. You will have to deal with:

- setting up home in another country
- being homesick
- understanding the cultural differences (socially and academically)
- working in a language that is not your native language
- facing, possibly, racist comments. Do report this if within the university.

External pressures are discussed in Activity 8.

NOTE   You are probably a happy and well-adjusted student even though you may have these added pressures. Please don't feel you have to be stressed out. If you are coping well, you may want to be alert to students in a similar situation to you who are not coping well and you may be able to give them some support (develop your emotional intelligence).

ACTIVITY 8 My external pressures

	Applies to me	Do I need to do anything?
Just returning to full-time education after many years and wonder how I will cope.		
I'm homesick (or may become).		
My English is not good enough.		
I'm not giving enough time to my family.		
I miss my friends back home.		
Can I cope?		

List more pressures that apply to you and check if you think you need to do something about it to keep them in check. What personality type are you – could this influence your reaction to stress? Are you proactive and use problem- and emotion-focused coping strategies (see Sections 4, 5 and 6 above)?

8 Stress-busting techniques: a maintenance strategy

In addition to the personal development and proactive strategies above, we can develop a maintenance programme that enables us to cope with on-going stress that hits us once in a while. Some basic techniques are:

- **Exercise**. This will help the physiological aspect of stress and the release of endorphins will give you a feeling of euphoria as well as help your heart. It is also ideal for getting rid of anger and frustrations. If you want to choose only one stress-busting technique, then choose this one.
- **Relax**. When you are feeling stressed out it is difficult to unwind. You may find you have to make a big effort to do this. It may be better to go to classes such as yoga or t'ai chi. Exercising also helps you to relax. If you want to develop your own relaxation techniques then try deep breathing or meditation. Go out with friends and have a good laugh.

- **Eat well**. Avoid junk food and too much alcohol – both of these can sap your energy and make you feel low.
- **Talk**. Open up to friends and family. They will feel honoured that you trust them enough to discuss your problems. Talking allows you to see things in perspective and get another view.
- **Stress diary**. By keeping a diary you start to articulate what your feelings are and what stresses you out. Once you do this you become conscious and self-aware, which is where you must start in order to cope. You can couple this with talking to your friends.
- **Focus**. When we are stressed we start to feel overwhelmed. Go back and look at the strategies for developing self-belief above and focus on each part of your plan.
- **Get support from others**. There are some problems you can't and shouldn't face on your own. Don't try and be superman or super-woman. Most Higher Education institutions are caring and will have support in place for you. You should make yourself familiar with what is available: for example, student services, Students Union, religious chaplains, counselling services, medical services, your personal tutor and, of course, your friends and family.

Exams – the special case

During revision:

- plan a realistic revision timetable – this will help you stay on top of things
- summarise your notes, make key points, highlight important information and use concept maps for quick overviews
- take breaks so you can stay alert.

During the exam:

- 'feel' calm – breathe slowly and deeply
- feel in control
- read the instructions carefully (very often students don't do this)
- read the questions calmly, underlining key aspects
- mark the questions you want to do first
- allocate time for each question
- allow time to check your work.

9 On reflection

Stress management, as you have seen, is much more than learning a few techniques; it is life changing. It cannot guarantee you a stress-free life, and would you want one? But it will enable you to manage it and keep the health-threatening aspects of stress under control.

Summary of this chapter

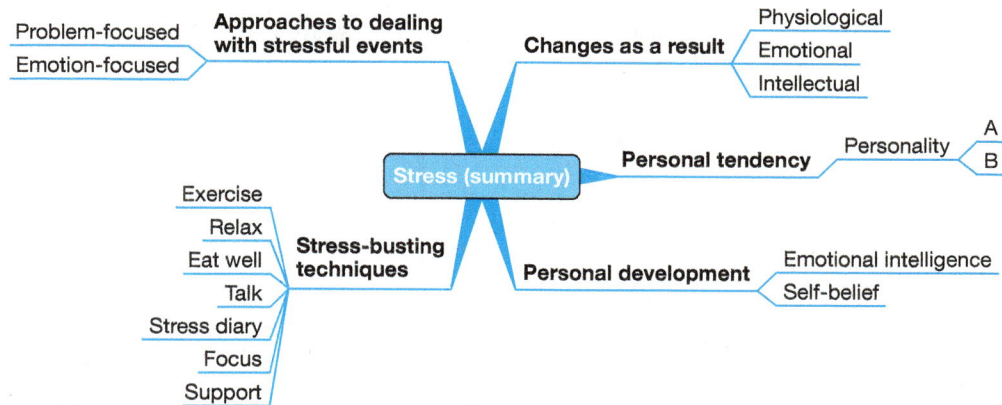

Now reflect on your current abilities to work through a stress management plan and consider what you need to do to improve. You may want to transfer this information to your own institution's PDP scheme.

ACTIVITY 9 Update your personal development planner

Having read this chapter, gauge your confidence again. How does this compare with your confidence levels at the start of the chapter? What can you do to improve? You can incorporate this into your own PDP and of course add anything else that you feel is appropriate.

Grade your confidence on a scale of 1–5 where 1 = poor and 5 = good.

My stress management plan	Confidence level 1–5	Plans to improve
Recognise how I react to stress. *Section 3*		
Check my self-belief. *Section 4*		
Improve my emotional intelligence. *Section 4*		
Recognise my personal tendency to being stressed (personality type A, B). *Section 5*		

My stress management plan	Confidence level 1–5	Plans to improve
Identify proactive strategies in dealing with stress that suit me best. *Section 6*		
Identify what stresses me. *Section 7*		
Identify and use the best stress-busting techniques for me. *Section 8*		

Date: _____

Getting extra help

- Talk to your university counsellor. He or she will be able to give advice on how best to deal with the common problems associated with the stresses of studying.
- Ask friends how they cope with stress – not only will you discover that it's more common than you think, but also they may have some useful stress-busting tips for you.

Consult a few interesting websites:

- **Student Mental Stress: Dstress**. This site is produced by Loughborough University and is full of useful information. It is a good interactive site. See: **www.d-stress.org.uk** [last accessed November 2008].
- **Mind: How to Cope with the Stress of Student Life**. Mind has a guide and a series of tips for getting help if you need it. Search on 'student stress' using the search engine: **www.mind.org.uk** [last accessed November 2008].
- **Channel 4, 4Health**, Student Stress, Wendy Moore. Search on 'stress' using the search engine. 'Most students will feel the effects of stress at some point in their studies and a small number of students may feel stressed or depressed for a lot of the time.' See: **www.channel4.com/health** [last accessed November 2008].

Feedback on activities

ACTIVITY 1 Identifying signs of stress

	Signs of stress	What he/she might be feeling	What he/she should do
Carlos	Becoming withdrawn. Not eating properly. On edge/irritable.	Emotional. This can be weepy, or aggressive. Emotional exhaustion.	Notice that things aren't right and something needs to be done before falling behind with his studies. Talk to someone he trusts – friend, tutor or counsellor. Make sure this doesn't go on for too long.
Lucy	Heavy drinking. Not sleeping well. Disinterested, forgetful.	Feeling unwell and possibly depressed from too much alcohol and not enough sleep. Mental exhaustion.	Be alert to a change in behaviour that is unhelpful. Identify the first thing that needs to be done, i.e. stop drinking. Seek help from a friend or counsellor to prevent serious alcohol damage.

NOTE In these case studies the key to moving on is being alert to your own stress patterns and recognising when they are becoming overwhelming. Seek help and allow your friends to help you. As a friend, you may have to help someone who is trying to push you away. Be patient and try not to abandon him or her during this difficult phase of your friendship.

ACTIVITY 2 Recognising your own symptoms of stress

Here are some symptoms of stress. Check the ones that you have identified. You may recognise more symptoms that you didn't realise indicated stress.

▶

How do you feel? (Include physical and emotional characteristics)	How do you act and behave?
Feeling overwhelmed.	You are disorganised and forgetful. You are over cautious and have difficulty making decisions. You panic. You have lost your confidence. You can't concentrate on your work. Mental exhaustion.
Feeling tired and exhausted.	You have no or little interest in things. You don't sleep well. You cry about things easily.
Feeling anxious and nervous.	You are moody, irritable, aggressive and get angry easily. You may resort to recreational drugs to alleviate symptoms.
Feeling very emotional and tearful.	You react emotionally and are often near to tears … emotional exhaustion.
Feeling sick/tight feeling in stomach/not hungry.	You have diarrhoea and/or lose interest in food.
Heart is pounding.	You perspire more than usual.
Feeling homesick.	You withdraw from your friends.
Being anti-social.	You want to be on your own. People irritate you and you get short tempered.
Feeling depressed.	Everything becomes too much and you have little interest in doing anything.

NOTE If your list was rather short, you might now recognise some of the symptoms you have. Add them to your list in this activity. Being aware of our stress symptoms is very important, as we saw in Activity 1.

ACTIVITY 3 Is it all down to fate?

	Comments
When things go wrong for me, it is just bad luck.	This means that you feel your behaviour doesn't contribute, or contribute much, to things that go wrong for you. You are placing the blame on something external – 'bad luck'.
It doesn't matter how well I plan, what's going to be, will be.	You feel you have no control as your whole life is already mapped out for you.
Friendships are a result of chemistry – they work or they don't.	Chemistry is definitely part of friendship, but not everything. If you don't work at finding and keeping friends, you will be on your own. Social well-being is very important in controlling stress.
Some people have all the luck.	See the first statement above. In this case you assume other people's successes are a result of 'good luck' rather than their efforts.
When things go wrong, I can usually find out who is to blame.	See the first statement above.

Statements of self-belief

I can influence what happens to me.
If I make specific short-term plans I know I will be able to keep to them.
I know friends are attracted to each other, but I can still influence how well I integrate with my friends. I have the interpersonal and emotional intelligence to do that.
When things go wrong, I work out why and sort it out so that it doesn't happen again.

ACTIVITY 7 Identifying your stressful events

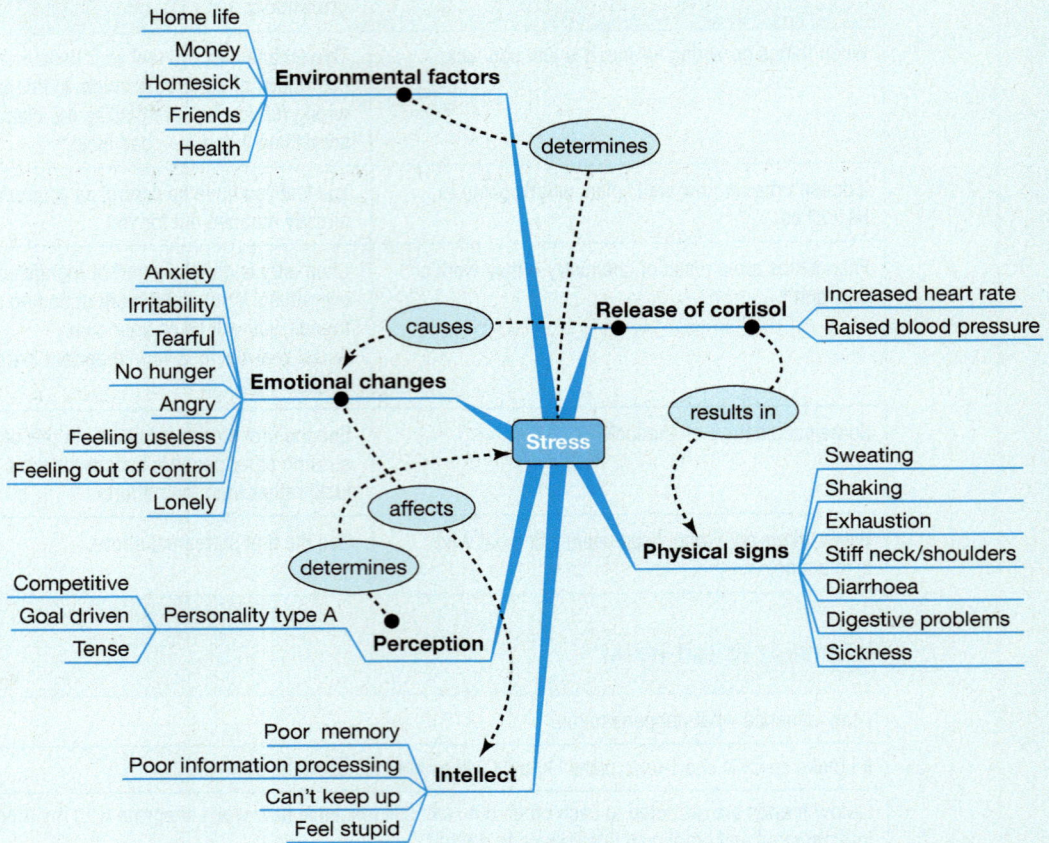

Map of study stressors – summary chart

References

- 6Seconds: Emotional Intelligence Network, available at: http://6seconds.org/index.php [last accessed November 2008].
- Bandura, A. (1997) *Self Efficacy in Changing Societies*. Cambridge, Cambridge University Press.
- BBC News (2004) 'One in seven students to drop out', 30 September, available at: http://news.bbc.co.uk/1/hi/education/3703468.stm [last accessed November 2008].
- Goleman, D. P. (1995) *Emotional Intelligence: Why It Can Matter More Than IQ for Character, Health and Lifelong Achievement*, New York, Bantam Books.
- Hennessy, K. (2002) 'All work and no play makes ... a student', *Guardian Unlimited*, 30 September, available at: http://education.guardian.co.uk/students/story/0,,802009,00.html [last accessed March 2009].
- Lazarus, R. S. and Cohen, J. B. (1977) 'Environmental Stress', in I. Altman and J. F. Wohlwill (eds), *Human Behavior and Environment*, Vol. 2. New York, Plenum.
- Lazarus, R. S. and Folkman, S. (1984) *Stress, Appraisal, and Coping*. New York, Springer.
- Unite, Student Experience Report 2006, MORI, available at: www.ipsos-mori.com [last accessed November 2008].

2 Managing your time

Managing our time is something like dieting. We know what we should eat, we know why we should eat that way and we know the benefits it will bring. However, how often do we start with good intentions and then let things slip? Time management can be similar. We know why we should manage our time, we often know what to do, but we just can't keep to it.

In this chapter you will learn how to:

1. identify your relationship with time and understand how this affects your time management
2. consider your life goals as part of your time management
3. manage your time efficiently and effectively.

USING THIS CHAPTER

Estimate your current levels of confidence. At the end of the chapter you will have the chance to reassess these levels where you can incorporate this into your personal development planner (PDP). Mark between 1 (poor) and 5 (good) for the following:

I can identify my relationship with time and understand how this affects my time management.	I can identify my life goals as part of my time management.	I can get the best out of my time.	I can manage my time effectively.

Date: _____

1 Introduction

How many of us have started each day by stumbling from lecture to seminar to the café, to the pub, and then to bed, only to do the same the next day with little thought of what we are doing? How many of us start the day by looking at the electronic messages and using that as a driver for the morning's activities? At the end of the day you get to bed exhausted because you have been so busy 'reacting'. But what have you actually done that is important in moving you forward? Are you a proactive time manager or a reactive one?

Our relationship to food, stress and time is very personal and in order to move on in all these areas we need to identify our relationship with them. This chapter enables you to identify your own relationship with time and recognise how you manage time now. You will look at the importance of the whole picture in order to fulfil all aspects of your life, not just your studies. Finally, we shall look at the mechanics of time management in order to make things happen.

Seeing time as a resource

We have only to look at the number of idioms in English that relate to time to see that we regard time as a resource. Most of these idioms refer to spending, wasting or saving time, as shown in the figure on the next page.

We are living with technological communications that give us instant access to information and we find ourselves in an environment that demands even quicker responses from us than ever before. We are living in

Short of time

Make up for lost time

Plenty of time

Play for time

Kill time

Waste of time

Can't afford the time

Time on your hands

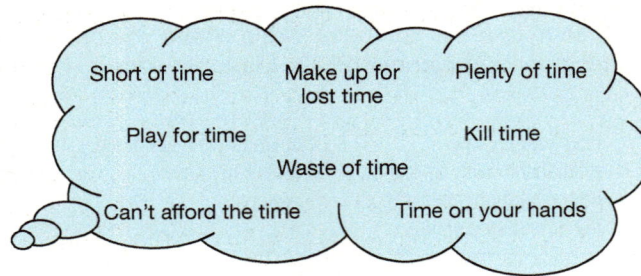

social cultures, be they industry, college or social spheres, where the volume of activity each week has rocketed. This can result in us feeling controlled by time. In a study of how North Americans use their time, the researchers found that 61% of the population reported never having excess time with 40% feeling that time is a bigger problem for them than money (work by Robinson and Godbey, 1997, cited in Boniwell, 2005).

The life of a student is tightly constrained by deadlines, time slots and timetables. How many times have fellow students you know complained about the amount of coursework they have to do and the bunching of deadlines? We increasingly work and play in environments that demand multi-tasking and that suits some and not others. Time affects us all, but how we **perceive time** and handle it varies between individuals.

2 Recognising your relationship with time

We can get an insight into how we deal with time by recognising if we generally 'look forward', 'look to the past', 'work to the wire' or finish one thing before starting the next. When we look at time like this, we realise there can be no 'one size fits all' as we have individual preferences.

First let us look at our preferences for particular time perspectives, as this is one aspect that affects our motivation to study.

Time perspectives

Philip Zimbardo, an award-winning social psychologist from the University of Stanford, looked at how our dominant orientation to the past, present and the future influences our behaviour and especially our ability to manage our time (Zimbardo and Boyd, 1999). Activity 1 helps you to identify some of these different time perspectives in other people.

ACTIVITY 1 Recognising different time perspectives in others

In this activity there are no absolute answers, and it is used to prepare you for recognising your own relationship with time later. Use the scenarios to give you a flavour of the characters and then estimate the following:

1. What time perspective dominates these students' lives at present: past, present or future? There could also be a mixture of these time perspectives.
2. Who do you think are multi-taskers and single-taskers?
3. Estimate their motivation to study.

Adrian is a second-year student living in a house with other students. He is very sociable and really enjoys his time with friends. The highlight of his week is Thursday night when he goes out with friends until the early hours of the morning. These Thursday nights have been so enjoyable he has started extending them to a few more nights as well, as Adrian's philosophy in life is 'to live for today'. Now, in the second semester, coursework and work difficulty is increasing and he is finding it hard to cope with everything, apart from his social life. He has had several warnings from tutors for late hand-ins, but just can't get around to doing more work, but he knows he has to. He finds it quite difficult to juggle social life and coursework.

Ismet is someone you can rely on to have a good time. He often arranges great evenings that are cheap but great fun. He is now in his third year and knows exactly what he wants to do when he finishes studying. His great planning abilities have helped him manage a busy social life and a challenging course. However, he knows he could probably have got a better degree grade if he had put more work in, but he gets such a buzz from juggling all these parts of his life that he is prepared to accept that. Although, having said that, he is heading for an upper-second degree classification.

Rachael always wanted to be an engineer and as a child was fascinated by those Victorian civil engineers who laid the foundations of our cities today. She knows it is tough, and is determined to get a good degree. She works very hard and is setting up volunteering and vacation work to get as much hands-on experience as possible. She also manages to have several pieces of coursework on the go at the same time and seems to be able to cope with it, although she gets a little irritated if she is interrupted while working. Her friends think she needs to relax a bit and at least take some time to enjoy herself now.

Student	Time perspective (past, present, future)	Preference to multi-tasking or single-tasking	Motivation to study (high, medium, low)	Estimated time management skills (poor, OK, good)
Adrian				
Ismet				
Rachael				

Check the feedback section at the end of the chapter.

Now, think about some of your friends. What time perspective dominates their lives? Do you think they are multi-taskers?

What's your time perspective?

Sometimes it is easier to recognise characteristics in others than ourselves, so now you've looked at others, it is time to take a look at yourself and see if you can identify which time perspective dominates you during semester time. In Activity 2 you can select several time perspectives. It would be interesting to see which one feels like you **now**.

ACTIVITY 2 Identifying your own time perspective

Look at the different time perspectives – which one(s) do you feel dominate(s) you during the semester?

Time persective 1	Time perspective 2
I tend to be impulsive and love excitement. I am happy to take risks as this makes life exciting. My motto is 'Live for today because I don't know what tomorrow will bring.'	My past life was not very pleasant and I too frequently recall events or things I regret doing and it can sometimes affect me now.
Time persective 3	**Time perspective 4**
I know where I want to go and I put plans in place to help me get there. I am prepared to work through boring pieces of coursework as I know it is laying a foundation for later work.	My motto is 'Whatever will be, will be.' I generally feel that I shouldn't worry too much about the future as it will take care of itself and luck plays a large part in how successful one is anyway.
Time persective 5	
I get a warm feeling when I think about the past, my family or cultural traditions. It makes me know who I am. It is very important for me to keep track of my old friends.	

Check the feedback section at the end of the chapter.

Consider how these time perspectives could effect your time management behaviour. Do you think you need to make adjustments to enable your studies?

Ideally we should be balanced between the different positive time perspectives, but not perspectives 2 and 4 as they have a negative effect on our life. Most successful people have a tendency to be 'future oriented' (perspective 3). When you are engaged in your academic studies this should motivate you sufficiently to encourage you to be future oriented. If you are not motivated, then it is going to be hard to engage with your learning or manage your time effectively. However, too much of this orientation can make you a workaholic, so you do need a balance.

We have seen that our time perspective affects our behaviour and our motivation to study and subsequently how we manage time. Our preference to being a multi- or linear tasker reflects our perception of time and how we manage time to complete tasks.

Are you comfortable multi-tasking or not?

An important anthropologist, Edward T. Hall, observed that different cultures had particular preferences when structuring their time. Cultures that see time as linear tend to emphasise the usage of time in discrete slots and complete tasks in a linear manner. Those cultures that see time as more fluid and less exact tend to carry out their tasks in a more non-linear manner and do lots of things at the same time. Work has continued in this field and these characteristics are also observed in individuals and particular jobs.

Different jobs have different time cultures where different time personalities can thrive. Those working with disaster teams, transport crews and surgical teams need people who can estimate time accurately and know what has to be done, when it has to be done, and do it. Those working in more creative fields may find such colleagues stifling. The academic time culture is deadline driven and many institutions will penalise you if your work is not handed in on time. If working to deadlines is not your preferred style then it is important to acknowledge that first and devise ways of coping.

With regard to individuals, those who prefer to do one task at a time are seen as 'linear taskers' while those happy to juggle lots of tasks at the same time are seen as 'multi-taskers'. If you see time as being discrete then you are able to identify slots in which to work and control your time. If, on the other hand, you see time as fluid and continuous you may not see much of a separation between work and your social life and you carry out tasks when the mood takes you rather than working to rigid time plans. How you think of time therefore can influence your tendency to multi-task or not. Activity 3 helps you to identify if you are a multi-tasker.

NOTE   If you want to learn some jargon, a multi-tasker is a **polychron** (a term first coined by Hall, 1959) and someone who focuses on one task at a time is a **monochron**! Can you recognise monochrons and polychrons in your friendship group?

ACTIVITY 3 Are you a multi-tasker?

Some of the key time management behaviours that can distinguish multi-taskers from others are: planning, focus and attention, reaction to change, and performing under pressure. You may already know if you are a multi-tasker, but have a look at a few of these statements and check the feedback. Remember: we can all be multi- or linear taskers but we prefer to operate in one or the other. Your preference will determine how you manage your time and how you meet your deadlines.

▶

	Ideally me	But in practice ... I do/don't do this ...
Planning		
1. I like to plan what I am going to do. Although I find it hard, I need to plan my time quite carefully. Without a plan, I feel a little bit lost. [linear tasker]		
2. I don't like working to a detailed time plan. It makes me feel constrained and irritable. [multi-tasker]		
Focus and attention		
3. Once I start on a task I give it my full attention and I dislike it when I am interrupted. [linear tasker]		
4. My focus and attention tends to be spread across lots of different tasks I am doing. It doesn't bother me if I am interrupted, I just deal with that and then carry on. [multi-tasker]		
Reaction to change		
5. Once I have worked out my plan of action, I get annoyed if I have to change it. [linear tasker]		
6. I can make rough plans, but happily change them too. [multi-tasker]		
Performance under pressure		
7. I like to keep track of the tasks I have to do and can prioritise very well. This gives me breathing space and so I can do the work before the pressure gets too strong. [linear tasker]		
8. I work best when I feel under time pressure. I am usually juggling several pieces of work to meet my deadlines. Prioritising is a last-minute approach for me, but I tend to get everything done. [multi-tasker]		
Is your preference multi-tasking or linear tasking?		

Check the feedback section at the end of this chapter for more information.

NOTE   These characteristics are just some indicators of multi- and linear tasking.

Advantages for the multi-tasker

You will probably feel less intimidated by the time pressure as you are able to juggle your coursework. You will probably find this stimulating. You may be a procrastinator as you are happy to leave things to the last minute and get started on many things simultaneously, but make sure you finish them! You have a very flexible working style and can deal with interruptions and changes to your schedule.

Dangers for the multi-tasker

Your preference for working under pressure and leaving things to the last minute does not allow for any mishaps. What if you suddenly realise you don't understand something the night before you hand in your coursework or that you should have completed a set of data before now? Since you can juggle lots of tasks, you may react to all your tasks in the same way. You must remember to plan and schedule and prioritise your activities, at least to some degree. If you try to do too much at one time you can be inefficient as you may just get overloaded and find you don't do anything very well. It may be better to allocate quality time for particularly difficult or important tasks. You may find you are a multi-tasker because you are an urgency addict (see Section 3 below). Now is your time to reveal your true colours!

Advantages for the linear tasker

You consciously want to have control over your time and if you are able to plan and identify time periods when things should be done, you can probably deal with the pressure. As a result of your prioritising and planning, you will be able to focus on key pieces of work.

Dangers for the linear tasker

Studying and the bunching of coursework deadlines can lead to a sense of time stress and the feeling that you can't do anything properly. You need to break down your tasks into smaller chunks and schedule at that level so you feel you are working in a linear mode. You may also need to be flexible enough to find those quality slots at short notice.

Checklist for dealing with your relationship with time

1. Identify your time preference.
2. Recognise if you are a multi- or a linear tasker.
3. Note if you can improve your relationship with time.
4. Recognise how this impacts on your time management.

3 Addressing your life goals: getting a balance

Time management is more than just organising ourselves and writing 'to-do lists'. We also need to make room for our wider goals in life, relationships, friends and family – we need a balance. Just planning and prioritising the tasks we have been given can be rather reactive and in order to account for all aspects of our life that are important to us, we also need to be proactive and ensure we work at them too. In our busy world there is a tendency to be 'urgency driven', reacting to all those demands that cross our path, rather than by those things that are important. We need to make sure we can plan, create and fit in all the things that are important to us in our life.

Traditionally time management training has been concerned with giving us tips to enable us to organise our time and deal with those ever-increasing urgent activities, generally in a very linear manner. Stephen Covey, father of nine children, professor of Business Management and an author of one of the most influential business books, *First Things First*, believes that we need to change our paradigm of time management from being addicted to dealing with what we perceive as urgent to proactively determining what is important. 'Importance' then becomes the new framework for managing our time.

The framework below was devised by Covey *et al.* (1994) to enable us to clarify what is urgent, not urgent, important and not important. Activity 4 asks what is important in your life.

	Urgent	**Not urgent**
Important	**I** Lectures, seminars, etc. Coursework preparation Assignment deadlines Crises	**II** Preparation – long-term goals Planning – long-term goals Relationship building Creating new ideas/plans Personal development
Not important	**III** Interruptions (some) Meetings (some) Some emails	**IV** Trivia Junk mail Time-wasting activities

Adapted from Covey, *et al.* (1994)

Quadrant I

Activities here are important and urgent; they have to be dealt with. To deal with activities here, we have to organise and prioritise what needs to be done. If we procrastinate with activities here, there will be serious consequences. In this quadrant we can feel driven and constrained by time, resulting in feeling stressed.

Quadrant II

This quadrant is where we deal with important issues such as planning (to keep quadrant I in check), creating new ideas and working towards our goals for both university and life in general. Keeping fit, doing exercise, broadening our mind, making intellectual leaps in our studies, volunteering, reading, helping friends and family, and developing meaningful relationships are all part of quadrant II. In this quadrant, we feel empowered and we need to deal proactively with the items in it. Don't neglect to do so.

Quadrant III

Many of us who are urgency addicted will deal with items that seem urgent but are not important. You may find you are reacting to other people's priorities at the expense of your own – try and keep a balance, and say 'no' to a few more non-urgent things.

Quadrant IV

This is where we generally waste our time. We might slump in front of the television, read trashy novels, etc. We are all in this quadrant from time to time, but try to limit how much time you spend here. You will find yourself in this quadrant often if you are driven by urgency as you will be stressed and exhausted and this is where you 'drop'. Also, when you procrastinate, you will find yourself in this quadrant.

ACTIVITY 4 What's important in your life?

You may feel very tempted to skip this activity. Please take time to think about it. The questions are quite challenging, but answers will come.

1. What things are important to me across my life?
2. What gives me a buzz?
3. What kind of work would I like to do after my studies? Do I need to be getting experience in place for that?

Now think of some of the steps you need to take in order to operationalise these goals. What could your plan look like if you include some of these things? Remember: these are your quadrant II activities and you need to be **proactive** in order to make them happen. Quadrant II activities are easier for those with a future time perspective.

This activity is something you need to do on an annual basis as your views do change, and it may need to be revitalised.

NOTE   You should be motivated to study and successfully completing your degree should be one of your life goals. If this does not appear in your list, you need to ask yourself why you are studying or if you are studying the wrong subject.

4 Organising yourself

Organising yourself involves planning your time and organising your study space. Your plan tells you what you should do and when you should do it and for how long. Your study space enables that to happen. If you are a multi-tasker you may want to skip this section, but stop and read it as you may be able to maintain your spontaneity and couple this with some degree of planning that can help you. In addition, you should be able to determine the kind of environment that gets the best out of you. Linear taskers will probably be competent planners by now but check where you best learn and ensure you can make that happen.

Of course your degree of motivation for this will depend, to some extent, on your time perspective. Planning encourages the development of a future orientation. If you are dominantly oriented towards the present, you will find it hard to fufil your plans even if you make them. Be careful of this.

How do you organise your time through planning?

Even the worst students of time management don't lurch unconsciously from one thing to another during the day, every day. There is always some degree of planning. However, what is your general pattern on time planning during a week? A plan will give you some idea of where all that time is going and how effective you are at getting those important things done (see Activities 5 and 6). Interestingly, a study in 1997 found that students at a particular university had more study work activity on Monday, Tuesday and Thursday, and fewer studied at weekends. The study found that typically students spend 38.8 hours on study-related tasks (the range was 34–48 hours depending on age, gender and year). Of that study time, 35.5% was spent on assessed work, 12.8% in lectures, 8% on non-assessed work, 7.6% of time in tutorials and 3.2% searching books in the library (Innis and Shaw, 1997).

ACTIVITY 5 Developing a weekly schedule

Look back on a typical week during semester time and try to remember how you spent your time. Include sleep, going out, paid work, private study, group/coursework, etc., as well as attendance at lectures/seminars. Note this down on the schedule below and estimate the time for your activities, using time slots. Are you happy with this or would you have liked it to be different? Is it similar or wildly different to the research above?

A typical week

Approximate times	Mon	Tues	Wed	Thurs	Fri	Sat	Sun
8.00–10.00am				9.00–10.00 Lecture			Catching up with sleep
10.00–12.00		11.00–12.00 Lecture	Seminar				Catching up with sleep
12.00–2.00pm						Paid work	Seeing friends
2.00–4.00pm			**Sport**				
4.00–6.00pm			**Sport**				
6.00–8.00pm			Paid work				
8.00–10.00pm			Paid work				
10.00–12.00pm							

Now think of next week and plan how you should spend your time, given the deadlines you have.

Approximate times	Mon	Tues	Wed	Thurs	Fri	Sat	Sun
6.00–8.00am	Sleep	Sleep	Sleep	Sleep	Sleep	Sleep	Sleep
8.00–10.00am				9.00–10.00 Lecture			Catching up with sleep
10.00–12.00		11.00–12.00 Lecture	Seminar				Catching up with sleep
12.00–2.00pm						Paid work	Seeing friends
2.00–4.00pm			**Sport**				
4.00–6.00pm			**Sport**				
6.00–8.00pm			Paid work				
8.00–10.00pm			Paid work				
10.00–12.00pm							

Next week my main goals are: _____

ACTIVITY 6 Balancing your time

Look at the activities on your weekly plan:

1. Can you identify the quadrants? Label them QI, QII, QIII and QIV.

    ■ Are any of your activities labelled QI really QIII? You can gain time by weeding out QIII-type activities.

2. Make a new empty weekly planner and start by putting in events/activities that are time sensitive, e.g. a lecture, as these are immovable.

3. Add QII-type activities in the free slots (these may not be on a weekly basis, but possibly a monthly basis). These will be taken from Activity 4, above, 'What's important in your life?' Remember to use the time slots to free up time to do things you want to do.

Organising your study space

You may have read in time management books that you need to have a clear desk (represents a clear head!), be somewhere quiet and not be disturbed. However, when you actually talk to students and ask them about their organisational preferences, it varies. What do you prefer? See Activity 7.

ACTIVITY 7 Your current and ideal study space

Imagine you have to complete a piece of coursework, which could, for example, be an essay or a laboratory report. You know you have to begin this piece of work today and so you sit down to start. Answer the questions in the table below. The examples are just prompts; you can also add your own. You may be happy with what you do: if so, then say so; if not, say what would be ideal for you.

	What you do currently	Is this ideal? If not, what is ideal?
1. Where do you prefer to work?	*At home, in the library.*	
2. Generally how is your work space organised?	*Cleared desk, work on top of other things, work on floor, have papers in a folder, have loose papers.*	
3. When you sit down to work do you find yourself getting up soon afterwards?	*You are hungry, thirsty, just need to sort something out quickly. Check the ritual you have before you finally get started.*	

	What you do currently	Is this ideal? If not, what is ideal?
4. How long do you think it takes you to feel settled and start work?		
5. Do you like to have music on at the same time as studying or have other people around you?	*Some people need to be alone and quiet and others need a certain background noise. What is your ambient preference?*	

There are no correct answers for this except to say that it is advisable to have all the papers you need to start an assignment at hand, as well as knowing **exactly** (not roughly) what you have to do and how long you have to do it. Having a messy desk and working with music and people around you may be what works for you. If so, then keep to it but do check you get the best out of this and it is not just a habit. The essence of this activity is for you to identify how you currently organise yourself, recognise your rituals (this is like doing stretches in the gym prior to your workout; you prime yourself for activity) and recognise that you are getting ready for work. However, if your 'rituals' go on for too long, you may be procrastinating. So be aware. If you are currently working in a space that is not conducive to your learning, now is the time to identify what the problems are and make changes.

Making a piece of work manageable

Some pieces of coursework can be rather daunting, so you need to create smaller chunks that are easier to manage:

- clarify what is needed in your coursework
  - identify any data you need from experimental or practical work
  - identify the pieces of information you need
- make a list of all the parts/chunks you need to complete
  - order the list
- check the hand-in date for your coursework
  - add a time frame to each chunk.

If you are a multi-tasker you may be happy with the main points. If you are a linear tasker, you may want to develop further the sub-points in your list.

5 Time management strategies

In the earlier sections we have looked at individual preferences with respect to our perceptions of time and how this influences the way we organise our time. In some cases time may be handled well and for others, the majority of us, there will be room for improvement.

Time is a resource that cannot be reused or recycled as with some other resources. We have a fixed number of hours in a semester and the only way of doing all those things we want to do and need to do is to manage this resource more efficiently. If you consider how much effort you put in each day you need to ask yourself what the net effect or outcome of all this effort is.

Mechanics of time management – planning, scheduling and using 'to-do' lists

To do this effectively you need to take different time frames and the most appropriate is the semester, the week and the day. Your semester plan enables you to see the overall picture for your studies and plan those important things that can get lost once the semester starts, e.g. develop a new sport, start up a new hobby, do some volunteering work or attending the careers advisory talks/workshops.

The weekly schedule fills in those time-constrained activities like lectures etc., leaving you slots for other important activities.

The 'to-do' list relates to each day and is where all your planning stops and the 'doing' takes place. This time frame is critical. If you consistently don't deliver within this time frame and you are predominantly a linear tasker, you start to feel overwhelmed and out of control. Multi-taskers may condense their 'to-do' lists in a flurry of activity, possibly at the last minute.

The table below gives some idea of how these time management aids work for your studies, but remember: this should also include important things you want to do outside of your studies.

NOTE 'To-do' lists are where the action happens and they should have a time frame and be able to support your goals. Make them SMART: Specific, Manageable, Relevant and Timely.

Recommending a time management strategy

Good time management is about working smart and not about working long hours. Your time is precious and you don't want to squander it on things that are not important, so be:

1. **S**pecific – identify precisely what you have to do. Goals that are too general rarely get finished.

2. **M**anageable – you will need to break large pieces of work down into smaller, manageable chunks so that you can tangibly feel small successes of a larger piece of work or project. By doing this you can more easily stay on track.

3. **A**ttainable – don't set yourself goals that are going to be difficult to achieve as this will only sap your self-confidence. Set sizeable goals that may be challenging, but attainable within the resources you have.

4. *R*elevant – the goal is working towards something you want or have to do within this time frame and for a particular project. Remain focused.

5. *T*imely – know when your task is done. What is your time frame? What needs to be done to make it complete?

Long-term planning	Mid-term planning	Short-term planning
Planning ⟶		Doing (outcome from your time planning)
Semester plan	Weekly schedule	Daily 'to-do' list
Identify your academic goals for this semester. Read unit descriptions to see what is expected of you.	This is similar to the weekly planner in Activity 5, above. Ensure items identified in your semester plan get transferred to the appropriate weekly planner.	This is your present time perspective. Apart from your time-sensitive slots, you should prioritise your other activities according to their importance.
Note assignments and hand-in dates for your courses.	Enter your time-sensitive items like lectures, tasks/event that satisfy your key goals and those urgent things that just must get done.	Start your day by setting your 'to-do' list and then **prioritising** tasks according to their **importance** and 'due date'.
Find out who you need to see regarding possible work placements, Erasmus exchange, etc.	Make sure your weekly planner includes your whole life and not just your studies. Many people are increasingly turning to electronic means for this through mobile phones or PDAs.*	PDAs usually have a 'to-do list' function, you may want to use that.
Note any software you need to learn or be expected to know and find out how you can train yourself.		Highlight the high priority tasks.
Promise yourself to complete your personal development planner as this will enable you to articulate what you are learning and identify where your strengths and weaknesses are.	Carefully estimate the time it will take you to complete tasks. This takes experience, but it is a characteristic of good time management.	

*PDA is a personal digital assistant. It can be integrated in your mobile phone or a standalone tool. There are also several desktop tools that can be used like a PDA, e.g. Google has a selection of tools and Microsoft Outlook has a PDA-like function built into it.

Checklist for developing good time management strategies

1. Balance short-term with long-term (life) goals.
2. Be importance rather than urgency driven.
3. Plan – in detail for linear tasker and roughly for multi-tasker.
4. Know how and where you learn best.
5. Understand your relationship with time.

ACTIVITY 8 Recommending time management strategies

How should the students below improve their time management skills? Can you identify their issues with regard to time management? A summary of time management is included below to help you work through this activity.

Jane is the first of her family to study at university and she is very excited by it. She lives with a long-term boyfriend who is just finishing a modern apprenticeship scheme. She is in her first year and, although she has worked before, she was not prepared for the amount of independent work she would have to do in addition to keeping her 'old life' together. Jane knows what her goals are, but finds the juggling of tasks difficult as there seems to be so many demands on her time.

Winston has been in the UK for about a year and is enjoying his studies. He knows what he wants to do when he finishes but has difficulty around exam times. He is fine during the year and manages to get his coursework in on time. Revision for exams is somehow different. He doesn't have a set place to revise and some days goes to the library, other times he sits on the floor of his bedroom or in the kitchen. He knows that when he starts to revise he will suddenly feel hungry and then goes to make something to eat. He will come back, ready to start, and then realises he hasn't made a promised phone call, so he does that. He is now ready to start, and a friend calls and they have a chat. By late afternoon he gets some work done but then his friends ring up and invite him out. Since he feels that his day is already wasted, he decides to go. He feels bad about this, but promises himself he will start revising properly tomorrow.

Can you write your own scenario?

NOTE If you are dyslexic you may have difficulty putting things (mentally and physically) in order. It is important for you to try and identify what you need to do and create a slot for it. If you have persistent problems with this, then it would be advisable to consult a learning differences unit at your institution as it is essential you find a strategy that suits you.

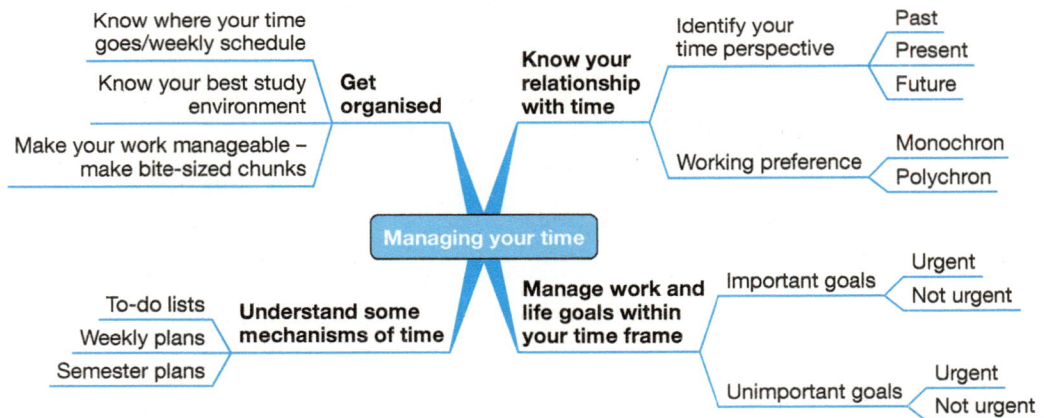

6 On reflection

Time management is about understanding your relationship with time and how that affects your ability to manage time. Looking forward motivates you and enables you to identify your life's goals. Keeping up with old friends, and enjoying yourself now, also balances your life.

Planning, scheduling and 'to-do' lists are mechanisms you can use to keep yourself on track, but ensure that your track is for important issues and not trivia. This will give you a sense of achievement and a feeling of control over your time.

Now, reflect on your own relationship with time and how you intend to adapt your behaviour so that you can spend your time more effectively. You may want to transfer this information to your own institution's personal development planner scheme.

ACTIVITY 9 Update your personal development planner

Having read this chapter, gauge your confidence again. How does this compare with your confidence levels at the start of the chapter? What can you do to improve? You can incorporate this into your own personal development planner. Add anything else you feel appropriate.

Grade your confidence on a scale of 1–5 where 1 = poor and 5 = good.

My time management plan	Confidence level 1–5	Plans to improve
I recognise that my relationship with time affects how I manage my time. *Section 2*		
I recognise that my life goals are as much a part of my time management as course deadlines. *Section 3*		
I know how to get the best out of my time as I know how I study best. *Section 4*		
I now know how I can manage my time effectively and can develop strategies that suit me. *Section 5*		

Date: _____

Getting extra help

At your institution:

- Consult the Careers Advisory Service or student services as they often hold key skill workshops on topics such as time management.
- Attend your institution's learning support unit (or similar) if you feel this is an issue for you.
- Check out your local Students Union as it often provides help in this area.

Books:

- Covey, S.R., Merrill, A. and Merrill, R. (1994) *First Things First: Coping with the Ever-increasing Demands of the Workplace*. London, Simon & Schuster.

A useful website:

- Mindtools, at: **www.mindtools.com** [last accessed November 2008].

Feedback on activities

ACTIVITY 1 Recognising different time perspectives in others

There are no absolute answers to this feedback. Here are some interpretations. If yours are different, it may be worth articulating your reasons.

Adrian

His time perspective is very much in the **present**, especially with respect to his social life and having a good time. From his short description, we might conclude that he is happier doing **one type of activity** at a time (his social life doesn't seem to vary much) rather than juggling a lot of different activities. His **motivation** to study appears to be **low**. His **time management skills** may be doubtful (poor).

Ismet

His time perspective is dominated by **present** and **future**. He is prepared to live now, but keeps his eye on coursework so that he doesn't fall behind. He seems to be a good organiser, and that takes some juggling. He has to do this as well as keep up with coursework, although it seems he pulls back on his social life to get some of his coursework completed. He seems to be a **multi-tasker** and quite **motivated** in his studies as well as **good at time management**.

Rachael

Her time perspective is very much in the **future** and very much at the expense of living now. She should be careful that she doesn't experience burn-out and needs to re-balance her life. She appears to be a **multi-tasker** when it comes to her studies, but the fact that she gets irritated when interrupted could mean that she prefers to focus on single aspects of her coursework – doing one piece at a time and liking to stay focused. She is **highly motivated** and probably a **good time manager** (motivated people usually manage their time better than non-motivated people).

ACTIVITY 2 Identifying your own time perspective

If you are dominated by time **perspective 1**, you are '**present oriented**'. You really focus on having a good time. For you, it is the now that counts. This is really a hedonistic perspective and we should all spend time in this perspective at some time during a week. If, however, it dominates you, you may find that you will be prone to giving up your work in favour of the addiction to seek excitement and having a good time. Being permanently in this time perspective is very unhealthy for your studies or career in the future as you succumb to temptations that appear more exciting at the time.

If you are dominated by time **perspective 4**, you are also '**present oriented**' but in a negative, fatalistic way. You feel that life is outside your control and nothing you do will change that. You have a general feeling of helplessness. Being predominantly in this time perspective zaps your motivation. You see no point in putting in the effort so your studies and future work will really suffer.

If you are dominated by **perspective 5**, you are '**past oriented**' in a positive way. Your happy memories have helped you develop a positive view of life and given you the stability to move on; we all need this. Research has shown that those in this perspective have a high sense of self-esteem (Boniwell, 2005).

If you are dominated by **perspective 2**, you are '**past oriented**' in a negative way and you may not be able to get over something that was unpleasant in your past. If that is the case, and you feel it is an issue, you may be advised to seek professional help. It is important to deal with negative experiences so they don't run your life. In terms of your studies, you may find you are not meeting your full potential. Negative past events don't have to be traumatic; getting consistently bad marks for essay writing or maths tests, for example, could be enough to determine how you deal with these now.

If you are dominated by time **perspective 3** you are '**future oriented**'. You have set out your goals and you make plans so that you can fulfil them. You seek out new challenges and opportunities where you can. Research has shown that this time perspective is associated with well-being, persistence and self-confidence (Boniwell, 2005). You can, however, be so concerned with achieving that you forget to enjoy yourself, become a workaholic, experience burn-out and forget to live in the present. You need a balance.

ACTIVITY 3 Are you a multi-tasker?

You will probably find academic life is very much a polychronic culture. More than likely your coursework assignments will be bunched towards the end of your course just when you are thinking of revising for your exams. In some cases you are finishing coursework and sitting exams in the same week. It is important to identify what your working preference is so that you can make adaptations to fit in with the actuality of study life.

If you have identified yourself as a multi-tasker then you will probably fit in well with academic structure. Be careful, however, that you give important pieces of coursework enough attention and don't leave things to the last minute.

If you have identified yourself as a linear tasker, then you need to prioritise your tasks, break them down into small tasks, create a time plan and carry out these smaller tasks in a linear way. You need to work in small chunks so you can get that piece of work finished within your schedule. This will keep you on track in a polychronic environment while you work in a linear fashion!

Multi-taskers (polychrons) prefer ...	Linear taskers (monochrons) prefer ...
time to be unstructured	structured time
not to make detailed plans	to work to detailed time plans
to work on tasks when they are in the mood	to work to their prioritised list of activities
to spread their focus and attention across lots of things	a very focused approach
to go with the flow and if they are interrupted it doesn't matter.	to work without interruption.

ACTIVITY 8 Recommending time management strategies

Jane may have sorted out her major goals and planned well, but she does not seem to be handling her 'to-do' list well. She needs to prioritise, and that includes her home life, and stick to her daily tasks. If she carries on like this, she may feel that she can't cope with her studies and leave. She must work smart and really do what is important.

Winston has problems revising for exams whereas structured assignments seem to be OK for him. He seems to be a classic procrastinator. He needs first to accept that this is what he is doing and then set himself small tasks. He should concentrate on the task at hand and not take or make phone calls during this period. He can then reward himself with a couple of hours out with his friends. He will feel good about himself and enjoy his time out a lot more.

References

■ Boniwell, L. (2005) 'Beyond time management: how the latest research on time perspectives and perceived time use can assist clients with time related concerns', *International Journal of Evidence Based Coaching and Mentoring*, 3(2), 61.

■ Covey, S. R., Merrill, A. and Merrill, R. (1994) *First Things First: Coping with the Ever-increasing Demands of the Workplace*. London, Simon & Schuster.

■ Hall, Edward, T. (1959) *The Silent Language*. New York, Garden City.

■ Innis, K. and Shaw, M. (1997) 'How do students spend their time?', *Quality Assurance in Education* 5(2), 85–89.

■ Robinson, J. P. and Godbey, G. (1997) *Time for Life: The Surprising Ways Americans Use their Time*. State College, The Pennsylvania State University Press.

■ Zimbardo, P. and Boyd, J. (1999) 'Putting time in perspective: a valid, reliable individual differences metric', *Journal of Personality and Social Psychology*, 77, 1271–1288.

4 Getting the most out of lectures

If you have to take notes in a lecture, the pace, rate of delivery and framework for presenting the information are all out of your hands. The pressure is on to think on your feet, to try to make sense of the thinking which has gone on behind the scenes in the preparation of the lecture and to be able to record information at speed – in other words, the ability to multi-task. Thus, it is vital that your listening skills and your note-making abilities are in tip-top condition to enable you to get the most out of lectures.

In this chapter you will:

1. assess your own interaction during lectures
2. explore the skills needed to get the most out of lectures
3. examine how to prepare for lectures to develop efficiency
4. develop keener listening skills.

USING THIS CHAPTER

Estimate your current levels of confidence. At the end of the chapter you will have the chance to reassess these levels where you can incorporate this into your personal development planner (PDP). Mark between 1 (poor) and 5 (good) for the following:

I know the skills needed to get the most out of lectures.	I know the different types and purposes of lectures.	I can listen effectively and differentiate the information I am listening to in lectures.

Date: _____

1 Are you a lecture sponge?

Lectures are a waste of time.

Angela, first-year student

A **sponge** learner is ready (or not so ready) to **soak up** information from tutors and lecturers. This sounds comfortable and relatively relaxing, but it is an ineffective way of learning. Did you know, for example, that if you listen to someone (e.g. a lecturer), without actively making notes or participating in some other activity, you will be doing well to remember 20% of what's been said?

There are many reasons why some students do not get as much out of lectures as they should. Often this is because they have not prepared sufficiently and have inappropriate expectations of lectures.

What do you expect to get out of a lecture?

Pitching your expectations high is one of the ways you can yield good results. If you intend to interact with the information you will receive during lectures, you need to have the right mindset (see Activity 1).

ACTIVITY 1 Am I a lecture sponge?

Answer true or false to each of the statements.

	True	False
1. The lecture (or series of lectures) should teach me all I need to know on that subject/topic.		
2. I want to go into the lecture and get all the information I need for my assignment.		
3. I should not need to take notes because the information is provided as handouts or online.		
4. I do not need to think in lectures; I just need to listen carefully.		
5. Lectures should contain pictures, video clips, etc., as well as written and oral communication.		

If you have answered 'true' to most of these statements, you will find that there is a gap between your expectations and what lectures offer. This is neither the fault of your lecturer nor of you. It is simply that the rules of the lecture game do not match what you expect. Most students want value for money from the lectures but it is important to understand the purpose of lectures as a teaching tool. This will help you to get the most out of them.

How to increase your capacity during lectures

Activity 2 explores some of the problems that students have expressed about lectures. Identify your problems and look at the solution hint so that you can go immediately to the appropriate section of this chapter.

ACTIVITY 2 What do I do in lectures?

Problem	Solution
Your expectations for the purpose of the lecture are inappropriate.	Look at the purpose of lectures so that you adjust your expectations.
You are unable to cope with the volume of information because it is **all** new to you.	You need to do some pre-lecture preparations.

Problem	Solution
You quickly go into information overload and give up taking notes.	You need to do some pre-lecture preparations to ensure that you are ready for listening and understanding the information more effectively and at greater speed. You need to sharpen up your listening and selection skills.
You do not recognise or understand some of the new terminology.	You need to do some pre-lecture preparations.
You cannot follow the gist of the lecture and seem to become muddled.	You need to have a tentative information framework upon which to hang the information. You need to do some pre-lecture preparations.
The information seems very detailed and in great depth.	You need to do some pre-lecture preparations so that you have your own framework or skeleton of information before going to the lecture.
Your questions are not answered during the lecture.	This may be the result of a misunderstanding of the lecture format. Have a look at the purpose of lectures.
You are distracted easily by other students who are talking or by rustling of paper.	Either choose where you sit very carefully (if possible) or learn how to cut out extraneous and unwanted noise. Develop more effective listening skills.
The lecturer's style may not match the way you take in information.	You need to be more aware of the way academic tutors present information so that you can choose an appropriate method to take in more information and also to get the information down more effectively. Try to increase your listening skills. Try to vary the format of the presentation of your notes.
Your lecture notes are not used later on.	Match up the purpose of the lecture, the type of lecture and your presentation format so that the notes will be helpful. Develop more effective listening skills.

2 The purpose of lectures

Lectures are not the same as seminars and group tutorials. They serve a different purpose, and consequently the anticipated outcomes for students are different. Lectures last between 40 and 50 minutes. As a teaching tool, they are intended to give information to groups of students. In some ways they are cost effective in that they can deliver information to large student cohorts. The size of the student group will depend upon the subject and the individual university. Some undergraduates are taken aback when they walk into a lecture theatre, and there are up to 500 students present. The size of the group can vary between 25 and 500.

Most departments organise a series of lectures to coincide with specific units of study. At the start of the unit, some students seem unaware of the purpose of lectures. However, this may be a case of crossed messages, and that the lecturers' intentions are not made explicit to students. For example, many lecturers do not usually expect to be interrupted by students' questions during a lecture. Some academics will tell you that they have set aside a little time at the end for questions but many will give their 'speech' and disappear. This is down to individual teaching style and delivery. However, be alert to the lecturer who sets aside time for questions. This may change your note-taking tactics during the lecture in terms of making your questions stand out in your notes as a memory jogger for later. Usually, you are expected to listen to the talk. Many lecturers use PowerPoint slides on a large screen to get across their points. Some lecturers may use an overhead projector (OHP) with transparencies (OHTs) containing information. These may be typed or handwritten. In some subjects, notably Mathematics, lecturers provide examples by writing mathematical workings at speed on a board.

There are various types of lectures, and the efficient student is aware of these types so that most use can be made of the information, format and style. This means that you may need to think on your feet quite quickly to spot the type and be flexible in your response in terms of expectations and note-taking.

Type of lecture	Purpose	Outcomes
Keynote	Keynote lecture is intended to raise issues/questions. Setting the scene and giving a broad overview.	To get you to question information and research. To inform you of the main issues.
Introductory	Introducing a series of lectures. Setting the scene and giving a broad overview.	To provide you with a framework of knowledge/ concepts upon which everything else will hinge.
Sequential	Each lecture builds upon the previous one.	An assumption of prior knowledge from previous lectures.
Focus	Takes a specific aspect of a topic and goes into detail. Provides information and detail about specific research.	To fill in or put flesh upon the framework which was provided in the introduction.
Conclusion	Sums up the key points of previous lectures. Draws all the threads together.	To give an overview which can be used in conjunction with introductory lecture notes.

The biggest problem for students is that often the lecturers do not specify which type of lecture they are delivering so you will have to think on your feet at the beginning of a lecture. Of course, you can make some judgements prior to the lecture. If you look at the unit/course handbook this will help you to work out the type of lecture you are listening to. By reading between the lines of the departmental guidance information you can decide upon the type.

Most experienced lecturers follow a logical framework for delivery. There will be a brief introduction, the main part of the lecture and summaries or conclusions. However, these components are discrete and many lecturers do not signal explicitly what is happening. However, you need to be alert to this hidden structure so that you can be prepared. For example, the introduction will help you to anticipate what is to come. Some lecturers will provide a quick overview of the structure, which will help you to be aware of when they are moving on to another section or sub-topic. It is worth making sure that you take down the summaries and conclusions so that you can use these as a check to find out if you have teased out the main points of the lecture. This alerting system will be examined in more detail in the section about listening skills.

3 What skills are involved?

Getting the most out of lectures hinges upon your ability to make connections. The efficient and effective student is able to take in and select the information, while at the same time fitting this into some internal scheme or mental jigsaw. The lecture sponge soaks up the information but does not realise that the facts and knowledge are part of a big picture and so has not developed the flexibility to fit new information into previous knowledge – so the connections are not made and the jigsaw is often incomplete. This will result in notes gathering dust in files or having to spend time trying to make sense of why you made the comments.

There are seven main skills which you need if you are to get the most out of your lectures:

- good listening skills
- concentration skills
- summary skills
- note-taking skills
- organisational skills – both on paper and in your thinking
- critical thinking skills
- multi-tasking skills – the ability to do many of the above at the same time and at speed.

Of course, lectures do not suit all types of learner. Some students' knowledge and understanding is increased by listening to someone tell them about a topic or explaining a concept. However, others do not get as much out of this oral method of getting information because it has no hooks to help them remember and process the information. Thus, you must ask yourself how you are going to bypass your preferred learning style if you rely upon visual and written note cues. Perhaps it is worth considering how you can develop greater efficiency so that lectures are a true source of information. See the sections on pre-lecture preparation and templates for taking down information – in particular the Cornell Method.

As was stated earlier, students who simply turn up for the lecture and listen for 40–50 minutes are missing opportunities. Some work in preparation for lectures is not time wasted. Similarly, reflection and consolidation after the lecture will reap benefits for revision and in helping you to obtain better grades in your coursework and examinations.

Efficient pre-lecture preparations

Spending time preparing for lectures is time well spent and will ensure that you learn more when you go to the lecture and that your note-taking is more effective and meaningful.

Your preparation will pay off because you will be able to recognise and begin to understand new terminology and ideas. This means that you know which key words to listen out for. This will help you to **focus your listening skills** so that you can take better notes. You will, therefore, be able to listen for the clues which are in the lecture to help you make sense of new information and concepts.

There are many sources of information which you can use to help you prepare effectively to get the most out of your lectures:

Source	How to make use of it
Course handbook	
Unit/session overviews	To give you an overview. To give you an idea of what to expect. To inform you of the purpose of specified lectures.
Lecture series titles	To help you to start building that framework or jigsaw of information.
Lecture titles	To enable you to make the connections and links.
Unit glossaries	To help prepare you for new terminology. To improve your listening skills – you know what to listen for. To help you to understand new concepts.
Indicative reading lists	Get hold of some of these and look at the sub-headings in chapters to get a sense of a new topic and to help you to develop your own internal map or jigsaw picture. See if there are any definitions of new terminology so that you are prepared for your lecture.

▶

Source	How to make use of it
Online information	
Department site	Check electronic information which is available. This may be in the form of PowerPoint notes or information sheets. Read this information in advance of the lecture to put you in the right frame of mind and to prepare you for key concepts and ideas.
Internet searches	Download background information to help you understand what the lecturer is getting at.
Library site	Check the subject section to find out what your subject librarian has loaded up for different courses/units.
Yourself	
	Make a list of questions which spring to mind about the topic. See if you can get the answers in the lecture. (If not, at least this is a checklist of things you need to find out.) Get your file/notes organised in advance to save time on the day. Anticipate some sub-headings for your notes.

Making effective use of pre-lecture notes and downloads

In the long term, pre-lecture preparations will help you to understand new concepts and ensure that you are ready to take in new terminology because you have had to engage with the information and have had to think about it. Think about athletes. They always perform warm-up activities to ensure that their muscles are flexed beforehand and to ensure that performance is high. Pre-lecture preparations have the same main purposes and act as a warm-up for the brain or to get you into the right frame of mind to absorb the lecturer's information more efficiently and effectively. The hidden side effects are explained in the following table.

Pre-lecture activity with collected or downloaded information	Purpose/use
You can go through the lecture notes carefully and highlight with a coloured marker pen important information.	This will increase your understanding. This will improve your memory skills. This will help you to retrieve the information later because crucial information stands out and provides a quick-access short cut for the brain.
You can also annotate those notes – make your own comments or questions in the margin.	This will increase your understanding. This will improve your memory skills.
You can highlight key terminology (and put a definition of meaning alongside if necessary).	By putting the definition in your own words, this will increase your understanding and memory – much more so than if you simply copy out someone else's definition.
You can scan the lecture notes into your your computer.	You can customise the layout so that you can make your own additional notes during the lecture alongside the lecturer's notes. (Some students prefer to customise printed lecture notes by double spacing for ease of access; or make space for your own notes parallel to the lecturer's notes.) Once again, reading and making decisions about what to do with the layout will provide valuable reinforcement.
You can scan the notes into your computer and make up your own concept map.	This is useful for those who prefer to have information in this alternative format rather than the traditional linear format. Making yourself do this activity can help you to develop your own map of the information.

Cautionary tale

I haven't got the time to do all this before each lecture. It's bad enough having to keep up with everything as it is.

Sharon, first-year History student

It is short-sighted to think that there is not enough time to do this type of pre-lecture preparation. It will save you time in the long run because you will get more out of the lecture in terms of your understanding; your notes will be of a better quality; and this in turn will boost your chances of doing a better assignment or remembering information for examinations. It boils down to ensuring that you organise your time as effectively as you can and add this element into your weekly schedules. Try out some of these activities over a semester and reflect upon your grasp of the topic and your ability to cope with the process of writing an assignment.

Supposing I did all of this beforehand. What would be the point in actually going to the lecture?

Jim, second-year English Studies student

Jim is not the only student who has made this comment. However, the point he is missing is that during lectures, tone of voice, emphasis and other body language will strengthen your understanding. Remember: some lecturers try to provoke thought by their tone of voice, and this does not come across in the impersonal notes. You can't get all of this from the two-dimensional downloads and information on screen. It is true that some lecturers are more memorable in their delivery than others but this human interface may spark off discussions with your friends, and you will not be able to participate in this further dimension to the purpose of lectures – to generate discussion and questions.

Post-lecture activities: what to do with the information after lectures

What do **you** do with your lecture notes after the lecture? Many students toss the notes into a file, often in a haphazard way. Some have a number of file pads which are used randomly for various lectures, and the notes are left there for filing at a later date. But what happens when you drop your bag, and the notes are scattered everywhere?

If your notes are of real value, you will need to do some work on them as soon after the lecture as you possibly can – while the information is still fresh in your mind. Your notes will be vital for assignment and examination success, so why not spend some valuable time in reviewing, consolidating, tidying up the loose ends and reflecting?

- The organisation of your filing system is personal but the system has to be maintained and each set of lecture notes needs to be carefully filed away into your system.
- Take time to read through your own notes to make sure they make sense to you. You may have to write in full some of the abbreviations you were forced to use in the lecture because of the speed of the lecturer's delivery. Tackling this soon after you have taken the notes means that you can draw upon recent memory of what the lecturer said to improve your notes and make them more understandable.
- Highlight key words and phrases so that they will stand out when you come back to the notes at a later date.
- If you have not had time to do sub-headings, read through a section and put a succinct title to it. Check your sub-heading titles and consider whether you need to change these so that the notes have greater cohesion and you will be able to recognise immediately the framework of the information at a later date when your memory of the lecture has faded.
- Write the key concepts in a different colour in the margin next to important information. This is termed annotating your notes.
- A4 Summary Sheet – if you can discipline yourself to do this, you will reap greater benefits. This is a bullet-point summary of the information and key points. By doing this, you will have to review, reflect and consolidate the knowledge and information and most importantly you will have to put it into your own words. This can be placed at the

beginning or the end of each notes section so that you can get a quick reference to what is contained in the notes to help you decide whether you need the information for an assignment at a later date. These Summary Sheets are also useful for revision purposes.

4 Lecture alerts: behind the scenes

Obviously, lecturers have their own style of delivery and quirky ways. However, there are some features that you might like to look out for in order to alert you to possible outcomes which could affect your concentration and selection of information.

Body language cues	Alert
Speaks very quickly	Need to have good listening skills. Look out for key words/information. It may simply be a sign of nervousness.
Speaks very softly at the beginning of the lecture	This may be used as a ploy to get students' attention and to calm down the 'audience'. If used for this purpose what is said at this point may not be vital.
Reads from notes	This type of lecture places greater pressure on your concentration skills because it can often be delivered in a monotone. The lecturer may be nervous or unsure of the information and needs to rely heavily on notes.
Says some things very slowly	This is a verbal method of underlining and putting information in bold. It is likely that the information is important so you need to record it in your notes.
Repeats phrases and sentences	It could be that the lecturer has lost his or her place in his or her notes! More often it is a way of emphasising important information so you need to record it in your notes.
Pauses occasionally	You have to decide if this is an individual/stylistic feature or not. It could be that the lecturer has lost his or her place in his or her notes! It may be a ploy to make a point that some students are talking during the lecture. It may be the lecturer's way of emphasising important information so you need to record it in your notes.
Turns to screen to go through slide information (be it OHT or PowerPoint)	This is the sign of an inexperienced lecturer. Sound levels will naturally drop so you need to be listening carefully.

▶

Body language cues	Alert
Paces up and down in front of 'audience'	This type of style of lecturing is often accompanied by lack of use of notes. The lecturer knows his or her stuff! It can be distracting for some students, so you must ensure that your concentration levels are high.
Use of rhetorical questions	You are not expected to answer these either by shouting out the answer or by raising your hand. They are used to get students to be critical or to demonstrate the current debates and issues. The lecturer then proceeds to answer his or her own questions. At times they are a device to vary the delivery so that students do not fall asleep in lectures!

Environmental features	Alert
PowerPoint slides	Where are the notes? Are hard copies available in the room? Was I expected to download them myself prior to the lecture?
PowerPoint slide usage	(i) As information handouts only (usually six slides per A4 page) to start off your notes. (ii) As an aide-memoire for note-taking (usually three or four slides per A4 page with lines for you to personalise the information). (iii) Some slides are for information only and are not talked about by the lecturer; others are brought up on screen and additional information is given. If a lecturer uses this style, you must be alert and concentrate so that you do not lose your place!
Overhead transparencies (OHTs)	This is an alternative to PowerPoint. It probably means that there is no electronic version available for download. Each slide contains succinct information which you are expected to record in some way.
Writes information on board	You need to take down this information because it may not be contained in any other source of notes.

An awareness of these features will ensure that you get even more out of your lectures.

5 Template for note-taking

Taking notes in lectures does rely upon the expertise of the lecturer. Style of delivery and expertise varies, and this can have an impact upon your ability to keep up with the notes but more importantly the need to be flexible. This applies to all formats of note-taking.

Your note-taking should ensure that you leave spaces for the lecture's afterthoughts and revisitings. Lecturers are only human and at times suddenly remember information that should have gone with an earlier section. At other times, lecturers can be imparting information from their notes and at the end of a section they want to bring you up-to-date information which they have just read about. This information has to be tacked on and you would need to try to place it in the appropriate section of your notes. If you have left no room, you should ensure that you link the information by arrows or colour coding when you are involved in the post-lecture activities.

On the other hand, one of the problems with making a note of what the lecturer has said in a linear manner is that there is less room for flexibility. A template for lecture notes could solve your problems.

The Cornell Method

This is a method which was developed over 40 years ago by Walter Pauk to help his students at Cornell University (Pauk, 2000). It was intended to increase efficiency and originally consisted of six stages. It was his intention that students:

- record information from lectures
- reduce their notes
- recite the information to aid recall and memory
- reflect
- review the information to make sure they understand it
- recapitulate and make a summary.

The following table shows how you could organise your note-taking, the Cornell way. As you can see, it is a template which could be prepared beforehand, using your word processor. Section A provides vital information to help you to identify your notes at a later stage. Section B is the space where you write your information during the lecture while Section C will allow you to reflect upon what you have learnt during the lecture and give you space to write up distilled and useful information. This could be essential for use in gathering information for your essay or as a start to producing effective revision notes. Of course, the active student will come away from the lecture with some questions unanswered and Section D will provide space for you to summarise the lecture to get a global or overview picture.

A. Lecture title:	Date:	Lecturer's name:	Page number:

B. Space for information taken down **during** lecture	C. Additional notes in post-lecture phase: key words; key concepts; key theorists/names. Additional information which you have remembered from the lecturer's talk which you didn't have time to record in the lecture.

D. Follow-up:
Questions you might have
Commentary

Uses

Its main advantage is that it is possible to cut down on redoing notes. Again, you have to be well prepared in advance for this way of taking notes. However, once you have got into the routine of preparing your pages in this way, you will quickly adapt and the lecture work space (B) will not seem restricted or limited. It will also provide you with more usable notes for revision. Similarly, if you are searching through your files for information to put into your essays, you need only glance at the summary section to find out if there is anything worth using.

6 Using a laptop during lectures

Electronic notes are now part of a student's life. Writing electronic notes during lectures is down to personal preference but also to the facilities which are available in your college or university. If you have a laptop computer with wireless connections you will have access to many facilities. However, not all lecture rooms are set up in this way at the moment. To help you to decide whether electronic notes are viable for you, consider Activity 3.

ACTIVITY 3 Should I use a laptop in lectures?

Which of the following statements apply to you? Answer true or false.

	True	False
1. I prefer not to work straight onto screen.		
2. I do not feel confident working on a computer under pressure.		

	True	False
3. My keyboard skills are slow.		
4. I am not sure about basic functions of my word processor.		
5. I do not like to read information straight from the screen.		
6. I feel embarrassed using a computer in front of other people.		
7. I am worried that I might press the wrong keys and wipe all my lecture notes.		

If your answers are mainly true, you really ought to consider whether you are ready or really want to make electronic notes during lectures and seminars. You need sophisticated skills of listening, summarising and multi-tasking when coping with lectures. Making electronic notes adds another dimension to this complexity. You need to ask yourself whether using an electronic format during the lecture is the right approach for you. The crucial questions you have to ask yourself are:

- Do I have the necessary skills?
- Is this way of note-taking going to support me or be a barrier to my learning?
- Do I want to take notes in this way?

Of course, if the answer to the final question is 'no', then you will eliminate this mode of 'writing'. However, you need to make sure that in the long term you are not closing doors for more efficient ways of working both at university and beyond.

You need to have a good **speed of typing** if you are going to stand a chance of keeping up in lectures. This may seem a trite remark but spending some time in a vacation or before you embark upon your course learning how to touch-type or improving your typing speed will be time well spent. The old adage 'practice makes perfect' has never been more true than in these circumstances. The more time you set aside to practise your skills, the quicker you will become. The best case scenario is that you are able to **touch-type**. This means that you can look at the slides and still type in your information. Being at this level of expertise also implies that you will not be slowed down looking for a specific key. If this happens, the lecturer will be three sentences ahead of you, and you will be constantly chasing your tail. Touch-typing does not imply that you use both hands – though this is better. Many students can type at speed only using two fingers on each hand. You need to ensure that your typing speeds and your knowledge of the word processing program are automatic so that you are not slowed down grappling with the technology!

Reviewing and consolidating your notes is easier on computer, and the final product will be clearer to read at a later date. However, a small amount of forethought can reap excellent rewards when you are under pressure to find information for an essay, for example. Thus, setting up a template on your laptop can be done in advance so that you can move around the document, placing the lecturer's information in its appropriate box or section.

7 Critical listening: ways to increase your listening skills

Listening to a lecture requires skills which you may need to practise in order to increase your efficiency. The student who develops **active listening** skills is the one who will understand and deal with new and challenging information more effectively and will also be able to remember the information for longer periods of time before having to rehearse the information in some way (see the section on exams in Chapter 8).

Baseline skills

These are:

- concentration
- anticipation
- questioning
- selection/elimination
- analysing
- summarising.

If you are questioning, selecting and summarising spoken information, you will be actively involved in the lecture. The result will be higher levels of **concentration** because you are being critical – not in the sense of negatively criticising your lecturer's voice or clothes but, more importantly, critical of what is being said. You can improve your concentration skills. It is all very well to be told not to daydream during lectures. It is natural for the mind to wander but you must make sure that you keep yourself in check. Prompting yourself with questions is a way of keeping your mind on the job in hand. Thus, if you think you are getting bored, instead of doodling, start analysing the information you are listening to.

Mental joggers – asking the right questions

These are:

- Why has the information been included?
- How does it link with the rest of the information?
- Is it essential or exemplar information?
- Is this a new section?
- Does what the lecturer is saying fit in with what you have already read or is it controversial?
- What point is the lecturer trying to make?

In addition to concentration, a vital skill to use is that of anticipation because it will set off your own questions, make you listen for the answers you need, and in this process you will be selecting information and tagging some parts of the lecture as being of higher priority than other parts (selection and elimination).

What to anticipate/what to listen out for	What is its use?
Introductory statements	May indicate an overview of the lecture structure so that you can be ready to organise your sub-headings and branches of information.
Signal language	This could get you ready for lists, for example. For more specific examples see below.
Summaries/conclusions	These will help you to develop a framework of information. They can be used as a checklist when you review your notes to make sure you didn't miss anything out. They can deepen your understanding.

8 How to hone your listening skills: we hear what we want to hear

The warm-up

You can double your listening capacity by doing the pre-lecture activities. These activities will make you aware of **key terminology** and give you a broad framework of information so that you go into a lecture with some hooks upon which to put the new and sometimes challenging information. Although these activities will increase your ability to make sense of new concepts and ideas, you need to do something slightly different to ensure that you prepare yourself for **hearing the information**.

- Pick out and list key terms, terms with which you are unfamiliar and terminology which seems to be used in a very specific way in the subject. (You will be aware of this because your understanding of the meaning of the word does not make sense in the specialist texts.)
- Check your understanding by defining the terms in your own words. Then, cross-check in a subject glossary to find out if you got them right.
- Say the words aloud or, better still, record them onto a disk and listen to them. This way you will be prepared for hearing the terms, and your brain will not have to slow down to process the information when you are in the lecture.
- If you are working electronically, you can enlist the help of your computer if you have appropriate software. You can type in your list (or cut and paste if you are working from departmental, electronic information), and get the computer to speak the words to you so that you hear them. Voice recognition software such as Text Help has this facility and will even let you decide whether you want to hear a male or female voice!

Now you are in a better position to listen out for the key words in the lecture because your mind has heard them and is looking out for them (Activity 4).

ACTIVITY 4 Listening for key words

Here is the script of part of a lecture. Get a friend to read the text to you or scan the text into your computer and get your computer to read the information to you and see if you can pick out the key words.

The topic of the talk is 'The Dangers of the Sun'.

This is a general talk by the Health Services and is open to all and any students.

Jot down what you would anticipate you will hear about this topic:
1.
2.
3.
4.

You will find answers at the end of the chapter.

Now jot down the key words/terminology which you would anticipate:
1.
2.
3.
4.
5.
6.

You will find answers at the end of the chapter.

Text extract: 'The Dangers of the Sun'

Pick out the key words and points while you listen to this extract:

For many years dermatologists have warned the public about the dangers of staying in the sun without protection. Exposure to the sun can have dramatic results, apart from the treasured tanned skin. There are three points which I wish to bring to your attention in this talk. Firstly, the sun can damage the layers of the skin. The outer layer can change its appearance. The texture can become leathery with a loss of elasticity. This can result in premature ageing of the skin, causing wrinkles and brown blotches. Secondly, over-exposure can result in skin cancer. The brown blotches may be the outer indicator of cancer. They appear as moles on the skin. Next, extreme exposure to the sun increases the possibility of breaking down our natural protection from the sun's radiation. The effects of UVA and UVB are becoming more well known. Tanning shops promise their customers that they can provide 'safe' tanning. They try to convince us that UVA is a lower level of radiation and therefore less harmful. This is not true! In fact, UVA has been proved responsible for damaging the deeper layers of the skin which destroy structural proteins and thus harming the immune systems ...

Check your notes with the answers at the end of the chapter to see if you picked out the main key words and points.

Listening for main points/ideas

This exercise will help you to improve your skills of selection and elimination. The task is best tackled as a listening exercise so get a friend to read the text to you or scan the text into your computer and get your computer to read the information to you and see if you can pick out the main points.

Text extract: 'Is a bulky diet of eucalyptus leaves the best option for the tiny Koala?'

Should Koalas change their diet? Are eucalyptus leaves a sensible choice in the changing environment? Is the Koalas' diet appropriate for the modern world? All these questions and more have been asked by biologists in their study of this diminutive and appealing little animal.

▶

The diet of the Koala is limited almost entirely to eating eucalyptus leaves. Environmental issues and the decrease in natural habitats apart, there are drawbacks and advantages to such a restricted diet. The size of the Koalas' digestive system, their metabolic structures and chemical make-up of eucalyptus leaves combine to provide a fascinating forum for discussion.

The dichotomy lies in the leaves and the digestive system. On the one hand the leaves are rich in fibre but contain high levels of lignin. Fibre is not conducive to digestion, and lignin, a woody material found in the cell walls of many plants, is indigestible. So why does the Koala have such a voracious appetite for this source of fuel? Another drawback is that the ratio of an animal's gut volume to its energy needs is dependent upon animal mass. Thus, this tiny creature does not have the capacity and its metabolic system has difficulty coping. The quality of the food is poor so this means that large quantities are needed in order to extract sufficient nutrients. So how does it manage to digest and process poor-quality food for its metabolic needs?

It would appear that the Koala has adapted its digestive system to cope with its roughage-laden diet. Scientists in New South Wales conducted a study in the early 1980s and uncovered three major factors.

Firstly, the Koala can regulate the passage of food through its system, like a rabbit. In this way it has developed a system which discriminates between different sized particles so that the smaller, more easily digested ones can be digested first while the coarser, indigestible matter is expelled almost immediately. This space-saving exercise allows the Koala to increase the rate at which the 'good' material can be put into the system.

Secondly, the Koala is a relatively slow-moving animal compared with others of a similar size so it is able to reduce the fuel it needs. It can be compared with the slow-moving, three-toed sloth.

Finally, eucalyptus leaves have hidden fuels. Although the woody, indigestible lignin is present, there is also a wealth of lipids and phenols which are rich sources of energy. However, the Koala's system cannot cope with phenols so these are excreted, leaving the lipids which provide useful carbohydrate energy in the form of starch and sugar.

So what seems an improbable system has been adapted to take account of animal size, metabolic rates and energy-saving adaptations.

See if you have picked out the main points in the answers at the end of the chapter.

Verbal cues and signals

Your listening skills can be greatly improved if you know what triggers to listen for and the significance of these signals.

Signal	What to expect
Start with	This may be signalling the introduction which will give overviews.
Lecture is divided into ...	Tells you the structure.
However, on the other hand, but, conversely, on the contrary, despite	These signal contrasting or opposing information and evidence.
In addition, in other words, put another way, also, as I said previously	These signal repetition of information or provides you with another definition or explanation.
For example, that is to say, furthermore, another example, such as	These alert you to the fact that what follows will be examples of a main point.
Especially, specifically, most importantly, I cannot stress enough	Lecturers will use these to signal emphasis so listen very carefully because they obviously think the information is vital/important.
Firstly, secondly (etc.), next, then, penultimate (last but one), ultimate, finally, in conclusion	Be ready for a number of points or lists.
Therefore, thus, because, consequently, accordingly, if ... then, as a result of this	Cause and effect.
I'll expand on this later ... I'll give you more detail about this later in the lecture ... I'll take this point up later ...	These mean that you must be on the alert to link up later information with this earlier point. You might even leave space in your notes to accommodate this.
In conclusion, let me summarise, let's recap, in short/in brief, to wrap up, the main points covered were ...	These are useful because they will help you to get the global/big picture because the lecturer has summarised the information for you.

The significance of knowing about these signals when you are listening to someone speak is that you are expecting and anticipating certain types of information to follow. This will aid your understanding and speed up your processing of the information so that ultimately your notes will be of a better quality.

Thus, by a more focused and active approach to your listening, you will be able to make more effective notes and overcome the problem of forgetting what you have heard.

9 Recording lectures

This section explores the use of electrical and electronic devices to record and store information from lectures and seminars. Before you rush off and buy some gizmo, you need to consider its uses, the advantages and disadvantages of different devices and likely academic tutors' attitudes and responses to usage (see Activity 5).

Activity 5 Recording lectures: myth or reality?

Look at the following comments made by students and decide whether you think they are true or false.

Statements made by students If I use some sort of recording device ...	True	False
It will take all the hard work out of lectures.		
It will save me time.		
It will mean I do not have to do anything.		
It will help me remember information.		
It will ensure that I understand my lectures.		
I can sell the information to other students who didn't make the lecture.		

To find out if you are correct, look at the answers at the end of the chapter. The implications for these statements are discussed in this section. Some students have been encouraged at school and sixth-form college to use dictaphone-type devices. They may have been useful and appropriate at that stage of study but you need to consider your academic demands now, and whether this type of method of recording is most suitable and appropriate to your individual needs.

Devices

There is a baffling array of gadgets available on the market. Which one you choose largely depends upon what you want to use it for:

- tape recorders
- mini-disk recorders
- mobile telephones
- PDAs (Personal Digital Assistants).

The pros and cons of these gadgets are discussed in the table below.

Device	Pros	Cons	Additional features worth considering
Tape recorders	Cheap to buy. Small and portable. Tape cassettes are inexpensive.	Not very versatile. Information on tape is not easily transferred to other systems. A one-hour lecture takes an expert two hours to transcribe. Sound quality is variable and can be dependent upon where you are sitting in relation to the lecturer.	Variable speed playback enables you to slow down playback so that you can take in information more effectively. There are different sizes of tape cassettes. If you intend to share with others you need to consider compatibility. Is there an advanced facility to 'mark' information while someone is speaking? It aids retrieval later.
Mini-disk recorders	Sound quality on play-back is excellent and not reliant upon sitting at the front for best results. Fairly cheap to buy. Small and portable. Mini-disks are fairly inexpensive. Mini-disk capacity is larger than tape cassette. Navigation is easier – therefore searching for specific information is quicker and less time consuming. Can be used for other purposes, e.g. recording music.	Attractive gadget and therefore stealable. A one-hour lecture takes an expert two hours to transcribe.	Variable speed playback option enables you to slow down playback so that you can take in information more effectively.
Solid-state recorders	Record information onto RAM chips or cards. Easier transfer of information from one system to another. Recording time is longer than both the above. Small and portable.	A one-hour lecture takes an expert two hours to transcribe.	
Mobile telephones	You probably already have one so no additional cost.	Recording space is limited. Only use in emergencies.	Check the memory capacity. Is there an option to plug in memory cards to boost facilities?
PDAs	Small and portable. Voice memo is available on more expensive models.	Expensive if you get one with the options you need for this type of activity. Limited capacity for recording speech. Need to be well organised and to back up information regularly onto another, more permanent system. Attractive gadget and therefore stealable.	Look for MP3 facility to enable you to listen to text.

A final consideration: some machines can record information in a way that is compatible with speech recognition software on your computer. However, your machine has to be set up to recognise the voice before it will download and transcribe recorded speech. This may seem like an excellent solution but the practicalities are such that **all** of your lecturers would have to take time out of their busy schedules to go through the voice recognition programme. However, if you have one lecturer for a lot of your time, it might be worth considering. But be ready for your lecturer to refuse, stating time pressures etc.

Recording protocols

If you wish to record the lectures in some way, apart from cost, utility and meeting your needs, you must also bear in mind other factors. It is important that you get **permission** to use your machine. This means that you might need to email lecturers before the start of their unit to ask for permission. It is also worth briefly reassuring your lecturer about the purpose to which you intend to put the recordings. Some students explain that they are auditory learners and take in information more readily if they hear it while reading handouts and notes. It might be that you need to request a temporary use of a recorder because you have broken the hand/arm with which you write. Many lecturers are uneasy about students recording their lectures. Some are openly hostile. You need to be aware of this so that you are not frustrated or upset by responses to your request. The reasons some lecturers do not want you to record their lectures often relate to copyright of intellectual property or the fact that they can no longer control how their information is used.

'What are they going to do with this information?' is a question frequently asked by lecturers. Some academic tutors are wary of giving permission because a lecture may contain off-the-cuff comments and responses which the lecturer would not want to be used for future purposes. It may be a reflection of the litigious society in which we live that lecturers are on their guard concerning recording of lectures because of the notion of 'evidence which could be used etc.'. That is not to say that this is commendable, but it is certainly understandable.

If you seek permission at the beginning of a unit, this usually means that you do not have to make the request at each lecture. Of course, if there is a stand-in lecturer, it is only polite to inform him or her that you have been given permission to record the lecture.

At university you will be expected to cope with the recording and the machine so that it does not interfere with the smooth running of the lecture. Academic tutors do not expect to be given the machine so that they can turn the recording on and off. This may have been the system at school but it is different in Higher Education settings. You will need to think about the ethics of selling your recordings to other students.

Summary of this chapter

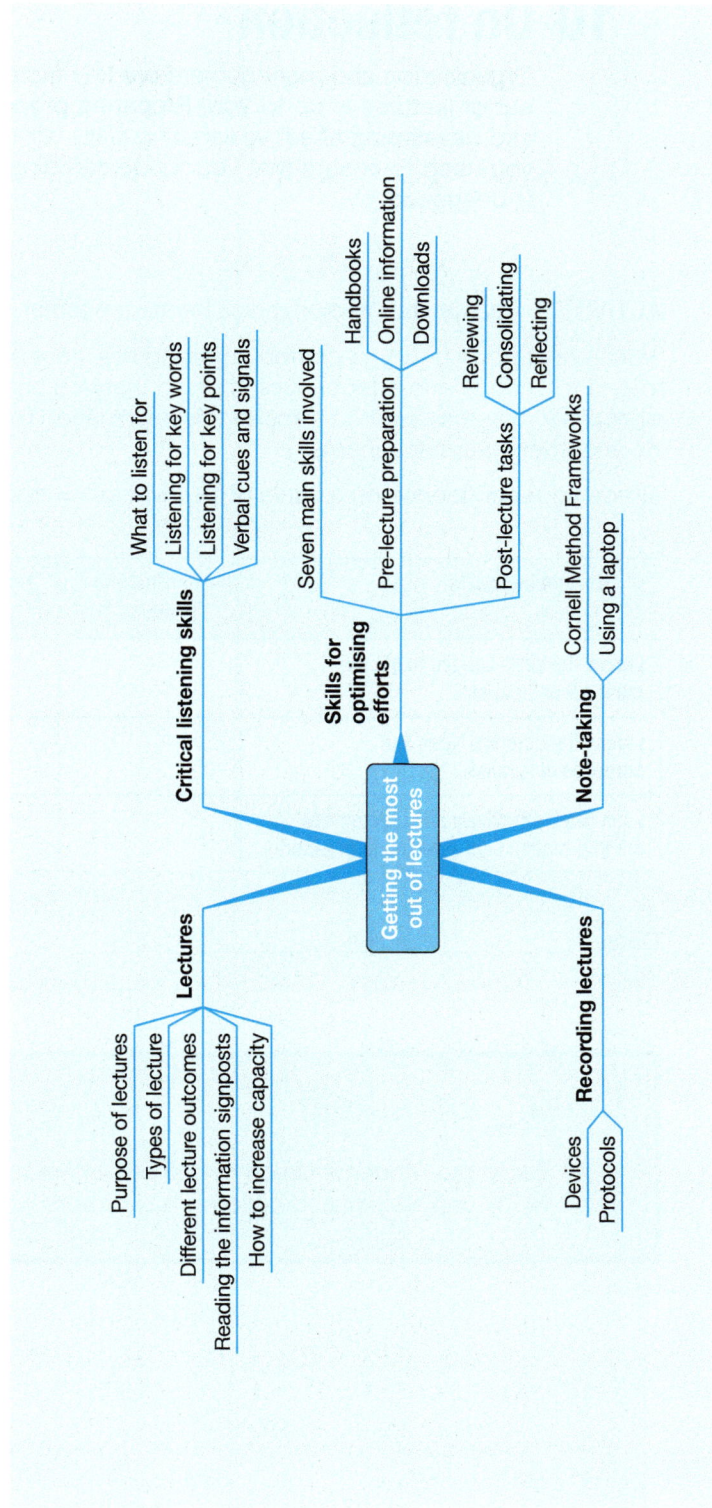

10 On reflection

Organisation and management are key factors to success. Getting the most out of lectures is up to you. Preparing properly, organising your note-taking and developing effective listening skills will help you to gain the added value you need to ensure that your understanding and knowledge of your subject is deepened.

ACTIVITY 6 Update your personal development planner

Now reflect upon how you go about getting the most out of lectures and how you intend to change and adapt your habits so that you can spend your time more effectively. You may want to transfer this information to your own institution's personal development planner scheme.

Grade your confidence on a scale of 1–5 where 1 = poor and 5 = good.

My developing skills	Confidence level: 1– 5	Plans to improve
I know the skills needed to get the most out of lectures.		
I know the different types and purposes of lectures.		
I can listen effectively and differentiate the information I am listening to in lectures.		

Date: _____

Getting extra help

Go to the Students Union to find out where to go for skill development. Many universities and colleges have tutors who provide this service.

Feedback on activities

ACTIVITY 4 Listening for key words

The talk: 'The Dangers of the Sun'

Jot down what you would anticipate you will hear about this topic:
1. Problems of over-exposure
2. Skin protection and radiation
3. Skin cancer
4. Ageing process

Now jot down the key words/terminology which you would anticipate:
1. Skin cancer
2. UVA/UVB
3. Dermatologist
4. Skin layers
5. Over-exposure
6. Cancerous moles

Sample notes

Dermatologists warned about the dangers of over-exposure without protection.

1. Sun damages layers of the skin, changing appearance:
   - (a) texture – leathery with a loss of elasticity
   - (b) result – premature ageing of the skin, causing wrinkles and brown blotches.

2. Secondly, over-exposure – skin cancer:
   - (a) brown blotches indicator of cancer
   - (b) appear as moles.

3. Extreme exposure – skin's natural protection from the sun's radiation destroyed:
   - (a) effects of UVA and UVB more well known
   - (b) tanning shops – UVA is a lower level of radiation and therefore less harmful (not true!)
     - (i) UVA responsible for damaging the deeper layers of the skin
     - (ii) structural proteins destroyed
     - (iii) immune systems damaged.

Text extract: 'Is a bulky diet of eucalyptus leaves the best option for the tiny Koala?'

Should Koalas change their diet? Are eucalyptus leaves a sensible choice in the changing environment? Is the Koalas' diet appropriate for the modern world? All these questions and more have been asked by biologists in their study of this diminutive and appealing little animal.

Koala diet: limited – eucalyptus leaves
+ & – to restricted diet.

The size of the Koalas' digestive system, their metabolic structures and chemical make-up of eucalyptus leaves combine to provide a fascinating forum for discussion.

Leaves and the digestive system

Leaves
- rich in fibre
- fibre not easily digested by Koalas
- but high levels of indigestible, woody lignin.

Digestive system
- gut volume to energy needed = animal mass
- Koala capacity = small
- eucalyptus nutrients poor so large quantity needed.

System adaptations

1. Koala can regulate food in system:
   (a) differentiates types of food
   (b) expels coarser indigestible matter
   (c) left with smaller, more easily digested particles.

2. Cut down on energy requirements:
   (a) slow moving
   (b) needs less energy
   (c) unlike other small animals
   (d) like three-toed sloth.

3. Koala extracts energy fuel carbohydrate from eucalyptus:
   (a) lipids – rich source of energy
   (b) expels phenols
   (c) gets starch and sugar for energy.

Reference

- Pauk, W. (2000) *How to Study in College*, 7th edn. New York, Houghton Mifflin.

1

Introduction: Themes in the Study of Life

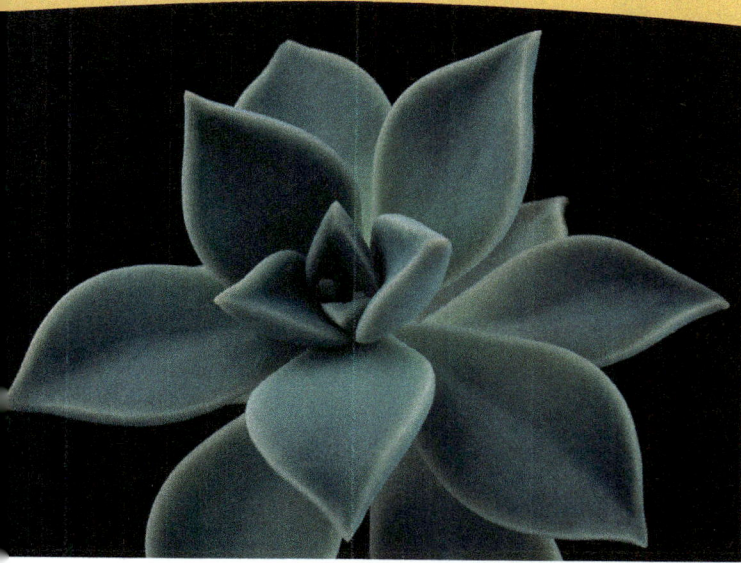

▲ **Figure 1.1 How is the mother-of-pearl plant adapted to its environment?**

OVERVIEW

Inquiring About Life

The mother-of-pearl plant, or ghost plant (**Figure 1.1**), is native to a single mountain in northeastern Mexico. Its fleshy, succulent leaves and other features allow this plant to store and conserve water. Even when rain falls, the plant's access to water is limited because it grows in crevices

of vertical rock walls, where little soil is present to hold rainwater (**Figure 1.2**). The plant's water-conserving characteristics help it survive and thrive in these nooks and crannies. Similar features are found in many plants that live in dry environments, allowing them to eke out a living where rain is unpredictable.

An organism's adaptations to its environment, such as adaptations for conserving water, are the result of **evolution**, the process of change that has transformed life on Earth from its earliest beginnings to the diversity of organisms living today. Evolution is the fundamental organizing principle of biology and the core theme of this book.

Although biologists know a great deal about life on Earth, many mysteries remain. For instance, what exactly led to the origin of flowering among plants such as the one pictured here? Posing questions about the living world and seeking science-based answers—scientific inquiry—are the central activities of **biology**, the scientific study of life. Biologists' questions can be ambitious. They may ask how a single tiny cell becomes a tree or a dog, how the human mind works, or how the different forms of life in a forest interact. Most people wonder about the organisms living around them, and many interesting questions probably occur to you when you are out-of-doors, surrounded by the natural world. When they do, you are already thinking like a biologist. More than anything else, biology is a quest, an ongoing inquiry about the nature of life.

What is life? Even a small child realizes that a dog or a plant is alive, while a rock or a lawn mower is not. Yet the phenomenon we call life defies a simple, one-sentence definition. We recognize life by what living things do. **Figure 1.3**, on the next page, highlights some of the properties and processes we associate with life.

While limited to a handful of images, Figure 1.3 reminds us that the living world is wondrously varied. How do biologists

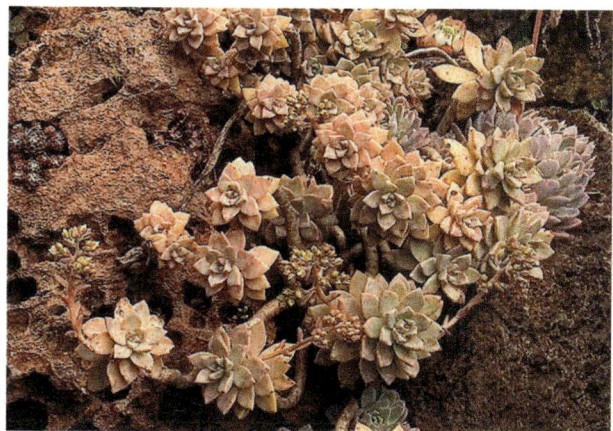

▲ **Figure 1.2 The mother-of-pearl plant (*Graptopetalum paraguayense*).** This plant's thick leaves hold water, enabling it to live where soil is scarce. The leaves vary in color, as seen here.

▼ **Order.** This close-up of a sunflower illustrates the highly ordered structure that characterizes life.

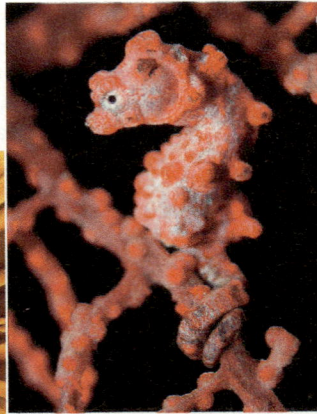

▲ **Response to the environment.** This Venus flytrap closed its trap rapidly in response to the environmental stimulus of a damselfly landing on the open trap.

▲ **Evolutionary adaptation.** The appearance of this pygmy sea horse camouflages the animal in its environment. Such adaptations evolve over many generations by the reproductive success of those individuals with heritable traits that are best suited to their environments.

▶ **Reproduction.** Organisms (living things) reproduce their own kind. Here, a baby giraffe stands close to its mother.

▲ **Regulation.** The regulation of blood flow through the blood vessels of this jackrabbit's ears helps maintain a constant body temperature by adjusting heat exchange with the surrounding air.

▲ **Energy processing.** This hummingbird obtains fuel in the form of nectar from flowers. The hummingbird will use chemical energy stored in its food to power flight and other work.

◀ **Growth and development.** Inherited information carried by genes controls the pattern of growth and development of organisms, such as this Nile crocodile.

▲ **Figure 1.3 Some properties of life.**

make sense of this diversity and complexity? This opening chapter sets up a framework for answering this question. The first part of the chapter provides a panoramic view of the biological "landscape," organized around some unifying themes. We then focus on biology's core theme, evolution, with an introduction to the reasoning that led Charles Darwin to his explanatory theory. Next, we look at scientific inquiry—how scientists raise and attempt to answer questions about the natural world. Finally, we address the culture of science and its effects on society.

CONCEPT **1.1**

The themes of this book make connections across different areas of biology

Biology is a subject of enormous scope, and news reports reveal exciting new biological discoveries being made every day. Simply memorizing the factual details of this huge subject is most likely not the best way to develop a coherent view of life. A better approach is to take a more active role by connecting the many things you learn to a set of themes that pervade all of biology. Focusing on a few big ideas—ways of thinking about life that will still hold true decades from now—will help you organize and make sense of all the information you'll encounter as you study biology. To help you, we have selected eight unifying themes to serve as touchstones as you proceed through this book.

Theme: New Properties Emerge at Each Level in the Biological Hierarchy

The study of life extends from the microscopic scale of the molecules and cells that make up organisms to the global scale of the entire living planet. We can divide this enormous range into different levels of biological organization.

Imagine zooming in from space to take a closer and closer look at life on Earth. It is spring in Ontario, Canada, and our destination is a local forest, where we will eventually explore a maple leaf right down to the molecular level. **Figure 1.4**, on the next two pages, narrates this journey into life, with the numbers leading you through the levels of biological organization illustrated by the photographs.

Emergent Properties

If we now zoom back out from the molecular level in Figure 1.4, we can see that novel properties emerge at each step, properties that are not present at the preceding level. These **emergent properties** are due to the arrangement and interactions of parts as complexity increases. For example, although photosynthesis occurs in an intact chloroplast, it will not take place in a disorganized test-tube mixture of chlorophyll and other chloroplast molecules. Photosynthesis requires a specific organization of these molecules in the chloroplast. To take another example, if a blow to the head disrupts the intricate architecture of a human brain, the mind may cease to function properly even though all of the brain tissues are still present. Our thoughts and memories are emergent properties of a complex network of nerve cells. At a much higher level of biological organization—at the ecosystem level—the recycling of chemical elements essential to life, such as carbon, depends on a network of diverse organisms interacting with each other and with the soil, water, and air.

Emergent properties are not unique to life. A box of bicycle parts won't take you anywhere, but if they are arranged in a certain way, you can pedal to your chosen destination. And while the graphite in a pencil "lead" and the diamond in a wedding ring are both pure carbon, they have very different appearances and properties due to the different arrangements of their carbon atoms. Both of these examples point out the importance of arrangement. Compared to such nonliving examples, however, the unrivaled complexity of biological systems makes the emergent properties of life especially challenging to study.

The Power and Limitations of Reductionism

Because the properties of life emerge from complex organization, scientists seeking to understand biological systems confront a dilemma. On the one hand, we cannot fully explain a higher level of order by breaking it down into its parts. A dissected animal no longer functions; a cell reduced to its chemical ingredients is no longer a cell. Disrupting a living system interferes with its functioning. On the other hand, something as complex as an organism or a cell cannot be analyzed without taking it apart.

Reductionism—the approach of reducing complex systems to simpler components that are more manageable to study—is a powerful strategy in biology. For example, by studying the molecular structure of DNA that had been extracted from cells, James Watson and Francis Crick inferred, in 1953, how this molecule could serve as the chemical basis of inheritance. The central role of DNA in cells and organisms became better understood, however, when scientists were able to study the interactions of DNA with other molecules. Biologists must balance the reductionist strategy with the larger-scale, holistic objective of understanding emergent properties—how the parts of cells, organisms, and higher levels of order, such as ecosystems, work together. This is the goal of an approach developed over the last 50 years called systems biology.

Systems Biology

A system is simply a combination of components that function together. A biologist can study a system at any level of organization. A single leaf cell can be considered a system, as can a frog, an ant colony, or a desert ecosytem. To understand how such systems work, it is not enough to have a "parts list," even a complete one. Realizing this, many researchers are now complementing the reductionist approach with new strategies for studying whole systems. This change in perspective is analogous to moving from ground level on a street corner, where you can observe local traffic, to a helicopter high above a city, from which you can see how variables such as time of day, construction projects, accidents, and traffic-signal malfunctions affect traffic throughout the city.

Systems biology is an approach that attempts to model the dynamic behavior of whole biological systems based on a study of the interactions among the system's parts. Successful models enable biologists to predict how a change in one or more variables will affect other components and the whole system. Thus, the systems approach enables us to pose new kinds of questions. How might a drug that lowers blood pressure affect the functioning of organs throughout the human body? How might increasing a crop's water supply affect processes in the plants, such as the storage of molecules essential for human nutrition? How might a gradual increase in atmospheric carbon dioxide alter ecosystems and the entire biosphere? The ultimate aim of systems biology is to answer large-scale questions like the last one.

Exploring Levels of Biological Organization

◄1 The Biosphere

As soon as we are near enough to Earth to make out its continents and oceans, we begin to see signs of life—in the green mosaic of the planet's forests, for example. This is our first view of the biosphere, which consists of all life on Earth and all the places where life exists—most regions of land, most bodies of water, the atmosphere to an altitude of several kilometers, and even sediments far below the ocean floor and rocks many kilometers below Earth's surface.

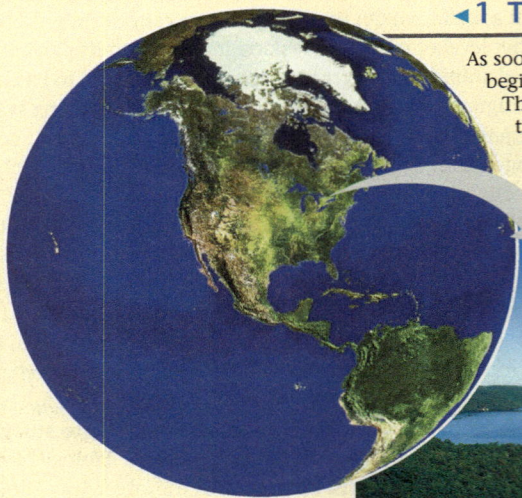

◄2 Ecosystems

As we approach Earth's surface for an imaginary landing in Ontario, we can begin to make out a forest with an abundance of trees that lose their leaves in one season and grow new ones in another (deciduous trees). Such a deciduous forest is an example of an ecosystem. Grasslands, deserts, and the ocean's coral reefs are other types of ecosystems. An ecosystem consists of all the living things in a particular area, along with all the nonliving components of the environment with which life interacts, such as soil, water, atmospheric gases, and light. All of Earth's ecosystems combined make up the biosphere.

►3 Communities

The entire array of organisms inhabiting a particular ecosystem is called a biological community. The community in our forest ecosystem includes many kinds of trees and other plants, a diversity of animals, various mushrooms and other fungi, and enormous numbers of diverse microorganisms, which are living forms, such as bacteria, that are too small to see without a microscope. Each of these forms of life is called a *species*.

►4 Populations

A population consists of all the individuals of a species living within the bounds of a specified area. For example, our Ontario forest includes a population of sugar maple trees and a population of white-tailed deer. We can now refine our definition of a community as the set of populations that inhabit a particular area.

▲5 Organisms

Individual living things are called organisms. Each of the maple trees and other plants in the forest is an organism, and so is each forest animal—whether deer, squirrel, frog, or beetle. The soil teems with microorganisms such as bacteria.

▼6 Organs and Organ Systems

The structural hierarchy of life continues to unfold as we explore the architecture of the more complex organisms. A maple leaf is an example of an organ, a body part that carries out a particular function in the body. Stems and roots are the other major organs of plants. Examples of human organs are the brain, heart, and kidney. The organs of humans, other complex animals, and plants are organized into organ systems, each a team of organs that cooperate in a larger function. For example, the human digestive system includes such organs as the tongue, stomach, and intestines. Organs consist of multiple tissues.

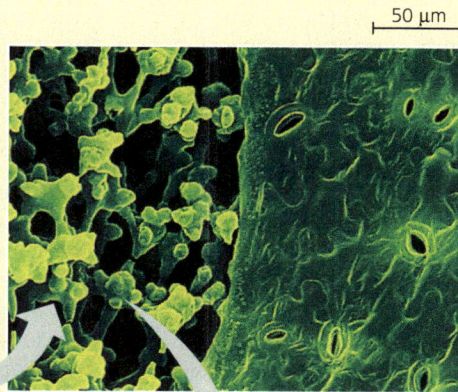

50 µm

◄7 Tissues

Our next scale change—to see the tissues of a leaf—requires a microscope. Each tissue is made up of a group of cells that work together, performing a specialized function. The leaf shown here has been cut on an angle. The honeycombed tissue in the interior of the leaf (left portion of photo) is the main location of photosynthesis, the process that converts light energy to the chemical energy of sugar and other food. We are viewing the sliced leaf from a perspective that also enables us to see the jigsaw puzzle–like "skin" on the surface of the leaf, a tissue called epidermis (right part of photo). The pores through the epidermis allow the gas carbon dioxide, a raw material for sugar production, to reach the photosynthetic tissue inside the leaf. At this scale, we can also see that each tissue has a distinct cellular structure.

Cell   10 µm

►9 Organelles

Chloroplasts are examples of organelles, the various functional components present in cells. In this image, a very powerful tool called an electron microscope brings a single chloroplast into sharp focus.

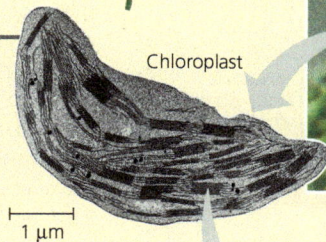

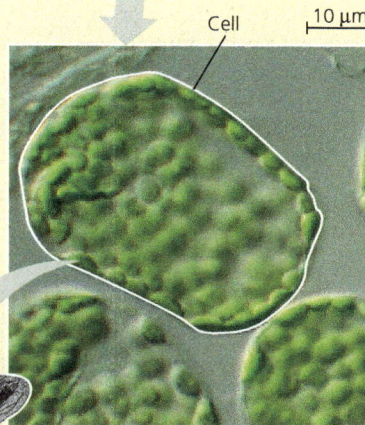

Chloroplast

1 µm

◄8 Cells

The cell is life's fundamental unit of structure and function. Some organisms, such as amoebas and most bacteria, are single cells. Other organisms, including plants and animals, are multicellular. Instead of a single cell performing all the functions of life, a multicellular organism has a division of labor among specialized cells. A human body consists of trillions of microscopic cells of many different kinds, such as muscle cells and nerve cells, which are organized into the various specialized tissues. For example, muscle tissue consists of bundles of muscle cells. In the photo at the upper left, we see a more highly magnified view of some cells in a leaf tissue. One cell is only about 40 micrometers (µm) across. It would take about 500 of these cells to reach across a small coin. As tiny as these cells are, you can see that each contains numerous green structures called chloroplasts, which are responsible for photosynthesis.

►10 Molecules

Our last scale change drops us into a chloroplast for a view of life at the molecular level. A molecule is a chemical structure consisting of two or more small chemical units called atoms, which are represented as balls in this computer graphic of a chlorophyll molecule. Chlorophyll is the pigment molecule that makes a maple leaf green. One of the most important molecules on Earth, chlorophyll absorbs sunlight during the first step of photosynthesis. Within each chloroplast, millions of chlorophyll molecules, together with accessory molecules, are organized into the equipment that converts light energy to the chemical energy of food.

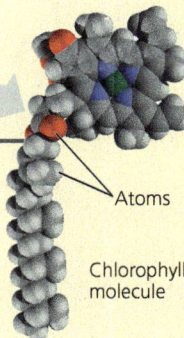

Atoms

Chlorophyll molecule

Systems biology is relevant to the study of life at all levels. During the early years of the 20th century, biologists studying how animal bodies function (animal physiology) began integrating data on how multiple organs coordinate processes such as the regulation of sugar concentration in the blood. And in the 1960s, scientists investigating ecosystems pioneered a more mathematically sophisticated systems approach with elaborate models diagramming the network of interactions between organisms and nonliving components of ecosystems, such as salt marshes. More recently, with the sequencing of DNA from many species, systems biology has taken hold at the cellular and molecular levels, as we'll describe later when we discuss DNA.

Theme: Organisms Interact with Other Organisms and the Physical Environment

Turn back again to Figure 1.4, this time focusing on the forest. In an ecosystem, each organism interacts continuously with its environment, which includes both other organisms and physical factors. The leaves of a tree, for example, absorb light from the sun, take in carbon dioxide from the air, and release oxygen to the air **(Figure 1.5)**. Both the organism and the environment are affected by the interactions between them. For example, a plant takes up water and minerals from the soil through its roots, and its roots help form soil by breaking up rocks. On a global scale, plants and other photosynthetic organisms have generated all the oxygen in the air.

A tree also interacts with other organisms, such as soil microorganisms associated with its roots, insects that live in the tree, and animals that eat its leaves and fruit. Interactions between organisms ultimately result in the cycling of nutrients in ecosystems. For example, minerals acquired by a tree will eventually be returned to the soil by other organisms that decompose leaf litter, dead roots, and other organic debris. The minerals are then available to be taken up by plants again.

Like all organisms, we humans interact with our environment. Unfortunately, our interactions sometimes have drastic consequences. For example, since the Industrial Revolution in the 1800s, the burning of fossil fuels (coal, oil, and gas) has been increasing at an ever-accelerating pace. This practice releases gaseous compounds into the atmosphere, including prodigious amounts of carbon dioxide (CO_2). About half the human-generated CO_2 stays in the atmosphere, acting like a layer of glass around the planet that admits radiation that warms the Earth but prevents heat from radiating into outer space. Scientists estimate that the average temperature of the planet has risen 1°C since 1900 due to this "greenhouse effect," and they project an additional rise in average global temperature of at least 3°C over the course of the 21st century.

This global warming, a major aspect of **global climate change**, has already had dire effects on life-forms and their habitats all over planet Earth. Polar bears have lost a significant portion of the ice platform from which they hunt, and there are examples of small rodents and plant species that have shifted their ranges to higher altitudes, as well as bird populations that have altered their migration schedules. Only time will reveal the consequences of these changes. Scientists predict that even if we stopped burning fossil fuels today, it would take several centuries to return to preindustrial CO_2 levels. That scenario is highly improbable, so it is imperative that we learn all we can about the effects of global climate change on Earth and its populations. Acting as the stewards of our planet, we must strive to find ways to address this problem.

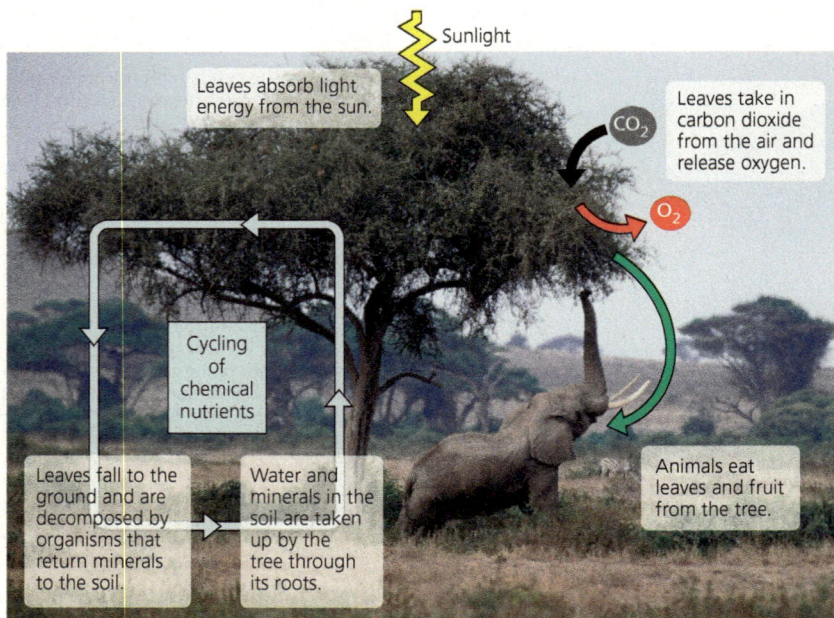

▲ **Figure 1.5 Interactions of an African acacia tree with other organisms and the physical environment.**

Theme: Life Requires Energy Transfer and Transformation

As you saw in Figure 1.5, a tree's leaves absorb sunlight. The input of energy from the sun makes life possible: A fundamental characteristic of living organisms is their use of energy to carry out life's activities. Moving, growing, reproducing, and the other activities of life are work, and work requires energy. In the business of living, organisms often

Sunlight

Producers absorb light energy and transform it into chemical energy.

Chemical energy

Chemical energy in food is transferred from plants to consumers.

(a) Energy flow from sunlight to producers to consumers

Heat

When energy is used to do work, some energy is converted to thermal energy, which is lost as heat.

An animal's muscle cells convert chemical energy from food to kinetic energy, the energy of motion.

A plant's cells use chemical energy to do work such as growing new leaves.

(b) Using energy to do work

▲ **Figure 1.6 Energy flow in an ecosystem.** This endangered Red Colobus monkey lives in Tanzania.

transform one form of energy to another. Chlorophyll molecules within the tree's leaves harness the energy of sunlight and use it to drive photosynthesis, converting carbon dioxide and water to sugar and oxygen. The chemical energy in sugar is then passed along by plants and other photosynthetic organisms (producers) to consumers. Consumers are organisms, such as animals, that feed on producers and other consumers **(Figure 1.6a)**.

An animal's muscle cells use sugar as fuel to power movements, converting chemical energy to kinetic energy, the energy of motion **(Figure 1.6b)**. The cells in a leaf use sugar to drive the process of cell proliferation during leaf growth, transforming stored chemical energy into cellular work. In both cases, some of the energy is converted to thermal energy, which dissipates to the surroundings as heat. In contrast to chemical nutrients, which recycle within an ecosystem, energy flows through an ecosystem, usually entering as light and exiting as heat.

Theme: Structure and Function Are Correlated at All Levels of Biological Organization

Another theme evident in Figure 1.4 is the idea that form fits function, which you'll recognize from everyday life. For example, a screwdriver is suited to tighten or loosen screws, a hammer to pound nails. How a device works is correlated with its structure. Applied to biology, this theme is a guide to the anatomy of life at all its structural levels. An example from Figure 1.4 is seen in the leaf: Its thin, flat shape maximizes the amount of sunlight that can be captured by its chloroplasts. Analyzing a biological structure gives us clues about what it does and how it works. Conversely, knowing the function of something provides insight into its construction. An example from the animal kingdom, the wing of a bird, provides additional instances of the structure-function theme **(Figure 1.7)**. In exploring life on its different structural levels, we discover functional beauty at every turn.

(a) A bird's wings have an aerodynamically efficient shape.

(b) Wing bones have a honeycombed internal structure that is strong but lightweight.

▲ **Figure 1.7 Form fits function in a gull's wing. (a)** The shape of a bird's wings and **(b)** the structure of its bones make flight possible.

❓ *How does form fit function in a human hand?*

Theme: The Cell Is an Organism's Basic Unit of Structure and Function

In life's structural hierarchy, the cell has a special place as the lowest level of organization that can perform all activities required for life. Moreover, the activities of organisms are all based on the activities of cells. For instance, the movement of your eyes as you read this line is based on activities of muscle and nerve cells. Even a global process such as the recycling of carbon is the cumulative product of cellular activities, including the photosynthesis that occurs in the chloroplasts of leaf cells. Understanding how cells work is a major focus of biological research.

All cells share certain characteristics. For example, every cell is enclosed by a membrane that regulates the passage of materials between the cell and its surroundings. And every cell uses DNA as its genetic information. However, we can distinguish between two main forms of cells: prokaryotic cells and eukaryotic cells. The cells of two groups of microorganisms, called bacteria (singular, *bacterium*) and archaea (singular, *archaean*), are prokaryotic. All other forms of life, including plants and animals, are composed of eukaryotic cells.

A **eukaryotic cell** is subdivided by internal membranes into various membrane-enclosed organelles **(Figure 1.8)**. In most eukaryotic cells, the largest organelle is the nucleus, which contains the cell's DNA. The other organelles are located in the cytoplasm, the entire region between the nucleus and outer membrane of the cell. The chloroplast you saw in Figure 1.4 is an organelle found in eukaryotic cells that carry out photosynthesis. Prokaryotic cells are much simpler and generally smaller than eukaryotic cells, as seen clearly in Figure 1.8. In a **prokaryotic cell**, the DNA is not separated from the rest of the cell by enclosure in a membrane-bounded nucleus. Prokaryotic cells also lack the other kinds of membrane-enclosed organelles that characterize eukaryotic cells. The properties of all organisms, whether prokaryotic or eukaryotic, are based in the structure and function of cells.

Theme: The Continuity of Life Is Based on Heritable Information in the Form of DNA

The division of cells to form new cells is the foundation for all reproduction and for the growth and repair of multicellular organisms. Inside the dividing cell in **Figure 1.9**, you can see structures called chromosomes, which are stained with a blue-glowing dye. The chromosomes have almost all of the cell's genetic material, its **DNA** (short for deoxyribonucleic acid). DNA is the substance of **genes**, the units of inheritance that transmit information from parents to offspring. Your blood group (A, B, AB, or O), for example, is the result of certain genes that you inherited from your parents.

DNA Structure and Function

Each chromosome contains one very long DNA molecule, with hundreds or thousands of genes arranged along its length. The genes encode the information necessary to build other molecules in the cell, most notably proteins. Proteins play structural roles and are also responsible for carrying out cellular work. They thus establish a cell's identity.

The DNA of chromosomes replicates as a cell prepares to divide, and each of the two cellular offspring inherits a complete set of genes, identical to that of the parent cell. Each of us began life as a single cell stocked with DNA inherited from our parents. Replication of that DNA with each round of cell division transmitted copies of the DNA to our trillions of cells. The DNA controls the development and maintenance of the entire organism and, indirectly, everything the organism does **(Figure 1.10)**. The DNA serves as a central database.

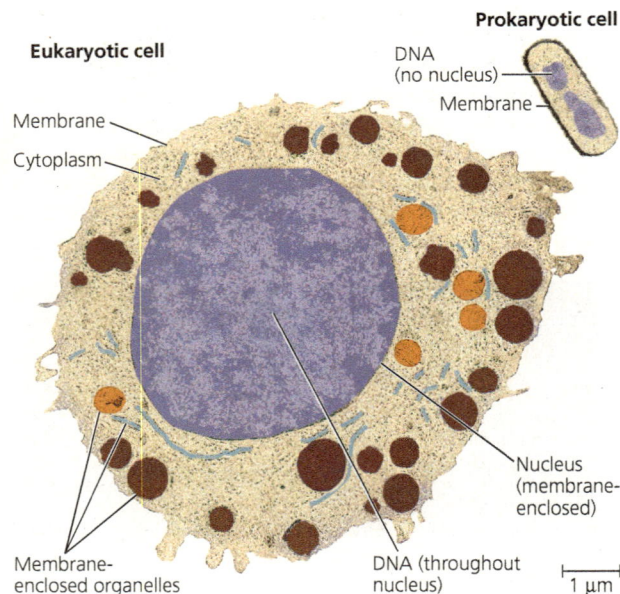
▲ **Figure 1.8 Contrasting eukaryotic and prokaryotic cells in size and complexity.**

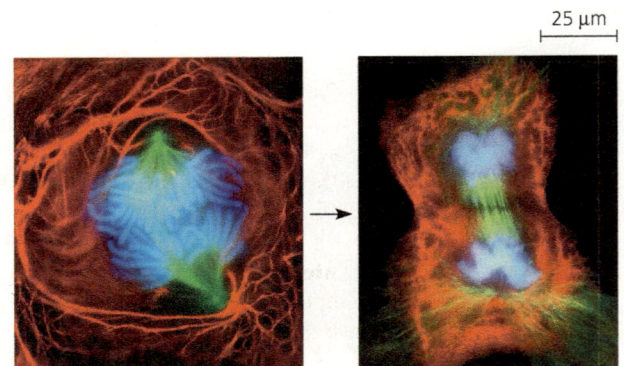
▲ **Figure 1.9 A lung cell from a newt divides into two smaller cells that will grow and divide again.**

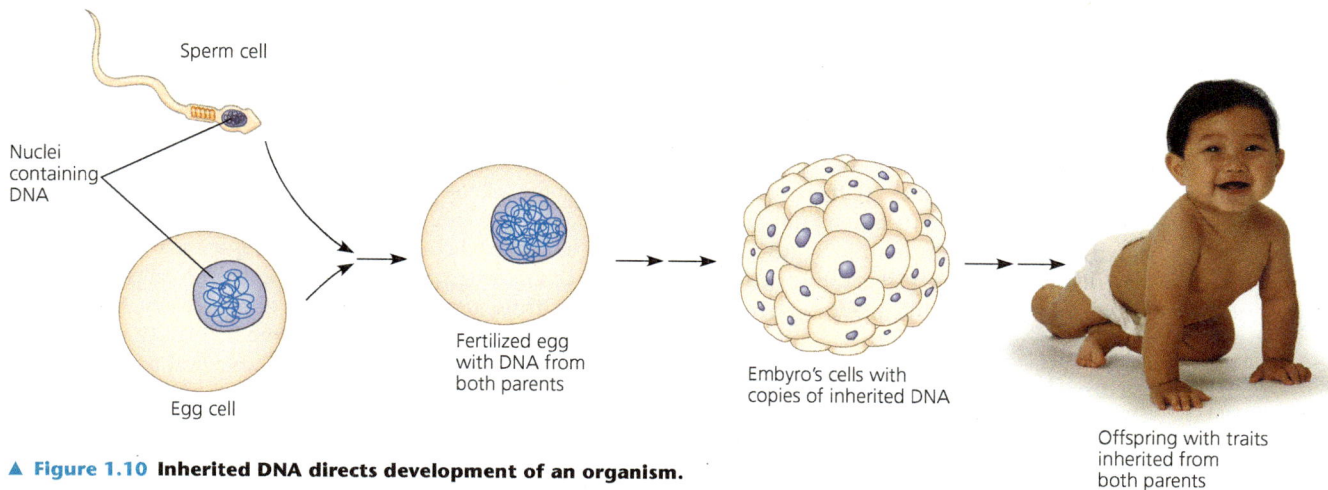

▲ **Figure 1.10 Inherited DNA directs development of an organism.**

The molecular structure of DNA accounts for its ability to store information. Each DNA molecule is made up of two long chains, called strands, arranged in a double helix. Each chain is made up of four kinds of chemical building blocks called nucleotides, abbreviated A, T, C, and G **(Figure 1.11)**. The way DNA encodes information is analogous to how we arrange the letters of the alphabet into precise sequences with specific meanings. The word *rat*, for example, evokes a rodent; the words *tar* and *art*, which contain the same letters, mean very different things. We can think of nucleotides as a four-letter alphabet of inheritance. Specific sequential arrangements of these four nucleotide letters encode the information in genes, which are typically hundreds or thousands of nucleotides long.

DNA provides the blueprints for making proteins, and proteins are the main players in building and maintaining the cell and carrying out its activities. For instance, the information carried in a bacterial gene may specify a certain protein in a bacterial cell membrane, while the information in a human gene may denote a protein hormone that stimulates growth. Other human proteins include proteins in a muscle cell that drive contraction and the defensive proteins called antibodies. Enzymes, which catalyze (speed up) specific chemical reactions, are mostly proteins and are crucial to all cells.

The DNA of genes controls protein production indirectly, using a related kind of molecule called RNA as an intermediary. The sequence of nucleotides along a gene is transcribed into RNA, which is then translated into a specific protein with a unique shape and function. This entire process, by which the information in a gene directs the production of a cellular product, is called **gene expression**. In translating genes into proteins, all forms of life employ essentially the same genetic code. A particular sequence of nucleotides says the same thing in one organism as it does in another. Differences between organisms reflect differences between their nucleotide sequences rather than between their genetic codes.

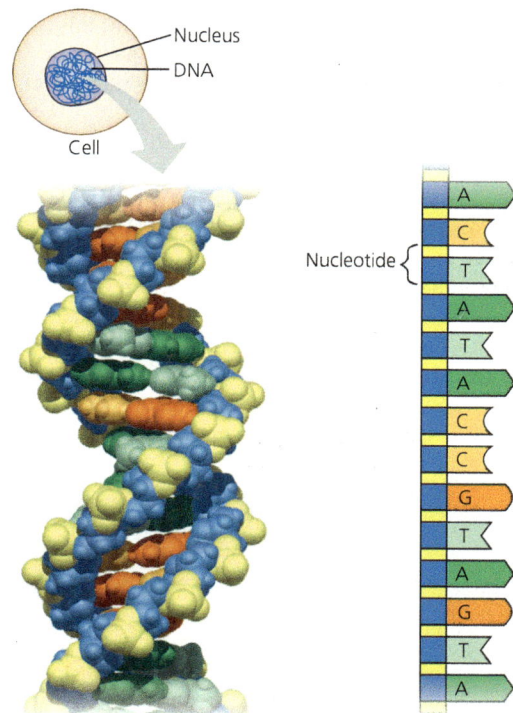

(a) DNA double helix. This model shows each atom in a segment of DNA. Made up of two long chains of building blocks called nucleotides, a DNA molecule takes the three-dimensional form of a double helix.

(b) Single strand of DNA. These geometric shapes and letters are simple symbols for the nucleotides in a small section of one chain of a DNA molecule. Genetic information is encoded in specific sequences of the four types of nucleotides. (Their names are abbreviated A, T, C, and G.)

▲ **Figure 1.11 DNA: The genetic material.**

Not all RNA molecules in the cell are translated into protein; some RNAs carry out other important tasks. We have known for decades that some types of RNA are actually components of the cellular machinery that manufactures proteins. Recently, scientists have discovered whole new classes of RNA that play other roles in the cell, such as regulating the functioning of protein-coding genes. All these RNAs are specified by genes, and the process of their transcription is also referred to as gene expression. By carrying the instructions for making proteins and RNAs and by replicating with each cell division, DNA ensures faithful inheritance of genetic information from generation to generation.

Genomics: Large-Scale Analysis of DNA Sequences

The entire "library" of genetic instructions that an organism inherits is called its **genome**. A typical human cell has two similar sets of chromosomes, and each set has DNA totaling about 3 billion nucleotide pairs. If the one-letter abbreviations for the nucleotides of one strand were written in letters the size of those you are now reading, the genetic text would fill about 600 books the size of this one. Within this genomic library of nucleotide sequences are genes for about 75,000 kinds of proteins and an as yet unknown number of RNA molecules that do not code for proteins.

Since the early 1990s, the pace at which we can sequence genomes has accelerated at an almost unbelievable rate, enabled by a revolution in technology. The development of new methods and DNA-sequencing machines, such as those shown in **Figure 1.12**, have led the charge. The entire sequence of nucleotides in the human genome is now known, along with the genome sequences of many other organisms, including bacteria, archaea, fungi, plants, and other animals.

The sequencing of the human genome was heralded as a scientific and technological achievement comparable to landing the *Apollo* astronauts on the moon in 1969. But it

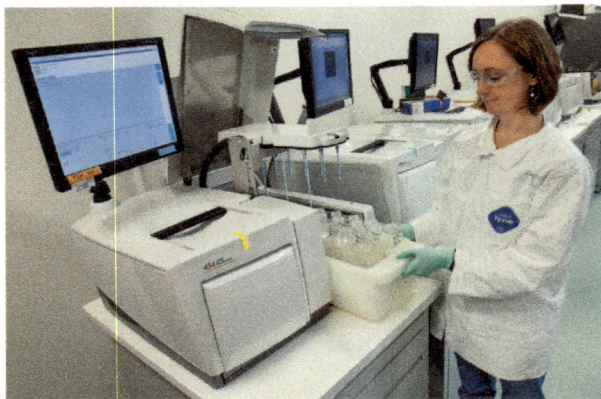

▲ **Figure 1.12 Biology as an information science.** Automatic DNA-sequencing machines and abundant computing power make the sequencing of genomes possible. This facility in Walnut Creek, California, is part of the Joint Genome Institute.

was only the beginning of an even bigger research endeavor, an effort to learn how the activities of the myriad proteins encoded by the DNA are coordinated in cells and whole organisms. To make sense of the deluge of data from genome-sequencing projects and the growing catalog of known protein functions, scientists are applying a systems approach at the cellular and molecular levels. Rather than investigating a single gene at a time, these researchers have shifted to studying whole sets of genes of a species as well as comparing genomes between species—an approach called **genomics**.

Three important research developments have made the genomic approach possible. One is "high-throughput" technology, tools that can analyze biological materials very rapidly and produce enormous amounts of data. The automatic DNA-sequencing machines that made the sequencing of the human genome possible are examples of high-throughput devices (see Figure 1.12). The second major development is **bioinformatics**, the use of computational tools to store, organize, and analyze the huge volume of data that result from high-throughput methods. The third key development is the formation of interdisciplinary research teams—melting pots of diverse specialists that may include computer scientists, mathematicians, engineers, chemists, physicists, and, of course, biologists from a variety of fields.

Theme: Feedback Mechanisms Regulate Biological Systems

Just as a coordinated control of traffic flow is necessary for a city to function smoothly, regulation of biological processes is crucial to the operation of living systems. Consider your muscles, for instance. When your muscle cells require more energy during exercise, they increase their consumption of the sugar molecules that serve as fuel. In contrast, when you rest, a different set of chemical reactions converts surplus sugar to storage molecules.

Like most of the cell's chemical processes, those that either decompose or store sugar are accelerated, or catalyzed, by proteins called enzymes. Each type of enzyme catalyzes a specific chemical reaction. In many cases, these reactions are linked into chemical pathways, each step with its own enzyme. How does the cell coordinate its various chemical pathways? In our example of sugar management, how does the cell match fuel supply to demand, regulating its opposing pathways of sugar consumption and storage? The key is the ability of many biological processes to self-regulate by a mechanism called feedback.

In feedback regulation, the output, or product, of a process regulates that very process. The most common form of regulation in living systems is **negative feedback**, in which accumulation of an end product of a process slows that process. For example, the cell's breakdown of sugar generates chemical energy in the form of a substance called ATP. When a cell makes more ATP than it can use, the excess ATP "feeds back"

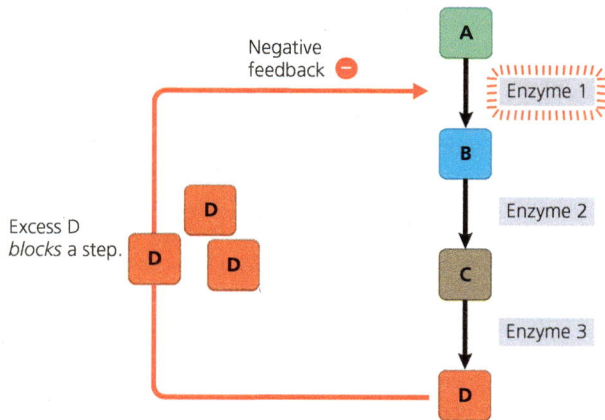

Negative feedback −

Excess D *blocks* a step.

(a) Negative feedback. This three-step chemical pathway converts substance A to substance D. A specific enzyme catalyzes each chemical reaction. Accumulation of the final product (D) inhibits the first enzyme in the sequence, thus slowing down production of more D.

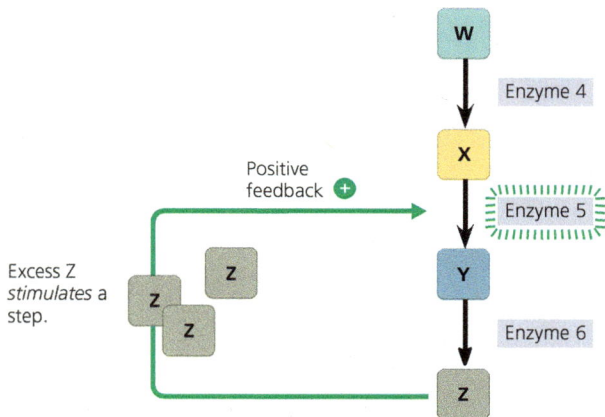

Positive feedback +

Excess Z *stimulates* a step.

(b) Positive feedback. In a biochemical pathway regulated by positive feedback, a product stimulates an enzyme in the reaction sequence, increasing the rate of production of the product.

▲ **Figure 1.13 Regulation by feedback mechanisms.**

? *What would happen to the feedback system if enzyme 2 were missing?*

and inhibits an enzyme near the beginning of the pathway **(Figure 1.13a)**.

Though less common than processes regulated by negative feedback, there are also many biological processes regulated by **positive feedback**, in which an end product *speeds up* its own production **(Figure 1.13b)**. The clotting of your blood in response to injury is an example. When a blood vessel is damaged, structures in the blood called platelets begin to aggregate at the site. Positive feedback occurs as chemicals released by the platelets attract *more* platelets. The platelet pileup then initiates a complex process that seals the wound with a clot.

Feedback is a regulatory motif common to life at all levels, from the molecular level to ecosystems and the biosphere.

Such regulation is an example of the integration that makes living systems much greater than the sum of their parts.

Evolution, the Overarching Theme of Biology

Having considered all the other themes that run through this book, let's now turn to biology's core theme—evolution. Evolution is the one idea that makes sense of everything we know about living organisms. Life has been evolving on Earth for billions of years, resulting in a vast diversity of past and present organisms. But along with the diversity we find many shared features. For example, while the sea horse, jackrabbit, hummingbird, crocodile, and giraffes in Figure 1.3 look very different, their skeletons are basically similar. The scientific explanation for this unity and diversity—and for the suitability of organisms for their environments—is evolution: the idea that the organisms living on Earth today are the modified descendants of common ancestors. In other words, we can explain traits shared by two organisms with the idea that they have descended from a common ancestor, and we can account for differences with the idea that heritable changes have occurred along the way. Many kinds of evidence support the occurrence of evolution and the theory that describes how it takes place. In the next section, we'll consider the fundamental concept of evolution in greater detail.

CONCEPT CHECK 1.1

1. For each biological level in Figure 1.4, write a sentence that includes the next "lower" level. Example: "A community consists of *populations* of the various species inhabiting a specific area."
2. What theme or themes are exemplified by (a) the sharp spines of a porcupine, (b) the cloning of a plant from a single cell, and (c) a hummingbird using sugar to power its flight?
3. **WHAT IF?** For each theme discussed in this section, give an example not mentioned in the book.

For suggested answers, see Appendix A.

CONCEPT 1.2

The Core Theme: Evolution accounts for the unity and diversity of life

EVOLUTION The list of biological themes discussed in Concept 1.1 is not absolute; some people might find a shorter or longer list more useful. There is consensus among biologists, however, as to the core theme of biology: It is evolution. To quote one of the founders of modern evolutionary theory, Theodosius Dobzhansky, "Nothing in biology makes sense except in the light of evolution."

In addition to encompassing a hierarchy of size scales from molecules to the biosphere, biology extends across the great diversity of species that have ever lived on Earth. To understand Dobzhansky's statement, we need to discuss how biologists think about this vast diversity.

Classifying the Diversity of Life

Diversity is a hallmark of life. Biologists have so far identified and named about 1.8 million species. To date, this diversity of life is known to include at least 100,000 species of fungi, 290,000 plant species, 52,000 vertebrate species (animals with backbones), and 1 million insect species (more than half of all known forms of life)—not to mention the myriad types of single-celled organisms. Researchers identify thousands of additional species each year. Estimates of the total number of species range from about 10 million to over 100 million. Whatever the actual number, the enormous variety of life

gives biology a very broad scope. Biologists face a major challenge in attempting to make sense of this variety.

Grouping Species: The Basic Idea

There is a human tendency to group diverse items according to their similarities and their relationships to each other. For instance, we may speak of "squirrels" and "butterflies," though we recognize that many different species belong to each group. We may even sort groups into broader categories, such as rodents (which include squirrels) and insects (which include butterflies). Taxonomy, the branch of biology that names and classifies species, formalizes this ordering of species into groups of increasing breadth, based on the degree to which they share characteristics **(Figure 1.14)**. You will learn more about the details of this taxonomic scheme in Chapter 26. For

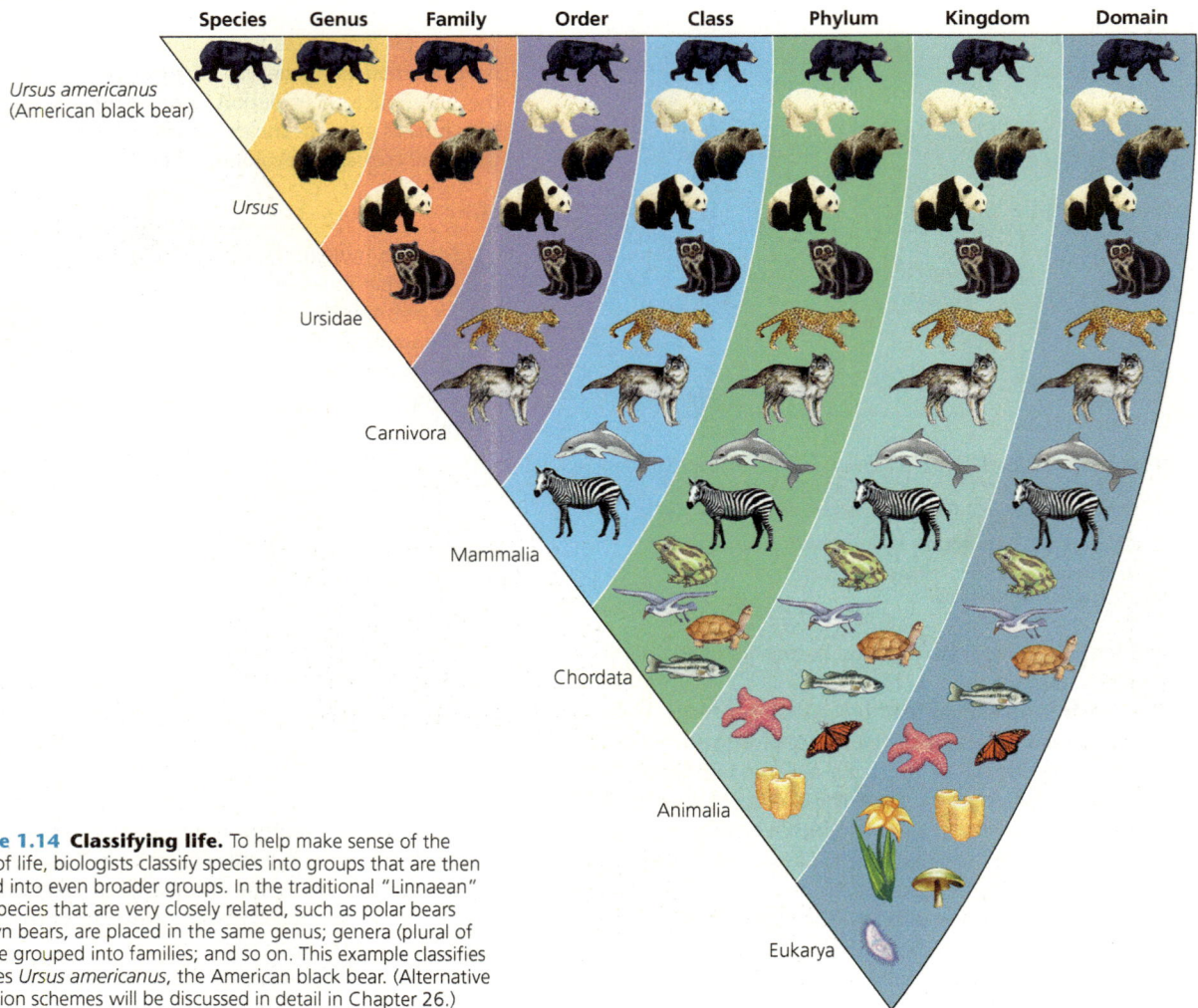

▲ **Figure 1.14 Classifying life.** To help make sense of the diversity of life, biologists classify species into groups that are then combined into even broader groups. In the traditional "Linnaean" system, species that are very closely related, such as polar bears and brown bears, are placed in the same genus; genera (plural of genus) are grouped into families; and so on. This example classifies the species *Ursus americanus*, the American black bear. (Alternative classification schemes will be discussed in detail in Chapter 26.)

now, we will focus on the big picture by considering the broadest units of classification, kingdoms and domains.

The Three Domains of Life

Historically, scientists have classified the diversity of life-forms into kingdoms and finer groupings by careful comparisons of structure, function, and other obvious features. In the last few decades, new methods of assessing species relationships, such as comparisons of DNA sequences, have led to an ongoing reevaluation of the number and boundaries of kingdoms. Researchers have proposed anywhere from six kingdoms to dozens of kingdoms. While debate continues at the kingdom level, there is consensus among biologists that the kingdoms of life can be grouped into three even higher

levels of classification called domains. The three domains are named Bacteria, Archaea, and Eukarya **(Figure 1.15)**.

The organisms making up two of the three domains—domain **Bacteria** and domain **Archaea**—are all prokaryotic. Most prokaryotes are single-celled and microscopic. Previously, bacteria and archaea were combined in a single kingdom because they shared the prokaryotic form of cell structure. But much evidence now supports the view that bacteria and archaea represent two very distinct branches of prokaryotic life, different in key ways that you'll learn about in Chapter 27. There is also evidence that archaea are at least as closely related to eukaryotic organisms as they are to bacteria.

All the eukaryotes (organisms with eukaryotic cells) are now grouped in domain **Eukarya**. This domain includes three kingdoms of multicellular eukaryotes: kingdoms Plantae,

▼ Figure 1.15 The three domains of life.

(a) Domain Bacteria

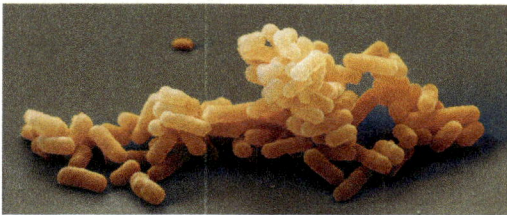

2 μm

Bacteria are the most diverse and widespread prokaryotes and are now classified into multiple kingdoms. Each rod-shaped structure in this photo is a bacterial cell.

(b) Domain Archaea

2 μm

Many of the prokaryotes known as **archaea** live in Earth's extreme environments, such as salty lakes and boiling hot springs. Domain Archaea includes multiple kingdoms. Each round structure in this photo is an archaeal cell.

(c) Domain Eukarya

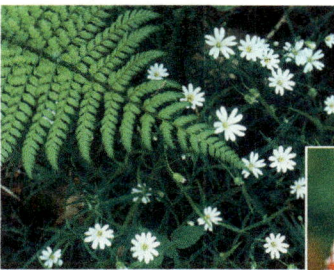

◀ **Kingdom Animalia** consists of multicellular eukaryotes that ingest other organisms.

100 μm

▲ **Kingdom Plantae** consists of terrestrial multicellular eukaryotes (land plants) that carry out photosynthesis, the conversion of light energy to the chemical energy in food.

▶ **Kingdom Fungi** is defined in part by the nutritional mode of its members (such as this mushroom), which absorb nutrients from outside their bodies.

▶ **Protists** are mostly unicellular eukaryotes and some relatively simple multicellular relatives. Pictured here is an assortment of protists inhabiting pond water. Scientists are currently debating how to classify protists in a way that accurately reflects their evolutionary relationships.

94   Life Sciences Foundation

Fungi, and Animalia. These three kingdoms are distinguished partly by their modes of nutrition. Plants produce their own sugars and other food molecules by photosynthesis. Fungi absorb dissolved nutrients from their surroundings; many decompose dead organisms and organic wastes (such as leaf litter and animal feces) and absorb nutrients from these sources. Animals obtain food by ingestion, which is the eating and digesting of other organisms. Animalia is, of course, the kingdom to which we belong. But neither animals, plants, nor fungi are as numerous or diverse as the single-celled eukaryotes we call protists. Although protists were once placed in a single kingdom, biologists now realize that they do not form a single natural group of species. And recent evidence shows that some protist groups are more closely related to multicellular eukaryotes such as animals and fungi than they are to each other. Thus, the recent taxonomic trend has been to split the protists into several groups.

Unity in the Diversity of Life

As diverse as life is, it also displays remarkable unity. Earlier we mentioned both the similar skeletons of different vertebrate animals and the universal genetic language of DNA (the genetic code). In fact, similarities between organisms are evident at all levels of the biological hierarchy. For example, unity is obvious in many features of cell structure **(Figure 1.16)**.

How can we account for life's dual nature of unity and diversity? The process of evolution, explained next, illuminates both the similarities and differences in the world of life and introduces another dimension of biology: historical time.

Charles Darwin and the Theory of Natural Selection

The history of life, as documented by fossils and other evidence, is the saga of a changing Earth billions of years old, inhabited by an evolving cast of living forms **(Figure 1.17)**. This evolutionary view of life came into sharp focus in November 1859, when Charles Robert Darwin published one of the most important and influential books ever written. Entitled *On the Origin of Species by Means of Natural Selection*, Darwin's book was an immediate bestseller and soon made "Darwinism," as it was dubbed at the time, almost synonymous with the concept of evolution **(Figure 1.18)**.

The Origin of Species articulated two main points. The first point was that contemporary species arose from a succession of ancestors, an idea that Darwin supported with a large amount of evidence. (We will discuss the evidence for evolution in detail in Chapter 22.) Darwin called this evolutionary history of species "descent with modification." It was an insightful phrase, as it captured the duality of life's unity and diversity—unity in the kinship among species that descended

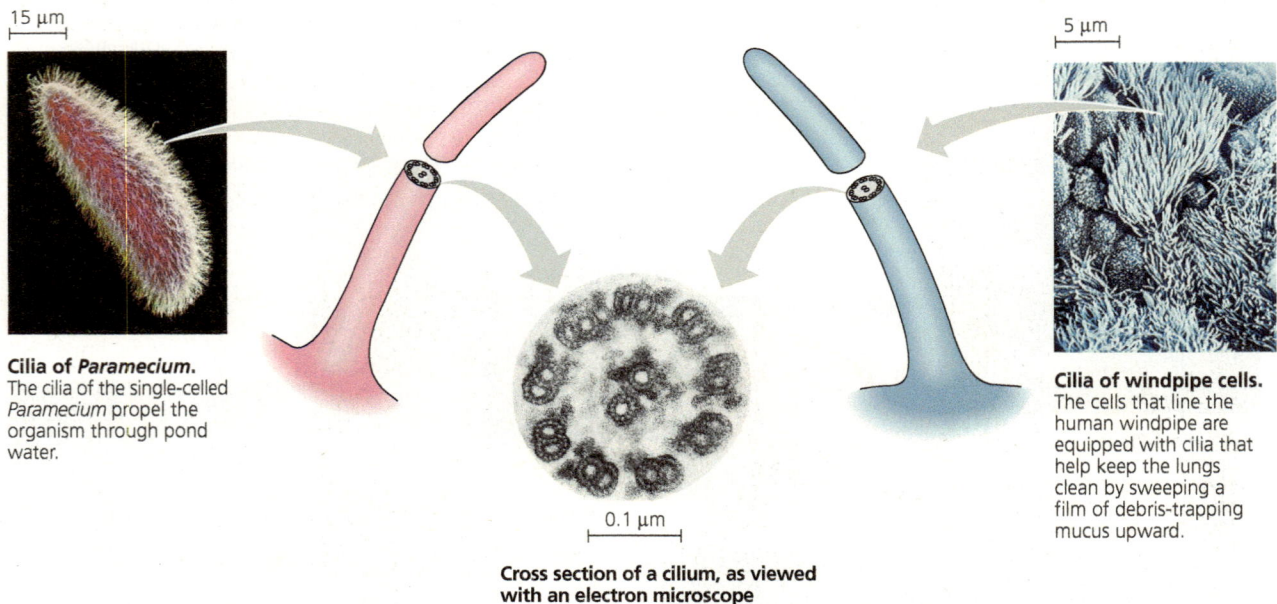

Cilia of *Paramecium*. The cilia of the single-celled *Paramecium* propel the organism through pond water.

Cross section of a cilium, as viewed with an electron microscope

Cilia of windpipe cells. The cells that line the human windpipe are equipped with cilia that help keep the lungs clean by sweeping a film of debris-trapping mucus upward.

▲ **Figure 1.16 An example of unity underlying the diversity of life: the architecture of cilia in eukaryotes.** Cilia (singular, *cilium*) are extensions of cells that function in locomotion. They occur in eukaryotes as diverse as *Paramecium* and humans. Even organisms so different share a common architecture for their cilia, which have an elaborate system of tubules that is striking in cross-sectional views.

▲ **Figure 1.17 Digging into the past.** Paleontologists carefully excavate the hind leg of a long-necked dinosaur (*Rapetosaurus krausei*) from rocks in Madagascar.

▲ **Figure 1.18 Charles Darwin as a young man.**

profound. Others had the pieces of the puzzle, but Darwin saw how they fit together. He started with the following three observations from nature: First, individuals in a population vary in their traits, many of which seem to be heritable (passed on from parents to offspring). Second, a population can produce far more offspring than can survive to produce offspring of their own. With more individuals than the environment is able to support, competition is inevitable. Third, species generally suit their environments—in other words, they are adapted to their environments. For instance, a common adaptation among birds with tough seeds as their major food source is that they have especially strong beaks.

Darwin made inferences from these observations to arrive at his theory of evolution. He reasoned that individuals with inherited traits that are best suited to the local environment are more likely to survive and reproduce than less suited individuals. Over many generations, a higher and higher proportion of individuals in a population will have the advantageous traits. Evolution occurs as the unequal reproductive success of individuals ultimately leads to adaptation to their environment, as long as the environment remains the same.

Darwin called this mechanism of evolutionary adaptation **natural selection** because the natural environment "selects" for the propagation of certain traits among naturally occurring variant traits in the population. The example

from common ancestors, diversity in the modifications that evolved as species branched from their common ancestors **(Figure 1.19)**. Darwin's second main point was a proposed mechanism for descent with modification. He called this evolutionary mechanism "natural selection."

Darwin synthesized his theory of natural selection from observations that by themselves were neither new nor

◄ **Figure 1.19 Unity and diversity in the orchid family.** These three orchids are variations on a common floral theme. For example, each of these flowers has a liplike petal that helps attract pollinating insects and provides a landing platform for the pollinators.

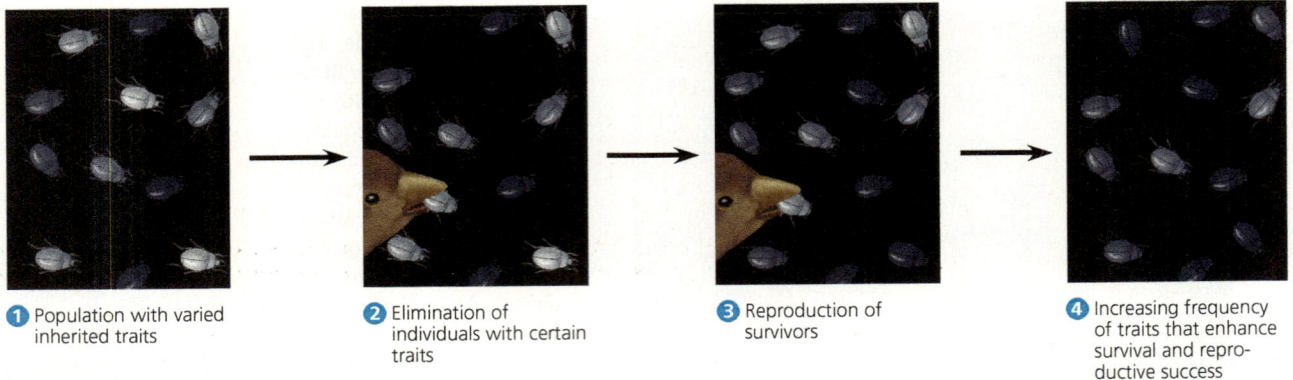

1 Population with varied inherited traits

2 Elimination of individuals with certain traits

3 Reproduction of survivors

4 Increasing frequency of traits that enhance survival and reproductive success

▲ **Figure 1.20 Natural selection.** This imaginary beetle population has colonized a locale where the soil has been blackened by a recent brush fire. Initially, the population varies extensively in the inherited coloration of the individuals, from very light gray to charcoal. For hungry birds that prey on the beetles, it is easiest to spot the beetles that are lightest in color.

in **Figure 1.20** illustrates the ability of natural selection to "edit" a population's heritable variations in color. We see the products of natural selection in the exquisite adaptations of various organisms to the special circumstances of their way of life and their environment. The wings of the bat shown in **Figure 1.21** are an excellent example of adaptation.

The Tree of Life

Take another look at the skeletal architecture of the bat's wings in Figure 1.21. These forelimbs, though adapted for flight, actually have all the same bones, joints, nerves, and blood vessels found in other limbs as diverse as the human arm, the horse's foreleg, and the whale's flipper. Indeed, all mammalian forelimbs are anatomical variations of a common architecture, much as the flowers in Figure 1.19 are variations on an underlying "orchid" theme. Such examples of kinship connect life's unity in diversity to the Darwinian

▲ **Figure 1.21 Evolutionary adaptation.** Bats, the only mammals capable of active flight, have wings with webbing between extended "fingers." In the Darwinian view of life, such adaptations are refined over time by natural selection.

concept of descent with modification. In this view, the unity of mammalian limb anatomy reflects inheritance of that structure from a common ancestor—the "prototype" mammal from which all other mammals descended. The diversity of mammalian forelimbs results from modification by natural selection operating over millions of generations in different environmental contexts. Fossils and other evidence corroborate anatomical unity in supporting this view of mammalian descent from a common ancestor.

Darwin proposed that natural selection, by its cumulative effects over long periods of time, could cause an ancestral species to give rise to two or more descendant species. This could occur, for example, if one population fragmented into several subpopulations isolated in different environments. In these separate arenas of natural selection, one species could gradually radiate into multiple species as the geographically isolated populations adapted over many generations to different sets of environmental factors.

The "family tree" of 14 finches in **Figure 1.22** illustrates a famous example of adaptive radiation of new species from a common ancestor. Darwin collected specimens of these birds during his 1835 visit to the remote Galápagos Islands, 900 kilometers (km) off the Pacific coast of South America. These relatively young, volcanic islands are home to many species of plants and animals found nowhere else in the world, though most Galápagos organisms are clearly related to species on the South American mainland. After volcanism built the Galápagos several million years ago, finches probably diversified on the various islands from an ancestral finch species that by chance reached the archipelago from elsewhere. (Once thought to have originated on the mainland of South America like many Galápagos organisms, the ancestral finches are now thought to have come from the West Indies—islands of the Caribbean that were once much closer to the Galápagos than they are now.)

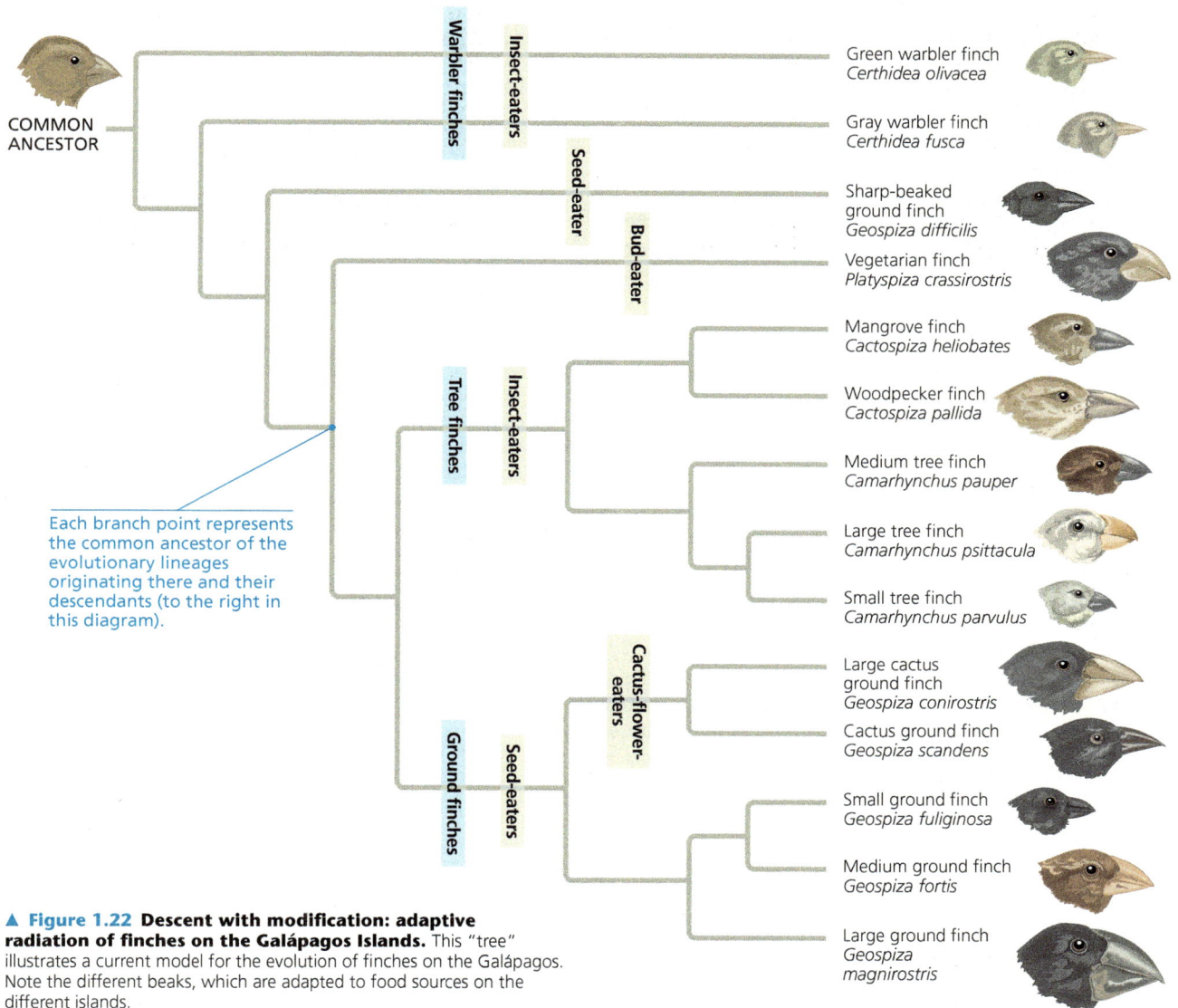

Each branch point represents the common ancestor of the evolutionary lineages originating there and their descendants (to the right in this diagram).

▲ **Figure 1.22 Descent with modification: adaptive radiation of finches on the Galápagos Islands.** This "tree" illustrates a current model for the evolution of finches on the Galápagos. Note the different beaks, which are adapted to food sources on the different islands.

Years after Darwin's collection of Galápagos finches, researchers began to sort out the relationships among the finch species, first from anatomical and geographic data and more recently with the help of DNA sequence comparisons.

Biologists' diagrams of evolutionary relationships generally take treelike forms, though today biologists usually turn the trees sideways as in Figure 1.22. Tree diagrams make sense: Just as an individual has a genealogy that can be diagrammed as a family tree, each species is one twig of a branching tree of life extending back in time through ancestral species more and more remote. Species that are very similar, such as the Galápagos finches, share a common ancestor at a relatively recent branch point on the tree of life. But through an ancestor that lived much farther back in time, finches are related to sparrows, hawks, penguins, and all other birds. And birds, mammals, and all other vertebrates share a common ancestor even more ancient. We find evidence of still broader relationships in such similarities as the identical construction of all eukaryotic cilia (see Figure 1.16). Trace life back far enough, and there are only fossils of the primeval prokaryotes that inhabited Earth over 3.5 billion years ago. We can recognize their vestiges in our own cells— in the universal genetic code, for example. All of life is connected through its long evolutionary history.

CONCEPT CHECK **1.2**

1. How is a mailing address analogous to biology's hierarchical taxonomic system?
2. Explain why "editing" is an appropriate metaphor for how natural selection acts on a population's heritable variation.
3. **WHAT IF?** The three domains you learned about in Concept 1.2 can be represented in the tree of life as the three main branches, with three subbranches on the eukaryotic branch being the kingdoms Plantae, Fungi, and Animalia. What if fungi and animals are more closely related to each other than either of these kingdoms is to plants—as recent evidence strongly suggests? Draw a simple branching pattern that symbolizes the proposed relationship between these three eukaryotic kingdoms.

For suggested answers, see Appendix A.

CONCEPT **1.3**

In studying nature, scientists make observations and then form and test hypotheses

The word *science* is derived from a Latin verb meaning "to know." **Science** is a way of knowing—an approach to understanding the natural world. It developed out of our curiosity about ourselves, other life-forms, our planet, and the universe. Striving to understand seems to be one of our basic urges.

At the heart of science is **inquiry**, a search for information and explanation, often focusing on specific questions. Inquiry drove Darwin to seek answers in nature for how species adapt to their environments. And today inquiry drives the genomic analyses that are helping us understand biological unity and diversity at the molecular level. In fact, the inquisitive mind is the engine that drives all progress in biology.

There is no formula for successful scientific inquiry, no single scientific method with a rule book that researchers must rigidly follow. As in all quests, science includes elements of challenge, adventure, and luck, along with careful planning, reasoning, creativity, cooperation, competition, patience, and the persistence to overcome setbacks. Such diverse elements of inquiry make science far less structured than most people realize. That said, it is possible to distill certain characteristics that help to distinguish science from other ways of describing and explaining nature.

Scientists attempt to understand how natural phenomena work using a process of inquiry that includes making observations, forming logical hypotheses, and testing them. The process is necessarily repetitive: In testing a hypothesis, more observations may force formation of a new hypothesis or revision of the original one, and further testing. In this way,

scientists circle closer and closer to their best estimation of the laws governing nature.

Making Observations

In the course of their work, scientists describe natural structures and processes as accurately as possible through careful observation and analysis of data. The observations are often valuable in their own right. For example, a series of detailed observations have shaped our understanding of cell structure, and another set of observations are currently expanding our databases of genomes of diverse species.

Types of Data

Observation is the use of the senses to gather information, either directly or indirectly with the help of tools such as microscopes that extend our senses. Recorded observations are called **data**. Put another way, data are items of information on which scientific inquiry is based.

The term *data* implies numbers to many people. But some data are *qualitative*, often in the form of recorded descriptions rather than numerical measurements. For example, Jane Goodall spent decades recording her observations of chimpanzee behavior during field research in a Tanzanian jungle **(Figure 1.23)**. She also documented her observations with photographs and movies. Along with these qualitative data, Goodall also enriched the field of animal behavior with volumes of *quantitative* data, which are generally recorded as

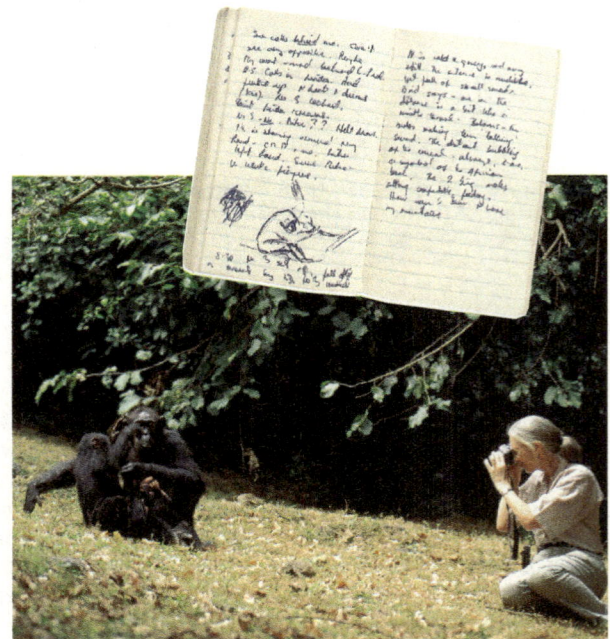

▲ **Figure 1.23 Jane Goodall collecting qualitative data on chimpanzee behavior.** Goodall recorded her observations in field notebooks, often with sketches of the animals' behavior.

measurements. Skim through any of the scientific journals in your college library, and you'll see many examples of quantitative data organized into tables and graphs.

Inductive Reasoning

Collecting and analyzing observations can lead to important conclusions based on a type of logic called **inductive reasoning**. Through induction, we derive generalizations from a large number of specific observations. "The sun always rises in the east" is an example. And so is "All organisms are made of cells." The latter generalization, part of the so-called cell theory, was based on two centuries of microscopic observations by biologists of cells in diverse biological specimens. Careful observations and data analyses, along with the generalizations reached by induction, are fundamental to our understanding of nature.

Forming and Testing Hypotheses

Observations and inductive reasoning stimulate us to seek natural causes and explanations for those observations. What *caused* the diversification of finches on the Galápagos Islands? What *causes* the roots of a plant seedling to grow downward and the leaf-bearing shoot to grow upward? What *explains* the generalization that the sun always rises in the east? In science, such inquiry usually involves the proposing and testing of hypothetical explanations—that is, hypotheses.

The Role of Hypotheses in Inquiry

In science, a **hypothesis** is a tentative answer to a well-framed question—an explanation on trial. It is usually a rational accounting for a set of observations, based on the available data and guided by inductive reasoning. A scientific hypothesis leads to predictions that can be tested by making additional observations or by performing experiments.

We all use hypotheses in solving everyday problems. Let's say, for example, that your flashlight fails during a camp-out. That's an observation. The question is obvious: Why doesn't the flashlight work? Two reasonable hypotheses based on your experience are that (1) the batteries in the flashlight are dead or (2) the bulb is burnt out. Each of these alternative hypotheses leads to predictions you can test with experiments. For example, the dead-battery hypothesis predicts that replacing the batteries will fix the problem. **Figure 1.24** diagrams this campground inquiry. Of course, we rarely dissect our thought processes this way when we are solving a problem using hypotheses, predictions, and experiments. But the hypothesis-based nature of science clearly has its origins in the human tendency to figure things out by trial and error.

Deductive Reasoning and Hypothesis Testing

A type of logic called deduction is built into the use of hypotheses in science. Deduction contrasts with induction,

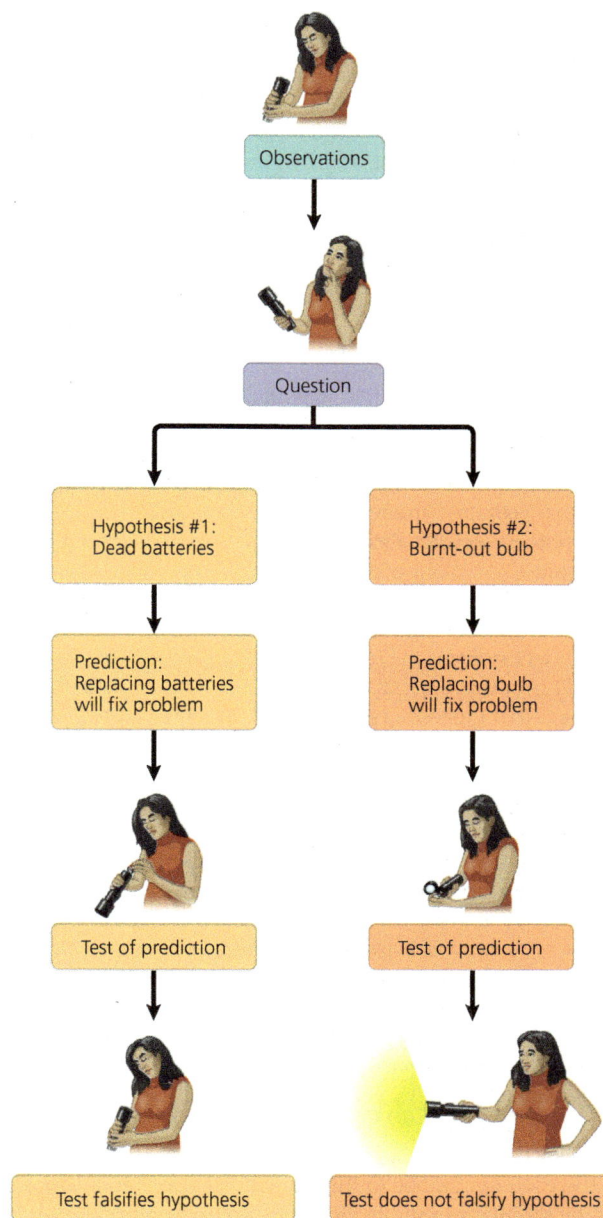

▲ **Figure 1.24 A campground example of hypothesis-based inquiry.**

which, remember, is reasoning from a set of specific observations to reach a general conclusion—a process that feeds into hypothesis formation. **Deductive reasoning** is generally used after the hypothesis has been developed and involves logic that flows in the opposite direction, from the general to the specific. From general premises, we extrapolate to the specific results we should expect if the premises are true. If all organisms are made of cells (premise 1), and humans are organisms (premise 2), then humans are composed of cells (deductive prediction about a specific case).

When using hypotheses in the scientific process, deductions usually take the form of predictions of experimental or observational results that will be found if a particular hypothesis (premise) is correct. We then test the hypothesis by carrying out the experiments or observations to see whether or not the results are as predicted. This deductive testing takes the form of "*If . . . then*" logic. In the case of the flashlight example: *If* the dead-battery hypothesis is correct and you replace the batteries with new ones, *then* the flashlight should work.

The flashlight inquiry demonstrates a key point about the use of hypotheses in science: that the initial observations may give rise to multiple hypotheses. The ideal is to design experiments to test all these candidate explanations. In addition to the two explanations tested in Figure 1.24, for instance, another of the many possible alternative hypotheses is that *both* the batteries *and* the bulb are bad. What does this hypothesis predict about the outcome of the experiments in Figure 1.24? What additional experiment would you design to test this hypothesis of multiple malfunctions?

We can mine the flashlight scenario for yet another important lesson about the scientific inquiry process. The burnt-out bulb hypothesis stands out as the most likely explanation, but notice that the testing supports that hypothesis *not* by proving that it is correct, but rather by not eliminating it through falsification (proving it false). Perhaps the first bulb was simply loose, so it wasn't making electrical contact, and the new bulb was inserted correctly. We could attempt to falsify the burnt-out bulb hypothesis by trying another experiment—removing the original bulb and carefully reinstalling it. If the flashlight still doesn't work, the burnt-out bulb hypothesis can stand. But no amount of experimental testing can *prove* a hypothesis beyond a shadow of doubt, because it is impossible to test *all* alternative hypotheses. A hypothesis gains credibility by surviving multiple attempts to falsify it while alternative hypotheses are eliminated (falsified) by testing.

Questions That Can and Cannot Be Addressed by Science

Scientific inquiry is a powerful way to learn about nature, but there are limitations to the kinds of questions it can answer. The flashlight example illustrates two important qualities of scientific hypotheses. First, a hypothesis must be *testable*; there must be some way to check the validity of the idea. Second, a hypothesis must be *falsifiable*; there must be some observation or experiment that could reveal if such an idea is actually *not* true. The hypothesis that dead batteries are the sole cause of the broken flashlight could be falsified by replacing the old batteries with new ones and finding that the flashlight still doesn't work.

Not all hypotheses meet the criteria of science: You wouldn't be able to devise a test to falsify the hypothesis that invisible campground ghosts are fooling with your flashlight! Because

science requires natural explanations for natural phenomena, it can neither support nor falsify hypotheses that angels, ghosts, or spirits, whether benevolent or evil, cause storms, rainbows, illnesses, and cures. Such supernatural explanations are simply outside the bounds of science, as are religious matters, which are issues of personal faith.

The Flexibility of the Scientific Method

The flashlight example of Figure 1.24 traces an idealized process of inquiry called *the scientific method*. We can recognize the elements of this process in most of the research articles published by scientists, but rarely in such structured form. Very few scientific inquiries adhere rigidly to the sequence of steps prescribed by the "textbook" scientific method. For example, a scientist may start to design an experiment, but then backtrack upon realizing that more preliminary observations are necessary. In other cases, puzzling observations simply don't prompt well-defined questions until other research places those observations in a new context. For example, Darwin collected specimens of the Galápagos finches, but it wasn't until years later, as the idea of natural selection began to gel, that biologists began asking key questions about the history of those birds.

Moreover, scientists sometimes redirect their research when they realize they have been asking the wrong question. For example, in the early 20th century, much research on schizophrenia and manic-depressive disorder (now called bipolar disorder) got sidetracked by focusing too much on the question of how life experiences might cause these serious maladies. Research on the causes and potential treatments became more productive when it was refocused on questions of how certain chemical imbalances in the brain contribute to mental illness. To be fair, we acknowledge that such twists and turns in scientific inquiry become more evident with the advantage of historical perspective.

It is important for you to get some experience with the power of the scientific method—by using it for some of the laboratory inquiries in your biology course, for example. But it is also important to avoid stereotyping science as a lock-step adherence to this method.

A Case Study in Scientific Inquiry: Investigating Mimicry in Snake Populations

Now that we have highlighted the key features of scientific inquiry—making observations and forming and testing hypotheses—you should be able to recognize these features in a case study of actual scientific research.

The story begins with a set of observations and inductive generalizations. Many poisonous animals are brightly colored, often with distinctive patterns that stand out against the background. This is called *warning coloration* because it apparently signals "dangerous species" to potential predators. But there are also mimics. These imposters look like poisonous species but are actually harmless. A question that follows from these observations is: What is the function of such mimicry? A reasonable hypothesis is that the "deception" is an evolutionary adaptation that reduces the harmless animal's risk of being eaten because predators mistake it for the poisonous species. This hypothesis was first formulated by British scientist Henry Bates in 1862.

As obvious as this hypothesis may seem, it has been relatively difficult to test, especially with field experiments. But in 2001, biologists David and Karin Pfennig, of the University of North Carolina, along with William Harcombe, an undergraduate, designed a simple but elegant set of field experiments to test Bates's mimicry hypothesis.

The team investigated a case of mimicry among snakes that live in North and South Carolina **(Figure 1.25)**. A venomous snake called the eastern coral snake has warning coloration: bold, alternating rings of red, yellow (or white), and black. (The word *venomous* is used when a poisonous species delivers their poison actively, by stinging, stabbing, or biting.) Predators rarely attack these coral snakes. It is unlikely that the predators learn this avoidance behavior by trial and error, as a first encounter with a coral snake is usually deadly. In areas where coral snakes live, natural selection has apparently increased the frequency of predators that have inherited an instinctive avoidance of the coral snake's coloration. A nonvenomous snake named the scarlet kingsnake mimics the ringed coloration of the coral snake.

Both types of snakes live in the Carolinas, but the kingsnakes' geographic range also extends into regions where no coral snakes are found (see Figure 1.25). The geographic distribution of the snakes made it possible to test the key prediction of the mimicry hypothesis. Avoiding snakes with warning coloration is an adaptation we expect to be present only in predator populations that evolved in areas where the venomous coral snakes are present. Therefore, mimicry should help protect kingsnakes from predators *only in regions where coral snakes also live*. The mimicry hypothesis predicts that predators adapted to the warning coloration of coral snakes will attack kingsnakes less frequently than will predators in areas where coral snakes are absent.

Field Experiments with Artificial Snakes

To test the prediction, Harcombe made hundreds of artificial snakes out of wire covered with plasticine. He fashioned two versions of fake snakes: an *experimental group* with the red, black, and white ring pattern of kingsnakes and a *control group* of plain brown artificial snakes as a basis of comparison **(Figure 1.26)**.

The researchers placed equal numbers of the two types of artificial snakes in field sites throughout North and South

Scarlet kingsnake (nonvenomous)

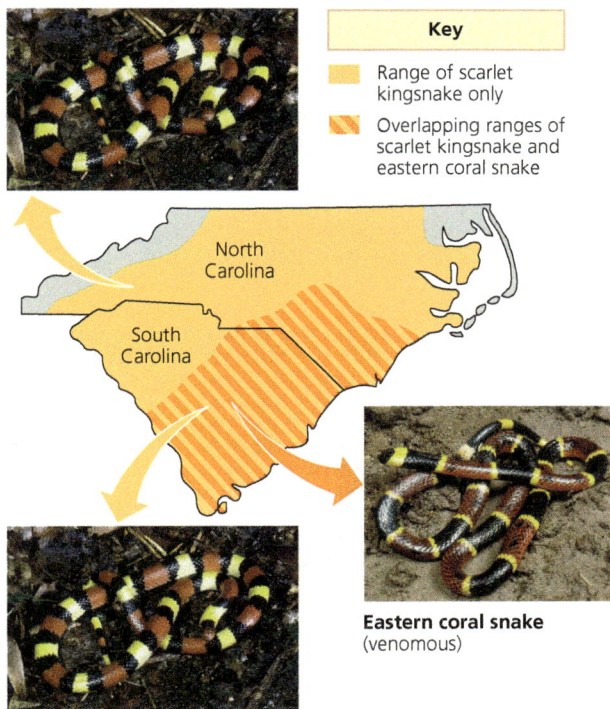

Key

Range of scarlet kingsnake only

Overlapping ranges of scarlet kingsnake and eastern coral snake

North Carolina

South Carolina

Eastern coral snake (venomous)

Scarlet kingsnake (nonvenomous)

▲ **Figure 1.25 The geographic ranges of a venomous snake and its mimic.** The scarlet kingsnake (*Lampropeltis triangulum*) mimics the warning coloration of the venomous eastern coral snake (*Micrurus fulvius*).

(a) Artificial kingsnake

(b) Brown artificial snake that has been attacked

▲ **Figure 1.26 Artificial snakes used in field experiments to test the mimicry hypothesis.** A bear has chewed on the brown artificial snake in **(b)**.

Carolina, including the region where coral snakes are absent. After four weeks, the scientists retrieved the fake snakes and recorded how many had been attacked by looking for bite or claw marks. The most common predators were foxes, coyotes, and raccoons, but black bears also attacked some of the artificial snakes (see Figure 1.26b).

The data fit the key prediction of the mimicry hypothesis. Compared to the brown artificial snakes, the ringed artificial snakes were attacked by predators less frequently only in field sites within the geographic range of the venomous coral snakes. **Figure 1.27** summarizes the field experiments that the researchers carried out. This figure also introduces a format we will use throughout the book for other examples of biological inquiry.

Experimental Controls and Repeatability

The snake mimicry experiment is an example of a **controlled experiment**, one that is designed to compare an experimental group (the artificial kingsnakes, in this case) with a control group (the brown artificial snakes). Ideally, the experimental and control groups differ only in the one factor the experiment is designed to test—in our example, the effect of the snakes' coloration on the behavior of predators. Without the control group, the researchers would not have been able to rule out other factors as causes of the more frequent attacks on the artificial kingsnakes—such as different numbers of predators or different temperatures in the different test areas. The clever experimental design left coloration as the only factor that could account for the low predation rate on the artificial kingsnakes placed within the range of coral snakes. It was not the absolute number of attacks on the artificial kingsnakes that counted, but the difference between that number and the number of attacks on the brown snakes.

A common misconception is that the term *controlled experiment* means that scientists control the experimental environment to keep everything constant except the one variable being tested. But that's impossible in field research and not realistic even in highly regulated laboratory environments. Researchers usually "control" unwanted variables not by *eliminating* them through environmental regulation, but by *canceling out* their effects by using control groups.

Another hallmark of science is that the observations and experimental results must be repeatable. Observations that can't be verified may be interesting or even entertaining, but they cannot count as evidence in scientific inquiry. The headlines of supermarket tabloids would have you believe that humans are occasionally born with the head of a dog and that some of your classmates are extraterrestrials. The unconfirmed eyewitness accounts and the computer-rigged photos are amusing but unconvincing. In science, evidence from observations and experiments is only convincing if it stands up to the criterion of repeatability. The scientists who investigated snake mimicry in the Carolinas obtained similar data when they

▼ **Figure 1.27**

INQUIRY

Does the presence of venomous coral snakes affect predation rates on their mimics, kingsnakes?

EXPERIMENT David Pfennig and his colleagues made artificial snakes to test a prediction of the mimicry hypothesis: that kingsnakes benefit from mimicking the warning coloration of venomous coral snakes only in regions where coral snakes are present. The researchers placed equal numbers of artificial kingsnakes (experimental group) and brown artificial snakes (control group) at 14 field sites, half in the area the two snakes cohabit and half in the area where coral snakes are absent. The researchers recovered the artificial snakes after four weeks and tabulated predation data based on teeth and claw marks on the snakes.

RESULTS In field sites where coral snakes are absent, most attacks were on artificial kingsnakes. Where coral snakes were present, most attacks were on brown artificial snakes.

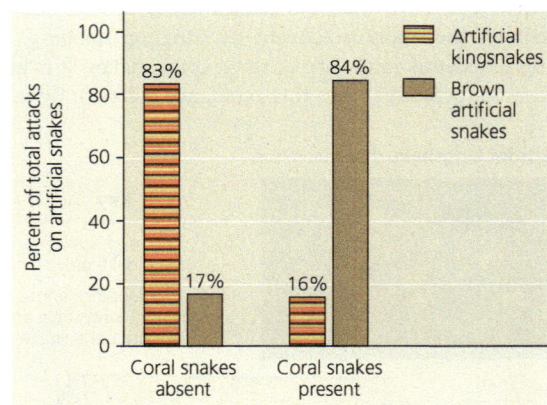

CONCLUSION The field experiments support the mimicry hypothesis by not falsifying the prediction, which was that mimicking coral snakes is effective only in areas where coral snakes are present. The experiments also tested an alternative hypothesis: that predators generally avoid all snakes with brightly colored rings. That hypothesis was falsified by the data showing that in areas without coral snakes, the ringed coloration failed to repel predators. (The fake kingsnakes may have been attacked more often in those areas because their bright pattern made them easier to spot than the brown fakes.)

SOURCE D. W. Pfennig, W. R. Harcombe, and K. S. Pfennig, Frequency-dependent Batesian mimicry, *Nature* 410:323 (2001).

INQUIRY IN ACTION Read and analyze the original paper in *Inquiry in Action: Interpreting Scientific Papers*.

(MB) See the related Experimental Inquiry Tutorial in MasteringBiology.

WHAT IF? What experimental results would you predict if predators throughout the Carolinas avoided all snakes with brightly colored ring patterns?

repeated their experiments with different species of coral snakes and kingsnakes in Arizona. And *you* should be able to obtain similar results if you were to repeat the snake experiments.

Theories in Science

"It's just a theory!" Our everyday use of the term *theory* often implies an untested speculation. But the term *theory* has a different meaning in science. What is a scientific theory, and how is it different from a hypothesis or from mere speculation?

First, a scientific **theory** is much broader in scope than a hypothesis. *This* is a hypothesis: "Mimicking the coloration of venomous snakes is an adaptation that protects nonvenomous snakes from predators." But *this* is a theory: "Evolutionary adaptations arise by natural selection." Darwin's theory of natural selection accounts for an enormous diversity of adaptations, including mimicry.

Second, a theory is general enough to spin off many new, specific hypotheses that can be tested. For example, two researchers at Princeton University, Peter and Rosemary Grant, were motivated by the theory of natural selection to test the specific hypothesis that the beaks of Galápagos finches evolve in response to changes in the types of available food. (Their results supported their hypothesis; see p. 515.)

And third, compared to any one hypothesis, a theory is generally supported by a much greater body of evidence. Those theories that become widely adopted in science (such as the theory of natural selection) explain a great diversity of observations and are supported by a vast accumulation of evidence. In fact, scrutiny of theories continues through testing of the specific, falsifiable hypotheses they spawn.

In spite of the body of evidence supporting a widely accepted theory, scientists must sometimes modify or even reject theories when new research methods produce results that don't fit. For example, the theory of biological diversity that lumped bacteria and archaea together as a kingdom of prokaryotes began to erode when new methods for comparing cells and molecules made it possible to test some of the hypothetical relationships between organisms that were based on the theory. If there is "truth" in science, it is conditional, based on the preponderance of available evidence.

CONCEPT CHECK 1.3

1. Contrast inductive reasoning with deductive reasoning.
2. In the snake mimicry experiment, what is the variable?
3. Why is natural selection called a theory?
4. **WHAT IF?** Suppose you extended the snake mimicry experiment to an area of Virginia where neither type of snake is known to live. What results would you predict at your field site?

For suggested answers, see Appendix A.

CONCEPT 1.4

Science benefits from a cooperative approach and diverse viewpoints

Movies and cartoons sometimes portray scientists as loners working in isolated labs. In reality, science is an intensely social activity. Most scientists work in teams, which often include both graduate and undergraduate students **(Figure 1.28)**. And to succeed in science, it helps to be a good communicator. Research results have no impact until shared with a community of peers through seminars, publications, and websites.

Building on the Work of Others

The great scientist Sir Isaac Newton once said: "To explain all nature is too difficult a task for any one man or even for any one age. 'Tis much better to do a little with certainty, and leave the rest for others that come after you. . . ." Anyone who becomes a scientist, driven by curiosity about how nature works, is sure to benefit greatly from the rich storehouse of discoveries by others who have come before.

Scientists working in the same research field often check one another's claims by attempting to confirm observations or repeat experiments. If experimental results cannot be repeated by scientific colleagues, this failure may reflect some underlying weakness in the original claim, which will then have to be revised. In this sense, science polices itself. Integrity and adherence to high professional standards in reporting results are central to the scientific endeavor. After all, the validity of experimental data is key to designing further lines of inquiry.

It is not unusual for several scientists to converge on the same research question. Some scientists enjoy the challenge of being first with an important discovery or key experiment, while others derive more satisfaction from cooperating with fellow scientists working on the same problem.

▲ **Figure 1.28 Science as a social process.** In laboratory meetings, lab members help each other interpret data, troubleshoot experiments, and plan future lines of inquiry.

Cooperation is facilitated when scientists use the same organism. Often it is a widely used **model organism**—a species that is easy to grow in the lab and lends itself particularly well to the questions being investigated. Because all organisms are evolutionarily related, lessons learned from a model organism are often widely applicable. For example, genetic studies of the fruit fly *Drosophila melanogaster* have taught us a lot about how genes work in other species, including humans. Some other popular model organisms are the mustard plant *Arabidopsis thaliana*, the soil worm *Caenorhabditis elegans*, the zebrafish *Danio rerio*, the mouse *Mus musculus*, and the bacterium *Escherichia coli*. As you read through this book, note the many contributions that these and other model organisms have made to the study of life.

Biologists may come at interesting questions from different angles. Some biologists focus on ecosystems, while others study natural phenomena at the level of organisms or cells. This book is divided into units that look at biology from different levels. Yet any given problem can be addressed from many perspectives, which in fact complement each other.

As a beginning biology student, you can benefit from making connections between the different levels of biology. You can begin to develop this skill by noticing when certain topics crop up again and again in different units. One such topic is sickle-cell disease, a well-understood genetic condition that is prevalent among native inhabitants of Africa and other warm regions and their descendants. Another topic viewed at different levels in this book is global climate change, mentioned earlier in this chapter. Sickle-cell disease and global climate change will appear in several units of the book, each time addressed at a new level. We hope these recurring topics will help you integrate the material you're learning and enhance your enjoyment of biology by helping you keep the "big picture" in mind.

Science, Technology, and Society

The biology community is part of society at large, embedded in the cultural milieu of the times. Some philosophers of science argue that scientists are so influenced by cultural and political values that science is no more objective than other ways of understanding nature. At the other extreme are people who speak of scientific theories as though they were natural laws instead of human interpretations of nature. The reality of science is probably somewhere in between—rarely perfectly objective, but continuously vetted through the expectation that observations and experiments be repeatable and hypotheses be testable and falsifiable.

The relationship of science to society becomes clearer when we add technology to the picture. Though science and technology sometimes employ similar inquiry patterns, their basic goals differ. The goal of science is to understand natural phenomena. In contrast, **technology** generally *applies* scientific knowledge for some specific purpose. Biologists and

▲ **Figure 1.29 DNA technology and crime scene investigation.** In 2008, forensic analysis of DNA samples from a crime scene led to the release of Charles Chatman from prison after he had served nearly 27 years for a rape he didn't commit. The photo shows Judge John Creuzot hugging Mr. Chatman after his conviction was overturned. The details of forensic analysis of DNA will be described in Chapter 20.

other scientists usually speak of "discoveries," while engineers and other technologists more usually speak of "inventions." And the beneficiaries of those inventions include scientists, who put new technology to work in their research. Thus, science and technology are interdependent.

The potent combination of science and technology can have dramatic effects on society. Sometimes, the applications of basic research that turn out to be the most beneficial come out of the blue, from completely unanticipated observations in the course of scientific exploration. For example, discovery of the structure of DNA by Watson and Crick 60 years ago and subsequent achievements in DNA science led to the technologies of DNA manipulation that are transforming applied fields such as medicine, agriculture, and forensics **(Figure 1.29)**. Perhaps Watson and Crick envisioned that their discovery would someday lead to important applications, but it is unlikely that they could have predicted exactly what all those applications would be.

The directions that technology takes depend less on the curiosity that drives basic science than on the current needs and wants of people and on the social environment of the times. Debates about technology center more on "*should* we do it" than "*can* we do it." With advances in technology come difficult choices. For example, under what circumstances is it acceptable to use DNA technology to find out if particular people have genes for hereditary diseases? Should such tests always be voluntary, or are there circumstances when genetic testing should be mandatory? Should insurance companies or employers have access to the information, as they do for many other types of personal health data? These questions are becoming much more urgent as the sequencing of individual genomes becomes quicker and cheaper.

Such ethical issues have as much to do with politics, economics, and cultural values as with science and technology. All citizens—not only professional scientists—have a responsibility to be informed about how science works and about the potential benefits and risks of technology. The relationship between science, technology, and society increases the significance and value of any biology course.

The Value of Diverse Viewpoints in Science

Many of the technological innovations with the most profound impact on human society originated in settlements along trade routes, where a rich mix of different cultures ignited new ideas. For example, the printing press, which helped spread knowledge to all social classes and ultimately led to the book in your hands, was invented by the German Johannes Gutenberg around 1440. This invention relied on several innovations from China, including paper and ink. Paper traveled along trade routes from China to Baghdad, where technology was developed for its mass production. This technology then migrated to Europe, as did water-based ink from China, which was modified by Gutenberg to become oil-based ink. We have the cross-fertilization of diverse cultures to thank for the printing press, and the same can be said for other important inventions.

Along similar lines, science stands to gain much from embracing a diversity of backgrounds and viewpoints among its practitioners. But just how diverse a population are scientists in relation to gender, race, ethnicity, and other attributes?

The scientific community reflects the cultural standards and behaviors of society at large. It is therefore not surprising that until recently, women and certain minorities have faced huge obstacles in their pursuit to become professional scientists in many countries around the world. Over the past 50 years, changing attitudes about career choices have increased the proportion of women in biology and some other sciences, so that now women constitute roughly half of undergraduate biology majors and biology Ph.D. students. The pace has been slow at higher levels in the profession, however, and women and many racial and ethnic groups are still significantly underrepresented in many branches of science. This lack of diversity hampers the progress of science. The more voices that are heard at the table, the more robust, valuable, and productive the scientific interchange will be. The authors of this textbook welcome all students to the community of biologists, wishing you the joys and satisfactions of this very exciting and satisfying field of science—biology.

CONCEPT CHECK 1.4

1. How does science differ from technology?
2. **WHAT IF?** The gene that causes sickle-cell disease is present in a higher percentage of residents of sub-Saharan Africa than it is among those of African descent living in the United States. The presence of this gene provides some protection from malaria, a serious disease that is widespread in sub-Saharan Africa. Discuss an evolutionary process that could account for the different percentages among residents of the two regions.

For suggested answers, see Appendix A.

---

1 CHAPTER REVIEW

SUMMARY OF KEY CONCEPTS

CONCEPT 1.1

The themes of this book make connections across different areas of biology (pp. 48–57)

- **Theme: New properties emerge at each level in the biological hierarchy**
  The hierarchy of life unfolds as follows: biosphere > ecosystem > community > population > organism > organ system > organ > tissue > cell > organelle > molecule > atom. With each step upward from atoms, new properties emerge as a result of interactions among components at the lower levels. In an approach called reductionism, complex systems are broken down to simpler components that are more manageable to study. In **systems biology**, scientists attempt to model the dynamic behavior of whole biological systems based on a study of the interactions among the system's parts.

- **Theme: Organisms interact with other organisms and the physical environment**
  Plants take up nutrients from the soil and chemicals from the air and use energy from the sun. Interactions between plants and other organisms result in cycling of chemical nutrients within an ecosystem. One harmful outcome of human interactions with the environment has been global climate change, caused by burning of fossil fuels and increasing atmospheric CO_2.

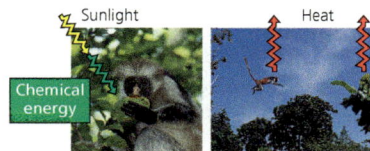

- **Theme: Life requires energy transfer and transformation**
  Energy flows through an ecosystem. All organisms must perform work, which requires energy. Energy from sunlight is converted to chemical energy by producers, which is then passed on to consumers.

- **Theme: Structure and function are correlated at all levels of biological organization**
  The form of a biological structure suits its function and vice versa.

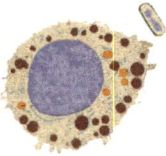

- **Theme: The cell is an organism's basic unit of structure and function**
  The cell is the lowest level of organization that can perform all activities required for life. Cells are either prokaryotic or eukaryotic. **Eukaryotic cells** contain membrane-enclosed organelles, including a DNA-containing nucleus. **Prokaryotic cells** lack such organelles.

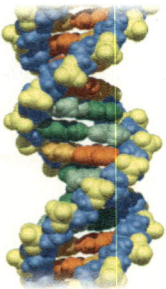

- **Theme: The continuity of life is based on heritable information in the form of DNA**
  Genetic information is encoded in the nucleotide sequences of **DNA**. It is DNA that transmits heritable information from parents to offspring. DNA sequences program a cell's protein production by being transcribed into RNA and then translated into specific proteins, a process called **gene expression**. Gene expression also results in RNAs that are not translated into protein but serve other important functions. **Genomics** is the large-scale analysis of the DNA sequences within a species as well as the comparison of sequences between species.

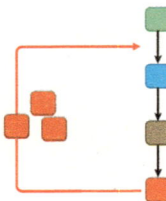

- **Theme: Feedback mechanisms regulate biological systems**
  In **negative feedback**, accumulation of an end product slows the process that makes that product. In **positive feedback**, the end product stimulates the production of more product. Feedback is a type of regulation common to life at all levels, from molecules to ecosystems.

- **Evolution, the Overarching Theme of Biology**
  Evolution accounts for the unity and diversity of life and also for the match of organisms to their environments.

? *Why is evolution considered the core theme of biology?*

CONCEPT 1.2

The Core Theme: Evolution accounts for the unity and diversity of life (pp. 57–64)

- Biologists classify species according to a system of broader and broader groups. Domain **Bacteria** and domain **Archaea** consist of prokaryotes. Domain **Eukarya**, the eukaryotes, includes various groups of protists and the kingdoms Plantae, Fungi, and Animalia. As diverse as life is, there is also evidence of remarkable unity, which is revealed in the similarities between different kinds of organisms.

- Darwin proposed **natural selection** as the mechanism for evolutionary adaptation of populations to their environments.

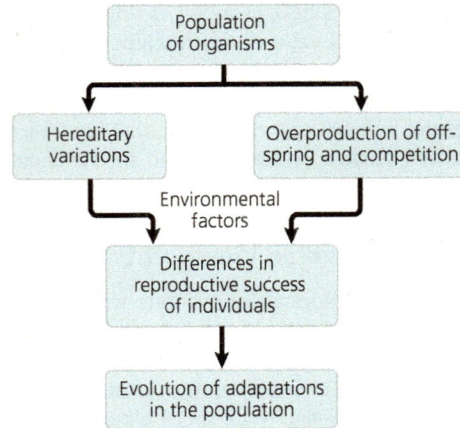

- Each species is one twig of a branching tree of life extending back in time through ancestral species more and more remote. All of life is connected through its long evolutionary history.

? *How could natural selection have led to the evolution of adaptations such as the thick, water-conserving leaves of the mother-of-pearl plant shown in Figures 1.1 and 1.2?*

CONCEPT 1.3

In studying nature, scientists make observations and then form and test hypotheses (pp. 64–69)

- In scientific **inquiry**, scientists make observations (collect **data**) and use **inductive reasoning** to draw a general conclusion, which can be developed into a testable **hypothesis**. **Deductive reasoning** makes predictions that can be used to test hypotheses: If a hypothesis is correct, and we test it, then we can expect the predictions to come true. Hypotheses must be testable and falsifiable; science can address neither the possibility of supernatural phenomena nor the validity of religious beliefs.

- **Controlled experiments**, such as the study investigating mimicry in snake populations, are designed to demonstrate the effect of one variable by testing control groups and experimental groups that differ in only that one variable.

- A scientific **theory** is broad in scope, generates new hypotheses, and is supported by a large body of evidence.

? *What are the roles of inductive and deductive reasoning in the process of scientific inquiry?*

CONCEPT 1.4

Science benefits from a cooperative approach and diverse viewpoints (pp. 69–71)

- Science is a social activity. The work of each scientist builds on the work of others that have come before. Scientists must be able to repeat each other's results, so integrity is key. Biologists approach questions at different levels; their approaches complement each other.

- **Technology** is a method or device that applies scientific knowledge for some specific purpose that affects society. The ultimate impact of basic research is not always immediately obvious.

- Diversity among scientists promotes progress in science.

? *Explain why different approaches and diverse backgrounds among scientists are important.*

TEST YOUR UNDERSTANDING

MB Multiple-choice Self-Quiz questions #1–10 can be found in the Study Area at www.masteringbiology.com.

11. **DRAW IT** With rough sketches, draw a biological hierarchy similar to the one in Figure 1.4 but using a coral reef as the ecosystem, a fish as the organism, its stomach as the organ, and DNA as the molecule. Include all levels in the hierarchy.

12. **EVOLUTION CONNECTION**
A typical prokaryotic cell has about 3,000 genes in its DNA, while a human cell has about 20,500 genes. About 1,000 of these genes are present in both types of cells. Based on your understanding of evolution, explain how such different organisms could have this same subset of genes. What sorts of functions might these shared genes have?

13. **SCIENTIFIC INQUIRY**
Based on the results of the snake mimicry case study, suggest another hypothesis researchers might use to extend the investigation.

14. **WRITE ABOUT A THEME**
Evolution In a short essay (100–150 words), discuss Darwin's view of how natural selection resulted in both unity and diversity of life on Earth. Include in your discussion some of his evidence. (See p. 15 for a suggested grading rubric. The rubric and tips for writing good essays can also be found in the Study Area of MasteringBiology.)

For selected answers, see Appendix A.

Mastering BIOLOGY   www.masteringbiology.com

1. MasteringBiology® Assignments
Experimental Inquiry Tutorial What Can You Learn About the Process of Science from Investigating a Cricket's Chirp?
Tutorial The Scientific Method
Activities The Levels of Life Card Game • Form Fits Function: Cells • Heritable Information: DNA • Introduction to Experimental Design • GraphIt!: An Introduction to Graphing
Questions Student Misconceptions • Reading Quiz • Multiple Choice • End-of-Chapter

2. eText
Read your book online, search, take notes, highlight text, and more.

3. The Study Area
Practice Tests • Cumulative Test • *BioFlix* 3-D Animations • MP3 Tutor Sessions • Videos • Activities • Investigations • Lab Media • Audio Glossary • Word Study Tools • Art

2

The Chemical Context of Life

▲ Figure 2.1 Who tends this "garden"?

KEY CONCEPTS

2.1 Matter consists of chemical elements in pure form and in combinations called compounds

2.2 An element's properties depend on the structure of its atoms

2.3 The formation and function of molecules depend on chemical bonding between atoms

2.4 Chemical reactions make and break chemical bonds

OVERVIEW

A Chemical Connection to Biology

The Amazon rain forest in South America is a showcase for the diversity of life on Earth. Colorful birds, insects, and other animals live in a densely-packed environment of trees, shrubs, vines, and wildflowers, and an excursion along a waterway or a forest path typically reveals a lush variety of plant life. Visitors traveling near the Amazon's headwaters in Peru are therefore surprised to come across tracts of forest like that seen in the foreground of the photo in **Figure 2.1**. This patch is almost completely dominated by a single plant species—a small flowering tree called *Duroia hirsuta*. Travelers may wonder if the plot of land is planted and maintained by local people, but the indigenous people are as mystified as the visitors. They call these stands of *Duroia* trees "devil's gardens," from a legend attributing them to an evil forest spirit.

Seeking a scientific explanation, a research team at Stanford University recently solved the "devil's garden" mystery. **Figure 2.2** describes their main experiment. The researchers showed that the "farmers" who create and maintain these gardens are actually ants that live in the hollow stems of the *Duroia* trees. The ants do not plant the *Duroia* trees, but they prevent other plant species from growing in the garden by injecting intruders with a poisonous chemical. In this way, the ants create space for the growth of the *Duroia* trees that serve as their home. With the ability to maintain and expand its habitat, a single colony of devil's garden ants can live for hundreds of years.

The chemical used by the ants to weed their garden turns out to be formic acid. This substance is produced by many species of ants and in fact got its name from the Latin word for ant, *formica*. For many ant species, the formic acid probably serves as a disinfectant that protects the ants against microbial parasites. The devil's garden ant is the first ant species found to use formic acid as an herbicide, an important addition to the list of functions mediated by chemicals in the insect world. Scientists have long known that chemicals play a major role in insect communication, attraction of mates, and defense against predators.

Research on devil's gardens is only one example of the relevance of chemistry to the study of life. Unlike a list of college courses, nature is not neatly packaged into the individual natural sciences—biology, chemistry, physics, and so forth. Biologists specialize in the study of life, but organisms and their environments are natural systems to which the concepts of chemistry and physics apply. Biology is a multidisciplinary science.

This unit of chapters introduces some basic concepts of chemistry that apply to the study of life. We will make many connections to the themes introduced in Chapter 1. One of these themes is the organization of life into a hierarchy of structural levels, with additional properties emerging at each successive level. In this unit, we will see how emergent properties are apparent at the lowest levels of biological organization—such as the ordering of atoms into molecules and the interactions of those molecules within cells. Somewhere in the transition from molecules to cells, we will cross the blurry boundary between nonlife and life. This chapter focuses on the chemical components that make up all matter.

▼ **Figure 2.2**

INQUIRY

What creates "devil's gardens" in the rain forest?

EXPERIMENT Working under Deborah Gordon and with Michael Greene, graduate student Megan Frederickson sought the cause of "devil's gardens," stands of a single species of tree, *Duroia hirsuta*. One hypothesis was that ants living in these trees, *Myrmelachista schumanni*, produce a poisonous chemical that kills trees of other species; another was that the *Duroia* trees themselves kill competing trees, perhaps by means of a chemical.

To test these hypotheses, Frederickson did field experiments in Peru. Two saplings of a local nonhost tree species, *Cedrela odorata*, were planted inside each of ten devil's gardens. At the base of one sapling, a sticky insect barrier was applied; the other was unprotected. Two more *Cedrela* saplings, with and without barriers, were planted about 50 meters outside each garden.

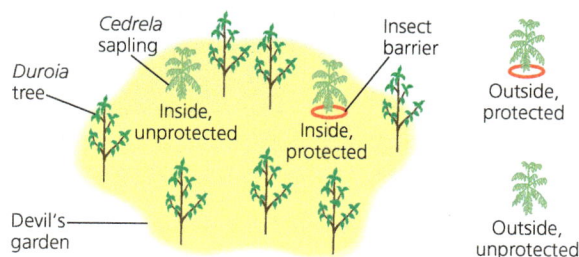

The researchers observed ant activity on the *Cedrela* leaves and measured areas of dead leaf tissue after one day. They also chemically analyzed contents of the ants' poison glands.

RESULTS The ants made injections from the tips of their abdomens into leaves of unprotected saplings in their gardens (see photo). Within one day, these leaves developed dead areas (see graph). The protected saplings were uninjured, as were the saplings planted outside the gardens. Formic acid was the only chemical detected in the poison glands of the ants.

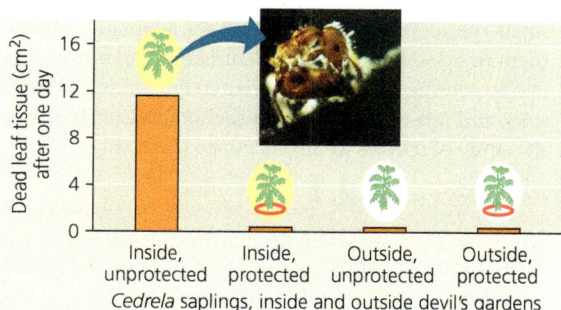

CONCLUSION Ants of the species *Myrmelachista schumanni* kill nonhost trees by injecting the leaves with formic acid, thus creating hospitable habitats (devil's gardens) for the ant colony.

SOURCE M. E. Frederickson, M. J. Greene, and D. M. Gordon, "Devil's gardens" bedevilled by ants, *Nature* 437:495–496 (2005).

INQUIRY IN ACTION Read and analyze the original paper in *Inquiry in Action: Interpreting Scientific Papers*.

WHAT IF? What would be the results if the unprotected saplings' inability to grow in the devil's gardens was caused by a chemical released by the *Duroia* trees rather than by the ants?

CONCEPT ## 2.1

Matter consists of chemical elements in pure form and in combinations called compounds

Organisms are composed of **matter**, which is defined as anything that takes up space and has mass.* Matter exists in many diverse forms. Rocks, metals, oils, gases, and humans are just a few examples of what seems an endless assortment of matter.

Elements and Compounds

Matter is made up of elements. An **element** is a substance that cannot be broken down to other substances by chemical reactions. Today, chemists recognize 92 elements occurring in nature; gold, copper, carbon, and oxygen are examples. Each element has a symbol, usually the first letter or two of its name. Some symbols are derived from Latin or German; for instance, the symbol for sodium is Na, from the Latin word *natrium*.

A **compound** is a substance consisting of two or more different elements combined in a fixed ratio. Table salt, for example, is sodium chloride (NaCl), a compound composed of the elements sodium (Na) and chlorine (Cl) in a 1:1 ratio. Pure sodium is a metal, and pure chlorine is a poisonous gas. When chemically combined, however, sodium and chlorine form an edible compound. Water (H_2O), another compound, consists of the elements hydrogen (H) and oxygen (O) in a 2:1 ratio. These are simple examples of organized matter having emergent properties: A compound has characteristics different from those of its elements (**Figure 2.3**).

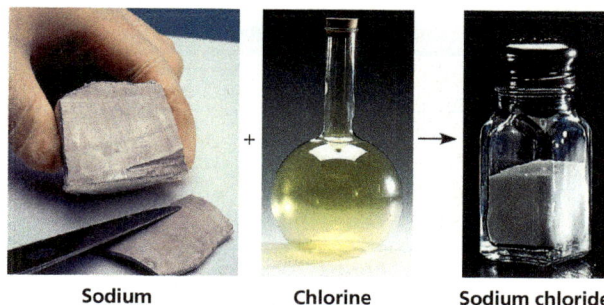

Sodium   **Chlorine**   **Sodium chloride**

▲ **Figure 2.3 The emergent properties of a compound.** The metal sodium combines with the poisonous gas chlorine, forming the edible compound sodium chloride, or table salt.

*Sometimes we substitute the term weight for mass, although the two are not identical. Mass is the amount of matter in an object, whereas the weight of an object is how strongly that mass is pulled by gravity. The weight of an astronaut walking on the moon is approximately 1/6 the astronaut's weight on Earth, but his or her mass is the same. However, as long as we are earthbound, the weight of an object is a measure of its mass; in everyday language, therefore, we tend to use the terms interchangeably.

The Elements of Life

Of the 92 natural elements, about 20–25% are **essential elements** that an organism needs to live a healthy life and reproduce. The essential elements are similar among organisms, but there is some variation—for example, humans need 25 elements, but plants need only 17.

Just four elements—oxygen (O), carbon (C), hydrogen (H), and nitrogen (N)—make up 96% of living matter. Calcium (Ca), phosphorus (P), potassium (K), sulfur (S), and a few other elements account for most of the remaining 4% of an organism's mass. **Trace elements** are required by an organism in only minute quantities. Some trace elements, such as iron (Fe), are needed by all forms of life; others are required only by certain species. For example, in vertebrates (animals with backbones), the element iodine (I) is an essential ingredient of a hormone produced by the thyroid gland. A daily intake of only 0.15 milligram (mg) of iodine is adequate for normal activity of the human thyroid. An iodine deficiency in the diet causes the thyroid gland to grow to abnormal size, a condition called goiter. Where it is available, eating seafood or iodized salt reduces the incidence of goiter. All the elements needed by the human body are listed in **Table 2.1**.

Some naturally occurring elements are toxic to organisms. In humans, for instance, the element arsenic has been linked to numerous diseases and can be lethal. In some areas of the world, arsenic occurs naturally and can make its way into the groundwater. As a result of using water from drilled wells in southern Asia, millions of people have been inadvertently exposed to arsenic-laden water. Efforts are under way to reduce arsenic levels in their water supply.

▲ **Figure 2.4 Serpentine plant community.** The plants in the large photo are growing on serpentine soil, which contains elements that are usually toxic to plants. The insets show a close-up of serpentine rock and one of the plants, a Tiburon Mariposa lily.

Case Study: Evolution of Tolerance to Toxic Elements

EVOLUTION Some species have become adapted to environments containing elements that are usually toxic. A compelling example is found in serpentine plant communities. Serpentine is a jade-like mineral that contains toxic elements such as chromium, nickel, and cobalt. Although most plants cannot survive in soil that forms from serpentine rock, a small number of plant species have adaptations that allow them to do so **(Figure 2.4)**. Presumably, variants of ancestral, nonserpentine species arose that could survive in serpentine soils, and subsequent natural selection resulted in the distinctive array of species we see in these areas today.

CONCEPT CHECK 2.1

1. **MAKE CONNECTIONS** Review the discussion of emergent properties in Chapter 1 (p. 49). Explain how table salt has emergent properties.
2. Is a trace element an essential element? Explain.
3. In humans, iron is a trace element required for the proper functioning of hemoglobin, the molecule that carries oxygen in red blood cells. What might be the effects of an iron deficiency?
4. **MAKE CONNECTIONS** Review the discussion of natural selection in Chapter 1 (pp. 60–62) and explain how natural selection might have played a role in the evolution of species that are tolerant of serpentine soils.

For suggested answers, see Appendix A.

Table 2.1 Elements in the Human Body		
Element	**Symbol**	**Percentage of Body Mass (including water)**
Oxygen	O	65.0%
Carbon	C	18.5%
Hydrogen	H	9.5%
Nitrogen	N	3.3%
Calcium	Ca	1.5%
Phosphorus	P	1.0%
Potassium	K	0.4%
Sulfur	S	0.3%
Sodium	Na	0.2%
Chlorine	Cl	0.2%
Magnesium	Mg	0.1%

Oxygen, Carbon, Hydrogen, Nitrogen: 96.3%

Calcium, Phosphorus, Potassium, Sulfur, Sodium, Chlorine, Magnesium: 3.7%

Trace elements (less than 0.01% of mass): Boron (B), chromium (Cr), cobalt (Co), copper (Cu), fluorine (F), iodine (I), iron (Fe), manganese (Mn), molybdenum (Mo), selenium (Se), silicon (Si), tin (Sn), vanadium (V), zinc (Zn)

CONCEPT **2.2**

An element's properties depend on the structure of its atoms

Each element consists of a certain type of atom that is different from the atoms of any other element. An **atom** is the smallest unit of matter that still retains the properties of an element. Atoms are so small that it would take about a million of them to stretch across the period printed at the end of this sentence. We symbolize atoms with the same abbreviation used for the element that is made up of those atoms. For example, the symbol C stands for both the element carbon and a single carbon atom.

Subatomic Particles

Although the atom is the smallest unit having the properties of an element, these tiny bits of matter are composed of even smaller parts, called *subatomic particles*. Physicists have split the atom into more than a hundred types of particles, but only three kinds of particles are relevant here: **neutrons**, **protons**, and **electrons**. Protons and electrons are electrically charged. Each proton has one unit of positive charge, and each electron has one unit of negative charge. A neutron, as its name implies, is electrically neutral.

Protons and neutrons are packed together tightly in a dense core, or **atomic nucleus**, at the center of an atom; protons give the nucleus a positive charge. The electrons form a sort of cloud of negative charge around the nucleus, and it is the attraction between opposite charges that keeps the electrons in the vicinity of the nucleus. **Figure 2.5** shows two commonly used models of the structure of the helium atom as an example.

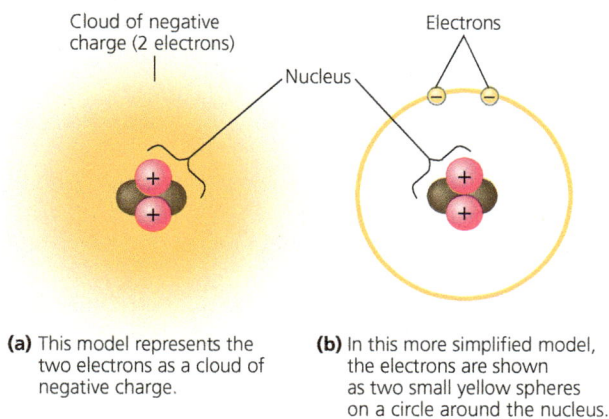

(a) This model represents the two electrons as a cloud of negative charge.

(b) In this more simplified model, the electrons are shown as two small yellow spheres on a circle around the nucleus.

▲ **Figure 2.5 Simplified models of a helium (He) atom.** The helium nucleus consists of 2 neutrons (brown) and 2 protons (pink). Two electrons (yellow) exist outside the nucleus. These models are not to scale; they greatly overestimate the size of the nucleus in relation to the electron cloud.

The neutron and proton are almost identical in mass, each about 1.7×10^{-24} gram (g). Grams and other conventional units are not very useful for describing the mass of objects so minuscule. Thus, for atoms and subatomic particles (and for molecules, too), we use a unit of measurement called the **dalton**, in honor of John Dalton, the British scientist who helped develop atomic theory around 1800. (The dalton is the same as the *atomic mass unit*, or *amu*, a unit you may have encountered elsewhere.) Neutrons and protons have masses close to 1 dalton. Because the mass of an electron is only about 1/2,000 that of a neutron or proton, we can ignore electrons when computing the total mass of an atom.

Atomic Number and Atomic Mass

Atoms of the various elements differ in their number of subatomic particles. All atoms of a particular element have the same number of protons in their nuclei. This number of protons, which is unique to that element, is called the **atomic number** and is written as a subscript to the left of the symbol for the element. The abbreviation $_2$He, for example, tells us that an atom of the element helium has 2 protons in its nucleus. Unless otherwise indicated, an atom is neutral in electrical charge, which means that its protons must be balanced by an equal number of electrons. Therefore, the atomic number tells us the number of protons and also the number of electrons in an electrically neutral atom.

We can deduce the number of neutrons from a second quantity, the **mass number**, which is the sum of protons plus neutrons in the nucleus of an atom. The mass number is written as a superscript to the left of an element's symbol. For example, we can use this shorthand to write an atom of helium as $_2^4$He. Because the atomic number indicates how many protons there are, we can determine the number of neutrons by subtracting the atomic number from the mass number: The helium atom, $_2^4$He, has 2 neutrons. For sodium (Na):

$$_{11}^{23}\text{Na}$$

Mass number = number of protons + neutrons
= 23 for sodium

Atomic number = number of protons
= number of electrons in a neutral atom
= 11 for sodium

Number of neutrons = mass number – atomic number
= 23 – 11 = 12 for sodium

The simplest atom is hydrogen, $_1^1$H, which has no neutrons; it consists of a single proton with a single electron.

As mentioned earlier, the contribution of electrons to mass is negligible. Therefore, almost all of an atom's mass is concentrated in its nucleus. Because neutrons and protons each have a mass very close to 1 dalton, the mass number is an approximation of the total mass of an atom, called its **atomic mass**. So we might say that the atomic mass of sodium ($_{11}^{23}$Na) is 23 daltons, although more precisely it is 22.9898 daltons.

Isotopes

All atoms of a given element have the same number of protons, but some atoms have more neutrons than other atoms of the same element and therefore have greater mass. These different atomic forms of the same element are called **isotopes** of the element. In nature, an element occurs as a mixture of its isotopes. For example, consider the three isotopes of the element carbon, which has the atomic number 6. The most common isotope is carbon-12, $^{12}_6C$, which accounts for about 99% of the carbon in nature. The isotope $^{12}_6C$ has 6 neutrons. Most of the remaining 1% of carbon consists of atoms of the isotope $^{13}_6C$, with 7 neutrons. A third, even rarer isotope, $^{14}_6C$, has 8 neutrons. Notice that all three isotopes of carbon have 6 protons; otherwise, they would not be carbon. Although the isotopes of an element have slightly different masses, they behave identically in chemical reactions. (The number usually given as the atomic mass of an element, such as 22.9898 daltons for sodium, is actually an average of the atomic masses of all the element's naturally occurring isotopes.)

Both ^{12}C and ^{13}C are stable isotopes, meaning that their nuclei do not have a tendency to lose particles. The isotope ^{14}C, however, is unstable, or radioactive. A **radioactive isotope** is one in which the nucleus decays spontaneously, giving off particles and energy. When the decay leads to a change in the number of protons, it transforms the atom to an atom of a different element. For example, when a radioactive carbon atom decays, it becomes an atom of nitrogen.

Radioactive isotopes have many useful applications in biology. In Chapter 25, you will learn how researchers use measurements of radioactivity in fossils to date these relics of past life. As shown in **Figure 2.6**, radioactive isotopes are also useful as tracers to follow atoms through metabolism, the chemical processes of an organism. Cells use the radioactive atoms as they would use nonradioactive isotopes of the same element, but the radioactive tracers can be readily detected.

Radioactive tracers are important diagnostic tools in medicine. For example, certain kidney disorders can be diagnosed by injecting small doses of substances containing radioactive isotopes into the blood and then measuring the amount of tracer excreted in the urine. Radioactive tracers are also used in combination with sophisticated imaging instruments. PET scanners, for instance, can monitor chemical processes, such as those involved in cancerous growth, as they actually occur in the body **(Figure 2.7)**.

Although radioactive isotopes are very useful in biological research and medicine, radiation from decaying isotopes also poses a hazard to life by damaging cellular molecules. The severity of this damage depends on the type and amount of radiation an organism absorbs. One of the most serious environmental threats is radioactive fallout from nuclear accidents. The doses of most isotopes used in medical diagnosis, however, are relatively safe.

▼ **Figure 2.6**   **RESEARCH METHOD**

Radioactive Tracers

APPLICATION Scientists use radioactive isotopes to label certain chemical compounds, creating tracers that allow them to follow a metabolic process or locate the compound within an organism. In this example, radioactive tracers are utilized to determine the effect of temperature on the rate at which cells make copies of their DNA.

TECHNIQUE

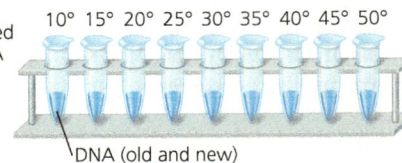

❶ Compounds used by cells to make DNA are added to human cells. One ingredient is labeled with ^3H, a radioactive isotope of hydrogen. Nine dishes of cells are incubated at different temperatures. The cells make new DNA, incorporating the radioactive tracer.

❷ Cells from each incubator are placed in tubes; their DNA is isolated; and unused labeled compounds are removed.

❸ A solution called scintillation fluid is added to the samples, which are then placed in a scintillation counter. As the ^3H in the newly made DNA decays, it emits radiation that excites chemicals in the scintillation fluid, causing them to give off light. Flashes of light are recorded by the scintillation counter.

RESULTS The frequency of flashes, which is recorded as counts per minute, is proportional to the amount of the radioactive tracer present, indicating the amount of new DNA. In this experiment, when the counts per minute are plotted against temperature, it is clear that temperature affects the rate of DNA synthesis; the most DNA was made at 35°C.

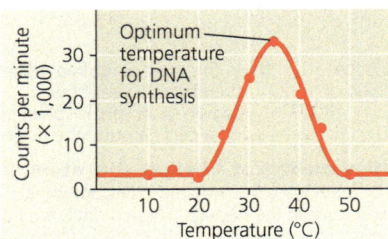

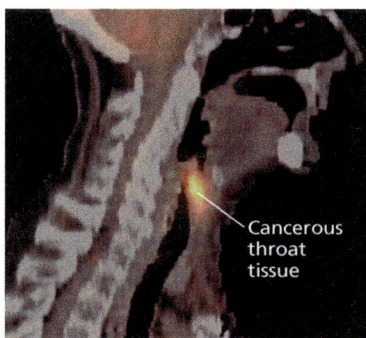

◄ **Figure 2.7 A PET scan, a medical use for radioactive isotopes.** PET, an acronym for positron-emission tomography, detects locations of intense chemical activity in the body. The bright yellow spot marks an area with an elevated level of radioactively labeled glucose, which in turn indicates high metabolic activity, a hallmark of cancerous tissue.

Cancerous throat tissue

(a) A ball bouncing down a flight of stairs provides an analogy for energy levels of electrons, because the ball can come to rest only on each step, not between steps.

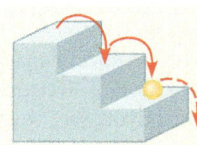

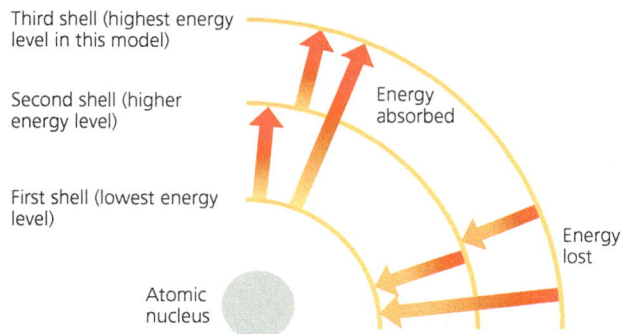

Third shell (highest energy level in this model)

Second shell (higher energy level)

First shell (lowest energy level)

Energy absorbed

Energy lost

Atomic nucleus

(b) An electron can move from one shell to another only if the energy it gains or loses is exactly equal to the difference in energy between the energy levels of the two shells. Arrows in this model indicate some of the stepwise changes in potential energy that are possible.

▲ **Figure 2.8 Energy levels of an atom's electrons.** Electrons exist only at fixed levels of potential energy called electron shells.

The Energy Levels of Electrons

The simplified models of the atom in Figure 2.5 greatly exaggerate the size of the nucleus relative to the volume of the whole atom. If an atom of helium were the size of a typical football stadium, the nucleus would be the size of a pencil eraser in the center of the field. Moreover, the electrons would be like two tiny gnats buzzing around the stadium. Atoms are mostly empty space.

When two atoms approach each other during a chemical reaction, their nuclei do not come close enough to interact. Of the three kinds of subatomic particles we have discussed, only electrons are directly involved in the chemical reactions between atoms.

An atom's electrons vary in the amount of energy they possess. **Energy** is defined as the capacity to cause change—for instance, by doing work. **Potential energy** is the energy that matter possesses because of its location or structure. For example, water in a reservoir on a hill has potential energy because of its altitude. When the gates of the reservoir's dam are opened and the water runs downhill, the energy can be used to do work, such as turning generators. Because energy has been expended, the water has less energy at the bottom of the hill than it did in the reservoir. Matter has a natural tendency to move to the lowest possible state of potential energy; in this example, the water runs downhill. To restore the potential energy of a reservoir, work must be done to elevate the water against gravity.

The electrons of an atom have potential energy because of how they are arranged in relation to the nucleus. The negatively charged electrons are attracted to the positively charged nucleus. It takes work to move a given electron farther away from the nucleus, so the more distant an electron is from the nucleus, the greater its potential energy. Unlike the continuous flow of water downhill, changes in the potential energy of electrons can occur only in steps of fixed amounts. An electron having a certain amount of energy is something like a ball on a staircase **(Figure 2.8a)**. The ball can have different amounts of potential energy, depending on which step it is

on, but it cannot spend much time between the steps. Similarly, an electron's potential energy is determined by its energy level. An electron cannot exist between energy levels.

An electron's energy level is correlated with its average distance from the nucleus. Electrons are found in different **electron shells**, each with a characteristic average distance and energy level. In diagrams, shells can be represented by concentric circles **(Figure 2.8b)**. The first shell is closest to the nucleus, and electrons in this shell have the lowest potential energy. Electrons in the second shell have more energy, and electrons in the third shell even more energy. An electron can change the shell it occupies, but only by absorbing or losing an amount of energy equal to the difference in potential energy between its position in the old shell and that in the new shell. When an electron absorbs energy, it moves to a shell farther out from the nucleus. For example, light energy can excite an electron to a higher energy level. (Indeed, this is the first step taken when plants harness the energy of sunlight for photosynthesis, the process that produces food from carbon dioxide and water.) When an electron loses energy, it "falls back" to a shell closer to the nucleus, and the lost energy is usually released to the environment as heat. For example, sunlight excites electrons in the surface of a car to higher energy levels. When the electrons fall back to their original levels, the car's surface heats up. This thermal energy can be transferred to the air or to your hand if you touch the car.

Electron Distribution and Chemical Properties

The chemical behavior of an atom is determined by the distribution of electrons in the atom's electron shells. Beginning with hydrogen, the simplest atom, we can imagine building the atoms of the other elements by adding 1 proton and 1 electron at a time (along with an appropriate number of neutrons). **Figure 2.9**, an abbreviated version of what is called the *periodic table of the elements*, shows this distribution of electrons for the first 18 elements, from hydrogen ($_1H$) to argon ($_{18}Ar$). The elements are arranged in three rows, or periods, corresponding to the number of electron shells in their atoms. The left-to-right sequence of elements in each row corresponds to the sequential addition of electrons and protons. (See Appendix B for the complete periodic table.)

Hydrogen's 1 electron and helium's 2 electrons are located in the first shell. Electrons, like all matter, tend to exist in the lowest available state of potential energy. In an atom, this state is in the first shell. However, the first shell can hold no more than 2 electrons; thus, hydrogen and helium are the only elements in the first row of the table. An atom with more than 2 electrons must use higher shells because the first shell

is full. The next element, lithium, has 3 electrons. Two of these electrons fill the first shell, while the third electron occupies the second shell. The second shell holds a maximum of 8 electrons. Neon, at the end of the second row, has 8 electrons in the second shell, giving it a total of 10 electrons.

The chemical behavior of an atom depends mostly on the number of electrons in its *outermost* shell. We call those outer electrons **valence electrons** and the outermost electron shell the **valence shell**. In the case of lithium, there is only 1 valence electron, and the second shell is the valence shell. Atoms with the same number of electrons in their valence shells exhibit similar chemical behavior. For example, fluorine (F) and chlorine (Cl) both have 7 valence electrons, and both form compounds when combined with the element sodium (see Figure 2.3). An atom with a completed valence shell is unreactive; that is, it will not interact readily with other atoms. At the far right of the periodic table are helium, neon, and argon, the only three elements shown in Figure 2.9 that have full valence shells. These elements are said to be *inert*, meaning chemically unreactive. All the other atoms in Figure 2.9 are chemically reactive because they have incomplete valence shells.

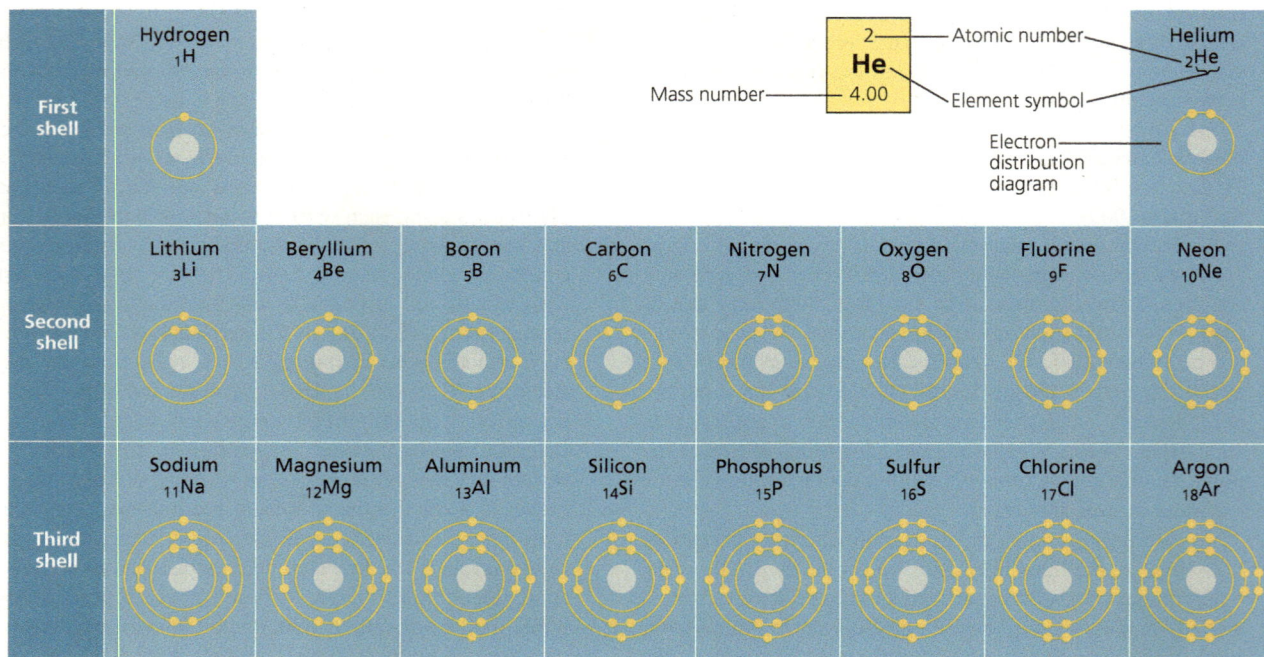

▲ **Figure 2.9 Electron distribution diagrams for the first 18 elements in the periodic table.** In a standard periodic table (see Appendix B), information for each element is presented as shown for helium in the inset. In the diagrams in this table, electrons are represented as yellow dots and electron shells as concentric circles. These diagrams are a convenient way to picture the distribution of an atom's electrons among its electron shells, but these simplified models do not accurately represent the shape of the atom or the location of its electrons. The elements are arranged in rows, each representing the filling of an electron shell. As electrons are added, they occupy the lowest available shell.

? *What is the atomic number of magnesium? How many protons and electrons does it have? How many electron shells? How many valence electrons?*

Electron Orbitals

In the early 1900s, the electron shells of an atom were visualized as concentric paths of electrons orbiting the nucleus, somewhat like planets orbiting the sun. It is still convenient to use two-dimensional concentric-circle diagrams, as in Figure 2.9, to symbolize three-dimensional electron

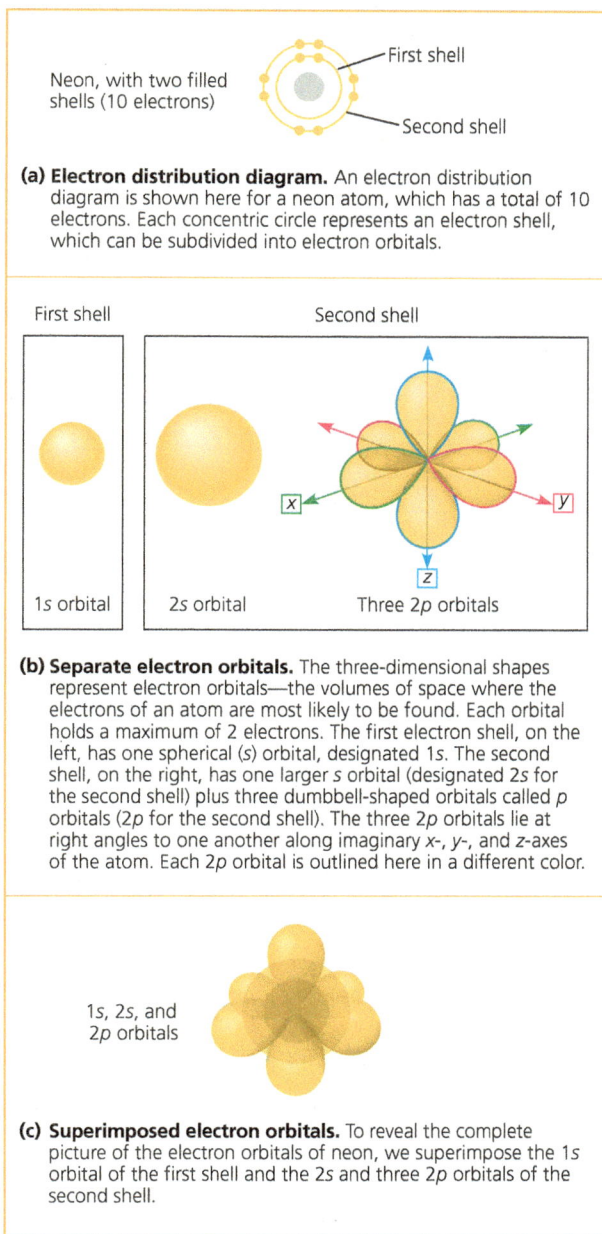

Neon, with two filled shells (10 electrons)

First shell
Second shell

(a) Electron distribution diagram. An electron distribution diagram is shown here for a neon atom, which has a total of 10 electrons. Each concentric circle represents an electron shell, which can be subdivided into electron orbitals.

First shell

Second shell

1s orbital   2s orbital   Three 2p orbitals

(b) Separate electron orbitals. The three-dimensional shapes represent electron orbitals—the volumes of space where the electrons of an atom are most likely to be found. Each orbital holds a maximum of 2 electrons. The first electron shell, on the left, has one spherical (s) orbital, designated 1s. The second shell, on the right, has one larger s orbital (designated 2s for the second shell) plus three dumbbell-shaped orbitals called p orbitals (2p for the second shell). The three 2p orbitals lie at right angles to one another along imaginary x-, y-, and z-axes of the atom. Each 2p orbital is outlined here in a different color.

1s, 2s, and 2p orbitals

(c) Superimposed electron orbitals. To reveal the complete picture of the electron orbitals of neon, we superimpose the 1s orbital of the first shell and the 2s and three 2p orbitals of the second shell.

▲ **Figure 2.10 Electron orbitals.**

shells. However, you need to remember that each concentric circle represents only the *average* distance between an electron in that shell and the nucleus. Accordingly, the concentric-circle diagrams do not give a real picture of an atom. In reality, we can never know the exact location of an electron. What we can do instead is describe the space in which an electron spends most of its time. The three-dimensional space where an electron is found 90% of the time is called an **orbital**.

Each electron shell contains electrons at a particular energy level, distributed among a specific number of orbitals of distinctive shapes and orientations. **Figure 2.10** shows the orbitals of neon as an example, with its electron distribution diagram for reference. You can think of an orbital as a component of an electron shell. The first electron shell has only one spherical s orbital (called 1s), but the second shell has four orbitals: one large spherical s orbital (called 2s) and three dumbbell-shaped p orbitals (called 2p orbitals). (The third shell and other higher electron shells also have s and p orbitals, as well as orbitals of more complex shapes.)

No more than 2 electrons can occupy a single orbital. The first electron shell can therefore accommodate up to 2 electrons in its s orbital. The lone electron of a hydrogen atom occupies the 1s orbital, as do the 2 electrons of a helium atom. The four orbitals of the second electron shell can hold up to 8 electrons, 2 in each orbital. Electrons in each of the four orbitals have nearly the same energy, but they move in different volumes of space.

The reactivity of atoms arises from the presence of unpaired electrons in one or more orbitals of their valence shells. As you will see in the next section, atoms interact in a way that completes their valence shells. When they do so, it is the *unpaired* electrons that are involved.

CONCEPT CHECK 2.2

1. A lithium atom has 3 protons and 4 neutrons. What is its atomic mass in daltons?
2. A nitrogen atom has 7 protons, and the most common isotope of nitrogen has 7 neutrons. A radioactive isotope of nitrogen has 8 neutrons. Write the atomic number and mass number of this radioactive nitrogen as a chemical symbol with a subscript and superscript.
3. How many electrons does fluorine have? How many electron shells? Name the orbitals that are occupied. How many electrons are needed to fill the valence shell?
4. **WHAT IF?** In Figure 2.9, if two or more elements are in the same row, what do they have in common? If two or more elements are in the same column, what do they have in common?

For suggested answers, see Appendix A.

CONCEPT 2.3

The formation and function of molecules depend on chemical bonding between atoms

Now that we have looked at the structure of atoms, we can move up the hierarchy of organization and see how atoms combine to form molecules and ionic compounds. Atoms with incomplete valence shells can interact with certain other atoms in such a way that each partner completes its valence shell: The atoms either share or transfer valence electrons. These interactions usually result in atoms staying close together, held by attractions called **chemical bonds**. The strongest kinds of chemical bonds are covalent bonds and ionic bonds.

Covalent Bonds

A **covalent bond** is the sharing of a pair of valence electrons by two atoms. For example, let's consider what happens when two hydrogen atoms approach each other. Recall that hydrogen has 1 valence electron in the first shell, but the shell's capacity is 2 electrons. When the two hydrogen atoms come close enough for their 1s orbitals to overlap, they can share their electrons (Figure 2.11). Each hydrogen atom is now associated with 2 electrons in what amounts

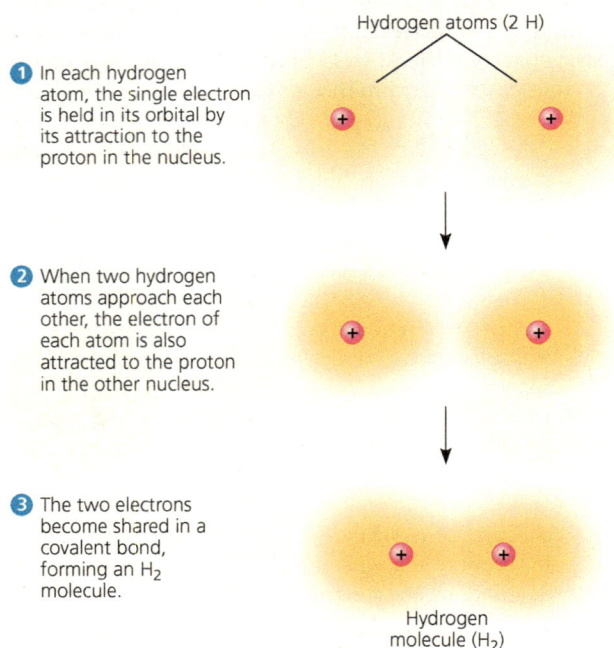

to a completed valence shell. Two or more atoms held together by covalent bonds constitute a **molecule**, in this case a hydrogen molecule.

Figure 2.12a shows several ways of representing a hydrogen molecule. Its *molecular formula*, H_2, simply indicates that the molecule consists of two atoms of hydrogen. Electron sharing can be depicted by an electron distribution diagram or by a *Lewis dot structure*, in which element symbols are surrounded by dots that represent the valence electrons (H:H). We can also use a *structural formula*, H—H, where the line represents a **single bond**, a pair of shared electrons. A space-filling model comes closest to representing the actual shape of the molecule.

Oxygen has 6 electrons in its second electron shell and therefore needs 2 more electrons to complete its valence shell. Two oxygen atoms form a molecule by sharing *two* pairs of valence electrons (Figure 2.12b). The atoms are thus joined by a **double bond** (O=O).

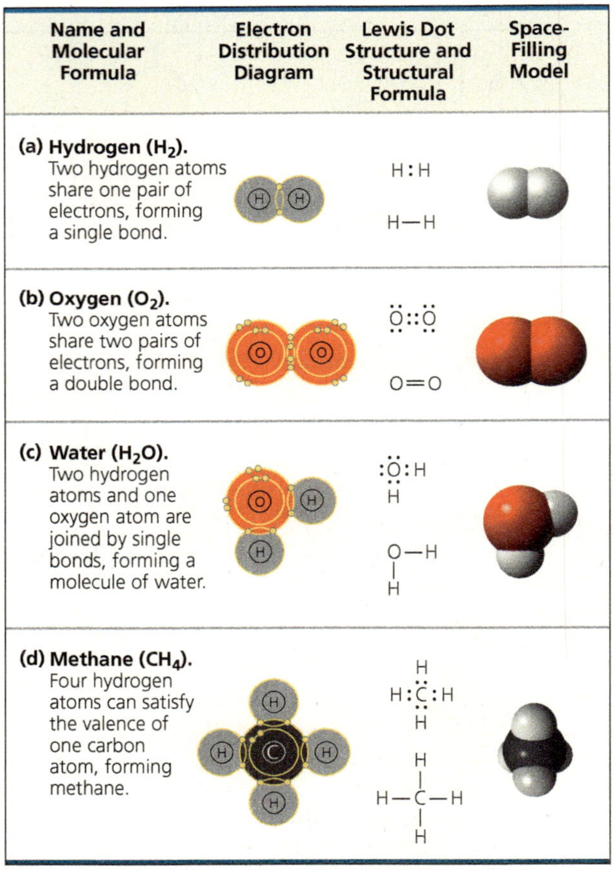

▲ Figure 2.11 **Formation of a covalent bond.**

1 In each hydrogen atom, the single electron is held in its orbital by its attraction to the proton in the nucleus.

2 When two hydrogen atoms approach each other, the electron of each atom is also attracted to the proton in the other nucleus.

3 The two electrons become shared in a covalent bond, forming an H_2 molecule.

▲ Figure 2.12 **Covalent bonding in four molecules.** The number of electrons required to complete an atom's valence shell generally determines how many covalent bonds that atom will form. This figure shows several ways of indicating covalent bonds.

(a) **Hydrogen (H_2).** Two hydrogen atoms share one pair of electrons, forming a single bond.

(b) **Oxygen (O_2).** Two oxygen atoms share two pairs of electrons, forming a double bond.

(c) **Water (H_2O).** Two hydrogen atoms and one oxygen atom are joined by single bonds, forming a molecule of water.

(d) **Methane (CH_4).** Four hydrogen atoms can satisfy the valence of one carbon atom, forming methane.

Each atom that can share valence electrons has a bonding capacity corresponding to the number of covalent bonds the atom can form. When the bonds form, they give the atom a full complement of electrons in the valence shell. The bonding capacity of oxygen, for example, is 2. This bonding capacity is called the atom's **valence** and usually equals the number of unpaired electrons required to complete the atom's outermost (valence) shell. See if you can determine the valences of hydrogen, oxygen, nitrogen, and carbon by studying the electron distribution diagrams in Figure 2.9. You can see that the valence of hydrogen is 1; oxygen, 2; nitrogen, 3; and carbon, 4. However, the situation is more complicated for elements in the third row of the periodic table. Phosphorus, for example, can have a valence of 3, as we would predict from the presence of 3 unpaired electrons in its valence shell. In some molecules that are biologically important, however, phosphorus can form three single bonds and one double bond. Therefore, it can also have a valence of 5.

The molecules H_2 and O_2 are pure elements rather than compounds because a compound is a combination of two or more *different* elements. Water, with the molecular formula H_2O, is a compound. Two atoms of hydrogen are needed to satisfy the valence of one oxygen atom. **Figure 2.12c** shows the structure of a water molecule. Water is so important to life that Chapter 3 is devoted entirely to its structure and behavior.

Methane, the main component of natural gas, is a compound with the molecular formula CH_4. It takes four hydrogen atoms, each with a valence of 1, to complement one atom of carbon, with its valence of 4 **(Figure 2.12d)**. We will look at many other compounds of carbon in Chapter 4.

Atoms in a molecule attract shared electrons to varying degrees, depending on the element. The attraction of a particular atom for the electrons of a covalent bond is called its **electronegativity**. The more electronegative an atom is, the more strongly it pulls shared electrons toward itself. In a covalent bond between two atoms of the same element, the electrons are shared equally because the two atoms have the same electronegativity—the tug-of-war is at a standoff. Such a bond is called a **nonpolar covalent bond**. For example, the single bond of H_2 is nonpolar, as is the double bond of O_2. However, when one atom is bonded to a more electronegative atom, the electrons of the bond are not shared equally. This type of bond is called a **polar covalent bond**. Such bonds vary in their polarity, depending on the relative electronegativity of the two atoms. For example, the bonds between the oxygen and hydrogen atoms of a water molecule are quite polar **(Figure 2.13)**.

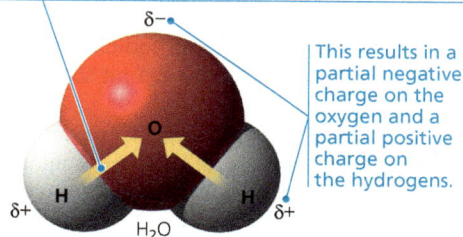

Because oxygen (O) is more electronegative than hydrogen (H), shared electrons are pulled more toward oxygen.

This results in a partial negative charge on the oxygen and a partial positive charge on the hydrogens.

$\delta-$

O

$\delta+$ H   H $\delta+$

H_2O

▲ **Figure 2.13 Polar covalent bonds in a water molecule.**

Oxygen is one of the most electronegative of all the elements, attracting shared electrons much more strongly than hydrogen does. In a covalent bond between oxygen and hydrogen, the electrons spend more time near the oxygen nucleus than they do near the hydrogen nucleus. Because electrons have a negative charge and are pulled toward oxygen in a water molecule, the oxygen atom has a partial negative charge (indicated by the Greek letter δ with a minus sign, $\delta-$, or "delta minus"), and each hydrogen atom has a partial positive charge ($\delta+$, or "delta plus"). In contrast, the individual bonds of methane (CH_4) are much less polar because the electronegativities of carbon and hydrogen are similar.

Ionic Bonds

In some cases, two atoms are so unequal in their attraction for valence electrons that the more electronegative atom strips an electron completely away from its partner. This is what happens when an atom of sodium ($_{11}Na$) encounters an atom of chlorine ($_{17}Cl$) **(Figure 2.14)**. A sodium atom has a total of 11 electrons, with its single valence electron in the third electron shell. A chlorine atom has a total of 17 electrons,

① The lone valence electron of a sodium atom is transferred to join the 7 valence electrons of a chlorine atom.

② Each resulting ion has a completed valence shell. An ionic bond can form between the oppositely charged ions.

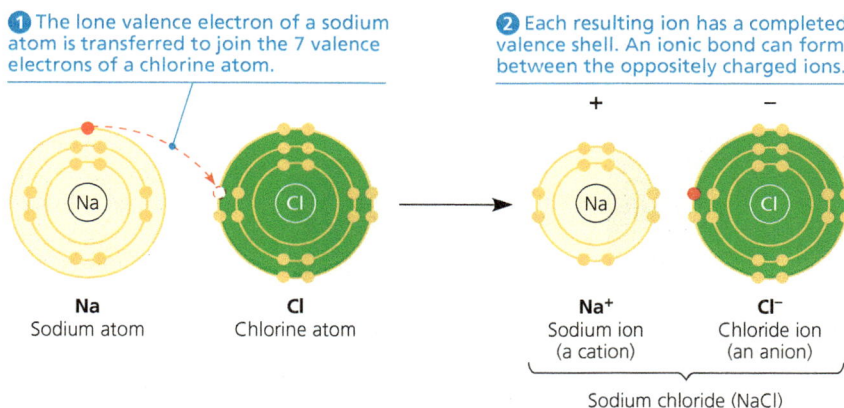

Na
Sodium atom

Cl
Chlorine atom

Na⁺
Sodium ion
(a cation)

Cl⁻
Chloride ion
(an anion)

Sodium chloride (NaCl)

▲ **Figure 2.14 Electron transfer and ionic bonding.** The attraction between oppositely charged atoms, or ions, is an ionic bond. An ionic bond can form between any two oppositely charged ions, even if they have not been formed by transfer of an electron from one to the other.

with 7 electrons in its valence shell. When these two atoms meet, the lone valence electron of sodium is transferred to the chlorine atom, and both atoms end up with their valence shells complete. (Because sodium no longer has an electron in the third shell, the second shell is now the valence shell.)

The electron transfer between the two atoms moves one unit of negative charge from sodium to chlorine. Sodium, now with 11 protons but only 10 electrons, has a net electrical charge of 1+. A charged atom (or molecule) is called an **ion**. When the charge is positive, the ion is specifically called a **cation**; the sodium atom has become a cation. Conversely, the chlorine atom, having gained an extra electron, now has 17 protons and 18 electrons, giving it a net electrical charge of 1−. It has become a chloride ion—an **anion**, or negatively charged ion. Because of their opposite charges, cations and anions attract each other; this attraction is called an **ionic bond**. The transfer of an electron is not the formation of a bond; rather, it allows a bond to form because it results in two ions of opposite charge. Any two ions of opposite charge can form an ionic bond. The ions do not need to have acquired their charge by an electron transfer with each other.

Compounds formed by ionic bonds are called **ionic compounds**, or **salts**. We know the ionic compound sodium chloride (NaCl) as table salt **(Figure 2.15)**. Salts are often found in nature as crystals of various sizes and shapes. Each salt crystal is an aggregate of vast numbers of cations and anions bonded by their electrical attraction and arranged in a three-dimensional lattice. Unlike a covalent compound, which consists of molecules having a definite size and number of atoms, an ionic compound does not consist of molecules. The formula for an ionic compound, such as NaCl, indicates only the ratio of elements in a crystal of the salt. "NaCl" by itself is not a molecule.

Not all salts have equal numbers of cations and anions. For example, the ionic compound magnesium chloride ($MgCl_2$) has two chloride ions for each magnesium ion. Magnesium ($_{12}Mg$) must lose 2 outer electrons if the atom is to have a complete valence shell, so it tends to become a cation with a net charge of 2+ (Mg^{2+}). One magnesium cation can therefore form ionic bonds with two chloride anions.

The term *ion* also applies to entire molecules that are electrically charged. In the salt ammonium chloride (NH_4Cl), for instance, the anion is a single chloride ion (Cl^-), but the cation is ammonium (NH_4^+), a nitrogen atom with four covalently bonded hydrogen atoms. The whole ammonium ion has an electrical charge of 1+ because it is 1 electron short.

Environment affects the strength of ionic bonds. In a dry salt crystal, the bonds are so strong that it takes a hammer and chisel to break enough of them to crack the crystal in two. If the same salt crystal is dissolved in water, however, the ionic bonds are much weaker because each ion is partially shielded by its interactions with water molecules. Most drugs are manufactured as salts because they are quite stable when dry but can dissociate (come apart) easily in water. In the next chapter, you will learn how water dissolves salts.

Weak Chemical Bonds

In organisms, most of the strongest chemical bonds are covalent bonds, which link atoms to form a cell's molecules. But weaker bonding within and between molecules is also indispensable in the cell, contributing greatly to the emergent properties of life. Many large biological molecules are held in their functional form by weak bonds. In addition, when two molecules in the cell make contact, they may adhere temporarily by weak bonds. The reversibility of weak bonding can be an advantage: Two molecules can come together, respond to one another in some way, and then separate.

Several types of weak chemical bonds are important in organisms. One is the ionic bond as it exists between ions dissociated in water, which we just discussed. Hydrogen bonds and van der Waals interactions are also crucial to life.

Hydrogen Bonds

Among the various kinds of weak chemical bonds, hydrogen bonds are so important in the chemistry of life that they deserve special attention. The partial positive charge on a hydrogen atom that is covalently bonded to an electronegative atom allows the hydrogen to be attracted to a different electronegative atom nearby. This noncovalent attraction between a hydrogen and an electronegative atom is called a **hydrogen bond**. In living cells, the electronegative partners are usually oxygen or nitrogen atoms. Refer to **Figure 2.16** to examine the simple case of hydrogen bonding between water (H_2O) and ammonia (NH_3).

Van der Waals Interactions

Even a molecule with nonpolar covalent bonds may have positively and negatively charged regions. Electrons are not always symmetrically distributed in such a molecule; at any

▲ **Figure 2.15 A sodium chloride (NaCl) crystal.** The sodium ions (Na⁺) and chloride ions (Cl⁻) are held together by ionic bonds. The formula NaCl tells us that the ratio of Na⁺ to Cl⁻ is 1:1.

Water (H_2O)

$\delta-$ $\delta+$

A hydrogen bond results from the attraction between the partial positive charge on the hydrogen atom of water and the partial negative charge on the nitrogen atom of ammonia.

$\delta+$
$\delta-$

Ammonia (NH_3)

$\delta+$ $\delta+$
$\delta+$

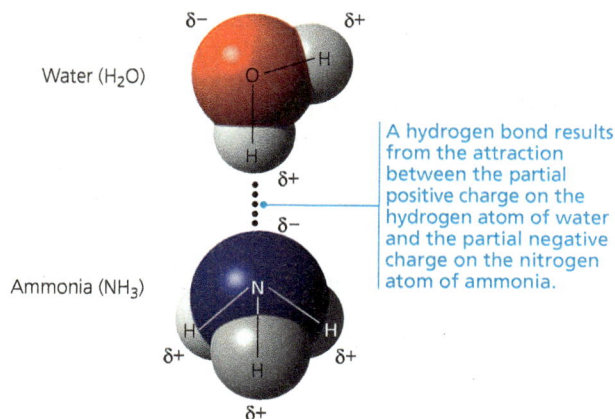

▲ **Figure 2.16 A hydrogen bond.**
DRAW IT *Draw five water molecules using structural formulas and indicating partial charges, and show how they can make hydrogen bonds with each other.*

instant, they may accumulate by chance in one part of the molecule or another. The results are ever-changing regions of positive and negative charge that enable all atoms and molecules to stick to one another. These **van der Waals interactions** are individually weak and occur only when atoms and molecules are very close together. When many such interactions occur simultaneously, however, they can be powerful: Van der Waals interactions are the reason a gecko lizard (right) can walk straight up a wall! Each gecko toe has hundreds of thousands of tiny hairs, with multiple projections at each hair's tip that increase surface area. Apparently, the van der Waals interactions between the hair tip molecules and the molecules of the wall's surface are so numerous that despite their individual weakness, together they can support the gecko's body weight.

Van der Waals interactions, hydrogen bonds, ionic bonds in water, and other weak bonds may form not only between molecules but also between parts of a large molecule, such as a protein. The cumulative effect of weak bonds is to reinforce the three-dimensional shape of the molecule. You will learn more about the very important biological roles of weak bonds in Chapter 5.

Molecular Shape and Function

A molecule has a characteristic size and shape. The precise shape of a molecule is usually very important to its function in the living cell.

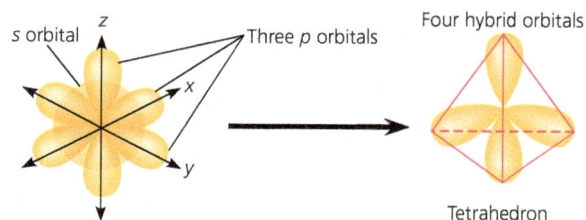

s orbital   *z*   Three *p* orbitals   Four hybrid orbitals

x
y

Tetrahedron

(a) Hybridization of orbitals. The single *s* and three *p* orbitals of a valence shell involved in covalent bonding combine to form four teardrop-shaped hybrid orbitals. These orbitals extend to the four corners of an imaginary tetrahedron (outlined in pink).

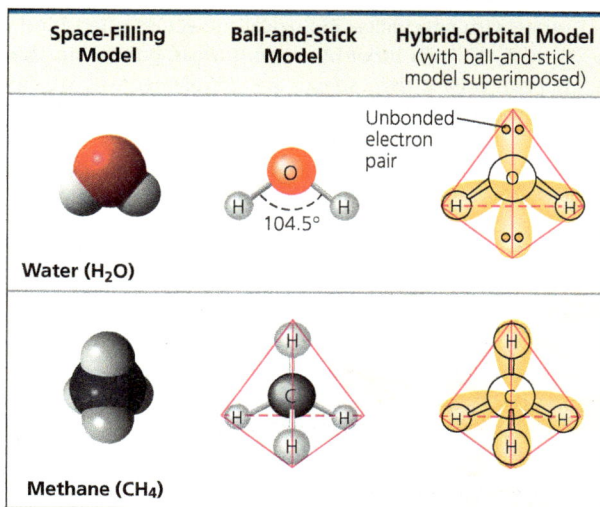

Space-Filling Model	Ball-and-Stick Model	Hybrid-Orbital Model (with ball-and-stick model superimposed)
Water (H_2O)	O H H 104.5°	Unbonded electron pair
Methane (CH_4)		

(b) Molecular-shape models. Three models representing molecular shape are shown for water and methane. The positions of the hybrid orbitals determine the shapes of the molecules.

▲ **Figure 2.17 Molecular shapes due to hybrid orbitals.**

A molecule consisting of two atoms, such as H_2 or O_2, is always linear, but most molecules with more than two atoms have more complicated shapes. These shapes are determined by the positions of the atoms' orbitals. When an atom forms covalent bonds, the orbitals in its valence shell undergo rearrangement. For atoms with valence electrons in both *s* and *p* orbitals (review Figure 2.10), the single *s* and three *p* orbitals form four new hybrid orbitals shaped like identical teardrops extending from the region of the atomic nucleus **(Figure 2.17a)**. If we connect the larger ends of the teardrops with lines, we have the outline of a geometric shape called a tetrahedron, a pyramid with a triangular base.

For the water molecule (H_2O), two of the hybrid orbitals in the oxygen atom's valence shell are shared with hydrogen atoms **(Figure 2.17b)**. The result is a molecule shaped roughly like a V, with its two covalent bonds spread apart at an angle of 104.5°.

The methane molecule (CH_4) has the shape of a completed tetrahedron because all four hybrid orbitals of the carbon atom are shared with hydrogen atoms (see Figure 2.17b). The carbon nucleus is at the center, with its four covalent bonds radiating to hydrogen nuclei at the corners of the tetrahedron. Larger molecules containing multiple carbon atoms, including many of the molecules that make up living matter, have more complex overall shapes. However, the tetrahedral shape of a carbon atom bonded to four other atoms is often a repeating motif within such molecules.

Molecular shape is crucial in biology because it determines how biological molecules recognize and respond to one another with specificity. Biological molecules often bind temporarily to each other by forming weak bonds, but this can happen only if their shapes are complementary. We can see this specificity in the effects of opiates, drugs derived from

opium. Opiates, such as morphine and heroin, relieve pain and alter mood by weakly binding to specific receptor molecules on the surfaces of brain cells. Why would brain cells carry receptors for opiates, compounds that are not made by our bodies? The discovery of endorphins in 1975 answered this question. Endorphins are signaling molecules made by the pituitary gland that bind to the receptors, relieving pain and producing euphoria during times of stress, such as intense exercise. It turns out that opiates have shapes similar to endorphins and mimic them by binding to endorphin receptors in the brain. That is why opiates (such as morphine) and endorphins have similar effects **(Figure 2.18)**. The role of molecular shape in brain chemistry illustrates the relationship between structure and function, one of biology's unifying themes.

CONCEPT CHECK 2.3

1. Why does the structure H—C≡C—H fail to make sense chemically?
2. What holds the atoms together in a crystal of magnesium chloride ($MgCl_2$)?
3. **WHAT IF?** If you were a pharmaceutical researcher, why would you want to learn the three-dimensional shapes of naturally occurring signaling molecules?

For suggested answers, see Appendix A.

CONCEPT 2.4

Chemical reactions make and break chemical bonds

The making and breaking of chemical bonds, leading to changes in the composition of matter, are called **chemical reactions**. An example is the reaction between hydrogen and oxygen molecules that forms water:

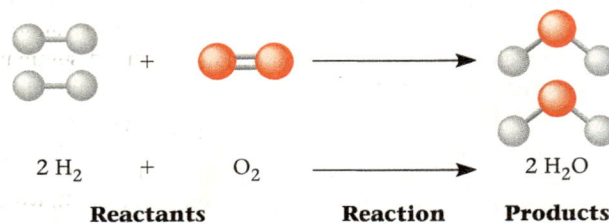

$$2\ H_2 \quad + \quad O_2 \quad \longrightarrow \quad 2\ H_2O$$

Reactants   **Reaction**   **Products**

This reaction breaks the covalent bonds of H_2 and O_2 and forms the new bonds of H_2O. When we write a chemical reaction, we use an arrow to indicate the conversion of the starting materials, called the **reactants**, to the **products**. The coefficients indicate the number of molecules involved; for example, the coefficient 2 in front of the H_2 means that

Key

■ Carbon   ■ Nitrogen
□ Hydrogen   ■ Sulfur
              ■ Oxygen

Natural endorphin

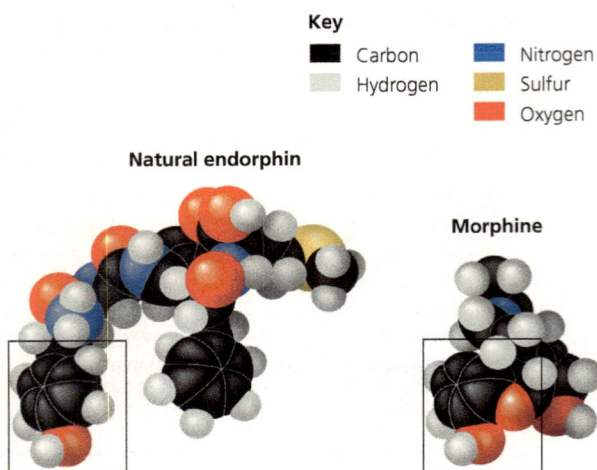

Morphine

(a) Structures of endorphin and morphine. The boxed portion of the endorphin molecule (left) binds to receptor molecules on target cells in the brain. The boxed portion of the morphine molecule (right) is a close match.

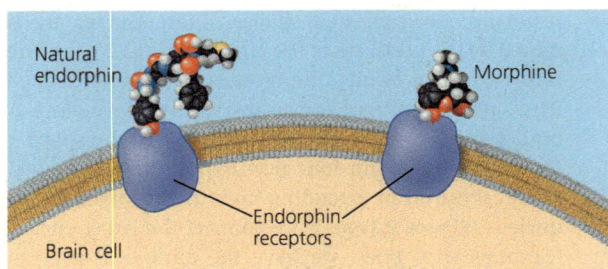

(b) Binding to endorphin receptors. Both endorphin and morphine can bind to endorphin receptors on the surface of a brain cell.

▲ **Figure 2.18 A molecular mimic.** Morphine affects pain perception and emotional state by mimicking the brain's natural endorphins.

▲ **Figure 2.19 Photosynthesis: a solar-powered rearrangement of matter.** *Elodea,* a freshwater plant, produces sugar by rearranging the atoms of carbon dioxide and water in the chemical process known as photosynthesis, which is powered by sunlight. Much of the sugar is then converted to other food molecules. Oxygen gas (O_2) is a by-product of photosynthesis; notice the bubbles of oxygen escaping from the leaves in the photo.

> **?** *Explain how this photo relates to the reactants and products in the equation for photosynthesis given in the text. (You will learn more about photosynthesis in Chapter 10.)*

the reaction starts with two molecules of hydrogen. Notice that all atoms of the reactants must be accounted for in the products. Matter is conserved in a chemical reaction: Reactions cannot create or destroy matter but can only rearrange it.

Photosynthesis, which takes place within the cells of green plant tissues, is a particularly important example of how chemical reactions rearrange matter. Humans and other animals ultimately depend on photosynthesis for food and oxygen, and this process is at the foundation of almost all ecosystems. The following chemical shorthand summarizes the process of photosynthesis:

$$6 CO_2 + 6 H_2O \rightarrow C_6H_{12}O_6 + 6 O_2$$

The raw materials of photosynthesis are carbon dioxide (CO_2), which is taken from the air, and water (H_2O), which is absorbed from the soil. Within the plant cells, sunlight powers the conversion of these ingredients to a sugar called glucose ($C_6H_{12}O_6$) and oxygen molecules (O_2), a by-product that the plant releases into the surroundings **(Figure 2.19)**. Although photosynthesis is actually a sequence of many chemical reactions, we still end up with the same number and types of atoms that we had when we started. Matter has simply been rearranged, with an input of energy provided by sunlight.

All chemical reactions are reversible, with the products of the forward reaction becoming the reactants for the reverse reaction. For example, hydrogen and nitrogen molecules can combine to form ammonia, but ammonia can also decompose to regenerate hydrogen and nitrogen:

$$3 H_2 + N_2 \rightleftharpoons 2 NH_3$$

The two opposite-headed arrows indicate that the reaction is reversible.

One of the factors affecting the rate of a reaction is the concentration of reactants. The greater the concentration of reactant molecules, the more frequently they collide with one another and have an opportunity to react and form products. The same holds true for products. As products accumulate, collisions resulting in the reverse reaction become more frequent. Eventually, the forward and reverse reactions occur at the same rate, and the relative concentrations of products and reactants stop changing. The point at which the reactions offset one another exactly is called **chemical equilibrium**. This is a dynamic equilibrium; reactions are still going on, but with no net effect on the concentrations of reactants and products. Equilibrium does *not* mean that the reactants and products are equal in concentration, but only that their concentrations have stabilized at a particular ratio. The reaction involving ammonia reaches equilibrium when ammonia decomposes as rapidly as it forms. In some chemical reactions, the equilibrium point may lie so far to the right that these reactions go essentially to completion; that is, virtually all the reactants are converted to products.

We will return to the subject of chemical reactions after more detailed study of the various types of molecules that are important to life. In the next chapter, we focus on water, the substance in which all the chemical processes of organisms occur.

CONCEPT CHECK 2.4

1. **MAKE CONNECTIONS** Consider the reaction between hydrogen and oxygen that forms water, shown with ball-and-stick models on page 88. Study Figure 2.12 and draw the Lewis dot structures representing this reaction.
2. Which type of chemical reaction occurs faster at equilibrium, the formation of products from reactants or reactants from products?
3. **WHAT IF?** Write an equation that uses the products of photosynthesis as reactants and the reactants of photosynthesis as products. Add energy as another product. This new equation describes a process that occurs in your cells. Describe this equation in words. How does this equation relate to breathing?

For suggested answers, see Appendix A.

2 CHAPTER REVIEW

SUMMARY OF KEY CONCEPTS

CONCEPT 2.1

Matter consists of chemical elements in pure form and in combinations called compounds (pp. 77–78)

- **Elements** cannot be broken down chemically to other substances. A **compound** contains two or more different elements in a fixed ratio. Oxygen, carbon, hydrogen, and nitrogen make up approximately 96% of living matter.

? *In what way does the need for iodine or iron in your diet differ from your need for calcium or phosphorus?*

CONCEPT 2.2

An element's properties depend on the structure of its atoms (pp. 79–83)

- An **atom**, the smallest unit of an element, has the following components:

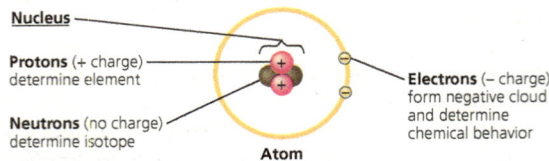

Nucleus

Protons (+ charge) determine element

Neutrons (no charge) determine isotope

Electrons (– charge) form negative cloud and determine chemical behavior

Atom

- An electrically neutral atom has equal numbers of electrons and protons; the number of protons determines the **atomic number**. The **atomic mass** is measured in **daltons** and is roughly equal to the sum of protons plus neutrons. **Isotopes** of an element differ from each other in neutron number and therefore mass. Unstable isotopes give off particles and energy as radioactivity.
- In an atom, electrons occupy specific **electron shells**; the electrons in a shell have a characteristic energy level. Electron distribution in shells determines the chemical behavior of an atom. An atom that has an incomplete outer shell, the **valence shell**, is reactive.
- Electrons exist in **orbitals**, three-dimensional spaces with specific shapes that are components of electron shells.

Electron orbitals

DRAW IT *Draw the electron distribution diagrams for neon ($_{10}$Ne) and argon ($_{18}$Ar). Use these diagrams to explain why these elements are chemically unreactive.*

CONCEPT 2.3

The formation and function of molecules depend on chemical bonding between atoms (pp. 84–88)

- **Chemical bonds** form when atoms interact and complete their valence shells. **Covalent bonds** form when pairs of electrons are shared.

H· + H· ⟶ H:H
Single covalent bond

:Ö· + ·Ö: ⟶ Ö::Ö
Double covalent bond

- **Molecules** consist of two or more covalently bonded atoms. The attraction of an atom for the electrons of a covalent bond is its **electronegativity**. If both atoms are the same, they have the same electronegativity and share a **nonpolar covalent bond**. Electrons of a **polar covalent bond** are pulled closer to the more electronegative atom.
- An **ion** forms when an atom or molecule gains or loses an electron and becomes charged. An **ionic bond** is the attraction between two oppositely charged ions.

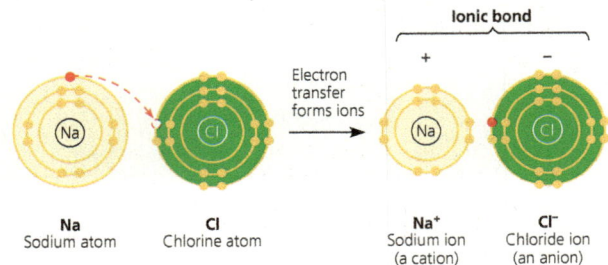

Ionic bond

Na   Cl   Na⁺   Cl⁻
Sodium atom Chlorine atom Sodium ion   Chloride ion
(a cation)   (an anion)

Electron transfer forms ions

- Weak bonds reinforce the shapes of large molecules and help molecules adhere to each other. A **hydrogen bond** is an attraction between a hydrogen atom carrying a partial positive charge ($\delta+$) and an electronegative atom ($\delta-$). **Van der Waals interactions** occur between transiently positive and negative regions of molecules.
- A molecule's shape is determined by the positions of its atoms' valence orbitals. Covalent bonds result in hybrid orbitals, which are responsible for the shapes of H_2O, CH_4, and many more complex biological molecules. Shape is usually the basis for the recognition of one biological molecule by another.

? *In terms of electron sharing between atoms, compare nonpolar covalent bonds, polar covalent bonds, and the formation of ions.*

CONCEPT 2.4

Chemical reactions make and break chemical bonds (pp. 88–89)

- **Chemical reactions** change **reactants** into **products** while conserving matter. All chemical reactions are theoretically reversible. **Chemical equilibrium** is reached when the forward and reverse reaction rates are equal.

? *What would happen to the concentration of products if more reactants were added to a reaction that was in chemical equilibrium? How would this addition affect the equilibrium?*

TEST YOUR UNDERSTANDING

(MB) Multiple-choice Self-Quiz questions #1–8 can be found in the Study Area at www.masteringbiology.com.

9. **DRAW IT** Draw Lewis dot structures for each hypothetical molecule shown below, using the correct number of valence electrons for each atom. Determine which molecule makes sense because each atom has a complete valence shell and each bond has the correct number of electrons. Explain what makes the other molecules nonsensical, considering the number of bonds each type of atom can make.

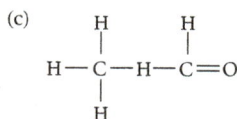

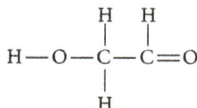

(a) O=C—H

(c)
```
      H      H
      |      |
  H—C—H—C=O
      |
      H
```

(b)
```
   H   H
   |   |
H—O—C—C=O
       |
       H
```

(d) H—N=H with O above N

10. **EVOLUTION CONNECTION**

The percentages of naturally occurring elements making up the human body (see Table 2.1) are similar to the percentages of these elements found in other organisms. How could you account for this similarity among organisms?

11. **SCIENTIFIC INQUIRY**

Female silkworm moths (*Bombyx mori*) attract males by emitting chemical signals that spread through the air. A male hundreds of meters away can detect these molecules and fly toward their source. The sensory organs responsible for this behavior are the comblike antennae visible in the photograph shown here. Each filament of an antenna is equipped with thousands of receptor cells that detect the sex attractant. Based on what you learned in this chapter, propose a hypothesis to account for the ability of the male moth to detect a specific molecule in the presence of many other molecules in the air. What predictions does your hypothesis make? Design an experiment to test one of these predictions.

12. **WRITE ABOUT A THEME**

Emergent Properties While waiting at an airport, Neil Campbell once overheard this claim: "It's paranoid and ignorant to worry about industry or agriculture contaminating the environment with their chemical wastes. After all, this stuff is just made of the same atoms that were already present in our environment." Drawing on your knowledge of electron distribution, bonding, and the theme of emergent properties (pp. 49–51), write a short essay (100–150 words) countering this argument.

For selected answers, see Appendix A.

MasteringBIOLOGY   www.masteringbiology.com

1. MasteringBiology® Assignments

Tutorials The Anatomy of Atoms • Atomic Number and Mass Number
Activities Structure of the Atomic Nucleus • Electron Arrangement • Covalent Bonds • Nonpolar and Polar Molecules • Ionic Bonds • Hydrogen Bonds
Questions Student Misconceptions • Reading Quiz • Multiple Choice • End-of-Chapter

2. eText

Read your book online, search, take notes, highlight text, and more.

3. The Study Area

Practice Tests • Cumulative Test • *BioFlix* 3-D Animations • MP3 Tutor Sessions • Videos • Activities • Investigations • Lab Media • Audio Glossary • Word Study Tools • Art

3

Water and Life

▲ **Figure 3.1** How does the habitat of a polar bear depend on the chemistry of water?

OVERVIEW

The Molecule That Supports All of Life

As astronomers study newly discovered planets orbiting distant stars, they hope to find evidence of water on these far-off celestial bodies, for water is the substance that makes possible life as we know it here on Earth. All organisms familiar to us are made mostly of water and live in an environment dominated by water. Water is the biological medium here on Earth, and possibly on other planets as well.

Three-quarters of Earth's surface is covered by water. Although most of this water is in liquid form, water is also present on Earth as a solid (ice) and a gas (water vapor). Water is the only common substance to exist in the natural environment in all three physical states of matter. Furthermore, the solid state of water floats on the liquid, a rare property emerging from the chemistry of the water molecule. Ice can thus provide a hunting platform for the polar bear in **Figure 3.1**.

The abundance of water is a major reason Earth is habitable. In a classic book called *The Fitness of the Environment*, ecologist Lawrence Henderson highlighted the importance of water to life. While acknowledging that life adapts to its environment through natural selection, Henderson emphasized that for life to exist at all, the environment must first be suitable.

Life on Earth began in water and evolved there for 3 billion years before spreading onto land. Modern life, even terrestrial (land-dwelling) life, remains tied to water. All living organisms require water more than any other substance. Human beings, for example, can survive for quite a few weeks without food, but only a week or so without water. Molecules of water participate in many chemical reactions necessary to sustain life. Most cells are surrounded by water, and cells themselves are about 70–95% water.

What properties of the simple water molecule make it so indispensable to life on Earth? In this chapter, you will learn how the structure of a water molecule allows it to interact with other molecules, including other water molecules. This ability leads to water's unique emergent properties that help make Earth suitable for life.

CONCEPT **3.1**

Polar covalent bonds in water molecules result in hydrogen bonding

Water is so common that it is easy to overlook the fact that it is an exceptional substance with many extraordinary qualities. Following the theme of emergent properties, we can trace water's unique behavior to the structure and interactions of its molecules.

Studied on its own, the water molecule is deceptively simple. It is shaped like a wide V, with its two hydrogen atoms joined to the oxygen atom by single covalent bonds. Oxygen is more electronegative than hydrogen, so the electrons of the covalent bonds spend more time closer to oxygen than to hydrogen; these are **polar covalent bonds** (see Figure 2.13). This unequal sharing of electrons and water's V-like shape make it a **polar molecule**, meaning that its overall charge is unevenly distributed: The oxygen region of the molecule has a partial negative charge ($\delta-$), and each hydrogen has a partial positive charge ($\delta+$).

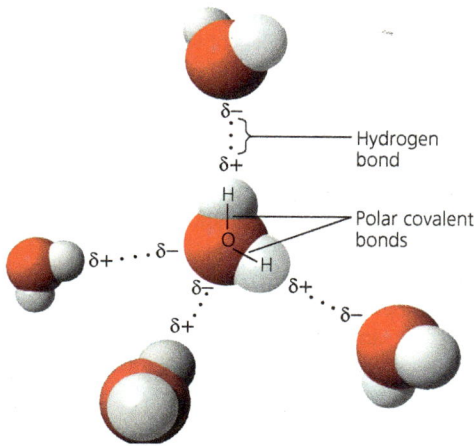

▲ **Figure 3.2 Hydrogen bonds between water molecules.** The charged regions in a water molecule are due to its polar covalent bonds. Oppositely charged regions of neighboring water molecules are attracted to each other, forming hydrogen bonds. Each molecule can hydrogen-bond to multiple partners, and these associations are constantly changing.

DRAW IT *Draw partial charges on all the atoms of the water molecule on the far left above, and draw two more water molecules hydrogen-bonded to it.*

The properties of water arise from attractions between oppositely charged atoms of different water molecules: The slightly positive hydrogen of one molecule is attracted to the slightly negative oxygen of a nearby molecule. The two molecules are thus held together by a hydrogen bond **(Figure 3.2)**. When water is in its liquid form, its hydrogen bonds are very fragile, each about 1/20 as strong as a covalent bond. The hydrogen bonds form, break, and re-form with great frequency. Each lasts only a few trillionths of a second, but the molecules are constantly forming new hydrogen bonds with a succession of partners. Therefore, at any instant, a substantial percentage of all the water molecules are hydrogen-bonded to their neighbors. The extraordinary qualities of water are emergent properties resulting in large part from the hydrogen bonding that organizes water molecules into a higher level of structural order.

CONCEPT CHECK 3.1

1. **MAKE CONNECTIONS** What is electronegativity, and how does it affect interactions between water molecules? Review p. 85 and Figure 2.13.
2. Why is it unlikely that two neighboring water molecules would be arranged like this?

$$O \diagdown \substack{H\ H} \diagup O$$
$$\diagup \substack{H\ H} \diagdown$$

3. **WHAT IF?** What would be the effect on the properties of the water molecule if oxygen and hydrogen had equal electronegativity?

For suggested answers, see Appendix A.

CONCEPT 3.2

Four emergent properties of water contribute to Earth's suitability for life

We will examine four emergent properties of water that contribute to Earth's suitability as an environment for life: cohesive behavior, ability to moderate temperature, expansion upon freezing, and versatility as a solvent.

Cohesion of Water Molecules

Water molecules stay close to each other as a result of hydrogen bonding. Although the arrangement of molecules in a sample of liquid water is constantly changing, at any given moment many of the molecules are linked by multiple hydrogen bonds. These linkages make water more structured than most other liquids. Collectively, the hydrogen bonds hold the substance together, a phenomenon called **cohesion**.

Cohesion due to hydrogen bonding contributes to the transport of water and dissolved nutrients against gravity in plants **(Figure 3.3)**. Water from the roots reaches the leaves through a network of water-conducting cells. As water evaporates from a

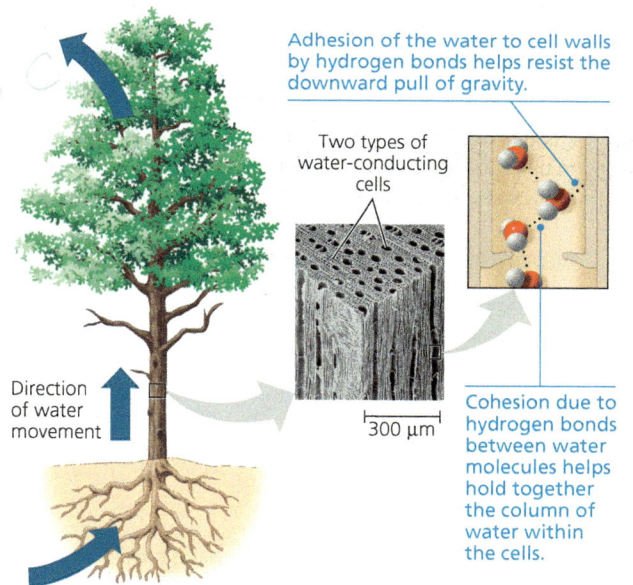

▲ **Figure 3.3 Water transport in plants.** Evaporation from leaves pulls water upward from the roots through water-conducting cells. Because of the properties of cohesion and adhesion, the tallest trees can transport water more than 100 m upward—approximately one-quarter the height of the Empire State Building in New York City.

ANIMATION **BioFlix** Visit the Study Area at www.masteringbiology.com for the BioFlix® 3-D Animation on Water Transport in Plants.

▲ Figure 3.4 Walking on water. The high surface tension of water, resulting from the collective strength of its hydrogen bonds, allows this raft spider to walk on the surface of a pond.

leaf, hydrogen bonds cause water molecules leaving the veins to tug on molecules farther down, and the upward pull is transmitted through the water-conducting cells all the way to the roots. **Adhesion**, the clinging of one substance to another, also plays a role. Adhesion of water to cell walls by hydrogen bonds helps counter the downward pull of gravity (see Figure 3.3).

Related to cohesion is **surface tension**, a measure of how difficult it is to stretch or break the surface of a liquid. Water has a greater surface tension than most other liquids. At the interface between water and air is an ordered arrangement of water molecules, hydrogen-bonded to one another and to the water below. This makes the water behave as though coated with an invisible film. You can observe the surface tension of water by slightly overfilling a drinking glass; the water will stand above the rim. In a more biological example, some animals can stand, walk, or run on water without breaking the surface **(Figure 3.4)**.

Moderation of Temperature by Water

Water moderates air temperature by absorbing heat from air that is warmer and releasing the stored heat to air that is cooler. Water is effective as a heat bank because it can absorb or release a relatively large amount of heat with only a slight change in its own temperature. To understand this capability of water, we must first look briefly at heat and temperature.

Heat and Temperature

Anything that moves has **kinetic energy**, the energy of motion. Atoms and molecules have kinetic energy because they are always moving, although not necessarily in any particular direction. The faster a molecule moves, the greater its kinetic energy. **Heat** is a form of energy. For a given body of matter, the amount of heat is a measure of the matter's *total* kinetic energy due to motion of its molecules; thus, heat depends in part on the matter's volume. Although heat is related to temperature, they are not the same thing. **Temperature** is a

measure of heat intensity that represents the *average* kinetic energy of the molecules, regardless of volume. When water is heated in a coffeemaker, the average speed of the molecules increases, and the thermometer records this as a rise in temperature of the liquid. The amount of heat also increases in this case. Note, however, that although the pot of coffee has a much higher temperature than, say, the water in a swimming pool, the swimming pool contains more heat because of its much greater volume.

Whenever two objects of different temperature are brought together, heat passes from the warmer to the cooler object until the two are the same temperature. Molecules in the cooler object speed up at the expense of the kinetic energy of the warmer object. An ice cube cools a drink not by adding coldness to the liquid, but by absorbing heat from the liquid as the ice itself melts.

In general, we will use the **Celsius scale** to indicate temperature. (Celsius degrees are abbreviated °C; Appendix C shows how to convert between Celsius and Fahrenheit.) At sea level, water freezes at 0°C and boils at 100°C. The temperature of the human body averages 37°C, and comfortable room temperature is about 20–25°C.

One convenient unit of heat used in this book is the **calorie (cal)**. A calorie is the amount of heat it takes to raise the temperature of 1 g of water by 1°C. Conversely, a calorie is also the amount of heat that 1 g of water releases when it cools by 1°C. A **kilocalorie (kcal)**, 1,000 cal, is the quantity of heat required to raise the temperature of 1 kilogram (kg) of water by 1°C. (The "calories" on food packages are actually kilocalories.) Another energy unit used in this book is the **joule (J)**. One joule equals 0.239 cal; one calorie equals 4.184 J.

Water's High Specific Heat

The ability of water to stabilize temperature stems from its relatively high specific heat. The **specific heat** of a substance is defined as the amount of heat that must be absorbed or lost for 1 g of that substance to change its temperature by 1°C. We already know water's specific heat because we have defined a calorie as the amount of heat that causes 1 g of water to change its temperature by 1°C. Therefore, the specific heat of water is 1 calorie per gram and per degree Celsius, abbreviated as 1 cal/g·°C. Compared with most other substances, water has an unusually high specific heat. For example, ethyl alcohol, the type of alcohol in alcoholic beverages, has a specific heat of 0.6 cal/g·°C; that is, only 0.6 cal is required to raise the temperature of 1 g of ethyl alcohol by 1°C.

Because of the high specific heat of water relative to other materials, water will change its temperature less when it absorbs or loses a given amount of heat. The reason you can burn your fingers by touching the side of an iron pot on the stove when the water in the pot is still lukewarm is that the specific heat of water is ten times greater than that of iron.

▲ **Figure 3.5 Effect of a large body of water on climate.** By absorbing or releasing heat, oceans moderate coastal climates. In this example from an August day in Southern California, the relatively cool ocean reduces coastal air temperatures by absorbing heat.

In other words, the same amount of heat will raise the temperature of 1 g of the iron much faster than it will raise the temperature of 1 g of the water. Specific heat can be thought of as a measure of how well a substance resists changing its temperature when it absorbs or releases heat. Water resists changing its temperature; when it does change its temperature, it absorbs or loses a relatively large quantity of heat for each degree of change.

We can trace water's high specific heat, like many of its other properties, to hydrogen bonding. Heat must be absorbed in order to break hydrogen bonds; by the same token, heat is released when hydrogen bonds form. A calorie of heat causes a relatively small change in the temperature of water because much of the heat is used to disrupt hydrogen bonds before the water molecules can begin moving faster. And when the temperature of water drops slightly, many additional hydrogen bonds form, releasing a considerable amount of energy in the form of heat.

What is the relevance of water's high specific heat to life on Earth? A large body of water can absorb and store a huge amount of heat from the sun in the daytime and during summer while warming up only a few degrees. At night and during winter, the gradually cooling water can warm the air. This is the reason coastal areas generally have milder climates than inland regions **(Figure 3.5)**. The high specific heat of water also tends to stabilize ocean temperatures, creating a favorable environment for marine life. Thus, because of its high specific heat, the water that covers most of Earth keeps temperature fluctuations on land and in water within limits that permit life. Also, because organisms are made primarily of water, they are better able to resist changes in their own temperature than if they were made of a liquid with a lower specific heat.

Evaporative Cooling

Molecules of any liquid stay close together because they are attracted to one another. Molecules moving fast enough to overcome these attractions can depart the liquid and enter the air as a gas. This transformation from a liquid to a gas is called vaporization, or *evaporation*. Recall that the speed of molecular movement varies and that temperature is the *average* kinetic energy of molecules. Even at low temperatures, the speediest molecules can escape into the air. Some evaporation occurs at any temperature; a glass of water at room temperature, for example, will eventually evaporate completely. If a liquid is heated, the average kinetic energy of molecules increases and the liquid evaporates more rapidly.

Heat of vaporization is the quantity of heat a liquid must absorb for 1 g of it to be converted from the liquid to the gaseous state. For the same reason that water has a high specific heat, it also has a high heat of vaporization relative to most other liquids. To evaporate 1 g of water at 25°C, about 580 cal of heat is needed—nearly double the amount needed to vaporize a gram of alcohol or ammonia. Water's high heat of vaporization is another emergent property resulting from the strength of its hydrogen bonds, which must be broken before the molecules can make their exodus from the liquid.

The high amount of energy required to vaporize water has a wide range of effects. On a global scale, for example, it helps moderate Earth's climate. A considerable amount of solar heat absorbed by tropical seas is consumed during the evaporation of surface water. Then, as moist tropical air circulates poleward, it releases heat as it condenses and forms rain. On an organismal level, water's high heat of vaporization accounts for the severity of steam burns. These burns are caused by the heat energy released when steam condenses into liquid on the skin.

As a liquid evaporates, the surface of the liquid that remains behind cools down. This **evaporative cooling** occurs because the "hottest" molecules, those with the greatest kinetic energy, are the most likely to leave as gas. It is as if the hundred fastest runners at a college transferred to another school; the average speed of the remaining students would decline.

Evaporative cooling of water contributes to the stability of temperature in lakes and ponds and also provides a mechanism that prevents terrestrial organisms from overheating. For example, evaporation of water from the leaves of a plant helps keep the tissues in the leaves from becoming too warm in the sunlight. Evaporation of sweat from human skin dissipates body heat and helps prevent overheating on a hot day or when excess heat is generated by strenuous activity. High humidity on a hot day increases discomfort because the high concentration of water vapor in the air inhibits the evaporation of sweat from the body.

Floating of Ice on Liquid Water

Water is one of the few substances that are less dense as a solid than as a liquid. In other words, ice floats on liquid water. While other materials contract and become denser when they solidify, water expands. The cause of this exotic behavior is, once again, hydrogen bonding. At temperatures above

▶ **Figure 3.6 Ice: crystalline structure and floating barrier.** In ice, each molecule is hydrogen-bonded to four neighbors in a three-dimensional crystal. Because the crystal is spacious, ice has fewer molecules than an equal volume of liquid water. In other words, ice is less dense than liquid water. Floating ice becomes a barrier that protects the liquid water below from the colder air. The marine organism shown here is a type of shrimp called krill; it was photographed beneath floating ice in the Southern Ocean near Antarctica.

WHAT IF? *If water did not form hydrogen bonds, what would happen to the shrimp's environment?*

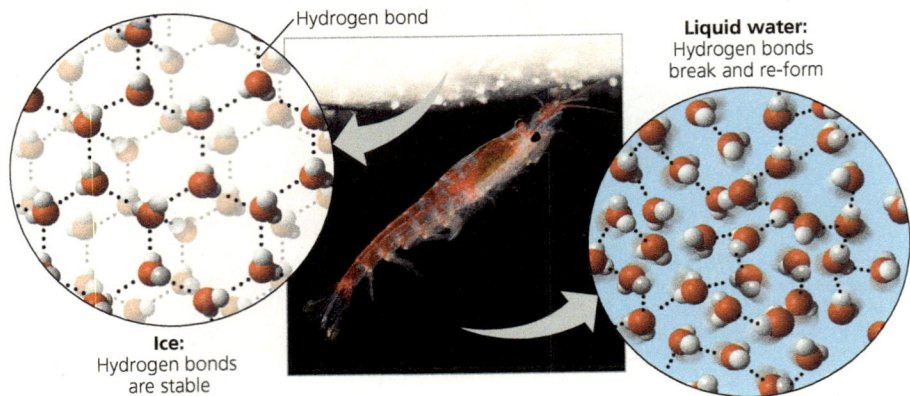

Hydrogen bond

Liquid water: Hydrogen bonds break and re-form

Ice: Hydrogen bonds are stable

4°C, water behaves like other liquids, expanding as it warms and contracting as it cools. As the temperature falls from 4°C to 0°C, water begins to freeze because more and more of its molecules are moving too slowly to break hydrogen bonds. At 0°C, the molecules become locked into a crystalline lattice, each water molecule hydrogen-bonded to four partners **(Figure 3.6)**. The hydrogen bonds keep the molecules at "arm's length," far enough apart to make ice about 10% less dense (10% fewer molecules for the same volume) than liquid water at 4°C. When ice absorbs enough heat for its temperature to rise above 0°C, hydrogen bonds between molecules are disrupted. As the crystal collapses, the ice melts, and molecules are free to slip closer together. Water reaches its greatest density at 4°C and then begins to expand as the molecules move faster. Even in liquid water, many of the molecules are connected by hydrogen bonds, though only transiently: The hydrogen bonds are constantly breaking and re-forming.

The ability of ice to float due to its lower density is an important factor in the suitability of the environment for life. If ice sank, then eventually all ponds, lakes, and even oceans would freeze solid, making life as we know it impossible on Earth. During summer, only the upper few inches of the ocean would thaw. Instead, when a deep body of water cools, the floating ice insulates the liquid water below, preventing it from freezing and allowing life to exist under the frozen surface, as shown in the photo in Figure 3.6. Besides insulating the water below, ice also provides solid habitat for some animals, such as polar bears and seals (see Figure 3.1).

Many scientists are worried that these bodies of ice are at risk of disappearing. Global warming, which is caused by carbon dioxide and other "greenhouse" gases in the atmosphere, is having a profound effect on icy environments around the globe. In the Arctic, the average air temperature has risen 1.4°C just since 1961. This temperature increase has affected the seasonal balance between Arctic sea ice and liquid water, causing ice to form later in the year, to melt earlier, and to cover a smaller area. The alarming rate at which glaciers and Arctic sea

ice are disappearing is posing an extreme challenge to animals that depend on ice for their survival.

Water: The Solvent of Life

A sugar cube placed in a glass of water will dissolve. The glass will then contain a uniform mixture of sugar and water; the concentration of dissolved sugar will be the same everywhere in the mixture. A liquid that is a completely homogeneous mixture of two or more substances is called a **solution**. The dissolving agent of a solution is the **solvent**, and the substance that is dissolved is the **solute**. In this case, water is the solvent and sugar is the solute. An **aqueous solution** is one in which water is the solvent.

The medieval alchemists tried to find a universal solvent, one that would dissolve anything. They learned that nothing works better than water. Yet, water is not a universal solvent; if it were, it would dissolve any container in which it was stored, including our cells. Water is a very versatile solvent, however, a quality we can trace to the polarity of the water molecule.

Suppose, for example, that a spoonful of table salt, the ionic compound sodium chloride (NaCl), is placed in water **(Figure 3.7)**. At the surface of each grain, or crystal, of salt, the sodium and chloride ions are exposed to the solvent. These ions and the water molecules have a mutual affinity owing to the attraction between opposite charges. The oxygen regions of the water molecules are negatively charged and are attracted to sodium cations. The hydrogen regions are positively charged and are attracted to chloride anions. As a result, water molecules surround the individual sodium and chloride ions, separating and shielding them from one another. The sphere of water molecules around each dissolved ion is called a **hydration shell**. Working inward from the surface of each salt crystal, water eventually dissolves all the ions. The result is a solution of two solutes, sodium cations and chloride anions, homogeneously mixed with water, the solvent. Other ionic compounds also dissolve in water. Seawater, for instance, contains a great variety of dissolved ions, as do living cells.

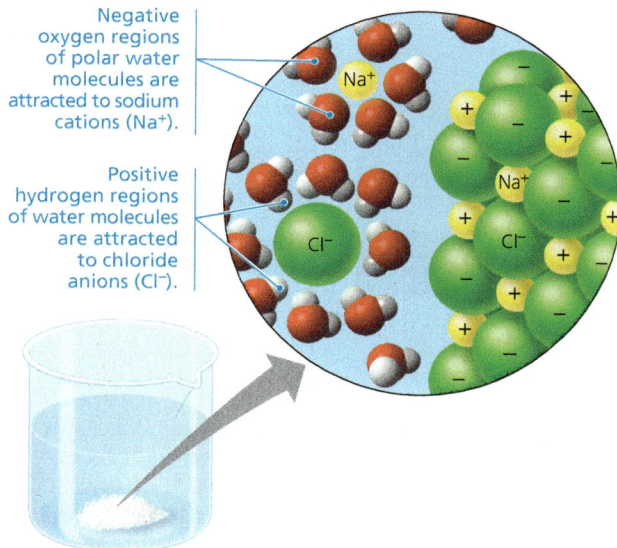

Negative oxygen regions of polar water molecules are attracted to sodium cations (Na+).

Positive hydrogen regions of water molecules are attracted to chloride anions (Cl−).

▲ **Figure 3.7 Table salt dissolving in water.** A sphere of water molecules, called a hydration shell, surrounds each solute ion.

WHAT IF? *What would happen if you heated this solution for a long time?*

A compound does not need to be ionic to dissolve in water; many compounds made up of nonionic polar molecules, such as sugars, are also water-soluble. Such compounds dissolve when water molecules surround each of the solute molecules, forming hydrogen bonds with them. Even molecules as large as proteins can dissolve in water if they have ionic and polar regions on their surface **(Figure 3.8)**. Many different kinds of polar compounds are dissolved (along with ions) in the water of such biological fluids as blood, the sap of plants, and the liquid within all cells. Water is the solvent of life.

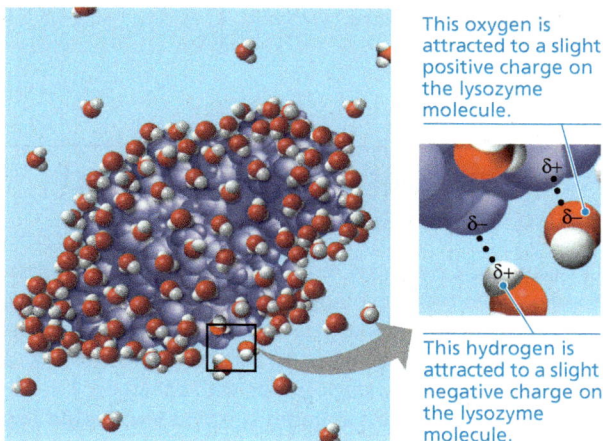

This oxygen is attracted to a slight positive charge on the lysozyme molecule.

This hydrogen is attracted to a slight negative charge on the lysozyme molecule.

▲ **Figure 3.8 A water-soluble protein.** Human lysozyme is a protein found in tears and saliva that has antibacterial action. This model shows the lysozyme molecule (purple) in an aqueous environment. Ionic and polar regions on the protein's surface attract water molecules.

Hydrophilic and Hydrophobic Substances

Any substance that has an affinity for water is said to be **hydrophilic** (from the Greek *hydro*, water, and *philios*, loving). In some cases, substances can be hydrophilic without actually dissolving. For example, some molecules in cells are so large that they do not dissolve. Instead, they remain suspended in the aqueous liquid of the cell. Such a mixture is an example of a **colloid**, a stable suspension of fine particles in a liquid. Another example of a hydrophilic substance that does not dissolve is cotton, a plant product. Cotton consists of giant molecules of cellulose, a compound with numerous regions of partial positive and partial negative charges that can form hydrogen bonds with water. Water adheres to the cellulose fibers. Thus, a cotton towel does a great job of drying the body, yet it does not dissolve in the washing machine. Cellulose is also present in the walls of water-conducting cells in a plant; you read earlier how the adhesion of water to these hydrophilic walls allows water transport to occur.

There are, of course, substances that do not have an affinity for water. Substances that are nonionic and nonpolar (or otherwise cannot form hydrogen bonds) actually seem to repel water; these substances are said to be **hydrophobic** (from the Greek *phobos*, fearing). An example from the kitchen is vegetable oil, which, as you know, does not mix stably with water-based substances such as vinegar. The hydrophobic behavior of the oil molecules results from a prevalence of relatively nonpolar covalent bonds, in this case bonds between carbon and hydrogen, which share electrons almost equally. Hydrophobic molecules related to oils are major ingredients of cell membranes. (Imagine what would happen to a cell if its membrane dissolved!)

Solute Concentration in Aqueous Solutions

Biological chemistry is "wet" chemistry. Most of the chemical reactions in organisms involve solutes dissolved in water. To understand such reactions, we must know how many atoms and molecules are involved and be able to calculate the concentration of solutes in an aqueous solution (the number of solute molecules in a volume of solution).

When carrying out experiments, we use mass to calculate the number of molecules. We know the mass of each atom in a given molecule, so we can calculate the **molecular mass**, which is simply the sum of the masses of all the atoms in a molecule. As an example, let's calculate the molecular mass of table sugar (sucrose), which has the molecular formula $C_{12}H_{22}O_{11}$. In round numbers of daltons, the mass of a carbon atom is 12, the mass of a hydrogen atom is 1, and the mass of an oxygen atom is 16. Thus, sucrose has a molecular mass of $(12 \times 12) + (22 \times 1) + (11 \times 16) = 342$ daltons. Of course, weighing out small numbers of molecules is not practical. For this reason, we usually measure substances in units called moles. Just as a dozen always means 12 objects, a **mole (mol)** represents an exact number of objects: 6.02×10^{23}, which is called Avogadro's number. Because of the way in which Avogadro's number and the unit *dalton* were originally defined, there are 6.02×10^{23} daltons in 1 g. This is significant because once we determine the molecular mass of a molecule such as sucrose, we can use the same number (342), but with the unit *gram*, to represent the mass of 6.02×10^{23} molecules of sucrose, or 1 mol of sucrose (this is sometimes called the *molar mass*). To obtain 1 mol of sucrose in the lab, therefore, we weigh out 342 g.

The practical advantage of measuring a quantity of chemicals in moles is that a mole of one substance has exactly the same number of molecules as a mole of any other substance. If the molecular mass of substance A is 342 daltons and that of substance B is 10 daltons, then 342 g of A will have the same number of molecules as 10 g of B. A mole of ethyl alcohol (C_2H_6O) also contains 6.02×10^{23} molecules, but its mass is only 46 g because the mass of a molecule of ethyl alcohol is less than that of a molecule of sucrose. Measuring in moles makes it convenient for scientists working in the laboratory to combine substances in fixed ratios of molecules.

How would we make a liter (L) of solution consisting of 1 mol of sucrose dissolved in water? We would measure out 342 g of sucrose and then gradually add water, while stirring, until the sugar was completely dissolved. We would then add enough water to bring the total volume of the solution up to 1 L. At that point, we would have a 1-molar (1 *M*) solution of sucrose. **Molarity**—the number of moles of solute per liter of solution—is the unit of concentration most often used by biologists for aqueous solutions.

Water's capacity as a versatile solvent complements the other properties discussed in this chapter. Since these remarkable properties allow water to support life on Earth so well, scientists who seek life elsewhere in the universe look for water as a sign that a planet might sustain life.

Possible Evolution of Life on Other Planets with Water

EVOLUTION Humans have probably always gazed skyward, wondering whether other living beings exist beyond Earth. And if life has arisen on other planets, into what form or forms has it evolved? Biologists who look for life elsewhere in the universe (known as *astrobiologists*) have concentrated their search on planets that might have water. To date, more than 200 planets have been found outside our solar system, and there is evidence for the presence of water vapor on one or two of them. In our own solar system, Mars has been most compelling to astrobiologists as a focus of study.

Like Earth, Mars has an ice cap at both poles. And in the decades since the age of space exploration began, scientists have found intriguing signs that water may exist elsewhere on Mars. Finally, in 2008, the robotic spacecraft *Phoenix* landed on Mars and began to sample its surface. Years of debate were

◄ **Figure 3.9 Subsurface ice and morning frost on Mars.** This photograph was taken by the Mars lander *Phoenix* in 2008. The trench was scraped by a robotic arm, uncovering ice (white in rectangle near bottom) below the surface material. Frost also appears as a white coating in several places in the upper half of the image. This photograph was colorized by NASA to highlight the ice.

resolved by the images sent back from *Phoenix*: Ice is definitely present just under Mars's surface, and enough water vapor is in the Martian atmosphere for frost to form **(Figure 3.9)**. This exciting finding has reinvigorated the search for signs of life, past or present, on Mars and other planets. If any life-forms or fossils are found, their study will shed light on the process of evolution from an entirely new perspective.

CONCEPT CHECK 3.2

1. Describe how properties of water contribute to the upward movement of water in a tree.
2. Explain the saying "It's not the heat; it's the humidity."
3. How can the freezing of water crack boulders?
4. The concentration of the appetite-regulating hormone ghrelin is about $1.3 \times 10^{-10} M$ in a fasting person. How many molecules of ghrelin are in 1 L of blood?
5. **WHAT IF?** A water strider (which can walk on water) has legs that are coated with a hydrophobic substance. What might be the benefit? What would happen if the substance were hydrophilic?

For suggested answers, see Appendix A.

CONCEPT 3.3

Acidic and basic conditions affect living organisms

Occasionally, a hydrogen atom participating in a hydrogen bond between two water molecules shifts from one molecule to the other. When this happens, the hydrogen atom leaves its electron behind, and what is actually transferred is a **hydrogen ion** (H^+), a single proton with a charge of 1+. The water molecule that lost a proton is now a **hydroxide ion** (OH^-), which has a charge of 1−. The proton binds to the other water molecule, making that molecule a **hydronium ion** (H_3O^+). We can picture the chemical reaction as shown at the top of the next page.

2 H$_2$O   Hydronium   Hydroxide
                           ion (H$_3$O$^+$)   ion (OH$^-$)

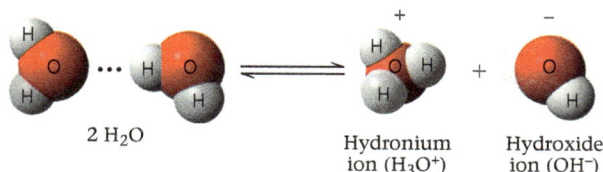

By convention, H$^+$ (the hydrogen ion) is used to represent H$_3$O$^+$ (the hydronium ion), and we follow that practice here. Keep in mind, though, that H$^+$ does not exist on its own in an aqueous solution. It is always associated with another water molecule in the form of H$_3$O$^+$.

As indicated by the double arrows, this is a reversible reaction that reaches a state of dynamic equilibrium when water molecules dissociate at the same rate that they are being re-formed from H$^+$ and OH$^-$. At this equilibrium point, the concentration of water molecules greatly exceeds the concentrations of H$^+$ and OH$^-$. In pure water, only one water molecule in every 554 million is dissociated; the concentration of each ion in pure water is 10^{-7} M (at 25°C). This means there is only one ten-millionth of a mole of hydrogen ions per liter of pure water and an equal number of hydroxide ions.

Although the dissociation of water is reversible and statistically rare, it is exceedingly important in the chemistry of life. H$^+$ and OH$^-$ are very reactive. Changes in their concentrations can drastically affect a cell's proteins and other complex molecules. As we have seen, the concentrations of H$^+$ and OH$^-$ are equal in pure water, but adding certain kinds of solutes, called acids and bases, disrupts this balance. Biologists use something called the pH scale to describe how acidic or basic (the opposite of acidic) a solution is. In the remainder of this chapter, you will learn about acids, bases, and pH and why changes in pH can adversely affect organisms.

Acids and Bases

What would cause an aqueous solution to have an imbalance in H$^+$ and OH$^-$ concentrations? When acids dissolve in water, they donate additional H$^+$ to the solution. An **acid** is a substance that increases the hydrogen ion concentration of a solution. For example, when hydrochloric acid (HCl) is added to water, hydrogen ions dissociate from chloride ions:

$$HCl \rightarrow H^+ + Cl^-$$

This source of H$^+$ (dissociation of water is the other source) results in an acidic solution—one having more H$^+$ than OH$^-$.

A substance that reduces the hydrogen ion concentration of a solution is called a **base**. Some bases reduce the H$^+$ concentration directly by accepting hydrogen ions. Ammonia (NH$_3$), for instance, acts as a base when the unshared electron pair in nitrogen's valence shell attracts a hydrogen ion from the solution, resulting in an ammonium ion (NH$_4^+$):

$$NH_3 + H^+ \rightleftharpoons NH_4{^+}$$

Other bases reduce the H$^+$ concentration indirectly by dissociating to form hydroxide ions, which combine with hydrogen ions and form water. One such base is sodium hydroxide (NaOH), which in water dissociates into its ions:

$$NaOH \rightarrow Na^+ + OH^-$$

In either case, the base reduces the H$^+$ concentration. Solutions with a higher concentration of OH$^-$ than H$^+$ are known as basic solutions. A solution in which the H$^+$ and OH$^-$ concentrations are equal is said to be neutral.

Notice that single arrows were used in the reactions for HCl and NaOH. These compounds dissociate completely when mixed with water, so hydrochloric acid is called a strong acid and sodium hydroxide a strong base. In contrast, ammonia is a relatively weak base. The double arrows in the reaction for ammonia indicate that the binding and release of hydrogen ions are reversible reactions, although at equilibrium there will be a fixed ratio of NH$_4^+$ to NH$_3$.

There are also weak acids, which reversibly release and accept back hydrogen ions. An example is carbonic acid:

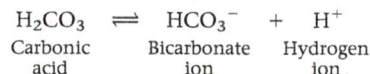

$$H_2CO_3 \rightleftharpoons HCO_3{^-} + H^+$$

Carbonic   Bicarbonate   Hydrogen
acid   ion   ion

Here the equilibrium so favors the reaction in the left direction that when carbonic acid is added to pure water, only 1% of the molecules are dissociated at any particular time. Still, that is enough to shift the balance of H$^+$ and OH$^-$ from neutrality.

The pH Scale

In any aqueous solution at 25°C, the *product* of the H$^+$ and OH$^-$ concentrations is constant at 10^{-14}. This can be written

$$[H^+][OH^-] = 10^{-14}$$

In such an equation, brackets indicate molar concentration. In a neutral solution at room temperature (25°C), $[H^+] = 10^{-7}$ and $[OH^-] = 10^{-7}$, so in this case, 10^{-14} is the product of $10^{-7} \times 10^{-7}$. If enough acid is added to a solution to increase $[H^+]$ to 10^{-5} M, then $[OH^-]$ will decline by an equivalent amount to 10^{-9} M (note that $10^{-5} \times 10^{-9} = 10^{-14}$). This constant relationship expresses the behavior of acids and bases in an aqueous solution. An acid not only adds hydrogen ions to a solution, but also removes hydroxide ions because of the tendency for H$^+$ to combine with OH$^-$, forming water. A base has the opposite effect, increasing OH$^-$ concentration but also reducing H$^+$ concentration by the formation of water. If enough of a base is added to raise the OH$^-$ concentration to 10^{-4} M, it will cause the H$^+$ concentration to drop to 10^{-10} M. Whenever we know the concentration of either H$^+$ or OH$^-$ in an aqueous solution, we can deduce the concentration of the other ion.

Because the H$^+$ and OH$^-$ concentrations of solutions can vary by a factor of 100 trillion or more, scientists have

pH Scale

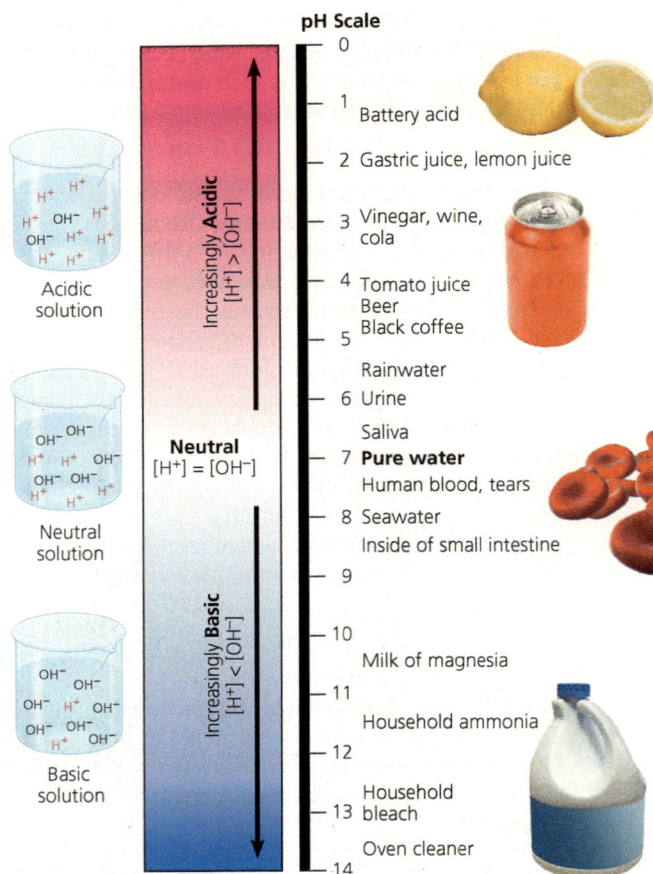

▲ **Figure 3.10 The pH scale and pH values of some aqueous solutions.**

developed a way to express this variation more conveniently than in moles per liter. The pH scale **(Figure 3.10)** compresses the range of H⁺ and OH⁻ concentrations by employing logarithms. The **pH** of a solution is defined as the negative logarithm (base 10) of the hydrogen ion concentration:

$$pH = -\log [H^+]$$

For a neutral aqueous solution, $[H^+]$ is 10^{-7} M, giving us

$$-\log 10^{-7} = -(-7) = 7$$

Notice that pH *declines* as H⁺ concentration *increases*. Notice, too, that although the pH scale is based on H⁺ concentration, it also implies OH⁻ concentration. A solution of pH 10 has a hydrogen ion concentration of 10^{-10} M and a hydroxide ion concentration of 10^{-4} M.

The pH of a neutral aqueous solution at 25°C is 7, the midpoint of the pH scale. A pH value less than 7 denotes an acidic solution; the lower the number, the more acidic the solution. The pH for basic solutions is above 7. Most biological fluids are within the range pH 6–8. There are a few exceptions, however,

including the strongly acidic digestive juice of the human stomach, which has a pH of about 2.

Remember that each pH unit represents a tenfold difference in H⁺ and OH⁻ concentrations. It is this mathematical feature that makes the pH scale so compact. A solution of pH 3 is not twice as acidic as a solution of pH 6, but a thousand times ($10 \times 10 \times 10$) more acidic. When the pH of a solution changes slightly, the actual concentrations of H⁺ and OH⁻ in the solution change substantially.

Buffers

The internal pH of most living cells is close to 7. Even a slight change in pH can be harmful, because the chemical processes of the cell are very sensitive to the concentrations of hydrogen and hydroxide ions. The pH of human blood is very close to 7.4, or slightly basic. A person cannot survive for more than a few minutes if the blood pH drops to 7 or rises to 7.8, and a chemical system exists in the blood that maintains a stable pH. If you add 0.01 mol of a strong acid to a liter of pure water, the pH drops from 7.0 to 2.0. If the same amount of acid is added to a liter of blood, however, the pH decrease is only from 7.4 to 7.3. Why does the addition of acid have so much less of an effect on the pH of blood than it does on the pH of water?

The presence of substances called buffers allows biological fluids to maintain a relatively constant pH despite the addition of acids or bases. A **buffer** is a substance that minimizes changes in the concentrations of H⁺ and OH⁻ in a solution. It does so by accepting hydrogen ions from the solution when they are in excess and donating hydrogen ions to the solution when they have been depleted. Most buffer solutions contain a weak acid and its corresponding base, which combine reversibly with hydrogen ions.

There are several buffers that contribute to pH stability in human blood and many other biological solutions. One of these is carbonic acid (H_2CO_3), formed when CO_2 reacts with water in blood plasma. As mentioned earlier, carbonic acid dissociates to yield a bicarbonate ion (HCO_3^-) and a hydrogen ion (H^+):

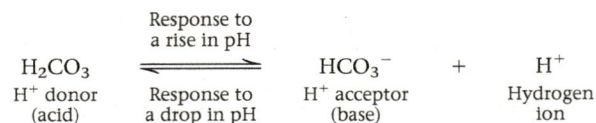

H_2CO_3	Response to a rise in pH ⇌ Response to a drop in pH	HCO_3^-	+	H^+
H⁺ donor (acid)		H⁺ acceptor (base)		Hydrogen ion

The chemical equilibrium between carbonic acid and bicarbonate acts as a pH regulator, the reaction shifting left or right as other processes in the solution add or remove hydrogen ions. If the H⁺ concentration in blood begins to fall (that is, if pH rises), the reaction proceeds to the right and more carbonic acid dissociates, replenishing hydrogen ions. But when H⁺ concentration in blood begins to rise (when pH drops), the reaction proceeds to the left, with HCO_3^- (the base) removing the hydrogen ions from the solution and forming H_2CO_3. Thus, the carbonic acid–bicarbonate buffering system consists of an acid and a base in equilibrium with each other. Most other buffers are also acid-base pairs.

Acidification: A Threat to Water Quality

Among the many threats to water quality posed by human activities is the burning of fossil fuels, which releases gaseous compounds into the atmosphere. When certain of these compounds react with water, the water becomes more acidic, altering the delicate balance of conditions for life on Earth.

Carbon dioxide is the main product of fossil fuel combustion. About 25% of human-generated CO_2 is absorbed by the oceans. In spite of the huge volume of water in the oceans, scientists worry that the absorption of so much CO_2 will harm marine ecosystems.

Recent data have shown that such fears are well founded. When CO_2 dissolves in seawater, it reacts with water to form carbonic acid, which lowers ocean pH, a process known as **ocean acidification**. Based on measurements of CO_2 levels in air bubbles trapped in ice over thousands of years, scientists calculate that the pH of the oceans is 0.1 pH unit lower now than at any time in the past 420,000 years. Recent studies predict that it will drop another 0.3–0.5 pH unit by the end of this century.

As seawater acidifies, the extra hydrogen ions combine with carbonate ions (CO_3^{2-}) to form bicarbonate ions (HCO_3^{-}), thereby reducing the carbonate concentration **(Figure 3.11)**.

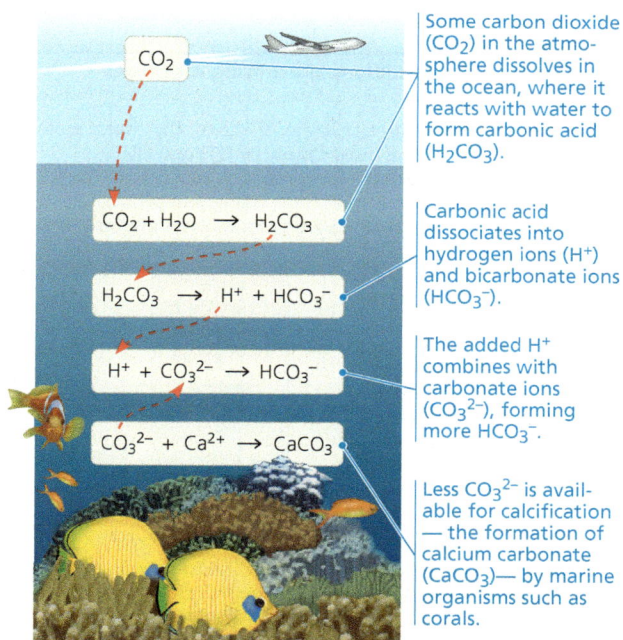

Some carbon dioxide (CO_2) in the atmosphere dissolves in the ocean, where it reacts with water to form carbonic acid (H_2CO_3).

$$CO_2 + H_2O \longrightarrow H_2CO_3$$

Carbonic acid dissociates into hydrogen ions (H^+) and bicarbonate ions (HCO_3^{-}).

$$H_2CO_3 \longrightarrow H^+ + HCO_3^{-}$$

The added H^+ combines with carbonate ions (CO_3^{2-}), forming more HCO_3^{-}.

$$H^+ + CO_3^{2-} \longrightarrow HCO_3^{-}$$

$$CO_3^{2-} + Ca^{2+} \longrightarrow CaCO_3$$

Less CO_3^{2-} is available for calcification — the formation of calcium carbonate $(CaCO_3)$ — by marine organisms such as corals.

▲ **Figure 3.11 Atmospheric CO₂ from human activities and its fate in the ocean.**

▼ Figure 3.12

IMPACT

The Threat of Ocean Acidification to Coral Reef Ecosystems

Recently, scientists have sounded the alarm about the effects of ocean acidification, the process in which oceans become more acidic due to increased atmospheric carbon dioxide levels (see Figure 3.11). They predict that the resulting decrease in the concentration of carbonate ion (CO_3^{2-}) will take a serious toll on coral reef calcification. Taking many studies into account, and including the effects of ocean warming as well, one group of scientists defined three scenarios for coral reefs during this century, depending on whether the concentration of atmospheric CO_2 (a) stays at today's level, (b) increases at the current rate, or (c) increases more rapidly. The photographs below show coral reefs resembling those predicted under each scenario.

(a)   (b)   (c)

The healthy coral reef in (a) supports a highly diverse group of species and bears little resemblance to the damaged coral reef in (c).

WHY IT MATTERS The disappearance of coral reef ecosystems would be a tragic loss of biological diversity. In addition, coral reefs provide shoreline protection, a feeding ground for many commercial fishery species, and a popular tourist draw, so coastal human communities would suffer from greater wave damage, collapsed fisheries, and reduced tourism.

FURTHER READING O. Hoegh-Guldberg et al., Coral reefs under rapid climate change and ocean acidification, *Science* 318:1737–1742 (2007). S. C. Doney, The dangers of ocean acidification, *Scientific American*, March 2006, 58–65.

WHAT IF? Would lowering the ocean's carbonate concentration have any effect, even indirectly, on organisms that don't form $CaCO_3$? Explain.

Scientists predict that ocean acidification will cause the carbonate concentration to decrease by 40% by the year 2100. This is of great concern because carbonate is required for calcification, the production of calcium carbonate $(CaCO_3)$ by many marine organisms, including reef-building corals and animals that build shells. Coral reefs are sensitive ecosystems that act as havens for a great diversity of marine life **(Figure 3.12)**.

The burning of fossil fuels is also a major source of sulfur oxides and nitrogen oxides. These compounds react with water in the air to form strong acids, which fall to Earth with rain or snow. **Acid precipitation** refers to rain, snow, or fog with a pH lower (more acidic) than 5.2. (Uncontaminated rain has a pH of about 5.6, which is slightly acidic due to the formation of carbonic acid from CO_2 and water.) Acid precipitation can damage life in lakes and streams, and it adversely affects plants on land by changing soil chemistry. To address this problem, the U.S. Congress amended the Clean Air Act in 1990, and the mandated improvements in industrial technologies have been largely responsible for improving the health of most North American lakes and forests.

If there is any reason for optimism about the future quality of water resources on our planet, it is that we have made progress in learning about the delicate chemical balances in oceans, lakes, and rivers. Continued progress can come only from the actions of informed individuals, like yourselves, who are concerned about environmental quality. This requires understanding the crucial role that water plays in the suitability of the environment for continued life on Earth.

CONCEPT CHECK 3.3

1. Compared with a basic solution at pH 9, the same volume of an acidic solution at pH 4 has ____ times as many hydrogen ions (H^+).
2. HCl is a strong acid that dissociates in water: $HCl \rightarrow H^+ + Cl^-$. What is the pH of 0.01 M HCl?
3. Acetic acid (CH_3COOH) can be a buffer, similar to carbonic acid. Write the dissociation reaction, identifying the acid, base, H^+ acceptor, and H^+ donor.
4. **WHAT IF?** Given a liter of pure water and a liter solution of acetic acid, what would happen to the pH if you added 0.01 mol of a strong acid to each? Use the reaction equation from question 3 to explain the result.

For suggested answers, see Appendix A.

3 CHAPTER REVIEW

SUMMARY OF KEY CONCEPTS

CONCEPT 3.1

Polar covalent bonds in water molecules result in hydrogen bonding (pp. 92–93)

- A hydrogen bond forms when the slightly negatively charged oxygen of one water molecule is attracted to the slightly positively charged hydrogen of a nearby water molecule. Hydrogen bonding between water molecules is the basis for water's properties.

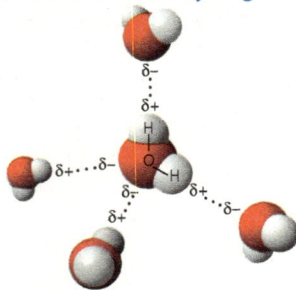

DRAW IT Label a hydrogen bond and a polar covalent bond in this figure. How many hydrogen bonds can each water molecule make?

CONCEPT 3.2

Four emergent properties of water contribute to Earth's suitability for life (pp. 93–98)

- Hydrogen bonding keeps water molecules close to each other, and this **cohesion** helps pull water upward in the microscopic water-conducting cells of plants. Hydrogen bonding is also responsible for water's **surface tension**.
- Water has a high **specific heat**: Heat is absorbed when hydrogen bonds break and is released when hydrogen bonds form. This helps keep temperatures relatively steady, within limits that permit life. **Evaporative cooling** is based on water's high **heat of vaporization**. The evaporative loss of the most energetic water molecules cools a surface.
- Ice floats because it is less dense than liquid water. This allows life to exist under the frozen surfaces of lakes and polar seas.

Ice: stable hydrogen bonds
Liquid water: transient hydrogen bonds

- Water is an unusually versatile **solvent** because its polar molecules are attracted to charged and polar substances capable of forming hydrogen bonds. **Hydrophilic** substances have an affinity for water; **hydrophobic** substances do not. **Molarity**, the number of moles of **solute** per liter of **solution**, is used as a measure of solute concentration in solutions. A **mole** is a certain number of molecules of a substance. The mass of a mole of a substance in grams is the same as the **molecular mass** in daltons.
- The emergent properties of water support life on Earth and may contribute to the potential for life to have evolved on other planets.

? *Describe how different types of solutes dissolve in water. Explain the difference between a solution and a colloid.*

CONCEPT 3.3

Acidic and basic conditions affect living organisms (pp. 98–102)

- A water molecule can transfer an H^+ to another water molecule to form H_3O^+ (represented simply by H^+) and OH^-.
- The concentration of H^+ is expressed as **pH**; pH = $-\log [H^+]$. **Buffers** in biological fluids resist changes in pH. A buffer consists of an acid-base pair that combines reversibly with hydrogen ions.
- The burning of fossil fuels increases the amount of CO_2 in the atmosphere. Some CO_2 dissolves in the oceans, causing **ocean acidification**, which has potentially grave consequences for coral reefs. The burning of fossil fuels also releases oxides of sulfur and nitrogen, leading to **acid precipitation**.

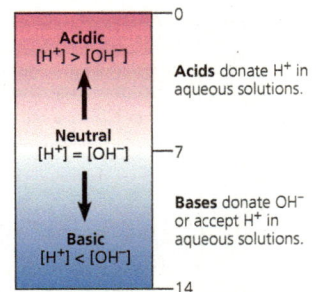

Acidic [H^+] > [OH^-]
Neutral [H^+] = [OH^-]
Basic [H^+] < [OH^-]

Acids donate H^+ in aqueous solutions.
Bases donate OH^- or accept H^+ in aqueous solutions.

? *Explain how increasing amounts of CO_2 dissolving in the ocean leads to ocean acidification. How does this change in pH affect carbonate ion concentration and the rate of calcification?*

TEST YOUR UNDERSTANDING

MB **Multiple-choice Self-Quiz questions #1–8 can be found in the Study Area at www.masteringbiology.com.**

9. **DRAW IT** Draw the hydration shells that form around a potassium ion and a chloride ion when potassium chloride (KCl) dissolves in water. Label the positive, negative, and partial charges on the atoms.

10. **MAKE CONNECTIONS** What do global warming (see Chapter 1, p. 52) and ocean acidification have in common?

11. In agricultural areas, farmers pay close attention to the weather forecast. Right before a predicted overnight freeze, farmers spray water on crops to protect the plants. Use the properties of water to explain how this method works. Be sure to mention why hydrogen bonds are responsible for this phenomenon.

12. **EVOLUTION CONNECTION**
This chapter explains how the emergent properties of water contribute to the suitability of the environment for life. Until fairly recently, scientists assumed that other physical requirements for life included a moderate range of temperature, pH, atmospheric pressure, and salinity, as well as low levels of toxic chemicals. That view has changed with the discovery of organisms known as extremophiles, which have been found flourishing in hot, acidic sulfur springs, around hydrothermal vents deep in the ocean, and in soils with high levels of toxic metals. Why would astrobiologists be interested in studying extremophiles? What does the existence of life in such extreme environments say about the possibility of life on other planets?

13. **SCIENTIFIC INQUIRY**
Design a controlled experiment to test the hypothesis that acid precipitation inhibits the growth of *Elodea*, a common freshwater plant (see Figure 2.19, p. 89).

14. **SCIENTIFIC INQUIRY**
In a study reported in 2000, C. Langdon and colleagues used an artificial coral reef system to test the effect of carbonate concentration on the rate of calcification by reef organisms. The graph on the right presents one set of their results. Describe what these data show. How do these results relate to the ocean acidification that is associated with increasing atmospheric CO_2 levels?

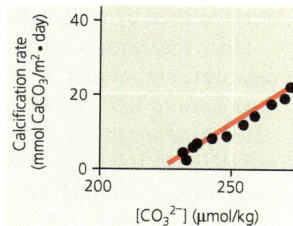

15. **SCIENCE, TECHNOLOGY, AND SOCIETY**
Agriculture, industry, and the growing populations of cities all compete, through political influence, for water. If you were in charge of water resources in an arid region, what would your priorities be for allocating the limited water supply for various uses? How would you try to build consensus among the different special-interest groups?

16. **WRITE ABOUT A THEME**
Emergent Properties Several emergent properties of water contribute to the suitability of the environment for life. In a short essay (100–150 words), describe how the ability of water to function as a versatile solvent arises from the structure of water molecules.

For selected answers, see Appendix A.

MasteringBIOLOGY www.masteringbiology.com

1. MasteringBiology® Assignments
Tutorials Hydrogen Bonding and Water • The pH Scale
Activities The Polarity of Water • Cohesion of Water • Dissociation of Water Molecules • Acids, Bases, and pH
Questions Student Misconceptions • Reading Quiz • Multiple Choice • End-of-Chapter
2. eText
Read your book online, search, take notes, highlight text, and more.
3. The Study Area
Practice Tests • Cumulative Test • *BioFlix* 3-D Animations • MP3 Tutor Sessions • Videos • Activities • Investigations • Lab Media • Audio Glossary • Word Study Tools • Art

4

Carbon and the Molecular Diversity of Life

▲ **Figure 4.1** What properties make carbon the basis of all life?

OVERVIEW

Carbon: The Backbone of Life

Water is the universal medium for life on Earth, but living organisms, such as the plants and Roosevelt elk in **Figure 4.1**, are made up of chemicals based mostly on the element carbon. Carbon enters the biosphere through the action of plants. Plants use solar energy to transform atmospheric CO_2 into the molecules of life, which are then taken in by plant-eating animals.

Of all chemical elements, carbon is unparalleled in its ability to form molecules that are large, complex, and varied, making possible the diversity of organisms that have evolved on Earth. Proteins, DNA, carbohydrates, and other molecules that distinguish living matter from inanimate material are all composed of carbon atoms bonded to one another and to atoms of other elements. Hydrogen (H), oxygen (O), nitrogen (N), sulfur (S), and phosphorus (P) are other common ingredients of these compounds, but it is the element carbon (C) that accounts for the enormous variety of biological molecules.

Large biological molecules, such as proteins, are the main focus of Chapter 5. In this chapter, we investigate the properties of smaller molecules. We will use these small molecules to illustrate concepts of molecular architecture that will help explain why carbon is so important to life, at the same time highlighting the theme that emergent properties arise from the organization of matter in living organisms.

CONCEPT 4.1

Organic chemistry is the study of carbon compounds

For historical reasons, compounds containing carbon are said to be organic, and the branch of chemistry that specializes in the study of carbon compounds is called **organic chemistry**. Organic compounds range from simple molecules, such as methane (CH_4), to colossal ones, such as proteins, with thousands of atoms. Most organic compounds contain hydrogen atoms in addition to carbon atoms.

The overall percentages of the major elements of life—C, H, O, N, S, and P—are quite uniform from one organism to another. Because of carbon's versatility, however, this limited assortment of atomic building blocks can be used to build an inexhaustible variety of organic molecules. Different species of organisms, and different individuals within a species, are distinguished by variations in their organic molecules.

Since the dawn of human history, people have used other organisms as sources of valued substances—from foods and medicines to fabrics. The science of organic chemistry originated in attempts to purify and improve the yield of such products. By the early 1800s, chemists had learned to make many simple compounds in the laboratory by combining elements under the right conditions. Artificial synthesis of the complex molecules extracted from living matter seemed impossible, however. At that time, the Swedish chemist Jöns Jakob Berzelius made the distinction between organic compounds, those thought to arise only in living organisms, and inorganic compounds, those found only in the nonliving world. *Vitalism*, the belief in a life force outside the jurisdiction of physical and chemical laws, provided the foundation for the new discipline of organic chemistry.

Chemists began to chip away at the support for vitalism when they finally learned to synthesize organic compounds in the laboratory. In 1828, Friedrich Wöhler, a German chemist who had studied with Berzelius, tried to make an "inorganic" salt, ammonium cyanate, by mixing solutions of ammonium ions (NH_4^+) and cyanate ions (CNO^-). Wöhler was astonished to find that instead he had made urea, an organic compound present in the urine of animals. Wöhler challenged the vitalists when he wrote, "I must tell you that I can prepare urea without requiring a kidney or an animal, either man or dog." However, one of the ingredients used in the synthesis, the cyanate, had been extracted from animal blood, and the vitalists were not swayed by Wöhler's discovery. A few years later, however, Hermann Kolbe, a student of Wöhler's, made the organic compound acetic acid from inorganic substances that could be prepared directly from pure elements. Vitalism crumbled completely after several decades of laboratory synthesis of increasingly complex organic compounds.

Organic Molecules and the Origin of Life on Earth

EVOLUTION In 1953, Stanley Miller, a graduate student of Harold Urey's at the University of Chicago, helped bring the abiotic (nonliving) synthesis of organic compounds into the context of evolution. Study **Figure 4.2** to learn about his classic experiment. From his results, Miller concluded that complex organic molecules could arise spontaneously under conditions thought to have existed on the early Earth. Miller also performed experiments designed to mimic volcanic conditions, with roughly similar results. In 2008, a former graduate student of Miller's discovered some samples from these experiments. Reanalyzing them using modern equipment, he identified additional organic compounds that had not been found by Miller. Although the jury is still out, these experiments support the idea that abiotic synthesis of organic compounds, perhaps near volcanoes, could have been an early stage in the origin of life (see Chapter 25).

The pioneers of organic chemistry helped shift the mainstream of biological thought from vitalism to *mechanism*, the view that physical and chemical laws govern all natural phenomena, including the processes of life. Organic chemistry was redefined as the study of carbon compounds, regardless of origin. Organisms produce most of the naturally occurring organic compounds, and these molecules represent a diversity and range of complexity unrivaled by inorganic compounds. However, the rules of chemistry apply to all molecules. The foundation of organic chemistry is not some intangible life force, but the unique chemical versatility of the element carbon.

CONCEPT CHECK 4.1

1. Why was Wöhler astonished to find he had made urea?
2. **WHAT IF?** When Miller tried his experiment without the electrical discharge, no organic compounds were found. What might explain this result?

For suggested answers, see Appendix A.

▼ Figure 4.2   **INQUIRY**

Can organic molecules form under conditions believed to simulate those on the early Earth?

EXPERIMENT In 1953, Stanley Miller set up a closed system to mimic conditions thought to have existed on the early Earth. A flask of water simulated the primeval sea. The water was heated so that some vaporized and moved into a second, higher flask containing the "atmosphere"—a mixture of gases. Sparks were discharged in the synthetic atmosphere to mimic lightning.

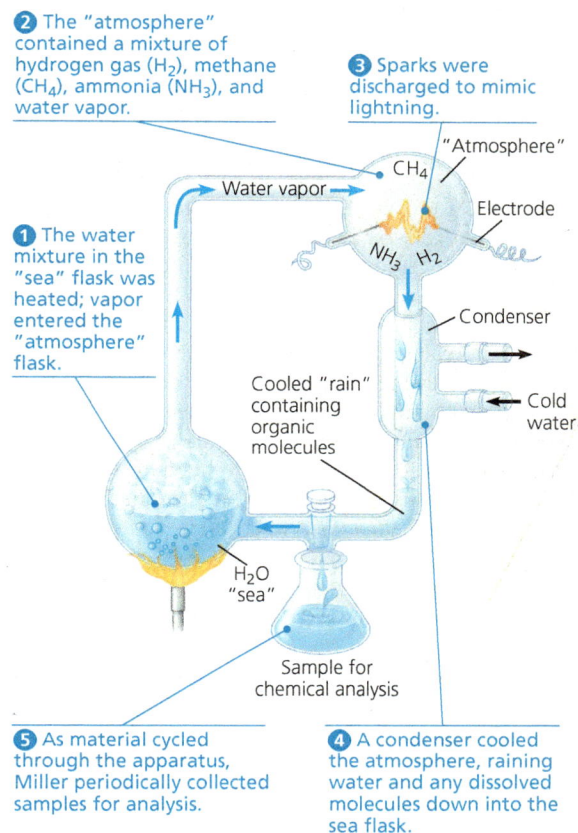

RESULTS Miller identified a variety of organic molecules that are common in organisms. These included simple compounds, such as formaldehyde (CH_2O) and hydrogen cyanide (HCN), and more complex molecules, such as amino acids and long chains of carbon and hydrogen known as hydrocarbons.

CONCLUSION Organic molecules, a first step in the origin of life, may have been synthesized abiotically on the early Earth. (We will explore this hypothesis in more detail in Chapter 25.)

SOURCE S. L. Miller, A production of amino acids under possible primitive Earth conditions, *Science* 117:528–529 (1953).

WHAT IF? If Miller had increased the concentration of NH_3 in his experiment, how might the relative amounts of the products HCN and CH_2O have differed?

CONCEPT 4.2

Carbon atoms can form diverse molecules by bonding to four other atoms

The key to an atom's chemical characteristics is its electron configuration. This configuration determines the kinds and number of bonds an atom will form with other atoms.

The Formation of Bonds with Carbon

Carbon has 6 electrons, with 2 in the first electron shell and 4 in the second shell; thus, it has 4 valence electrons in a shell that holds 8 electrons. A carbon atom usually completes its valence shell by sharing its 4 electrons with other atoms so that 8 electrons are present. Each pair of shared electrons constitutes a covalent bond (see Figure 2.12d). In organic molecules, carbon usually forms single or double covalent bonds. Each carbon atom acts as an intersection point from which a molecule can branch off in as many as four directions. This ability is one facet of carbon's versatility that makes large, complex molecules possible.

When a carbon atom forms four single covalent bonds, the arrangement of its four hybrid orbitals causes the bonds to angle toward the corners of an imaginary tetrahedron (see Figure 2.17b). The bond angles in methane (CH_4) are 109.5° **(Figure 4.3a)**, and they are roughly the same in any group of atoms where carbon has four single bonds. For example,

ethane (C_2H_6) is shaped like two overlapping tetrahedrons **(Figure 4.3b)**. In molecules with more carbons, every grouping of a carbon bonded to four other atoms has a tetrahedral shape. But when two carbon atoms are joined by a double bond, as in ethene (C_2H_4), the atoms joined to those carbons are in the same plane as the carbons **(Figure 4.3c)**. We find it convenient to write molecules as structural formulas, as if the molecules being represented are two-dimensional, but keep in mind that molecules are three-dimensional and that the shape of a molecule often determines its function.

The electron configuration of carbon gives it covalent compatibility with many different elements. **Figure 4.4** shows the valences of carbon and its most frequent partners—hydrogen, oxygen, and nitrogen. These are the four major atomic components of organic molecules. These valences are the basis for the rules of covalent bonding in organic chemistry—the building code for the architecture of organic molecules.

Let's consider how the rules of covalent bonding apply to carbon atoms with partners other than hydrogen. We'll look at two examples, the simple molecules carbon dioxide and urea.

In the carbon dioxide molecule (CO_2), a single carbon atom is joined to two atoms of oxygen by double covalent bonds. The structural formula for CO_2 is shown here:

$$O{=}C{=}O$$

Each line in a structural formula represents a pair of shared electrons. Thus, the two double bonds in CO_2 have the same number of shared electrons as four single bonds. The arrangement completes the valence shells of all atoms in the molecule.

Name and Comment	Molecular Formula	Structural Formula	Ball-and-Stick Model (molecular shape in pink)	Space-Filling Model
(a) Methane. When a carbon atom has four single bonds to other atoms, the molecule is tetrahedral.	CH_4			
(b) Ethane. A molecule may have more than one tetrahedral group of single-bonded atoms. (Ethane consists of two such groups.)	C_2H_6			
(c) Ethene (ethylene). When two carbon atoms are joined by a double bond, all atoms attached to those carbons are in the same plane; the molecule is flat.	C_2H_4			

▲ **Figure 4.3 The shapes of three simple organic molecules.**

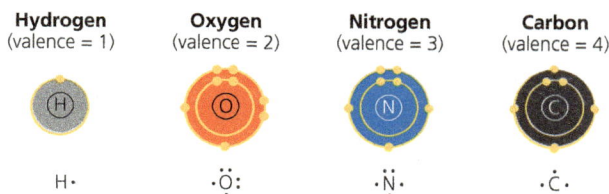

Hydrogen (valence = 1)   **Oxygen** (valence = 2)   **Nitrogen** (valence = 3)   **Carbon** (valence = 4)

H·   ·Ö: ·Ṅ·   ·Ç·

▲ **Figure 4.4 Valences of the major elements of organic molecules.** Valence is the number of covalent bonds an atom can form. It is generally equal to the number of electrons required to complete the valence (outermost) shell (see Figure 2.9). All the electrons are shown for each atom in the electron distribution diagrams (top). Only the valence shell electrons are shown in the Lewis dot structures (bottom). Note that carbon can form four bonds.

MAKE CONNECTIONS *Refer to Figure 2.9 (p. 82) and draw the Lewis dot structures for sodium, phosphorus, sulfur, and chlorine.*

Because CO_2 is a very simple molecule and lacks hydrogen, it is often considered inorganic, even though it contains carbon. Whether we call CO_2 organic or inorganic, however, it is clearly important to the living world as the source of carbon for all organic molecules in organisms.

Urea, $CO(NH_2)_2$, is the organic compound found in urine that Wöhler synthesized in the early 1800s. Again, each atom has the required number of covalent bonds. In this case, one carbon atom participates in both single and double bonds.

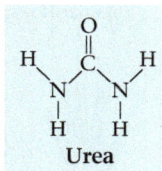
Urea

Urea and carbon dioxide are molecules with only one carbon atom. But as Figure 4.3 shows, a carbon atom can also use one or more valence electrons to form covalent bonds to other carbon atoms, linking the atoms into chains of seemingly infinite variety.

Molecular Diversity Arising from Carbon Skeleton Variation

Carbon chains form the skeletons of most organic molecules. The skeletons vary in length and may be straight, branched, or arranged in closed rings **(Figure 4.5)**. Some carbon skeletons have double bonds, which vary in number and location. Such variation in carbon skeletons is one important source of the molecular complexity and diversity that characterize living matter. In addition, atoms of other elements can be bonded to the skeletons at available sites.

Hydrocarbons

All of the molecules shown in Figures 4.3 and 4.5 are **hydrocarbons**, organic molecules consisting of only carbon and hydrogen. Atoms of hydrogen are attached to the carbon skeleton wherever electrons are available for covalent bonding. Hydrocarbons are the major components of petroleum, which is called a fossil fuel because it consists of the partially decomposed remains of organisms that lived millions of years ago.

▼ **Figure 4.5 Four ways that carbon skeletons can vary.**

(a) Length
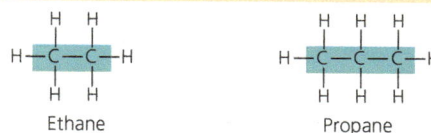
Ethane   Propane
Carbon skeletons vary in length.

(b) Branching
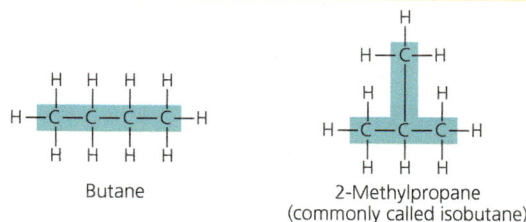
Butane   2-Methylpropane (commonly called isobutane)
Skeletons may be unbranched or branched.

(c) Double bond position
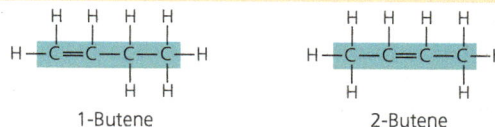
1-Butene   2-Butene
The skeleton may have double bonds, which can vary in location.

(d) Presence of rings
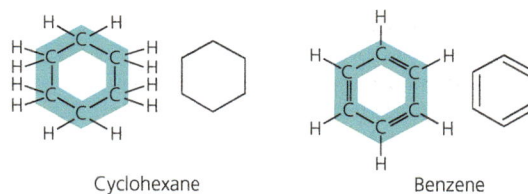
Cyclohexane   Benzene
Some carbon skeletons are arranged in rings. In the abbreviated structural formula for each compound (at the right), each corner represents a carbon and its attached hydrogens.

Although hydrocarbons are not prevalent in most living organisms, many of a cell's organic molecules have regions consisting of only carbon and hydrogen. For example, the molecules known as fats have long hydrocarbon tails attached to a nonhydrocarbon component **(Figure 4.6,** on the next page). Neither petroleum nor fat dissolves in water; both are hydrophobic compounds because the great majority of their bonds are relatively nonpolar carbon-to-hydrogen linkages. Another characteristic of hydrocarbons is that they can undergo reactions that release a relatively large amount of energy. The gasoline that fuels a car consists of hydrocarbons, and the hydrocarbon tails of fats serve as stored fuel for animals.

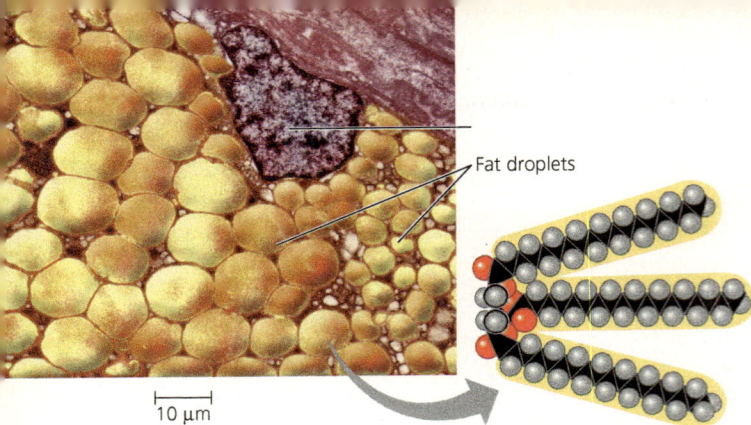

/ Fat droplets

┠──┨
10 μm

(a) Part of a human adipose cell **(b) A fat molecule**

▲ **Figure 4.6 The role of hydrocarbons in fats.** **(a)** Mammalian adipose cells stockpile fat molecules as a fuel reserve. This colorized TEM shows part of a human adipose cell with many fat droplets, each containing a large number of fat molecules. **(b)** A fat molecule consists of a small, nonhydrocarbon component joined to three hydrocarbon tails that account for the hydrophobic behavior of fats. The tails can be broken down to provide energy. (Black = carbon; gray = hydrogen; red = oxygen.)

MAKE CONNECTIONS *How do the tails account for the hydrophobic nature of fats? (See Concept 3.2, p. 97.)*

Isomers

Variation in the architecture of organic molecules can be seen in **isomers**, compounds that have the same numbers of atoms of the same elements but different structures and hence different properties. We will examine three types of isomers: structural isomers, *cis-trans* isomers, and enantiomers.

Structural isomers differ in the covalent arrangements of their atoms. Compare, for example, the two five-carbon compounds in **Figure 4.7a**. Both have the molecular formula C_5H_{12}, but they differ in the covalent arrangement of their carbon skeletons. The skeleton is straight in one compound but branched in the other. The number of possible isomers increases tremendously as carbon skeletons increase in size. There are only three forms of C_5H_{12} (two of which are shown in Figure 4.7a), but there are 18 variations of C_8H_{18} and 366,319 possible structural isomers of $C_{20}H_{42}$. Structural isomers may also differ in the location of double bonds.

In ***cis-trans*** isomers (formerly called *geometric isomers*), carbons have covalent bonds to the same atoms, but these atoms differ in their spatial arrangements due to the inflexibility of double bonds. Single bonds allow the atoms they join to rotate freely about the bond axis without changing the compound. In contrast, double bonds do not permit such rotation. If a double bond joins two carbon atoms, and each C also has two different atoms (or groups of atoms) attached to it, then two distinct *cis-trans* isomers are possible. Consider a simple molecule with two double-bonded carbons, each of which has an H and an X attached to it **(Figure 4.7b)**. The arrangement with both Xs on the same side of the double bond is called a *cis isomer*, and that with the Xs on opposite sides is called a *trans* isomer. The subtle difference in shape between such isomers can dramatically affect the biological activities of organic molecules. For example, the biochem-

▼ **Figure 4.7 Three types of isomers, compounds with the same molecular formula but different structures.**

(a) Structural isomers

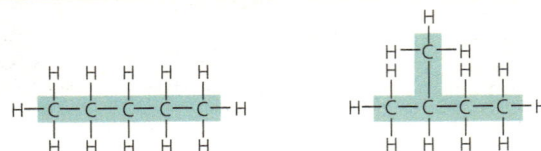

Structural isomers differ in covalent partners, as shown in this example of two isomers of C_5H_{12}: pentane (left) and 2-methyl butane (right).

(b) *Cis-trans* isomers

cis isomer: The two Xs are on the same side.

trans isomer: The two Xs are on opposite sides.

Cis-trans isomers differ in arrangement about a double bond. In these diagrams, X represents an atom or group of atoms attached to a double-bonded carbon.

(c) Enantiomers

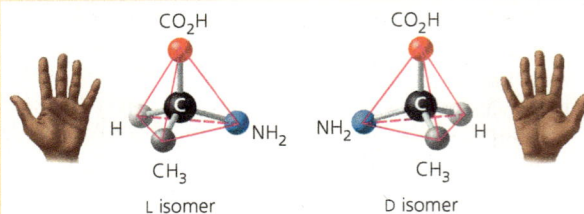

L isomer   D isomer

Enantiomers differ in spatial arrangement around an asymmetric carbon, resulting in molecules that are mirror images, like left and right hands. The two isomers are designated the L and D isomers from the Latin for "left" and "right" (*levo* and *dextro*). Enantiomers cannot be superimposed on each other.

DRAW IT *There are three structural isomers of C_5H_{12}; draw the one not shown in (a).*

istry of vision involves a light-induced change of rhodopsin, a chemical compound in the eye, from the *cis* isomer to the *trans* isomer (see Figure 50.17). Another example involves *trans* fats, which are discussed in Chapter 5.

Enantiomers are isomers that are mirror images of each other and that differ in shape due to the presence of an *asymmetric carbon*, one that is attached to four different atoms or groups of atoms. (See the middle carbon in the ball-and-stick models shown in **Figure 4.7c**.) The four groups can be arranged in space around the asymmetric carbon in two different ways that are mirror images. Enantiomers are, in a way, left-handed and right-handed versions of the molecule. Just as your right hand won't fit into a left-handed glove, a "right-handed" molecule won't fit into the same space as the "left-handed" version.

Drug	Condition	Effective Enantiomer	Ineffective Enantiomer
Ibuprofen	Pain; inflammation	S-Ibuprofen	R-Ibuprofen
Albuterol	Asthma	R-Albuterol	S-Albuterol

▲ **Figure 4.8 The pharmacological importance of enantiomers.** Ibuprofen and albuterol are examples of drugs whose enantiomers have different effects. (S and R are letters used in one system to distinguish between enantiomers.) Ibuprofen reduces inflammation and pain. It is commonly sold as a mixture of the two enantiomers. The S enantiomer is 100 times more effective than the other. Albuterol is used to relax bronchial muscles, improving airflow in asthma patients. Only R-albuterol is synthesized and sold as a drug; the S form counteracts the active R form.

Usually, only one isomer is biologically active because only that form can bind to specific molecules in an organism.

The concept of enantiomers is important in the pharmaceutical industry because the two enantiomers of a drug may not be equally effective, as is the case for both ibuprofen and the asthma medication albuterol (**Figure 4.8**). Methamphetamine also occurs in two enantiomers that have very different effects. One enantiomer is the highly addictive stimulant drug known as "crank," sold illegally in the street drug trade. The other has a much weaker effect and is even found as an ingredient in an over-the-counter vapor inhaler for treatment of nasal congestion! The differing effects of enantiomers in the body demonstrate that organisms are sensitive to even the most subtle variations in molecular architecture. Once again, we see that molecules have emergent properties that depend on the specific arrangement of their atoms.

CONCEPT CHECK 4.2

1. **DRAW IT** Draw a structural formula for C_2H_4.
2. Which molecules in Figure 4.5 are isomers? For each pair, identify the type of isomer.
3. How are gasoline and fat chemically similar?
4. **WHAT IF?** Can propane (C_3H_8) form isomers?

For suggested answers, see Appendix A.

CONCEPT 4.3

A few chemical groups are key to the functioning of biological molecules

The distinctive properties of an organic molecule depend not only on the arrangement of its carbon skeleton but also on the chemical groups attached to that skeleton. We can think of hydrocarbons, the simplest organic molecules, as the underlying framework for more complex organic molecules. A number of chemical groups can replace one or more of the hydrogens bonded to the carbon skeleton of the hydrocarbon. (Some groups include atoms of the carbon skeleton, as we will see.) These groups may participate in chemical reactions or may contribute to function indirectly by their effects on molecular shape. The number and arrangement of the groups help give each molecule its unique properties.

The Chemical Groups Most Important in the Processes of Life

Consider the differences between estradiol (a type of estrogen) and testosterone. These compounds are female and male sex hormones, respectively, in humans and other vertebrates. Both are steroids, organic molecules with a common carbon skeleton in the form of four fused rings. These sex hormones differ only in the chemical groups attached to the rings (shown here in abbreviated form); the distinctions in molecular architecture are shaded in blue:

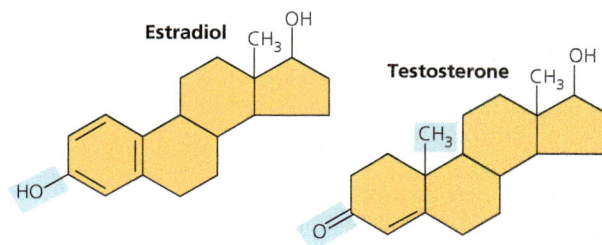

The different actions of these two molecules on many targets throughout the body help produce the contrasting anatomical and physiological features of male and female vertebrates. Thus, even our sexuality has its biological basis in variations of molecular architecture.

In the example of sex hormones, different chemical groups contribute to function by affecting the molecule's shape. In other cases, the chemical groups affect molecular function by being directly involved in chemical reactions; these important chemical groups are known as **functional groups**. Each functional group participates in chemical reactions in a characteristic way from one organic molecule to another.

The seven chemical groups most important in biological processes are the hydroxyl, carbonyl, carboxyl, amino, sulfhydryl, phosphate, and methyl groups. The first six groups can act as functional groups; they are also hydrophilic and thus increase the solubility of organic compounds in water. The methyl group is not reactive, but instead often serves as a recognizable tag on biological molecules. Before reading further, study **Figure 4.9** on the next two pages to familiarize yourself with these biologically important chemical groups.

▼ Figure 4.9

Exploring Some Biologically Important Chemical Groups

CHEMICAL GROUP	Hydroxyl	Carbonyl	Carboxyl
STRUCTURE	—OH (may be written HO—) In a **hydroxyl group** (—OH), a hydrogen atom is bonded to an oxygen atom, which in turn is bonded to the carbon skeleton of the organic molecule. (Do not confuse this functional group with the hydroxide ion, OH⁻.)	The **carbonyl group** (>CO) consists of a carbon atom joined to an oxygen atom by a double bond.	When an oxygen atom is double-bonded to a carbon atom that is also bonded to an —OH group, the entire assembly of atoms is called a **carboxyl group** (—COOH).
NAME OF COMPOUND	**Alcohols** (Their specific names usually end in -ol.)	**Ketones** if the carbonyl group is within a carbon skeleton **Aldehydes** if the carbonyl group is at the end of the carbon skeleton	**Carboxylic acids**, or organic acids
EXAMPLE	**Ethanol**, the alcohol present in alcoholic beverages	**Acetone**, the simplest ketone **Propanal**, an aldehyde	**Acetic acid**, which gives vinegar its sour taste
FUNCTIONAL PROPERTIES	• Is polar as a result of the electrons spending more time near the electronegative oxygen atom. • Can form hydrogen bonds with water molecules, helping dissolve organic compounds such as sugars. (Sugars are shown in Figure 5.3.)	• A ketone and an aldehyde may be structural isomers with different properties, as is the case for acetone and propanal. • Ketone and aldehyde groups are also found in sugars, giving rise to two major groups of sugars: ketoses (containing ketone groups) and aldoses (containing aldehyde groups).	• Acts as an acid; can donate an H⁺ because the covalent bond between oxygen and hydrogen is so polar: Nonionized Ionized • Found in cells in the ionized form with a charge of 1− and called a carboxylate ion.

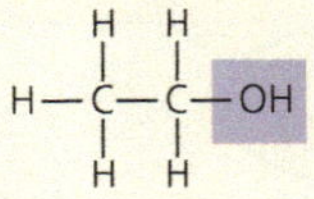

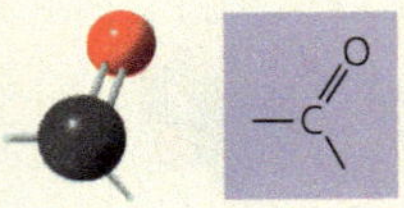

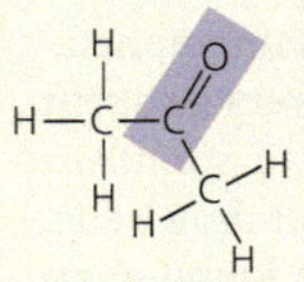

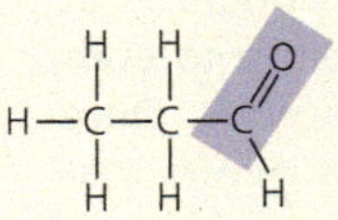

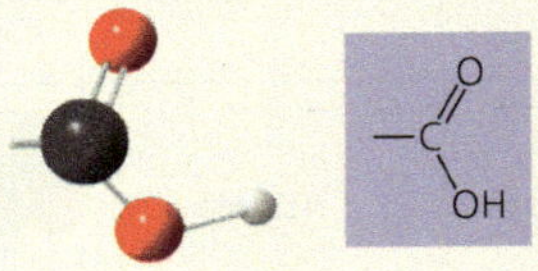

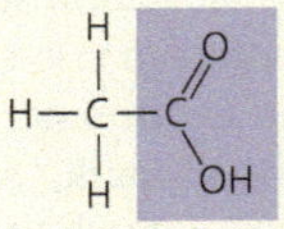

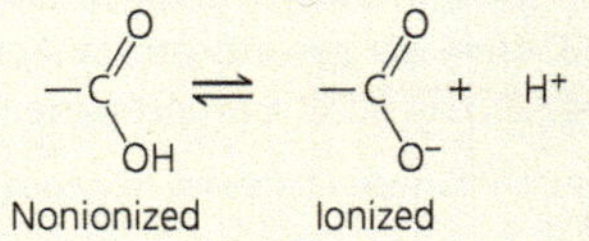

Amino	Sulfhydryl	Phosphate	Methyl
The **amino group** (—NH$_2$) consists of a nitrogen atom bonded to two hydrogen atoms and to the carbon skeleton.	The **sulfhydryl group** (—SH) consists of a sulfur atom bonded to an atom of hydrogen; it resembles a hydroxyl group in shape. (may be written HS —)	In the **phosphate group** shown here, a phosphorus atom is bonded to four oxygen atoms; one oxygen is bonded to the carbon skeleton; two oxygens carry negative charges (—OPO$_3^{2-}$). In this text, (P) represents an attached phosphate group.	A **methyl group** (—CH$_3$) consists of a carbon bonded to three hydrogen atoms. The carbon of a methyl group may be attached to a carbon or to a different atom.
Amines	**Thiols**	**Organic phosphates**	**Methylated compounds**
Glycine, a compound that is both an amine and a carboxylic acid because it has both an amino group and a carboxyl group; compounds with both groups are called **amino acids**	**Cysteine**, an important sulfur-containing amino acid	**Glycerol phosphate**, which takes part in many important chemical reactions in cells; glycerol phosphate also provides the backbone for phospholipids, the most prevalent molecules in cell membranes	**5-Methyl cytidine**, a component of DNA that has been modified by addition of a methyl group
• Acts as a base; can pick up an H$^+$ from the surrounding solution (water, in living organisms): H$^+$ + —N(H)(H) ⇌ —$^+$N—H (H)(H) Nonionized Ionized • Found in cells in the ionized form with a charge of 1+.	• Two sulfhydryl groups can react, forming a covalent bond. This "cross-linking" helps stabilize protein structure (see Figure 5.20, Tertiary Structure). • Cross-linking of cysteines in hair proteins maintains the curliness or straightness of hair. Straight hair can be "permanently" curled by shaping it around curlers and then breaking and re-forming the cross-linking bonds.	• Contributes negative charge to the molecule of which it is a part (2− when at the end of a molecule, as above; 1− when located internally in a chain of phosphates). • Molecules containing phosphate groups have the potential to react with water, releasing energy.	• Addition of a methyl group to DNA, or to molecules bound to DNA, affects the expression of genes. • Arrangement of methyl groups in male and female sex hormones affects their shape and function (see p. 109).

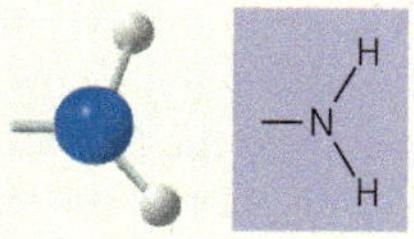

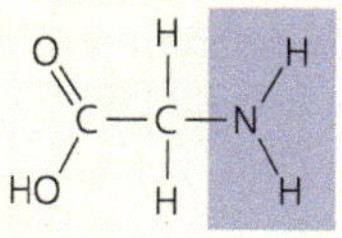

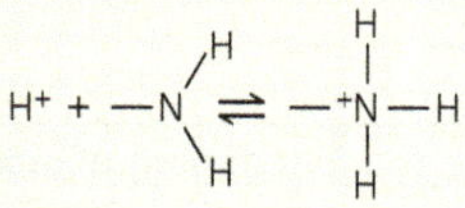

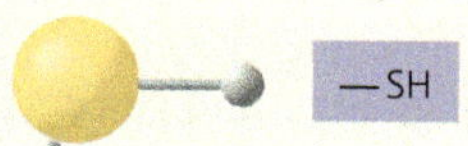

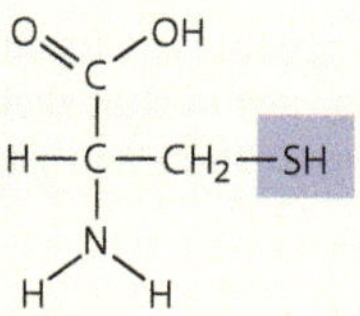

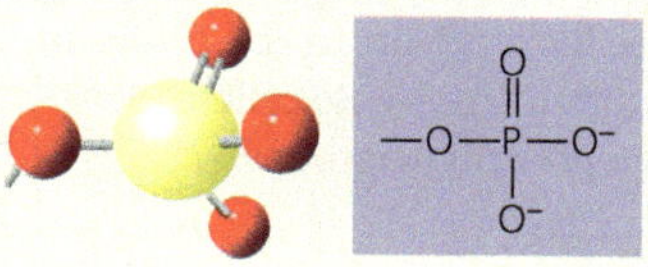

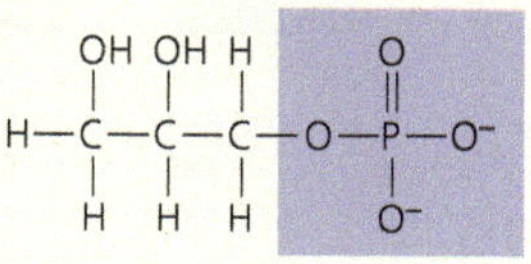

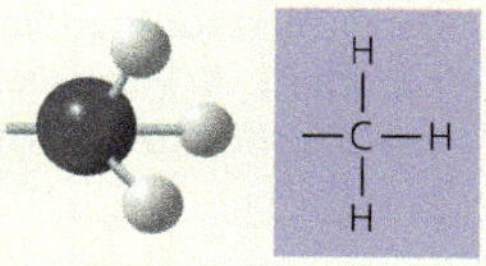

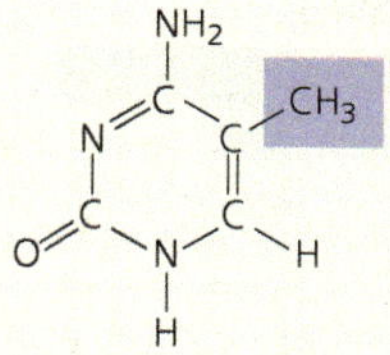

MAKE CONNECTIONS *Given the information in this figure and what you know about the electronegativity of oxygen (see Concept 2.3, p. 85), predict which of the following molecules would be the stronger acid (see Concept 3.3, p. 99). Explain your answer.*

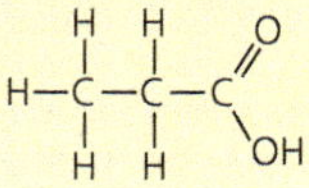

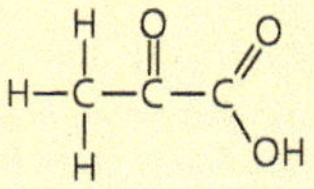

ATP: An Important Source of Energy for Cellular Processes

The "Phosphate" column in Figure 4.9 shows a simple example of an organic phosphate molecule. A more complicated organic phosphate, **adenosine triphosphate**, or **ATP**, is worth mentioning here because its function in the cell is so important. ATP consists of an organic molecule called adenosine attached to a string of three phosphate groups:

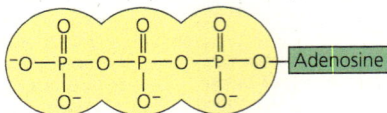

Where three phosphates are present in series, as in ATP, one phosphate may be split off as a result of a reaction with water. This inorganic phosphate ion, $HOPO_3^{2-}$, is often abbreviated P_i in this book. Having lost one phosphate, ATP becomes adenosine *di*phosphate, or ADP. Although ATP is sometimes said to store energy, it is more accurate to think of it as storing the potential to react with water. This reaction releases energy that can be used by the cell. You will learn about this in more detail in Chapter 8.

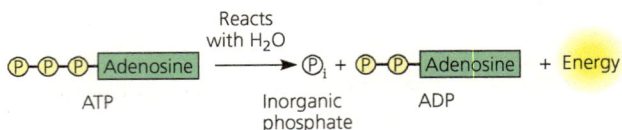

The Chemical Elements of Life: *A Review*

Living matter, as you have learned, consists mainly of carbon, oxygen, hydrogen, and nitrogen, with smaller amounts of sulfur and phosphorus. These elements all form strong covalent bonds, an essential characteristic in the architecture of complex organic molecules. Of all these elements, carbon is the virtuoso of the covalent bond. The versatility of carbon makes possible the great diversity of organic molecules, each with particular properties that emerge from the unique arrangement of its carbon skeleton and the chemical groups appended to that skeleton. At the foundation of all biological diversity lies this variation at the molecular level.

4 CHAPTER REVIEW

SUMMARY OF KEY CONCEPTS

CONCEPT 4.1

Organic chemistry is the study of carbon compounds (pp. 104–105)

- Living matter is made mostly of carbon, oxygen, hydrogen, and nitrogen, with some sulfur and phosphorus. Biological diversity has its molecular basis in carbon's ability to form a huge number of molecules with particular shapes and chemical properties.
- Organic compounds were once thought to arise only within living organisms, but this idea (vitalism) was disproved when chemists were able to synthesize organic compounds in the laboratory.

  ? *How did Stanley Miller's experiments extend the idea of mechanism to the origin of life?*

CONCEPT 4.2

Carbon atoms can form diverse molecules by bonding to four other atoms (pp. 106–109)

- Carbon, with a valence of 4, can bond to various other atoms, including O, H, and N. Carbon can also bond to other carbon atoms, forming the carbon skeletons of organic compounds.

These skeletons vary in length and shape and have bonding sites for atoms of other elements. **Hydrocarbons** consist only of carbon and hydrogen.
- **Isomers** are compounds with the same molecular formula but different structures and properties. Three types of isomers are **structural isomers**, *cis-trans* **isomers**, and **enantiomers**.

  ? *Refer back to Figure 4.9. What type of isomers are acetone and propanal? How many asymmetric carbons are present in acetic acid, glycine, and glycerol phosphate? Can these three molecules exist as forms that are enantiomers?*

CONCEPT 4.3

A few chemical groups are key to the functioning of biological molecules (pp. 109–112)

- Chemical groups attached to the carbon skeletons of organic molecules participate in chemical reactions (**functional groups**) or contribute to function by affecting molecular shape (see Figure 4.9).
- **ATP (adenosine triphosphate)** consists of adenosine attached to three phosphate groups. ATP can react with water, forming inorganic phosphate and ADP (adenosine diphosphate). This reaction releases energy that can be used by the cell (see the equation at the top of the next page).

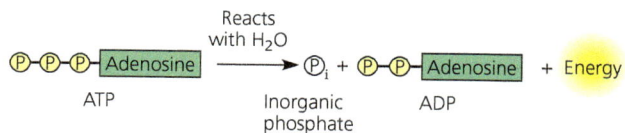

ATP → Inorganic phosphate + ADP + Energy

Reacts with H_2O

? *In what ways does a methyl group differ chemically from the other six important chemical groups shown in Figure 4.9?*

TEST YOUR UNDERSTANDING

(MB) **Multiple-choice Self-Quiz questions #1–7 can be found in the Study Area at www.masteringbiology.com.**

8. Which of the following molecules has an asymmetric carbon? Which carbon is asymmetric?

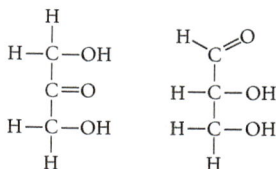

9. **EVOLUTION CONNECTION**

DRAW IT Some scientists think that life elsewhere in the universe might be based on the element silicon, rather than on carbon, as on Earth. Look at the electron distribution diagram for silicon in Figure 2.9 and draw the Lewis dot structure for silicon. What properties does silicon share with carbon that would make silicon-based life more likely than, say, neon-based life or aluminum-based life?

10. **SCIENTIFIC INQUIRY**

Thalidomide achieved notoriety 50 years ago because of a wave of birth defects among children born to women who took this drug during pregnancy as a treatment for morning sickness. Thalidomide is a mixture of two enantiomers; one reduces morning sickness, but the other causes severe birth defects. (Although the beneficial enantiomer can be synthesized and given to patients, it is converted in the body to the harmful enantiomer.) The U.S. Food and Drug Administration (FDA) withheld approval of thalidomide in 1960. Since then, however, the FDA has approved this drug for the treatment of conditions associated with Hansen's disease (leprosy) and newly diagnosed multiple myeloma, a blood and bone marrow cancer. In clinical trials, thalidomide also shows promise as a treatment for AIDS, tuberculosis, inflammatory diseases, and some other types of cancer. Assuming that molecules related to thalidomide could be synthesized in the laboratory, describe in a broad way the type of experiments you would do to improve the benefits of this drug and minimize its harmful effects.

11. **WRITE ABOUT A THEME**

Structure and Function In 1918, an epidemic of sleeping sickness caused an unusual rigid paralysis in some survivors, similar to symptoms of advanced Parkinson's disease. Years later, L-dopa (below, left), a chemical used to treat Parkinson's disease, was given to some of these patients, as dramatized in the movie *Awakenings*, starring Robin Williams. L-dopa was remarkably effective at eliminating the paralysis, at least temporarily. However, its enantiomer, D-dopa (right), was subsequently shown to have no effect at all, as is the case for Parkinson's disease. In a short essay (100–150 words), discuss how the effectiveness of one enantiomer and not the other illustrates the theme of structure and function.

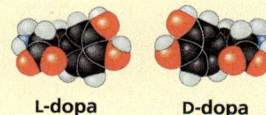

L-dopa   D-dopa

For selected answers, see Appendix A.

MasteringBIOLOGY www.masteringbiology.com

1. MasteringBiology® Assignments
Tutorial Carbon Bonding and Functional Groups
Activities Diversity of Carbon-Based Molecules • Isomers • Functional Groups
Questions Student Misconceptions • Reading Quiz • Multiple Choice • End-of-Chapter

2. eText
Read your book online, search, take notes, highlight text, and more.

3. The Study Area
Practice Tests • Cumulative Test • **BioFlix** 3-D Animations • MP3 Tutor Sessions • Videos • Activities • Investigations • Lab Media • Audio Glossary • Word Study Tools • Art

22

Descent with Modification: A Darwinian View of Life

▲ **Figure 22.1 How can this beetle survive in the desert, and what is it doing?**

OVERVIEW

Endless Forms Most Beautiful

In the coastal Namib desert of southwestern Africa, a land where fog is common but virtually no rain falls, lives the beetle *Onymacris unguicularis*. To obtain the water it needs to survive, this insect relies on a peculiar "headstanding" behavior (Figure 22.1). Tilting head-downward, the beetle faces into the winds that blow fog across the dunes. Droplets of moisture from the fog collect on the beetle's body and run down into its mouth.

Interesting in its own right, this headstander beetle is also a member of an astonishingly diverse group: the more than 350,000 species of beetles. In fact, nearly one of every five known species is a beetle. These beetles all share similar features, such as six pairs of legs, a hard outer surface, and two pairs of wings. But they also differ from one another. How did there come to be so many beetles, and what causes their similarities and differences?

The headstander beetle and its many close relatives illustrate three key observations about life:

- the striking ways in which organisms are suited for life in their environments*
- the many shared characteristics (unity) of life
- the rich diversity of life

A century and a half ago, Charles Darwin was inspired to develop a scientific explanation for these three broad observations. When he published his hypothesis in *The Origin of Species*, Darwin ushered in a scientific revolution—the era of evolutionary biology.

For now, we will define **evolution** as *descent with modification*, a phrase Darwin used in proposing that Earth's many species are descendants of ancestral species that were different from the present-day species. Evolution can also be defined more narrowly as a change in the genetic composition of a population from generation to generation, as discussed further in Chapter 23.

Whether it is defined broadly or narrowly, we can view evolution in two related but different ways: as a pattern and as a process. The *pattern* of evolutionary change is revealed by data from a range of scientific disciplines, including biology, geology, physics, and chemistry. These data are facts—they are observations about the natural world. The *process* of evolution consists of the mechanisms that produce the observed pattern of change. These mechanisms represent natural causes of the natural phenomena we observe. Indeed, the power of evolution as a unifying theory is its ability to explain and connect a vast array of observations about the living world.

As with all general theories in science, we continue to test our understanding of evolution by examining whether it can account for new observations and experimental results. In this and the following chapters, we'll examine how ongoing discoveries shape what we know about the pattern and process of evolution. To set the stage, we'll first retrace Darwin's quest to explain the adaptations, unity, and diversity of what he called life's "endless forms most beautiful."

---

*Here and throughout this book, the term *environment* refers to other organisms as well as to the physical aspects of an organism's surroundings.

1809
Lamarck publishes his hypothesis of evolution.

1798
Malthus publishes "Essay on the Principle of Population."

1795
Hutton proposes his principle of gradualism.

1812
Cuvier publishes his extensive studies of vertebrate fossils.

1830
Lyell publishes *Principles of Geology*.

1858
While studying species in the Malay Archipelago, Wallace sends Darwin his hypothesis of natural selection.

1790

1809
Charles Darwin is born.

1831–36
Darwin travels around the world on HMS *Beagle*.

1844
Darwin writes his essay on descent with modification.

1859
On the Origin of Species is published.

1870

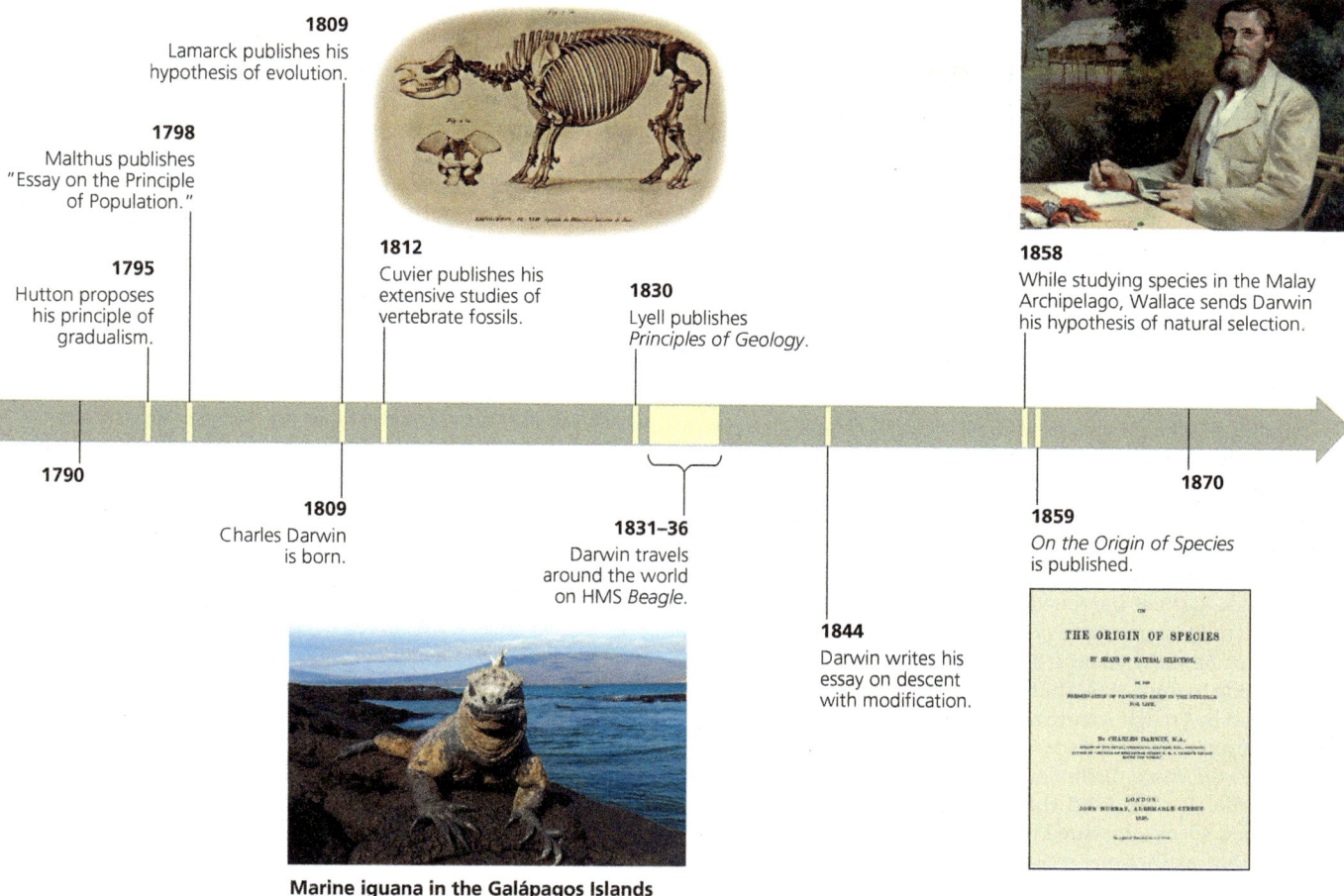

Marine iguana in the Galápagos Islands

▲ **Figure 22.2 The intellectual context of Darwin's ideas.**

CONCEPT 22.1

The Darwinian revolution challenged traditional views of a young Earth inhabited by unchanging species

What impelled Darwin to challenge the prevailing views about Earth and its life? Darwin's revolutionary proposal developed over time, influenced by the work of others and by his travels **(Figure 22.2)**. As we'll see, his ideas had deep historical roots.

Scala Naturae and Classification of Species

Long before Darwin was born, several Greek philosophers suggested that life might have changed gradually over time. But one philosopher who greatly influenced early Western science, Aristotle (384–322 BCE), viewed species as fixed (un-

changing). Through his observations of nature, Aristotle recognized certain "affinities" among organisms. He concluded that life-forms could be arranged on a ladder, or scale, of increasing complexity, later called the *scala naturae* ("scale of nature"). Each form of life, perfect and permanent, had its allotted rung on this ladder.

These ideas were generally consistent with the Old Testament account of creation, which holds that species were individually designed by God and therefore perfect. In the 1700s, many scientists interpreted the often remarkable match of organisms to their environment as evidence that the Creator had designed each species for a particular purpose.

One such scientist was Carolus Linnaeus (1707–1778), a Swedish physician and botanist who sought to classify life's diversity, in his words, "for the greater glory of God." Linnaeus developed the two-part, or *binomial*, format for naming species (such as *Homo sapiens* for humans) that is still used today. In contrast to the linear hierarchy of the *scala naturae*, Linnaeus adopted a nested classification system, grouping similar species into increasingly general categories. For example, similar species are grouped in the same genus, similar genera (plural of genus) are grouped in the same family, and so on (see Figure 1.14).

Linnaeus did not ascribe the resemblances among species to evolutionary kinship, but rather to the pattern of their creation. A century later, however, Darwin argued that classification should be based on evolutionary relationships. He also noted that scientists using the Linnaean system often grouped organisms in ways that reflected those relationships.

Ideas About Change over Time

Darwin drew from the work of scientists studying **fossils**, the remains or traces of organisms from the past. Many fossils are found in sedimentary rocks formed from the sand and mud that settle to the bottom of seas, lakes, swamps, and other aquatic habitats **(Figure 22.3)**. New layers of sediment cover older ones and compress them into superimposed layers of rock called **strata** (singular, *stratum*). The fossils in a particular stratum provide a glimpse of some of the organisms that populated Earth at the time that layer formed. Later, erosion may carve through upper (younger) strata, revealing deeper (older) strata that had been buried.

Paleontology, the study of fossils, was developed in large part by French scientist Georges Cuvier (1769–1832). In examining strata near Paris, Cuvier noted that the older the stratum, the more dissimilar its fossils were to current life-forms. He also observed that from one layer to the next, some new species appeared while others disappeared. He inferred that extinctions must have been a common occurrence in the history of life. Yet Cuvier staunchly opposed the idea of evolution. To explain his observations, he advocated **catastrophism**, the principle that events in the past occurred suddenly and were caused by mechanisms different from those operating in the present. Cuvier speculated that each boundary between strata represented a catastrophe, such as a flood, that had destroyed many of the species living at that time. He proposed that these periodic catastrophes were usually confined to local regions, which were later repopulated by different species immigrating from other areas.

In contrast, other scientists suggested that profound change could take place through the cumulative effect of slow but continuous processes. In 1795, Scottish geologist James Hutton (1726–1797) proposed that Earth's geologic features could be explained by gradual mechanisms still operating today. For example, he suggested that valleys were often formed by rivers wearing through rocks and that rocks containing marine fossils were formed when sediments that had eroded from the land were carried by rivers to the sea, where they buried dead marine organisms. The leading geologist of Darwin's time, Charles Lyell (1797–1875), incorporated Hutton's thinking into his principle of **uniformitarianism**, which stated that mechanisms of change are constant over time. Lyell proposed that the same geologic processes are operating today as in the past, and at the same rate.

Hutton and Lyell's ideas strongly influenced Darwin's thinking. Darwin agreed that if geologic change results from slow, continuous actions rather than from sudden events, then Earth must be much older than the widely accepted age of a few thousand years. It would, for example, take a very long time for a river to carve a canyon by erosion. He later reasoned that perhaps similarly slow and subtle processes could produce substantial biological change. Darwin was not the first to apply the idea of gradual change to biological evolution, however.

Lamarck's Hypothesis of Evolution

During the 18th century, several naturalists (including Darwin's grandfather, Erasmus Darwin) suggested that life evolves as environments change. But only one of Charles Darwin's predecessors proposed a mechanism for *how* life changes over time: French biologist Jean-Baptiste de Lamarck (1744–1829). Alas, Lamarck is primarily remembered today *not* for his visionary recognition that evolutionary change explains patterns in fossils and the match of organisms to their environments, but for the incorrect mechanism he proposed to explain how evolution occurs.

Lamarck published his hypothesis in 1809, the year Darwin was born. By comparing living species with fossil forms, Lamarck had found what appeared to be several lines of descent, each a chronological series of older to younger fossils leading to a living species. He explained his findings using two principles that were widely accepted at the time. The first was *use and disuse*, the idea that parts of the body that are used

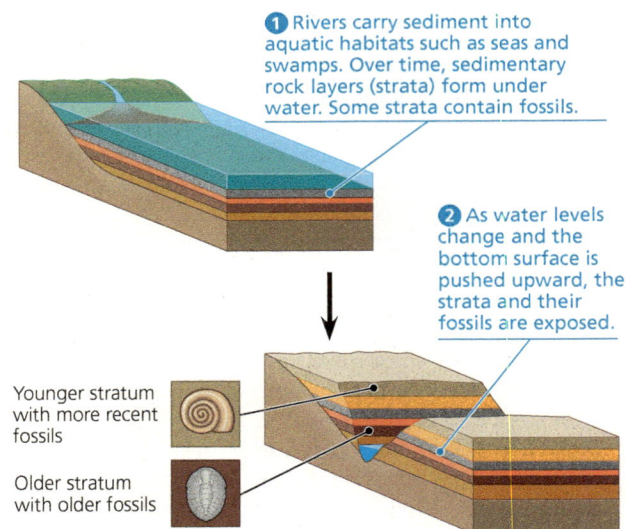

❶ Rivers carry sediment into aquatic habitats such as seas and swamps. Over time, sedimentary rock layers (strata) form under water. Some strata contain fossils.

❷ As water levels change and the bottom surface is pushed upward, the strata and their fossils are exposed.

Younger stratum with more recent fossils

Older stratum with older fossils

▲ **Figure 22.3 Formation of sedimentary strata with fossils.**

▲ **Figure 22.4 Acquired traits cannot be inherited.** This bonsai tree was "trained" to grow as a dwarf by pruning and shaping. However, seeds from this tree would produce offspring of normal size.

extensively become larger and stronger, while those that are not used deteriorate. Among many examples, he cited a giraffe stretching its neck to reach leaves on high branches. The second principle, *inheritance of acquired characteristics*, stated that an organism could pass these modifications to its offspring. Lamarck reasoned that the long, muscular neck of the living giraffe had evolved over many generations as giraffes stretched their necks ever higher.

Lamarck also thought that evolution happens because organisms have an innate drive to become more complex. Darwin rejected this idea, but he, too, thought that variation was introduced into the evolutionary process in part through inheritance of acquired characteristics. Today, however, our understanding of genetics refutes this mechanism: Experiments show that traits acquired by use during an individual's life are not inherited in the way proposed by Lamarck **(Figure 22.4)**.

Lamarck was vilified in his own time, especially by Cuvier, who denied that species ever evolve. In retrospect, however, Lamarck did recognize that the match of organisms to their environments can be explained by gradual evolutionary change, and he did propose a testable explanation for how this change occurs.

CONCEPT CHECK 22.1

1. How did Hutton's and Lyell's ideas influence Darwin's thinking about evolution?
2. **MAKE CONNECTIONS** In Concept 1.3 (pp. 65–66), you read that scientific hypotheses must be testable and falsifiable. Applying these criteria, are Cuvier's explanation of the fossil record and Lamarck's hypothesis of evolution scientific? Explain your answer in each case.

For suggested answers, see Appendix A.

Descent with modification by natural selection explains the adaptations of organisms and the unity and diversity of life

As the 19th century dawned, it was generally thought that species had remained unchanged since their creation. A few clouds of doubt about the permanence of species were beginning to gather, but no one could have forecast the thundering storm just beyond the horizon. How did Charles Darwin become the lightning rod for a revolutionary view of life?

Darwin's Research

Charles Darwin (1809–1882) was born in Shrewsbury, in western England. Even as a boy, he had a consuming interest in nature. When he was not reading nature books, he was fishing, hunting, and collecting insects. Darwin's father, a physician, could see no future for his son as a naturalist and sent him to medical school in Edinburgh. But Charles found medicine boring and surgery before the days of anesthesia horrifying. He quit medical school and enrolled at Cambridge University, intending to become a clergyman. (At that time in England, many scholars of science belonged to the clergy.)

At Cambridge, Darwin became the protégé of the Reverend John Henslow, a botany professor. Soon after Darwin graduated, Henslow recommended him to Captain Robert FitzRoy, who was preparing the survey ship HMS *Beagle* for a long voyage around the world. Darwin would pay his own way and serve as a conversation partner to the young captain. FitzRoy, who was himself an accomplished scientist, accepted Darwin because he was a skilled naturalist and because they were of the same social class and close in age.

The Voyage of the Beagle

Darwin embarked from England on the *Beagle* in December 1831. The primary mission of the voyage was to chart poorly known stretches of the South American coastline. While the ship's crew surveyed the coast, Darwin spent most of his time on shore, observing and collecting thousands of South American plants and animals. He noted the characteristics of plants and animals that made them well suited to such diverse environments as the humid jungles of Brazil, the expansive grasslands of Argentina, and the towering peaks of the Andes.

Darwin observed that the plants and animals in temperate regions of South America more closely resembled species living in the South American tropics than species living in temperate regions of Europe. Furthermore, the fossils he found, though clearly different from living species, were distinctly South American in their resemblance to the living organisms of that continent.

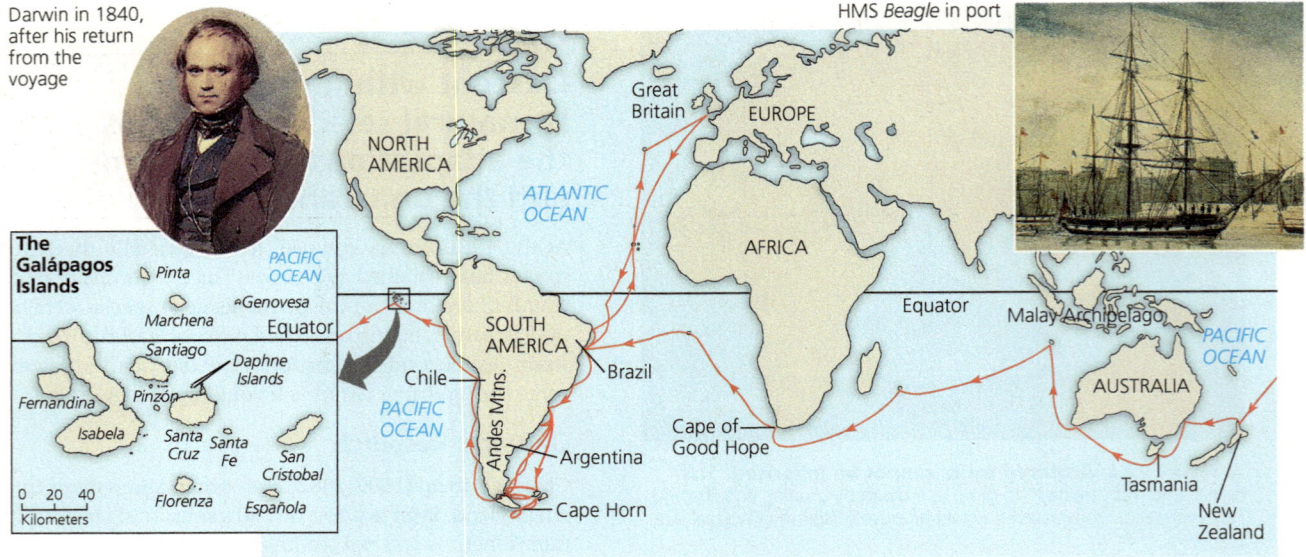

▲ **Figure 22.5 The voyage of HMS *Beagle*.**

Darwin also spent much time thinking about geology. Despite bouts of seasickness, he read Lyell's *Principles of Geology* while aboard the *Beagle*. He experienced geologic change firsthand when a violent earthquake rocked the coast of Chile, and he observed afterward that rocks along the coast had been thrust upward by several feet. Finding fossils of ocean organisms high in the Andes, Darwin inferred that the rocks containing the fossils must have been raised there by many similar earthquakes. These observations reinforced what he had learned from Lyell: The physical evidence did not support the traditional view that Earth was only a few thousand years old.

Darwin's interest in the geographic distribution of species was further stimulated by the *Beagle*'s stop at the Galápagos, a group of volcanic islands located near the equator about 900 km west of South America **(Figure 22.5)**. Darwin was fascinated by the unusual organisms there. The birds he collected included the finches mentioned in Chapter 1 and several kinds of mockingbirds. These mockingbirds, though similar to each other, seemed to be different species. Some were unique to individual islands, while others lived on two or more adjacent islands. Furthermore, although the animals on the Galápagos resembled species living on the South American mainland, most of the Galápagos species were not known from anywhere else in the world. Darwin hypothesized that the Galápagos had been colonized by organisms that had strayed from South America and then diversified, giving rise to new species on the various islands.

Darwin's Focus on Adaptation

During the voyage of the *Beagle*, Darwin observed many examples of **adaptations**, inherited characteristics of organisms that enhance their survival and reproduction in specific environments. Later, as he reassessed his observations, he began to perceive adaptation to the environment and the origin of new species as closely related processes. Could a new species arise from an ancestral form by the gradual accumulation of adaptations to a different environment? From studies made years after Darwin's voyage, biologists have concluded that this is indeed what happened to the diverse group of Galápagos finches (see Figure 1.22). The finches' various beaks and behaviors are adapted to the specific foods available on their home islands **(Figure 22.6)**. Darwin realized that explaining such adaptations was essential to understanding evolution. As we'll explore further, his explanation of how adaptations arise centered on **natural selection**, a process in which individuals that have certain inherited traits tend to survive and reproduce at higher rates than other individuals *because of* those traits.

By the early 1840s, Darwin had worked out the major features of his hypothesis. He set these ideas on paper in 1844, when he wrote a long essay on descent with modification and its underlying mechanism, natural selection. Yet he was still reluctant to publish his ideas, apparently because he anticipated the uproar they would cause. During this time, Darwin continued to compile evidence in support of his hypothesis. By the mid-1850s, he had described his ideas to Lyell and a few others. Lyell, who was not yet convinced of evolution, nevertheless urged Darwin to publish on the subject before someone else came to the same conclusions and published first.

In June 1858, Lyell's prediction came true. Darwin received a manuscript from Alfred Russel Wallace (1823–1913), a British naturalist working in the South Pacific islands of the Malay

(a) **Cactus-eater.** The long, sharp beak of the cactus ground finch (*Geospiza scandens*) helps it tear and eat cactus flowers and pulp.

(b) **Insect-eater.** The green warbler finch (*Certhidea olivacea*) uses its narrow, pointed beak to grasp insects.

(c) **Seed-eater.** The large ground finch (*Geospiza magnirostris*) has a large beak adapted for cracking seeds that fall from plants to the ground.

▲ **Figure 22.6 Three examples of beak variation in Galápagos finches.** The Galápagos Islands are home to more than a dozen species of closely related finches, some found only on a single island. The most striking differences among them are their beaks, which are adapted for specific diets.

MAKE CONNECTIONS *Review Figure 1.22 (p. 63). To which of the other two species shown above is the cactus-eater more closely related (that is, with which does it share a more recent common ancestor)?*

Archipelago (see Figure 22.2). Wallace had developed a hypothesis of natural selection nearly identical to Darwin's. He asked Darwin to evaluate his paper and forward it to Lyell if it merited publication. Darwin complied, writing to Lyell: "Your words have come true with a vengeance. . . . I never saw a more striking coincidence . . . so all my originality, whatever it may amount to, will be smashed." On July 1, 1858, Lyell and a colleague presented Wallace's paper, along with extracts from Darwin's unpublished 1844 essay, to the Linnean Society of London. Darwin quickly finished his book, titled *On the Origin of Species by Means of Natural Selection* (commonly referred to as *The Origin of Species*), and published it the next year. Although Wallace had submitted his ideas for publication first, he admired Darwin and thought that Darwin had developed the idea of natural selection so extensively that he should be known as its main architect.

Within a decade, Darwin's book and its proponents had convinced most scientists that life's diversity is the product of evolution. Darwin succeeded where previous evolutionists had failed, mainly by presenting a plausible scientific mechanism with immaculate logic and an avalanche of evidence.

The Origin of Species

In his book, Darwin amassed evidence that descent with modification by natural selection explains the three broad observations about nature listed in the Overview: the unity of life, the diversity of life, and the match between organisms and their environments.

Descent with Modification

In the first edition of *The Origin of Species*, Darwin never used the word *evolution* (although the final word of the book is

"evolved"). Rather, he discussed *descent with modification*, a phrase that summarized his view of life. Organisms share many characteristics, leading Darwin to perceive unity in life. He attributed the unity of life to the descent of all organisms from an ancestor that lived in the remote past. He also thought that as the descendants of that ancestral organism lived in various habitats over millions of years, they accumulated diverse modifications, or adaptations, that fit them to specific ways of life. Darwin reasoned that over long periods of time, descent with modification eventually led to the rich diversity of life we see today.

Darwin viewed the history of life as a tree, with multiple branchings from a common trunk out to the tips of the youngest twigs **(Figure 22.7).** The tips of the twigs represent the diversity of organisms living in the present. Each fork of the tree represents the most recent common ancestor of all the lines of evolution that subsequently branch from that point. As an example, consider the three living species of elephants: the Asian elephant (*Elephas maximus*) and African elephants

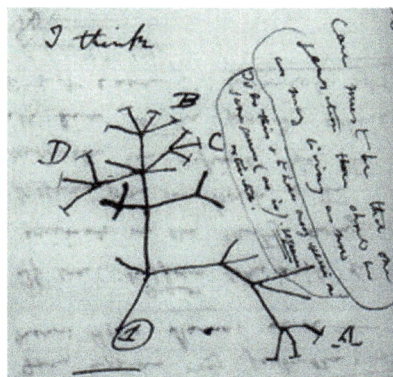

◀ **Figure 22.7 "I think. . ."** In this 1837 sketch, Darwin envisioned the branching pattern of evolution.

(*Loxodonta africana* and *L. cyclotis*). These closely related species are very similar because they shared the same line of descent until a relatively recent split from their common ancestor, as shown in the tree diagram in **Figure 22.8**. Note that seven lineages related to elephants have become extinct over the past 32 million years. As a result, there are no living species that fill the gap between the elephants and their nearest relatives today, the hyraxes and manatees. Such extinctions are not uncommon. In fact, many evolutionary branches, even some major ones, are dead ends: Scientists estimate that over 99% of all species that have ever lived are now extinct. As in Figure 22.8, fossils of extinct species can document the divergence of present-day groups by "filling in" gaps between them.

In his efforts at classification, Linnaeus had realized that some organisms resemble each other more closely than others, but he had not linked these resemblances to evolution. Nonetheless, because he had recognized that the great diversity of organisms could be organized into "groups subordinate to groups" (Darwin's phrase), Linnaeus's system meshed well with Darwin's hypothesis. To Darwin, the Linnaean hierarchy reflected the branching history of life, with organisms at the various levels related through descent from common ancestors.

Artificial Selection, Natural Selection, and Adaptation

Darwin proposed the mechanism of natural selection to explain the observable patterns of evolution. He crafted his argument carefully, to persuade even the most skeptical readers. First he discussed familiar examples of selective breeding of domesticated plants and animals. Humans have modified other species over many generations by selecting and breeding individuals that possess desired traits, a process called **artificial selection (Figure 22.9)**. As a result of artificial selection, crops, livestock animals, and pets often bear little resemblance to their wild ancestors.

Darwin then argued that a similar process occurs in nature. He based his argument on two observations, from which he drew two inferences:

Observation #1: Members of a population often vary in their inherited traits **(Figure 22.10)**.

Observation #2: All species can produce more offspring than their environment can support **(Figure 22.11)**, and many of these offspring fail to survive and reproduce.

Inference #1: Individuals whose inherited traits give them a higher probability of surviving and reproducing in a given environment tend to leave more offspring than other individuals.

Inference #2: This unequal ability of individuals to survive and reproduce will lead to the accumulation of favorable traits in the population over generations.

Darwin saw an important connection between natural selection and the

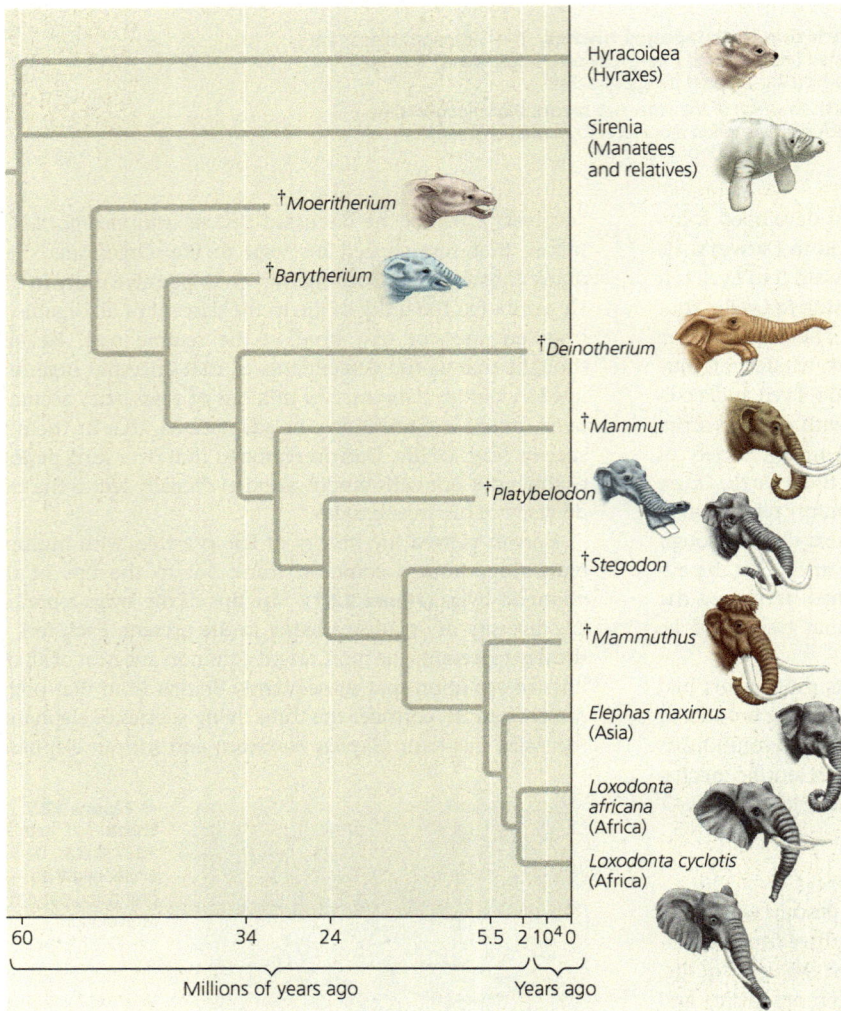

▲ **Figure 22.8 Descent with modification.** This evolutionary tree of elephants and their relatives is based mainly on fossils—their anatomy, order of appearance in strata, and geographic distribution. Note that most branches of descent ended in extinction (denoted by the dagger symbol †). (Time line not to scale.)

? *Based on the tree shown here, approximately when did the most recent ancestor shared by Mammuthus (woolly mammoths), Asian elephants, and African elephants live?*

► **Figure 22.9 Artificial selection.** These different vegetables have all been selected from one species of wild mustard. By selecting variations in different parts of the plant, breeders have obtained these divergent results.

▲ **Figure 22.10 Variation in a population.** Individuals in this population of Asian ladybird beetles vary in color and spot pattern. Natural selection may act on these variations only if (1) they are heritable and (2) they affect the beetles' ability to survive and reproduce.

► **Figure 22.11 Overproduction of offspring.** A single puffball fungus can produce billions of offspring. If all of these offspring and their descendants survived to maturity, they would carpet the surrounding land surface.

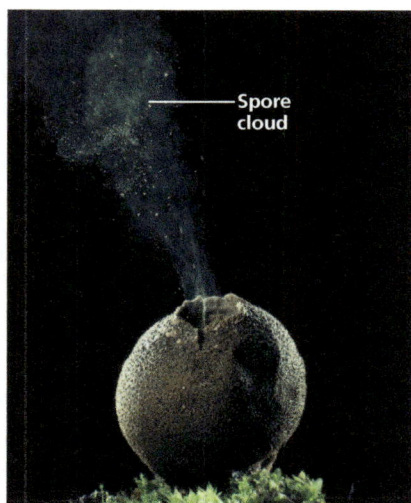

capacity of organisms to "overreproduce." He began to make this connection after reading an essay by economist Thomas Malthus, who contended that much of human suffering—disease, famine, and war—was the inescapable consequence of the human population's potential to increase faster than food supplies and other resources. Darwin realized that the capacity to overreproduce was characteristic of all species. Of the many eggs laid, young born, and seeds spread, only a tiny fraction complete their development and leave offspring of their own. The rest are eaten, starved, diseased, unmated, or unable to tolerate physical conditions of the environment such as salinity or temperature.

An organism's heritable traits can influence not only its own performance, but also how well its offspring cope with environmental challenges. For example, an organism might have a trait that gives its offspring an advantage in escaping predators, obtaining food, or tolerating physical conditions. When such advantages increase the number of offspring that survive and reproduce, the traits that are favored will likely appear at a greater frequency in the next generation. Thus, over time, natural selection resulting from factors such as predators, lack of food, or adverse physical conditions can lead to an increase in the proportion of favorable traits in a population.

How rapidly do such changes occur? Darwin reasoned that if artificial selection can bring about dramatic change in a relatively short period of time, then natural selection should be capable of substantial modification of species over many hundreds of generations. Even if the advantages of some heritable traits over others are slight, the advantageous variations will gradually accumulate in the population, and less favorable variations will diminish. Over time, this process will increase the frequency of individuals with favorable adaptations and hence refine the match between organisms and their environment (see Figure 1.20).

Natural Selection: A Summary

Let's now recap the main ideas of natural selection:

- Natural selection is a process in which individuals that have certain heritable traits survive and reproduce at a higher rate than other individuals because of those traits.
- Over time, natural selection can increase the match between organisms and their environment **(Figure 22.12)**.
- If an environment changes, or if individuals move to a new environment, natural selection may result in adaptation to these new conditions, sometimes giving rise to new species.

One subtle but important point is that although natural selection occurs through interactions between individual organisms and their environment, *individuals do not evolve*. Rather, it is the population that evolves over time.

A second key point is that natural selection can amplify or diminish only those heritable traits that differ among the individuals in a population. Thus, even if a trait is heritable, if all the individuals in a population are genetically identical for that trait, evolution by natural selection cannot occur.

Third, remember that environmental factors vary from place to place and over time. A trait that is favorable in one place or time may be useless—or even detrimental—in other places or times. Natural selection is always operating, but which traits are favored depends on the context in which a species lives and mates.

Next, we'll survey the wide range of observations that support a Darwinian view of evolution by natural selection.

CONCEPT CHECK 22.2

1. How does the concept of descent with modification explain both the unity and diversity of life?
2. **WHAT IF?** If you discovered a fossil of an extinct mammal that lived high in the Andes, would you predict that it would more closely resemble present-day mammals from South American jungles or present-day mammals that live high in African mountains? Explain.
3. **MAKE CONNECTIONS** Review Figures 14.4 and 14.6 (pp. 311 and 313) on the relationship between genotype and phenotype. In a particular pea population, suppose that flowers with the white phenotype are favored by natural selection. Predict what would happen over time to the frequency of the *p* allele in the population, and explain your reasoning.

For suggested answers, see Appendix A.

CONCEPT 22.3

Evolution is supported by an overwhelming amount of scientific evidence

In *The Origin of Species*, Darwin marshaled a broad range of evidence to support the concept of descent with modification. Still—as he readily acknowledged—there were instances in which key evidence was lacking. For example, Darwin referred to the origin of flowering plants as an "abominable mystery," and he lamented the lack of fossils showing how earlier groups of organisms gave rise to new groups.

In the last 150 years, new discoveries have filled many of the gaps that Darwin identified. The origin of flowering plants, for example, is much better understood (see Chapter 30), and many fossils have been discovered that signify the origin of new groups of organisms (see Chapter 25). In this section, we'll consider four types of data that document the pattern of evolution and illuminate the processes by which it occurs: direct observations of evolution, homology, the fossil record, and biogeography.

Direct Observations of Evolutionary Change

Biologists have documented evolutionary change in thousands of scientific studies. We'll examine many such studies throughout this unit, but let's look at two examples here.

(a) A flower mantid in Malaysia

(b) A leaf mantid in Borneo

▲ **Figure 22.12 Camouflage as an example of evolutionary adaptation.** Related species of the insects called mantids have diverse shapes and colors that evolved in different environments.

? *Explain how these mantids demonstrate the three key observations about life introduced in this chapter's Overview: the match between organisms and their environments, unity, and diversity.*

Natural Selection in Response to Introduced Plant Species

Animals that eat plants, called herbivores, often have adaptations that help them feed efficiently on their primary food sources. What happens when herbivores begin to feed on a plant species with different characteristics than their usual food source?

An opportunity to study this question in nature is provided by soapberry bugs, which use their "beak," a hollow, needle-like mouthpart, to feed on seeds located within the fruits of various plants. In southern Florida, the soapberry bug *Jadera haematoloma* feeds on the seeds of a native plant, the balloon vine (*Cardiospermum corindum*). In central Florida, however, balloon vines have become rare. Instead, soapberry bugs in that region now feed on goldenrain tree (*Koelreuteria elegans*), a species recently introduced from Asia.

Soapberry bugs feed most effectively when their beak length closely matches the depth at which the seeds are found within the fruit. Goldenrain tree fruit consists of three flat lobes, and its seeds are much closer to the fruit surface than the seeds of the plump, round native balloon vine fruit. Researchers at the University of Utah predicted that in populations that feed on goldenrain tree, natural selection would result in beaks that are *shorter* than those in populations that feed on balloon vine (**Figure 22.13**). Indeed, beak lengths are shorter in the populations that feed on goldenrain tree.

Researchers have also studied beak length evolution in soapberry bug populations that feed on plants introduced to Louisiana, Oklahoma, and Australia. In each of these locations, the fruit of the introduced plants is larger than the fruit of the native plant. Thus, in populations feeding on introduced species in these regions, the researchers predicted that natural selection would result in the evolution of *longer* beak length. Again, data collected in field studies upheld this prediction.

The adaptation observed in these soapberry bug populations had important consequences: In Australia, for example, the increase in beak length nearly doubled the success with which soapberry bugs could eat the seeds of the introduced species. Furthermore, since historical data show that the goldenrain tree reached central Florida just 35 years before the scientific studies were initiated, the results demonstrate that natural selection can cause rapid evolution in a wild population.

The Evolution of Drug-Resistant Bacteria

An example of ongoing natural selection that dramatically affects humans is the evolution of drug-resistant pathogens (disease-causing organisms and viruses). This is a particular problem with bacteria and viruses because resistant strains of these pathogens can proliferate very quickly.

Consider the evolution of drug resistance in the bacterium *Staphylococcus aureus*. About one in three people harbor this species on their skin or in their nasal passages with no negative effects. However, certain genetic varieties (strains) of this species, known as methicillin-resistant *S. aureus* (MRSA), are

▼ **Figure 22.13**

INQUIRY

Can a change in a population's food source result in evolution by natural selection?

FIELD STUDY Soapberry bugs (*Jadera haematoloma*) feed most effectively when the length of their "beak" closely matches the depth within the fruits of the seeds they eat. Scott Carroll and his colleagues measured beak lengths in soapberry bug populations in southern Florida feeding on the native balloon vine. They also measured beak lengths in populations in central Florida feeding on the introduced goldenrain tree, which has a flatter fruit shape than the balloon vine. The researchers then compared the measurements to those of museum specimens collected in the two areas before the goldenrain tree was introduced.

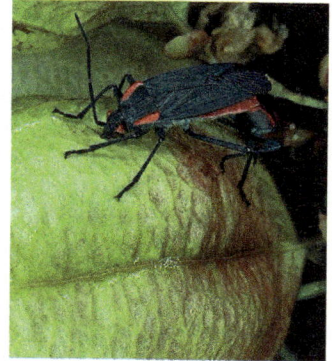

Soapberry bug with beak inserted in balloon vine fruit

RESULTS Beak lengths were shorter in populations feeding on the introduced species than in populations feeding on the native species, in which the seeds are buried more deeply. The average beak length in museum specimens from each population (indicated by red arrows) was similar to beak lengths in populations feeding on native species.

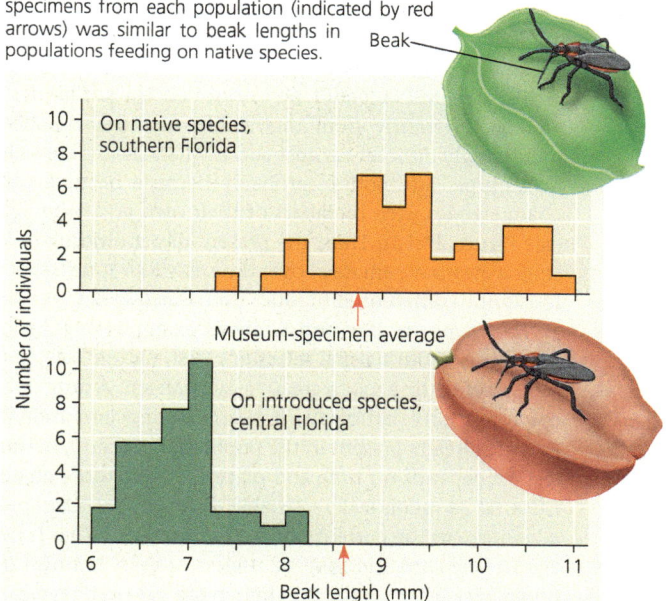

CONCLUSION Museum specimens and contemporary data suggest that a change in the size of the soapberry bug's food source can result in evolution by natural selection for matching beak size.

SOURCE S. P. Carroll and C. Boyd, Host race radiation in the soapberry bug: natural history with the history, *Evolution* 46: 1052–1069 (1992).

WHAT IF? When soapberry bug eggs from a population fed on balloon vine fruits were reared on goldenrain tree fruits (or vice versa), the beak lengths of the adult insects matched those in the population from which the eggs were obtained. Interpret these results.

formidable pathogens. The past decade has seen an alarming increase in virulent forms of MRSA such as clone USA300, a strain that can cause "flesh-eating disease" and potentially fatal infections **(Figure 22.14)**. How did clone USA300 and other strains of MRSA become so dangerous?

The story begins in 1943, when penicillin became the first widely used antibiotic. Since then, penicillin and other antibiotics have saved millions of lives. However, by 1945, more than 20% of the *S. aureus* strains seen in hospitals were already resistant to penicillin. These bacteria had an enzyme, penicillinase, that could destroy penicillin. Researchers responded by developing antibiotics that were not destroyed by penicillinase, but some *S. aureus* populations developed resistance to each new drug within a few years.

In 1959, doctors began using the powerful antibiotic methicillin, but within two years, methicillin-resistant strains of *S. aureus* appeared. How did these resistant strains emerge? Methicillin works by deactivating a protein that bacteria use to synthesize their cell walls. However, *S. aureus* populations exhibited variations in how strongly their members were affected by the drug. In particular, some individuals were able to synthesize their cell walls using a different protein that was not affected by methicillin. These individuals survived the methicillin treatments and reproduced at higher rates than did other individuals. Over time, these resistant individuals became increasingly common, leading to the spread of MRSA.

Initially, MRSA could be controlled by antibiotics that worked differently from methicillin. But this has become increasingly difficult because some MRSA strains are resistant to multiple antibiotics—probably because bacteria can exchange genes with members of their own and other species (see Figure 27.13). Thus, the present-day multidrug-resistant strains may have emerged over time as MRSA strains that were resistant to different antibiotics exchanged genes.

The soapberry bug and *S. aureus* examples highlight two key points about natural selection. First, natural selection is a process of editing, not a creative mechanism. A drug does not *create* resistant pathogens; it *selects for* resistant individuals that are already present in the population. Second, natural selection depends on time and place. It favors those characteristics in a genetically variable population that provide advantage in the current, local environment. What is beneficial in one situation may be useless or even harmful in another. Beak lengths arise that match the size of the typical fruit eaten by a particular soapberry bug population. However, a beak length suitable for fruit of one size can be disadvantageous when the bug is feeding on fruit of another size.

Homology

A second type of evidence for evolution comes from analyzing similarities among different organisms. As we've discussed, evolution is a process of descent with modification: Characteristics present in an ancestral organism are altered (by natural

▼ **Figure 22.14**
IMPACT

The Rise of MRSA

Most methicillin-resistant *Staphylococcus aureus* (MRSA) infections are caused by recently appearing strains such as clone USA300. Resistant to multiple antibiotics and highly contagious, this strain and its close relatives can cause lethal infections of the skin, lungs, and blood. Researchers have identified key areas of the USA300 genome that code for its particularly virulent properties.

The circular chromosome of clone USA300 has been sequenced and contains 2,872,769 base pairs of DNA.

The highlighted regions contain genes that increase the strain's virulence (see the key).

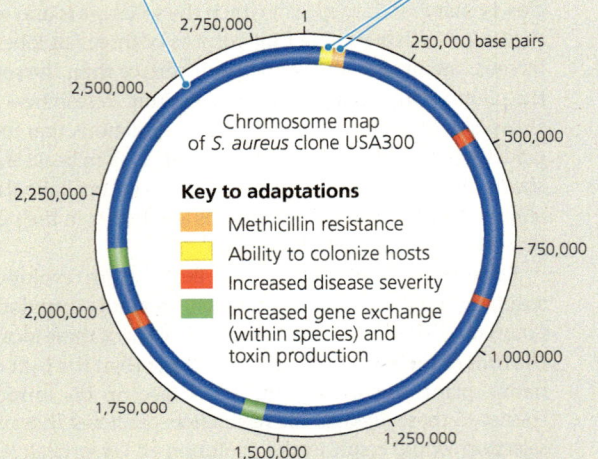

Chromosome map of *S. aureus* clone USA300

Key to adaptations
- Methicillin resistance
- Ability to colonize hosts
- Increased disease severity
- Increased gene exchange (within species) and toxin production

WHY IT MATTERS MRSA infections have proliferated dramatically in the past few decades, and the annual death toll in the United States is in the tens of thousands. There is grave concern about the continuing evolution of drug resistance and the resulting difficulty of treating MRSA infections. Ongoing studies of how MRSA strains colonize their hosts and cause disease may help scientists develop drugs to combat MRSA.

FURTHER READING General information about MRSA can be found on the Centers for Disease Control and Prevention (CDC) website (www.cdc.gov/mrsa) and in G. Taubes, The bacteria fight back, *Science* 321:356–361 (2008).

WHAT IF? Efforts are underway to develop drugs that target *S. aureus* specifically and to develop drugs that slow the growth of MRSA but do not kill it. Based on how natural selection works and on the fact that bacterial species can exchange genes, explain why each of these strategies might be effective.

selection) in its descendants over time as they face different environmental conditions. As a result, related species can have characteristics that have an underlying similarity yet function differently. Similarity resulting from common ancestry is known as **homology**. As this section will explain, an understanding of homology can be used to make testable predictions and explain observations that are otherwise puzzling.

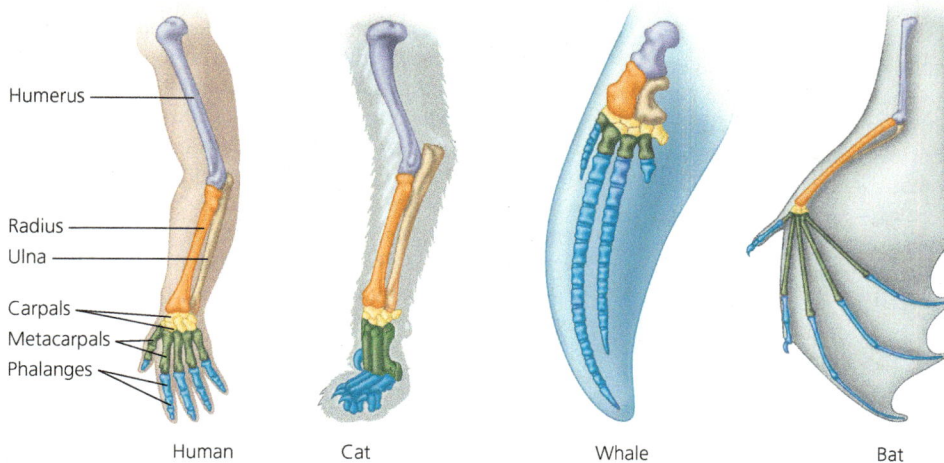

◄ **Figure 22.15 Mammalian forelimbs: homologous structures.** Even though they have become adapted for different functions, the forelimbs of all mammals are constructed from the same basic skeletal elements: one large bone (purple), attached to two smaller bones (orange and tan), attached to several small bones (gold), attached to several metacarpals (green), attached to approximately five digits, or phalanges (blue).

Humerus
Radius
Ulna
Carpals
Metacarpals
Phalanges

Human   Cat   Whale   Bat

Anatomical and Molecular Homologies

The view of evolution as a remodeling process leads to the prediction that closely related species should share similar features—and they do. Of course, closely related species share the features used to determine their relationship, but they also share many other features. Some of these shared features make little sense except in the context of evolution. For example, the forelimbs of all mammals, including humans, cats, whales, and bats, show the same arrangement of bones from the shoulder to the tips of the digits, even though these appendages have very different functions: lifting, walking, swimming, and flying **(Figure 22.15)**. Such striking anatomical resemblances would be highly unlikely if these structures had arisen anew in each species. Rather, the underlying skeletons of the arms, forelegs, flippers, and wings of different mammals are **homologous structures** that represent variations on a structural theme that was present in their common ancestor.

Comparing early stages of development in different animal species reveals additional anatomical homologies not visible in adult organisms. For example, at some point in their development, all vertebrate embryos have a tail located posterior to (behind) the anus, as well as structures called pharyngeal (throat) pouches **(Figure 22.16)**. These homologous throat pouches ultimately develop into structures with very different functions, such as gills in fishes and parts of the ears and throat in humans and other mammals.

Some of the most intriguing homologies concern "leftover" structures of marginal, if any, importance to the organism. These **vestigial structures** are remnants of features that served important functions in the organism's ancestors. For instance, the skeletons of some snakes retain vestiges of the pelvis and leg bones of walking ancestors. Another example is provided by eye remnants that are buried under scales in blind species of cave fishes. We would not expect to see

these vestigial structures if snakes and blind cave fishes had origins separate from other vertebrate animals.

Biologists also observe similarities among organisms at the molecular level. All forms of life use the same genetic language of DNA and RNA, and the genetic code is essentially universal. Thus, it is likely that all species descended from common ancestors that used this code. But molecular homologies go beyond a shared code. For example, organisms as dissimilar as humans and bacteria share genes inherited from a very distant common ancestor. Some of these homologous genes have acquired new functions, while others, such as those coding for the ribosomal subunits used in protein synthesis (see Figure 17.17), have retained their original functions. It is also common for organisms to have genes that have lost their function, even though the homologous genes in related species may be fully functional. Like vestigial structures, it appears that such inactive "pseudogenes" may be present simply because a common ancestor had them.

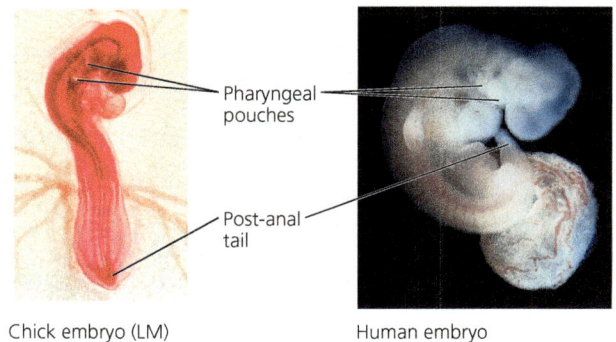

Pharyngeal pouches
Post-anal tail
Chick embryo (LM)   Human embryo

▲ **Figure 22.16 Anatomical similarities in vertebrate embryos.** At some stage in their embryonic development, all vertebrates have a tail located posterior to the anus (referred to as a post-anal tail), as well as pharyngeal (throat) pouches. Descent from a common ancestor can explain such similarities.

Homologies and "Tree Thinking"

Some homologous characteristics, such as the genetic code, are shared by all species because they date to the deep ancestral past. In contrast, homologous characteristics that evolved more recently are shared only within smaller groups of organisms. Consider the *tetrapods* (from the Greek *tetra*, four, and *pod*, foot), the vertebrate group that consists of amphibians, mammals, and reptiles (including birds—see Figure 22.17). All tetrapods have limbs with digits (see Figure 22.15), whereas other vertebrates do not. Thus, homologous characteristics form a nested pattern: All life shares the deepest layer, and each successive smaller group adds its own homologies to those it shares with larger groups. This nested pattern is exactly what we would expect to result from descent with modification from a common ancestor.

Biologists often represent the pattern of descent from common ancestors and the resulting homologies with an **evolutionary tree**, a diagram that reflects evolutionary relationships among groups of organisms. We will explore in detail how evolutionary trees are constructed in Chapter 26, but for now, let's consider how we can interpret and use such trees.

Figure 22.17 is an evolutionary tree of tetrapods and their closest living relatives, the lungfishes. In this diagram, each branch point represents the common ancestor of all species that descended from it. For example, lungfishes and all tetrapods descended from ancestor ❶, whereas mammals, lizards and snakes, crocodiles, and birds all descended from ancestor ❸. As expected, the three homologies shown on the tree—limbs with digits, the amnion (a protective embryonic membrane), and feathers—form a nested pattern. Limbs with digits were present in common ancestor ❷ and hence are found in all of the descendants of that ancestor (the tetrapods). The amnion was present only in ancestor ❸ and hence is shared only by some tetrapods (mammals and reptiles). Feathers were present only in common ancestor ❻ and hence are found only in birds.

To explore "tree thinking" further, note that in Figure 22.17, mammals are positioned closer to amphibians than to birds. As a result, you might conclude that mammals are more closely related to amphibians than they are to birds. However, mammals are actually more closely related to birds than to amphibians because mammals and birds share a more recent common ancestor (ancestor ❸) than do mammals and amphibians (ancestor ❷). Ancestor ❷ is also the most recent common ancestor of birds and amphibians, making mammals and birds equally related to amphibians. Finally, note that the tree in Figure 22.17 shows the relative timing of evolutionary events but not their actual dates. Thus, we can conclude that ancestor ❷ lived before ancestor ❸, but we do not know when that was.

Evolutionary trees are hypotheses that summarize our current understanding of patterns of descent. Our confidence in these relationships, as with any hypothesis, depends on the strength of the supporting data. In the case of Figure 22.17, the tree is supported by a variety of independent data sets, including both anatomical and DNA sequence data. As a result, biologists feel confident that it accurately reflects evolutionary history. As you will read in Chapter 26, scientists can use such well-supported evolutionary trees to make specific and sometimes surprising predictions about organisms.

A Different Cause of Resemblance: Convergent Evolution

Although organisms that are closely related share characteristics because of common descent, distantly related organisms can resemble one another for a different reason: **convergent evolution**, the independent evolution of similar features in different lineages. Consider marsupial mammals, many of which live in Australia. Marsupials are distinct from another group of mammals—the eutherians—few of which live in Australia. (Eutherians complete their embryonic development in the uterus, whereas marsupials

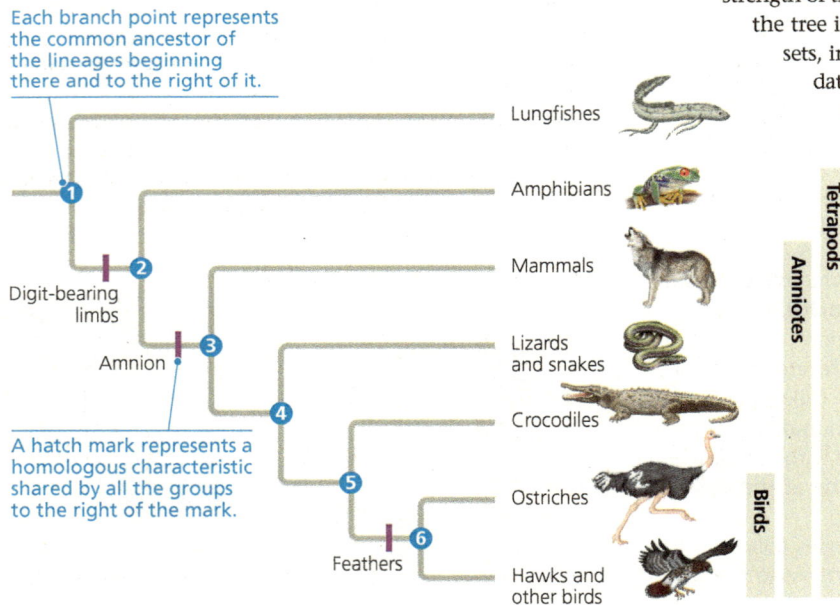

▲ **Figure 22.17 Tree thinking: information provided in an evolutionary tree.** This evolutionary tree for tetrapods and their closest living relatives, the lungfishes, is based on anatomical and DNA sequence data. The purple bars indicate the origin of three important homologies, each of which evolved only once. Birds are nested within and evolved from reptiles; hence, the group of organisms called "reptiles" technically includes birds.

❓ *Are crocodiles more closely related to lizards or birds? Explain your answer.*

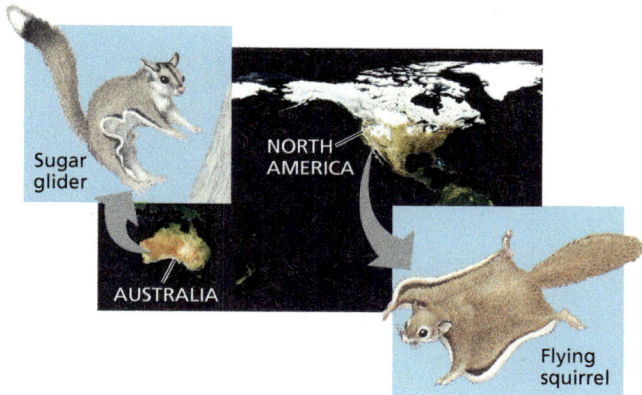

▲ **Figure 22.18 Convergent evolution.** The ability to glide through the air evolved independently in these two distantly related mammals.

are born as embryos and complete their development in an external pouch.) Some Australian marsupials have eutherian look-alikes with superficially similar adaptations. For instance, a forest-dwelling Australian marsupial called the sugar glider is superficially very similar to flying squirrels, gliding eutherians that live in North American forests (Figure 22.18). But the sugar glider has many other characteristics that make it a marsupial, much more closely related to kangaroos and other Australian marsupials than to flying squirrels or other eutherians. Once again, our understanding of evolution can explain these observations. Although they evolved independently from different ancestors, these two mammals have adapted to similar environments in similar ways. In such examples in which species share features because of convergent evolution, the resemblance is said to be **analogous**, not homologous. Analogous features share similar function, but not common ancestry, while homologous features share common ancestry, but not necessarily similar function.

The Fossil Record

A third type of evidence for evolution comes from fossils. As Chapter 25 discusses in more detail, the fossil record documents the pattern of evolution, showing that past organisms differed from present-day organisms and that many species have become extinct. Fossils also show the evolutionary changes that have occurred in various groups of organisms. To give one of hundreds of possible examples, researchers found that the pelvic bone in fossil stickleback fish became greatly reduced in size over time in a number of different lakes. The consistent nature of this change sug-

gests that the reduction in the size of the pelvic bone may have been driven by natural selection.

Fossils can also shed light on the origins of new groups of organisms. An example is the fossil record of cetaceans, the mammalian order that includes whales, dolphins, and porpoises. Some of these fossils provided an unexpected line of support for a hypothesis based on DNA data: that cetaceans are closely related to even-toed ungulates, a group that includes deer, pigs, camels, and cows (Figure 22.19). What else can fossils tell us about cetacean origins? The earliest cetaceans lived 50–60 million years ago. The fossil record indicates that prior to that time, most mammals were terrestrial. Although scientists had long realized that whales and other cetaceans originated from land mammals, few fossils had been found that revealed how cetacean limb structure had changed over time, leading eventually to the loss of hind limbs and the development of flippers and tail flukes. In the past few decades, however, a series of remarkable fossils have been discovered in Pakistan, Egypt, and North America. These fossils document steps in the transition from life on land to life in the sea, filling in some of the gaps between ancestral and living cetaceans (Figure 22.20, on the next page).

Collectively, the recent fossil discoveries document the formation of new species and the origin of a major new group of mammals, the cetaceans. These discoveries also show that cetaceans and their close living relatives (hippopotamuses, pigs, deer, and

▲ *Diacodexis*, an early even-toed ungulate

other even-toed ungulates) are much more different from each other than were *Pakicetus* and early even-toed ungulates, such as *Diacodexis*. Similar patterns are seen in fossils documenting the origins of other major new groups of organisms, including

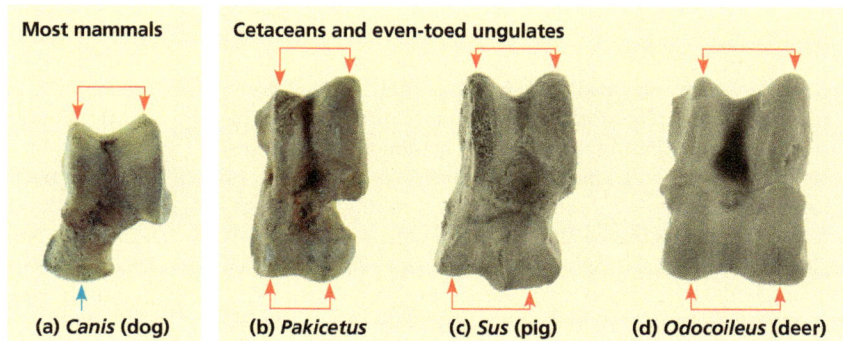

(a) *Canis* (dog)   (b) *Pakicetus*   (c) *Sus* (pig)   (d) *Odocoileus* (deer)

Most mammals | Cetaceans and even-toed ungulates

▲ **Figure 22.19 Ankle bones: one piece of the puzzle.** Comparing fossils and present-day examples of the astragalus (a type of ankle bone) provides one line of evidence that cetaceans are closely related to even-toed ungulates. **(a)** In most mammals, the astragalus is shaped like that of a dog, with a double hump on one end (indicated by the red arrows) but not at the opposite end (blue arrow). **(b)** Fossils show that the early cetacean *Pakicetus* had an astragalus with double humps at both ends, a unique shape that is otherwise found only in even-toed ungulates, as shown here for **(c)** a pig and **(d)** a deer.

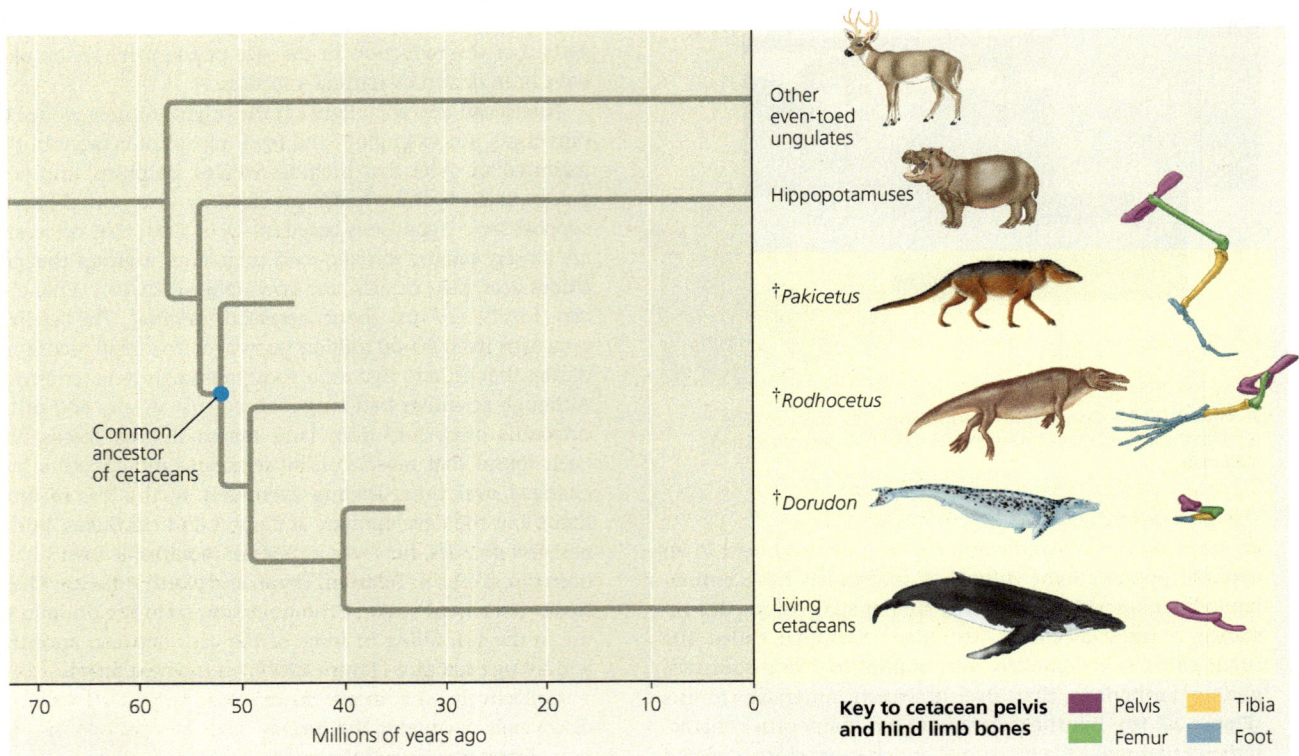

▲ **Figure 22.20 The transition to life in the sea.** Multiple lines of evidence support the hypothesis that cetaceans evolved from terrestrial mammals. Fossils document the reduction over time in the pelvis and hind limb bones of extinct cetacean ancestors, including *Pakicetus*, *Rodhocetus*, and *Dorudon*. DNA sequence data support the hypothesis that cetaceans are most closely related to hippopotamuses, even-toed ungulates.

? *Which happened first during the evolution of cetaceans: changes in hind limb structure or the origin of tail flukes?*

mammals (see Chapter 25), flowering plants (see Chapter 30), and tetrapods (see Chapter 34). In each of these cases, the fossil record shows that over time, descent with modification produced increasingly large differences among related groups of organisms, ultimately resulting in the diversity of life we see today.

Biogeography

A fourth type of evidence for evolution comes from **biogeography**, the geographic distribution of species. The geographic distribution of organisms is influenced by many factors, including *continental drift*, the slow movement of Earth's continents over time. About 250 million years ago, these movements united all of Earth's landmasses into a single large continent called **Pangaea** (see Figure 25.14). Roughly 200 million years ago, Pangaea began to break apart; by 20 million years ago, the continents we know today were within a few hundred kilometers of their present locations.

We can use our understanding of evolution and continental drift to predict where fossils of different groups of organisms might be found. For example, scientists have constructed evolutionary trees for horses based on anatomical data. These trees and the ages of fossils of horse ancestors suggest that present-day horse species originated 5 million years ago in North America. At that time, North and South America were close to their present locations, but they were not yet connected, making it difficult for horses to travel between them. Thus, we would predict that the oldest horse fossils should be found only on the continent on which horses originated—North America. This prediction and others like it for different groups of organisms have been upheld, providing more evidence for evolution.

We can also use our understanding of evolution to explain biogeographic data. For example, islands generally have many species of plants and animals that are **endemic**, which means they are found nowhere else in the world. Yet, as Darwin described in *The Origin of Species*, most island species are closely related to species from the nearest mainland or a neighboring island. He explained this observation by suggesting that islands are colonized by species from the nearest mainland. These colonists eventually give rise to new species as they adapt to their new environments. Such a process also explains why two islands with similar environments in distant parts of the world tend to be populated not by species that are closely related to each other, but rather by species related to those of the nearest mainland, where the environment is often quite different.

What Is Theoretical About Darwin's View of Life?

Some people dismiss Darwin's ideas as "just a theory." However, as we have seen, the *pattern* of evolution—the observation that life has evolved over time—has been documented directly and is supported by a great deal of evidence. In addition, Darwin's explanation of the *process* of evolution—that natural selection is the primary cause of the observed pattern of evolutionary change—makes sense of massive amounts of data. The effects of natural selection also can be observed and tested in nature.

What, then, is theoretical about evolution? Keep in mind that the scientific meaning of the term *theory* is very different from its meaning in everyday use. The colloquial use of the word *theory* comes close to what scientists mean by a hypothesis. In science, a theory is more comprehensive than a hypothesis. A theory, such as the theory of evolution by natural selection, accounts for many observations and explains and integrates a great variety of phenomena. Such a unifying theory does not become widely accepted unless its predictions stand up to thorough and continual testing by experiment and additional observation (see Chapter 1). As the next three chapters demonstrate, this has certainly been the case with the theory of evolution by natural selection.

The skepticism of scientists as they continue to test theories prevents these ideas from becoming dogma. For example, although Darwin thought that evolution was a very slow process, we now know that this isn't always true. New species can form in relatively short periods of time (a few thousand years or less; see Chapter 24). Furthermore, as we'll explore throughout this unit, evolutionary biologists now recognize that natural selection is not the only mechanism responsible for evolution. Indeed, the study of evolution today is livelier than ever as scientists find more ways to test predictions based on natural selection and other evolutionary mechanisms.

Although Darwin's theory attributes the diversity of life to natural processes, the diverse products of evolution nevertheless remain elegant and inspiring. As Darwin wrote in the final sentence of *The Origin of Species*, "There is grandeur in this view of life . . . [in which] endless forms most beautiful and most wonderful have been, and are being, evolved."

CONCEPT CHECK 22.3

1. Explain how the following statement is inaccurate: "Antibiotics have created drug resistance in MRSA."
2. How does evolution account for (a) the similar mammalian forelimbs with different functions shown in Figure 22.15 and (b) the similar lifestyle of the two distantly related mammals shown in Figure 22.18?
3. **WHAT IF?** The fossil record shows that dinosaurs originated 200–250 million years ago. Would you expect the geographic distribution of early dinosaur fossils to be broad (on many continents) or narrow (on one or a few continents only)? Explain.

For suggested answers, see Appendix A.

22 CHAPTER REVIEW

SUMMARY OF KEY CONCEPTS

CONCEPT 22.1

The Darwinian revolution challenged traditional views of a young Earth inhabited by unchanging species (pp. 499–501)

- Darwin proposed that life's diversity arose from ancestral species through natural selection, a departure from prevailing views.
- In contrast to **catastrophism** (the principle that events in the past occurred suddenly by mechanisms not operating today), Hutton and Lyell thought that geologic change results from mechanisms that operated in the past in the same manner as at the present time (**uniformitarianism**).
- Lamarck hypothesized that species evolve, but the underlying mechanisms he proposed are not supported by evidence.

? *Why was the age of Earth important for Darwin's ideas about evolution?*

CONCEPT 22.2

Descent with modification by natural selection explains the adaptations of organisms and the unity and diversity of life (pp. 501–506)

- Darwin's experiences during the voyage of the *Beagle* gave rise to his idea that new species originate from ancestral forms through the accumulation of **adaptations**. He refined his theory for many years and finally published it in 1859 after learning that Wallace had come to the same idea.
- In *The Origin of Species*, Darwin proposed that evolution occurs by **natural selection**.

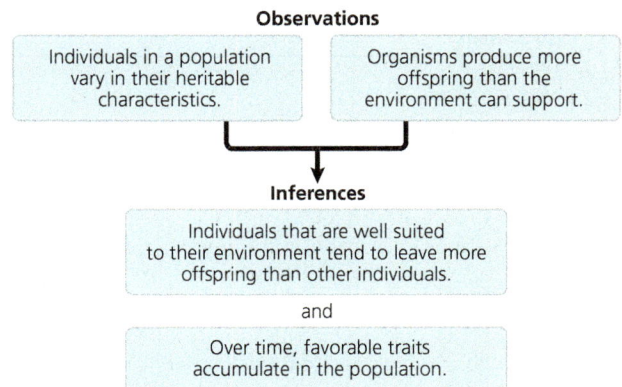

Observations

| Individuals in a population vary in their heritable characteristics. | Organisms produce more offspring than the environment can support. |

Inferences

Individuals that are well suited to their environment tend to leave more offspring than other individuals.

and

Over time, favorable traits accumulate in the population.

? *Describe how overreproduction and heritable variation relate to evolution by natural selection.*

CONCEPT **22.3**

Evolution is supported by an overwhelming amount of scientific evidence (pp. 506–513)

- Researchers have directly observed natural selection leading to adaptive evolution in many studies, including research on soapberry bug populations and on MRSA.
- Organisms share characteristics because of common descent (**homology**) or because natural selection affects independently evolving species in similar environments in similar ways (**convergent evolution**).
- Fossils show that past organisms differed from living organisms, that many species have become extinct, and that species have evolved over long periods of time; fossils also document the origin of major new groups of organisms.
- Evolutionary theory can explain biogeographic patterns.

? *Summarize the different lines of evidence supporting the hypothesis that cetaceans descended from land mammals and are closely related to even-toed ungulates.*

TEST YOUR UNDERSTANDING

MB Multiple-choice Self-Quiz questions #1–5 can be found in the Study Area at www.masteringbiology.com.

6. EVOLUTION CONNECTION

Explain why anatomical and molecular features often fit a similar nested pattern. In addition, describe a process that can cause this not to be the case.

7. SCIENTIFIC INQUIRY

DRAW IT Mosquitoes resistant to the pesticide DDT first appeared in India in 1959, but now are found throughout the world. (a) Graph the data in the table below. (b) Examining the graph, hypothesize why the percentage of mosquitoes resistant to DDT rose rapidly. (c) Suggest an explanation for the global spread of DDT resistance.

Month	0	8	12
Mosquitoes Resistant* to DDT	4%	45%	77%

Source: C. F. Curtis et al., Selection for and against insecticide resistance and possible methods of inhibiting the evolution of resistance in mosquitoes, *Ecological Entomology* 3:273–287 (1978).
*Mosquitoes were considered resistant if they were not killed within 1 hour of receiving a dose of 4% DDT.

8. WRITE ABOUT A THEME

Environmental Interactions Write a short essay (about 100–150 words) evaluating whether changes to an organism's physical environment are likely to result in evolutionary change. Use an example to support your reasoning.

For selected answers, see Appendix A.

Mastering**BIOLOGY** www.masteringbiology.com

1. MasteringBiology® Assignments:

Tutorial Evidence for Evolution
Activities Artificial Selection • Darwin and the Galápagos Islands • The Voyage of the *Beagle*: Darwin's Trip Around the World • Discovery Channel Video: Charles Darwin • Natural Selection for Antibiotic Resistance • Reconstructing Forelimbs
Questions Student Misconceptions • Reading Quiz • Multiple Choice • End-of-Chapter

2. eText

Read your book online, search, take notes, highlight text, and more.

3. The Study Area

Practice Tests • Cumulative Test • *BioFlix* 3-D Animations • MP3 Tutor Sessions • Videos • Activities • Investigations • Lab Media • Audio Glossary • Word Study Tools • Art

26

Phylogeny and the Tree of Life

▲ **Figure 26.1 What is this organism?**

OVERVIEW

Investigating the Tree of Life

Look closely at the organism in **Figure 26.1**. Although it resembles a snake, this animal is actually an Australian legless lizard known as the common scaly-foot (*Pygopus lepidopodus*). Why isn't the scaly-foot considered a snake? More generally, how do biologists distinguish and categorize the millions of species on Earth?

An understanding of evolutionary relationships suggests one way to address these questions: We can decide in which "container" to place a species by comparing its traits with those of potential close relatives. For example, the scaly-foot does not have a fused eyelid, a highly mobile jaw, or a short tail posterior to the anus, three traits shared by all snakes. These and other characteristics suggest that despite a superficial resemblance, the scaly-foot is not a snake. Furthermore, a survey of the lizards reveals that the scaly-foot is not alone; the legless condition has evolved independently in several different groups of lizards. Most legless lizards are burrowers or live in grasslands, and like snakes, these species lost their legs over generations as they adapted to their environments.

Snakes and lizards are part of the continuum of life extending from the earliest organisms to the great variety of species alive today. In this unit, we will survey this diversity and describe hypotheses regarding how it evolved. As we do so, our emphasis will shift from the *process* of evolution (the evolutionary mechanisms described in Unit Four) to its *pattern* (observations of evolution's products over time).

To set the stage for surveying life's diversity, in this chapter we consider how biologists trace **phylogeny**, the evolutionary history of a species or group of species. A phylogeny of lizards and snakes, for example, indicates that both the scaly-foot and snakes evolved from lizards with legs—but that they evolved from different lineages of legged lizards. Thus, it appears that their legless conditions evolved independently.

To construct phylogenies, biologists utilize **systematics**, a discipline focused on classifying organisms and determining their evolutionary relationships. Systematists use data ranging from fossils to molecules and genes to infer evolutionary relationships **(Figure 26.2)**. This information is enabling biologists to construct a tree of all life, which will continue to be refined as additional data are collected.

▲ **Figure 26.2 An unexpected family tree.** What are the evolutionary relationships between a human, a mushroom, and a tulip? A phylogeny based on DNA data reveals that—despite appearances—animals (including humans) and fungi (including mushrooms) are more closely related to each other than either is to plants.

Phylogenies show evolutionary relationships

As we discussed in Chapter 22, organisms share homologous characteristics because of common ancestry. As a result, we can learn a great deal about a species if we know its evolutionary history. For example, an organism is likely to share many of its genes, metabolic pathways, and structural proteins with its close relatives. We'll consider practical applications of such information at the close of this section, but first we'll examine how organisms are named and classified, the scientific discipline of **taxonomy**. We'll also look at how we can interpret and use diagrams that represent evolutionary history.

Binomial Nomenclature

Common names for organisms—such as monkey, finch, and lilac—convey meaning in casual usage, but they can also cause confusion. Each of these names, for example, refers to more than one species. Moreover, some common names do not accurately reflect the kind of organism they signify. Consider these three "fishes": jellyfish (a cnidarian), crayfish (a small lobsterlike crustacean), and silverfish (an insect). And of course, a given organism has different names in different languages.

To avoid ambiguity when communicating about their research, biologists refer to organisms by Latin scientific names. The two-part format of the scientific name, commonly called a **binomial**, was instituted in the 18th century by Carolus Linnaeus (see Chapter 22). The first part of a binomial is the name of the **genus** (plural, *genera*) to which the species belongs. The second part, called the specific epithet, is unique for each species within the genus. An example of a binomial is *Panthera pardus*, the scientific name for the large cat commonly called the leopard. Notice that the first letter of the genus is capitalized and the entire binomial is italicized. (Newly created scientific names are also "latinized": You can name an insect you discover after a friend, but you must add a Latin ending.) Many of the more than 11,000 binomials assigned by Linnaeus are still used today, including the optimistic name he gave our own species—*Homo sapiens*, meaning "wise man."

Hierarchical Classification

In addition to naming species, Linnaeus also grouped them into a hierarchy of increasingly inclusive categories. The first grouping is built into the binomial: Species that appear to be closely related are grouped into the same genus. For example, the leopard (*Panthera pardus*) belongs to a genus that also includes the African lion (*Panthera leo*), the tiger (*Panthera tigris*), and the jaguar (*Panthera onca*). Beyond genera, taxonomists employ progressively more comprehensive categories of classification. The taxonomic system named after Linnaeus, the

Linnaean system, places related genera in the same **family**, families into **orders**, orders into **classes**, classes into **phyla** (singular, *phylum*), phyla into **kingdoms**, and, more recently, kingdoms into **domains** (Figure 26.3). The resulting biological classification of a particular organism is somewhat like a postal address identifying a person in a particular apartment, in a building with many apartments, on a street with many apartment buildings, in a city with many streets, and so on.

The named taxonomic unit at any level of the hierarchy is called a **taxon** (plural, *taxa*). In the leopard example, *Panthera* is a taxon at the genus level, and Mammalia is a taxon at the class level that includes all the many orders of mammals. Note that in the Linnaean system, taxa broader than the genus are not italicized, though they are capitalized.

Classifying species is a way to structure our human view of the world. We lump together various species of trees to which we give the common name of pines and distinguish them from other trees that we call firs. Taxonomists have decided

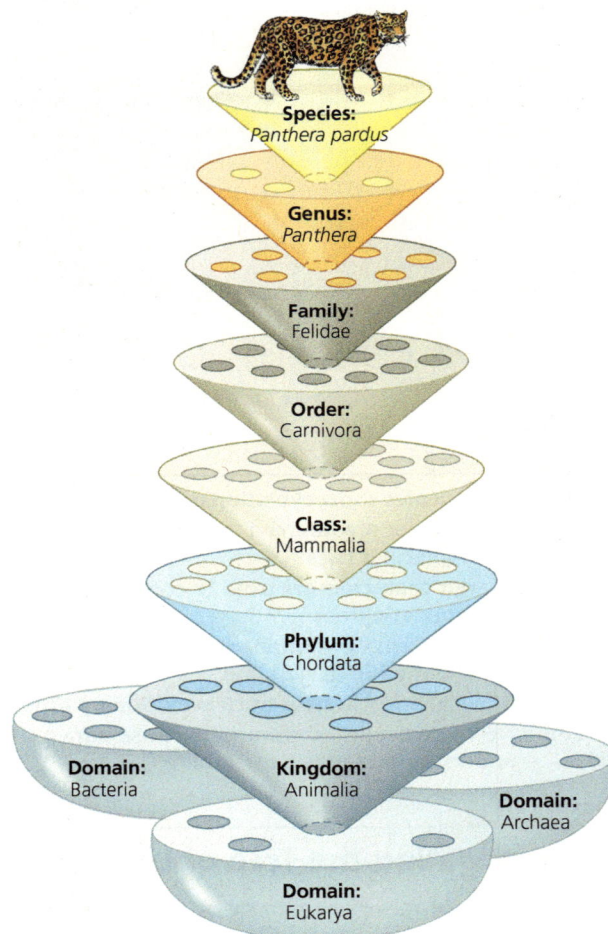

▲ **Figure 26.3 Linnaean classification.** At each level, or "rank," species are placed in groups within more inclusive groups.

that pines and firs are different enough to be placed in separate genera, yet similar enough to be grouped into the same family, Pinaceae. As with pines and firs, higher levels of classification are usually defined by particular characters chosen by taxonomists. However, characters that are useful for classifying one group of organisms may not be appropriate for other organisms. For this reason, the larger categories often are not comparable between lineages; that is, an order of snails does not exhibit the same degree of morphological or genetic diversity as an order of mammals. Furthermore, as we'll see, the placement of species into orders, classes, and so on, does not necessarily reflect evolutionary history.

Linking Classification and Phylogeny

The evolutionary history of a group of organisms can be represented in a branching diagram called a **phylogenetic tree**. As in **Figure 26.4**, the branching pattern often matches how taxonomists have classified groups of organisms nested within more inclusive groups. Sometimes, however, taxonomists have placed a species within a genus (or other group) to which it is *not* most closely related. One reason for misclassification might be that over the course of evolution, a species has lost a key feature shared by its close relatives. If DNA or other new evidence indicates that such a mistake has occurred, the organism may be reclassified to accurately reflect its evolutionary

history. Another issue is that while the Linnaean system may distinguish groups, such as mammals, reptiles, birds, and other classes of vertebrates, it tells us nothing about these groups' evolutionary relationships to one another.

In fact, such difficulties in aligning Linnaean classification with phylogeny have led some systematists to propose that classification be based entirely on evolutionary relationships. A system called **PhyloCode**, for example, only names groups that include a common ancestor and all of its descendants. While PhyloCode would change the way taxa are defined and recognized, the taxonomic names of most species would remain the same. But groups would no longer have "ranks" attached to them, such as family or class. Also, some commonly recognized groups would become part of other groups previously of the same rank. For example, because birds evolved from a group of reptiles, Aves (the Linnaean class to which birds are assigned) would be considered a subgroup of Reptilia (also a class in the Linnaean system). Although PhyloCode is controversial, many systematists are adopting the phylogenetic approach on which it is based.

Whether groups are named according to PhyloCode or according to Linnaean classification, a phylogenetic tree represents a hypothesis about evolutionary relationships. These relationships often are depicted as a series of dichotomies, or two-way **branch points**. Each branch point represents the divergence of two evolutionary lineages from a common ancestor. In **Figure 26.5**, for example, branch point ❸ represents the common ancestor of taxa A, B, and C. The position of branch point ❹ to the right of ❸ indicates that taxa B and C diverged after their shared lineage split from that of taxon A. (Tree branches can be rotated around a branch point without changing their evolutionary relationships.)

In Figure 26.5, taxa B and C are **sister taxa**, groups of organisms that share an immediate common ancestor (branch

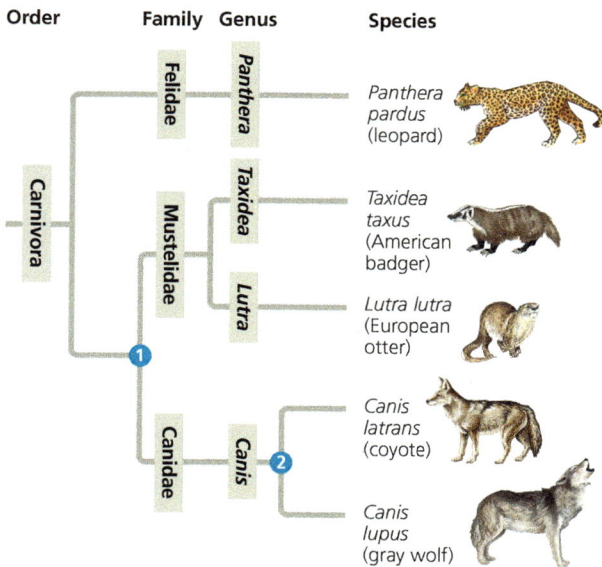

▲ **Figure 26.4 The connection between classification and phylogeny.** Hierarchical classification can reflect the branching patterns of phylogenetic trees. This tree traces possible evolutionary relationships between some of the taxa within order Carnivora, itself a branch of class Mammalia. The branch point ❶ represents the most recent common ancestor of all members of the weasel (Mustelidae) and dog (Canidae) families. The branch point ❷ represents the most recent common ancestor of coyotes and gray wolves.

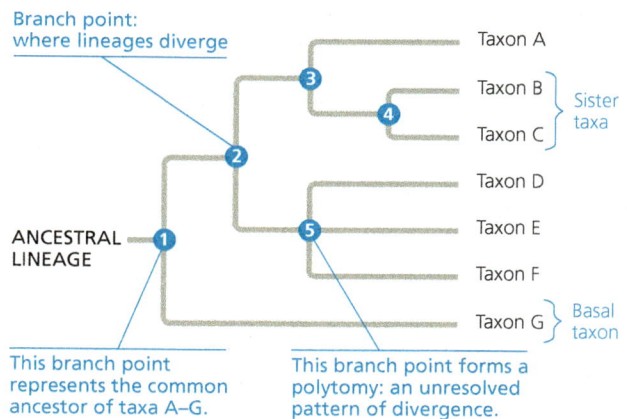

▲ **Figure 26.5 How to read a phylogenetic tree.**

DRAW IT Redraw this tree, rotating the branches around branch points ❷ and ❹. Does your new version tell a different story about the evolutionary relationships between the taxa? Explain.

point **4**) and hence are each other's closest relatives. Note also that this tree, like most of the phylogenetic trees in this book, is **rooted**, which means that a branch point within the tree (often drawn farthest to the left) represents the most recent common ancestor of all taxa in the tree. The term **basal taxon** refers to a lineage that diverges early in the history of a group and hence, like taxon G in Figure 26.5, lies on a branch that originates near the common ancestor of the group. Finally, the lineage leading to taxa D–F includes a **polytomy**, a branch point from which more than two descendant groups emerge. A polytomy signifies that evolutionary relationships among the taxa are not yet clear.

What We Can and Cannot Learn from Phylogenetic Trees

Let's summarize three key points about phylogenetic trees. First, they are intended to show patterns of descent, not phenotypic similarity. Although closely related organisms often resemble one another due to their common ancestry, they may not if their lineages have evolved at different rates or faced very different environmental conditions. For example, even though crocodiles are more closely related to birds than to lizards (see Figure 22.17), they look more like lizards because morphology has changed dramatically in the bird lineage.

Second, the sequence of branching in a tree does not necessarily indicate the actual (absolute) ages of the particular species. For example, the tree in Figure 26.4 does not indicate that the wolf evolved more recently than the European otter; rather, the tree shows only that the most recent common ancestor of the wolf and otter (branch point **1**) lived before the most recent common ancestor of the wolf and coyote (**2**). To indicate when wolves and otters evolved, the tree would need to include additional divergences in each evolutionary lineage, as well as the dates when those splits occurred. Generally, unless given specific information about what the branch lengths in a phylogenetic tree mean—for example, that they are proportional to time—we should interpret the diagram solely in terms of patterns of descent. No assumptions should be made about when particular species evolved or how much change occurred in each lineage.

Third, we should not assume that a taxon on a phylogenetic tree evolved from the taxon next to it. Figure 26.4 does not indicate that wolves evolved from coyotes or vice versa. We can infer only that the lineage leading to wolves and the lineage leading to coyotes both evolved from the common ancestor **2**. That ancestor, which is now extinct, was neither a wolf nor a coyote. However, its descendants include the two *extant* (living) species shown here, wolves and coyotes.

Applying Phylogenies

Understanding phylogeny can have practical applications. Consider maize (corn), which originated in the Americas and is

now an important food crop worldwide. From a phylogeny of maize based on DNA data, researchers have been able to identify two species of wild grasses that may be maize's closest living relatives. These two close relatives may be useful as "reservoirs" of beneficial alleles that can be transferred to cultivated maize by cross-breeding or genetic engineering (see Chapter 20).

A different use of phylogenetic trees is described in **Figure 26.6**: investigating whether whale meat samples had

▼ **Figure 26.6**   **INQUIRY**

What is the species identity of food being sold as whale meat?

EXPERIMENT C. S. Baker, then at the University of Auckland, New Zealand, and S. R. Palumbi, then at the University of Hawaii, purchased 13 samples of "whale meat" from Japanese fish markets. They sequenced a specific part of the mitochondrial DNA from each sample and compared their results with the comparable DNA sequence from known whale species. To infer the species identity of each sample, Baker and Palumbi constructed a *gene tree*, a phylogenetic tree that shows patterns of relatedness among DNA sequences rather than among taxa.

RESULTS The analysis yielded the following gene tree:

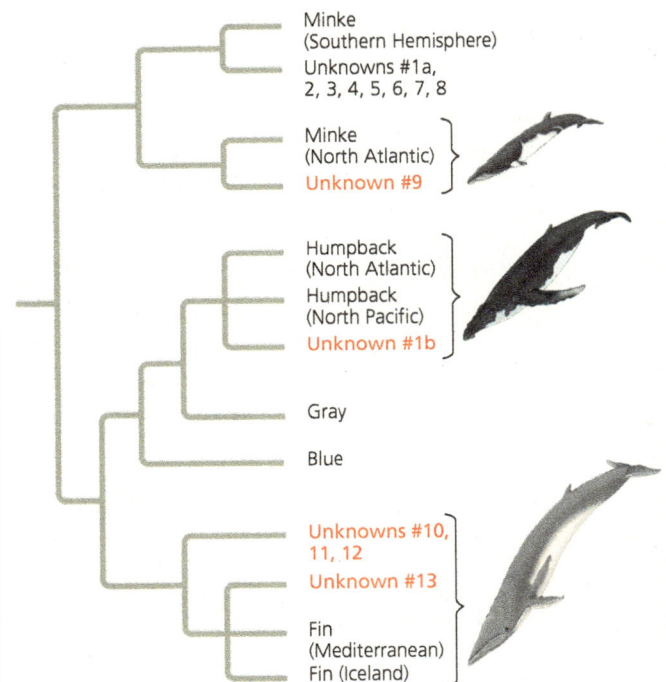

CONCLUSION This analysis indicated that DNA sequences of six of the unknown samples (in red) were most closely related to DNA sequences of whales that are not legal to harvest.

SOURCE C. S. Baker and S. R. Palumbi, Which whales are hunted? A molecular genetic approach to monitoring whaling, *Science* 265:1538–1539 (1994).

WHAT IF? What different results would have indicated that the whale meat had *not* been illegally harvested?

been illegally harvested from whale species protected under international law—rather than from species that can be harvested legally, such as Minke whales caught in the Southern Hemisphere. This phylogeny indicated that meat from humpback, fin, and Minke whales caught in the Northern Hemisphere was being sold illegally in some Japanese fish markets.

How do researchers construct trees like those we've considered here? In the next section, we'll begin to answer that question by examining the data used to determine phylogenies.

CONCEPT CHECK 26.1

1. Which levels of the classification in Figure 26.3 do humans share with leopards?
2. What does the phylogenetic tree in Figure 26.4 indicate about the evolutionary relationships of the leopard, badger, and wolf?
3. Which of the trees shown here depicts an evolutionary history different from the other two? Explain.

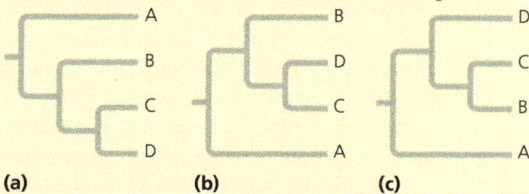

(a)   (b)   (c)

4. **WHAT IF?** Suppose new evidence indicates that taxon E in Figure 26.5 is the sister taxon of a group consisting of taxa D and F. Redraw the tree to accommodate this new finding.

For suggested answers, see Appendix A.

CONCEPT 26.2

Phylogenies are inferred from morphological and molecular data

To infer phylogeny, systematists must gather as much information as possible about the morphology, genes, and biochemistry of the relevant organisms. It is important to focus on features that result from common ancestry, because only such features reflect evolutionary relationships.

Morphological and Molecular Homologies

Recall that phenotypic and genetic similarities due to shared ancestry are called *homologies*. For example, the similarity in the number and arrangement of bones in the forelimbs of mammals is due to their descent from a common ancestor with the same bone structure; this is an example of a morphological homology (see Figure 22.15). In the same way, genes or other DNA sequences are homologous if they are descended from sequences carried by a common ancestor.

In general, organisms that share very similar morphologies or similar DNA sequences are likely to be more closely related than organisms with vastly different structures or sequences. In some cases, however, the morphological divergence between related species can be great and their genetic divergence small (or vice versa). Consider the Hawaiian silversword plants discussed in Chapter 25. These species vary dramatically in appearance throughout the islands. Some are tall, twiggy trees, and others are dense, ground-hugging shrubs (see Figure 25.20). But despite these striking phenotypic differences, the silverswords' genes are very similar. Based on these small molecular divergences, scientists estimate that the silversword group began to diverge 5 million years ago, which is also about the time when the oldest of the current islands formed. We'll discuss how scientists use molecular data to estimate such divergence times later in this chapter.

Sorting Homology from Analogy

A potential red herring in constructing a phylogeny is similarity due to convergent evolution—called **analogy**—rather than to shared ancestry (homology). As you read in Chapter 22, convergent evolution occurs when similar environmental pressures and natural selection produce similar (analogous) adaptations in organisms from different evolutionary lineages. For example, the two mole-like animals illustrated in **Figure 26.7** are very similar in their external appearance. However, their internal anatomy, physiology, and reproductive systems are very dissimilar. Australian "moles" are marsupials; their young complete their embryonic development in a pouch on the outside of the mother's body. North American moles, in contrast, are eutherians; their young complete

▲ **Figure 26.7 Convergent evolution of analogous burrowing characteristics.** An elongated body, enlarged front paws, small eyes, and a pad of thickened skin that protects a tapered nose all evolved independently in the marsupial Australian "mole" (top) and a eutherian North American mole (bottom).

their embryonic development in the uterus within the mother's body. Indeed, genetic comparisons and the fossil record provide evidence that the common ancestor of these moles lived 140 million years ago, about the time the marsupial and eutherian mammals diverged. This common ancestor and most of its descendants were not mole-like, but analogous characteristics evolved independently in these two mole lineages as they became adapted to similar lifestyles.

Distinguishing between homology and analogy is critical in reconstructing phylogenies. To see why, consider bats and birds, both of which have adaptations that enable flight. This superficial resemblance might imply that bats are more closely related to birds than they are to cats, which cannot fly. But a closer examination reveals that a bat's wing is far more similar to the forelimbs of cats and other mammals than to a bird's wing. Bats and birds descended from a common tetrapod ancestor that lived about 320 million years ago. This common ancestor could not fly. Thus, although the underlying skeletal systems of bats and birds are homologous, their *wings* are not. Flight is enabled in different ways—stretched membranes in the bat wing versus feathers in the bird wing. Fossil evidence also documents that bat wings and bird wings arose independently from the forelimbs of different tetrapod ancestors. Thus, with respect to flight, a bat's wing is *analogous*, not homologous, to a bird's wing. Analogous structures that arose independently are also called **homoplasies** (from the Greek, meaning "to mold in the same way").

Besides corroborative similarities and fossil evidence, another clue to distinguishing between homology and analogy is the complexity of the characters being compared. The more elements that are similar in two complex structures, the more likely it is that they evolved from a common ancestor. For instance, the skulls of an adult human and an adult chimpanzee both consist of many bones fused together. The compositions of the skulls match almost perfectly, bone for bone. It is highly improbable that such complex structures, matching in so many details, have separate origins. More likely, the genes involved in the development of both skulls were inherited from a common ancestor. The same argument applies to comparisons at the gene level. Genes are sequences of thousands of nucleotides, each of which represents an inherited character in the form of one of the four DNA bases: A (adenine), G (guanine), C (cytosine), or T (thymine). If genes in two organisms share many portions of their nucleotide sequences, it is likely that the genes are homologous.

Evaluating Molecular Homologies

Comparisons of DNA molecules often pose technical challenges for researchers. The first step after sequencing the molecules is to align comparable sequences from the species being studied. If the species are very closely related, the sequences probably differ at only one or a few sites. In contrast, comparable nucleic acid sequences in distantly related species usually have different bases at many sites and may have different lengths. This is because insertions and deletions accumulate over long periods of time.

Suppose, for example, that certain noncoding DNA sequences near a particular gene are very similar in two species, except that the first base of the sequence has been deleted in one of the species. The effect is that the remaining sequence shifts back one notch. A comparison of the two sequences that does not take this deletion into account would overlook what in fact is a very good match. To address such problems, researchers have developed computer programs that estimate the best way to align comparable DNA segments of differing lengths **(Figure 26.8)**.

Such molecular comparisons reveal that many base substitutions and other differences have accumulated in the comparable genes of an Australian mole and a North American mole. The many differences indicate that their lineages have diverged greatly since their common ancestor; thus, we say that the living species are not closely related. In contrast, the high degree of gene sequence similarity among the silverswords indicates that they are all very closely related, in spite of their considerable morphological differences.

Just as with morphological characters, it is necessary to distinguish homology from analogy in evaluating molecular similarities for evolutionary studies. Two sequences that resemble each other at many points along their length most likely are

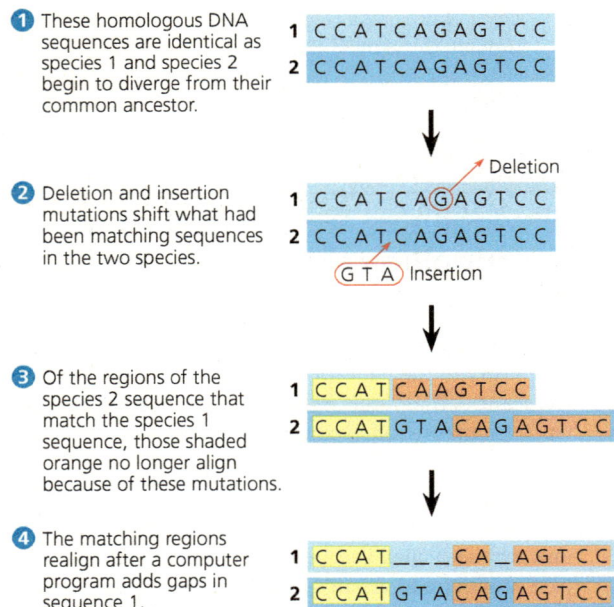

1 These homologous DNA sequences are identical as species 1 and species 2 begin to diverge from their common ancestor.

1 CCATCAGAGTCC
2 CCATCAGAGTCC

2 Deletion and insertion mutations shift what had been matching sequences in the two species.

Deletion

1 CCATCA(G)AGTCC
2 CCATCAGAGTCC
(G T A) Insertion

3 Of the regions of the species 2 sequence that match the species 1 sequence, those shaded orange no longer align because of these mutations.

1 CCATCAAGTCC
2 CCATGTACAGAGTCC

4 The matching regions realign after a computer program adds gaps in sequence 1.

1 CCAT___CA_AGTCC
2 CCATGTACAGAGTCC

▲ **Figure 26.8 Aligning segments of DNA.** Systematists search for similar sequences along DNA segments from two species (only one DNA strand is shown for each species). In this example, 11 of the original 12 bases have not changed since the species diverged. Hence, those portions of the sequences still align once the length is adjusted.

ACGGATAGTCCACTAGGCACTA
TCACCGACAGGTCTTTGACTAG

▲ **Figure 26.9 A molecular homoplasy.** These two DNA sequences from organisms that are not closely related coincidentally share 25% of their bases. Statistical tools have been developed to determine whether DNA sequences that share more than 25% of their bases do so because they are homologous.

? *Why might you expect organisms that are not closely related to nevertheless share roughly 25% of their bases?*

homologous (see Figure 26.8). But in organisms that do not appear to be closely related, the bases that their otherwise very different sequences happen to share may simply be coincidental matches, called molecular homoplasies **(Figure 26.9)**. Scientists have developed statistical tools that can help distinguish "distant" homologies from such coincidental matches in extremely divergent sequences.

To date, researchers have sequenced more than 110 billion bases of DNA from thousands of species. This enormous collection of data has fueled a boom in the study of phylogeny. The new data have supported earlier hypotheses regarding many evolutionary relationships, such as that between Australian and North American moles, and have clarified other relationships, such as those between the various silverswords. In the rest of this unit, you will see how our understanding of phylogeny has been transformed by **molecular systematics**, the discipline that uses data from DNA and other molecules to determine evolutionary relationships.

CONCEPT CHECK 26.2

1. Decide whether each of the following pairs of structures more likely represents analogy or homology, and explain your reasoning: (a) a porcupine's quills and a cactus's spines; (b) a cat's paw and a human's hand; (c) an owl's wing and a hornet's wing.
2. **WHAT IF?** Suppose that species 1 and species 2 have similar appearances but very divergent gene sequences and that species 2 and species 3 have very different appearances but similar gene sequences. Which pair of species is more likely to be closely related: 1 and 2, or 2 and 3? Explain.

For suggested answers, see Appendix A.

CONCEPT 26.3

Shared characters are used to construct phylogenetic trees

In reconstructing phylogenies, the first step is to distinguish homologous features from analogous ones (since only homology reflects evolutionary history). Next we must choose a method of inferring phylogeny from these homologous characters. A widely used set of methods is known as cladistics.

Cladistics

In the approach to systematics called **cladistics**, common ancestry is the primary criterion used to classify organisms. Using this methodology, biologists attempt to place species into groups called **clades**, each of which includes an ancestral species and all of its descendants **(Figure 26.10a)**. Clades, like

▼ **Figure 26.10 Monophyletic, paraphyletic, and polyphyletic groups.**

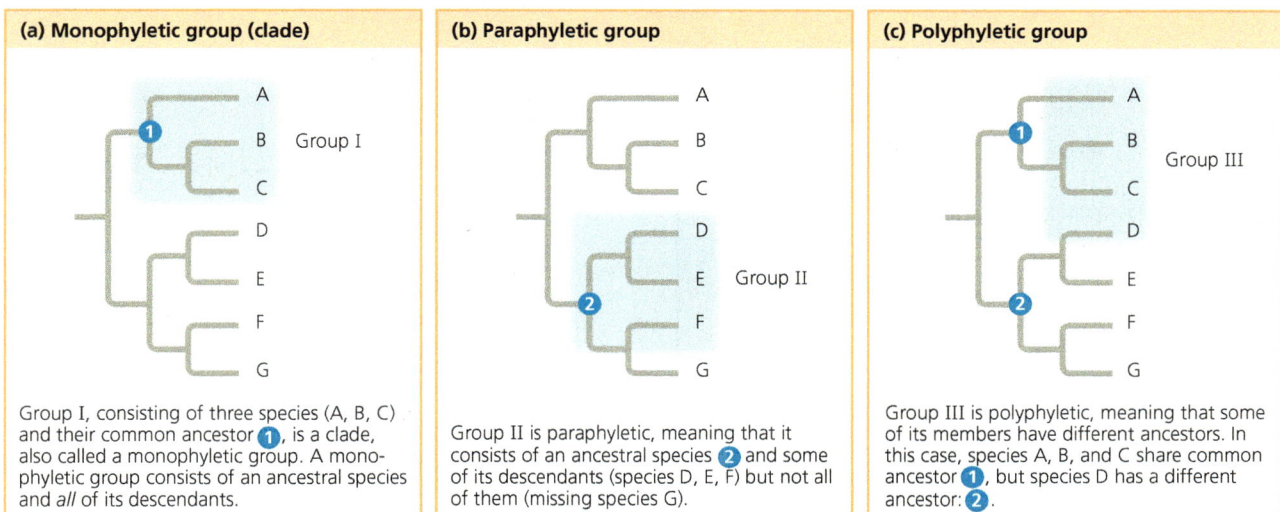

(a) Monophyletic group (clade)

Group I, consisting of three species (A, B, C) and their common ancestor ❶, is a clade, also called a monophyletic group. A monophyletic group consists of an ancestral species and *all* of its descendants.

(b) Paraphyletic group

Group II is paraphyletic, meaning that it consists of an ancestral species ❷ and some of its descendants (species D, E, F) but not all of them (missing species G).

(c) Polyphyletic group

Group III is polyphyletic, meaning that some of its members have different ancestors. In this case, species A, B, and C share common ancestor ❶, but species D has a different ancestor: ❷.

taxonomic ranks, are nested within larger clades. In Figure 26.4, for example, the cat group (Felidae) represents a clade within a larger clade (Carnivora) that also includes the dog group (Canidae). However, a taxon is equivalent to a clade only if it is **monophyletic** (from the Greek, meaning "single tribe"), signifying that it consists of an ancestral species and all of its descendants (see Figure 26.10a). Contrast this with a **paraphyletic** ("beside the tribe") group, which consists of an ancestral species and some, but not all, of its descendants **(Figure 26.10b)**, or a **polyphyletic** ("many tribes") group, which includes taxa with different ancestors **(Figure 26.10c)**. Next we'll discuss how clades are identified using shared derived characters.

Shared Ancestral and Shared Derived Characters

As a result of descent with modification, organisms both share characteristics with their ancestors and differ from them. For example, all mammals have backbones, but a backbone does not distinguish mammals from other vertebrates because *all* vertebrates have backbones. The backbone predates the branching of mammals from other vertebrates. Thus for mammals, the backbone is a **shared ancestral character**, a character that originated in an ancestor of the taxon. In contrast, hair is a character shared by all mammals but *not* found in their ancestors. Thus, in mammals, hair is considered a **shared derived character**, an evolutionary novelty unique to a clade.

Note that it is a relative matter whether a particular character is considered ancestral or derived. A backbone can also qualify as a shared derived character, but only at a deeper branch point that distinguishes all vertebrates from other animals. Among mammals, a backbone is considered a shared ancestral character because it was present in the ancestor common to all mammals.

Inferring Phylogenies Using Derived Characters

Shared derived characters are unique to particular clades. Because all features of organisms arose at some point in the history of life, it should be possible to determine the clade in which each shared derived character first appeared and to use that information to infer evolutionary relationships.

To see how this analysis is done, consider the set of characters shown in **Figure 26.11a** for each of five vertebrates—a leopard, turtle, frog, bass, and lamprey (a jawless aquatic vertebrate). As a basis of comparison, we need to select an outgroup. An **outgroup** is a species or group of species from an evolutionary lineage that is known to have diverged before the lineage that includes the species we are studying (the **ingroup**). A suitable outgroup can be determined based on evidence from morphology, paleontology, embryonic development, and gene sequences. An appropriate outgroup for our example is the lancelet, a small animal that lives in mudflats and (like vertebrates) is a member of Chordata. Unlike the vertebrates, however, the lancelet does not have a backbone.

By comparing members of the ingroup with each other and with the outgroup, we can determine which characters were derived at the various branch points of vertebrate evolution. For example, *all* of the vertebrates in the ingroup have backbones: This character was present in the ancestral vertebrate, but not in the outgroup. Now note that hinged jaws are a character absent in lampreys but present in other members of the ingroup; this character helps us to identify an early branch point in the vertebrate clade. Proceeding in this way, we can translate the data in our table of characters into a phylogenetic tree that groups all the ingroup taxa into a hierarchy based on their shared derived characters **(Figure 26.11b)**.

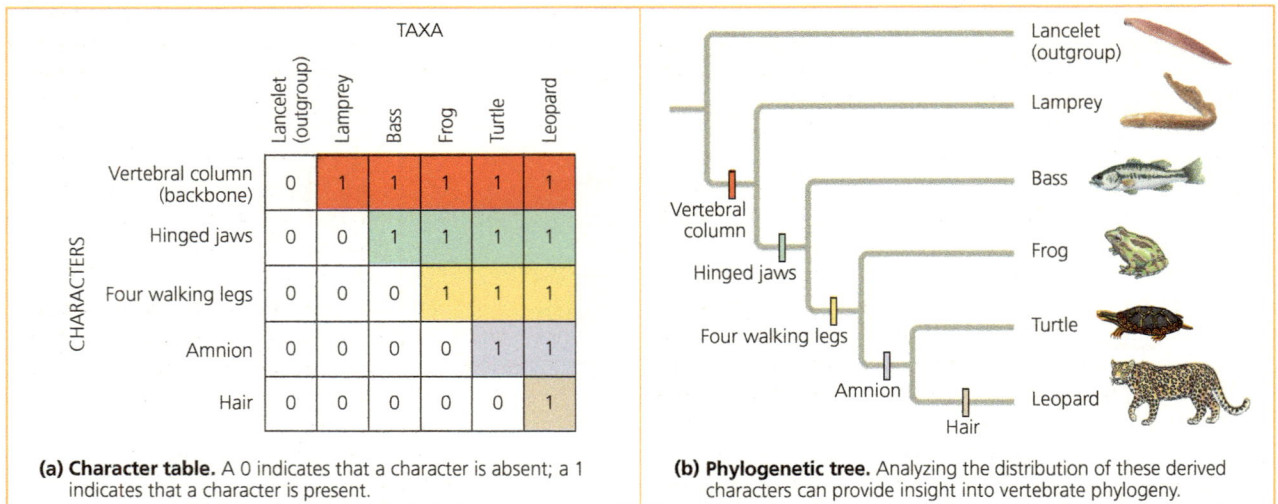

(a) Character table. A 0 indicates that a character is absent; a 1 indicates that a character is present.

(b) Phylogenetic tree. Analyzing the distribution of these derived characters can provide insight into vertebrate phylogeny.

▲ **Figure 26.11 Constructing a phylogenetic tree.** The characters used here include the amnion, a membrane that encloses the embryo inside a fluid-filled sac (see Figure 34.25).

DRAW IT *In (b), circle the most inclusive clade for which a hinged jaw is a shared ancestral character.*

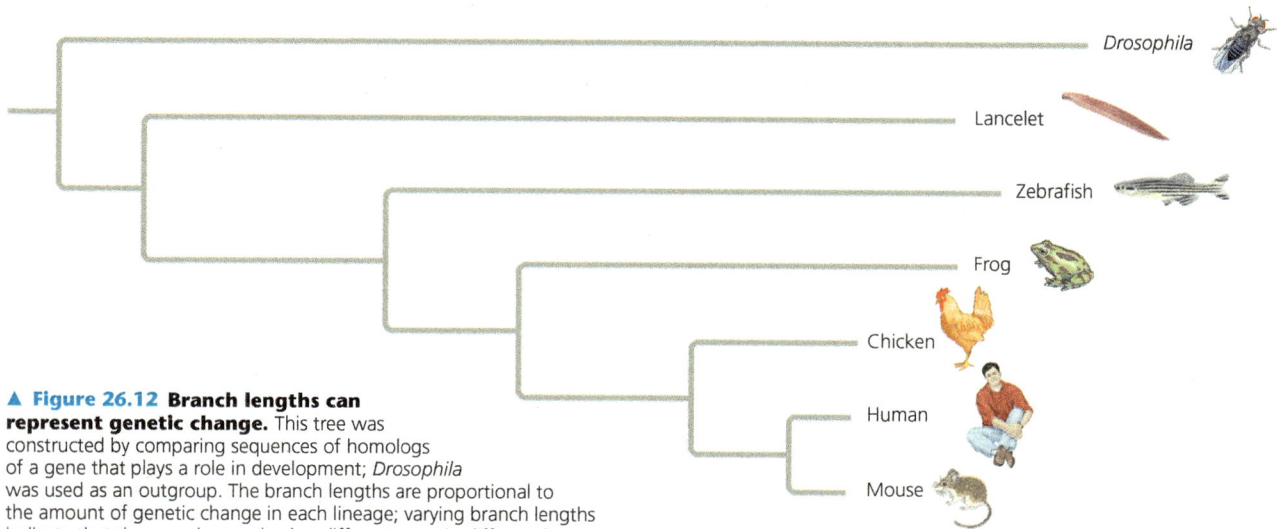

▲ **Figure 26.12 Branch lengths can represent genetic change.** This tree was constructed by comparing sequences of homologs of a gene that plays a role in development; *Drosophila* was used as an outgroup. The branch lengths are proportional to the amount of genetic change in each lineage; varying branch lengths indicate that the gene has evolved at different rates in different lineages.

? *In which vertebrate lineage has the studied gene evolved most rapidly? Explain.*

Phylogenetic Trees with Proportional Branch Lengths

In the phylogenetic trees we have presented so far, the lengths of the tree's branches do not indicate the degree of evolutionary change in each lineage. Furthermore, the chronology represented by the branching pattern of the tree is relative (earlier versus later) rather than absolute (how many millions of years ago). But in some tree diagrams, branch lengths are proportional to amount of evolutionary change or to the times at which particular events occurred.

In **Figure 26.12**, for example, the branch length of the phylogenetic tree reflects the number of changes that have taken place in a particular DNA sequence in that lineage. Note that the total length of the horizontal lines from the base of the tree to the mouse is less than that of the line leading to the outgroup species, the fruit fly *Drosophila*. This implies that in the time since the mouse and fly diverged from a common ancestor, more genetic changes have occurred in the *Drosophila* lineage than in the mouse lineage.

Even though the branches of a phylogenetic tree may have different lengths, among organisms alive today, all the different lineages that descend from a common ancestor have survived for the same number of years. To take an extreme example, humans and bacteria had a common ancestor that lived over 3 billion years ago. Fossils and genetic evidence indicate that this ancestor was a single-celled prokaryote. Even though bacteria have apparently changed little in their morphology since that common ancestor, there have nonetheless been 3 billion years of evolution in the bacterial lineage, just as there have been 3 billion years of evolution in the eukaryotic lineage that includes humans.

These equal spans of chronological time can be represented in a phylogenetic tree whose branch lengths are proportional to time **(Figure 26.13)**. Such a tree draws on fossil data to place branch points in the context of geologic time. Additionally, it is possible to combine these two types of trees by labeling branch points with information about rates of genetic change or dates of divergence.

Maximum Parsimony and Maximum Likelihood

As the growing database of DNA sequences enables us to study more species, the difficulty of building the phylogenetic tree that best describes their evolutionary history also grows. What if you are analyzing data for 50 species? There are 3×10^{76} different ways to arrange 50 species into a tree! And which tree in this huge forest reflects the true phylogeny? Systematists can never be sure of finding the most accurate tree in such a large data set, but they can narrow the possibilities by applying the principles of maximum parsimony and maximum likelihood.

According to the principle of **maximum parsimony**, we should first investigate the simplest explanation that is consistent with the facts. (The parsimony principle is also called "Occam's razor" after William of Occam, a 14th-century English philosopher who advocated this minimalist problem-solving approach of "shaving away" unnecessary complications.) In the case of trees based on morphology, the most parsimonious tree requires the fewest evolutionary events, as measured by the origin of shared derived morphological characters. For phylogenies based on DNA, the most parsimonious tree requires the fewest base changes.

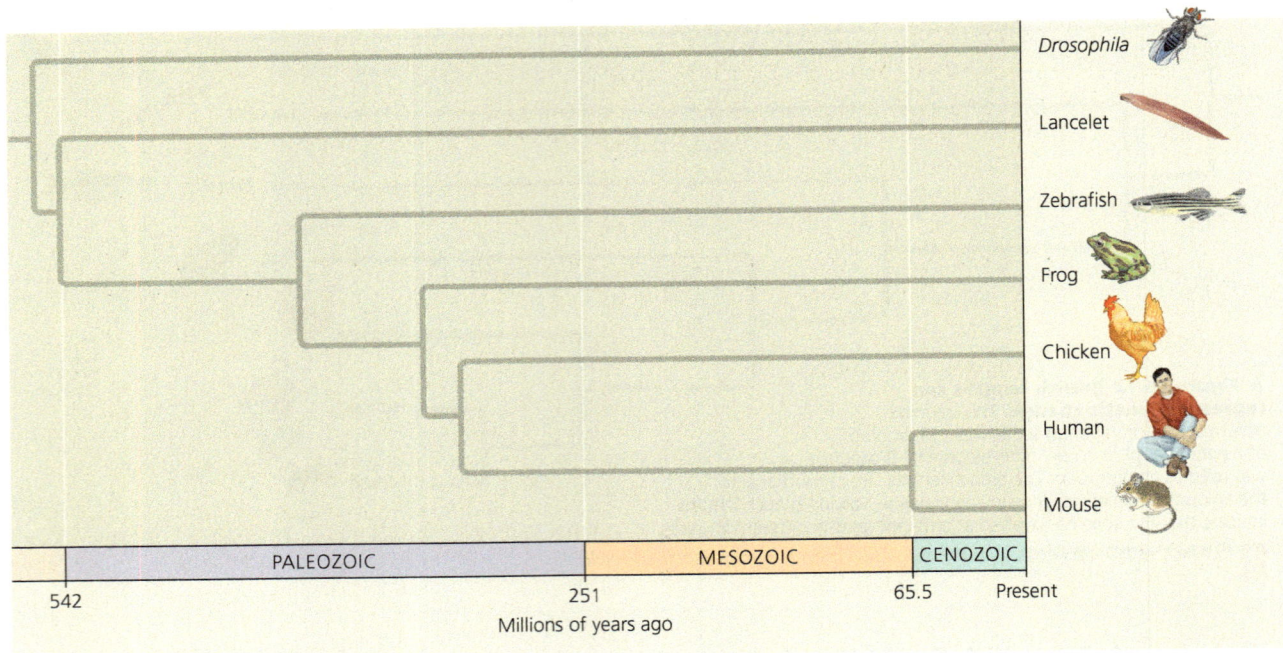

▲ **Figure 26.13 Branch lengths can indicate time.** This tree is based on the same molecular data as the tree in Figure 26.12, but here the branch points are mapped to dates based on fossil evidence. Thus, the branch lengths are proportional to time. Each lineage has the same total length from the base of the tree to the branch tip, indicating that all the lineages have diverged from the common ancestor for equal amounts of time.

(a) Percentage differences between sequences

	Human	Mushroom	Tulip
Human	0	30%	40%
Mushroom		0	40%
Tulip			0

Tree 1: More likely   Tree 2: Less likely

(b) Comparison of possible trees

The principle of **maximum likelihood** states that given certain probability rules about how DNA sequences change over time, a tree can be found that reflects the most likely sequence of evolutionary events. Maximum-likelihood methods are complex, but as a simple example, let us return to the phylogenetic relationships between a human, a mushroom, and a tulip. **Figure 26.14** shows two possible, equally parsimonious trees for this trio. Tree 1 is more likely if we assume that DNA changes have occurred at equal rates along all the branches of the tree from the common ancestor. Tree 2 requires assuming that the rate of evolution slowed greatly in the mushroom lineage and sped up greatly in the tulip lineage. Thus, assuming that equal rates are more common than unequal rates, tree 1 is more likely. We will soon see that many genes do evolve at approximately equal rates in different lineages. But note that if we find new evidence of unequal rates, tree 2 might be more likely! The likelihood of a tree depends on the assumptions on which it is based.

Scientists have developed many computer programs to search for trees that are parsimonious and likely. When a large amount of accurate data is available, the methods used in these programs usually yield similar trees. As an example of one

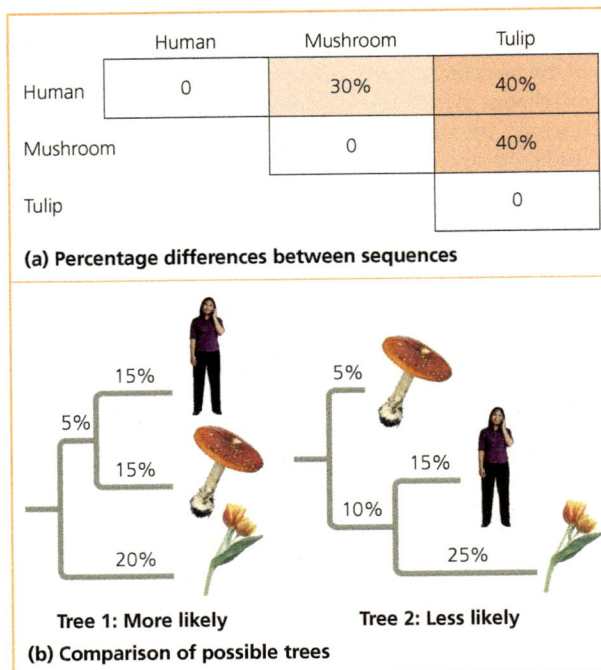

▲ **Figure 26.14 Trees with different likelihoods.** Based on percentage differences between genes in a human, a mushroom, and a tulip **(a)**, there are two phylogenetic trees with the same total branch length **(b)**. The sum of the percentages from a point of divergence in a tree equals the percentage differences in (a). For example, in tree 1, the human–tulip divergence is 15% + 5% + 20% = 40%. In tree 2, this divergence also equals 40% (15% + 25%). If the genes have evolved at the same rate in the different branches, tree 1 is more likely.

▼ **Figure 26.15**

RESEARCH METHOD

Applying Parsimony to a Problem in Molecular Systematics

APPLICATION In considering possible phylogenies for a group of species, systematists compare molecular data for the species. An efficient way to begin is by identifying the most parsimonious hypothesis—the one that requires the fewest evolutionary events (molecular changes) to have occurred.

TECHNIQUE Follow the numbered steps as we apply the principle of parsimony to a hypothetical phylogenetic problem involving three closely related bird species.

Species I   Species II   Species III

Three phylogenetic hypotheses:

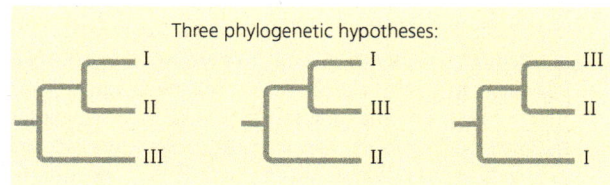

1 First, draw the three possible phylogenies for the species. (Although only 3 trees are possible when ordering 3 species, the number of possible trees increases rapidly with the number of species: There are 15 trees for 4 species and 34,459,425 trees for 10 species.)

	Site 1	Site 2	Site 3	Site 4
Species I	C	T	A	T
Species II	C	T	T	C
Species III	A	G	A	C
Ancestral sequence	A	G	T	T

2 Tabulate the molecular data for the species. In this simplified example, the data represent a DNA sequence consisting of just four nucleotide bases. Data from several outgroup species (not shown) were used to infer the ancestral DNA sequence.

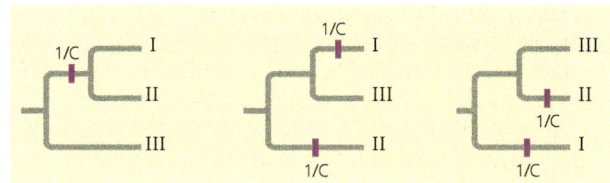

3 Now focus on site 1 in the DNA sequence. In the tree on the left, a single base-change event, represented by the purple hatchmark on the branch leading to species I and II (and labeled 1/C, indicating a change at site 1 to nucleotide C), is sufficient to account for the site 1 data. In the other two trees, two base-change events are necessary.

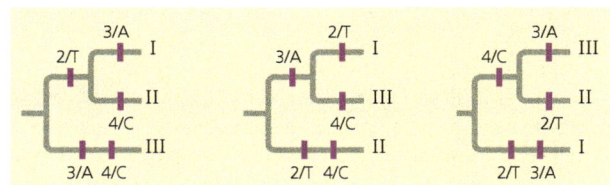

4 Continuing the comparison of bases at sites 2, 3, and 4 reveals that each of the three trees requires a total of five additional base-change events (purple hatchmarks).

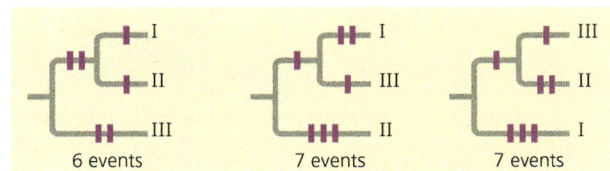

RESULTS To identify the most parsimonious tree, we total all of the base-change events noted in steps 3 and 4. We conclude that the first tree is the most parsimonious of the three possible phylogenies. (In a real example, many more sites would be analyzed. Hence, the trees would often differ by more than one base-change event.)

6 events   7 events   7 events

method, **Figure 26.15**, on the facing page, walks you through the process of identifying the most parsimonious molecular tree for a three-species problem. Computer programs use the principle of parsimony to estimate phylogenies in a similar way: They examine large numbers of possible trees and select the tree or trees that require fewest evolutionary changes.

Phylogenetic Trees as Hypotheses

This is a good place to reiterate that any phylogenetic tree represents a hypothesis about how the various organisms in the tree are related to one another. The best hypothesis is the one that best fits all the available data. A phylogenetic hypothesis may be modified when new evidence compels systematists to revise their trees. Indeed, while many older phylogenetic hypotheses have been supported by new morphological and molecular data, others have been changed or rejected.

Thinking of phylogenies as hypotheses also allows us to use them in a powerful way: We can make and test predictions based on the assumption that a phylogeny—our hypothesis—is correct. For example, in an approach known as *phylogenetic bracketing*, we can predict (by parsimony) that features shared by two groups of closely related organisms are present in their common ancestor and all of its descendants unless independent data indicate otherwise. (Note that "prediction" can refer to unknown past events as well as to evolutionary changes yet to occur.)

This approach has been used to make novel predictions about dinosaurs. For example, there is evidence that birds descended from the theropods, a group of bipedal saurischian dinosaurs. As seen in **Figure 26.16**, the closest living relatives of birds are crocodiles. Birds and crocodiles share numerous features: They have four-chambered hearts, they "sing" to defend territories and attract mates (although a crocodile's "song" is more like a bellow), and they build nests. Both birds and crocodiles also care for their eggs by *brooding*, a behavior in which a parent warms the eggs with its body. Birds brood by sitting on their eggs, whereas crocodiles cover their eggs with their neck. Reasoning that any feature shared by birds and crocodiles is likely to have been present in their common ancestor (denoted by the blue dot in Figure 26.16) and *all* of its descendants, biologists predicted that dinosaurs had four-chambered hearts, sang, built nests, and exhibited brooding.

Internal organs, such as the heart, rarely fossilize, and it is, of course, difficult to test whether dinosaurs sang to defend territories and attract mates. However, fossilized dinosaur eggs and nests have provided evidence supporting the prediction of brooding in dinosaurs. First, a fossil embryo of an *Oviraptor* dinosaur was found, still inside its egg. This egg was identical to those found in another fossil, one that showed an *Oviraptor* adult crouching over a group of eggs in a posture similar to that in brooding birds today **(Figure 26.17)**. Researchers suggested that the *Oviraptor* dinosaur preserved in this second fossil died while incubating or protecting its eggs. The broader conclusion that emerged from this work—that

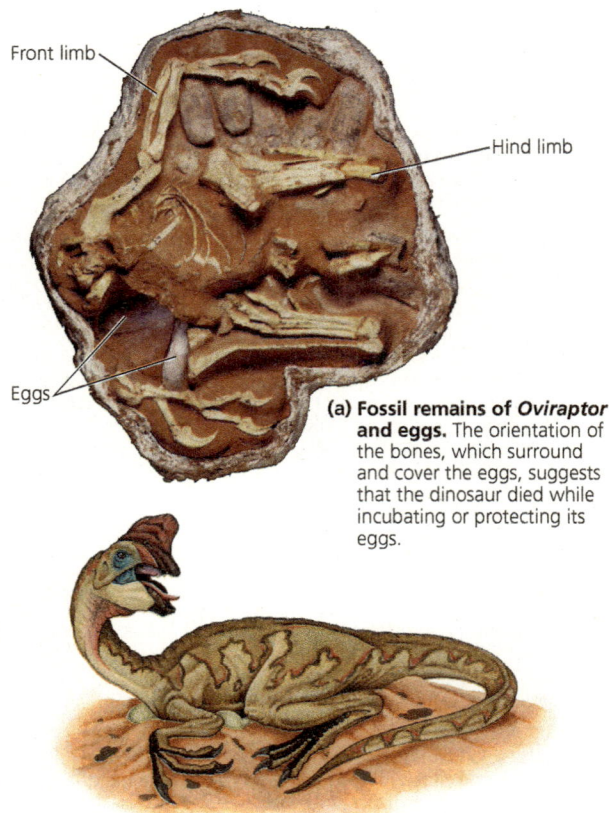

(a) **Fossil remains of *Oviraptor* and eggs.** The orientation of the bones, which surround and cover the eggs, suggests that the dinosaur died while incubating or protecting its eggs.

(b) Artist's reconstruction of the dinosaur's posture based on the fossil findings.

▲ **Figure 26.17 Fossil support for a phylogenetic prediction: Dinosaurs built nests and brooded their eggs.**

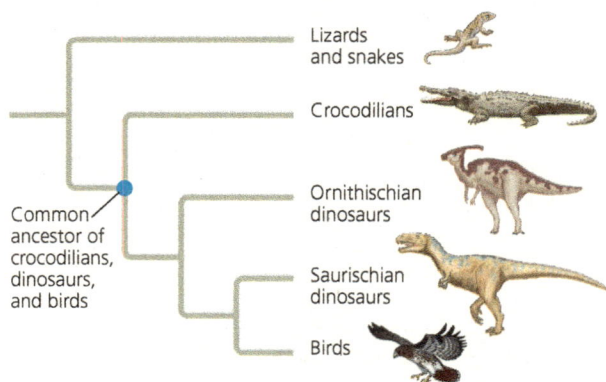

▲ **Figure 26.16 A phylogenetic tree of birds and their close relatives.**

? *What is the most basal taxon represented in this tree?*

dinosaurs built nests and exhibited brooding—has since been strengthened by additional fossil discoveries that show that other species of dinosaurs built nests and sat on their eggs. Finally, by supporting predictions based on the phylogenetic hypothesis shown in Figure 26.16, fossil discoveries of nests and brooding in dinosaurs provide independent data that suggest that the hypothesis is correct.

CONCEPT CHECK 26.3

1. To distinguish a particular clade of mammals within the larger clade that corresponds to class Mammalia, would hair be a useful character? Why or why not?
2. The most parsimonious tree of evolutionary relationships can be inaccurate. How can this occur?
3. **WHAT IF?** Draw a phylogenetic tree that includes the relationships from both Figure 25.6 and Figure 26.16. Traditionally, all the taxa shown besides birds and mammals were classified as reptiles. Would a cladistic approach support that classification? Explain.

For suggested answers, see Appendix A.

CONCEPT 26.4

An organism's evolutionary history is documented in its genome

As you have seen in this chapter, molecular systematics—using comparisons of nucleic acids or other molecules to deduce relatedness—is a valuable approach for tracing evolutionary history. The molecular approach helps us understand phylogenetic relationships that cannot be determined by nonmolecular methods such as comparative anatomy. For example, molecular systematics helps us uncover evolutionary relationships between groups that have little common ground for morphological comparison, such as animals and fungi. And molecular methods allow us to reconstruct phylogenies among groups of present-day organisms for which the fossil record is poor or lacking entirely. Overall, molecular biology has helped to extend systematics to evolutionary relationships far above and below the species level, ranging from the major branches of the tree of life to its finest twigs.

Different genes evolve at different rates, even in the same evolutionary lineage. As a result, molecular trees can represent short or long periods of time, depending on which genes are used. For example, the DNA that codes for ribosomal RNA (rRNA) changes relatively slowly. Therefore, comparisons of DNA sequences in these genes are useful for investigating relationships between taxa that diverged hundreds of millions of years ago. Studies of rRNA sequences indicate, for instance, that fungi are more closely related to animals than to green plants (see Figure 26.2). In contrast, mitochondrial DNA (mtDNA) evolves relatively rapidly and can be used to ex-

plore recent evolutionary events. One research team has traced the relationships among Native American groups through their mtDNA sequences. The molecular findings corroborate other evidence that the Pima of Arizona, the Maya of Mexico, and the Yanomami of Venezuela are closely related, probably descending from the first of three waves of immigrants that crossed the Bering land bridge from Asia to the Americas about 15,000 years ago.

Gene Duplications and Gene Families

What does molecular systematics reveal about the evolutionary history of genome change? Consider gene duplication, which plays a particularly important role in evolution because it increases the number of genes in the genome, providing more opportunities for further evolutionary changes. Molecular techniques now allow us to trace the phylogenies of gene duplications and the influence of these duplications on genome evolution. These molecular phylogenies must account for repeated duplications that have resulted in *gene families*, groups of related genes within an organism's genome (see Figure 21.11). Accounting for such duplications leads us to distinguish two types of homologous genes: orthologous genes and paralogous genes. **Orthologous genes** (from the Greek *orthos*, exact) are those found in different species, and their divergence traces back to the speciation events that produced the species (Figure 26.18a). The cytochrome *c* genes (which code for an electron transport chain protein) in humans and dogs are orthologous. In **paralogous genes** (from the Greek *para*, in parallel), the homology results from gene duplication; hence, multiple copies of these genes have diverged from one another within a species (Figure 26.18b). In Chapter 23, you encountered the example of olfactory receptor genes, which have undergone many gene duplications in vertebrates. Humans and mice both have huge families of more than 1,000 of these paralogous genes.

Note that orthologous genes can only diverge after speciation has taken place, that is, after the genes are found in separate gene pools. For example, although the cytochrome *c* genes in humans and dogs serve the same function, the gene's sequence in humans has diverged from that in dogs in the time since these species last shared a common ancestor. Paralogous genes, on the other hand, can diverge within a species because they are present in more than one copy in the genome. The paralogous genes that make up the olfactory receptor gene family in humans have diverged from each other during our long evolutionary history. They now specify proteins that confer sensitivity to a wide variety of molecules, ranging from food odors to sex pheromones.

Genome Evolution

Now that we can compare the entire genomes of different organisms, including our own, two patterns have emerged. First, lineages that diverged long ago can share orthologous genes. For

▼ **Figure 26.18 Two types of homologous genes.** Colored bands mark regions of the genes where differences in base sequences have accumulated.

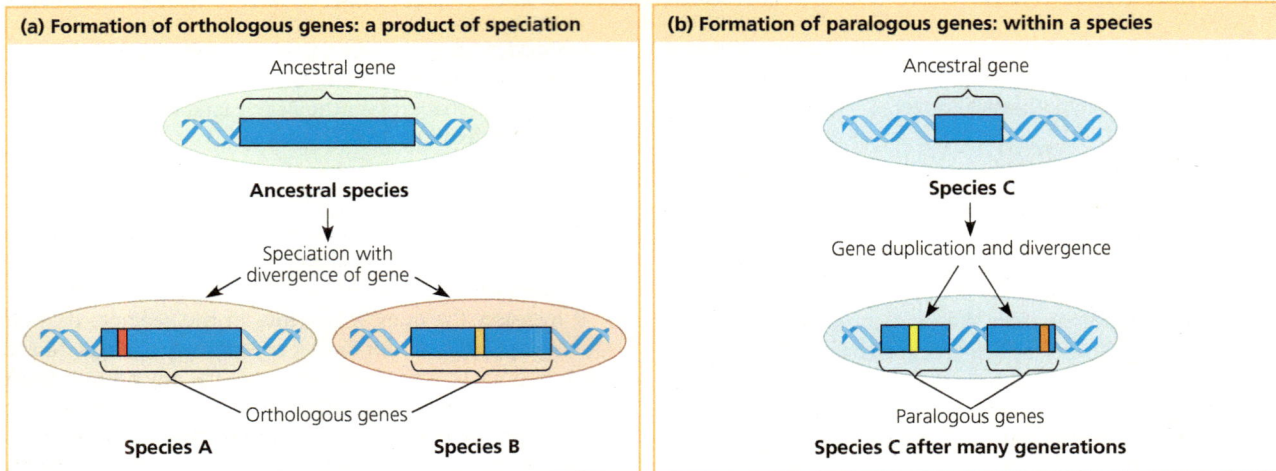

(a) Formation of orthologous genes: a product of speciation

Ancestral gene

Ancestral species

Speciation with divergence of gene

Orthologous genes

Species A   Species B

(b) Formation of paralogous genes: within a species

Ancestral gene

Species C

Gene duplication and divergence

Paralogous genes

Species C after many generations

example, though the human and mouse lineages diverged about 65 million years ago, 99% of the genes of humans and mice are orthologous. And 50% of human genes are orthologous with those of yeast, despite 1 billion years of divergent evolution. Such commonalities explain why disparate organisms nevertheless share many biochemical and developmental pathways.

Second, the number of genes a species has doesn't seem to increase through duplication at the same rate as perceived phenotypic complexity. Humans have only about four times as many genes as yeast, a single-celled eukaryote, even though—unlike yeast—we have a large, complex brain and a body with more than 200 different types of tissues. Evidence is emerging that many human genes are more versatile than those of yeast: A single human gene can encode multiple proteins that perform different tasks in various body tissues. Unraveling the mechanisms that cause this genomic versatility and phenotypic variation is an exciting challenge.

CONCEPT CHECK 26.4

1. Explain how comparing proteins of two species can yield data about the species' evolutionary relationship.
2. **WHAT IF?** Suppose gene A is orthologous in species 1 and species 2, and gene B is paralogous to gene A in species 1. Suggest a sequence of two evolutionary events that could result in the following: Gene A differs considerably between species, yet gene A and gene B show little divergence from each other.
3. **MAKE CONNECTIONS** Review Figure 18.13 (p. 409); then suggest how a particular gene could have different functions in different tissues within an organism.

For suggested answers, see Appendix A.

CONCEPT 26.5

Molecular clocks help track evolutionary time

One of the long-term goals of evolutionary biology is to understand the relationships among all organisms, including those for which there is no fossil record. When we extend molecular phylogenies beyond the fossil record, however, we must rely on an important assumption about how change occurs at the molecular level.

Molecular Clocks

We stated earlier that researchers have estimated that the common ancestor of Hawaiian silversword plants lived about 5 million years ago. How did they make this estimate? They relied on the concept of a **molecular clock**, a yardstick for measuring the absolute time of evolutionary change based on the observation that some genes and other regions of genomes appear to evolve at constant rates. The assumption underlying the molecular clock is that the number of nucleotide substitutions in orthologous genes is proportional to the time that has elapsed since the species branched from their common ancestor (divergence time). In the case of paralogous genes, the number of substitutions is proportional to the time since the ancestral gene was duplicated.

We can calibrate the molecular clock of a gene that has a reliable average rate of evolution by graphing the number of genetic differences—for example, nucleotide, codon, or amino acid differences—against the dates of evolutionary branch points that are known from the fossil record

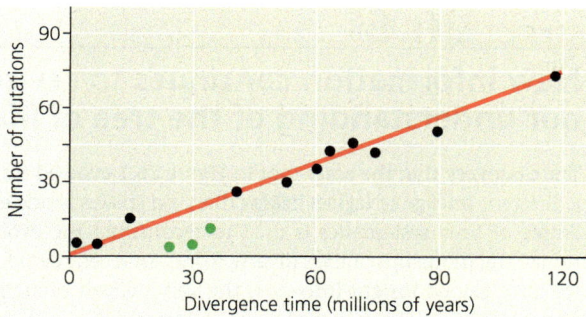

▲ **Figure 26.19** **A molecular clock for mammals.** The number of accumulated mutations in seven proteins has increased over time in a consistent manner for most mammal species. The three green data points represent primate species, whose proteins appear to have evolved more slowly than those of other mammals. The divergence time for each data point was based on fossil evidence.

? *Use the graph to estimate the divergence time for a mammal with a total of 30 mutations in the seven proteins.*

(Figure 26.19). The average rates of genetic change inferred from such graphs can then be used to estimate the dates of events that cannot be discerned from the fossil record, such as the origin of the silverswords discussed earlier.

Of course, no gene marks time with complete precision. In fact, some portions of the genome appear to have evolved in irregular bursts that are not at all clocklike. And even those genes that seem to act as reliable molecular clocks are accurate only in the statistical sense of showing a fairly smooth *average* rate of change. Over time, there may still be deviations from that average rate. Furthermore, the same gene may evolve at different rates in different groups of organisms. And even among genes that are clocklike, the rate of the clock may vary greatly from one gene to another; some genes evolve a million times faster than others.

Neutral Theory

The observed regularity of change that enables us to use some genes as molecular clocks raises the possibility that many of the changes in these sequences result from mutations that have become fixed in a population by genetic drift (see Chapter 23) and that the changes are selectively neutral—neither beneficial nor detrimental. In the 1960s, Motoo Kimura, at the Japanese National Institute of Genetics, and Jack King and Thomas Jukes, at the University of California, Berkeley, independently published papers describing this **neutral theory**— that much evolutionary change in genes and proteins has no effect on fitness and therefore is not influenced by natural selection. Kimura pointed out that many new mutations are harmful and are removed quickly. But if most of the rest are neutral and have little or no effect on fitness, then the rate of molecular change should indeed be regular, like a clock. Differences in the clock rate for different genes are a function of how important a gene is. If the exact sequence of amino

acids that a gene specifies is essential to survival, most of the mutational changes will be harmful and only a few will be neutral. As a result, such genes change only slowly. But if the exact sequence of amino acids is less critical, fewer of the new mutations will be harmful and more will be neutral. Such genes change more quickly.

Problems with Molecular Clocks

In fact, molecular clocks do not run as smoothly as neutral theory predicts. Many irregularities are likely to be the result of natural selection in which certain DNA changes are favored over others. Consequently, some scientists question the utility of molecular clocks for timing evolution. Their skepticism is part of a broader debate about the extent to which neutral genetic variation can account for some kinds of DNA diversity. Indeed, evidence suggests that almost half the amino acid differences in proteins of two *Drosophila* species, *D. simulans* and *D. yakuba*, are not neutral but have resulted from directional natural selection. But because the direction of natural selection may change repeatedly over long periods of time (and hence may average out), some genes experiencing selection can nevertheless serve as approximate markers of elapsed time.

Another question arises when researchers attempt to extend molecular clocks beyond the time span documented by the fossil record. Although some fossils are more than 3 billion years old, these are very rare. An abundant fossil record extends back only about 550 million years, but molecular clocks have been used to date evolutionary divergences that occurred a billion or more years ago. These estimates assume that the clocks have been constant for all that time. Such estimates are highly uncertain.

In some cases, problems may be avoided by calibrating molecular clocks with many genes rather than just one or a few genes (as is often done). By using many genes, fluctuations in evolutionary rate due to natural selection or other factors that vary over time may average out. For example, one group of researchers constructed molecular clocks of vertebrate evolution from published sequence data for 658 nuclear genes. Despite the broad period of time covered (nearly 600 million years) and the fact that natural selection probably affected some of these genes, their estimates of divergence times agreed closely with fossil-based estimates.

Applying a Molecular Clock: The Origin of HIV

Researchers have used a molecular clock to date the origin of HIV infection in humans. Phylogenetic analysis shows that HIV, the virus that causes AIDS, is descended from viruses that infect chimpanzees and other primates. (Most of these viruses do not cause AIDS-like diseases in their native hosts.) When did HIV jump to humans? There is no simple answer, because the virus has spread to humans more than once. The multiple origins of HIV are reflected in the variety of strains

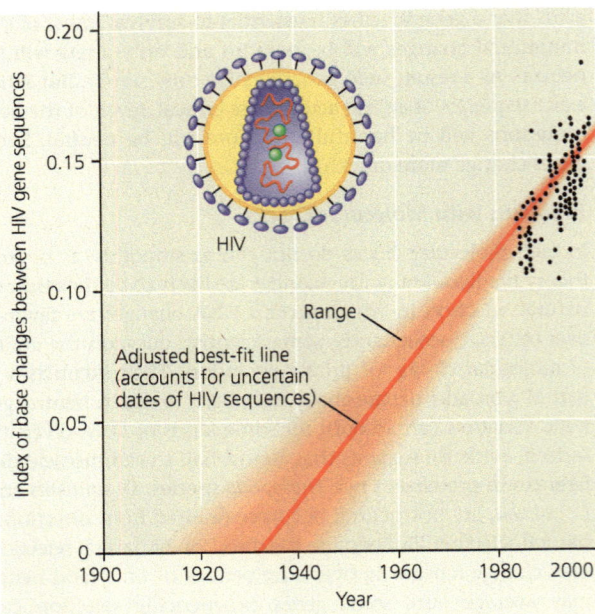

▲ **Figure 26.20 Dating the origin of HIV-1 M with a molecular clock.** The black data points are based on DNA sequences of an HIV gene in blood samples collected from patients. (The dates when these individual HIV gene sequences arose are not known with certainty because a person can harbor the virus for years before symptoms occur.) Projecting the gene's rate of change in the 1980s and 1990s backward in time suggests that the virus originated in the 1930s.

(genetic types) of the virus. HIV's genetic material is made of RNA, and like other RNA viruses, it evolves quickly.

The most widespread strain in humans is HIV-1 M. To pinpoint the earliest HIV-1 M infection, researchers compared samples of the virus from various times during the epidemic, including a sample from 1959. A comparison of gene sequences showed that the virus has evolved in a clocklike fashion **(Figure 26.20)**. Extrapolating backward in time using the molecular clock indicates that the HIV-1 M strain first spread to humans during the 1930s.

CONCEPT CHECK 26.5

1. What is a molecular clock? What assumption underlies the use of a molecular clock?
2. **MAKE CONNECTIONS** Review Concept 17.5 (pp. 390–392). Then explain how numerous base changes could occur in an organism's DNA yet have no effect on its fitness.
3. **WHAT IF?** Suppose a molecular clock dates the divergence of two taxa at 80 million years ago, but new fossil evidence shows that the taxa diverged at least 120 million years ago. Explain how this could happen.

For suggested answers, see Appendix A.

CONCEPT 26.6

New information continues to revise our understanding of the tree of life

The discovery that the scaly-foot in Figure 26.1 evolved from a different lineage of legless lizards than did snakes is one example of how systematics is used to reconstruct the evolutionary relationships of life's diverse forms. In recent decades, we have gained insight into even the very deepest branches of the tree of life through molecular systematics.

From Two Kingdoms to Three Domains

Early taxonomists classified all known species into two kingdoms: plants and animals. Even with the discovery of the diverse microbial world, the two-kingdom system persisted: Noting that bacteria had a rigid cell wall, taxonomists placed them in the plant kingdom. Eukaryotic unicellular organisms with chloroplasts were also considered plants. Fungi, too, were classified as plants, partly because most fungi, like most plants, are unable to move about (never mind the fact that fungi are not photosynthetic and have little in common structurally with plants!). In the two-kingdom system, unicellular eukaryotes that move and ingest food—protozoans—were classified as animals. Those such as *Euglena* that move and are photosynthetic were claimed by both botanists and zoologists and showed up in both kingdoms.

Taxonomic schemes with more than two kingdoms gained broad acceptance in the late 1960s, when many biologists recognized five kingdoms: Monera (prokaryotes), Protista (a diverse kingdom consisting mostly of unicellular organisms), Plantae, Fungi, and Animalia. This system highlighted the two fundamentally different types of cells, prokaryotic and eukaryotic, and set the prokaryotes apart from all eukaryotes by placing them in their own kingdom, Monera.

However, phylogenies based on genetic data soon began to reveal a problem with this system: Some prokaryotes differ as much from each other as they do from eukaryotes. Such difficulties have led biologists to adopt a three-domain system. The three domains—Bacteria, Archaea, and Eukarya—are a taxonomic level higher than the kingdom level. The validity of these domains is supported by many studies, including a recent study that analyzed nearly 100 completely sequenced genomes.

The domain Bacteria contains most of the currently known prokaryotes, including the bacteria closely related to chloroplasts and mitochondria. The second domain, Archaea, consists of a diverse group of prokaryotic organisms that inhabit a wide variety of environments. Some archaea can use hydrogen as an energy source, and others were the chief source of the natural gas deposits that are found throughout Earth's crust. As you will read in Chapter 27, bacteria differ from archaea in many structural, biochemical, and physiological characteristics. The third domain, Eukarya, consists of all the organisms that have cells containing true nuclei. This domain includes many groups of single-celled organisms (see Chapter 28) as well as multicellular plants (Chapters 29 and 30), fungi (Chapter 31), and animals (Chapters 32–34). **Figure 26.21** represents one possible phylogenetic tree for the three domains and the many lineages they encompass.

The three-domain system highlights the fact that much of the history of life has been about single-celled organisms. The two prokaryotic domains consist entirely of single-celled organisms, and even in Eukarya, only the branches shown in red (plants, fungi, and animals) are dominated by multicellular organisms. Of the five kingdoms previously recognized by taxonomists, most biologists continue to recognize Plantae, Fungi, and Animalia, but not Monera and Protista. The kingdom Monera is obsolete because it would have members in

two different domains. As you'll read in Chapter 28, the kingdom Protista has also crumbled because it is polyphyletic—it includes members that are more closely related to plants, fungi, or animals than to other protists.

A Simple Tree of All Life

The evolutionary relationships shown in Figure 26.21 can be summarized in a simpler tree (see the figure legend question). In this tree, the first major split in the history of life occurred when bacteria diverged from other organisms. If this tree is correct, eukaryotes and archaea are more closely related to each other than either is to bacteria.

This reconstruction of the tree of life is based largely on sequence comparisons of rRNA genes, which code for the RNA components of ribosomes. Because ribosomes are fundamental to the workings of the cell, rRNA genes have evolved so slowly that homologies between distantly related organisms

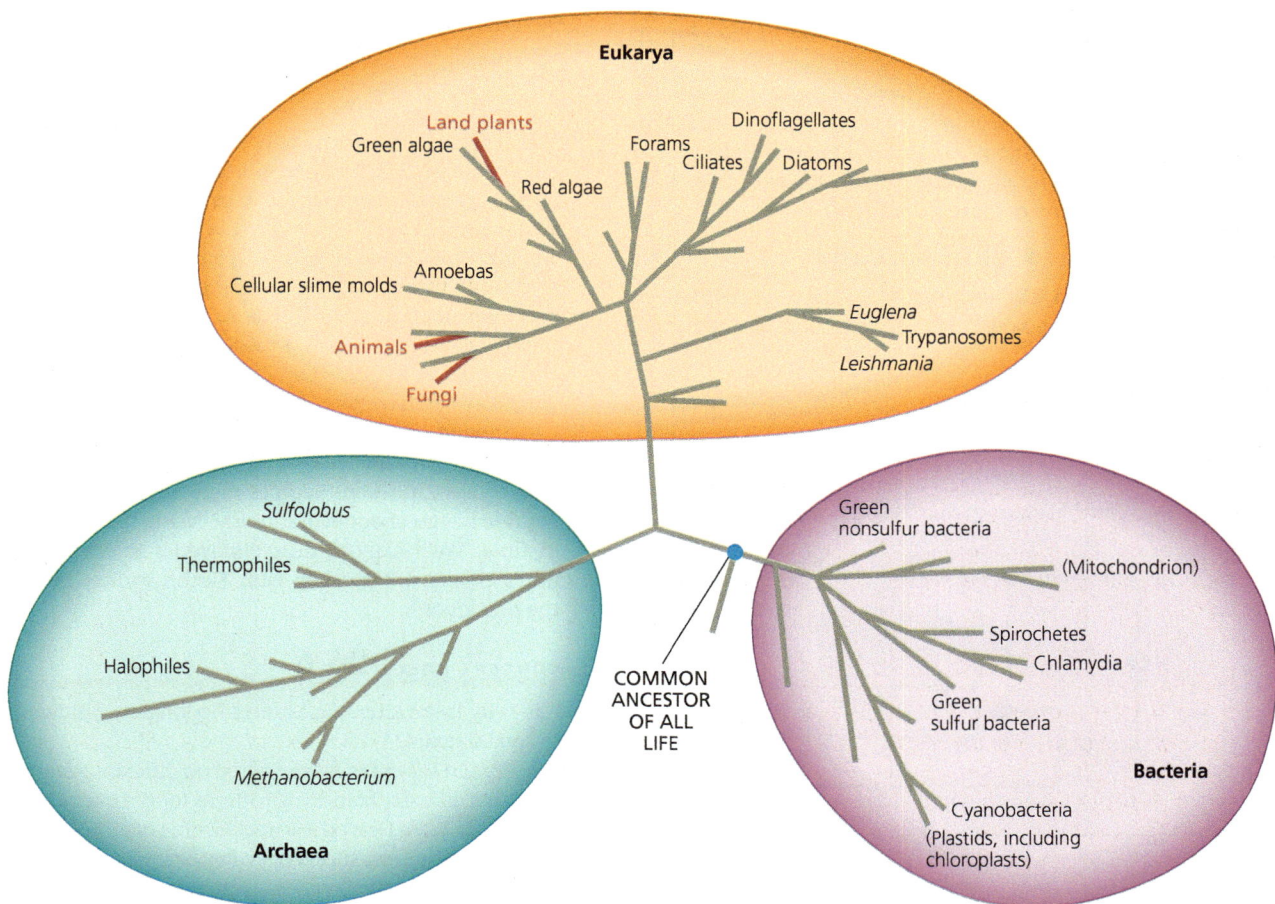

▲ **Figure 26.21 The three domains of life.** The phylogenetic tree shown here is based on rRNA gene sequences. Branch lengths are proportional to the amount of genetic change in each lineage. (To simplify the figure, only some branches are labeled.) In this diagram, the lineages within Eukarya that are dominated by multicellular organisms (plants, fungi, and animals) are shown in red. All other lineages consist solely or primarily of single-celled organisms.

DRAW IT *Redraw this tree as a horizontal tree that has just three branches, one for each domain. Which domain was the first to diverge? Which is the sister domain to Eukarya?*

can still be detected—making these genes very useful for determining evolutionary relationships between deep branches in the history of life. However, other genes reveal a different set of relationships. For example, researchers have found that many of the genes that influence metabolism in yeast (a unicellular eukaryote) are more similar to genes in the domain Bacteria than they are to genes in the domain Archaea—a finding that suggests that the eukaryotes may share a more recent common ancestor with bacteria than with archaea.

Comparisons of complete genomes from the three domains show that there have been substantial movements of genes between organisms in the different domains **(Figure 26.22)**. These took place through **horizontal gene transfer**, a process in which genes are transferred from one genome to another through mechanisms such as exchange of transposable elements and plasmids, viral infection (see Chapter 19), and perhaps fusions of organisms. Recent research reinforces the view that horizontal gene transfer is important. For example, a 2008 analysis indicated that, on average, 80% of the genes in 181 prokaryotic genomes had moved between species at some point during the course of evolution. Because phylogenetic trees are based on the assumption that genes are passed vertically from one generation to the next, the occurrence of such horizontal transfer events helps to explain why trees built using different genes can give inconsistent results.

Is the Tree of Life Really a Ring?

Some biologists have argued that horizontal gene transfer was so common that the early history of life should be represented

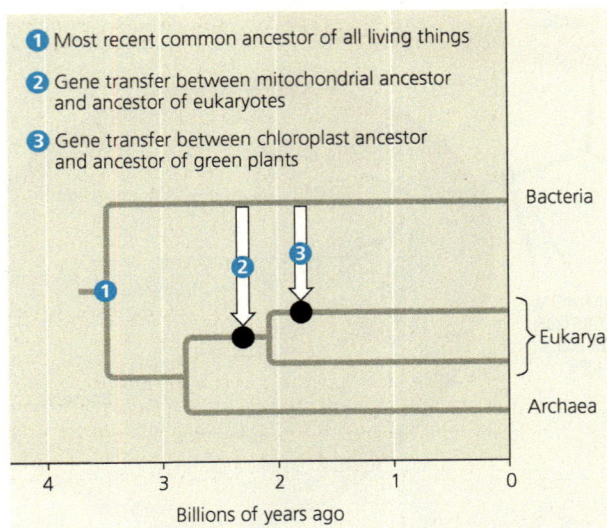

1 Most recent common ancestor of all living things

2 Gene transfer between mitochondrial ancestor and ancestor of eukaryotes

3 Gene transfer between chloroplast ancestor and ancestor of green plants

▲ **Figure 26.22 The role of horizontal gene transfer in the history of life.** This tree shows two major episodes of horizontal gene transfer, the dates of which are uncertain. It is known that many more such events occurred. (Because the tree is horizontal, the arrows representing "horizontal" transfer are vertical here.)

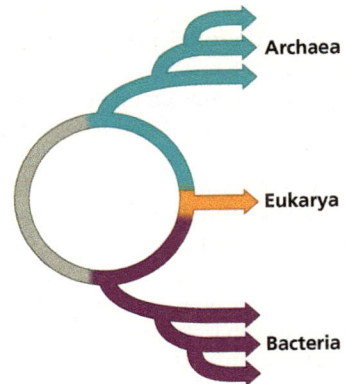

▲ **Figure 26.23 A ring of life.** In this hypothesis, the eukaryote lineage (orange) arose when an early archaean (teal) fused with an early bacterium (purple). Such an event is consistent with a "ring of life" but not with a tree of life. Three great domains (Archaea, Eukarya, and Bacteria) emerged from the ring and gave rise to the tremendous diversity of life we observe today.

as a tangled network of connected branches—not a simple, dichotomously branching tree like that in Figure 26.22. Others have suggested that relationships among early organisms are best represented by a ring, not a tree **(Figure 26.23)**. In an analysis based on hundreds of genes, these researchers hypothesized that eukaryotes arose as a fusion between an early bacterium and an early archaean. If correct, eukaryotes are simultaneously most closely related to bacteria *and* archaea—an evolutionary relationship that cannot be depicted in a tree of life, but can be depicted in a *ring* of life.

Although scientists continue to debate whether early steps in the history of life are best represented as a tree, a ring, or a tangled web, in recent decades there have been many exciting discoveries about evolutionary events that occurred later in time. We'll explore such discoveries in the rest of this unit's chapters, beginning with Earth's earliest inhabitants, the prokaryotes.

CONCEPT CHECK 26.6

1. Why is the kingdom Monera no longer considered a valid taxon?
2. Explain why phylogenies based on different genes can yield different branching patterns for the tree of all life.
3. **WHAT IF?** Draw the three possible dichotomously branching trees showing evolutionary relationships for the domains Bacteria, Archaea, and Eukarya. Two of these trees have been supported by genetic data. Is it likely that the third tree might also receive such support? Explain your answer.

For suggested answers, see Appendix A.

26 CHAPTER REVIEW

SUMMARY OF KEY CONCEPTS

CONCEPT 26.1

Phylogenies show evolutionary relationships (pp. 583–586)

- Linnaeus's **binomial** classification system gives organisms two-part names: a **genus** plus a specific epithet.
- In the Linnaean system, species are grouped in increasingly broad taxa: Related genera are placed in the same family, families in orders, orders in classes, classes in phyla, phyla in kingdoms, and (more recently) kingdoms in domains.
- Systematists depict evolutionary relationships as branching **phylogenetic trees**. Many systematists propose that classification be based entirely on evolutionary relationships.

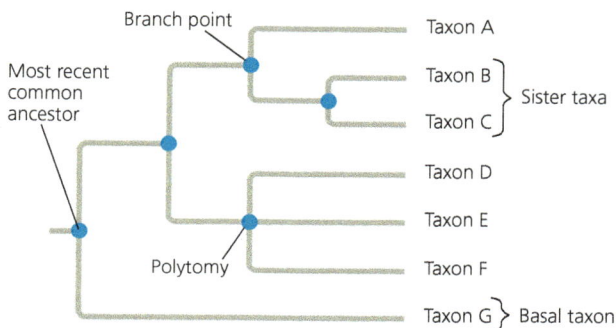

- Unless branch lengths are proportional to time or amount of genetic change, a phylogenetic tree indicates only patterns of descent.
- Much information can be learned about a species from its evolutionary history; hence, phylogenies are useful in a wide range of applications.

? *Humans and chimpanzees are sister species. Explain what that means.*

CONCEPT 26.2

Phylogenies are inferred from morphological and molecular data (pp. 586–588)

- Organisms with similar morphologies or DNA sequences are likely to be more closely related than organisms with very different structures and genetic sequences.
- To infer phylogeny, **homology** (similarity due to shared ancestry) must be distinguished from **analogy** (similarity due to convergent evolution).
- Computer programs are used to align comparable DNA sequences and to distinguish molecular homologies from coincidental matches between taxa that diverged long ago.

? *Why is it necessary to distinguish homology from analogy to infer phylogeny?*

CONCEPT 26.3

Shared characters are used to construct phylogenetic trees (pp. 588–594)

- A **clade** is a monophyletic grouping that includes an ancestral species and all of its descendants.

- Clades can be distinguished by their **shared derived characters**.

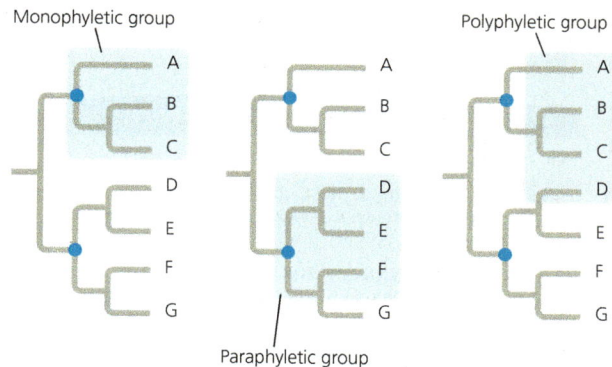

- Branch lengths can be drawn proportional to the amount of evolutionary change or time.
- Among phylogenies, the most parsimonious tree is the one that requires the fewest evolutionary changes. The most likely tree is the one based on the most likely pattern of changes.
- Well-supported phylogenetic hypotheses are consistent with a wide range of data.

? *Explain the logic of using shared derived characters to infer phylogeny.*

CONCEPT 26.4

An organism's evolutionary history is documented in its genome (pp. 594–595)

- **Orthologous genes** are homologous genes found in different species as a result of speciation. **Paralogous genes** are homologous genes within a species that result from gene duplication; such genes can diverge and potentially take on new functions.
- Distantly related species can have orthologous genes. The small variation in gene number in organisms of varying complexity suggests that genes are versatile and may have multiple functions.

? *When reconstructing phylogenies, is it better to compare orthologous or paralogous genes? Explain.*

CONCEPT 26.5

Molecular clocks help track evolutionary time (pp. 595–597)

- Some regions of DNA change at a rate consistent enough to serve as a **molecular clock**, in which the amount of genetic change is used to estimate the date of past evolutionary events. Other DNA regions change in a less predictable way.
- A molecular clock analysis suggests that the most common strain of HIV jumped from primates to humans in the 1930s.

? *Describe some assumptions and limitations of molecular clocks.*

CONCEPT 26.6

New information continues to revise our understanding of the tree of life (pp. 597–599)

- Past classification systems have given way to the current view of the tree of life, which consists of three great **domains**: Bacteria, Archaea, and Eukarya.

- Phylogenies based on rRNA genes suggest that eukaryotes are most closely related to archaea, while data from some other genes suggest a closer relationship to bacteria.
- Other genetic analyses suggest that eukaryotes arose as a fusion between a bacterium and an archaean, leading to a "ring of life" in which eukaryotes are equally closely related to bacteria and archaea.

? *Why was the five-kingdom system abandoned for a three-domain system?*

TESTING YOUR UNDERSTANDING

(MB) Multiple-choice Self-Quiz questions #1–7 can be found in the Study Area at www.masteringbiology.com.

8. EVOLUTION CONNECTION
Darwin suggested looking at a species' close relatives to learn what its ancestors may have been like. How does his suggestion anticipate recent methods, such as phylogenetic bracketing and the use of outgroups in cladistic analysis?

9. SCIENTIFIC INQUIRY
DRAW IT (a) Draw a phylogenetic tree based on the first five characters in the table below. Place hatch marks on the tree to indicate the origin(s) of each of the six characters.
(b) Assume that tuna and dolphins are sister species and redraw the phylogenetic tree accordingly. Place hatch marks on the tree to indicate the origin(s) of each of the six characters.
(c) How many evolutionary changes are required in each tree? Which tree is most parsimonious?

Character	Lancelet (outgroup)	Lamprey	Tuna	Salamander	Turtle	Leopard	Dolphin
Backbone	0	1	1	1	1	1	1
Hinged jaw	0	0	1	1	1	1	1
Four limbs	0	0	0	1	1	1	1*
Amnion	0	0	0	0	1	1	1
Milk	0	0	0	0	0	1	1
Dorsal fin	0	0	1	0	0	0	1

*Although adult dolphins have only two obvious limbs (their flippers), as embryos they have two hind-limb buds, for a total of four limbs.

10. WRITE ABOUT A THEME
The Cellular Basis of Life; The Genetic Basis of Life In a short essay (100–150 words), explain how these two themes—along with the process of descent with modification (see Chapter 22)—enable scientists to construct phylogenies that extend hundreds of millions of years back in time.

For selected answers, see Appendix A.

MasteringBIOLOGY www.masteringbiology.com

1. MasteringBiology® Assignments
Video Tutor Session Phylogenetic Trees
Tutorial Constructing Phylogenetic Trees
Activity Classification Schemes
Questions Student Misconceptions • Reading Quiz • Multiple Choice • End-of-Chapter
2. eText
Read your book online, search, take notes, highlight text, and more.
3. The Study Area
Practice Tests • Cumulative Test • *BioFlix* 3-D Animations • MP3 Tutor Sessions • Videos • Activities • Investigations • Lab Media • Audio Glossary • Word Study Tools • Art

35

Plant Structure, Growth, and Development

▲ Figure 35.1 **Computer art?**

OVERVIEW

Are Plants Computers?

The object in **Figure 35.1** is not the creation of a computer genius with a flair for the artistic. It is a head of romanesco, an edible relative of broccoli. Romanesco's mesmerizing beauty is attributable to the fact that each of its smaller buds resembles in miniature the entire vegetable. (Mathematicians refer to such repetitive patterns as *fractals*.) Romanesco looks as if it were generated by a computer because its growth pattern follows a repetitive sequence of instructions. As in most plants, the growing shoot tips lay down a pattern of leaf . . . bud . . . stem, over and over again. These repetitive developmental patterns are genetically determined and subject to natural selection. For example, a mutation that shortens the stem segments between leaves will generate a bushier plant. If this altered architecture enhances the plant's ability to access resources such as light and, by doing so, to leave more offspring, then this trait will occur more frequently in later generations—evolution will have occurred.

Romanesco is unusual in adhering so rigidly to its basic body organization. Most plants show much greater diversity in their individual forms because the growth of most plants, much more than in animals, is affected by local environmental conditions. All lions, for example, have four legs and are of roughly the same size, but oak trees vary in the number and arrangement of their branches. This is because lions and other animals respond to challenges and opportunities in their local environment by movement, whereas plants respond by altering their growth. Illumination of a plant from the side, for example, creates asymmetries in its basic body plan. Branches grow more quickly from the illuminated side of a shoot than from the shaded side, an architectural change of obvious benefit for photosynthesis. Recognizing the highly adaptive development of plants is critical for understanding how plants interact with their environment.

Chapters 29 and 30 described the evolution of plants from green algae to angiosperms (flowering plants). In Unit Six, we focus primarily on angiosperms because they serve as the primary producers in many ecosystems and are of great agricultural importance. We begin by discussing the structure of flowering plants and how these plants develop.

CONCEPT 35.1

Plants have a hierarchical organization consisting of organs, tissues, and cells

Plants, like most animals, have organs composed of different tissues, which in turn are composed of different cell types. A **tissue** is a group of cells, consisting of one or more cell types, that together perform a specialized function. An **organ** consists of several types of tissues that together carry out particular functions. In looking at the hierarchy of plant organs, tissues, and cells, we begin with organs because they are the most familiar and easily observed plant structures. As you learn about the hierarchy of plant structure, keep in mind how natural selection has produced plant forms that fit plant function at all levels of organization.

The Three Basic Plant Organs: Roots, Stems, and Leaves

The basic morphology of vascular plants reflects their evolutionary history as terrestrial organisms that inhabit and draw resources from two very different environments—below the ground and above the ground. They must absorb water and minerals from below the ground surface and CO_2 and light from above the ground surface. The ability to acquire these resources efficiently is traceable to the evolution of three basic organs—roots, stems, and leaves. These organs form a **root system** and a **shoot system**, the latter consisting of stems and leaves **(Figure 35.2)**. With few exceptions, vascular plants rely completely on both systems for survival. Roots typically are not photosynthetic; they starve unless *photosynthates*, the sugars and other carbohydrates produced during photosynthesis, are imported from the shoot system. Conversely, the shoot system depends on the water and minerals that roots absorb from the soil.

Vegetative growth—production of nonreproductive leaves, stems, and roots—is only one stage in a plant's life. Most plants also undergo growth relating to sexual reproduction. In angiosperms, reproductive shoots bear flowers, which consist of leaves that are highly modified for sexual reproduction.

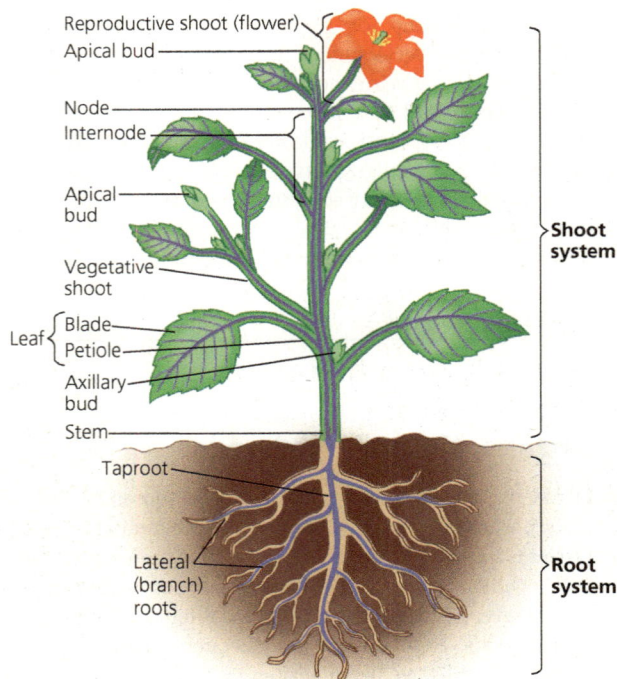

▲ **Figure 35.2 An overview of a flowering plant.** The plant body is divided into a root system and a shoot system, connected by vascular tissue (purple strands in this diagram) that is continuous throughout the plant. The plant shown is an idealized eudicot.

Later in this chapter, we'll discuss the transition from vegetative shoot formation to reproductive shoot formation.

In describing plant organs, we'll draw examples mainly from the two major groups of angiosperms: monocots and eudicots (see Figure 30.13).

Roots

A **root** is an organ that anchors a vascular plant in the soil, absorbs minerals and water, and often stores carbohydrates. Most eudicots and gymnosperms have a *taproot system*, consisting of one main vertical root, the **taproot**, which develops from an embryonic root. The taproot gives rise to **lateral roots**, also called branch roots (see Figure 35.2). Taproot systems generally penetrate deeply and are therefore well adapted to deep soils, where the groundwater is not close to the surface.

In most monocots, such as grasses, the embryonic root dies early on and does not form a taproot. Instead, many small roots emerge from the stem. Such roots are said to be *adventitious* (from the Latin *adventicus*, extraneous), a term describing a plant organ that grows in an unusual location, such as roots arising from stems or leaves. Each small root forms its own lateral roots. The result is a *fibrous root system*—a mat of generally thin roots spreading out below the soil surface (see Figure 30.13). Fibrous root systems usually do not penetrate deeply and are therefore best adapted to shallow soils or regions where rainfall is light and does not moisten the soil much below the surface layer. Most grasses have shallow roots, concentrated in the upper few centimeters of the soil. Because these shallow roots hold the topsoil in place, grass makes excellent ground cover for preventing erosion.

Although the entire root system helps anchor a plant, in most plants the absorption of water and minerals occurs primarily near the tips of roots, where vast numbers of **root hairs** emerge and increase the surface area of the root enormously **(Figure 35.3)**. A root hair is a thin, tubular extension of a root epidermal cell. It should not be confused with a lateral root, which is an organ. Despite their great surface

◄ **Figure 35.3 Root hairs of a radish seedling.** Root hairs grow by the thousands just behind the tip of each root. By increasing the root's surface area, they greatly enhance the absorption of water and minerals from the soil.

area, root hairs, unlike lateral roots, contribute little to plant anchorage. Their main function is absorption.

Many plants have root adaptations with specialized functions **(Figure 35.4)**. Some of these arise from the roots, and others are adventitious, developing from stems or, in rare cases, leaves. Some modified roots add support and anchorage. Others store water and nutrients or absorb oxygen from the air.

▼ **Figure 35.4 Evolutionary adaptations of roots.**

◀ **Storage roots.** Many plants, such as the common beet, store food and water in their roots.

▲ **Prop roots.** The aerial roots of hala trees are examples of prop roots, so named because they support the tall, top-heavy trees. Hala trees grow along coastal areas in the South Pacific where the sandy soils are shallow and unstable.

▲ **Pneumatophores.** Also known as air roots, pneumatophores are produced by trees such as mangroves that inhabit tidal swamps. By projecting above the water's surface, they enable the root system to obtain oxygen, which is lacking in the thick, waterlogged mud.

Stems

A **stem** is an organ that raises or separates leaves, exposing them to sunlight. Stems also raise reproductive structures, facilitating dispersal of pollen and fruit. Each stem consists of an alternating system of **nodes**, the points at which leaves are attached, and **internodes**, the stem segments between nodes (see Figure 35.2). In the upper angle (axil) formed by each leaf and the stem is an **axillary bud**, a structure that can form a lateral shoot, commonly called a branch. Young axillary buds typically grow very slowly: Most of the growth of a young shoot is concentrated near the shoot tip, which consists of an **apical bud**, or terminal bud, that is composed of developing leaves and a compact series of nodes and internodes.

The proximity of the axillary buds to the apical bud is partly responsible for their dormancy. The inhibition of axillary buds by an apical bud is called **apical dominance**. If an animal eats the end of the shoot or if shading results in

◀ **"Strangling" aerial roots.** The seeds of this strangler fig germinate in the branches of tall trees of other species and send numerous aerial roots to the ground. These snakelike roots gradually wrap around the host tree and objects such as this Cambodian temple ruin. Eventually, the host tree dies of shading by the fig leaves.

▼ **Buttress roots.** Because of moist conditions in the tropics, root systems of many of the tallest trees are surprisingly shallow. Aerial roots that look like buttresses, such as seen in this ceiba tree in Central America, give architectural support to the trunks of such trees.

the light being more intense to the side of the shoot, axillary buds break dormancy; that is, they start growing. A growing axillary bud gives rise to a lateral shoot, complete with its own apical bud, leaves, and axillary buds. Removing the apical bud stimulates the growth of axillary buds, resulting in more lateral shoots. That is why pruning trees and shrubs and pinching back houseplants will make them bushier. The hormonal changes underlying apical dominance are discussed in Chapter 39.

Some plants have stems with additional functions, such as food storage and asexual reproduction. These modified stems, which include rhizomes, bulbs, stolons, and tubers, are often mistaken for roots **(Figure 35.5)**.

▼ **Figure 35.5 Evolutionary adaptations of stems.**

◀ **Rhizomes.** The base of this iris plant is an example of a rhizome, a horizontal shoot that grows just below the surface. Vertical shoots emerge from axillary buds on the rhizome.

▶ **Bulbs.** Bulbs are vertical underground shoots consisting mostly of the enlarged bases of leaves that store food. You can see the many layers of modified leaves attached to the short stem by slicing an onion bulb lengthwise.

▶ **Stolons.** Shown here on a strawberry plant, stolons are horizontal shoots that grow along the surface. These "runners" enable a plant to reproduce asexually, as plantlets form at nodes along each runner.

◀ **Tubers.** Tubers, such as these potatoes, are enlarged ends of rhizomes or stolons specialized for storing food. The "eyes" of a potato are clusters of axillary buds that mark the nodes.

Leaves

In most vascular plants, the **leaf** is the main photosynthetic organ, although green stems also perform photosynthesis. Leaves vary extensively in form but generally consist of a flattened **blade** and a stalk, the **petiole**, which joins the leaf to the stem at a node (see Figure 35.2). Grasses and many other monocots lack petioles; instead, the base of the leaf forms a sheath that envelops the stem.

Monocots and eudicots differ in the arrangement of **veins**, the vascular tissue of leaves. Most monocots have parallel major veins that run the length of the blade. Eudicots generally have a branched network of major veins (see Figure 30.13).

In identifying angiosperms according to structure, taxonomists rely mainly on floral morphology, but they also use variations in leaf morphology, such as leaf shape, the branching pattern of veins, and the spatial arrangement of leaves. **Figure 35.6** illustrates a difference in leaf shape: simple versus compound. Many leaves, such as those of poison ivy, are

▼ **Figure 35.6 Simple versus compound leaves.**

Simple leaf

A simple leaf has a single, undivided blade. Some simple leaves are deeply lobed, as shown here.

Axillary bud

Petiole

Compound leaf

In a compound leaf, the blade consists of multiple leaflets. A leaflet has no axillary bud at its base.

Leaflet

Axillary bud

Petiole

Doubly compound leaf

In a doubly compound leaf, each leaflet is divided into smaller leaflets.

Axillary bud

Leaflet

Petiole

compound or doubly compound. This structural adaptation may enable leaves to withstand strong wind with less tearing. It may also confine some pathogens (disease-causing organisms and viruses) that invade the leaf to a single leaflet, rather than allowing them to spread to the entire leaf.

Almost all leaves are specialized for photosynthesis. However, some species have leaves with adaptations that enable them to perform additional functions, such as support, protection, storage, or reproduction **(Figure 35.7)**.

▼ **Figure 35.7 Evolutionary adaptations of leaves.**

▶ **Tendrils.** The tendrils by which this pea plant clings to a support are modified leaves. After it has "lassoed" a support, a tendril forms a coil that brings the plant closer to the support. Tendrils are typically modified leaves, but some tendrils are modified stems, as in grapevines.

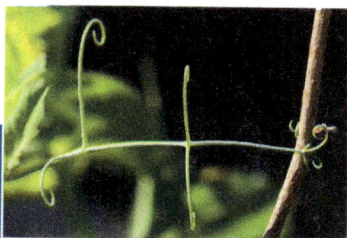

◀ **Spines.** The spines of cacti, such as this prickly pear, are actually leaves; photosynthesis is carried out by the fleshy green stems.

◀ **Storage leaves.** Most succulents, such as this ice plant, have leaves adapted for storing water.

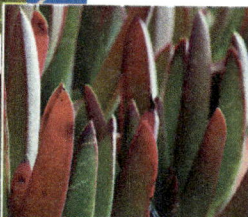

◀ **Reproductive leaves.** The leaves of some succulents, such as *Kalanchoë daigremontiana*, produce adventitious plantlets, which fall off the leaf and take root in the soil.

▶ **Bracts.** Often mistaken for petals, the red parts of the poinsettia are actually modified leaves called bracts that surround a group of flowers. Such brightly colored leaves attract pollinators.

Dermal, Vascular, and Ground Tissues

Each plant organ—root, stem, or leaf—has dermal, vascular, and ground tissues. Each of these three categories forms a **tissue system**, a functional unit connecting all of the plant's organs. Although each tissue system is continuous throughout the plant, specific characteristics of the tissues and their spatial relationships to one another vary in different organs **(Figure 35.8)**.

The **dermal tissue system** is the plant's outer protective covering. Like our skin, it forms the first line of defense against physical damage and pathogens. In nonwoody plants, it is usually a single tissue called the **epidermis**, a layer of tightly packed cells. In leaves and most stems, the **cuticle**, a waxy coating on the epidermal surface, helps prevent water loss. In woody plants, protective tissues called **periderm** replace the epidermis in older regions of stems and roots. In addition to protecting the plant from water loss and disease, the epidermis has specialized characteristics in each organ. For example, a root hair is an extension of an epidermal cell near the tip of a root. *Trichomes* are hairlike outgrowths of the shoot epidermis. In some desert species, they reduce water loss and reflect excess light, but their most common function

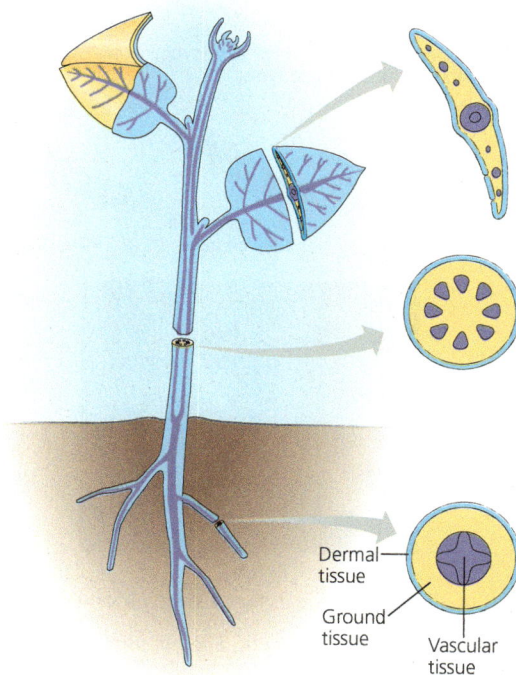

Dermal tissue

Ground tissue

Vascular tissue

▲ **Figure 35.8 The three tissue systems.** The dermal tissue system (blue) provides a protective cover for the entire body of a plant. The vascular tissue system (purple), which transports materials between the root and shoot systems, is also continuous throughout the plant, but is arranged differently in each organ. The ground tissue system (yellow), which is responsible for most of the plant's metabolic functions, is located between the dermal tissue and the vascular tissue in each organ.

is to provide defense against insects by forming a barrier or by secreting sticky fluids or toxic compounds. For instance, the trichomes on aromatic leaves such as mint secrete oils that protect the plants from herbivores and disease. **Figure 35.9** describes an investigation of the relationship between trichome density on soybean pods and damage by beetles.

▼ **Figure 35.9**

INQUIRY

Do soybean pod trichomes deter herbivores?

EXPERIMENT Bean leaf beetles (*Cerotoma trifurcata*) feed on developing legume pods, causing pod scarring and decreased seed quality. W. F. Lam and L. P. Pedigo, of Purdue University, investigated whether the stiff trichomes on soybean pods (*Glycine max*) physically deter these beetles. The researchers placed hungry beetles in muslin bags and sealed the bags around the pods of adjacent plants expressing different pod hairiness. The amount of damage to the pods was assessed after 24 hours.

Very hairy pod
(10 trichomes/
mm²)

Slightly hairy pod
(2 trichomes/
mm²)

Bald pod
(no trichomes)

RESULTS Beetle damage to very hairy soybean pods was much lower than damage to the other pod types.

Very hairy pod:
10% damage

Slightly hairy pod:
25% damage

Bald pod:
40% damage

CONCLUSION Soybean pod trichomes protect against beetle damage.

SOURCE W. F. Lam and L. P. Pedigo, Effect of trichome density on soybean pod feeding by adult bean leaf beetles (Coleoptera: Chrysomelidae), *Journal of Economic Entomology* 94:1459–1463 (2001).

WHAT IF? The pod trichomes of most soybean varieties are white, but some varieties have tan-colored trichomes. Suppose that the effects of trichome density on beetle feeding were observed only in tan-haired varieties. What might this finding suggest about how these trichomes deter beetles?

The **vascular tissue system** carries out long-distance transport of materials between the root and shoot systems. The two types of vascular tissues are xylem and phloem. **Xylem** conducts water and dissolved minerals upward from roots into the shoots. **Phloem** transports sugars, the products of photosynthesis, from where they are made (usually the leaves) to where they are needed—usually roots and sites of growth, such as developing leaves and fruits. The vascular tissue of a root or stem is collectively called the **stele** (the Greek word for "pillar"). The arrangement of the stele varies, depending on the species and organ. In angiosperms, for example, the root stele is a solid central *vascular cylinder* of xylem and phloem, whereas the stele of stems and leaves consists of *vascular bundles*, separate strands containing xylem and phloem (see Figure 35.8). Both xylem and phloem are composed of a variety of cell types, including cells that are highly specialized for transport or support.

Tissues that are neither dermal nor vascular are part of the **ground tissue system**. Ground tissue that is internal to the vascular tissue is known as **pith**, and ground tissue that is external to the vascular tissue is called **cortex**. The ground tissue system is not just filler. It includes various cells specialized for functions such as storage, photosynthesis, and support.

Common Types of Plant Cells

Like any multicellular organism, a plant is characterized by cell differentiation, the specialization of cells in structure and function. Cell differentiation may involve changes both in the cytoplasm and its organelles and in the cell wall. **Figure 35.10**, on the next two pages, focuses on the major types of plant cells: parenchyma cells, collenchyma cells, sclerenchyma cells, the water-conducting cells of the xylem, and the sugar-conducting cells of the phloem. Notice the structural adaptations in the different cells that make their specific functions possible. You may also wish to review Figures 6.9 and 6.28, which show basic plant cell structure.

CONCEPT CHECK 35.1

1. How does the vascular tissue system enable leaves and roots to function together in supporting growth and development of the whole plant?
2. What plant structure is each of the following? (a) brussels sprouts; (b) celery; (c) onions; (d) carrots
3. **WHAT IF?** If humans were photoautotrophs, making food by capturing light energy for photosynthesis, how might our anatomy be different?
4. **MAKE CONNECTIONS** Explain how central vacuoles and cellulose cell walls contribute to plant growth (see Chapter 6, pp. 154 and 164–165).

For suggested answers, see Appendix A.

▼ **Figure 35.10**

Exploring Examples of Differentiated Plant Cells

Parenchyma Cells

Mature **parenchyma cells** have primary walls that are relatively thin and flexible, and most lack secondary walls. (See Figure 6.28 to review primary and secondary cell walls.) When mature, parenchyma cells generally have a large central vacuole. Parenchyma cells perform most of the metabolic functions of the plant, synthesizing and storing various organic products. For example, photosynthesis occurs within the chloroplasts of parenchyma cells in the leaf. Some parenchyma cells in stems and roots have color-less plastids that store starch. The fleshy tissue of many fruits is composed mainly of parenchyma cells. Most parenchyma cells retain the ability to divide and differentiate into other types of plant cells under particular conditions—during wound repair, for example. It is even possible to grow an entire plant from a single parenchyma cell.

Parenchyma cells in *Elodea* leaf, with chloroplasts (LM)   60 µm

Collenchyma Cells

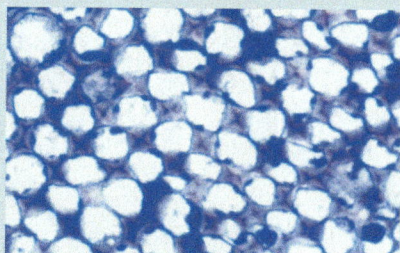

Grouped in strands, **collenchyma cells** (seen here in cross section) help support young parts of the plant shoot. Collenchyma cells are generally elongated cells that have thicker primary walls than parenchyma cells, though the walls are unevenly thickened. Young stems and petioles often have strands of collenchyma cells just below their epidermis (for example, the "strings" of a celery stalk, which is a petiole). Collenchyma cells provide flex-ible support without restraining growth. At maturity, these cells are living and flexible, elongating with the stems and leaves they support—unlike sclerenchyma cells, which we discuss next.

Collenchyma cells (in *Helianthus* stem) (LM)   5 µm

Sclerenchyma Cells

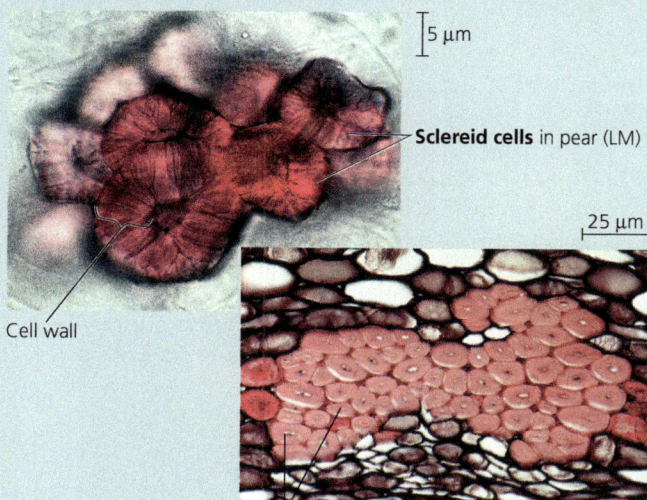

5 µm

Sclereid cells in pear (LM)

25 µm

Cell wall

Fiber cells (cross section from ash tree) (LM)

Sclerenchyma cells also function as supporting elements in the plant, but are much more rigid than collenchyma cells. The secondary walls of sclerenchyma cells are thick and contain large amounts of lignin. This relatively indigestible strengthen-ing polymer accounts for more than a quarter of the dry mass of wood. Lignin is present in all vascular plants, but not in bryophytes. Mature sclerenchyma cells cannot elongate, and they occur in regions of the plant that have stopped growing in length. Sclerenchyma cells are so specialized for support that many are dead at functional maturity, but they produce second-ary walls before the protoplast (the living part of the cell) dies. The rigid walls remain as a "skeleton" that supports the plant, in some cases for hundreds of years.

Two types of sclerenchyma cells, known as **sclereids** and **fibers**, are specialized entirely for support and strengthening. Sclereids, which are boxier than fibers and irregular in shape, have very thick, lignified secondary walls. Sclereids impart the hardness to nutshells and seed coats and the gritty texture to pear fruits. Fibers, which are usually grouped in strands, are long, slender, and tapered. Some are used commercially, such as hemp fibers for making rope and flax fibers for weaving into linen.

Water-Conducting Cells of the Xylem

The two types of water-conducting cells, **tracheids** and **vessel elements**, are tubular, elongated cells that are dead at functional maturity. Tracheids are in the xylem of nearly all vascular plants. In addition to tracheids, most angiosperms, as well as a few gymnosperms and a few seedless vascular plants, have vessel elements. When the living cellular contents of a tracheid or vessel element disintegrate, the cell's thickened walls remain behind, forming a nonliving conduit through which water can flow. The secondary walls of tracheids and vessel elements are often interrupted by pits, thinner regions where only primary walls are present (see Figure 6.28 to review primary and secondary walls). Water can migrate laterally between neighboring cells through pits.

Tracheids are long, thin cells with tapered ends. Water moves from cell to cell mainly through the pits, where it does not have to cross thick secondary walls.

Vessel elements are generally wider, shorter, thinner walled, and less tapered than the tracheids. They are aligned end to end, forming long micropipes known as **vessels**. The end walls of vessel elements have perforation plates that enable water to flow freely through the vessels.

The secondary walls of tracheids and vessel elements are hardened with lignin. This hardening prevents collapse under the tensions of water transport and also provides support.

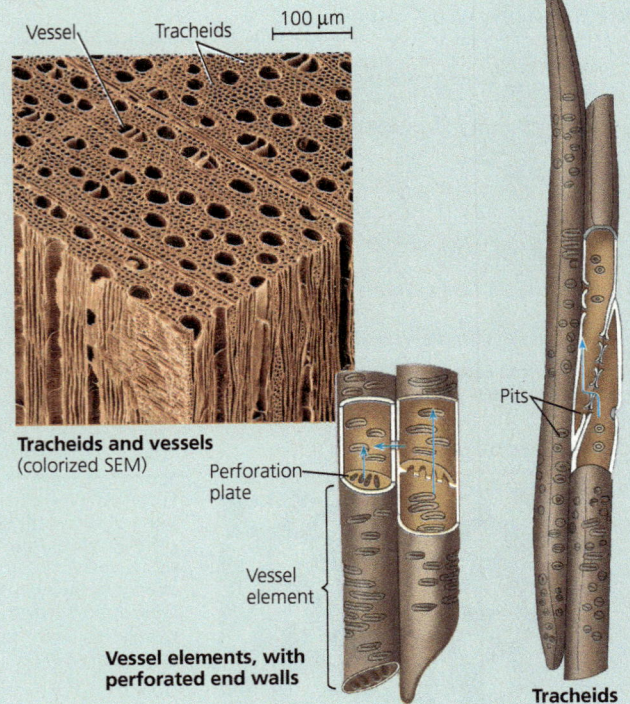

Tracheids and vessels
(colorized SEM)

Vessel elements, with
perforated end walls

Tracheids

Sugar-Conducting Cells of the Phloem

Unlike the water-conducting cells of the xylem, the sugar-conducting cells of the phloem are alive at functional maturity. In seedless vascular plants and gymnosperms, sugars and other organic nutrients are transported through long, narrow cells called sieve cells. In the phloem of angiosperms, these nutrients are transported through sieve tubes, which consist of chains of cells called **sieve-tube elements**, or sieve-tube members.

Though alive, sieve-tube elements lack a nucleus, ribosomes, a distinct vacuole, and cytoskeletal elements. This reduction in cell contents enables nutrients to pass more easily through the cell. The end walls between sieve-tube elements, called **sieve plates**, have pores that facilitate the flow of fluid from cell to cell along the sieve tube. Alongside each sieve-tube element is a nonconducting cell called a **companion cell**, which is connected to the sieve-tube element by numerous channels called plasmodesmata (see Figure 6.28). The nucleus and ribosomes of the companion cell serve not only that cell itself but also the adjacent sieve-tube element. In some plants, the companion cells in leaves also help load sugars into the sieve-tube elements, which then transport the sugars to other parts of the plant.

ANIMATION **BioFlix** Visit the Study Area at www.masteringbiology.com for the BioFlix® 3-D Animation called Tour of a Plant Cell.

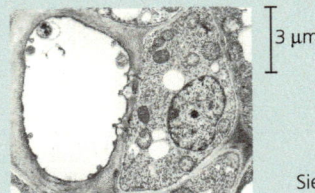

Sieve-tube element (left)
and companion cell:
cross section (TEM)

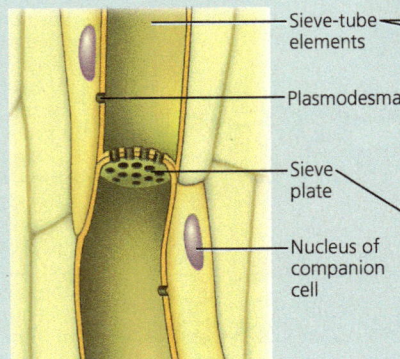

Sieve-tube elements:
longitudinal view

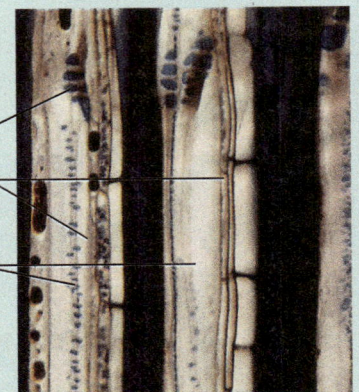

Sieve-tube elements:
longitudinal view (LM)

Sieve plate

Companion cells

Sieve-tube elements

Plasmodesma

Sieve plate

Nucleus of companion cell

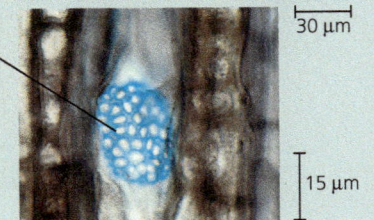

Sieve plate with pores (LM)

Meristems generate cells for primary and secondary growth

How do plant cells and tissues develop into mature organs? A major difference between plants and most animals is that plant growth is not limited to an embryonic or juvenile period. Instead, growth occurs throughout the plant's life, a process known as **indeterminate growth**. At any given time, a typical plant has embryonic, developing, and mature organs. Except for dormant periods, most plants grow continuously. In contrast, most animals and some plant organs—such as leaves, thorns, and flowers—undergo **determinate growth**; that is, they stop growing after reaching a certain size.

Plants are capable of indeterminate growth because they have perpetually undifferentiated tissues called **meristems** that divide when conditions permit, leading to new cells that can elongate. There are two main types of meristems: apical meristems and lateral meristems **(Figure 35.11)**. **Apical meristems**, located at the tips of roots and shoots and in axillary buds of shoots, provide additional cells that enable growth in length, a process known as **primary growth**. Primary growth allows roots to extend throughout the soil and shoots to increase their exposure to light. In herbaceous (non-woody) plants, primary growth produces all, or almost all, of the plant body. Woody plants, however, also grow in circumference in the parts of stems and roots that no longer grow in length. This growth in thickness, known as **secondary growth**, is caused by **lateral meristems** called the vascular

cambium and cork cambium. These cylinders of dividing cells extend along the length of roots and stems. The **vascular cambium** adds layers of vascular tissue called secondary xylem (wood) and secondary phloem. The **cork cambium** replaces the epidermis with the thicker, tougher periderm.

The cells within meristems divide relatively frequently, generating additional cells. Some new cells remain in the meristem and produce more cells, while others differentiate and are incorporated into tissues and organs of the growing plant. Cells that remain as sources of new cells have traditionally been called *initials* but are increasingly being called *stem cells* to correspond to animal stem cells that also perpetually divide and remain undifferentiated. The new cells displaced from the meristem, called *derivatives*, divide until the cells they produce become specialized in mature tissues.

The relationship between primary and secondary growth is clearly seen in the winter twig of a deciduous tree. At the shoot tip is the dormant apical bud, enclosed by scales that protect its apical meristem **(Figure 35.12)**. In spring, the bud sheds its scales and begins a new spurt of primary growth, producing a series of nodes and internodes. Along each growth segment, nodes are marked by scars that were left when leaves fell. Above each leaf scar is an axillary bud or a branch formed by an axillary bud. Farther down the twig are bud scars from the whorls of scales that enclosed the apical bud during the previous winter. During each growing season, primary growth extends the shoots, and secondary growth thickens the parts that formed in previous years.

Although plants grow throughout their lives, they do die, of course. Based on the length of their life cycle, flowering

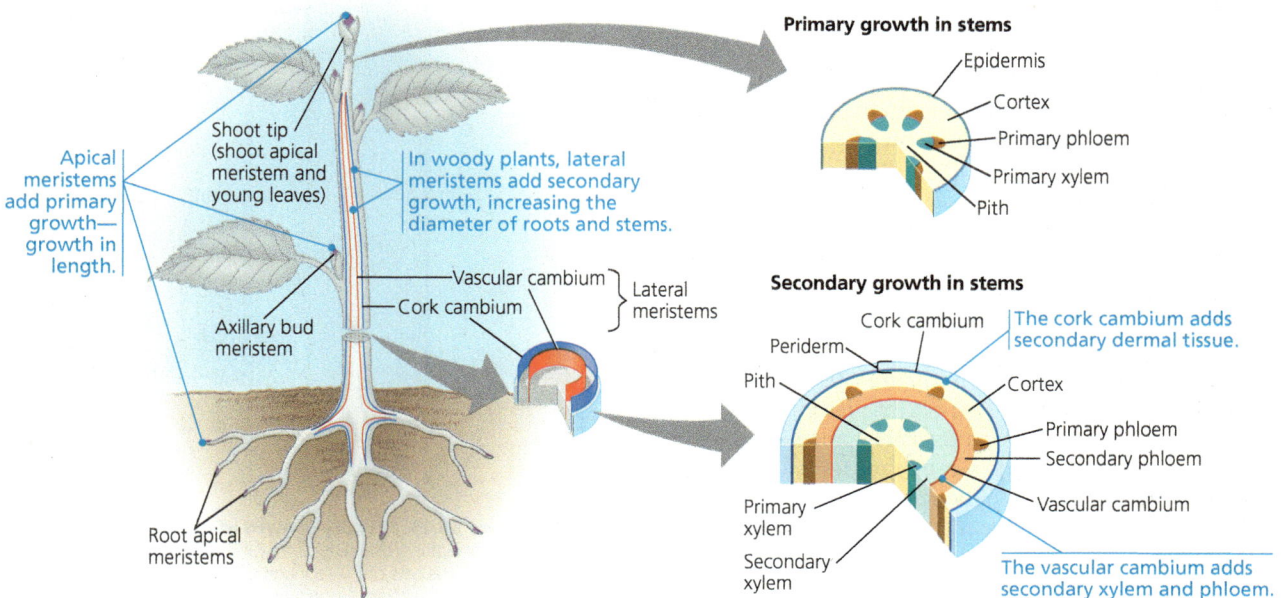

▲ **Figure 35.11 An overview of primary and secondary growth.**

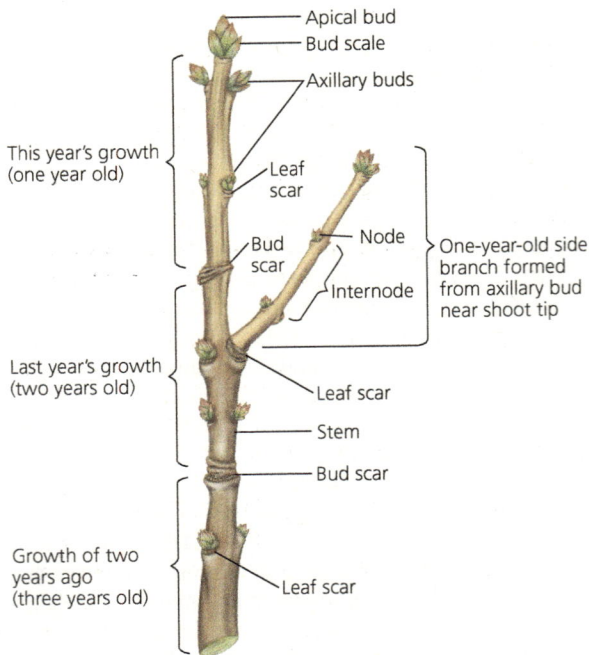

▲ **Figure 35.12 Three years' growth in a winter twig.**

plants can be categorized as annuals, biennials, or perennials. *Annuals* complete their life cycle—from germination to flowering to seed production to death—in a single year or less. Many wildflowers are annuals, as are most staple food crops, including legumes and cereal grains such as wheat and rice. *Biennials*, such as turnips, generally require two growing seasons to complete their life cycle, flowering and fruiting only in their second year. *Perennials* live many years and include trees, shrubs, and some grasses. Some buffalo grass of the North American plains is thought to have been growing for 10,000 years from seeds that sprouted at the close of the last ice age.

CONCEPT CHECK 35.2

1. Distinguish between primary and secondary growth.
2. Cells in lower layers of your skin divide and replace dead cells sloughed from the surface. Are such regions of cell division comparable to a plant meristem? Explain your answer.
3. Roots and stems grow indeterminately, but leaves do not. How might this benefit the plant?
4. **WHAT IF?** Suppose a gardener uproots some carrots after one season and sees they are too small. Carrots are biennials, and so the gardener leaves the remaining plants in the ground, thinking their roots will grow larger during their second year. Is this a good idea? Explain.

For suggested answers, see Appendix A.

CONCEPT 35.3

Primary growth lengthens roots and shoots

As you have learned, primary growth arises directly from cells produced by apical meristems. In herbaceous plants, the entire plant consists of primary growth, whereas in woody plants, only the nonwoody, more recently formed parts of the plant are primary growth. Although the elongation of both roots and shoots arises from cells derived from apical meristems, the primary growth of roots and primary growth of shoots differ in many ways.

Primary Growth of Roots

The tip of a root is covered by a thimble-like **root cap**, which protects the delicate apical meristem as the root pushes through the abrasive soil during primary growth. The root cap also secretes a polysaccharide slime that lubricates the soil around the tip of the root. Growth occurs just behind the tip in three overlapping zones of cells at successive stages of primary growth. These are the zones of cell division, elongation, and differentiation (Figure 35.13).

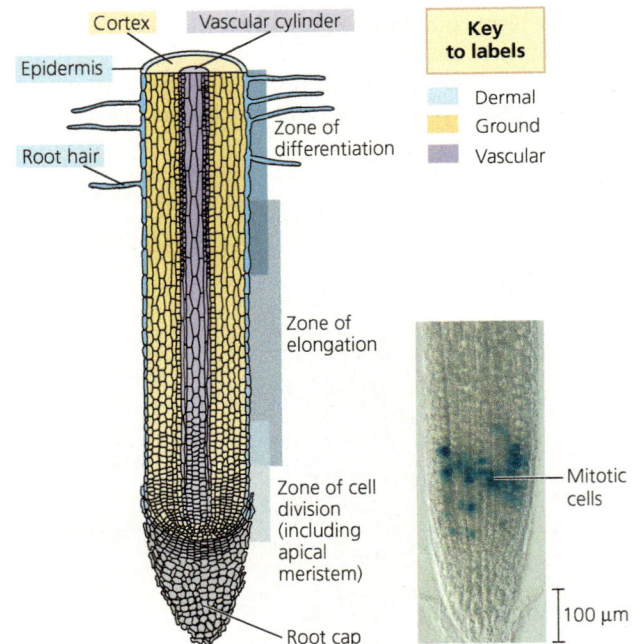

▲ **Figure 35.13 Primary growth of a root.** The diagram depicts the anatomical features of the tip of a typical eudicot root. The apical meristem produces all the cells of the root and the root cap. Most lengthening of the root occurs in the zone of elongation. In the micrograph, cells undergoing mitosis in the apical meristem are revealed by staining for cyclin, a protein that plays an important role in cell division (LM).

The *zone of cell division* includes the root apical meristem and its derivatives. New root cells are produced in this region, including cells of the root cap. Typically, a few millimeters behind the tip of the root is the *zone of elongation*, where most of the growth occurs as root cells elongate—sometimes to more than ten times their original length. Cell elongation in this zone pushes the tip farther into the soil. Meanwhile, the root apical meristem keeps adding cells to the younger end of the zone of elongation. Even before the root cells finish lengthening, many begin specializing in structure and function. In the *zone of differentiation*, or zone of maturation, cells complete their differentiation and become distinct cell types.

The primary growth of a root produces its epidermis, ground tissue, and vascular tissue. **Figure 35.14** shows in cross section the three primary tissue systems in the young roots of a eudicot (*Ranunculus*, buttercup) and a monocot (*Zea*, maize). Water and minerals absorbed from the soil must enter through the root's epidermis. Root hairs, which account for much of this absorption, enhance this process by greatly increasing the surface area of the epidermis.

In angiosperm roots, the stele is a vascular cylinder, consisting of a solid core of xylem and phloem **(Figure 35.14a)**. In most eudicot roots, the xylem has a starlike appearance in cross section and the phloem occupies the indentations between the arms of the xylem "star." In many monocot roots, the vascular tissue consists of a central core of parenchyma cells surrounded by a ring of xylem and a ring of phloem **(Figure 35.14b)**.

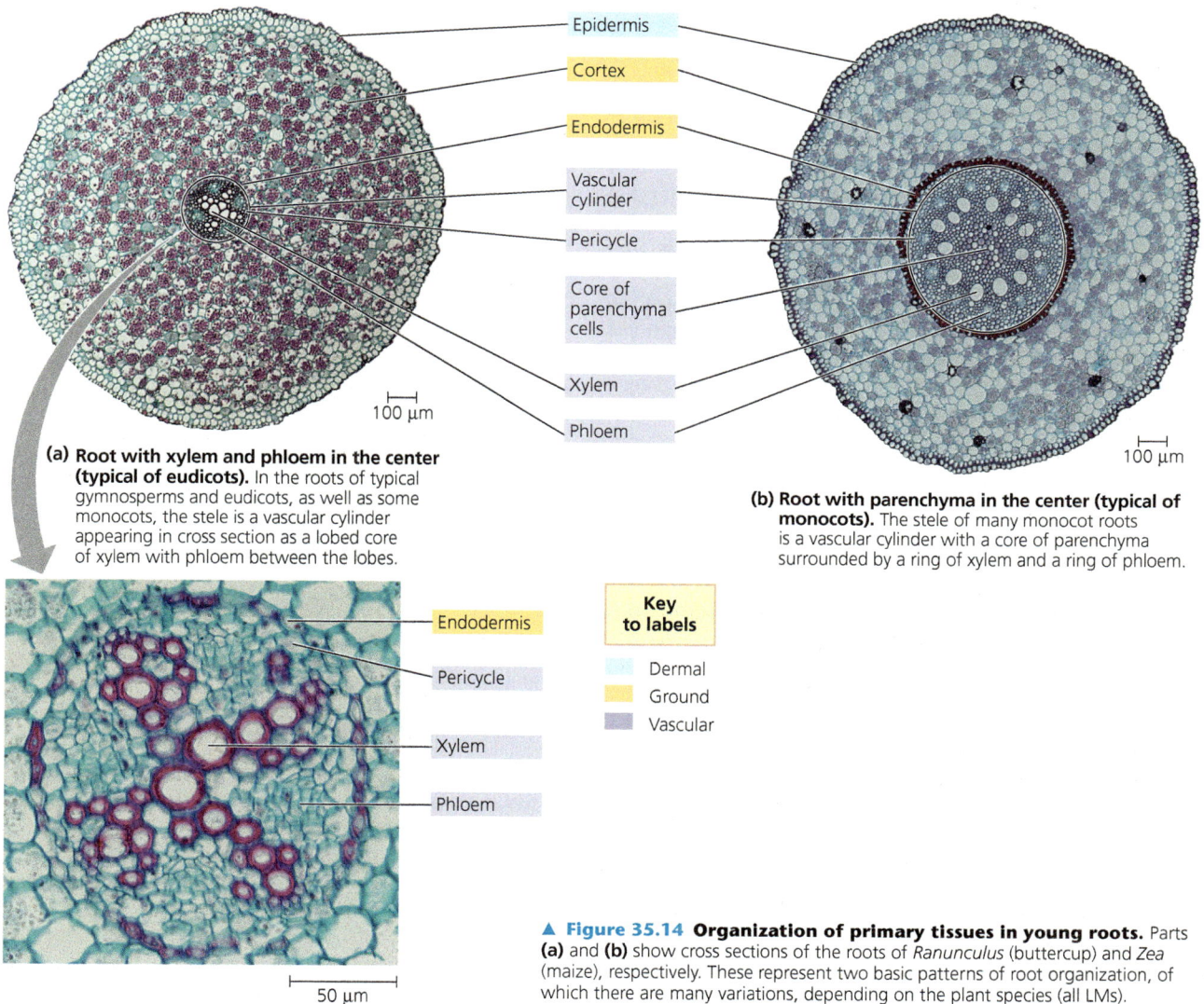

(a) Root with xylem and phloem in the center (typical of eudicots). In the roots of typical gymnosperms and eudicots, as well as some monocots, the stele is a vascular cylinder appearing in cross section as a lobed core of xylem with phloem between the lobes.

(b) Root with parenchyma in the center (typical of monocots). The stele of many monocot roots is a vascular cylinder with a core of parenchyma surrounded by a ring of xylem and a ring of phloem.

Key to labels
Dermal
Ground
Vascular

▲ **Figure 35.14 Organization of primary tissues in young roots.** Parts **(a)** and **(b)** show cross sections of the roots of *Ranunculus* (buttercup) and *Zea* (maize), respectively. These represent two basic patterns of root organization, of which there are many variations, depending on the plant species (all LMs).

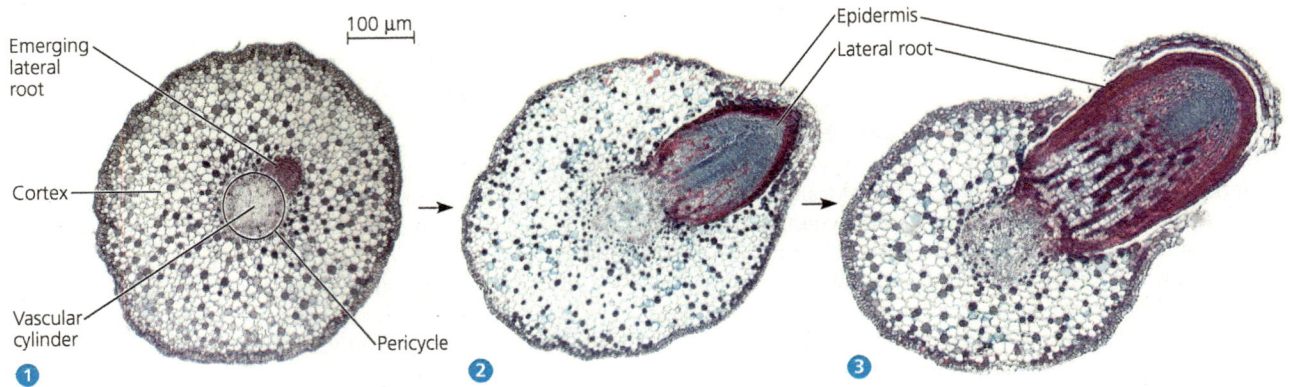

▲ **Figure 35.15 The formation of a lateral root.** A lateral root originates in the pericycle, the outermost layer of the vascular cylinder of a root, and grows out through the cortex and epidermis. In this series of light micrographs, the view of the original root is a cross section, while the view of the lateral root is a longitudinal section.

The ground tissue of roots, consisting mostly of parenchyma cells, fills the cortex, the region between the vascular cylinder and epidermis. Cells within the ground tissue store carbohydrates and absorb water and minerals from the soil. The innermost layer of the cortex is called the **endodermis**, a cylinder one cell thick that forms the boundary with the vascular cylinder. As you will see in Chapter 36, the endodermis is a selective barrier that regulates passage of substances from the soil into the vascular cylinder.

Lateral roots arise from the **pericycle**, the outermost cell layer in the vascular cylinder, which is adjacent to and just inside the endodermis (see Figure 35.14). A lateral root pushes through the cortex and epidermis until it emerges from the established root **(Figure 35.15)**.

Primary Growth of Shoots

A shoot apical meristem is a dome-shaped mass of dividing cells at the shoot tip **(Figure 35.16)**. Leaves develop from **leaf primordia** (singular, *primordium*), finger-like projections along the sides of the apical meristem. Within a bud, young leaves are spaced close together because the internodes are very short. Shoot elongation is due to the lengthening of internode cells below the shoot tip.

Branching, which is also part of primary growth, arises from the activation of axillary buds. Within each axillary bud is a shoot apical meristem. Its dormancy depends mainly on its proximity to an active apical bud. Generally, the closer an axillary bud is to an active apical bud, the more inhibited it is.

In some monocots, particularly grasses, meristematic activity occurs at the bases of stems and leaves. These areas, called *intercalary meristems*, allow damaged leaves to rapidly regrow, which accounts for the ability of lawns to grow following mowing. The ability of grasses to regrow leaves by intercalary meristems enables the plant to recover more effectively from damage incurred from grazing herbivores.

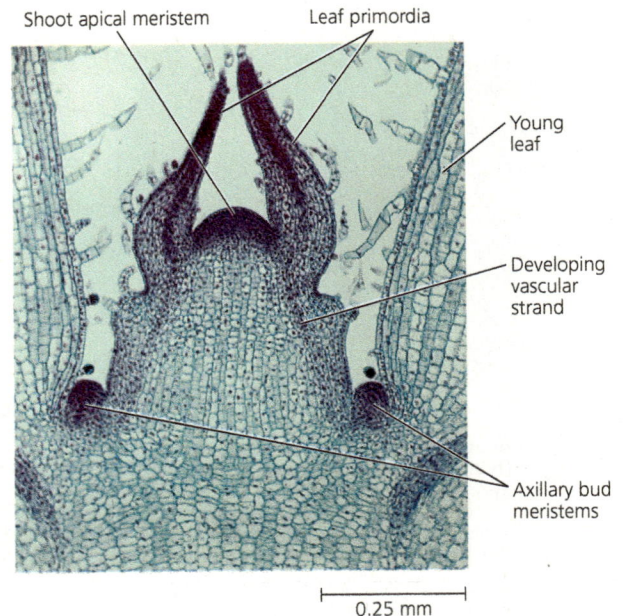

▲ **Figure 35.16 The shoot tip.** Leaf primordia arise from the flanks of the dome of the apical meristem. This is a longitudinal section of the shoot tip of *Coleus* (LM).

Tissue Organization of Stems

The epidermis covers stems as part of the continuous dermal tissue system. Vascular tissue runs the length of a stem in vascular bundles. Unlike lateral roots, which arise from vascular tissue deep within a root and disrupt the vascular cylinder, cortex, and epidermis as they emerge (see Figure 35.15), lateral shoots develop from axillary bud meristems on the stem's surface and disrupt no other tissues (see Figure 35.16). The vascular bundles of the stem converge with the root's vascular cylinder in a zone of transition located near the soil surface.

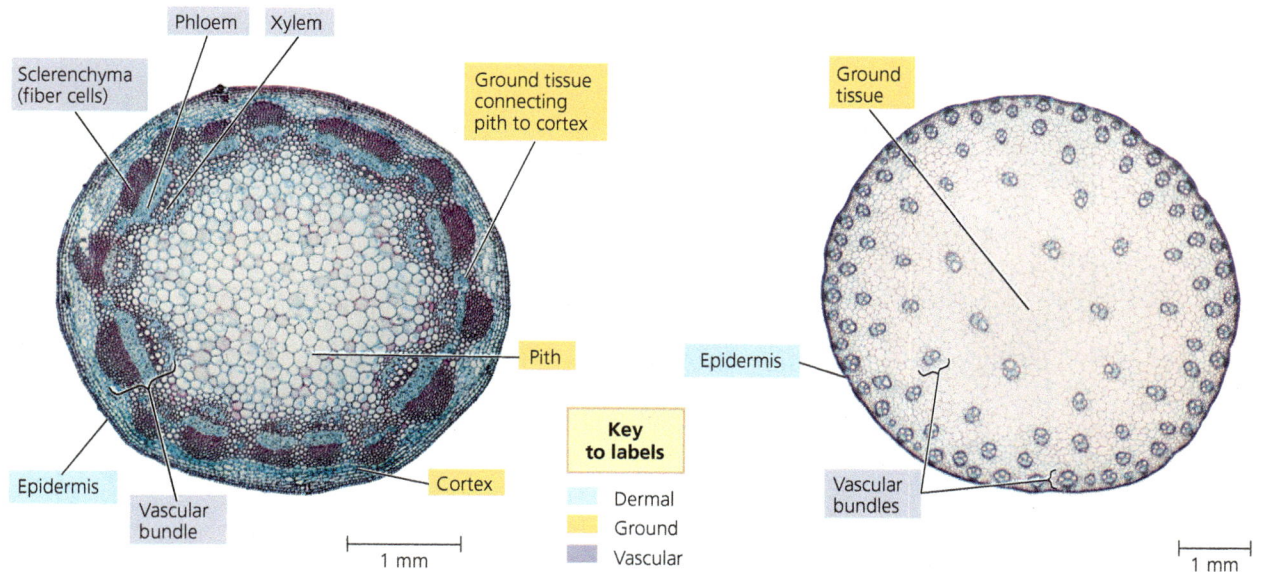

Phloem   Xylem

Sclerenchyma
(fiber cells)

Ground tissue
connecting
pith to cortex

Pith

Epidermis

Vascular
bundle

Cortex

**Key
to labels**

Dermal

Ground

Vascular

1 mm

**(a) Cross section of stem with vascular bundles forming a
ring (typical of eudicots).** Ground tissue toward the
inside is called pith, and ground tissue toward the outside is
called cortex (LM).

Ground
tissue

Epidermis

Vascular
bundles

1 mm

**(b) Cross section of stem with scattered vascular bundles
(typical of monocots).** In such an arrangement, ground tissue is
not partitioned into pith and cortex (LM).

▲ **Figure 35.17 Organization of primary tissues in young stems.**

? *Why aren't the terms* pith *and* cortex *used to describe the ground tissue of monocot stems?*

In most eudicot species, the vascular tissue consists of vascular bundles arranged in a ring **(Figure 35.17a)**. The xylem in each vascular bundle is adjacent to the pith, and the phloem in each bundle is adjacent to the cortex. In most monocot stems, the vascular bundles are scattered throughout the ground tissue rather than forming a ring **(Figure 35.17b)**. In the stems of both monocots and eudicots, the ground tissue consists mostly of parenchyma cells. However, collenchyma cells just beneath the epidermis strengthen many stems. Sclerenchyma cells, especially fiber cells, also provide support in those parts of the stems that are no longer elongating.

Tissue Organization of Leaves

Figure 35.18 provides an overview of leaf structure. The epidermis is interrupted by pores called **stomata** (singular, *stoma*), which allow exchange of CO_2 and O_2 between the surrounding air and the photosynthetic cells inside the leaf. In addition to regulating CO_2 uptake for photosynthesis, stomata are major avenues for the evaporative loss of water. The term *stoma* can refer to the stomatal pore or to the entire stomatal complex consisting of a pore flanked by two **guard cells**, which regulate the opening and closing of the pore. We'll discuss stomata in detail in Chapter 36.

The ground tissue of a leaf, a region called the **mesophyll** (from the Greek *mesos*, middle, and *phyll*, leaf), is sandwiched

between the upper and lower epidermal layers. Mesophyll consists mainly of parenchyma cells specialized for photosynthesis. The mesophylls of many eudicots have two distinct layers: palisade mesophyll and spongy mesophyll. *Palisade mesophyll* consists of one or more layers of elongated parenchyma cells on the upper part of the leaf. *Spongy mesophyll* is below the palisade mesophyll. These parenchyma cells are more loosely arranged, with a labyrinth of air spaces through which CO_2 and oxygen circulate around the cells and up to the palisade region. The air spaces are particularly large in the vicinity of stomata, where CO_2 is taken up from the outside air and O_2 is discharged.

The vascular tissue of each leaf is continuous with the vascular tissue of the stem. Veins subdivide repeatedly and branch throughout the mesophyll. This network brings xylem and phloem into close contact with the photosynthetic tissue, which obtains water and minerals from the xylem and loads its sugars and other organic products into the phloem for transport to other parts of the plant. The vascular structure also functions as a framework that reinforces the shape of the leaf. Each vein is enclosed by a protective *bundle sheath*, consisting of one or more layers of cells, usually parenchyma cells. Bundle sheath cells are particularly prominent in leaves of plant species that undergo C_4 photosynthesis (see Chapter 10).

▼ **Figure 35.18 Leaf anatomy.**

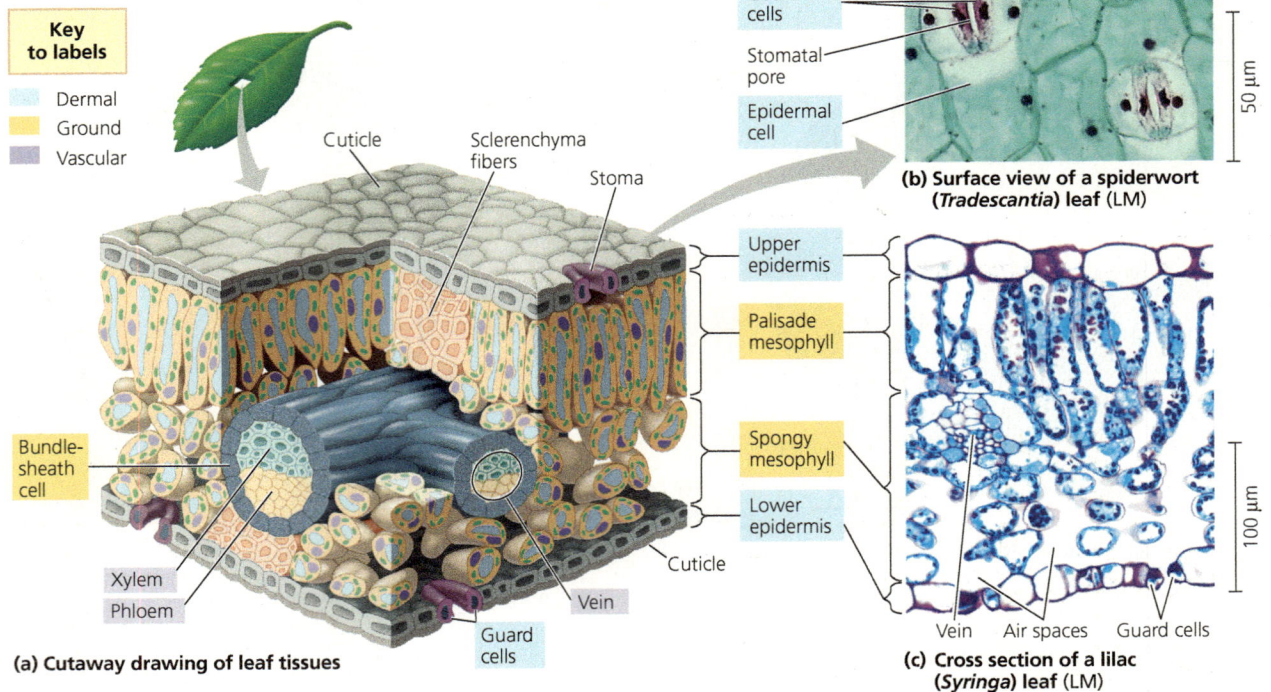

Key to labels

- Dermal
- Ground
- Vascular

Cuticle
Sclerenchyma fibers
Stoma

Bundle-sheath cell

Xylem
Phloem

Guard cells

(a) Cutaway drawing of leaf tissues

Guard cells
Stomatal pore
Epidermal cell

(b) Surface view of a spiderwort (*Tradescantia*) leaf (LM)

50 µm

Upper epidermis
Palisade mesophyll
Spongy mesophyll
Lower epidermis
Cuticle

Vein   Air spaces   Guard cells

(c) Cross section of a lilac (*Syringa*) leaf (LM)

100 µm

CONCEPT CHECK 35.3

1. Contrast primary growth in roots and shoots.
2. **WHAT IF?** If a plant species has vertically oriented leaves, would you expect its mesophyll to be divided into spongy and palisade layers? Explain.
3. **MAKE CONNECTIONS** How are root hairs and microvilli analogous structures? (See Figure 6.8 on p. 146 and the discussion of analogy on p. 586 of Concept 26.2.)

For suggested answers, see Appendix A.

CONCEPT 35.4

Secondary growth increases the diameter of stems and roots in woody plants

As you have seen, primary growth arises from apical meristems and involves the production and elongation of roots, stems, and leaves. In contrast, secondary growth, the growth in thickness produced by lateral meristems, occurs in stems and roots of woody plants, but rarely in leaves. Secondary growth consists of the tissues produced by the vascular cambium and cork cambium. The vascular cambium adds secondary xylem (wood) and secondary phloem, thereby increasing vascular flow and support for the shoots. The cork cambium produces a tough, thick covering consisting mainly of wax-impregnated cells that protect the stem from water loss and from invasion by insects, bacteria, and fungi. All gymnosperm species and many eudicot species undergo secondary growth, but it is rare in monocots.

In woody plants, primary growth and secondary growth occur simultaneously. As primary growth adds leaves and lengthens stems and roots in the younger regions of a plant, secondary growth thickens stems and roots in older regions where primary growth has stopped. The process is similar in shoots and roots. **Figure 35.19**, on the next page, provides an overview of growth in a woody stem.

The Vascular Cambium and Secondary Vascular Tissue

The vascular cambium is a cylinder of meristematic cells, often only one cell thick. It increases in circumference and also adds layers of secondary xylem to its interior and secondary phloem to its exterior. Each layer has a larger diameter than the previous layer (see Figure 35.19). In this way, the vascular cambium thickens roots and stems.

In a typical woody stem, the vascular cambium consists of a continuous cylinder of undifferentiated parenchyma cells, located outside the pith and primary xylem and to the inside of the cortex and primary phloem. In a typical woody root, the vascular cambium forms to the exterior of the primary xylem and interior to the primary phloem and pericycle.

(a) Primary and secondary growth in a two-year-old woody stem

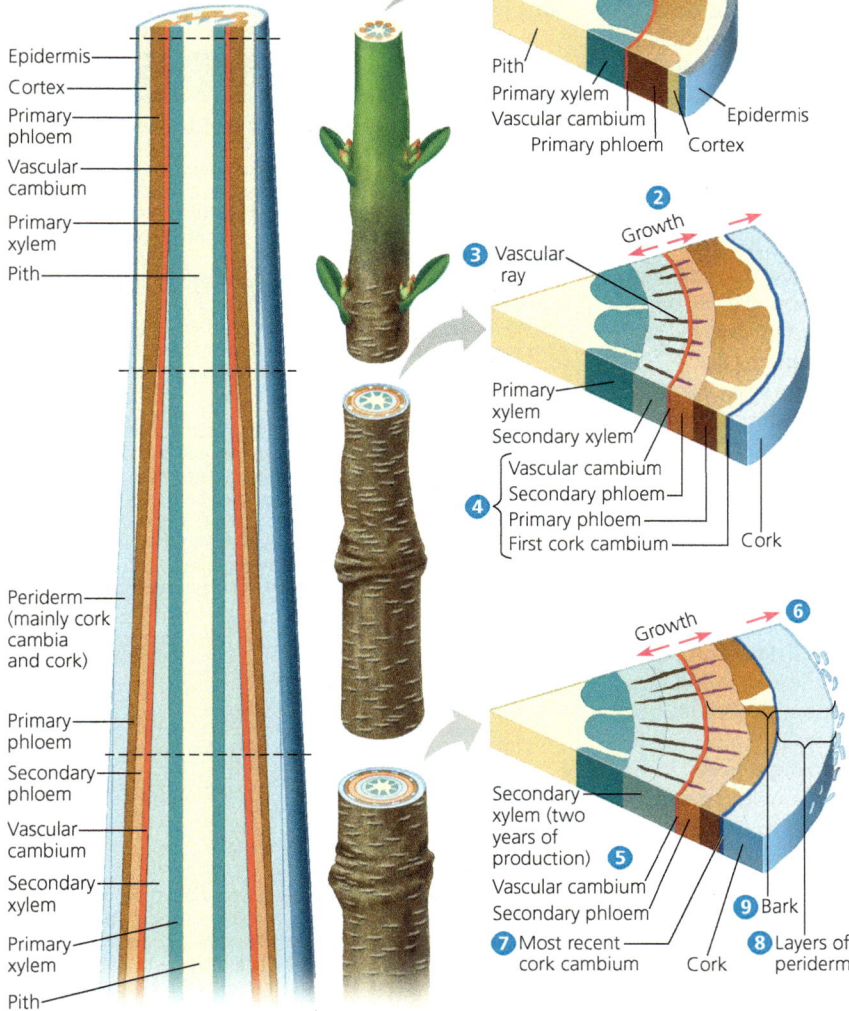

Epidermis

Cortex

Primary phloem

Vascular cambium

Primary xylem

Pith

Periderm (mainly cork cambia and cork)

Primary phloem

Secondary phloem

Vascular cambium

Secondary xylem

Primary xylem

Pith

Pith
Primary xylem
Vascular cambium
Primary phloem
Epidermis
Cortex

2 Growth

3 Vascular ray

Primary xylem
Secondary xylem
Vascular cambium
Secondary phloem
Primary phloem
First cork cambium
Cork

Growth **6**

Secondary xylem (two years of production) **5**
Vascular cambium
Secondary phloem
7 Most recent cork cambium
Cork
9 Bark
8 Layers of periderm

1 Primary growth from the activity of the apical meristem is nearing completion. The vascular cambium has just formed.

2 Although primary growth continues in the apical bud, only secondary growth occurs in this region. The stem thickens as the vascular cambium forms secondary xylem to the inside and secondary phloem to the outside.

3 Some initials of the vascular cambium give rise to vascular rays (see next page).

4 As the vascular cambium's diameter increases, the secondary phloem and other tissues external to the cambium can't keep pace because their cells no longer divide. As a result, these tissues, including the epidermis, will eventually rupture. A second lateral meristem, the cork cambium, develops from parenchyma cells in the cortex. The cork cambium produces cork cells, which replace the epidermis.

5 In year 2 of secondary growth, the vascular cambium produces more secondary xylem and phloem, and the cork cambium produces more cork.

6 As the stem's diameter increases, the outermost tissues exterior to the cork cambium rupture and are sloughed off.

7 In many cases, the cork cambium re-forms deeper in the cortex. When none of the cortex is left, the cambium develops from phloem parenchyma cells.

8 Each cork cambium and the tissues it produces form a layer of periderm.

9 Bark consists of all tissues exterior to the vascular cambium.

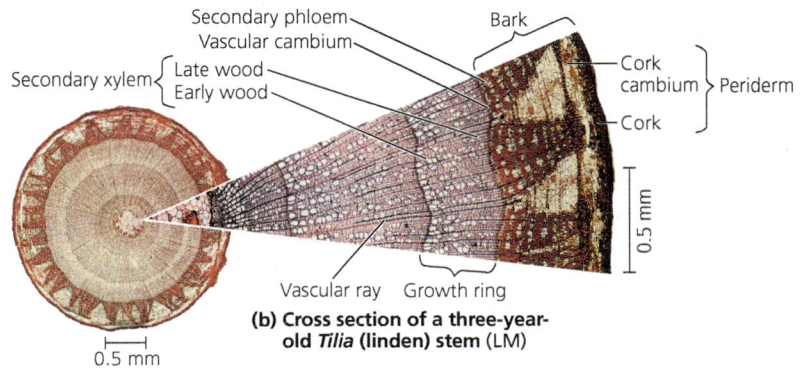

Secondary phloem
Vascular cambium
Bark
Secondary xylem { Late wood / Early wood
Cork cambium } Periderm
Cork
Vascular ray   Growth ring
0.5 mm

(b) Cross section of a three-year-old *Tilia* (linden) stem (LM)

0.5 mm

▲ **Figure 35.19 Primary and secondary growth of a woody stem.** The progress of secondary growth can be tracked by examining the sections through sequentially older parts of the stem.

? *How does the vascular cambium cause some tissues to rupture?*

Viewed in cross section, the vascular cambium appears as a ring of initials (stem cells). As these meristematic cells divide, they increase the circumference of the vascular cambium and also add secondary xylem to the inside of the cambium and secondary phloem to the outside (Figure 35.20). Some initials are elongated and are oriented with their long axis parallel to the axis of the stem or root. They produce cells such as the tracheids, vessel elements, and fibers of the xylem, as well as the sieve-tube elements, companion cells, axially oriented parenchyma, and fibers of the phloem. The other initials are shorter and are oriented perpendicular to the axis of the stem or root. They produce *vascular rays*—radial files of mostly parenchyma cells that connect the secondary xylem and phloem (see Figure 35.19b). The cells of a vascular ray move water and nutrients between the secondary xylem and phloem, store carbohydrates, and aid in wound repair.

As secondary growth continues over many years, layers of secondary xylem (wood) accumulate, consisting mainly of tracheids, vessel elements, and fibers (see Figure 35.10). Gymnosperms have only tracheids, whereas most angiosperms have tracheids and vessel elements. The walls of secondary xylem cells are heavily lignified and account for the hardness and strength of wood. In temperate regions, wood that develops early in the spring, known as early (or spring) wood, usually consists of secondary xylem cells with relatively large diameters and thin cell walls (see Figure 35.19b). This structure maximizes delivery of water to new leaves. Wood produced during the rest of the growing season is called late (or summer) wood. It is composed of thick-walled cells that do not transport as much water but provide more support.

In temperate regions, the vascular cambium becomes inactive during winter, and after growth resumes in spring, there is a marked contrast between the large cells of the new early wood and the smaller cells of the late wood of the previous growing season. A year's growth appears as a distinct ring in the cross sections of most tree trunks and roots. Therefore, researchers can estimate a tree's age by counting its annual rings. *Dendrochronology* (from the Greek *dendron*, trees) is the science of analyzing tree ring growth patterns. Rings can vary in thicknesses, depending on seasonal growth. Trees grow well in wet and warm years but may grow hardly at all in cold or dry years. Because a thick ring indicates a warm year and a thin ring indicates a cold or dry one, scientists can use ring patterns to study climate changes (Figure 35.21).

▼ Figure 35.21 **RESEARCH METHOD**

Using Dendrochronology to Study Climate

APPLICATION Dendrochronology, the science of analyzing tree rings, is useful in studying climate change. Most scientists attribute recent global warming to the burning of fossil fuels and release of CO_2 and other greenhouse gases, whereas a minority think it is a natural variation. Studying climate patterns requires comparing past and present temperatures, but instrumental climate records span only the last two centuries and apply only to some regions. By examining growth rings of Mongolian conifers dating back to the mid-1500s, G. C. Jacoby and Rosanne D'Arrigo, of the Lamont-Doherty Earth Observatory, and colleagues sought to learn whether Mongolia experienced similar warm periods in the past.

TECHNIQUE Researchers can analyze patterns of rings in living and dead trees. They can even study wood used for building long ago by matching samples with those from naturally situated specimens of overlapping age. Core samples, each about the diameter of a pencil, are taken from the bark to the center of the trunk. Each sample is dried and sanded to reveal the rings. By comparing, aligning, and averaging many samples from the Mongolian conifers, the researchers compiled a chronology. In this way, the trees served as a chronicle of environmental change.

RESULTS

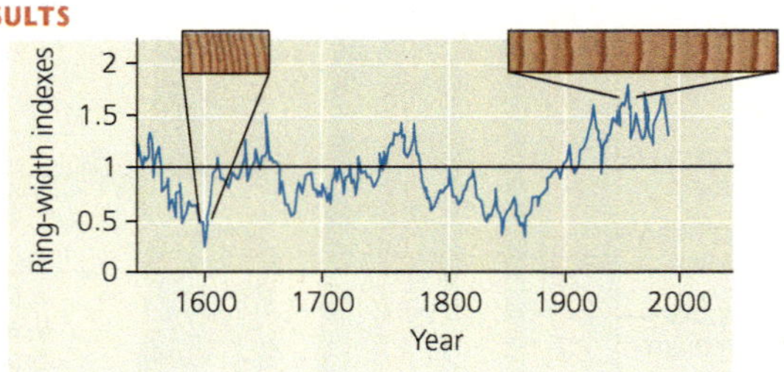

This graph summarizes a composite record of ring-width indexes for the Mongolian conifers from 1550 to 1993. Higher indexes indicate wider rings and higher temperatures. The highest growth period was from 1974 to 1993, and 17 of the 20 highest-growth years occurred since 1946, suggesting unusual warming during the 1900s.

SOURCE G. C. Jacoby et al., Mongolian Tree Rings and 20th-Century Warming, *Science* 273:771–773 (1996).

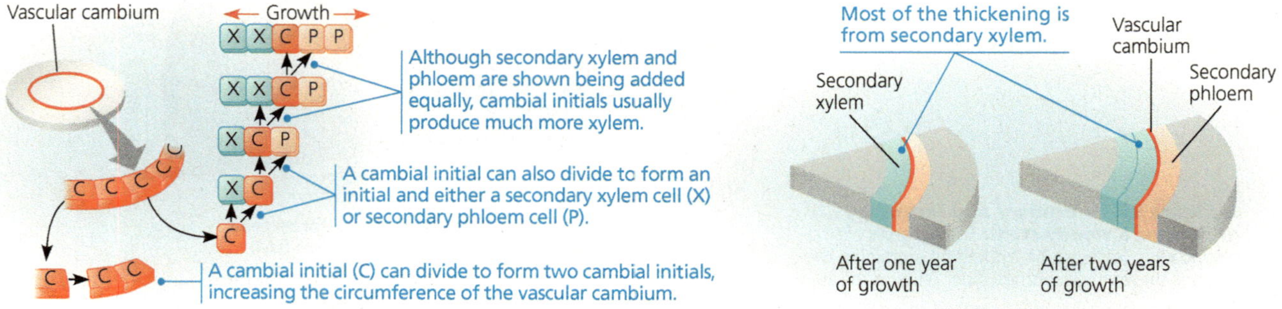

Although secondary xylem and phloem are shown being added equally, cambial initials usually produce much more xylem.

A cambial initial can also divide to form an initial and either a secondary xylem cell (X) or secondary phloem cell (P).

A cambial initial (C) can divide to form two cambial initials, increasing the circumference of the vascular cambium.

▲ Figure 35.20 **Secondary growth produced by the vascular cambium.**

Most of the thickening is from secondary xylem. Secondary xylem. Vascular cambium. Secondary phloem. After one year of growth. After two years of growth.

As a tree or woody shrub ages, the older layers of secondary xylem no longer transport water and minerals (a solution called xylem sap). These layers are called *heartwood* because they are closer to the center of a stem or root **(Figure 35.22)**. The newest, outer layers of secondary xylem still transport xylem sap and are therefore known as *sapwood*. That is why a large tree can survive even if the center of its trunk is hollow **(Figure 35.23)**. Because each new layer of secondary xylem has a larger circumference, secondary growth enables the xylem to transport more sap each year, supplying an increasing number of leaves. The heartwood is generally darker than sapwood because of resins and other compounds that permeate the cell cavities and help protect the core of the tree from fungi and wood-boring insects.

Only the youngest secondary phloem, closest to the vascular cambium, functions in sugar transport. As a stem or root increases in circumference, the older secondary phloem is sloughed off, which is one reason secondary phloem does not accumulate as extensively as secondary xylem.

The Cork Cambium and the Production of Periderm

During the early stages of secondary growth, the epidermis is pushed outward, causing it to split, dry, and fall off the stem or root. It is replaced by two tissues produced by the first cork cambium, a cylinder of dividing cells that arises in the outer cortex of stems (see Figure 35.19a) and in the outer layer of the pericycle in roots. One tissue, called *phelloderm*, is a thin layer of parenchyma cells that forms to the interior of the cork cambium. The other tissue consists of cork cells that accumulate to the exterior of the cork cambium. As cork cells mature, they deposit a waxy, hydrophobic material called *suberin* in their walls and then die. The cork tissue then functions as a barrier that helps protect the stem or root from water loss, physical damage, and pathogens. Each cork cambium and the tissues it produces comprise a layer of periderm.

Because cork cells have suberin and are usually compacted together, most of the periderm is impermeable to water and gases, unlike the epidermis. In most plants, therefore, water and minerals are absorbed primarily in the youngest parts of roots. The older parts of roots anchor the plant and transport water and solutes between the soil and shoots. Dotting the periderm are small, raised areas called **lenticels**, in which there is more space between cork cells, enabling living cells within a woody stem or root to exchange gases with the outside air. Lenticels often appear as horizontal slits, as shown on the stem in Figure 35.19a.

The thickening of a stem or root often splits the first cork cambium, which loses its meristematic activity and differentiates into cork cells. A new cork cambium forms to the inside, resulting in another layer of periderm. As this process continues, older layers of periderm are sloughed off, as you can see in the cracked, peeling bark of many tree trunks.

There is a popular misconception that bark consists only of the protective outer covering of a woody stem or root. Actually, **bark** includes all tissues external to the vascular cambium. Moving outward, its main components are the secondary phloem (produced by the vascular cambium), the most recent periderm, and all the older layers of periderm (see Figure 35.22).

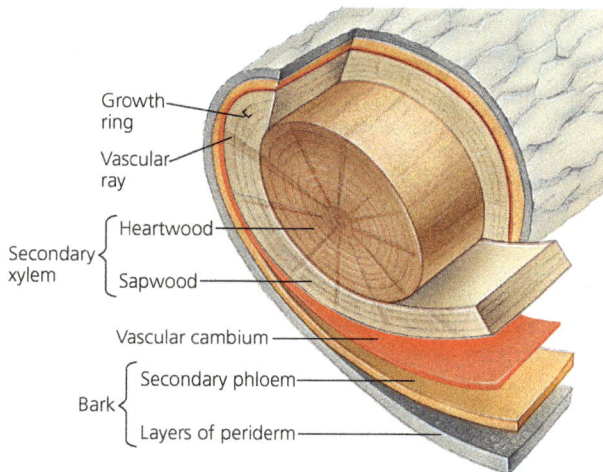

▲ **Figure 35.22 Anatomy of a tree trunk.**

◀ **Figure 35.23 Is this tree living or dead?** The Wawona Sequoia tunnel in Yosemite National Park in California was cut in 1881 as a tourist attraction. This giant sequoia (*Sequoiadendron giganteum*) lived for another 88 years before falling during a severe winter. It was 71.3 m tall and estimated to be 2,100 years old. Though conservation policies today would forbid the mutilation of such an important specimen, the Wawona Sequoia did teach a valuable botanical lesson: Trees can survive the excision of large portions of their heartwood.

Evolution of Secondary Growth

EVOLUTION Although the genome of one tree species, the poplar (*Populus trichocarpa*), has been sequenced, studying the molecular biology of secondary growth is difficult because woody plants take years to develop and require large areas to grow. Surprisingly, some insights into the evolution of secondary growth have been achieved by studying the herbaceous plant *Arabidopsis thaliana*. Researchers have found that they can stimulate some secondary growth in *Arabidopsis* stems by adding weights to the plant. These findings suggest that weight carried by the stem activates a developmental program leading to wood formation. Moreover, several developmental genes that regulate shoot apical meristems in *Arabidopsis* have been found to regulate vascular cambium activity in *Populus*. This suggests that the processes of primary and secondary growth are evolutionarily more closely related than previously thought.

CONCEPT CHECK 35.4

1. A sign is hammered into a tree 2 m from the tree's base. If the tree is 10 m tall and elongates 1 m each year, how high will the sign be after 10 years?
2. Stomata and lenticels are both involved in exchange of CO_2 and O_2. Why do stomata need to be able to close, but lenticels do not?
3. Would you expect a tropical tree to have distinct growth rings? Why or why not?
4. **WHAT IF?** If a complete ring of bark is removed around a tree trunk (a process called girdling), the tree usually dies. Explain why.

For suggested answers, see Appendix A.

CONCEPT 35.5

Growth, morphogenesis, and cell differentiation produce the plant body

As you'll recall, the specific series of changes by which cells form tissues, organs, and organisms is called **development**. Development unfolds according to the genetic information that an organism inherits from its parents but is also influenced by the external environment. A single genotype can produce different phenotypes in different environments. For example, the aquatic plant called the fanwort (*Cabomba caroliniana*) forms two very different types of leaves, depending on whether or not the shoot apical meristem is submerged **(Figure 35.24)**. This ability to alter form in response to local environmental conditions is called *developmental plasticity*. Dramatic examples of plasticity, as in *Cabomba,* are much more common in plants than in animals and may help compensate for plants' inability to escape adverse conditions by moving.

Let's briefly review the three overlapping processes in development: growth, morphogenesis, and cell differentiation. **Growth** is an irreversible increase in size. **Morphogenesis** (from the Greek *morphê*, shape, and *genesis*, creation) is the

▲ **Figure 35.24 Developmental plasticity in the aquatic plant *Cabomba caroliniana*.** The underwater leaves of *Cabomba* are feathery, an adaptation that protects them from damage by lessening their resistance to moving water. In contrast, the surface leaves are pads that aid in flotation. Both leaf types have genetically identical cells, but their different environments result in the turning on or off of different genes during leaf development.

process that gives a tissue, organ, or organism its shape and determines the positions of cell types. Cell **differentiation** is the process by which cells with the same genes become different from one another. We'll examine these three processes in turn, but first we'll discuss how applying techniques of modern molecular biology to model organisms, particularly *Arabidopsis thaliana*, has revolutionized the study of plant development.

Model Organisms: Revolutionizing the Study of Plants

As in other branches of biology, molecular biological techniques and a focus on model organisms such as *Arabidopsis thaliana* have catalyzed a research explosion in the last two decades. *Arabidopsis*, a tiny weed in the mustard family, has no inherent agricultural value but is a favored model organism of plant geneticists and molecular biologists for many reasons. It is so small that thousands of plants can be cultivated in a few square meters of lab space. It also has a short generation time, taking about six weeks for a seed to grow into a mature plant that produces more seeds. This rapid maturation enables biologists to conduct genetic cross experiments in a relatively short time frame. One plant can produce over 5,000 seeds, another property that makes *Arabidopsis* useful for genetic analysis.

Beyond these basic traits, the plant's genome makes it particularly well suited for analysis by molecular genetic methods. The *Arabidopsis* genome, which includes about 27,400 protein-encoding genes, is among the smallest known in plants. Furthermore, the plant has only five pairs

Table 35.1 *Arabidopsis thaliana* **Gene Functions**

Gene Function	Number of Genes	Percent of Total*
Unknown function	9,967	36%
Protein metabolism	3,204	12%
Transport	2,253	8%
Transcription	2,039	7%
Response to stress	1,811	7%
Development	1,627	6%
Environmental sensing	1,627	6%
Cell division and organization	1,201	4%
Signal transduction	1,097	4%
Nucleic acid metabolism	333	1%
Energy pathways	304	1%
Other cellular processes	8,959	33%
Other metabolic processes	8,476	31%
Other biological processes	1,592	6%

Source: The *Arabidopsis* Information Resource, 2010
*The percentages total more than 100% because some genes are listed in more than one category.

of chromosomes, making it easier for geneticists to locate specific genes. Because *Arabidopsis* has such a small genome, it was the first plant to have its entire genome sequenced—a six-year, multinational effort (Table 35.1).

Another property that makes *Arabidopsis* attractive to molecular biologists is that the plant's cells are easy to transform with foreign DNA. The transformation of *Arabidopsis* cells is useful for studying how genes function and interact with other genes. Biologists usually transform plant cells by infecting them with genetically altered varieties of the bacterium *Agrobacterium tumefaciens* (see Figure 20.26). *Arabidopsis* researchers also use a variation of this technique to create a plant with a particular mutation. Studying the effect of a mutation in a gene often yields important information about the gene's normal function. Because *Agrobacterium* inserts its transforming DNA randomly into the genome, the DNA may be inserted in the middle of a gene. Such an insertion usually destroys the function of the disrupted gene, resulting in a "knock-out mutant."

Large-scale projects using this technique are under way to determine the function of every gene in *Arabidopsis*. By identifying each gene's function and tracking every biochemical pathway, researchers aim to determine the blueprints for plant development, a major goal of systems biology. It may one day be possible to create a computer-generated "virtual plant" that enables researchers to visualize which genes are activated in different parts of the plant as the plant develops.

Basic research involving model organisms such as *Arabidopisis* has accelerated the pace of discovery in the plant sciences, including the identification of the complex genetic pathways underlying plant structure. As you read more about this, you'll be able to appreciate not just the power of studying model organisms but also the rich history of plant investigation that underpins all modern plant research.

Growth: Cell Division and Cell Expansion

Cell division enhances the potential for growth by increasing the number of cells, but plant growth itself is brought about by cell enlargement. The process of plant cell division is described more fully in Chapter 12 (see Figure 12.10), and Chapter 39 discusses the process of cell elongation (see Figure 39.8). Here we are more concerned with how these processes contribute to plant form.

The Plane and Symmetry of Cell Division

The new cell walls that bisect plant cells during cytokinesis develop from the cell plate (see Figure 12.10). The precise plane of cell division, determined during late interphase, usually corresponds to the shortest path that will halve the volume of the parent cell. The first sign of this spatial orientation is rearrangement of the cytoskeleton. Microtubules in the cytoplasm become concentrated into a ring called the *preprophase band* (Figure 35.25). The band disappears before metaphase but predicts the future plane of cell division.

It has long been thought that the plane of cell division provides the foundation for the forms of plant organs, but studies of an internally disorganized maize mutant called *tangled-1* have led researchers to question that view. In wild-type maize plants, leaf cells divide either transversely (crosswise) or longitudinally relative to the axis of the parent cell. Transverse divisions are associated with leaf elongation, and longitudinal divisions are associated with leaf broadening. In *tangled-1* leaves, transverse divisions are normal, but most longitudinal divisions are oriented abnormally, leading to cells that are crooked or curved (Figure 35.26). However, these abnormal cell divisions do not affect leaf shape. Mutant leaves grow more slowly than wild-type leaves, but their overall shapes remain normal, indicating that leaf shape does not depend solely on precise spatial control of cell division. In addition,

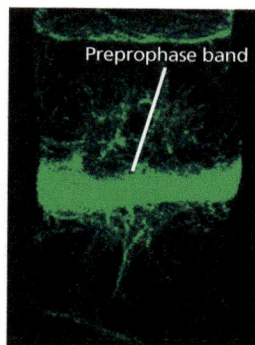

◄ **Figure 35.25 The preprophase band and the plane of cell division.** The location of the preprophase band predicts the plane of cell division. In this light micrograph, the preprophase band has been stained with green fluorescent protein bound to a microtubule-associated protein.

Preprophase band

7 μm

Leaf epidermal cells of wild-type maize

Leaf epidermal cells of *tangled-1* maize mutant

▲ **Figure 35.26 Cell division patterns in wild-type versus mutant maize plants.** Compared with the epidermal cells of wild-type maize plants (left), the epidermal cells of the *tangled-1* mutant of maize (right) are highly disordered. Nevertheless, *tangled-1* maize plants produce normal-looking leaves.

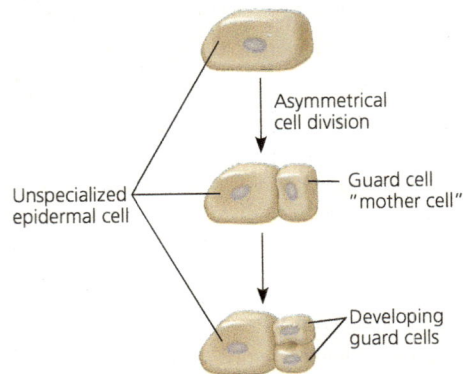

▲ **Figure 35.27 Asymmetrical cell division and stomatal development.** An asymmetrical cell division precedes the development of epidermal guard cells, the cells that border stomata (see Figure 35.18).

recent evidence suggests that the shape of the shoot apex in *Arabidopsis* depends not on the plane of cell division but on microtubule-dependent mechanical stresses stemming from the "crowding" associated with cell proliferation and growth.

Although the *plane* of cell division does not determine the shape of plant organs, the *symmetry* of cell division—the distribution of cytoplasm between daughter cells—is important in determining cell fate. Not all plant cells divide into two equal halves during mitosis. Although chromosomes are allocated to daughter cells equally during mitosis, the cytoplasm may sometimes divide asymmetrically. *Asymmetrical cell division*, in which one daughter cell receives more cytoplasm than the other during mitosis, usually signals a key event in development. For example, the formation of guard cells typically involves both an asymmetrical cell division and a change in the plane of cell division. An epidermal cell divides asymmetrically, forming a large cell that remains an unspecialized epidermal cell and a small cell that becomes the guard cell "mother cell." Guard cells form when this small mother cell divides in a plane perpendicular to the first cell division (Figure 35.27). Thus, asymmetrical cell division generates cells with different fates—that is, cells that mature into different types.

Asymmetrical cell divisions also play a role in the establishment of **polarity**, the condition of having structural or chemical differences at opposite ends of an organism. Plants typically have an axis, with a root end and a shoot end. Such polarity is most obvious in morphological differences, but it is also apparent in physiological properties, including the movement of the hormone auxin in a single direction and the emergence of adventitious roots and shoots from "cuttings." Adventitious roots form within the root end of a stem cutting, and adventitious shoots arise from the shoot end of a root cutting.

The first division of a plant zygote is normally asymmetrical, initiating polarization of the plant body into shoot and root. This polarity is difficult to reverse experimentally, indicating that the proper establishment of axial polarity is a critical step in a plant's morphogenesis. In the *gnom* (from the German for a dwarf and misshapen creature) mutant of *Arabidopsis*, the establishment of polarity is defective. The first cell division of the zygote is abnormal because it is symmetrical, and the resulting ball-shaped plant has neither roots nor leaves (Figure 35.28).

Orientation of Cell Expansion

Before discussing how cell expansion contributes to plant form, it is useful to consider the difference in cell expansion between plants and animals. Animal cells grow mainly by synthesizing protein-rich cytoplasm, a metabolically expensive process. Growing plant cells also produce additional protein-rich material in their cytoplasm, but water uptake typically accounts for about 90% of expansion. Most of this

◀ **Figure 35.28 Establishment of axial polarity.** The normal *Arabidopsis* seedling (left) has a shoot end and a root end. In the *gnom* mutant (right), the first division of the zygote was not asymmetrical; as a result, the plant is ball-shaped and lacks leaves and roots. The defect in *gnom* mutants has been traced to an inability to transport the hormone auxin in a polar manner.

water is packaged in the large central vacuole. Vacuolar sap is very dilute and nearly devoid of the energetically expensive macromolecules that are found in great abundance in the rest of the cytoplasm. Large vacuoles are therefore a "cheap" way of filling space, enabling a plant to grow rapidly and economically. Bamboo shoots, for instance, can elongate more than 2 m per week. Rapid and efficient extensibility of shoots and roots was an important evolutionary adaptation that increased their exposure to light and soil.

Plant cells rarely expand equally in all directions. Their greatest expansion is usually oriented along the plant's main axis. For example, cells near the tip of the root may elongate up to 20 times their original length, with relatively little increase in width. The orientation of cellulose microfibrils in the innermost layers of the cell wall causes this differential growth. The microfibrils do not stretch, so the cell expands mainly perpendicular to the main orientation of the microfibrils, as shown in **Figure 35.29**. As with the plane of cell division, microtubules play a key role in regulating the plane of cell expansion. It is the orientation of microtubules in the cell's outermost cytoplasm that determines the orientation of cellulose microfibrils, the basic structural units of the cell wall.

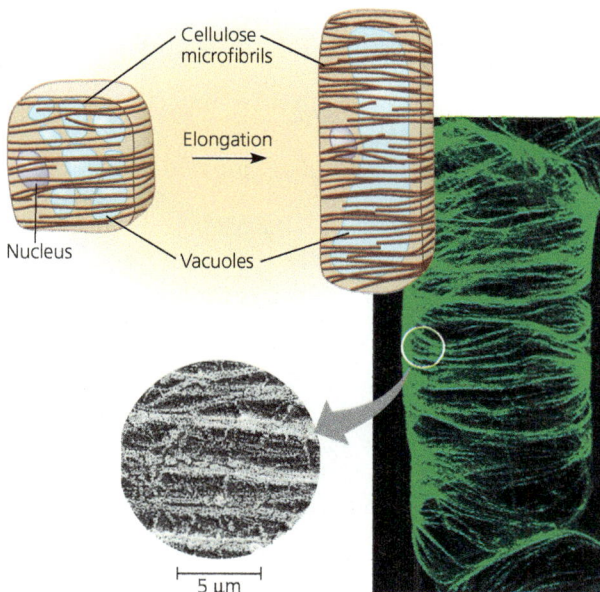

▲ **Figure 35.29 The orientation of plant cell expansion.**
Growing plant cells expand mainly through water uptake. In a growing cell, enzymes weaken cross-links in the cell wall, allowing it to expand as water diffuses into the vacuole by osmosis; at the same time, more microfibrils are made. The orientation of cell growth is mainly in the plane perpendicular to the orientation of cellulose microfibrils in the wall. The orientation of microtubules in the cell's outermost cytoplasm determines the orientation of the cellulose microfibrils (fluorescent LM). The microfibrils are embedded in a matrix of other (noncellulose) polysaccharides, some of which form the cross-links visible in the TEM.

Morphogenesis and Pattern Formation

A plant's body is more than a collection of dividing and expanding cells. During morphogenesis, cells acquire different identities in an ordered spatial arrangement. For example, dermal tissue forms on the exterior, and vascular tissue in the interior—never the other way around. The development of specific structures in specific locations is called **pattern formation**.

Two types of hypotheses have been put forward to explain how the fate of plant cells is determined during pattern formation. Hypotheses based on *lineage-based mechanisms* propose that cell fate is determined early in development and that cells pass on this destiny to their progeny. According to this view, the basic pattern of cell differentiation is mapped out according to the directions in which meristematic cells divide and expand. On the other hand, hypotheses based on *position-based mechanisms* propose that the cell's final position in an emerging organ determines what kind of cell it will become. In support of this view, experimental manipulations of cell positions by surgically destroying certain cells with lasers have demonstrated that a plant cell's fate is established late in development and largely depends on signaling from neighboring cells.

In contrast, cell fate in animals is largely determined by lineage-dependent mechanisms involving transcription factors. The homeotic (*Hox*) genes that encode such transcription factors are critical for the proper number and placement of embryonic structures, such as legs and antennae, in the fruit fly *Drosophila* (see Figure 18.19). Interestingly, maize has a homolog of *Hox* genes called *KNOTTED-1*, but unlike its counterparts in the animal world, *KNOTTED-1* does not affect the proper number or placement of plant organs. As you will see, an unrelated class of transcription factors called *MADS-box* proteins plays that role in plants. *KNOTTED-1* is, however, important in the development of leaf morphology, including the production of compound leaves. If the *KNOTTED-1* gene is expressed in greater quantity than normal in the genome of tomato plants, the normally compound leaves become "super-compound" **(Figure 35.30)**.

▲ **Figure 35.30 Overexpression of a *Hox*-like gene in leaf formation.** *KNOTTED-1* is a gene involved in leaf and leaflet formation. An increase in its expression in tomato plants results in leaves that are "super-compound" (right) compared with normal leaves (left).

Gene Expression and Control of Cell Differentiation

Cells of a developing organism can synthesize different proteins and diverge in structure and function even though they share a common genome. If a mature cell removed from a root or leaf can dedifferentiate in tissue culture and give rise to the diverse cell types of a plant, then it must possess all the genes necessary to make any kind of plant cell (see Figure 20.17). Therefore, cell differentiation depends, to a large degree, on the control of gene expression—the regulation of transcription and translation, resulting in the production of specific proteins.

Although cell differentiation depends on the control of gene expression, the fate of a plant cell is determined by its final position in the developing organ, not by cell lineage. If an undifferentiated cell is displaced, it will differentiate into a cell type appropriate to its new position. One aspect of plant cell interaction is the communication of positional information from one cell to another.

Evidence suggests that the activation or inactivation of specific genes involved in cell differentiation depends largely on cell-to-cell communication. For example, two cell types arise in the root epidermis of *Arabidopsis*: root hair cells and hairless epidermal cells. Cell fate is associated with the position of the epidermal cells. The immature epidermal cells that are in contact with two underlying cells of the root cortex differentiate into root hair cells, whereas the immature epidermal cells in contact with only one cortical cell differentiate into mature hairless cells. Differential expression of a homeotic gene called *GLABRA-2* (from the Latin *glaber*, bald) is required for appropriate root hair distribution **(Figure 35.31)**. Researchers have

demonstrated this by coupling the *GLABRA-2* gene to a "reporter gene" that causes every cell expressing *GLABRA-2* in the root to turn pale blue following a certain treatment. The *GLABRA-2* gene is normally expressed only in epidermal cells that will not develop root hairs.

Shifts in Development: Phase Changes

Multicellular organisms generally pass through developmental stages. In humans, these are infancy, childhood, adolescence, and adulthood, with puberty as the dividing line between the nonreproductive and reproductive stages. Plants also pass through stages, developing from a juvenile stage to an adult vegetative stage to an adult reproductive stage. In animals, the developmental changes take place throughout the entire organism, such as when a larva develops into an adult animal. In contrast, plant developmental stages, called *phases*, occur within a single region, the shoot apical meristem. The morphological changes that arise from these transitions in shoot apical meristem activity are called **phase changes**. During the transition from a juvenile phase to an adult phase, the most obvious morphological changes typically occur in leaf size and shape **(Figure 35.32)**. Juvenile nodes and internodes

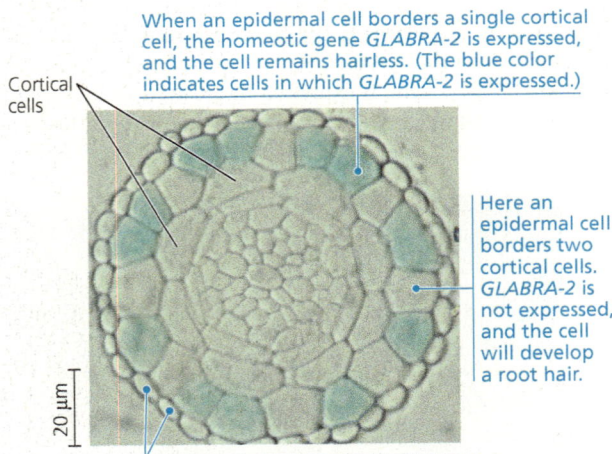

When an epidermal cell borders a single cortical cell, the homeotic gene *GLABRA-2* is expressed, and the cell remains hairless. (The blue color indicates cells in which *GLABRA-2* is expressed.)

Cortical cells

Here an epidermal cell borders two cortical cells. *GLABRA-2* is not expressed, and the cell will develop a root hair.

20 μm

The root cap cells external to the epidermal layer will be sloughed off before root hairs emerge.

▲ **Figure 35.31 Control of root hair differentiation by a homeotic gene** (LM).

WHAT IF? *What would the roots look like if GLABRA-2 were rendered dysfunctional by a mutation?*

Leaves produced by adult phase of apical meristem

Leaves produced by juvenile phase of apical meristem

▲ **Figure 35.32 Phase change in the shoot system of *Acacia koa*.** This native of Hawaii has compound juvenile leaves, consisting of many small leaflets, and simple mature leaves. This dual foliage reflects a phase change in the development of the apical meristem of each shoot. Once a node forms, the developmental phase—juvenile or adult—is fixed; that is, compound leaves do not mature into simple leaves.

retain their juvenile status even after the shoot continues to elongate and the shoot apical meristem has changed to the adult phase. Therefore, any *new* leaves that develop on branches that emerge from axillary buds at juvenile nodes will also be juvenile, even though the apical meristem of the stem's main axis may have been producing mature nodes for years.

If environmental conditions permit, an adult plant is induced to flower. Biologists have made great progress in explaining the genetic control of floral development—the topic of the next section.

Genetic Control of Flowering

Flower formation involves a phase change from vegetative growth to reproductive growth. This transition is triggered by a combination of environmental cues, such as day length, and internal signals, such as hormones. (You will learn more about the roles of these signals in flowering in Chapter 39.) Unlike vegetative growth, which is indeterminate, floral growth is determinate: The production of a flower by a shoot apical meristem stops the primary growth of that shoot. The transition from vegetative growth to flowering is associated with the switching on of floral **meristem identity genes**. The protein products of these genes are transcription factors that regulate the genes required for the conversion of the indeterminate vegetative meristems to determinate floral meristems.

When a shoot apical meristem is induced to flower, the order of each primordium's emergence determines its development into a specific type of floral organ—a sepal, petal, stamen, or carpel (see Figure 30.7 to review basic flower structure). These floral organs form four whorls that can be described roughly as concentric "circles" when viewed from above. Sepals form the first (outermost) whorl; petals form the second; stamens form the third; and carpels form the fourth (innermost) whorl. Plant biologists have identified several **organ identity genes** belonging to the *MADS-box* family that encode transcription factors that regulate the development of this characteristic floral pattern. Positional information determines which organ identity genes are expressed in a particular floral organ primordium. The result is the development of an emerging floral primordium into a specific floral organ. A mutation in a plant organ identity gene can cause abnormal floral development, such as petals growing in place of stamens **(Figure 35.33)**. Some homeotic mutants with increased petal numbers produce showier flowers that are prized by gardeners.

By studying mutants with abnormal flowers, researchers have identified and cloned three

classes of floral organ identity genes, and their studies are beginning to reveal how these genes function. **Figure 35.34a** shows a simplified version of the **ABC hypothesis** of flower formation, which proposes that three classes of genes direct the formation of the four types of floral organs. According to the ABC hypothesis, each class of organ identity genes is switched on in two specific whorls of the floral meristem. Normally, *A* genes are switched on in the two outer whorls (sepals and petals); *B* genes are switched on in the two middle whorls (petals and stamens); and *C* genes are switched on in the two inner whorls (stamens and carpels). Sepals arise from those parts of the floral meristems in which only *A* genes are active; petals arise where *A* and *B* genes are active; stamens where *B* and *C* genes are active; and carpels where only *C* genes are active. The ABC hypothesis can account for the phenotypes of mutants lacking *A*, *B*, or *C* gene activity, with one addition: Where gene *A* activity is present, it inhibits *C*, and vice versa. If either *A* or *C* is missing, the other takes its place. **Figure 35.34b** shows the floral patterns of mutants lacking each of the three classes of organ identity genes and depicts how the hypothesis accounts for the floral phenotypes. By constructing such hypotheses and designing experiments to test them, researchers are tracing the genetic basis of plant development.

(a) **Normal *Arabidopsis* flower.** *Arabidopsis* normally has four whorls of flower parts: sepals (Se), petals (Pe), stamens (St), and carpels (Ca).

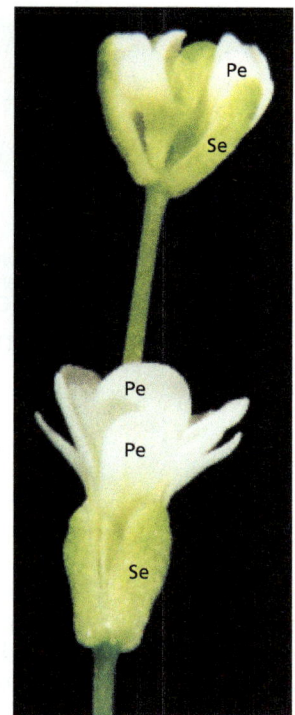

(b) **Abnormal *Arabidopsis* flower.** Researchers have identified several mutations of organ identity genes that cause abnormal flowers to develop. This flower has an extra set of petals in place of stamens and an internal flower where normal plants have carpels.

▲ **Figure 35.33 Organ identity genes and pattern formation in flower development.**

MAKE CONNECTIONS *Review Concept 18.4 on pages 412–419, and provide another example of a homeotic gene mutation that leads to organs being produced in the wrong place.*

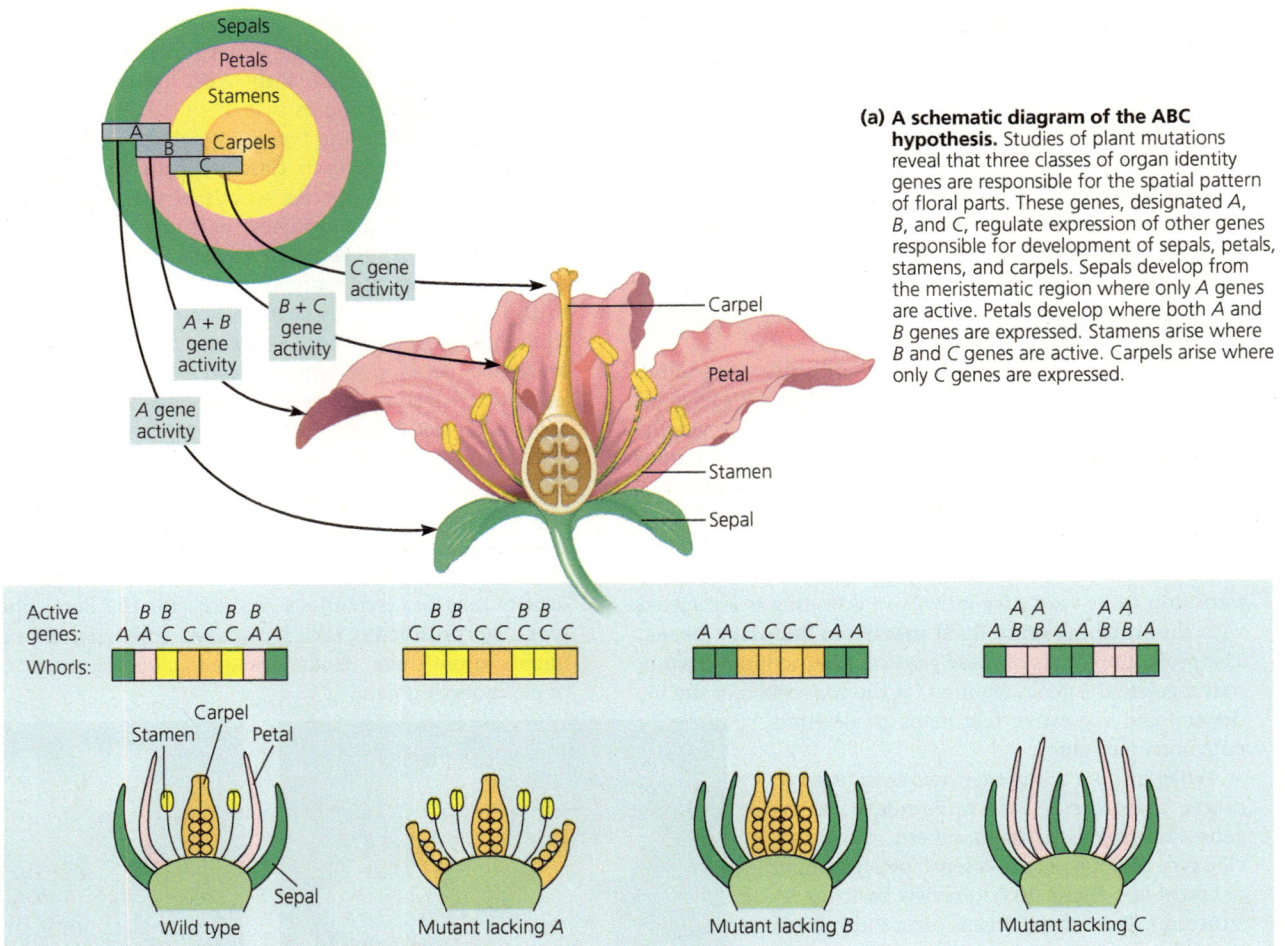

(a) **A schematic diagram of the ABC hypothesis.** Studies of plant mutations reveal that three classes of organ identity genes are responsible for the spatial pattern of floral parts. These genes, designated *A*, *B*, and *C*, regulate expression of other genes responsible for development of sepals, petals, stamens, and carpels. Sepals develop from the meristematic region where only *A* genes are active. Petals develop where both *A* and *B* genes are expressed. Stamens arise where *B* and *C* genes are active. Carpels arise where only *C* genes are expressed.

(b) **Side view of flowers with organ identity mutations.** The phenotype of mutants lacking a functional *A*, *B*, or *C* organ identity gene can be explained by combining the model in part (a) with the rule that if *A* or *C* activity is missing, the other activity occurs through all four whorls.

▲ **Figure 35.34 The ABC hypothesis for the functioning of organ identity genes in flower development.**

WHAT IF? *What would a flower look like if the* A *genes and* B *genes were inactivated?*

In dissecting the plant to examine its parts, as we have done in this chapter, we must remember that the whole plant functions as an integrated organism. In the following chapters, you'll learn more about how materials are transported within vascular plants (Chapter 36), how plants obtain nutrients (Chapter 37), how plants reproduce (Chapter 38, focusing on flowering plants), and how plant functions are coordinated (Chapter 39). As you read further, your understanding of plants will be enhanced by bearing in mind that the plant structures largely reflect evolutionary adaptations to the challenges of a photoautotrophic existence on land.

CONCEPT CHECK 35.5

1. How can two cells in a plant have vastly different structures even though they have the same genome?
2. What are three differences between animal development and plant development?
3. **WHAT IF?** In some species, sepals look like petals, and both are collectively called "tepals." Suggest an extension to the ABC hypothesis that could hypothetically account for the origin of tepals.

For suggested answers, see Appendix A.

35 CHAPTER REVIEW

SUMMARY OF KEY CONCEPTS

CONCEPT 35.1

Plants have a hierarchical organization consisting of organs, tissues, and cells (pp. 784–791)

- Vascular plants have shoots consisting of **stems**, **leaves**, and, in angiosperms, flowers. **Roots** anchor the plant, absorb and conduct water and minerals, and store food. Leaves are attached to stem **nodes** and are the main **organs** of photosynthesis. **Axillary buds**, in axils of leaves and stems, give rise to branches. Plant organs may be adapted for specialized functions.
- Vascular plants have three **tissue systems**—dermal, vascular, and ground—which are continuous throughout the plant. **Dermal tissue** protects against pathogens, herbivores, and drought and aids in the absorption of water, minerals, and carbon dioxide. **Vascular tissues** (**xylem** and **phloem**) facilitate the long-distance transport of substances. **Ground tissues** function in storage, metabolism, and regeneration.
- **Parenchyma cells** are relatively unspecialized and thin-walled cells that retain the ability to divide; they perform most of the plant's metabolic functions of synthesis and storage. **Collenchyma cells** have unevenly thickened walls; they support young, growing parts of the plant. **Sclerenchyma cells**—fibers and sclereids—have thick, lignified walls that help support mature, nongrowing parts of the plant. **Tracheids** and **vessel elements**, the water-conducting cells of xylem, have thick walls and are dead at functional maturity. **Sieve-tube elements** are living but highly modified cells that are largely devoid of internal organelles; they function in the transport of sugars through the phloem of angiosperms.

? *Describe at least three specializations in plant organs and plant cells that are adaptations to life on land.*

CONCEPT 35.2

Meristems generate cells for primary and secondary growth (pp. 792–793)

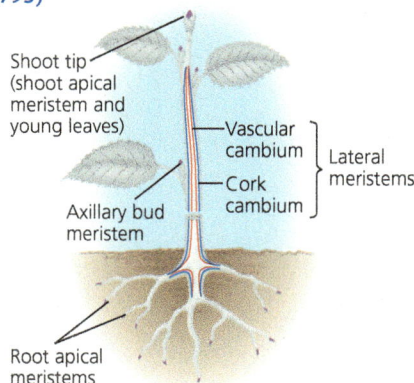

Shoot tip (shoot apical meristem and young leaves)
Vascular cambium
Cork cambium
Lateral meristems
Axillary bud meristem
Root apical meristems

? *Which plant organs originate from the activity of meristems?*

CONCEPT 35.3

Primary growth lengthens roots and shoots (pp. 793–797)

- The root **apical meristem** is located near the tip of the root, where it generates cells for the growing root axis and the **root cap**.
- The apical meristem of a shoot is located in the **apical bud**, where it gives rise to alternating **internodes** and leaf-bearing nodes.

? *How does branching differ in roots versus stems?*

CONCEPT 35.4

Secondary growth increases the diameter of stems and roots in woody plants (pp. 797–801)

- The **vascular cambium** is a meristematic cylinder that produces secondary xylem and secondary phloem during **secondary growth**. Older layers of secondary xylem (heartwood) become inactive, whereas younger layers (sapwood) still conduct water.
- The **cork cambium** gives rise to a thick protective covering called the periderm, which consists of the cork cambium plus the layers of cork cells it produces.

? *What advantages did plants gain from the evolution of secondary growth?*

CONCEPT 35.5

Growth, morphogenesis, and cell differentiation produce the plant body (pp. 801–807)

- Cell division and cell expansion are the primary determinants of **growth**. A preprophase band of microtubules determines where a cell plate will form in a dividing cell. Microtubule orientation also affects the direction of cell elongation by controlling the orientation of cellulose microfibrils in the cell wall.
- **Morphogenesis**, the development of body shape and organization, depends on cells responding to positional information from its neighbors.
- **Cell differentiation**, arising from differential gene activation, enables cells within the plant to assume different functions despite having identical genomes. The way in which a plant cell differentiates is determined largely by the cell's position in the developing plant.
- Internal or environmental cues may cause a plant to switch from one developmental stage to another—for example, from developing juvenile leaves to developing mature leaves. Such morphological changes are called **phase changes**.
- Research on **organ identity genes** in developing flowers provides a model system for studying **pattern formation**. The **ABC hypothesis** identifies how three classes of organ identity genes control formation of sepals, petals, stamens, and carpels.

? *By what mechanism do plant cells tend to elongate along one axis instead of expanding like a balloon in all directions?*

TEST YOUR UNDERSTANDING

(MB) Multiple-choice Self-Quiz questions #1–7 can be found in the Study Area at www.masteringbiology.com.

8.   **DRAW IT**   On this cross section from a woody eudicot, label a growth ring, late wood, early wood, and a vessel element. Then draw an arrow in the pith-to-cork direction.

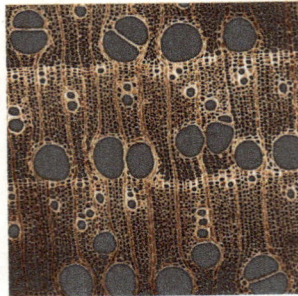

9. **EVOLUTION CONNECTION**

Evolutionary biologists have coined the term *exaptation* to describe a common occurrence in the evolution of life: A limb or organ evolves in a particular context but over time takes on a new function (see Chapter 25). What are some examples of exaptations in plant organs?

10. **SCIENTIFIC INQUIRY**

Grasslands typically do not flourish when large herbivores are removed. In fact, they are soon replaced by broad-leaved herbaceous eudicots, shrubs, and trees. Based on your knowledge of the structure and growth habits of monocots versus eudicots, suggest a reason why.

11. **SCIENCE, TECHNOLOGY, AND SOCIETY**

Hunger and malnutrition are urgent problems for many poor countries, and yet plant biologists in wealthy nations have focused most of their research efforts on *Arabidopsis thaliana*. Some people have argued that if plant biologists are truly concerned about fighting world hunger, they should focus their studies on crops such as cassava and plantain because they are staples for many of the world's poor. If you were an *Arabidopsis* researcher, how might you respond to these arguments?

12. **WRITE ABOUT A THEME**

Structure and Function   In a short essay (100–150 words), explain how the evolution of lignin affected vascular plant structure and function.

For selected answers, see Appendix A.

MasteringBIOLOGY   www.masteringbiology.com

1. MasteringBiology® Assignments:
BioFlix   **Tutorial** Tour of a Plant Cell
Tutorials Primary and Secondary Growth in Plants •
Developmental Biology of Plants
Activities Root, Stem, and Leaf Sections • Plant Growth • Primary and Secondary Growth
Questions Student Misconceptions • Reading Quiz • Multiple Choice • End-of-Chapter

2. eText
Read your book online, search, take notes, highlight text, and more.

3. The Study Area
Practice Tests • Cumulative Test • **BioFlix**   3-D Animations • MP3 Tutor Sessions • Videos • Activities • Investigations • Lab Media • Audio Glossary • Word Study Tools • Art

52

An Introduction to Ecology and the Biosphere

▲ Figure 52.1 **What threatens this amphibian's survival?**

KEY CONCEPTS

52.1 **Earth's climate varies by latitude and season and is changing rapidly**

52.2 **The structure and distribution of terrestrial biomes are controlled by climate and disturbance**

52.3 **Aquatic biomes are diverse and dynamic systems that cover most of Earth**

52.4 **Interactions between organisms and the environment limit the distribution of species**

OVERVIEW

Discovering Ecology

When University of Delaware undergraduate Justin Yeager spent his summer abroad in Costa Rica, all he wanted was to see the tropical rain forest and to practice his Spanish. Instead, he rediscovered the variable harlequin toad (*Atelopus varius*), a species thought to be extinct in the mountain slopes of Costa

Rica and Panama where it once lived (**Figure 52.1**). During the 1980s and 1990s, roughly two-thirds of the 82 known species of harlequin toads vanished. Scientists think that a disease-causing chytrid fungus, *Batrachochytrium dendrobatidis* (see Figure 31.26), contributed to many of these extinctions. Why was the fungus suddenly thriving in the rain forest? Cloudier days and warmer nights associated with global warming appear to have created an environment ideal for its success. As of 2009, the species that Yeager found was surviving as a single known population of fewer than 100 individuals.

What environmental factors limit the geographic distribution of harlequin toads? How do variations in their food supply or interactions with other species, such as pathogens, affect the size of their population? Questions like these are the subject of **ecology** (from the Greek *oikos*, home, and *logos*, study), the scientific study of the interactions between organisms and the environment. Ecological interactions occur at a hierarchy of scales that ecologists study, from single organisms to the globe (**Figure 52.2**).

Ecology's roots are in our basic human interest in observing other organisms. Naturalists, including Aristotle and Darwin, have long studied the living world and systematically recorded their observations. However, modern ecology involves more than observation. It is a rigorous experimental science that requires a breadth of biological knowledge. Ecologists generate hypotheses, manipulate environmental variables, and observe the outcome. In this unit, you will encounter many examples of ecological experiments, whose complex challenges have made ecologists innovators in experimental design and statistical inference.

In addition to providing a conceptual framework for understanding the field of ecology, Figure 52.2 provides the organizational framework for our final unit. In this chapter, we first describe Earth's climate and the importance of climate and other physical factors in determining the location of major life zones on land and in the oceans. We then examine how ecologists determine what controls the distribution and abundance of individual species. The next three chapters investigate population, community, and ecosystem ecology in detail, including approaches for restoring degraded ecosystems. The final chapter explores conservation biology and global ecology as we consider how ecologists apply biological knowledge to predict the global consequences of human activities and to conserve Earth's biodiversity.

CONCEPT 52.1

Earth's climate varies by latitude and season and is changing rapidly

The most significant influence on the distribution of organisms on land and in the oceans is **climate**, the long-term, prevailing weather conditions in a given area. Four physical

▼ **Figure 52.2**

Exploring The Scope of Ecological Research

Ecologists work at different levels of the biological hierarchy, from individual organisms to the planet. Here we present a sample research question for each level of the hierarchy.

Global Ecology

The **biosphere** is the global ecosystem—the sum of all the planet's ecosystems and landscapes. **Global ecology** examines how the regional exchange of energy and materials influences the functioning and distribution of organisms across the biosphere.

◄ How does ocean circulation affect the global distribution of crustaceans?

Landscape Ecology

A **landscape** (or seascape) is a mosaic of connected ecosystems. Research in **landscape ecology** focuses on the factors controlling exchanges of energy, materials, and organisms across multiple ecosystems.

◄ To what extent do the trees lining a river serve as corridors of dispersal for animals?

Ecosystem Ecology

An **ecosystem** is the community of organisms in an area and the physical factors with which those organisms interact. **Ecosystem ecology** emphasizes energy flow and chemical cycling between organisms and the environment.

◄ What factors control photosynthetic productivity in a temperate grassland ecosystem?

Community Ecology

A **community** is a group of populations of different species in an area. **Community ecology** examines how interactions between species, such as predation and competition, affect community structure and organization.

◄ What factors influence the diversity of species that make up a forest?

Population Ecology

A **population** is a group of individuals of the same species living in an area. **Population ecology** analyzes factors that affect population size and how and why it changes through time.

◄ What environmental factors affect the reproductive rate of locusts?

Organismal Ecology

Organismal ecology, which includes the subdisciplines of physiological, evolutionary, and behavioral ecology, is concerned with how an organism's structure, physiology, and behavior meet the challenges posed by its environment.

How do hammerhead sharks select a mate?

▼ Figure 52.3
Exploring Global Climate Patterns

Latitudinal Variation in Sunlight Intensity

Earth's curved shape causes latitudinal variation in the intensity of sunlight. Because sunlight strikes the **tropics** (those regions that lie between 23.5° north latitude and 23.5° south latitude) most directly, more heat and light per unit of surface area are delivered there. At higher latitudes, sunlight strikes Earth at an oblique angle, and thus the light energy is more diffuse on Earth's surface.

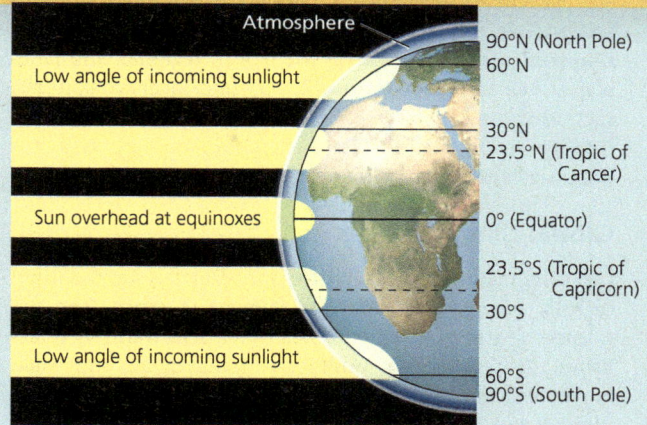

Atmosphere
90°N (North Pole)
60°N
Low angle of incoming sunlight
30°N
23.5°N (Tropic of Cancer)
Sun overhead at equinoxes
0° (Equator)
23.5°S (Tropic of Capricorn)
30°S
Low angle of incoming sunlight
60°S
90°S (South Pole)

Global Air Circulation and Precipitation Patterns

Intense solar radiation near the equator initiates a global pattern of air circulation and precipitation. High temperatures in the tropics evaporate water from Earth's surface and cause warm, wet air masses to rise (blue arrows) and flow toward the poles. The rising air masses release much of their water content, creating abundant precipitation in tropical regions. The high-altitude air masses, now dry, descend (tan arrows) toward Earth around 30° north and south, absorbing moisture from the land and creating an arid climate conducive to the development of the deserts that are common at those latitudes. Some of the descending air then flows toward the poles. At latitudes around 60° north and south, the air masses again rise and release abundant precipitation (though less than in the tropics). Some of the cold, dry rising air then flows to the poles, where it descends and flows back toward the equator, absorbing moisture and creating the comparatively rainless and bitterly cold climates of the polar regions.

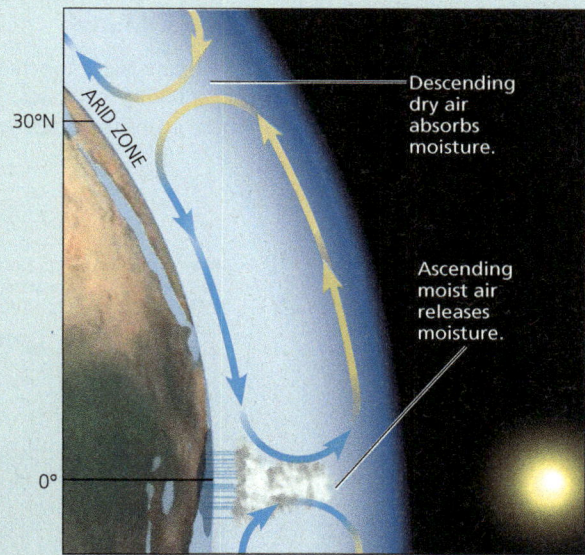

ARID ZONE
30°N
0°
Descending dry air absorbs moisture.
Ascending moist air releases moisture.

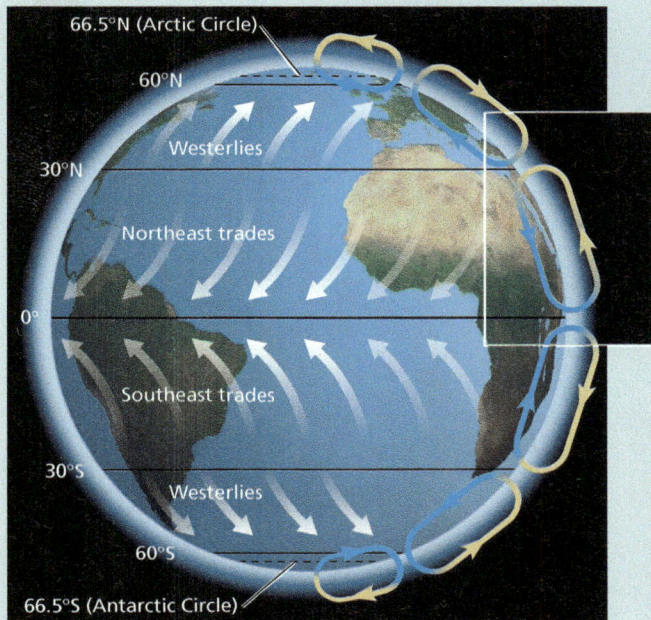

66.5°N (Arctic Circle)
60°N
Westerlies
30°N
Northeast trades
0°
Southeast trades
30°S
Westerlies
60°S
66.5°S (Antarctic Circle)

Air flowing close to Earth's surface creates predictable global wind patterns. As Earth rotates on its axis, land near the equator moves faster than that at the poles, deflecting the winds from the vertical paths shown above and creating the more easterly and westerly flows shown at left. Cooling trade winds blow from east to west in the tropics; prevailing westerlies blow from west to east in the temperate zones, defined as the regions between the Tropic of Cancer and the Arctic Circle and between the Tropic of Capricorn and the Antarctic Circle.

factors—temperature, precipitation, sunlight, and wind—are particularly important components of climate. In this section, we will describe climate patterns at two scales: **macroclimate**, patterns on the global, regional, and landscape level; and **microclimate**, very fine, localized patterns, such as those encountered by the community of organisms that live in the microhabitat beneath a fallen log. First let's examine Earth's macroclimate.

Global Climate Patterns

Global climate patterns are determined largely by the input of solar energy and Earth's movement in space. The sun warms the atmosphere, land, and water. This warming establishes the temperature variations, cycles of air and water movement, and evaporation of water that cause dramatic latitudinal variations in climate. **Figure 52.3** summarizes Earth's climate patterns and how they are formed.

Regional and Local Effects on Climate

Climate patterns can be modified by many factors, including seasonal variation in climate, large bodies of water, and mountain ranges. We will examine each of these factors in more detail.

Seasonality

As described in **Figure 52.4**, Earth's tilted axis of rotation and its annual passage around the sun cause strong seasonal cycles in middle to high latitudes. In addition to these global changes in day length, solar radiation, and temperature, the changing angle of the sun over the course of the year affects local environments. For example, the belts of wet and dry air on either side of the equator move slightly northward and southward with the changing angle of the sun, producing marked wet and dry seasons around 20° north and 20° south latitude, where many tropical deciduous forests grow. In addition, seasonal changes in wind patterns alter ocean currents, sometimes causing the upwelling of cold water from deep ocean layers. This nutrient-rich water stimulates the growth of surface-dwelling phytoplankton and the organisms that feed on them.

Bodies of Water

Ocean currents influence climate along the coasts of continents by heating or cooling overlying air masses that pass across the land. Coastal regions are also generally wetter than inland areas at the same latitude. The cool, misty climate produced by the cold California Current that flows southward

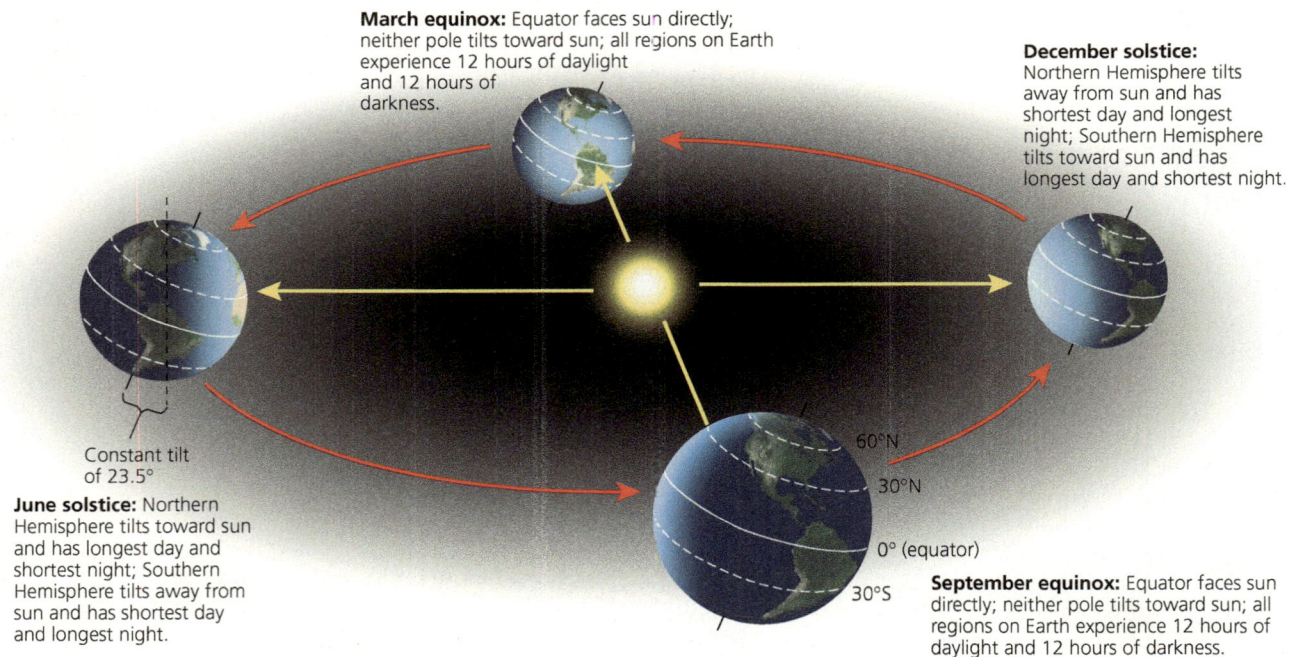

March equinox: Equator faces sun directly; neither pole tilts toward sun; all regions on Earth experience 12 hours of daylight and 12 hours of darkness.

December solstice: Northern Hemisphere tilts away from sun and has shortest day and longest night; Southern Hemisphere tilts toward sun and has longest day and shortest night.

Constant tilt of 23.5°

June solstice: Northern Hemisphere tilts toward sun and has longest day and shortest night; Southern Hemisphere tilts away from sun and has shortest day and longest night.

60°N
30°N
0° (equator)
30°S

September equinox: Equator faces sun directly; neither pole tilts toward sun; all regions on Earth experience 12 hours of daylight and 12 hours of darkness.

▲ **Figure 52.4 Seasonal variation in sunlight intensity.** Because Earth is tilted on its axis relative to its plane of orbit around the sun, the intensity of solar radiation varies seasonally. This variation is smallest in the tropics and increases toward the poles.

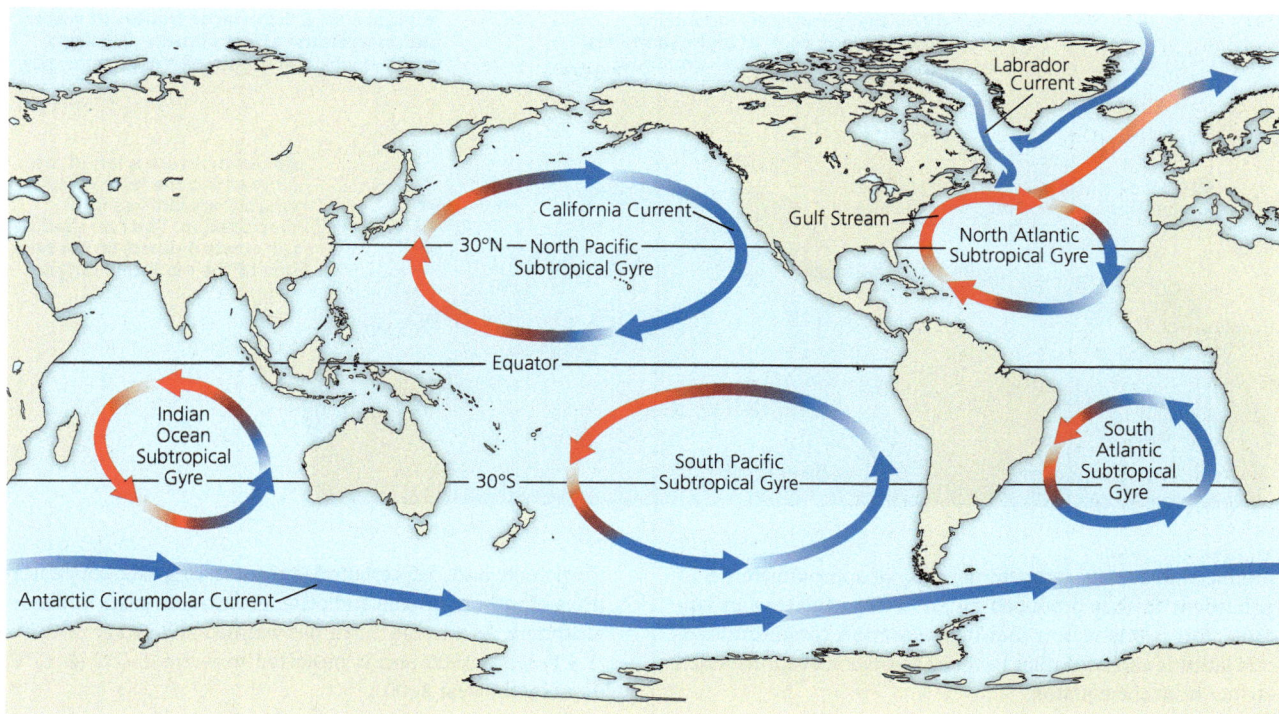

▲ **Figure 52.5 Global circulation of surface water in the oceans.** Water is warmed at the equator and flows north and south toward the poles, where it cools. Note the similarities between the direction of water circulation in the gyres and the direction of the trade winds in Figure 52.3.

along western North America supports a coniferous rain forest ecosystem along much of the continent's Pacific coast and large redwood groves farther south. Conversely, the west coast of northern Europe has a mild climate because the Gulf Stream carries warm water from the equator to the North Atlantic **(Figure 52.5)**. As a result, northwestern Europe is warmer during winter than southeastern Canada, which is farther south but is cooled by the Labrador Current flowing south from the coast of Greenland.

Because of the high specific heat of water (see Chapter 3), oceans and large lakes tend to moderate the climate of nearby land. During a hot day, when land is warmer than the water, air over the land heats up and rises, drawing a cool breeze from the water across the land **(Figure 52.6)**. In contrast, because temperatures drop more quickly over land than over water at night, air over the now warmer water rises, drawing cooler air from the land back out over the water and replacing it with warmer air from offshore. This local moderation of climate can be limited to the coast itself, however. In regions such as southern California and southwestern Australia, cool, dry ocean breezes in summer are warmed when they contact the land, absorbing moisture and creating a hot, arid climate just a few kilometers inland (see Figure 3.5). This

climate pattern also occurs around the Mediterranean Sea, which gives it the name *Mediterranean climate.*

Mountains

Like large bodies of water, mountains influence air flow over land. When warm, moist air approaches a mountain, the air rises and cools, releasing moisture on the windward side of the peak (see Figure 52.6). On the leeward side, cooler, dry air descends, absorbing moisture and producing a "rain shadow." This leeward rain shadow determines where many deserts are found, including the Great Basin and the Mojave Desert of western North America, the Gobi Desert of Asia, and the small deserts found in the southwest corners of some Caribbean islands.

Mountains also affect the amount of sunlight reaching an area and thus the local temperature and rainfall. South-facing slopes in the Northern Hemisphere receive more sunlight than north-facing slopes and are therefore warmer and drier. These physical differences influence species distributions locally. In many mountains of western North America, spruce and other conifers grow on the cooler north-facing slopes, but shrubby, drought-resistant plants inhabit the south-facing slopes. In addition, every 1,000-m increase in elevation

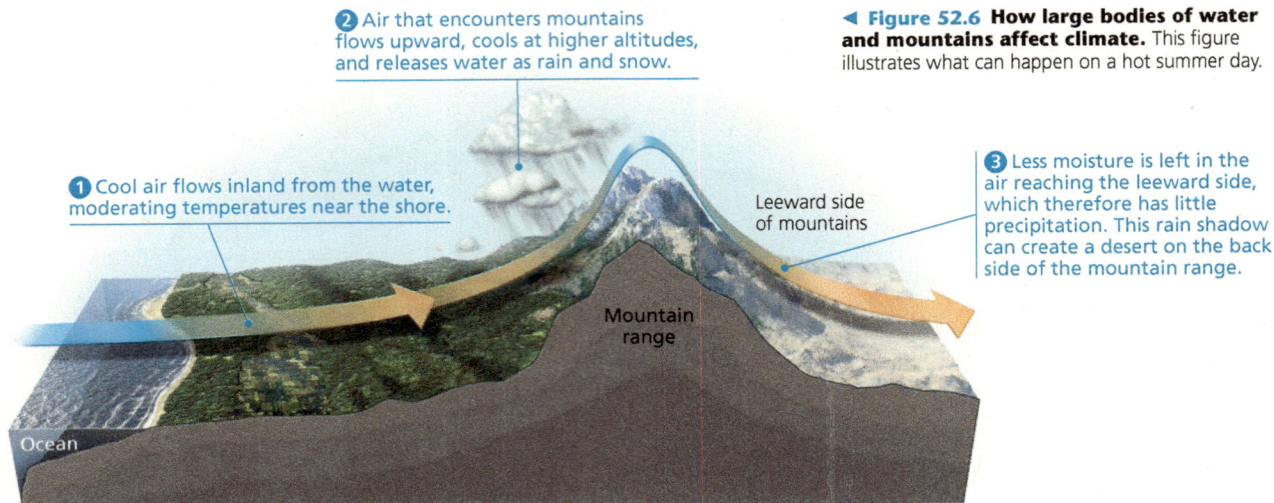

② Air that encounters mountains flows upward, cools at higher altitudes, and releases water as rain and snow.

◀ **Figure 52.6 How large bodies of water and mountains affect climate.** This figure illustrates what can happen on a hot summer day.

① Cool air flows inland from the water, moderating temperatures near the shore.

③ Less moisture is left in the air reaching the leeward side, which therefore has little precipitation. This rain shadow can create a desert on the back side of the mountain range.

Leeward side of mountains

Mountain range

Ocean

produces an average temperature drop of approximately 6°C, equivalent to that produced by an 880-km increase in latitude. This is one reason that high-elevation communities at one latitude can be similar to those at lower elevations much farther from the equator.

Microclimate

Many features in the environment influence microclimate by casting shade, altering evaporation from soil, or changing wind patterns. Forest trees often moderate the microclimate below them. Cleared areas therefore typically experience greater temperature extremes than the forest interior because of greater solar radiation and wind currents that arise from the rapid heating and cooling of open land. Within a forest, low-lying ground is usually wetter than higher ground and tends to be occupied by different tree species. A log or large stone can shelter organisms such as salamanders, worms, and insects, buffering them from the extremes of temperature and moisture. Every environment on Earth is characterized by a mosaic of small-scale differences in **abiotic**, or nonliving, factors, the chemical and physical attributes, such as temperature, light, water, and nutrients, that influence the distribution and abundance of organisms. Later in this chapter, we will also examine how all of the **biotic**, or living, factors—the other organisms that are part of an individual's environment—similarly influence the distribution and abundance of life on Earth.

Global Climate Change

Because climatic variables affect the geographic ranges of most plants and animals, any large-scale change in Earth's climate profoundly affects the biosphere. In fact, such a large-scale climate "experiment" is already under way, a topic we will examine in more detail in Chapter 56. The burning of

fossil fuels and deforestation are increasing the concentrations of carbon dioxide and other greenhouse gases in the atmosphere. As a result, Earth has warmed an average of 0.8°C (1.4°F) since 1900 and is projected to warm 1–6°C (2–11°F) more by the year 2100.

One way to predict the possible effects of future climate change on geographic ranges is to look back at the changes that have occurred in temperate regions since the last ice age ended. Until about 16,000 years ago, continental glaciers covered much of North America and Eurasia. As the climate warmed and the glaciers retreated, tree distributions expanded northward. A detailed record of these changes is captured in fossil pollen deposited in lakes and ponds. (Recall from Chapter 38 that wind and animals sometimes disperse pollen and seeds over great distances.) If researchers can determine the climatic limits of current distributions of organisms, they can make predictions about how those distributions may change with continued climatic warming.

A fundamental question when applying this approach to plants is whether seeds can disperse quickly enough to sustain the range shift of each species as climate changes. Fossil pollen shows that species with winged seeds that disperse relatively far from a parent tree, such as the sugar maple (*Acer saccharum*), expanded rapidly into the northeastern United States and Canada after the last ice age ended. In contrast, the northward range expansion of the eastern hemlock (*Tsuga canadensis*), whose seeds lack wings, was delayed nearly 2,500 years compared with the shift in suitable habitat.

Will plants and other species be able to keep up with the much more rapid warming projected for this century? Ecologists have attempted to answer this question for the American beech (*Fagus grandifolia*). Their models predict that the northern limit of the beech's range may move 700–900 km northward in the next century, and its southern range limit will

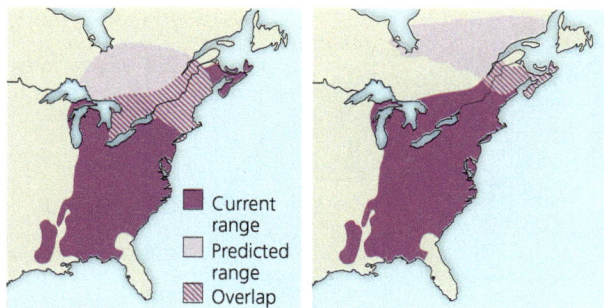

(a) 4.5°C warming over next century

(b) 6.5°C warming over next century

▲ **Figure 52.7 Current range and predicted range for the American beech under two climate-change scenarios.**

? *The predicted range in each scenario is based on climate factors alone. What other factors might alter the distribution of this species?*

shift even more. The current and predicted geographic ranges of this species under two different climate-change scenarios are illustrated in **Figure 52.7**. If these predictions are even approximately correct, the beech's range must shift 7–9 km northward per year to keep pace with the warming climate. However, since the end of the last ice age, the beech has moved at a rate of only 0.2 km per year. Without human help in moving to new habitats, species such as the American beech may have much smaller ranges or even become extinct.

Changes in the distributions of species are already evident in many well-studied groups of terrestrial, marine, and freshwater organisms, consistent with the signature of a warmer world. Ecologist Camille Parmesan of the University of Texas in Austin has studied range changes in European butterfly species, including the silver-washed fritillary (*Argynnis paphia*; see **Figure 52.8**). Parmesan and her colleagues found that the

northern range limits of 22 of the 35 butterfly species studied had shifted farther north by 35–240 km over the time periods for which records exist, in some cases beginning in 1900. And other scientists have reported that a Pacific diatom species, *Neodenticula seminae*, recently has colonized the Atlantic Ocean for the first time in 800,000 years. As Arctic sea ice has receded in the past decade, the increased flow of water from the Pacific has swept these diatoms around Canada and into the Atlantic, where they quickly became established. The observation that many species are on the move in the face of climate change illustrates the importance of climate in determining species distributions, a topic we will explore further in the next section.

CONCEPT CHECK 52.1

1. Explain how the sun's unequal heating of Earth's surface leads to the development of deserts around 30° north and south of the equator.
2. What are some of the differences in microclimate between an unplanted agricultural field and a nearby stream corridor with trees?
3. **WHAT IF?** Changes in Earth's climate at the end of the last ice age happened gradually, taking centuries to thousands of years. If the current global warming happens very quickly, as predicted, how may this rapid climate change affect the ability of long-lived trees to evolve, compared with annual plants, which have much shorter generation times?
4. **MAKE CONNECTIONS** In Concept 10.4 (pp. 245–247), you learned about the important differences between C_3 and C_4 plants. Focusing just on the effects of temperature, would you expect the global distribution of C_4 plants to expand or contract as Earth becomes warmer? Why?

For suggested answers, see Appendix A.

CONCEPT 52.2

The structure and distribution of terrestrial biomes are controlled by climate and disturbance

Throughout this book, you have seen many examples of how climate and other factors influence where individual species are found on Earth (see Figure 30.5, for instance). We turn now to the role of climate in determining the nature and location of Earth's **biomes**, major life zones characterized by vegetation type (in terrestrial biomes) or by the physical environment (in aquatic biomes). We first examine the influence of climate on terrestrial biomes, surveying aquatic systems later in the chapter.

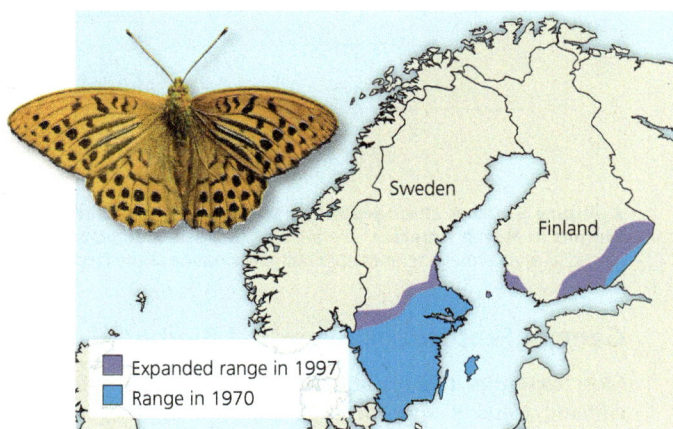

▲ **Figure 52.8 Northward range expansion of the silver-washed fritillary in Sweden and Finland.** This butterfly is one of many European species whose northern range limits have moved farther north in recent decades.

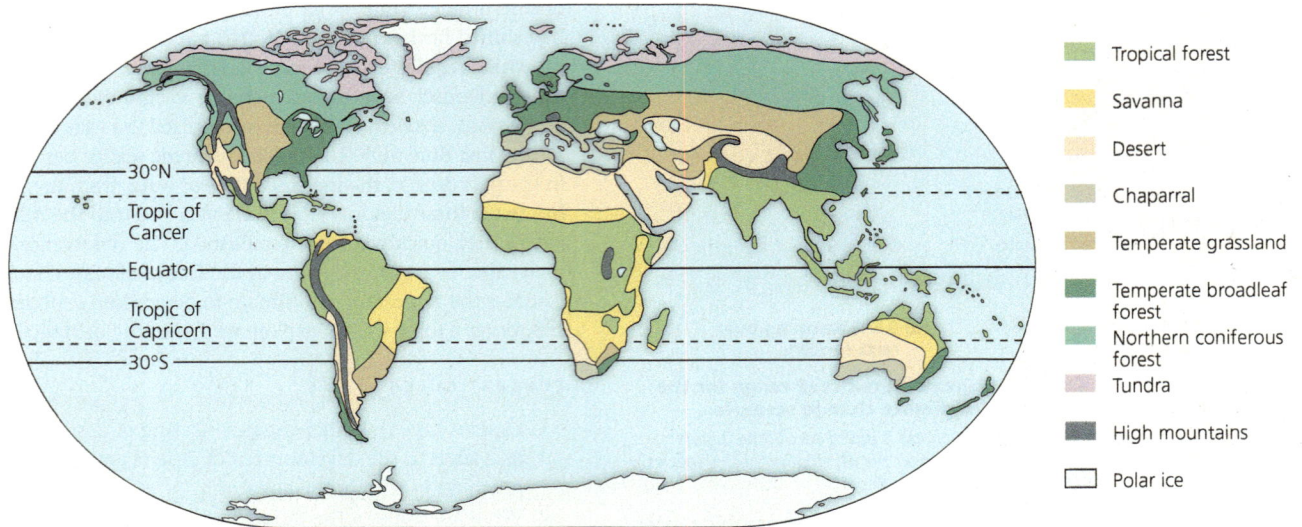

▲ **Figure 52.9 The distribution of major terrestrial biomes.** Although biomes are mapped here with sharp boundaries, biomes actually grade into one another, sometimes over large areas.

Climate and Terrestrial Biomes

Because of the latitudinal patterns of climate described in Figure 52.3, terrestrial biomes show strong latitudinal patterns in where they are found **(Figure 52.9)**. One way to highlight the importance of climate on the distribution of biomes is to construct a **climograph**, a plot of the annual mean temperature and precipitation in a particular region. **Figure 52.10** is a climograph for some of the biomes found in North America. Notice, for instance, that the range of precipitation in northern coniferous and temperate forests is similar but that temperate forests are generally warmer. Grasslands are typically drier than either kind of forest, and deserts are drier still.

Factors other than mean temperature and precipitation also play a role in determining where biomes exist. For example, some areas in North America with a particular combination of temperature and precipitation support a temperate broadleaf forest, but other areas with similar values for these variables support a coniferous forest (see the overlap in Figure 52.10). How might we explain this variation? First, remember that the climograph is based on annual *averages*. Often, however, the *pattern* of climatic variation is as important as the average climate. Some areas may receive regular precipitation throughout the year, whereas other areas may have distinct wet and dry seasons. A similar phenomenon may occur for temperature. In addition, other abiotic characteristics, such as the type of bedrock in an area, may greatly affect mineral nutrient availability and soil structure, which in turn affect the kind of vegetation that can grow.

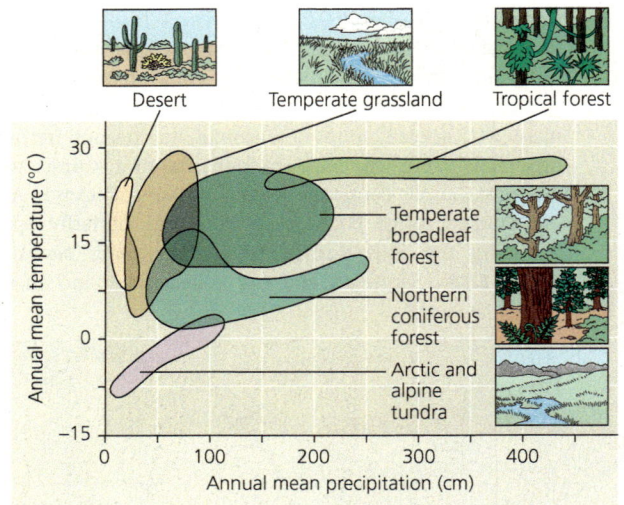

▲ **Figure 52.10 A climograph for some major types of biomes in North America.** The areas plotted here encompass the ranges of annual mean temperature and precipitation in the biomes.

General Features of Terrestrial Biomes

Most terrestrial biomes are named for major physical or climatic features and for their predominant vegetation. Temperate grasslands, for instance, are generally found in middle latitudes, where the climate is more moderate than in the tropics or polar regions, and are dominated by various grass species (see Figure 52.9). Each biome is also characterized by microorganisms, fungi, and animals adapted to that particular environment. Temperate grasslands are usually more likely than temperate forests to be populated by large grazing mammals and to have arbuscular mycorrhizal fungi (see Figure 37.13).

Although Figure 52.9 shows distinct boundaries between the biomes, terrestrial biomes usually grade into each other without sharp boundaries. The area of intergradation, called an **ecotone**, may be wide or narrow.

Vertical layering is an important feature of terrestrial biomes, and the shapes and sizes of plants largely define that layering. In many forests, the layers from top to bottom consist of the upper **canopy**, the low-tree layer, the shrub understory, the ground layer of herbaceous plants, the forest floor (litter layer), and the root layer. Nonforest biomes have similar, though usually less pronounced, layers. Grasslands have an herbaceous layer of grasses and forbs (small broadleaf plants), a litter layer, and a root layer. Layering of vegetation provides many different habitats for animals, which sometimes exist in well-defined feeding groups, from the insectivorous birds and bats that feed above canopies to the small mammals, numerous worms, and arthropods that search for food in the litter and root layers below.

The species composition of each kind of biome varies from one location to another. For instance, in the northern coniferous forest (taiga) of North America, red spruce is common in the east but does not occur in most other areas, where black spruce and white spruce are abundant. As **Figure 52.11** shows, cacti living in deserts of North and South America appear very

similar to plants called euphorbs found in African deserts. But since cacti and euphorbs belong to different evolutionary lineages, their similarities are due to convergent evolution (see Concept 22.3).

Disturbance and Terrestrial Biomes

Biomes are dynamic, and disturbance rather than stability tends to be the rule. In ecological terms, **disturbance** is an event such as a storm, fire, or human activity that changes a community, removing organisms from it and altering resource availability. For instance, frequent fires can kill woody plants and keep a savanna from becoming the woodland that climate alone would support. Hurricanes and other storms create openings for new species in many tropical and temperate forests. Fires and outbreaks of pests, such as pine beetles and spruce budworms, produce gaps in northern coniferous forests that allow deciduous species, including aspen and birch, to grow. As a result of disturbances, biomes often exhibit extensive patchiness, with several different communities represented in a single area.

In many biomes, even the dominant plants depend on periodic disturbance. Natural wildfires are an integral component of grasslands, savannas, chaparral, and many coniferous forests. In North America, fires are no longer common across much of the Great Plains because tallgrass prairie ecosystems have been converted to agricultural fields that rarely burn. Before agricultural and urban development, much of the southeastern United States was dominated by a single conifer species, the longleaf pine. Without periodic burning, broadleaf trees tended to replace the pines. Forest managers now use fire as a tool to help maintain many coniferous forests.

Figure 52.12, on the next four pages, summarizes the major features of terrestrial biomes. As you read about the characteristics of each biome, remember that humans have altered much of Earth's surface, replacing natural communities with urban and agricultural ones. Most of the eastern United States, for example, is classified as temperate broadleaf forest, but little of that original forest remains.

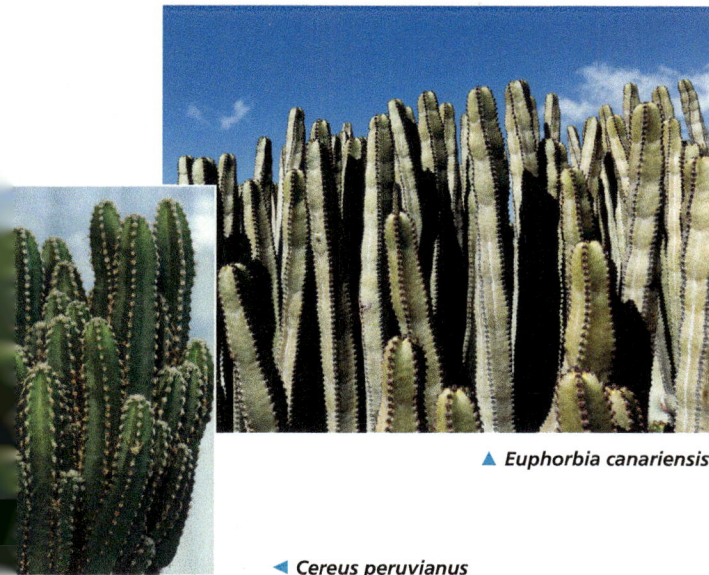

▲ *Euphorbia canariensis*

◄ *Cereus peruvianus*

▲ **Figure 52.11 Convergent evolution in a cactus and a euphorb.** *Cereus peruvianus*, a cactus, is found in the Americas; *Euphorbia canariensis*, a euphorb, is native to the Canary Islands, off the northwest coast of Africa.

CONCEPT CHECK 52.2

1. Based on the climograph in Figure 52.10, what mainly differentiates temperate grassland from temperate broadleaf forest?
2. Identify the natural biome in which you live, and summarize its abiotic and biotic characteristics. Do these reflect your actual surroundings? Explain.
3. **WHAT IF?** If global warming increases average temperatures on Earth by 4°C in this century, predict which biome is most likely to replace tundra in some locations as a result. Explain your answer.

For suggested answers, see Appendix A.

▼ Figure 52.12

Exploring **Terrestrial Biomes**

Tropical Forest

Distribution Equatorial and subequatorial regions

Precipitation In **tropical rain forests**, rainfall is relatively constant, about 200–400 cm annually. In **tropical dry forests**, precipitation is highly seasonal, about 150–200 cm annually, with a six- to seven-month dry season.

Temperature High year-round, averaging 25–29°C with little seasonal variation

Plants Tropical forests are vertically layered, and competition for light is intense. Layers in rain forests include emergent trees that grow above a closed canopy, the canopy trees, one or two layers of subcanopy trees, and layers of shrubs and herbs (small, nonwoody plants). There are generally fewer layers in tropical dry forests. Broadleaf evergreen trees are dominant in tropical rain forests, whereas many tropical dry forest trees drop their leaves during the dry season.

Epiphytes such as bromeliads and orchids generally cover tropical forest trees but are less abundant in dry forests. Thorny shrubs and succulent plants are common in some tropical dry forests.

Animals Earth's tropical forests are home to millions of species, including an estimated 5–30 million still undescribed species of insects, spiders, and other arthropods. In fact, animal diversity is higher in tropical forests than in any other terrestrial biome. The animals, including amphibians, birds and other reptiles, mammals, and arthropods, are adapted to the vertically layered environment and are often inconspicuous.

Human Impact Humans long ago established thriving communities in tropical forests. Rapid population growth leading to agriculture and development is now destroying many tropical forests.

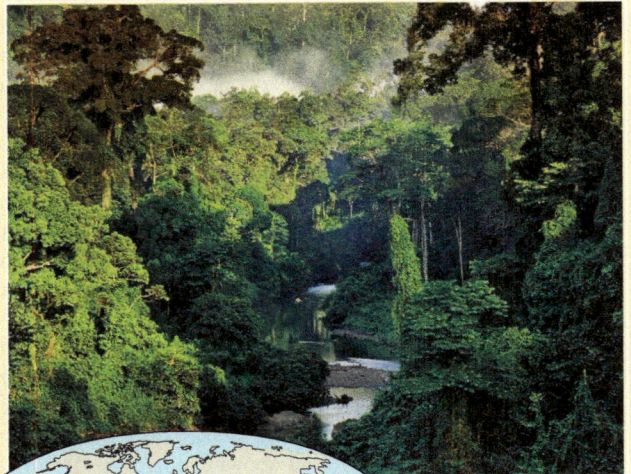

A tropical rain forest in Borneo

Desert

A desert in Jordan

Distribution **Deserts** occur in bands near 30° north and south latitude or at other latitudes in the interior of continents (for instance, the Gobi Desert of north-central Asia).

Precipitation Precipitation is low and highly variable, generally less than 30 cm per year.

Temperature Temperature is variable seasonally and daily. Maximum air temperature in hot deserts may exceed 50°C; in cold deserts air temperature may fall below –30°C.

Plants Desert landscapes are dominated by low, widely scattered vegetation; the proportion of bare ground is high compared with other terrestrial biomes. The plants include succulents such as cacti or euphorbs, deeply rooted shrubs, and herbs that grow during the infrequent moist periods. Desert plant adaptations include heat and desiccation

tolerance, water storage, and reduced leaf surface area. Physical defenses, such as spines, and chemical defenses, such as toxins in the leaves of shrubs, are common. Many of the plants exhibit C_4 or CAM photosynthesis (see Chapter 10).

Animals Common desert animals include snakes and lizards, scorpions, ants, beetles, migratory and resident birds, and seed-eating rodents. Many species are nocturnal. Water conservation is a common adaptation, with some species surviving solely on water from breaking down carbohydrates in seeds.

Human Impact Long-distance transport of water and deep groundwater wells have allowed humans to maintain substantial populations in deserts. Urbanization and conversion to irrigated agriculture have reduced the natural biodiversity of some deserts.

▼ **Figure 52.12 (continued)**

Exploring Terrestrial Biomes

Savanna

A savanna in Kenya

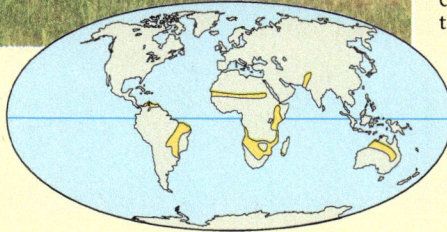

Distribution   Equatorial and subequatorial regions

Precipitation   Rainfall, which is seasonal, averages 30–50 cm per year. The dry season can last up to eight or nine months.

Temperature   The **savanna** is warm year-round, averaging 24–29°C, but with somewhat more seasonal variation than in tropical forests.

Plants   The scattered trees found at different densities in the savanna often are thorny and have small leaves, an apparent adaptation to the relatively dry conditions. Fires are common in the dry season, and the dominant plant species are fire-adapted and tolerant of seasonal drought. Grasses and small nonwoody plants called forbs, which make up most of the ground cover, grow rapidly in response to seasonal rains and are tolerant of grazing by large mammals and other herbivores.

Animals   Large plant-eating mammals, such as wildebeests and zebras, and predators, including lions and hyenas, are common inhabitants. However, the dominant herbivores are actually insects, especially termites. During seasonal droughts, grazing mammals often migrate to parts of the savanna with more forage and scattered watering holes.

Human Impact   There is evidence that the earliest humans lived in savannas. Fires set by humans may help maintain this biome, though overly frequent fires reduce tree regeneration by killing the seedlings and saplings. Cattle ranching and overhunting have led to declines in large-mammal populations.

Chaparral

Distribution   This biome occurs in midlatitude coastal regions on several continents, and its many names reflect its far-flung distribution: **chaparral** in North America, *matorral* in Spain and Chile, *garigue* and *maquis* in southern France, and *fynbos* in South Africa.

Precipitation   Precipitation is highly seasonal, with rainy winters and dry summers. Annual precipitation generally falls within the range of 30–50 cm.

Temperature   Fall, winter, and spring are cool, with average temperatures in the range of 10–12°C. Average summer temperature can reach 30°C, and daytime maximum temperature can exceed 40°C.

Plants   Chaparral is dominated by shrubs and small trees, along with many kinds of grasses and herbs. Plant diversity is high, with many species confined to a specific, relatively small geographic area. Adaptations to drought include the tough evergreen leaves of woody plants, which reduce water loss. Adaptations to fire are also prominent. Some of the shrubs produce seeds that will germinate only after a hot fire; food reserves stored in their fire-resistant roots enable them to resprout quickly and use nutrients released by the fire.

Animals   Native mammals include browsers, such as deer and goats, that feed on twigs and buds of woody vegetation, and a high diversity of small mammals. Chaparral areas also support many species of amphibians, birds and other reptiles, and insects.

Human Impact   Chaparral areas have been heavily settled and reduced through conversion to agriculture and urbanization. Humans contribute to the fires that sweep across the chaparral.

Typical fynbos vegetation in the Cape of Good Hope Nature Reserve, South Africa

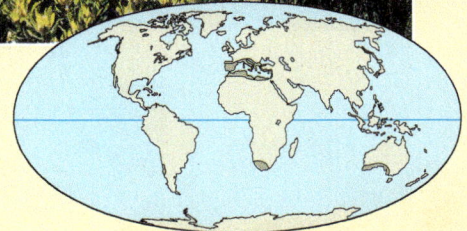

Temperate Grassland

Distribution The veldts of South Africa, the *puszta* of Hungary, the pampas of Argentina and Uruguay, the steppes of Russia, and the plains and prairies of central North America are examples of **temperate grasslands**.

Precipitation Precipitation is often highly seasonal, with relatively dry winters and wet summers. Annual precipitation generally averages between 30 and 100 cm. Periodic drought is common.

Temperature Winters are generally cold, with average temperatures frequently falling well below –10°C. Summers, with average temperatures often approaching 30°C, are hot.

Plants The dominant plants are grasses and forbs, which vary in height from a few centimeters to 2 m in tallgrass prairie. Many grassland plants have adaptations that help them survive periodic, protracted droughts and fire. For example, grasses can sprout quickly following fire. Grazing by large mammals helps prevent establishment of woody shrubs and trees.

Animals Native mammals include large grazers such as bison and wild horses. Temperate grasslands are also inhabited by a wide variety of burrowing mammals, such as prairie dogs in North America.

Human Impact Deep, fertile soils make temperate grasslands ideal places for agriculture, especially for growing grains. As a consequence, most grassland in North America and much of Eurasia has been converted to farmland. In some drier grasslands, cattle and other grazers have turned parts of the biome into desert.

Grasslands National Park, Saskatchewan

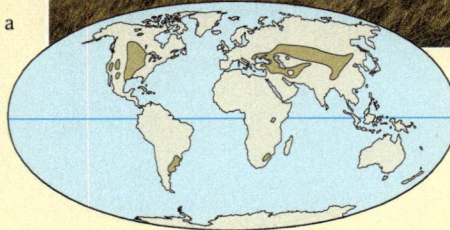

Northern Coniferous Forest

A forest in Norway

Distribution Extending in a broad band across northern North America and Eurasia to the edge of the arctic tundra, the **northern coniferous forest**, or *taiga*, is the largest terrestrial biome on Earth.

Precipitation Annual precipitation generally ranges from 30 to 70 cm, and periodic droughts are common. However, some coastal coniferous forests of the U.S. Pacific Northwest are temperate rain forests that may receive over 300 cm of annual precipitation.

Temperature Winters are usually cold; summers may be hot. Some areas of coniferous forest in Siberia typically range in temperature from –50°C in winter to over 20°C in summer.

Plants Northern coniferous forests are dominated by cone-bearing trees, such as pine, spruce, fir, and hemlock, some of which depend on fire to regenerate. The conical shape of many conifers prevents too much snow from accumulating and breaking their branches, and their needle- or scale-like leaves reduce water loss. The diversity of plants in the shrub and herb layers of these forests is lower than in temperate broadleaf forests.

Animals While many migratory birds nest in northern coniferous forests, other species reside there year-round. The mammals of this biome, which include moose, brown bears, and Siberian tigers, are diverse. Periodic outbreaks of insects that feed on the dominant trees can kill vast tracts of trees.

Human Impact Although they have not been heavily settled by human populations, northern coniferous forests are being logged at an alarming rate, and the old-growth stands of these trees may soon disappear.

▼ **Figure 52.12 (continued)**
Exploring Terrestrial Biomes

Temperate Broadleaf Forest

An area of temperate broadleaf forest in the French Alps in autumn

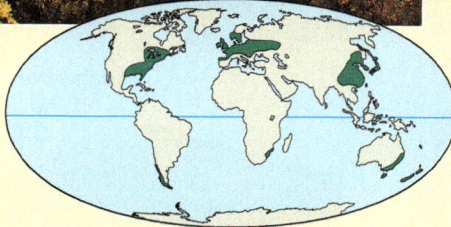

Distribution Found mainly at midlatitudes in the Northern Hemisphere, with smaller areas in Chile, South Africa, Australia, and New Zealand

Precipitation Precipitation can average from about 70 to over 200 cm annually. Significant amounts fall during all seasons, including summer rain and, in some forests, winter snow.

Temperature Winter temperatures average around 0°C. Summers, with maximum temperatures near 35°C, are hot and humid.

Plants A mature **temperate broadleaf forest** has distinct vertical layers, including a closed canopy, one or two strata of understory trees, a shrub layer, and an herb layer. There are few epiphytes. The dominant plants in the Northern Hemisphere are deciduous trees, which drop their leaves before winter, when low temperatures would reduce photosynthesis and make water uptake from frozen soil difficult. In Australia, evergreen eucalyptus trees dominate these forests.

Animals In the Northern Hemisphere, many mammals hibernate in winter, while many bird species migrate to warmer climates. Mammals, birds, and insects make use of all the vertical layers of the forest.

Human Impact Temperate broadleaf forest has been heavily settled on all continents. Logging and land clearing for agriculture and urban development have destroyed virtually all the original deciduous forests in North America. However, owing to their capacity for recovery, these forests are returning over much of their former range.

Tundra

Distribution **Tundra** covers expansive areas of the Arctic, amounting to 20% of Earth's land surface. High winds and low temperatures produce similar plant communities, called *alpine tundra*, on very high mountaintops at all latitudes, including the tropics.

Precipitation Precipitation averages from 20 to 60 cm annually in arctic tundra but may exceed 100 cm in alpine tundra.

Temperature Winters are cold, with averages in some areas below −30°C. Summers temperatures generally average less than 10°C.

Plants The vegetation of tundra is mostly herbaceous, consisting of a mixture of mosses, grasses, and forbs, along with some dwarf shrubs and trees and lichens. A permanently frozen layer of soil called permafrost restricts the growth of plant roots.

Animals Large grazing musk oxen are resident, while caribou and reindeer are migratory. Predators include bears, wolves, and foxes. Many bird species migrate to the tundra for summer nesting.

Human Impact Tundra is sparsely settled but has become the focus of significant mineral and oil extraction in recent years.

Tundra in Sarek National Park, Sweden

CONCEPT **52.3**

Aquatic biomes are diverse and dynamic systems that cover most of Earth

Now that we have examined terrestrial biomes, let's turn to aquatic biomes. Unlike terrestrial biomes, aquatic biomes are characterized primarily by their physical environment. They also show far less latitudinal variation, with all types found across the globe. Ecologists distinguish between freshwater and marine biomes on the basis of physical and chemical differences. Marine biomes generally have salt concentrations that average 3%, whereas freshwater biomes are usually characterized by a salt concentration of less than 0.1%.

The oceans make up the largest marine biome, covering about 75% of Earth's surface. Because of their vast size, they greatly impact the biosphere. Water evaporated from the oceans provides most of the planet's rainfall, and ocean temperatures have a major effect on global climate and wind patterns (see Figure 52.3). Marine algae and photosynthetic bacteria also supply a substantial portion of the world's oxygen and consume large amounts of atmospheric carbon dioxide.

Freshwater biomes are closely linked to the soils and biotic components of the surrounding terrestrial biome. The particular characteristics of a freshwater biome are also influenced by the patterns and speed of water flow and the climate to which the biome is exposed.

Zonation in Aquatic Biomes

Many aquatic biomes are physically and chemically stratified (layered), vertically and horizontally, as illustrated for both a lake and a marine environment in **Figure 52.13**. Light is absorbed by the water itself and by photosynthetic organisms, so its intensity decreases rapidly with depth. Ecologists distinguish between the upper **photic zone**, where there is sufficient light for photosynthesis, and the lower **aphotic zone**, where little light penetrates. The photic and aphotic zones together make up the **pelagic zone**. Deep in the aphotic zone lies the **abyssal zone**, the part of the ocean 2,000–6,000 m below the surface. At the bottom of all aquatic biomes, deep or shallow, is the **benthic zone**. Made up of sand and organic and inorganic sediments, the benthic zone is occupied by communities of organisms collectively called the **benthos**. A major source of food for many benthic species is dead organic matter called **detritus**, which "rains" down from the productive surface waters of the photic zone.

Thermal energy from sunlight warms surface waters to whatever depth the sunlight penetrates, but the deeper waters remain quite cold. In the ocean and in most lakes, a narrow layer of abrupt temperature change called a **thermocline**

▼ **Figure 52.13 Zonation in aquatic environments.**

(a) Zonation in a lake

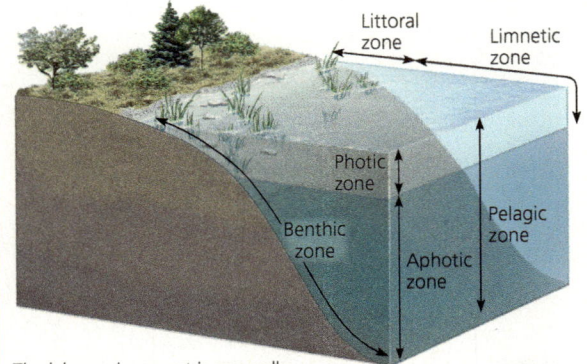

The lake environment is generally classified on the basis of three physical criteria: light penetration (photic and aphotic zones), distance from shore and water depth (littoral and limnetic zones), and whether the environment is open water (pelagic zone) or bottom (benthic zone).

(b) Marine zonation

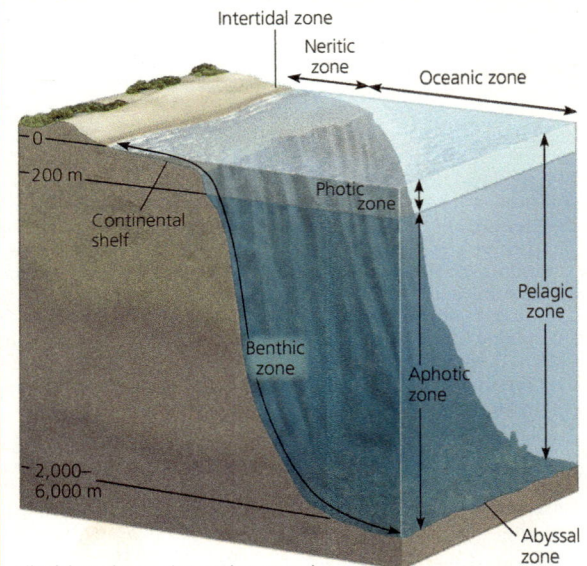

Like lakes, the marine environment is generally classified on the basis of light penetration (photic and aphotic zones), distance from shore and water depth (intertidal, neritic, and oceanic zones), and whether the environment is open water (pelagic zone) or bottom (benthic and abyssal zones).

separates the more uniformly warm upper layer from more uniformly cold deeper waters. Lakes tend to be particularly layered with respect to temperature, especially during summer and winter, but many temperate lakes undergo a semiannual mixing of their waters as a result of changing temperature

❶ In winter, the coldest water in the lake (0°C) lies just below the surface ice; water becomes progressively warmer at deeper levels of the lake, typically 4°C at the bottom.

❷ In spring, as the ice melts, the surface water warms to 4°C and mixes with the formerly cooler layers below, eliminating thermal stratification. Spring winds help mix the water, bringing oxygen to the bottom waters and nutrients to the surface.

❸ In summer, the lake regains a distinctive thermal profile, with warm surface water separated from cold bottom water by a narrow vertical zone of abrupt temperature change, called a thermocline.

❹ In autumn, as surface water cools rapidly, it sinks beneath the underlying layers, remixing the water until the surface begins to freeze and the winter temperature profile is reestablished.

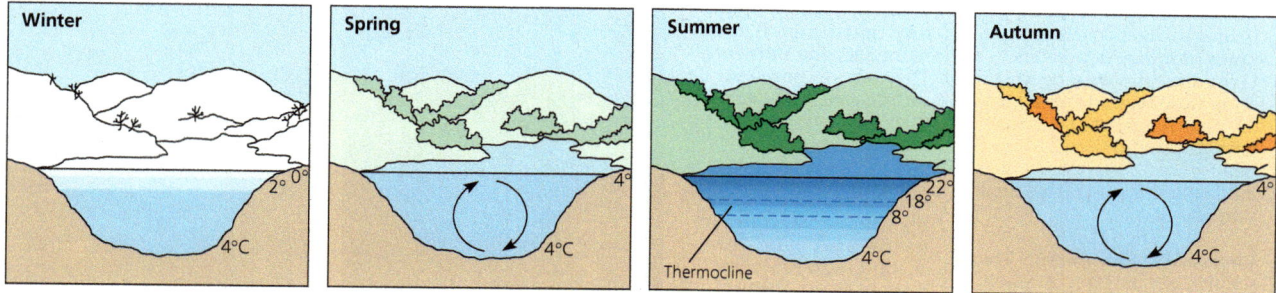

▲ **Figure 52.14 Seasonal turnover in lakes with winter ice cover.** Because of the seasonal turnover shown here, lake waters are well oxygenated at all depths in spring and autumn; in winter and summer, when the lake is stratified by temperature, oxygen concentrations are lower in deeper waters and higher near the surface of the lake.

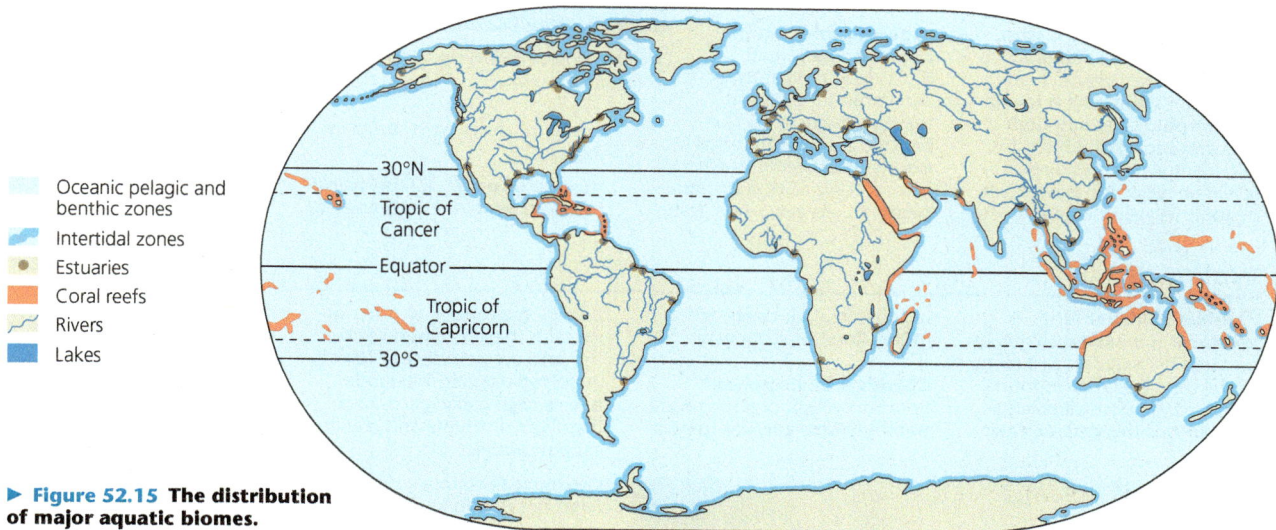

Oceanic pelagic and benthic zones
Intertidal zones
Estuaries
Coral reefs
Rivers
Lakes

▶ **Figure 52.15 The distribution of major aquatic biomes.**

profiles **(Figure 52.14)**. This **turnover**, as it is called, sends oxygenated water from a lake's surface to the bottom and brings nutrient-rich water from the bottom to the surface in both spring and autumn. These cyclic changes in the abiotic properties of lakes are essential for the survival and growth of organisms at all levels within this ecosystem.

In both freshwater and marine environments, communities are distributed according to water depth, degree of light penetration, distance from shore, and whether they are found in open water or near the bottom. Marine communities, in particular, illustrate the limitations on species distribution that result from these abiotic factors. Plankton and many fish species occur in the relatively shallow photic zone (see Figure 52.13b). Because water absorbs light so well and the ocean is so deep, most of the ocean volume is virtually devoid of light (the aphotic zone) and harbors relatively little life, except for microorganisms and relatively sparse populations of fishes and invertebrates. Similar factors limit species distribution in deep lakes as well.

Figure 52.15 shows the locations of Earth's major aquatic biomes. **Figure 52.16**, on the next four pages, explores their main characteristics.

▼ Figure 52.16

Exploring Aquatic Biomes

Lakes

Physical Environment
Standing bodies of water range from ponds a few square meters in area to lakes covering thousands of square kilometers. Light decreases with depth, creating stratification (see Figure 52.13a). Temperate lakes may have a seasonal thermocline (see Figure 52.14); tropical lowland lakes have a thermocline year-round.

Chemical Environment   The salinity, oxygen concentration, and nutrient content differ greatly among lakes and can vary with season. **Oligotrophic lakes** are nutrient-poor and generally oxygen-rich; **eutrophic lakes** are nutrient-rich and often depleted of oxygen in the deepest zone in summer and if covered with ice in winter. The amount of decomposable organic matter in bottom sediments is low in oligotrophic lakes and high in eutrophic lakes; high rates of decomposition in deeper layers of eutrophic lakes cause periodic oxygen depletion.

Geologic Features
Oligotrophic lakes may become more eutrophic over time as runoff adds sediments and nutrients. They tend to have less surface area relative to their depth than eutrophic lakes.

Photosynthetic Organisms   Rooted and floating aquatic plants live in the **littoral zone**, the shallow, well-lit waters close to shore. Farther from shore, where water is too deep to support rooted aquatic plants, the **limnetic zone** is inhabited by a variety of phytoplankton, including cyanobacteria.

Heterotrophs   In the limnetic zone, small drifting heterotrophs, or zooplankton, graze on the phytoplankton. The benthic zone is inhabited by assorted invertebrates whose species composition depends partly on oxygen levels. Fishes live in all zones with sufficient oxygen.

Human Impact   Runoff from fertilized land and dumping of wastes lead to nutrient enrichment, which can produce algal blooms, oxygen depletion, and fish kills.

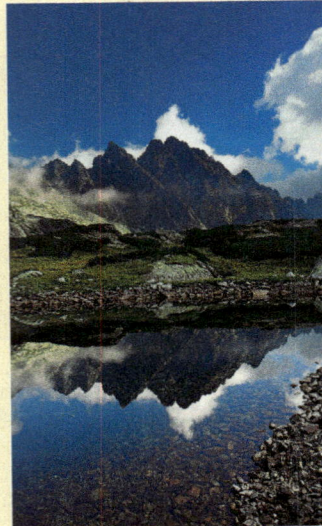

An oligotrophic lake in the Tatra Mountains, Slovakia

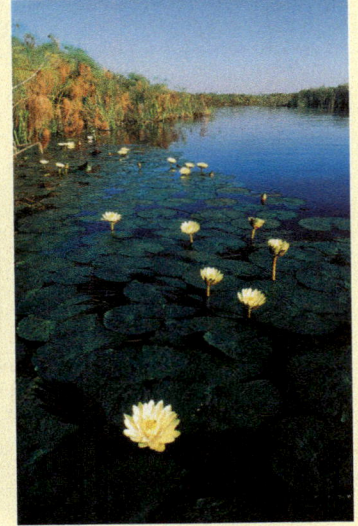

A eutrophic lake in the Okavango Delta, Botswana

Wetlands

Physical Environment   A **wetland** is a habitat that is inundated by water at least some of the time and that supports plants adapted to water-saturated soil. Some wetlands are inundated at all times, whereas others flood infrequently.

Chemical Environment
Because of high organic production by plants and decomposition by microbes and other organisms, both the water and the soils are periodically low in dissolved oxygen. Wetlands have a high capacity to filter dissolved nutrients and chemical pollutants.

Geologic Features   Basin wetlands develop in shallow basins, ranging from upland depressions to filled-in lakes and ponds. Riverine wetlands develop along shallow and periodically flooded banks of rivers and streams. Fringe wetlands occur along the coasts of large lakes and seas, where water flows back and forth because of rising lake levels or tidal action. Thus, fringe wetlands include both freshwater and marine biomes.

Photosynthetic Organisms
Wetlands are among the most productive biomes on Earth. Their water-saturated soils favor the growth of plants such as floating pond lilies and emergent cattails, many sedges, tamarack, and black spruce, which have adaptations enabling them to grow in water or in soil that is periodically anaerobic owing to the presence of unaerated water. Woody plants dominate the vegetation of swamps, while bogs are dominated by sphagnum mosses.

Heterotrophs   Wetlands are home to a diverse community of invertebrates, birds, and many other organisms. Herbivores, from crustaceans and aquatic insect larvae to muskrats, consume algae, detritus, and plants. Carnivores are also varied and may include dragonflies, otters, frogs, alligators, and herons.

Human Impact   Draining and filling have destroyed up to 90% of wetlands, which help purify water and reduce peak flooding.

A basin wetland in the United Kingdom

▼ **Figure 52.16 (continued)**
Exploring Aquatic Biomes

Streams and Rivers

Physical Environment The most prominent physical characteristic of streams and rivers is their current. Headwater streams are generally cold, clear, turbulent, and swift. Farther downstream, where numerous tributaries may have joined, forming a river, the water is generally warmer and more turbid because of suspended sediment. Streams and rivers are stratified into vertical zones.

Chemical Environment The salt and nutrient content of streams and rivers increases from the headwaters to the mouth. Headwaters are generally rich in oxygen. Downstream water may also contain substantial oxygen, except where there has been organic enrichment. A large fraction of the organic matter in rivers consists of dissolved or highly fragmented material that is carried by the current from forested streams.

Geologic Features Headwater stream channels are often narrow, have a rocky bottom, and alternate between shallow sections and deeper pools. The downstream stretches of rivers are generally wide and meandering. River bottoms are often silty from sediments deposited over long periods of time.

Photosynthetic Organisms Headwater streams that flow through grasslands or deserts may be rich in phytoplankton or rooted aquatic plants.

Heterotrophs A great diversity of fishes and invertebrates inhabit unpolluted rivers and streams, distributed according to, and throughout, the vertical zones. In streams flowing through temperate or tropical forests, organic matter from terrestrial vegetation is the primary source of food for aquatic consumers.

Human Impact Municipal, agricultural, and industrial pollution degrade water quality and kill aquatic organisms. Damming and flood control impair the natural functioning of stream and river ecosystems and threaten migratory species such as salmon.

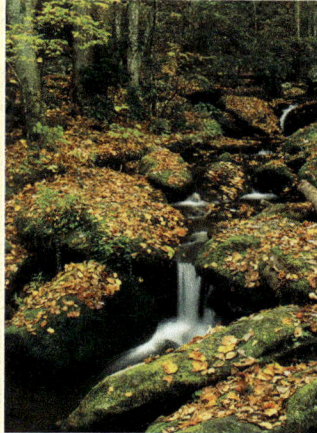

A headwater stream in the Great Smoky Mountains

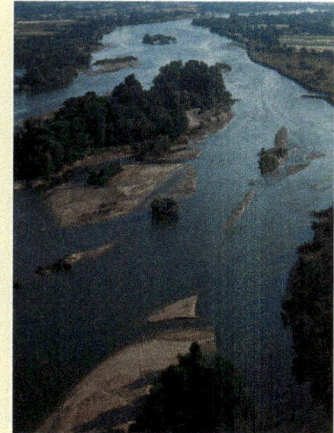

The Loire River (in France) far from its headwaters

Estuaries

The Menderes River estuary in Turkey

Physical Environment An **estuary** is a transition area between river and sea. Seawater flows up the estuary channel during a rising tide and flows back down during the falling tide. Often, higher-density seawater occupies the bottom of the channel and mixes little with the lower-density river water at the surface.

Chemical Environment Salinity varies spatially within estuaries, from nearly that of fresh water to that of seawater. Salinity also varies with the rise and fall of the tides. Nutrients from the river make estuaries, like wetlands, among the most productive biomes.

Geologic Features Estuarine flow patterns combined with the sediments carried by river and tidal waters create a complex network of tidal channels, islands, natural levees, and mudflats.

Photosynthetic Organisms Saltmarsh grasses and algae, including phytoplankton, are the major producers in estuaries.

Heterotrophs Estuaries support an abundance of worms, oysters, crabs, and many fish species that humans consume. Many marine invertebrates and fishes use estuaries as a breeding ground or migrate through them to freshwater habitats upstream. Estuaries are also crucial feeding areas for waterfowl and some marine mammals.

Human Impact Filling, dredging, and pollution from upstream have disrupted estuaries worldwide.

Intertidal Zones

Physical Environment An **intertidal zone** is periodically submerged and exposed by the tides, twice daily on most marine shores. Upper zones experience longer exposures to air and greater variations in temperature and salinity. Changes in physical conditions from the upper to the lower intertidal zones limit the distributions of many organisms to particular strata, as shown in the photograph.

Chemical Environment Oxygen and nutrient levels are generally high and are renewed with each turn of the tides.

Geologic Features The substrates of intertidal zones, which are generally either rocky or sandy, select for particular behavior and anatomy among intertidal organisms. The configuration of bays or coastlines influences the magnitude of tides and the relative exposure of intertidal organisms to wave action.

Photosynthetic Organisms A high diversity and biomass of attached marine algae inhabit rocky intertidal zones, especially in the lower zone. Sandy intertidal zones exposed to vigorous wave action generally lack attached plants or algae, while sandy intertidal zones in protected bays or lagoons often support rich beds of sea grass and algae.

Heterotrophs Many of the animals in rocky intertidal environments have structural adaptations that enable them to attach to the hard substrate. The composition, density, and diversity of animals change markedly from the upper to the lower intertidal zones. Many of the animals in sandy or muddy intertidal zones, such as worms, clams, and predatory crustaceans, bury themselves and feed as the tides bring sources of food. Other common animals are sponges, sea anemones, echinoderms, and small fishes.

Human Impact Oil pollution has disrupted many intertidal areas. The construction of rock walls and barriers to reduce erosion from waves and storm surges has disrupted this zone in some locations.

Rocky intertidal zone on the Oregon coast

Oceanic Pelagic Zone

Physical Environment The **oceanic pelagic zone** is a vast realm of open blue water, constantly mixed by wind-driven oceanic currents. Because of higher water clarity, the photic zone extends to greater depths than in coastal marine waters.

Chemical Environment Oxygen levels are generally high. Nutrient concentrations are generally lower than in coastal waters. Because they are thermally stratified year-round, some tropical areas of the oceanic pelagic zone have lower nutrient concentrations than temperate oceans. Turnover between fall and spring renews nutrients in the photic zones of temperate and high-latitude ocean areas.

Geologic Features This biome covers approximately 70% of Earth's surface and has an average depth of nearly 4,000 m. The deepest point in the ocean is more than 10,000 m beneath the surface.

Photosynthetic Organisms The dominant photosynthetic organisms are phytoplankton, including photosynthetic bacteria, that drift with the oceanic currents. Spring turnover renews nutrients in temperate oceans producing a surge of phytoplankton growth. Because of the large extent of this biome, photosynthetic plankton account for about half of the photosynthetic activity on Earth.

Heterotrophs The most abundant heterotrophs in this biome are zooplankton. These protists, worms, copepods, shrimp-like krill, jellies, and small larvae of invertebrates and fishes graze on photosynthetic plankton. The oceanic pelagic zone also includes free-swimming animals, such as large squids, fishes, sea turtles, and marine mammals.

Human Impact Overfishing has depleted fish stocks in all Earth's oceans, which have also been polluted by waste dumping.

Open ocean off the island of Hawaii

▼ **Figure 52.16 (continued)**

Exploring Aquatic Biomes

Coral Reefs

Physical Environment **Coral reefs** are formed largely from the calcium carbonate skeletons of corals. Shallow reef-building corals live in the photic zone of relatively stable tropical marine environments with high water clarity, primarily on islands and along the edge of some continents. They are sensitive to temperatures below about 18–20°C and above 30°C. Deep-sea coral reefs, found between 200 and 1,500 m deep, are less known than their shallow counterparts but harbor as much diversity as many shallow reefs do.

Chemical Environment Corals require high oxygen levels and are excluded by high inputs of fresh water and nutrients.

Geologic Features Corals require a solid substrate for attachment. A typical coral reef begins as a *fringing reef* on a young, high island, forming an offshore *barrier reef* later in the history of the island and becoming a *coral atoll* as the older island submerges.

Photosynthetic Organisms Unicellular algae live within the tissues of the corals, forming a mutualistic relationship that provides the corals with organic molecules. Diverse multicellular red and green algae growing on the reef also contribute substantial amounts of photosynthesis.

Heterotrophs Corals, a diverse group of cnidarians (see Chapter 33), are themselves the predominant animals on coral reefs. However, fish and invertebrate diversity is exceptionally high. Overall animal diversity on coral reefs rivals that of tropical forests.

Human Impact Collecting of coral skeletons and overfishing have reduced populations of corals and reef fishes. Global warming and pollution may be contributing to large-scale coral death. Development of coastal mangroves for aquaculture has also reduced spawning grounds for many species of reef fishes.

A coral reef in the Red Sea

Marine Benthic Zone

A deep-sea hydrothermal vent community

Physical Environment The **marine benthic zone** consists of the seafloor below the surface waters of the coastal, or **neritic**, zone and the offshore, pelagic zone (see Figure 52.13b). Except for shallow, near-coastal areas, the marine benthic zone receives no sunlight. Water temperature declines with depth, while pressure increases. As a result, organisms in the very deep benthic, or abyssal, zone are adapted to continuous cold (about 3°C) and very high water pressure.

Chemical Environment Except in areas of organic enrichment, oxygen is usually present at sufficient concentrations to support diverse animal life.

Geologic Features Soft sediments cover most of the benthic zone. However, there are areas of rocky substrate on reefs, submarine mountains, and new oceanic crust.

Autotrophs Photosynthetic organisms, mainly seaweeds and filamentous algae, are limited to shallow benthic areas with sufficient light to support them. Unique assemblages of organisms, such as those shown in the photo, are found near **deep-sea hydrothermal vents** on mid-ocean ridges. In these dark, hot environments, the food producers are chemoautotrophic prokaryotes (see Chapter 27) that obtain energy by oxidizing H_2S formed by a reaction of the hot water with dissolved sulfate (SO_4^{2-}).

Heterotrophs Neritic benthic communities include numerous invertebrates and fishes. Beyond the photic zone, most consumers depend entirely on organic matter raining down from above. Among the animals of the deep-sea hydrothermal vent communities are giant tube worms (pictured at left), some more than 1 m long. They are nourished by chemoautotrophic prokaryotes that live as symbionts within their bodies. Many other invertebrates, including arthropods and echinoderms, are also abundant around the hydrothermal vents.

Human Impact Overfishing has decimated important benthic fish populations, such as the cod of the Grand Banks off Newfoundland. Dumping of organic wastes has created oxygen-deprived benthic areas.

CONCEPT CHECK 52.3

The first two questions refer to Figure 52.16.

1. Why are phytoplankton, and not benthic algae or rooted aquatic plants, the dominant photosynthetic organisms of the oceanic pelagic zone?
2. **MAKE CONNECTIONS** Many organisms living in estuaries experience freshwater and saltwater conditions each day with the rising and falling of tides. Based on what you learned in Concept 44.1 (pp. 999–1004), explain how these changing conditions challenge the survival of these organisms.
3. **WHAT IF?** Water leaving a reservoir behind a dam is often taken from deep layers of the reservoir. Would you expect fish found in a river below a dam in summer to be species that prefer colder or warmer water than fish found in an undammed river? Explain.

For suggested answers, see Appendix A.

CONCEPT 52.4

Interactions between organisms and the environment limit the distribution of species

So far in this chapter we've examined Earth's climate and the characteristics of terrestrial and aquatic biomes. We've also introduced the range of biological levels at which ecologists work (see Figure 52.2). In this section, we will examine how ecologists determine what factors control the distribution of species, such as the harlequin toad shown in Figure 52.1.

Species distributions are a consequence of both ecological and evolutionary interactions through time. The differential survival and reproduction of individuals that lead to evolution occur in *ecological time*, the minute-to-minute time frame of interactions between organisms and the environment. Through natural selection, organisms adapt to their environment over the time frame of many generations, in *evolutionary time*. One example of how events in ecological time have led to evolution is the selection for beak depth in Galápagos finches (see Figures 23.1 and 23.2). On the island of Daphne Major, finches with larger, deeper beaks were better able to survive during a drought because they could eat the large, hard seeds that were available. Finches with shallower beaks, which required smaller, softer seeds that were in short supply, were less likely to survive and reproduce. Because beak depth is hereditary in this species, the generation of finches born after the drought had beaks that were deeper than those of previous generations.

Biologists have long recognized global and regional patterns in the distribution of organisms (see the discussion of biogeography in Chapter 22). Kangaroos, for instance, are found in Australia but nowhere else on Earth. Ecologists ask not only *where* species occur, but also *why* species occur where they do: What factors determine their distribution? In seeking to answer this question, ecologists focus on both biotic and abiotic factors that influence the distribution and abundance of organisms.

Figure 52.17 presents an example of how both kinds of factors might affect the distribution of a species, in this case the red kangaroo (*Macropus rufus*). As the figure shows, red kangaroos are most abundant in a few areas in the interior of Australia, where precipitation is relatively sparse and variable. They are not found around most of the periphery of the continent,

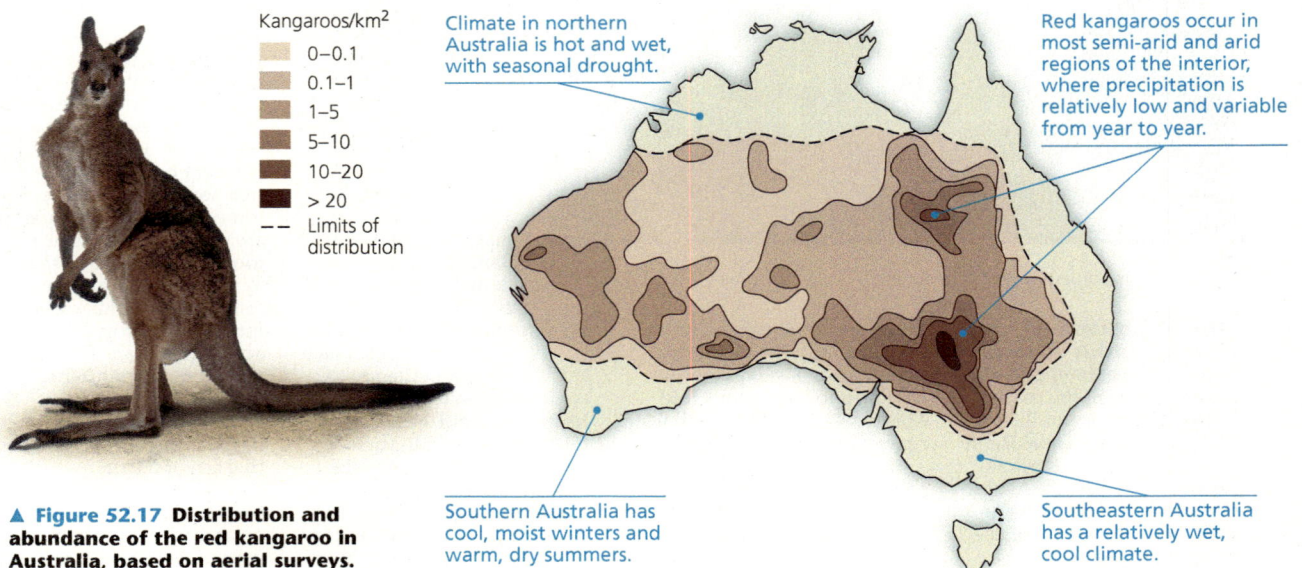

▲ **Figure 52.17 Distribution and abundance of the red kangaroo in Australia, based on aerial surveys.**

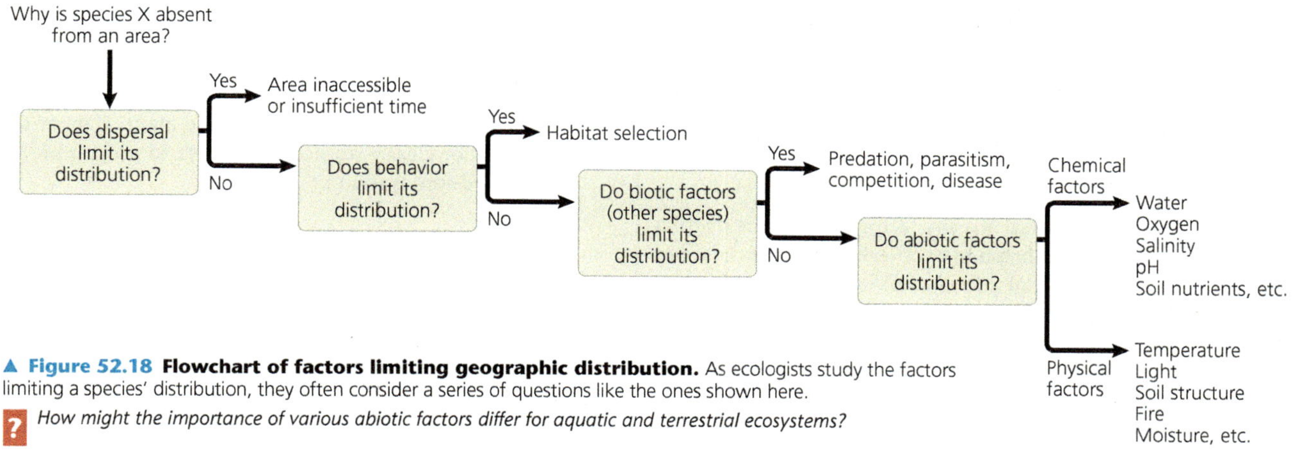

▲ **Figure 52.18 Flowchart of factors limiting geographic distribution.** As ecologists study the factors limiting a species' distribution, they often consider a series of questions like the ones shown here.

❓ *How might the importance of various abiotic factors differ for aquatic and terrestrial ecosystems?*

where the climate is wetter. At first glance, this distribution might suggest that an abiotic factor—the amount and variability of precipitation—directly determines where red kangaroos live. However, climate may also influence red kangaroo populations indirectly through biotic factors, such as pathogens, parasites, predators, competitors, and food availability. Ecologists generally need to consider multiple factors and alternative hypotheses when attempting to explain the distribution of species.

To see how ecologists might arrive at such an explanation, let's work our way through the series of questions in the flowchart in **Figure 52.18.**

Dispersal and Distribution

One factor that contributes greatly to the global distribution of organisms is **dispersal**, the movement of individuals or gametes away from their area of origin or from centers of high population density. A biogeographer who studies the distributions of species in the context of evolutionary theory might consider dispersal in hypothesizing why there are no kangaroos in North America: A barrier may have kept them from reaching the continent. While land-bound kangaroos have not reached North America under their own power, other organisms that disperse more readily, such as some birds, have. The dispersal of organisms is critical to understanding the role of geographic isolation in evolution (see Chapter 24) as well as the broad patterns of species distribution we see today, including that of the Pacific diatom discussed earlier in this chapter.

Natural Range Expansions and Adaptive Radiation

EVOLUTION The importance of dispersal is most evident when organisms reach an area where they did not exist previously. For instance, 200 years ago, the cattle egret (*Bubulcus ibis*) was found only in Africa and southwestern Europe. But in the late 1800s, some of these birds managed to cross the Atlantic Ocean and colonize northeastern South America.

From there, cattle egrets gradually spread southward and also northward through Central America and into North America, reaching Florida by 1960 **(Figure 52.19)**. Today they have breeding populations as far west as the Pacific coast of the United States and as far north as southern Canada.

In rare cases, such long-distance dispersal can lead to adaptive radiation, the rapid evolution of an ancestral species into new species that fill many ecological niches (see Chapter 25). The incredible diversity of Hawaiian silverswords is an example of adaptive radiation that was possible only with the long-distance dispersal of an ancestral tarweed from North America (see Figure 25.20).

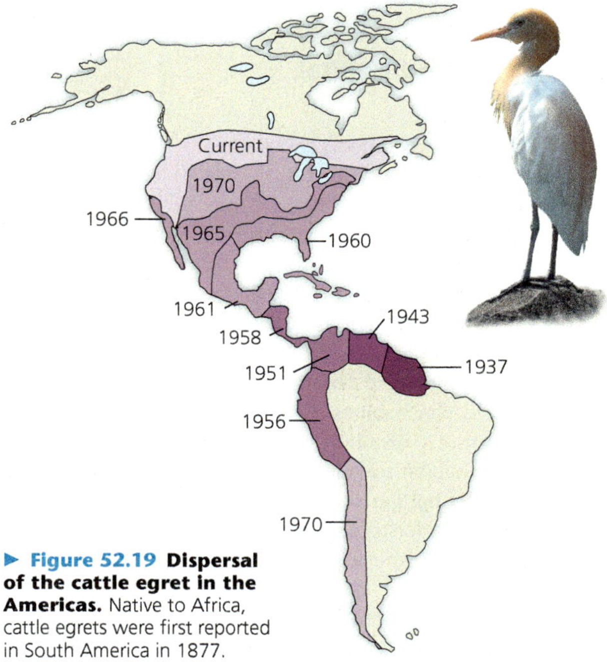

► **Figure 52.19 Dispersal of the cattle egret in the Americas.** Native to Africa, cattle egrets were first reported in South America in 1877.

Natural range expansions clearly show the influence of dispersal on distribution. However, opportunities to observe such dispersal directly are rare, so ecologists often turn to experimental methods to better understand the role of dispersal in limiting the distribution of species.

Species Transplants

To determine if dispersal is a key factor limiting the distribution of a species, ecologists may observe the results of intentional or accidental transplants of the species to areas where it was previously absent. For a transplant to be considered successful, some of the organisms must not only survive in the new area but also reproduce there sustainably. If a transplant is successful, then we can conclude that the *potential* range of the species is larger than its *actual* range; in other words, the species *could* live in certain areas where it currently does not.

Species introduced to new geographic locations often disrupt the communities and ecosystems to which they have been introduced and spread far beyond the area of introduction (see Chapter 56). Consequently, ecologists rarely move species to new geographic regions. Instead, they document the outcome when a species has been transplanted for other purposes, such as to introduce game animals or predators of pest species, or when a species has been accidentally transplanted.

Behavior and Habitat Selection

As transplant experiments show, some organisms do not occupy all of their potential range, even though they may be physically able to disperse into the unoccupied areas. To follow our line of questioning from Figure 52.18, does behavior play a role in limiting distribution in such cases? When individuals seem to avoid certain habitats, even when the habitats are suitable, the organism's distribution may be limited by habitat selection behavior.

Although habitat selection is one of the least understood of all ecological processes, some instances in insects have been closely studied. Female insects often deposit eggs only in response to a very narrow set of stimuli, which may restrict distribution of the insects to certain host plants. Larvae of the European corn borer, for example, can feed on a wide variety of plants but are found almost exclusively on corn (maize) because egg-laying females are attracted by odors produced by the plant. Habitat selection behavior clearly restricts this insect to geographic locations where corn is found.

Biotic Factors

If behavior does not limit the distribution of a species, our next question is whether biotic factors—other species—are responsible. Often, negative interactions with predators (organisms that kill their prey) or herbivores (organisms that eat plants or algae) restrict the ability of a species to survive and reproduce. **Figure 52.20** describes a specific case of an herbivore, a sea urchin, limiting the distribution of a food species.

▼ **Figure 52.20**

INQUIRY

Does feeding by sea urchins limit seaweed distribution?

EXPERIMENT W. J. Fletcher, of the University of Sydney, Australia, reasoned that if sea urchins are a limiting biotic factor in a particular ecosystem, then more seaweeds should invade an area from which sea urchins have been removed. To isolate the effect of sea urchins from that of a seaweed-eating mollusc, the limpet, he removed only urchins, only limpets, or both from study areas adjacent to a control site.

RESULTS Fletcher observed a large difference in seaweed growth between areas with and without sea urchins.

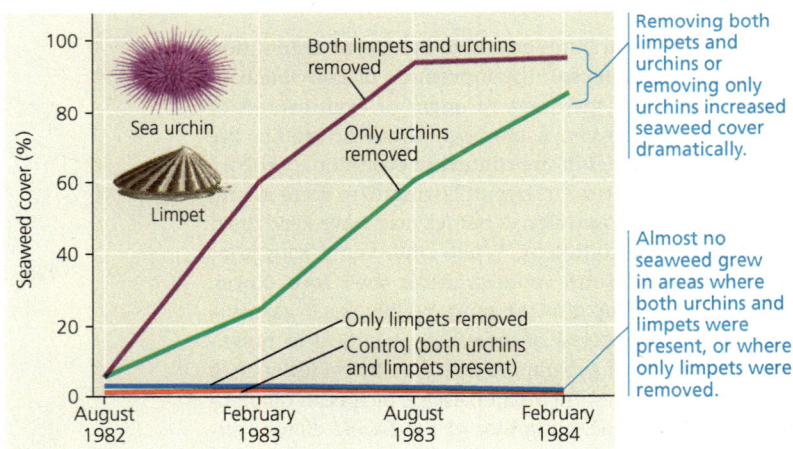

CONCLUSION Removing both limpets and urchins resulted in the greatest increase in seaweed cover, indicating that both species have some influence on seaweed distribution. But since removing only urchins greatly increased seaweed growth while removing only limpets had little effect, Fletcher concluded that sea urchins have a much greater effect than limpets in limiting seaweed distribution.

SOURCE W. J. Fletcher, Interactions among subtidal Australian sea urchins, gastropods, and algae: effects of experimental removals, *Ecological Monographs* 57:89–109 (1989).

WHAT IF? Seaweed cover increased the most when both urchins *and* limpets were removed. How might you explain this result?

In certain marine ecosystems, there is often an inverse relationship between the abundance of sea urchins and seaweeds (multicellular algae, such as kelp). Where urchins that graze on seaweeds and other algae are common, large stands of seaweeds do not become established. As described in Figure 52.20, Australian researchers have tested the hypothesis that sea urchins are a biotic factor limiting seaweed distribution. When sea urchins were removed from experimental plots, seaweed cover increased dramatically, showing that urchins limited the distribution of seaweeds.

In addition to predation and herbivory, the presence or absence of pollinators, food resources, parasites, pathogens, and competing organisms can act as a biotic limitation on species distribution. Some of the most striking cases of limitation occur when humans accidentally or intentionally introduce exotic predators or pathogens into new areas and wipe out native species. You will encounter examples of these impacts in Chapter 56, where we discuss conservation biology.

Abiotic Factors

The last question in the flowchart in Figure 52.18 considers whether abiotic factors, such as temperature, water, oxygen, salinity, sunlight, or soil, might be limiting a species' distribution. If the physical conditions at a site do not allow a species to survive and reproduce, then the species will not be found there. Throughout this discussion, keep in mind that most abiotic factors vary substantially in space and time. Daily and annual fluctuations of abiotic factors may either blur or accentuate regional distinctions. Furthermore, organisms can avoid some stressful conditions temporarily through behaviors such as dormancy or hibernation.

Temperature

Environmental temperature is an important factor in the distribution of organisms because of its effect on biological processes. Cells may rupture if the water they contain freezes (at temperatures below 0°C), and the proteins of most organisms denature at temperatures above 45°C. Most organisms function best within a specific range of environmental temperature. Temperatures outside that range may force some animals to expend energy regulating their internal temperature, as mammals and birds do (see Chapter 40). Extraordinary adaptations enable certain organisms, such as thermophilic prokaryotes (see Chapter 27), to live outside the temperature range habitable by other life.

Water and Oxygen

The dramatic variation in water availability among habitats is another important factor in species distribution. Species living at the seashore or in tidal wetlands can desiccate (dry out) as the tide recedes. Terrestrial organisms face a nearly constant threat of desiccation, and the distribution of terrestrial species reflects their ability to obtain and conserve water. Many amphibians, such as the harlequin toad in Figure 52.1, are particularly vulnerable to drying because they use their moist, delicate skin for gas exchange. Desert organisms exhibit a variety of adaptations for acquiring and conserving water in dry environments, as described in Chapter 44.

Water affects oxygen availability in aquatic environments and in flooded soils. Because oxygen diffuses slowly in water, its concentration can be low in certain aquatic systems and soils, limiting cellular respiration and other physiological processes. Oxygen concentrations can be particularly low in both deep ocean and deep lake waters and sediments where organic matter is abundant. Flooded wetland soils may also have low oxygen content. Mangroves and other trees have specialized roots that project above the water and help the root system obtain oxygen (see Figure 35.4). Unlike many flooded wetlands, the surface waters of streams and rivers tend to be well oxygenated because of rapid exchange of gases with the atmosphere.

Salinity

As you learned in Chapter 7, the salt concentration of water in the environment affects the water balance of organisms through osmosis. Most aquatic organisms are restricted to either freshwater or saltwater habitats by their limited ability to osmoregulate (see Chapter 44). Although most terrestrial organisms can excrete excess salts from specialized glands or in feces or urine, salt flats and other high-salinity habitats typically have few species of plants or animals.

Salmon that migrate between freshwater streams and the ocean use both behavioral and physiological mechanisms to osmoregulate. They adjust the amount of water they drink to help balance their salt content, and their gills switch from taking up salt in fresh water to excreting salt in the ocean.

Sunlight

Sunlight absorbed by photosynthetic organisms provides the energy that drives most ecosystems, and too little sunlight can limit the distribution of photosynthetic species. In forests, shading by leaves in the treetops makes competition for light especially intense, particularly for seedlings growing on the forest floor. In aquatic environments, every meter of water depth selectively absorbs about 45% of the red light and about 2% of the blue light passing through it. As a result, most photosynthesis in aquatic environments occurs relatively near the surface.

▲ **Figure 52.21 Alpine tree line in Banff National Park, Canada.** Organisms living at high elevations are exposed not only to high levels of ultraviolet radiation but also to freezing temperatures, moisture deficits, and strong winds. Above the tree line, the combination of such factors restricts the growth and survival of trees.

Too much light can also limit the survival of organisms. In some ecosystems, such as deserts, high light levels can increase temperature stress if animals and plants are unable to avoid the light or to cool themselves through evaporation (see Chapter 40). At high elevations, the sun's rays are more likely to damage DNA and proteins because the atmosphere is thinner, absorbing less ultraviolet (UV) radiation. Damage from UV radiation, combined with other abiotic stresses, prevents trees from surviving above a certain elevation, resulting in the appearance of a tree line on mountain slopes **(Figure 52.21)**.

Rocks and Soil

In terrestrial environments, the pH, mineral composition, and physical structure of rocks and soil limit the distribution of plants and thus of the animals that feed on them, contributing to the patchiness of terrestrial ecosystems. The pH of soil can limit the distribution of organisms directly, through extreme acidic or basic conditions, or indirectly, by affecting the solubility of nutrients and toxins.

In a river, the composition of the rocks and soil that make up the substrate (riverbed) can affect water chemistry, which in turn influences the resident organisms. In freshwater and marine environments, the structure of the substrate determines the organisms that can attach to it or burrow into it.

Throughout this chapter, you have seen how the distributions of biomes and organisms depend on abiotic and biotic factors. In the next chapter, we continue to work our way through the hierarchy outlined in Figure 52.2, focusing on how abiotic and biotic factors influence the ecology of populations.

CONCEPT CHECK 52.4

1. Give examples of human actions that could expand a species' distribution by changing its (a) dispersal or (b) biotic interactions.
2. **WHAT IF?** You suspect that deer are restricting the distribution of a tree species by preferentially eating the seedlings of the tree. How might you test this hypothesis?
3. **MAKE CONNECTIONS** As you saw in Figure 25.20 (p. 571), Hawaiian silverswords underwent a remarkable adaptive radiation after their ancestor reached Hawaii, while the islands were still young. Would you expect the cattle egret to undergo a similar adaptive radiation in the Americas (see Figure 52.19)? Explain.

For suggested answers, see Appendix A.

52 CHAPTER REVIEW

SUMMARY OF KEY CONCEPTS

CONCEPT 52.1

Earth's climate varies by latitude and season and is changing rapidly (pp. 1190–1196)

- Global **climate** patterns are largely determined by the input of solar energy and Earth's revolution around the sun.
- The changing angle of the sun over the year, bodies of water, and mountains exert seasonal, regional, and local effects on **macroclimate**.
- Fine-scale differences in **abiotic** (nonliving) factors, such as sunlight and temperature, determine **microclimate**.
- Increasing greenhouse gas concentrations in the air are warming Earth and altering the distributions of many species. Some species will not be able to shift their ranges quickly enough to reach suitable habitat in the future.

? *Suppose global air circulation suddenly reversed, with most air ascending at 30° north and south latitude and descending at the equator. At what latitude would you most likely find deserts in this scenario?*

CONCEPT 52.2

The structure and distribution of terrestrial biomes are controlled by climate and disturbance (pp. 1196–1202)

- **Climographs** show that temperature and precipitation are correlated with **biomes**. Because other factors also play roles in biome location, biomes overlap.
- Terrestrial biomes are often named for major physical or climatic factors and for their predominant vegetation. Vertical layering is an important feature of terrestrial biomes.
- **Disturbance**, both natural and human-induced, influences the type of vegetation found in biomes. Humans have altered much of Earth's surface, replacing the natural terrestrial communities described and depicted in Figure 52.12 with urban and agricultural ones.

? *Some arctic tundra ecosystems receive as little rainfall as deserts but have much more dense vegetation. Based on Figure 52.10, what climatic factor might explain this difference? Explain.*

CONCEPT 52.3

Aquatic biomes are diverse and dynamic systems that cover most of Earth (pp. 1203–1209)

- Aquatic biomes are characterized primarily by their physical environment rather than by climate and are often layered with regard to light penetration, temperature, and community structure. Marine biomes have a higher salt concentration than freshwater biomes.
- In the ocean and in most lakes, an abrupt temperature change called a **thermocline** separates a more uniformly warm upper layer from more uniformly cold deeper waters.

? *In which aquatic biomes might you find an aphotic zone?*

CONCEPT 52.4

Interactions between organisms and the environment limit the distribution of species (pp. 1209–1213)

- Ecologists want to know not only *where* species occur but also *why* those species occur where they do.

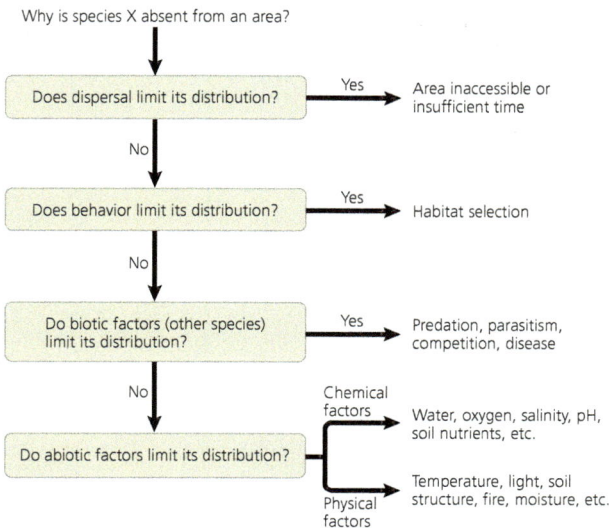

Why is species X absent from an area?

Does dispersal limit its distribution? — Yes → Area inaccessible or insufficient time

No ↓

Does behavior limit its distribution? — Yes → Habitat selection

No ↓

Do biotic factors (other species) limit its distribution? — Yes → Predation, parasitism, competition, disease

No ↓

Do abiotic factors limit its distribution? — Chemical factors → Water, oxygen, salinity, pH, soil nutrients, etc.
Physical factors → Temperature, light, soil structure, fire, moisture, etc.

- The distribution of species may be limited by **dispersal**, the movement of individuals away from their area of origin; behavior; **biotic** (living) factors; and abiotic factors, such as temperature extremes, salinity, and water availability.

? *If you were an ecologist studying the chemical and physical limits to the distributions of species, how might you rearrange the flowchart preceding this question?*

TEST YOUR UNDERSTANDING

(MB) **Multiple-choice Self-Quiz questions #1–10 can be found in the Study Area at www.masteringbiology.com.**

11. **DRAW IT** After reading about the experiment of W. J. Fletcher described in Figure 52.20, you decide to study feeding relationships among sea otters, sea urchins, and kelp on your own. You know that sea otters prey on sea urchins and that urchins eat kelp. At four coastal sites, you measure kelp abundance. Then you spend one day at each site and mark whether otters are present or absent every 5 minutes during daylight hours. Make a graph that shows how otter density depends on kelp abundance, using the data shown below. Then formulate a hypothesis to explain the pattern you observed.

Site	Kelp Abundance (% cover)	Otter Density (# sightings per day)
1	75	98
2	15	18
3	60	85
4	25	36

12. **EVOLUTION CONNECTION**
Discuss how the concept of time applies to ecological situations and evolutionary changes. Do ecological time and evolutionary time ever overlap? If so, what are some examples?

13. **SCIENTIFIC INQUIRY**
Jens Clausen and colleagues, at the Carnegie Institution of Washington, studied how the size of yarrow plants (*Achillea lanulosa*) growing on the slopes of the Sierra Nevada varied with elevation. They found that plants from low elevations were generally taller than plants from high elevations, as shown in the diagram on the next page.
Clausen and colleagues proposed two hypotheses to explain this variation within a species: (1) There are genetic differences between populations of plants found at different elevations. (2) The species has developmental flexibility and can assume tall or short growth forms, depending on local abiotic factors. If you had seeds from yarrow plants found at low and high elevations, what experiments would you perform to test these hypotheses?

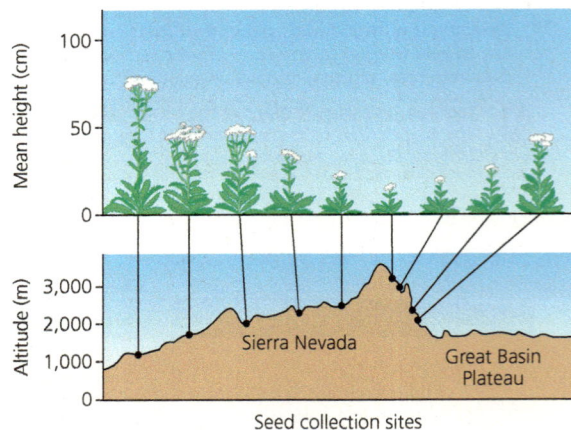

Source: J. Clausen et al., Experimental studies on the nature of species. III. Environmental responses of climatic races of *Achillea*, Carnegie Institution of Washington Publication No. 581 (1948).

14. **WRITE ABOUT A THEME**

Feedback Regulation Global warming is occurring rapidly in Arctic marine and terrestrial ecosystems, including tundra and northern coniferous forests. In such locations, reflective white snow and ice cover are melting more quickly and extensively, uncovering darker-colored ocean water, plants, and rocks. In a short essay (100–150 words), explain how this process might represent a positive-feedback loop.

For selected answers, see Appendix A.

2 Using Math:
Keep it in Proportion

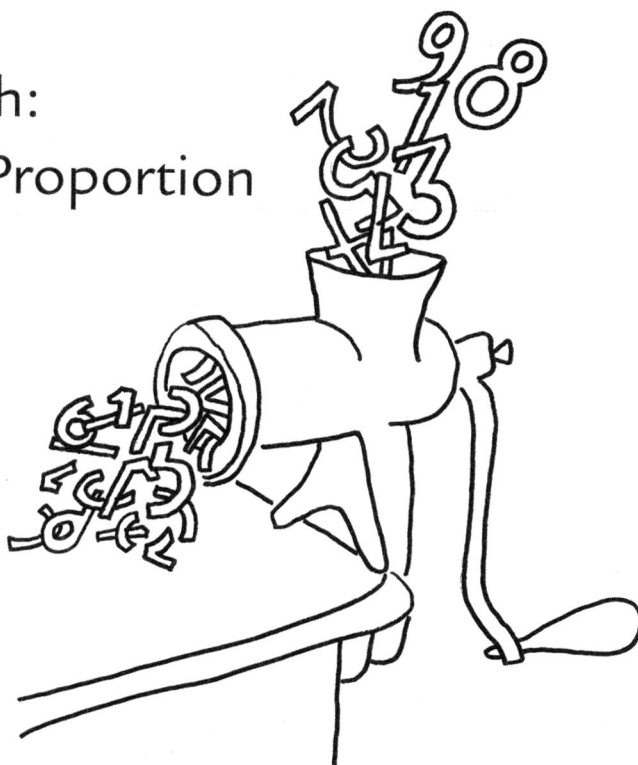

When you complete this chapter, you should be able to:

▓ Employ basic mathematical operations, traditionally or by use of a calculator.

▓ Solve simultaneous linear equations or quadratic equations.

▓ Simplify complex fractions.

▓ Use basic right-angle trigonometry.

▓ Work with logarithms and exponentials.

▓ Work with ratios and proportions of various kinds.

▓ Understand the use of significant figures, scientific notation, and useful prefixes.

▓ Be able to use vectors and calculate vector components.

▓ Construct graphs, and find the slope of a line and the area under a line.

Your Starting Point

Do You Still Remember These?

Answer the following questions to assess your basic math skills.

1. $\sqrt{100} = $ _____ or _____.

2. $x + 2 = 6.5; x = $ _____.

3. $\dfrac{1}{2} + \dfrac{1}{3} = $ _____.

4. $\begin{cases} 2x + 3y = 3 \\ 3x + 2y = 7 \end{cases} x = $ _____, $y = $ _____.

5. $\dfrac{1}{p} + \dfrac{1}{4} = \dfrac{1}{2}; p = $ _____.

6. $PV = 18, V = 2; P = $ _____.

For 7 and 8, use Figure 2.1.

7. Leave in fraction form: $\cos \theta = $ _____.

8. Leave in fraction form: $\tan \theta = $ _____.

9. Solve $x^2 + x - 12 = 0$ for x; $x = $ _____ or $x = $ _____.

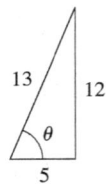

FIGURE 2.1 Triangle for questions 7 and 8.

10. Simplify $\dfrac{\dfrac{a+b}{1-ab}+b}{1+\dfrac{b(a-b)}{1-ab}}$.

Math in Physics

An ancient Egyptian clay tablet on which a student was solving a word problem—incorrectly—has survived through the years to be found by archeologists. Science has depended on mathematical representations of physical phenomena ever since ancient societies observed the regularities in the motions of the sun, moon, and planets; began to predict eclipses and when to plant; and started to form theories of the nature of matter. Modern physics may be said to have begun when Pythagoras (born approximately 497 BCE) found a relationship between ratios of lengths of strings and consonant musical intervals. (The simpler the fraction expressing that ratio, the more harmonious the sound.) We could say that Pythagoras, who had observed the simple right triangles the ancient Egyptians used to divide arable farmland areas after the annual flooding of the Nile, had learned how to use *data* (results of experiments) to explain phenomena (natural occurrences). But note one thing: Pythagoras first played with string lengths and string tensions before arriving at the need for math.

Physics, the first of the sciences to isolate phenomena and so to obtain correspondences between numbers and physical quantities that could be varied controllably, found success by summarizing the data in laws, equations giving mathematical representations of physical regularities. This book is intended for two groups of students: those who plan to take the physics course for health science majors and those who plan to take the calculus-based physics course for engineering and other science majors. At some schools, all students take the calculus-based course. The good news is that if you possess the basic arithmetical skills—including adding, multiplying, dividing fractions, and working with least common denominators—you should be well equipped to tackle physics concepts. Much of first-year physics will involve working with proportional relationships, inverse as well as direct; fairly simple equations, linear and quadratic; and right-angle trigonometry. Only the electricity and magnetism part of the calculus-based course will make extensive use of calculus.

This chapter will include a quick review of basic arithmetical operations and will then concentrate on the math skills you need for either the algebra-trig or calculus-based physics courses.

Basic Math Operations

Calculators are both a blessing and a curse: blessing, because with a calculator you don't need to memorize many multiplication tables or do long divisions; curse, because through using a calculator you lose the ability to estimate whether or not an answer is correct from its magnitude.

I will assume that everyone knows how to use a calculator to obtain $28 \times 53 = 1484$ and also knows that $28 \times 53 = 53 \times 28$. (Both addition and multiplication are commutative. You can add or multiply a series of numbers in any order. But be careful with subtraction: $6 - 2 \neq 2 - 6$.) What you absolutely need to be able to do is recognize a wrong result if, without realizing it, you hit the divide button on the calculator instead of the multiply button.

WORKED EXAMPLE 2.1

For practice, estimate the result below *without* using a calculator:

$$\frac{(343)(587)}{(727)(296)} = \qquad\qquad \text{Eqn. 2.1}$$

Before you pick up a calculator to check, follow the reasoning here, which uses rounding:

$$\frac{(343)(587)}{(727)(296)} \approx \frac{(300)(600)}{(700)(300)} = \frac{6}{7} \approx 1$$

Because the exact answer of our modified example is 0.936, while $\frac{6}{7} = 0.857$, we see that our answer is within $\frac{0.857 - 0.936}{0.936} \times 100 = -8.4\%$ of the correct answer. This value, 8.4%, is the percent error of our estimate from the known value. The *deviation* is the difference 0.857 – 0.936, the result minus the known value. The *fractional error* is the deviation divided by the known value, and the percent error is the fractional error multiplied by 100.

Also note the following approach:
$\frac{343}{727} \approx \frac{1}{2}$, $\frac{587}{296} \approx 2$, so $\left(\frac{343}{727}\right) \times \left(\frac{587}{296}\right) \approx \left(\frac{1}{2}\right) \times 2 = 1$. No matter how we do the estimation, we can definitely find the order of magnitude of an answer, in other words, whether it is in single digits, 10s, 100s, and so on.

TIME TO TRY

Estimate

(a) $\dfrac{(222)(333)}{(555)(777)} =$

(b) $\dfrac{(8.574)(7.458)}{(3.672)} =$

(c) What method was used to simplify calculations in the previous estimates?

Answers: (a) $\left(\frac{2}{6}\right) \times \left(\frac{3}{8}\right) \approx \frac{1}{8} = 0.13$; the exact result is 0.17.
(b) $\frac{9 \cdot 7}{4} = \frac{63}{4} = \frac{60}{4} + \frac{3}{4} = 15.8$; the exact result is 17.4. (c) The numbers were rounded to one significant digit and zeroes, or estimated as simple fractions. This means we need to look more carefully at rounding and significant digits in a number.

ROUNDING

Not all measurements we make or numbers we calculate are meaningful. The number of digits we keep in a result are those within the margin of error. We call these *significant* figures. We will study rounding numbers here, and deal more extensively with significant figures and experimental errors later. For now, remember that significant figures do not include initial or ending zeroes that serve only to indicate the scale of a number.

✔ **QUICK CHECK**

Round the number 95168226 to

(a) 7 significant figures: _____.

(b) 6 significant figures: _____.

(c) 5 significant figures: _____.

(d) 4 significant figures: _____.

(e) 3 significant figures: _____.

(e) 95200000.

Answers: (a) 95168230. (b) 95168200. (c) 95168000. (d) 95170000.

When rounding to six figures, 26 (formed by the last two digits) represents less than half of 100, so we round the last three digits down to 200. When rounding to four figures, 8226 (the last four digits) represents one-half or more of 10,000, so we round up to 95170000.

When do we round up, and when do we round down?

If the quantity to be rounded is 0% to 49% of the rightmost column that will keep a digit, don't change the number in that column (see [b] and [c]). If the quantity to be rounded is 50% or more of the number in the column being kept, increase that number by 1 (see [a], [d], and [e]).

SIGNIFICANT FIGURES To see why we need to round numbers consider how well you can measure a length with a ruler. How accurately can you measure liquids with a kitchen measuring cup? The smallest subdivisions on a ruler in centimeters are usually millimeters. You can estimate a length to about half a millimeter. A kitchen measuring cup is usually calibrated in ounces. You might be able to estimate a quantity to about a quarter of an ounce.

Use the following exercises to either review or acquaint yourself with how to determine and express significant figures. Pay particular attention to the rules determining the number of significant figures. The terms *accuracy* and *precision* will be illustrated in the following examples.

✔ QUICK CHECK

1. In a bio lab, a mite travels a distance of 4.7 cm (centimeters) in 3.00 s (seconds). What is its average speed?

2. You have counted scintillations in two separate experiments where the counts were limited to one-half hour to avoid eye strain. The first result was 5,824; the second was 6,017. What is the average number of scintillations per hour?

3. A result depends on the difference between 8,457 and 8,226. How many significant figures does the result have?

4. The result of an experiment depends on the difference between 5, 723, known to four significant figures, and 3, 550, known to three significant figures. How many significant figures are there in the result?

Answers: 1. The mite's average speed is $\dfrac{\text{distance}}{\text{time interval}} = \dfrac{4.7\ \text{cm}}{3.00\ \text{s}} = 1.6\ \dfrac{\text{cm}}{\text{s}}$. The answer a calculator gives, 1.566667 cm/s, is not correct, because the distance is only given to two digits. 2. The answer is the average of the two half-hour measurements (5,824 and 6,017) multiplied by 2. That comes out to the sum of the two counts, and is 11,841. However, 2 × 5,824 = 11,648 and 2 × 6,017 = 12,034. The first differs from the average counts per hour by 11,648 − 11,841 = −193 and the second by 12,034 − 11,841 = +193. This means that there is an uncertainty of ±193 in the answer. Therefore, we round it off to 11,800 ± 200. The result 11,800 indicates the accuracy of the result. The error ±200 indicates the precision. 3. Because 8,457 − 8,226 = 231, there are only three significant figures in the result. 4. Because 5,723 − 3,550 = 2,173 cannot have more significant figures than the number with the smaller number of significant figures, this should be rounded to 2,170 and have three significant figures.

When multiplying or dividing numbers, the answer only has as many significant digits as the number with the fewest digits. ▪

The result of a sum is rounded to the column with the last significant digit in the number with the smallest number of significant figures. ▪

When subtracting one number from another, the result will have no more significant figures than the number with the fewest significant figures. When one or more columns disappear(s) in the subtraction, the result has that many fewer significant figures. ▪

Roughly, the total number of significant figures gives us the accuracy. The number to which the last significant figure, or last few significant figures, is known gives us the precision.

TIME TO TRY

An agribusiness quotes the number of egg-laying hens in its barns as 86,732 ± 110. How many significant figures should this number have?

Answer: There may be as many as 86,842 or as few as 86,622 hens in the barns. This number should be quoted as 86,700 ± 100 to convey a true account of the accuracy—three significant figures—and the precision, represented by the ±100.

Use of Calculators

When calculating the answer to Equation 2.1, did you notice that as long as you hit the multiply key before entering 587 and the divide key before entering 727 or 296, the order didn't matter? That's one of the advantages in using a simple scientific calculator. The minimum calculator for most physics courses must add, subtract, multiply, and divide; square numbers and take square roots; provide sine, cosine, and tangent functions and inverse trig functions; give logs to base 10 and natural logarithms and their inverses; give exponentials and their inverses; and provide y^x and $y^{1/x}$ functions. If the calculator has a special key for π, that's useful, but not necessary. (If you have had a math course that required a more complicated calculator with parentheses having to be entered, etc., be sure you mastered its use.) ▪

MULTIPLE OPERATIONS

Determine the solution to the following multiple operation problem.

$$\text{The value of } 81 - \left[\frac{(28)(4-x)}{7}\right] \text{ when } x + 5 = 7 \text{ is } \underline{\hspace{1cm}}.$$

The easiest way to solve this is to find $x = 7 - 5 = 2$, and then solve $81 - \left[\frac{(28)(4-2)}{7}\right]$. Note that the order in which operations are performed is important. Start with the innermost parentheses and work outward:

$$4 - 2 = 2$$
$$28(2) = 56$$
$$\frac{56}{7} = 8$$
$$81 - 8 = 73$$

Alternatively,

$$4 - 2 = 2$$
$$\frac{28}{7} = 4$$
$$4 \cdot 2 = 8$$
$$81 - 8 = 73$$

Order of Multiple Operations

1. Do all operations inside parentheses or brackets first. Work from the innermost to the outermost parentheses.

2. Do all multiplications and divisions in each term in the order previously indicated.

3. Finally, add and subtract the terms as indicated by their signs. ▨

CANCELLATION

Is the following cancellation correct? $\dfrac{64}{16} = \dfrac{\cancel{6}4}{1\cancel{6}} = 4$. Right? WRONG! Although the answer is correct, the result is accidental, as we see from $\dfrac{3\cancel{2}}{\cancel{2}} = 3$, which is obviously wrong because $2 \times 16 = 32$. You can't cancel digits within numbers, only entire numbers for which the complete sets of digits cancel.

TIME TO TRY

Simplify the following fraction by canceling numbers where possible:

$$\frac{(537)(60)}{(15)(537)} = \underline{\hspace{3cm}}.$$

Answer: $\dfrac{(537)(60)}{(15)(537)} = \dfrac{(15)(537)}{(1)(60)} = \dfrac{(15)}{(60)} = 4$

Scientific Notation

Scientists and workers in scientific fields must be able to communicate without ambiguity. A difference of a factor of ten in a heart medication may be the difference between life and death for a patient. Scientific notation removes all ambiguity in numbers.

For instance, what is the difference between 3,330, 3,330., and 3,330.0? The implication is that we know 3330. to four decimal places, and 3,330.0 to five, but 3330 could be accurate to one, two, three, or four places. To remove any such uncertainty, we place a decimal point after the first digit, add all other digits that are known to be accurate, and multiply by a power of 10 to correct for the decimal placement. This method of expression is called scientific notation.

✔ QUICK CHECK

1. If 53,353 is known to five significant figures, express it in scientific notation.

2. Express 8,275,000 m in scientific notation. Only the first four digits are known to be accurate.

3. Express 0.00287 in scientific notation.

Answers: 1. It should be 5.3353 × 10⁴. Note that the exponent in 10⁴ tells how many decimal places to the left the decimal point has been moved. 2. This is 8.275 × 10⁶. We drop the place-holder zeroes when they contain no information about the accuracy or precision of the number. 3. This is 2.87 × 10⁻³. Here the 0.00 only gives the decimal order of magnitude—the power of ten—of the number. We never write 0002.87 × 10⁻³, because the initial zeroes are meaningless.

Note that scientific notation is easy to work with if you understand the rules for exponents. (See Laws of Exponents on pages 100–101.)

COMMON PREFIXES

Some decimal orders of magnitude, particular powers of 10, occur so often that they are indicated by prefixes. Table 2.1 gives a list of these. You will encounter others later in science courses, but the ones given in the table should be memorized. That will give you a good head start so you won't use the wrong power of ten when converting micrograms or milligrams to grams.

TABLE 2.1 **The most common decimal prefixes.**

Prefix	Symbol	Decimal Equivalent	Exponential Equivalent
giga	G	1,000,000,000	10^9
mega	M	1,000,000	10^6
kilo	k	1,000	10^3
deka	D	10	10^1
		1	10^0
demi	d	0.1	10^{-1}
centi	c	0.01	10^{-2}
milli	m	0.001	10^{-3}
micro	μ	0.000 001	10^{-6}
nano	n	0.000 000 001	10^{-9}
pico	p	0.000 000 000 001	10^{-12}

✔ **QUICK CHECK**

Refer to Table 2.1.

1. What is a deciliter?

2. What is a megavolt?

Answers: 1. A deciliter is 10^{-1} liter, or one-tenth of a liter. 2. A megavolt is 10^6 volts, or one million volts.

Algebra

SIMULTANEOUS LINEAR EQUATIONS

WORKED EXAMPLE 2.2

Given $\begin{cases} 8x - 5y = 28 \\ -3x + 6y = 6 \end{cases}$, solve for x and y.

The basic technique for solving simultaneous linear equations is to multiply each equation by a (different, occasionally equal) number such that either the terms in x or the terms in y sum to zero. Here $\begin{cases} 3[8x - 5y] = 3(28) \\ 8[-3x + 6y] = 8(6) \end{cases}$ so

$\begin{cases} 24x - 15y = 84 \\ -24x + 48y = 48 \end{cases}$ and $0 + 33y = 132$, with $y = 4$.

Substitute the value of y in either equation to find x:

$$8x - 5(4) = 28$$
$$8x = 48$$
$$x = 6$$

Solve the same two simultaneous equations by eliminating y:

Answer: Use $\begin{aligned} 6[8x - 5y] = 6(28) \\ 5[-3x + 6y] = 5(6) \end{aligned}$

Warning: If one equation is a multiple of the other equation, we have only one equation and cannot solve it.

Example: $2x + 3y = 5$ and $4x + 6y = 10$ are the same equation because the second equation is the first one multiplied by 2.

✔ QUICK CHECK

Solve for x and y:

1. $\begin{cases} 5x + 2y = 6 \\ 3x + 4y = 12 \end{cases}$

Solve for I_1, I_2, and I_3:

2. $\begin{cases} 2I_1 + 3I_2 - 6I_3 = 4 \\ 4I_1 - 2I_2 + 4I_3 = 8 \\ I_1 + I_2 - 4I_3 = 1 \end{cases}$

Note: Equations like these can arise when solving Kirchoff's laws for currents, I, in multi-loop resistive circuits. This example also illustrates the fact that we use many different symbols in physics, which makes it difficult to recognize math that we already know. That issue will be addressed later in this chapter.

Answers: 1. $x = 0$, $y = 3$. 2. $I_1 = 2$, $I_2 = 1$, $I_3 = \frac{1}{2}$. (Quick Check example 2 can be solved by the same method as Quick Check example 1, by eliminating one unknown quantity first, and then a second one, to be able to solve for the third unknown quantity.)

QUADRATIC EQUATIONS

Remember that quadratic equations are equations that contain the square of a quantity. Equations of the form $ax^2 = b$ are trivial because $x = \pm\sqrt{\frac{b}{a}}$. Therefore, we will review equations of the form $ax^2 + bx + c = 0$.

Some quadratic equations can be factored fairly easily into the form $(x - p)(x - q) = 0$. Solve $x^2 - 7x + 12 = 0$ for x: $x =$ _____ or _____.

If you notice that $4 + 3 = 7$ and $4 \times 3 = 12$, you can see that $x^2 - 7x + 12 = (x - 3)(x - 4) = 0$ so $x = 3$ or $x = 4$. (Because either factor may be zero, either factor yields a solution to the equation.)

Write any quadratic equation in the form $ax^2 + bx + c = 0$ and divide by a. We now have $(1)x^2 + b'x + c' = 0$. The previous example showed that $b' = -(p + q)$ and $c' = +pq$. When p and q are small integers, it is often possible to see what they are by inspecting b' and c'. ▨

When you cannot find the solution by inspection, you must use the quadratic formula:

$$x = \frac{-b \pm \sqrt{b^2 - 4ac}}{2a}.$$

✔ **QUICK CHECK**

1. Solve $x^2 + 3x - 10 = 0$ for x.

2. Solve for x: $x^2 + 4x - 21 = 0$.

3. Solve for t: $4t^2 - 16t + 15 = 0$.

4. Solve $2x^2 + 8x + 6 = 0$ by the quadratic formula.

Answers: 1. Because this is the same as $(x + 5)(x - 2) = 0$, $x = -5$ or $x = 2$.

2. $x = 3$, $x = -7$. 3. $t = \frac{3}{2}$, $t = \frac{5}{2}$. 4. $x = \frac{-8 \mp \sqrt{64 - 4(12)}}{4}$

$= \frac{-8 \mp \sqrt{64 - 48}}{4} = \frac{-8 \mp \sqrt{16}}{4} = \frac{-8 \mp 4}{4}$, so $x = -3$ or $x = -1$. In

factored form this equation is $2(x + 1)(x + 3) = 0$.

In 4, did you note that all the terms were multiples of 2, so the equation could have been simplified to $x^2 + 4x + 3 = 0$? Always look for ways of simplifying what you have to solve.

TIME TO TRY

1. Solve for ω: $9\omega^2 = 25$. (The Greek letter ω, omega, often represents angular velocity.)

2. Solve for t: $4t^2 - 2t - 6 = 0$. (The letter t usually represents time.)

3. Solve for x: $x^2 - 9abx + 20a^2b^2 = 0$. (This example illustrates the fact that equations may include symbols as well as numbers. In physics these may be well-known symbols, such as that for the speed of light. We can then insert numbers in the solution to replace the symbols.)

Answers: 1. $\omega = \pm\dfrac{5}{3}$. 2. $t = -1$ or $t = \dfrac{3}{2}$. 3. $x = 4ab$ or $x = 5ab$.

It's worth memorizing the quadratic formula even though many calculators are set up to solve quadratic equations. You should keep in mind that if you are in a class where you are not allowed to use alphanumeric calculators or preprogrammed solutions, this one formula will be very useful. And you can then use it to check that you entered the constants in your calculator correctly. ▪

More Complex Operations

COMMON DENOMINATORS

When asked to find a common denominator for two fractions, most students can do it. However, when the need to do so arises in the course of a physics problem, many students are unable to continue because the knowledge is compartmentalized as "math," not "science." (This stumbling block was already mentioned in the second practice exercise.) Keep this in mind when you have to add or subtract fractions in a physics problem. Remember, "Common denom is a known phenom (enon.)"

Try another example: Add $\dfrac{1}{3} + \dfrac{1}{4} = $ _____.

250 Life Sciences Foundation

First multiply each number by 1, so $\frac{1}{3}(1) + \frac{1}{4}(1) =$ _____. Then multiply $\frac{1}{3}$ by $\frac{4}{4}$ in place of 1 and multiply $\frac{1}{4}$ by $\frac{3}{3}$ in place of 1.

This results in $\frac{1}{3}\left(\frac{4}{4}\right) + \frac{1}{4}\left(\frac{3}{3}\right) = \frac{4}{12} + \frac{3}{12} = \frac{7}{12}$.

In this process each denominator became $3 \times 4 = 12$. Alternatively, you can multiply the two denominators together to get a common denominator and multiply each numerator by the other fraction's denominator. Use whichever method works for you.

Now try this with symbols rather than numbers: $\frac{1}{a} + \frac{1}{b} =$ _____.

Answer: $\frac{1b}{ab} + \frac{1a}{ba} = \frac{a+b}{ab}$

✔ **QUICK CHECK**

1. $\frac{1}{3} - \frac{1}{4} =$ _____.

2. $\frac{1}{a} - \frac{1}{b} =$ _____.

3. $\frac{5}{6} - \frac{2}{3} =$ _____.

4. $\frac{3}{p} + \frac{5}{q} =$ _____.

5. $\frac{p}{q^2} - \frac{2q}{p} =$ _____.

Answers: 1. $\frac{1}{12}$. 2. $\frac{b-a}{ab}$. 3. $\frac{1}{6}$. 4. $\frac{5p+3q}{pq}$. 5. $\frac{p^2-2q^3}{pq^2}$.

SIMPLIFYING COMPLEX FRACTIONS

See if you remember how to divide one fraction by another. Simplify:

$$\frac{\left(\frac{a}{b}\right)}{\left(\frac{c}{d}\right)} =$$ _____.

Here it is best to use a general formula before proceeding to specific cases and rules:

$$\frac{\left(\dfrac{a}{b}\right)}{\left(\dfrac{c}{d}\right)} = \frac{\left(\dfrac{a}{b}\right)\left(\dfrac{b}{1}\right)}{\left(\dfrac{c}{d}\right)\left(\dfrac{b}{1}\right)} = \frac{\left(\dfrac{a}{1}\right)}{\left(\dfrac{cb}{d}\right)} = \frac{\left(\dfrac{a}{1}\right)\left(\dfrac{d}{1}\right)}{\left(\dfrac{cb}{d}\right)\left(\dfrac{d}{1}\right)} = \frac{\left(\dfrac{ad}{1}\right)}{\left(\dfrac{bc}{1}\right)}.$$

Because anything divided by one is equal to itself, $\dfrac{ad}{1} = ad$ and $\dfrac{bc}{1} = bc$. Finally,

$$\frac{\left(\dfrac{a}{b}\right)}{\left(\dfrac{c}{d}\right)} = \frac{ad}{bc}.$$

But this is the same result you would get by multiplying $\dfrac{a}{b}$ by $\dfrac{d}{c}$ instead of dividing it by $\dfrac{c}{d}$.

The rule for dividing fractions is to invert the fraction in the denominator (bottom) first, and then multiply the fraction in the numerator (top) by this inverted fraction. ▪

✔ **QUICK CHECK**

1. $\dfrac{\dfrac{2}{5}}{\dfrac{8}{7}} = $ _____ .

Answer: 1. $\dfrac{\dfrac{2}{5}}{\dfrac{8}{7}} = \dfrac{2}{5} \times \dfrac{7}{8} = \dfrac{14}{40} = \dfrac{7}{20}$

All difficulties in simplifying fractions vanish if you pay close attention to parentheses and find common denominators as needed. But you will also need to know how to divide one fraction by another.

Simplify $\dfrac{1 - \dfrac{\dfrac{2}{3} + \dfrac{1}{4}}{\dfrac{1}{3} - \dfrac{1}{4}}}{1 + \dfrac{\dfrac{2}{3} - \dfrac{1}{4}}{\dfrac{1}{3} + \dfrac{1}{4}}}$ = _____.

You may want to say "forget it!" if it's been a while since complex fractions were taken up in a math class. However, go as far as you can by using the rule in the previous key statement before checking with the following step-by-step solution.

First, note the implied parentheses and brackets:

$$\dfrac{1 - \dfrac{\dfrac{2}{3} + \dfrac{1}{4}}{\dfrac{1}{3} - \dfrac{1}{4}}}{1 + \dfrac{\dfrac{2}{3} - \dfrac{1}{4}}{\dfrac{1}{3} + \dfrac{1}{4}}} = \dfrac{1 - \left[\dfrac{\left(\dfrac{2}{3} + \dfrac{1}{4}\right)}{\left(\dfrac{1}{3} - \dfrac{1}{4}\right)}\right]}{1 + \left[\dfrac{\left(\dfrac{2}{3} - \dfrac{1}{4}\right)}{\left(\dfrac{1}{3} + \dfrac{1}{4}\right)}\right]}.$$

By finding common denominators we obtain

$$\dfrac{1 - \left[\dfrac{\dfrac{11}{12}}{\dfrac{1}{12}}\right]}{1 + \left[\dfrac{\dfrac{5}{12}}{\dfrac{7}{12}}\right]} = \dfrac{1 - 11}{1 + \dfrac{5}{7}} = \dfrac{-10}{\dfrac{12}{7}} = \dfrac{-70}{12} = \dfrac{-35}{6}.$$

✔ **QUICK CHECK**

1. $\dfrac{\dfrac{1}{a^2} - \dfrac{1}{b^2}}{\dfrac{1}{a} - \dfrac{1}{b}} = $ _____.

2. $\dfrac{\dfrac{1+x}{1-x} - x}{1 + \dfrac{x(1+x)}{1-x}} = $ _____.

PROPORTIONS

PICTURE THIS

Owing to the economic downturn, a school has been forced to cancel the band for the senior prom unless the students can raise the money themselves for the band. To do this, some students plan on having a bake sale. A cookbook states that a basic puff pastry recipe of 2 cups of flour and $\frac{1}{2}$ pound of unsalted butter will make 60 palm cookies (also called elephant ears). The students want to make 510 cookies.

How many cups of flour will they need? How many pounds of butter will they need?

A ratio is a comparison between two numbers, usually written as $a:b$ or $\frac{a}{b}$. Our ratio of flour to cookies is $\dfrac{2 \text{ cups flour}}{60 \text{ cookies}}$ and of butter to cookies is $\dfrac{\frac{1}{2} \text{ cup butter}}{60 \text{ cookies}}$. In this recipe, the ratio of butter to flour, $\dfrac{\frac{1}{2} \text{ cup butter}}{2 \text{ cups flour}}$, remains the same no matter how many cookies you make.

If the students need 2 cups of flour for 60 cookies, then they need an unknown number of cups, x, for 510 cookies, but the amount of flour for each cookie is the same. "For each" is sometimes written as "per," and we can then say that the amount of flour "per" cookie is the same. Thus, $\dfrac{2 \text{ cups flour}}{60 \text{ cookies}} = \dfrac{x}{510 \text{ cookies}}$ and

$x = \dfrac{1020}{60}$ cups of flour = 17 cups of flour. An equality of two ratios, such as $\dfrac{2 \text{ cups flour}}{60 \text{ cookies}} = \dfrac{x}{510 \text{ cookies}}$ is called a proportion.

To find the number of cups of butter that the students will need, we use the same method:

The proportion is $\dfrac{\frac{1}{2} \text{ cup butter}}{60 \text{ cookies}} = \dfrac{x}{510 \text{ cookies}}$, so $x = \dfrac{255}{60}$ pounds of butter = 4.25 pounds of butter.

Note: this example has been kept simple by omitting the third ingredient, salt, and the details of preparation. Check a cookbook, not a physics book, to make cookies.

WORKED EXAMPLE 2.3

1. If a department store sells 187 pairs of men's socks in a week, how many pairs must the buyer order each year?

   Use the proportion $\dfrac{187}{1} = \dfrac{x}{52}$. Then $x = 52 \times 187 = 9{,}724$ pairs of socks. Note that this should be rounded to 9.72×10^3 in scientific notation because 52 is an absolute number and 187 has three significant figures.

2. Because class sizes vary from very small to very large, a university building committee uses a rule of thumb that one classroom is needed for each 25 students. How many classrooms are needed for 1,200 students?

Use the proportion $\frac{1}{25} = \frac{x}{12,000}$, so $x = 480$ classrooms.

3. The same university committee also follows a rule that they need one large classroom for every seven small classrooms. How many small classrooms does this 1,200-student university have?

Let s stand for the number of small classrooms and ℓ stand for the number of large classrooms. From (2) we already know that $s + \ell = 480$. From the information in this problem we know that $\frac{\ell}{s} = \frac{1}{7}$. Therefore, $s + \frac{s}{7} = 480$ and $s = \frac{3360}{8} = 420$. (Write out the missing intermediate step between the last two equations for practice.) That means $\ell = 480 - s = 480 - 420 = 60$. Alternatively, we could have solved $\ell + 7\ell = 480$ to find $\ell = 60$ directly, and then have found s. Would you have read the harder first method if we had started with the easier alternative method? Possibly, but keep in mind that it's always better to understand all possible problem-solving methods.

TIME TO TRY

These problems illustrate more abstract situations where symbols stand for invisible atoms or for general numbers.

1. There are twice as many hydrogen atoms as oxygen atoms in any quantity of water, H_2O. If there are 270,000 molecules of water in a test tube, how many hydrogen atoms does it contain?

2. A proportion can be written symbolically as $\frac{a}{b} = \frac{c}{d}$. Show that $\frac{b}{a} = \frac{d}{c}$.

Answers: 1. Let h stand for the number of hydrogen atoms and w for the number of water molecules. Then, $\frac{w}{h} = \frac{1}{2}$. But $w = 270,000$, so $h = 540,000$ hydrogen atoms. 2. Multiply the numerators by the product of the denominators: $\frac{b}{c}(bd) = \frac{d}{c}(bd)$, so $ad = bc$. Now divide by ac, the product of the original numerators: $\frac{ad}{ac} = \frac{bc}{ac}$, so $\frac{d}{c} = \frac{b}{a}$, which is the same as $\frac{b}{a} = \frac{d}{c}$.

DIRECT PROPORTIONS When we have a simple equation such as that for the number of cups of flour, c, as a function of the number of cookies, N, we can write $\frac{1}{30} = \frac{c}{N}$ or $c = \frac{1}{30}N$. When an unknown, or dependent quantity, c, is a simple multiple of a known, or independent, quantity, N, we have a direct proportion. No matter what symbols are used, this is always represented in the form $y = ax$ where the value of y depends on the value of x multiplied by a constant a. Note that the equation of a straight line, $y = mx + b$, is a direct proportion only when $b = 0$. When $b \neq 0$, we have a linear relationship, but not a direct proportion.

✔ **QUICK CHECK**

Which of the following are direct proportions and which are linear relationships? Look at the form of the equations: the symbols represent physical quantities. Also note that x and y are used in physics for representations of position along a coordinate axis.

1. $v = v_0 + at$. (v and t are variables, v_0 and a are constants.)

2. $v_{tang} = \omega r$. (v_{tang} and ω are variables, r is a constant.)

3. $S = \dfrac{E^2}{c}$. (S and E are variables, c is a constant.)

Answers: 1. Linear relationship (it is of the form $y = b + mx$). 2. Direct proportion. 3. Direct proportion (S is proportional to the quantity E^2 rather than to E).

THE GOLDEN MEAN When the proportion between three quantities is such that $\dfrac{a}{b} = \dfrac{b}{c}$, then b is the "golden mean" between a and c. This ratio occurs in nature and is used by artists and architects, among others.

CONTINUED PROPORTIONS Suppose a car drives 44 miles on 1.6 gallons of gas. How many gallons should the gas tank hold if the car is to be able to drive 330 miles without stopping for gas? We need to know how many miles the car gets to the gallon to be able to determine how many gallons it needs to travel 330 miles.

This calculation involves two steps. You will have to solve many problems that involve more than one step. Many students want to be able to look for the equation that solves the problem, but physics is about how you solve problems when you do not know the answer ahead of time. Study this problem carefully. It is a very simple example of the sort of solution that is needed frequently.

We first set up a proportion to find the miles per gallon: $\dfrac{44 \text{ mi}}{1.6 \text{ gal}} = \dfrac{x}{1 \text{ gal}}$, so $x = 27.5 \dfrac{\text{mi}}{\text{gal}}$. Then we follow with a second proportion: $\dfrac{1 \text{ gal}}{27.5 \text{ mi}} = \dfrac{y}{330 \text{ mi}}$, so $y = 12$ gal. This illustrates how the result of one proportion may become the basic information used for solving another proportion. Similarly, the solution of one linear or other equation may become the input of another equation. After you become used to such problems, you will be able to omit the intermediate step and immediately write $\dfrac{1.6 \text{ gal}}{44 \text{ mi}} = \dfrac{y}{330 \text{ mi}}$.

WORKED EXAMPLE 2.4

Let's apply this approach to another situation. You are riding in a long railroad car that is moving at a constant velocity of $10\,\dfrac{\text{m}}{\text{s}}$ (meter per second = meters covered in each second of movement). You start at the midpoint of the car and run backward relative to the car at $0.5\,\dfrac{\text{m}}{\text{s}}$ for 5.0 s. Your friend starts at the same point but runs forward at $0.5\,\dfrac{\text{m}}{\text{s}}$.

1. How far have you moved relative to the ground outside at the end of 5.0 s?

   The train moves 10 m in one second, so it moves 50 m in 5.0 seconds (proportional reasoning). You move $\left(0.5\,\dfrac{\text{m}}{\text{s}}\right)(5.0 \text{ s}) = 2.5 \text{ m}$ backward. Therefore, relative to the ground outside you moved 50 m forward and 2.5 m backward, or 47.5 m forward.

2. How far has your friend moved relative to the ground outside at the end of 5.0 s?

   The answer is reached similarly to (a), but your friend moves 50 m + 2.5 m = 52.5 m forward relative to the ground outside.

3. How far apart are you and your friend at that time, according to another passenger in the train?

> You each moved 2.5 m away from the center, so you are 5.0 m apart.

4. How far apart are you and your friend, according to an observer looking in from a station platform as the train passes by?

> The person outside also sees you as 5.0 m apart. When the person looks in the windows of the train at the end of the 5.0 s time interval, she sees exactly where you are in the train. Imagine that meters are indicated on the station platform. Then she can read your positions and determine how far apart you are.

INVERSE PROPORTIONS We have an inverse proportion when the product of two quantities remains constant even though the quantities themselves vary. For a fixed voltage drop V_0 across varying resistance R, the current I in the circuit is always such that $IR = V_0$. Because V_0 is constant, we write this as $I = \dfrac{V_0}{R}$. In notation you might see in a math class it would be written as $y = \dfrac{c}{x}$, where x varies independently and c is a constant.

Graphs

When you start to solve physics problems, you will be encouraged to use several different methods for representing the information. A picture that shows positions of objects in initial and final states is usually very helpful. Because we model objects as point particles, you will then produce a simplified picture: a diagrammatic representation. When you have sufficient data or equations, you may find that a graph is the best representation to use.

GRAPHS OF DIRECT PROPORTIONS AND LINEAR RELATIONSHIPS

Graphs can represent linear relationships between variables, including direct proportions.

WORKED EXAMPLE 2.5

As you solve these examples, remember that a y-intercept on a graph is the value of y when $x = 0$.

1. Graph $y = 2x$ on the axes in Figure 2.2.

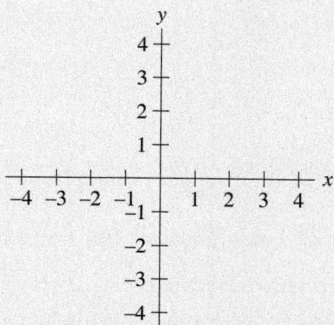

FIGURE 2.2   Axes for the graph of $y = 2x$.

This is a direct proportion. Because y is a constant times x for any direct proportion, no matter what x and y represent, the graph of a direct proportion always goes through the origin.

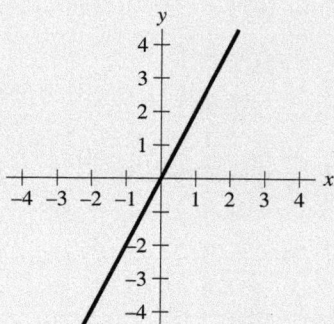

FIGURE 2.3   The graph of $y = 2x$.

2. Graph $y = 2x - 1$ on the axes in Figure 2.4.

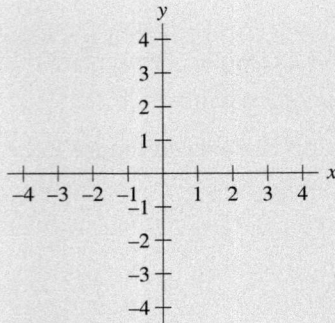

FIGURE 2.4   Axes for the graph of y = 2x – 1.

This is a graph of a straight line, but not a direct proportion. The ratio $\frac{y}{x}$ is not constant because $\frac{y}{x} = 2 - \frac{1}{x}$. The added constant –1 displaces the line from the origin so it has a y-intercept of –1.

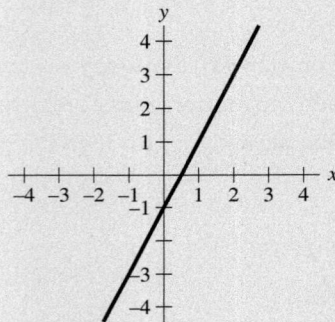

FIGURE 2.5   The graph of y = 2x – 1.

TIME TO TRY

1. Graph $y = -3x$.

2. Graph $y = -3x + 2$.

The lines in (1) and (2) have the same slopes and make the same angle with the x-axis, but they cross the y-axis at different points. They have different y-intercept values (values of y when x = 0).

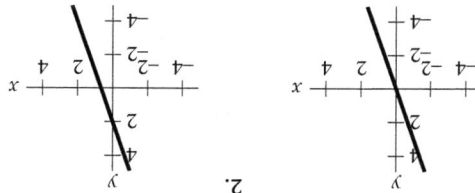

Answers: 1.   2.

The equation of a direct proportion $y = cx$ is a straight line through the origin. The equation of a straight line that does not go through the origin has the form $y = mx + b$, where m is the slope and b is the y-intercept. A direct proportion is a special case of a linear relationship because $b = 0$. ▨

WORKED EXAMPLE 2.6

1. Find the slope of the line in the graph in Figure 2.6.

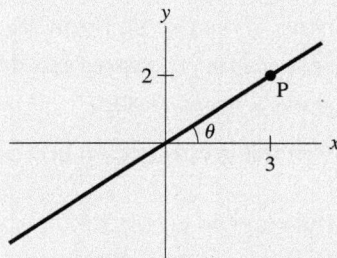

FIGURE 2.6 Graph of a line through the points (0,0) and (3,2).

To find the slope, we pick any two points sufficiently far apart on the line. For this line we know the coordinates of two points, the origin (0,0), and the point (3,2). In this notation, 3 stands for the x-coordinate and 2 for the y-coordinate. The slope, usually symbolized by the letter m, is given by the difference in the y-coordinates divided by the difference in the x-coordinates. We can call it the "rise," $\Delta y = y_A - y_B$, over the "run," $\Delta x = x_A - x_B$, for any two points A and B. The Greek letter Δ, "delta," applied to any symbol instructs us to take the difference of its values at two different points. Thus

$$m = \frac{\Delta y}{\Delta x} = \frac{y_P - y_O}{x_P - x_O} = \frac{2 - 0}{3 - 0} = \frac{2}{3}.$$

2. Find the slope of the line in the graph in Figure 2.7.

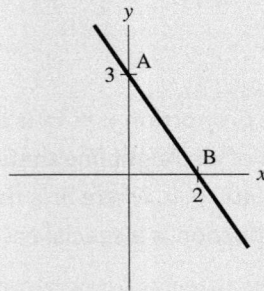

FIGURE 2.7 Graph of a line through the point (0,3) and (2,0).

We calculate the slope the same way we did in (1):

$$m = \frac{\Delta y}{\Delta x} = \frac{y_A - y_B}{x_A - x_B} = \frac{3 - 0}{0 - 2} = -\frac{3}{2}.$$ Note how important it is to keep the coordinates of the two points in the correct order when calculating the slope. Because y increases as x decreases and becomes negative, this line has a negative slope.

3. Find the angle θ in the graph shown in worked example (1).

See the copy of the graph in Figure 2.8.

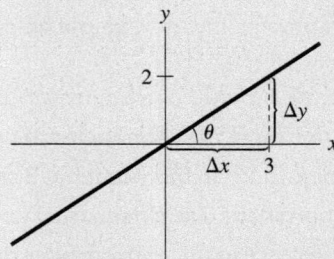

FIGURE 2.8 Graph of $y = \frac{2}{3}x$ with Δx and Δy shown.

The vertical dashed line is Δy, and the horizontal dashed line is Δx. But they are also the opposite and adjacent, respectively, for the angle θ.

Therefore, $\tan \theta = \dfrac{\text{OPP}}{\text{ADJ}} = \dfrac{\Delta y}{\Delta x} = \dfrac{2}{3}$. This is the slope of the line.

The slope is the tangent of the angle the line makes with the x-axis. We can use our calculators to find $\tan^{-1}\left(\dfrac{2}{3}\right) = 33.7°$.

On any straight line, pick any two points sufficiently far apart and find the ratio of the differences in their y- and x-values: that is the slope $m = \dfrac{\Delta y}{\Delta x} = \dfrac{y_A - y_B}{x_A - x_B}$. The slope is also the tangent of the angle the line makes with the x-axis. ▪

Trigonometry is reviewed later in this chapter.

AREA UNDER A GRAPH

The area under the curve in a graph often has a direct physical meaning. For instance, the area under a graph of velocity versus time represents the displacement of an object. For this reason it is important to be able to calculate the area under any such graph.

WORKED EXAMPLE 2.7

1. What is the area under the graph shown in Figure 2.9, from $x = 0$ to $x = 6$?

   The area is a triangle with the origin at one vertex, the point (6,0) at another vertex, and the point (6,4) at the third vertex. The area of a triangle is one-half the base times the height. Because this is a right triangle, the height is the right side of the triangle from (6,0) to (6,4), or 4 units of length. The base is the distance from the origin to (6,4), or 6 units of length. Therefore, $A = \dfrac{1}{2}bh = \dfrac{1}{2}(6) \cdot (4) = 12$.

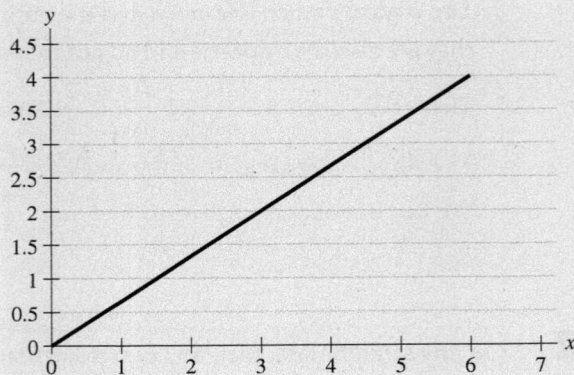

FIGURE 2.9 Graph of the line $y = \dfrac{2}{3}x$.

2. Compute the area under the graph in Figure 2.10 from $x = 0$ to $x = 4$.

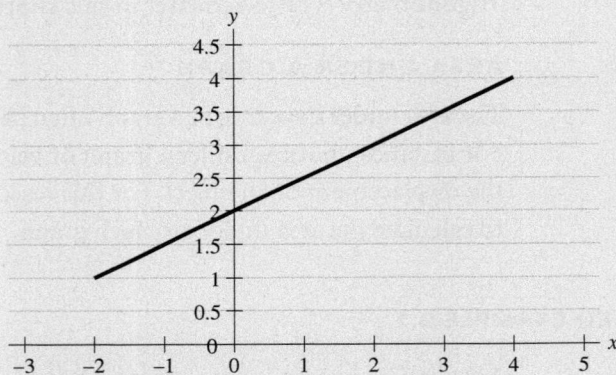

FIGURE 2.10 Graph of the line $y = \dfrac{1}{2}x + 2$.

The area between this line and the x-axis consists of a triangle with vertices (0,2), (4,2), and (4,4) and a rectangle with vertices (0,0), (0,2), (4,2), and (4,0). Draw the triangle and the rectangle in the figure. Can you see that the area of the triangle is $A = \dfrac{1}{2}(4) \cdot (2) = 4$ and that the area of the rectangle is $A = (4) \cdot (2) = 8$ so that the total area under the line is 12 units of area?

3. What is the area under the graph in Figure 2.11, from $x = 0$ to $x = 4$?

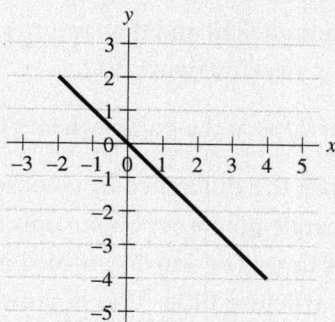

Graph of the line $y = -x$.

Here the line extends below the x-axis and the triangle has vertices $(0,0)$, $(4,0)$, and $(4,-4)$. Therefore the area is $A = \frac{1}{2}bh = \frac{1}{2}(4) \cdot (-4) = -8$ units of area. Remember that our base is $\Delta x = x_{(4,0)} - x_{(0,0)} = 4$, but our height is $\Delta y = y_{(4,-4)} - y_{(4,0)} = -4$. Can you show that the angle between the line and the x-axis is $-45°$?

GRAPHS PROPORTIONAL TO A POWER OF A QUANTITY

We often encounter relationships where the dependent quantity is proportional to or linearly related to a power of another quantity. Examples are electric power proportional to resistance times the square of the current ($P = RI^2$); the probability per unit length of finding a particle at the point x on the x-axis in quantum mechanics, which is proportional to the square of the normalized wave function $\psi(x)$: $P = |\psi(x)|^2$; and kinetic energy, which is equal to one-half the mass of a particle times its velocity squared ($K = \frac{1}{2}mv^2$). These examples also illustrate a danger: because the alphabet is limited, the same letter symbol sometimes has to represent more than one concept. Here P stand for power in one example and for probability density—probability per unit length—in another.

NONLINEAR GRAPHS

An example of a nonlinear graph is the graph of vertical height versus time when we throw an object straight up into the air. The object reaches a maximum height and then returns to your hand. An example of such a graph is given in Figure 2.12.

Can you find the slope at the points where t is 1, 2, 3, 4, and 5 seconds?

Answer: If we use the difference in y-coordinates and t-coordinates between two separate points, we obtain only a sort of average value, not the value at that time. The way to proceed is to draw a line tangent to the point at a particular time. This is shown for the second point in Figure 2.13.

If we take the coordinates where the tangent line crosses the y-axis and the $y = 50$ m line for the rise over the run, we find that $\Delta y = 30$ m and $\Delta t = 3$ s, so the slope is $m = \dfrac{\Delta y}{\Delta t} = \dfrac{30 \text{ m}}{3 \text{ s}} = 10 \dfrac{\text{m}}{\text{s}}$. You can find the slopes at the other times by drawing in the tangent lines at those points. You should find that the values in m/s from 1 s through 5 s are 20, 10, 0, −10, and −20.

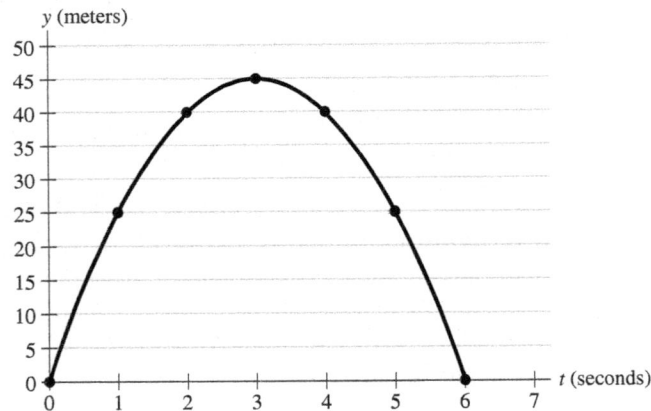

FIGURE 2.12 Height in meters versus time in seconds for an object thrown straight up with an initial velocity of $30\,\dfrac{\text{m}}{\text{s}}$. The value of the acceleration due to gravity has been rounded to $10\,\dfrac{\text{m}}{\text{s}^2}$.

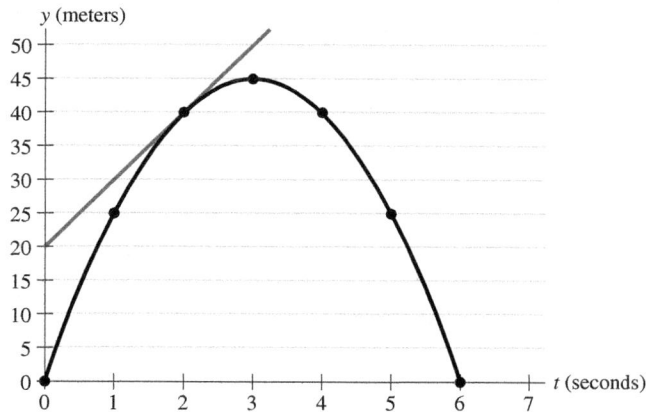

FIGURE 2.13   Height in meters versus time in seconds for an object thrown straight up with an initial velocity of $30\,\dfrac{m}{s}$, with a line drawn tangent to the point (2m, 40s) on the graph.

We now can find the slope of a line by taking the rise over the run. For a curve, we draw a straight line tangent to the curve at the point where we want to know the slope, and take the rise over the run for that tangent line. We can find the area under a straight line by using the coordinate values and the areas of triangles and rectangles. We won't usually need the area under a curve in an introductory course. ▪

PRACTICE

1. Figure 2.14 shows a circle with its center at the origin. What is the slope of the lines tangent to the circle at the following points?

    a) (4,0)   b) (0, 4)   c) (–4, 0)   d) (0, –4)

2. Figure 2.15 shows a possible velocity versus time curve for a car. What is the slope when *t* varies from

    a) 0 s to 2 s?

    b) 2 s to 4 s?

    c) 4 s to 8 s?

    d) 8s to 10 s?

    e) 10 s to 12 s?

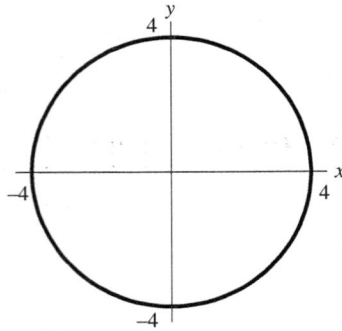

FIGURE 2.14 A circle with the x- and y-coordinates of the points where the circle crosses the axes shown.

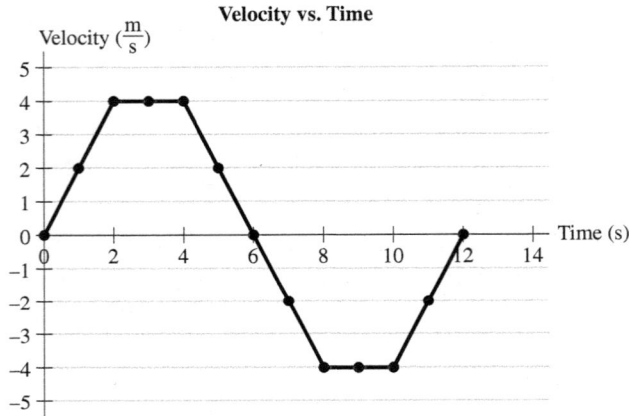

FIGURE 2.15 Graph of velocity versus time for a car.

Answers: 1. a) ∞; b) ∞; c) 0; d) 0 2. a) 2 $\frac{m}{s^2}$; b) 0; c) $-2\frac{m}{s^2}$; d) 0; e) 2 $\frac{m}{s^2}$.

Trigonometry

If you will be taking physics for a health science or other major that does not require calculus, the right angle trigonometry presented here is all you will need. If you are taking physics for an engineering or science major that requires calculus, your calculus courses will review most other trigonometry you might need besides that presented here.

Therefore, we will review only the trigonometric relations that are used frequently, and a few other relationships you will need.

A trigonometric ratio is defined by the ratio of two sides of a right triangle. (One of the angles of a right triangle is 90°.) There are six such ratios: sine, cosine, tangent, secant, cosecant, and cotangent. Greek letters, such as θ (theta) and ϕ (phi)—pronounced thay-tuh and fie, respectively—are used to represent angles, figures formed by two intersecting sides. In any right triangle, there are two sides that form the right angle, and the hypotenuse, the side opposite to the right, or 90°, angle. Opposite means the side that is not one of the two sides forming the angle. Of the two sides forming an angle other than the 90° angle, the adjacent is the side other than the hypotenuse. See Figure 2.16.

✔ **QUICK CHECK**

Given the right triangle here, what are

1. $\sin \theta$?

2. $\cos \theta$?

3. $\tan \theta$?

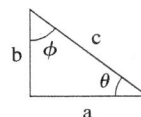

Answers: 1. $\frac{b}{c}$, 2. $\frac{a}{c}$, 3. $\frac{b}{a}$.

Use the following shorthand: OPP = opposite, ADJ = adjacent, and HYP = hypotenuse. Then we define

$$\sin \theta = \frac{\text{OPP}}{\text{HYP}} \text{ (sine);}$$

$$\cos \theta = \frac{\text{ADJ}}{\text{HYP}} \text{ (cosine);}$$

$$\tan \theta = \frac{\text{OPP}}{\text{ADJ}} \text{ (tangent).}$$

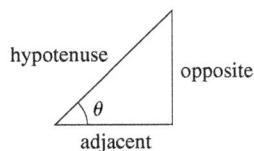

FIGURE 2.16   The sides of a right triangle in reference to the angle θ.

A mnemonic (memory device) to help with these is SOHCAHTOA for sin = opp/hyp; cos = adj/hyp; tan = opp/adj.

Used much less often but sometimes needed are

$$\operatorname{cosec} \theta = \frac{HYP}{OPP} = \frac{1}{\sin \theta} \text{ (cosecant)};$$

$$\sec \theta = \frac{HYP}{ADJ} = \frac{1}{\cos \theta} \text{ (secant)};$$

$$\cotan \theta = \frac{ADJ}{OPP} = \frac{1}{\tan \theta} \text{ (cotangent)}.$$

✔ **QUICK CHECK**

Use the definitions just given to find the sine, cosine, and tangent of angle ϕ in the triangle in the previous Quick Check.

Answers: 1. $\frac{a}{c}$; 2. $\frac{b}{c}$; 3. $\frac{a}{b}$.

TIME TO TRY

Given the right triangle shown, find the following:

1. $\sin \theta$

2. $\cos \theta$

3. $\tan \theta$

4. $\sin \phi$

5. $\cos \phi$

6. $\cot \phi$

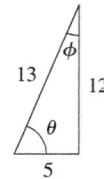

Answers: 1. $\frac{12}{13}$; 2. $\frac{5}{13}$; 3. $\frac{12}{5}$; 4. $\frac{5}{13}$; 5. $\frac{12}{13}$; 6. $\frac{5}{12}$.

The functions defined previously and their inverses—the angles found from the value of the trig functions, which we review in the Using Calculators for Finding Trig Functions section—cover most uses of trigonometry in the first physics course. However, you will also benefit from being familiar with some relations between trigonometric functions.

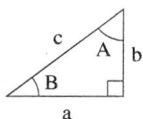

A standard right triangle.

TRIGONOMETRIC IDENTITIES

In this section, we look at the basic trig identities. There are many more than those given here, but these should cover almost any problem that might arise in an introductory physics course. The first one is based on Pythagoras's theorem: For the triangle shown in Figure 2.17, $a^2 + b^2 = c^2$.   Therefore, $1 = \dfrac{a^2}{c^2} + \dfrac{b^2}{c^2} = \left(\dfrac{a}{c}\right)^2 + \left(\dfrac{b}{c}\right)^2 = \sin^2\theta + \cos^2\theta$.

Note the distinction between $\sin 2\theta = \sin(2\theta)$ and $\sin^2\theta = (\sin\theta) \times (\sin\theta)$. You should also be aware that we can prove

$$\sin(A \pm B) = \sin A \cos B \pm \cos A \sin B \text{ and}$$
$$\cos(A \pm B) = \cos A \cos B \mp \sin A \sin B$$

for any two angles A and B, not necessarily those in a right triangle.

You will encounter $2\sin\theta\cos\theta = \sin\theta\cos\theta + \cos\theta\sin\theta = \sin(2\theta)$ when studying projectile motion.

For completeness, let a, b, and c be sides in any triangle, not necessarily a right triangle, and let A, B, and C be the angles opposite to those sides. Then the law of cosines is $c^2 = a^2 + b^2 - 2ab\cos C$, with equivalent equations for sides a or b, and the law of sines is $\dfrac{\sin A}{a} = \dfrac{\sin B}{b} = \dfrac{\sin C}{c}$.

WORKED EXAMPLE 2.8

1. One side of a right triangle is 6.0 m (meter) and the angle opposite to that side is 30°. Find the length of the hypotenuse, the other acute angle in the right triangle, and the length of the third side.

Answer: See the right triangle shown here.
Because $\sin(30°) = \dfrac{\text{OPP}}{\text{HYP}} = \dfrac{6.0\text{ m}}{h}$,
$h = 6.0\text{ m} \times \sin(30°) = 3.0\text{ m}$.

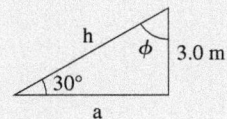

Because $\cos \phi = \dfrac{ADJ}{HYP} = \dfrac{3.0 \text{ m}}{6.0 \text{ m}} = 0.5$, $\phi = 60°$. (See the following Using Calculators for Finding Trig Functions section.) You could also have noticed that if one angle is 90° and the second one is 30°, the third angle must be 60° because the sum of the angles in a triangle is 180°. Finally, we can use Pythagoras's Theorem to find the third side, but let's practice using trig functions. Because $\cos 30° = \dfrac{ADJ}{HYP} = \dfrac{a}{6.0 \text{ m}}$, we can use a calculator to find that $a = 5.2$ m. Check this by using Pythagoras's theorem.

2. The law of refraction of light at a boundary between two different substances, such as air and glass, states that $n_1 \sin \theta_1 = n_2 \sin \theta_2$, where n_1 and n_2 are the indices of refraction of the first substance and the second substance, respectively, that light passes through; θ_1 is the angle between the light ray in the first substance and the line perpendicular to the boundary between the two substances; and θ_2 is the angle the light ray in the second substance makes with the same perpendicular line. See Figure 2.18.

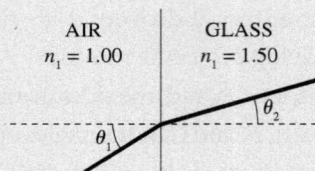

FIGURE 2.18 The refraction of light as it passes from air into glass.

If $\theta_1 = 45°$, find θ_2.

Answer: We solve $n_1 \sin \theta_1 = n_2 \sin \theta_2$ for $\sin \theta_2$, and then use a calculator to find θ_2.

$$\sin \theta_2 = \frac{n_1}{n_2} \sin \theta_1 = \frac{1.00}{1.50} \sin 45° = \frac{0.707}{1.50} = 0.4714.$$

We keep an extra significant figure in our solution than within our equation because trig functions vary rapidly with angle. To determine θ_2, we need to find the inverse sine of 0.4714 or $\sin^{-1}(0.4714)$. If you press the second function key and then the sine key on your standard scientific calculator, you will find that $\theta_2 = 28.1°$ to three significant figures.

What was found here was an inverse to the sine of the angle. The sine of the angle is the function. The inverse sine, the inverse of the function, is the angle. In the next section, you will practice finding inverse trig functions.

USING CALCULATORS FOR FINDING TRIG FUNCTIONS AND INVERSE TRIG FUNCTIONS

TRIG FUNCTIONS To find $\sin\theta$, $\cos\theta$, and $\tan\theta$, be sure that your calculator is set for degrees, enter the value of the angle, and press the appropriate key. To find the other three trig functions, use

$$\operatorname{cosec}\theta = \frac{1}{\sin\theta}; \sec\theta = \frac{1}{\cos\theta}; \text{ and } \cot\theta = \frac{1}{\tan\theta}.$$

✔ **QUICK CHECK**

Find the sine, cosine, tangent, secant, cosecant, and cotangent of 22.5°.

Answer: sine 22.5° = 0.383; cosine 22.5° = 0.924; tangent 22.5° = 0.414; secant 22.5° = 1.082; cosecant 22.5° = 2.61; cotangent 22.5° = 2.41.

INVERSE TRIG FUNCTIONS Difficulties arise in going from the value of the trig function back to the angle, because trig functions are multiple-valued; more than one angle results in the same value of the function. Therefore, additional information is needed when finding an inverse. For example, $\sin 60° = \sin 120° = 0.8660$ and $\cos 60° = \cos(-60°) = 0.5000$. Given $0.8660 = \sin\theta$ and asked to find the angle, we need to know the quadrant the angle is in to determine the answer. Otherwise there are two possibilities. The quadrants are shown in Figure 2.19 in a plane defined by the x and y axes.

The best way to understand this is to try some examples.

y

II   I

————————————— x

III   IV

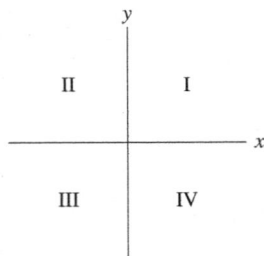

FIGURE 2.19   Quadrant positions of angles associated with trig functions.

TIME TO TRY

1. Given $\sin \theta = 0.8000$, find the possible angles θ.

2. Given $\sin \theta = -0.5000$, find the possible angles θ.

3. Given $\tan \theta = 1.0000$, find the possible angles θ.

Answers: 1. $\theta = 53.1°$ or $\theta = 180° - 53.1° = 126.9°$. 2. $\theta = -30.0°$ or $\theta = 180.0° + 30.0° = 210.0°$. Note that $-30.0°$ is the same as $+330.0°$. 3. $\theta = 45.0°$ or $\theta = 180.0° + 45.0° = 235°$.

Sketch these angles in the x-y plane to see why this is the case. Look up http://www.mathwizz.com/algebra/help/help29.htm or an equivalent site on the Web for more information on quadrants and the values of trig functions.

VECTORS AND VECTOR COMPONENTS

The quantities you will use in pictorial, diagrammatic, and mathematical representations of physical interactions will have directions as well as magnitudes. A quantity with a magnitude and a direction is called a vector. Changes in position, called displacements, forces, velocities, electric fields, and many others all have both direction and magnitude. First, you will work with vectors relative to coordinate axes. Then the following section will show how to calculate the projections of vectors on coordinate axes, these projections being the components of the vectors.

Any vector, such as displacement, may be drawn as a directed line or arrow. Place the coordinate origin at the *tail* of the arrow and draw in x and y axes, as in Figure 2.20.

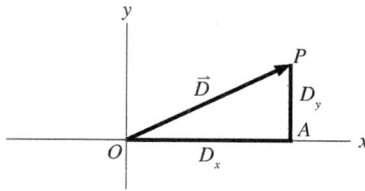

FIGURE 2.20 The scalar components of a vector.

The displacement, $\vec{D}$, is shown as a directed line. In addition, the line AP is drawn perpendicular to the x-axis. The segment of the positive x-axis cut off by the line AP is OA. OA, labeled D_x, is the projection of $\vec{D}$ on the x-axis. D_x is called the x-component of the vector $\vec{D}$.

Drop a perpendicular line from the head of $\vec{D}$ to the y-axis. Label the point where it cuts the y-axis point B. How does the length OB compare to the length AP?

The length OB is equal to AP. AP is labeled D_y. OB, or AP, is called the y-component of the vector $\vec{D}$. D_x and D_y are *scalar* components because they do not have arrows attached.

In Figure 2.21, OA and AP are vectors. They are called vector components of $\vec{D}$ because they have directions. They are the vectors $\vec{D}_x$ and $\vec{D}_y$.

Walk from O to A and then from A to P. You have undergone two displacements, $\vec{D}_x$ and $\vec{D}_y$, and have ended up at P. If you start at O and walk directly to P, the single displacement $\vec{D}$ will get you there. $\vec{D}$ is equivalent to the instruction "displacement $\vec{D}_x$ followed by displacement $\vec{D}_y$." Therefore,

$$\vec{D} = \vec{D}_x + \vec{D}_y.$$

Any vector is equal to the sum of its vector components along the x- and y-axes.

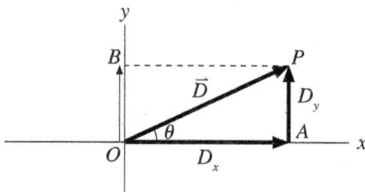

FIGURE 2.21 The vector components of a vector.

WORKED EXAMPLE 2.9

1. Suppose the magnitude of $\vec{D}_x$ is 3 m, and the magnitude of $\vec{D}_y$ is 4 m. Find the magnitude of $\vec{D}$.

   We find D from the Pythagorean theorem.
   $D^2 = D_x^2 + D_y^2 = (3 \text{ m})^2 + (4 \text{ m})^2 = (5 \text{ m})^2$ so $D = 5$ m.

2. Suppose the magnitude of $\vec{D}$ is 10 m, and it is 53.1° counter-clockwise from the x-axis. Find D_x and D_y.

   For this vector, $D_x = (10 \text{ m}) \cos 53.1° = (10 \text{ m})(.8) = 8$ m and
   $D_y = (10 \text{ m}) \sin 53.1° = (10 \text{ m})(.6) = 6$ m.

3. Given the magnitudes of $\vec{D}_x$ and $\vec{D}_y$, find $\vec{D}$. Given $\vec{D}$, find the magnitudes of $\vec{D}_x$ and $\vec{D}_y$.

   We use the same process we used before, but now in symbols:
   $D^2 = D_x^2 + D_y^2$. To find D_x and D_y, we use $D_x = D \cos \theta$ and
   $D_y = D \sin \theta$.

   To see this, look at Figure 2.21, in which $\sin \theta = \dfrac{D_y}{D}$ and $\cos \theta = \dfrac{D_x}{D}$.
   Thus, $D_x = D \cos \theta$, $D_y = D \sin \theta$. If you know D and θ, you know D_x
   and D_y. If you divide $D_y = D \sin \theta$ by $D_x = D \cos \theta$ you get
   $\tan \theta = \dfrac{D_y}{D_x}$. In addition, Pythagoras's theorem gives $D_x^2 + D_y^2 = D^2$.
   If you know D_x and D_y, you know D and θ. These equations are sum-marized here:

   $$D_x = D \cos \theta$$

   $$D_y = D \sin \theta$$

   $$\tan \theta = \frac{D_y}{D_x}$$

   $$D^2 = D_x^2 + D_y^2.$$

These equations hold for vectors in any quadrant as long as θ is always measured counterclockwise from the positive x-axis. Always measure θ consistently from the x-axis. That way you'll always get correct values for D_x and D_y from your calculator.

TIME TO TRY

Find the *x*- and *y*-components of the following vectors:

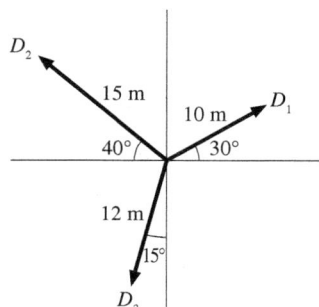

FIGURE 2.22   Three vectors in the *xy*-plane.

Answers: $D_{1x} = 10.0$ m cos $(30°) = 8.66$ m, $D_{1y} = 10.0$ m sin $(30°) = 5.0$ m, $D_{2x} = 15.0$ m cos $(140°) = -11.5$ m, $D_{2y} = 15.0$ m sin $(140°) = 9.64$ m, $D_{3x} = 12.0$ m cos $(255°) = -3.11$ m, $D_{3y} = 12.0$ m sin $(255°) = -11.6$ m

If you ride your bicycle to a class and then over to the cafeteria, we need to add the two displacements to get your net displacement. That means adding vectors. We do it by placing the tail of the second vector at the head of the first vector, as in Figure 2.23. It's like dogs sniffing: the head of the first dog at the second dog's tail.

What happens if you walk backward? You change direction. The negative of a vector has the same length but the opposite direction. We subtract vector 2 from vector 1 by adding the negative of vector 2 to vector 1 as in Figure 2.24.

To find the length of vectors added or subtracted in this way requires a ruler and a protractor, and is not accurate. It turns out that you can add vectors by adding their components. We can subtract vectors by

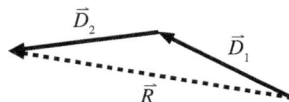

FIGURE 2.23   The dashed arrow shows the sum of the other two displacements.

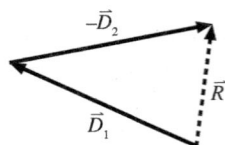

FIGURE 2.24 The result of subtracting vector 2 from vector 1.

subtracting components. You will use the resultant components to find the vector as in the previous examples.

Exponents, Logarithms, and Exponentials

If you know that 2 "squared" is four and that 3 "squared" is 9, you already know the most basic rule of exponents. "Square" is an instruction, written as the superscript 2, to multiply a quantity by itself. Thus, $2^2 = 4$ and $3^2 = 9$. In short, an exponent p is an instruction to multiply a number a or a symbol such as x by itself p times. If $a = 2$ and $p = 4$, $a^p = 2^4 = 2 \times 2 \times 2 \times 2 = 16$.

What is 2^6?

Answer:

$$2^6 = \underbrace{\frac{2 \times 2 \times 2 \times 2 \times 2 \times 2}{}}_{6 \text{ times}} = 4 \times 4 \times 4 = 8 \times 8 = 64$$

LAWS OF EXPONENTS

A number of laws follow from this basic definition of exponents.

Law of Exponents I. $a^p \times a^q = a^{p+q}$, because

$$\underbrace{(a \times a \times a...a)}_{p \text{ times}} \times \underbrace{(a \times a \times a...a)}_{q \text{ times}} = \underbrace{(a \times a \times a...a)}_{p + q \text{ times}}.$$

Law of Exponents II. $\dfrac{a^p}{a^q} = a^{p-q}$ because $\dfrac{\underbrace{(a \times a \times a...a)}_{p \text{ times}}}{\underbrace{(a \times a \times a...a)}_{q \text{ times}}} =$

$\underbrace{(a \times a \times a...a)}_{p - q \text{ times}}$ owing to the q cancellations.

This assumes $p > q$.

From these we can deduce that $a^{-n} = \dfrac{1}{a^n}$, and $a^0 = 1$.

✔ **QUICK CHECK**

1. Show that $a^0 = 1$. (Hint: Use Law II.)

2. Show that $a^{\frac{1}{2}} = \sqrt{a}$. (Hint: Use Law I.)

3. What is $2^{2.5}$?

4. What is 2^{-4}?

Answers: 1. Because $1 = \dfrac{a^n}{a^n} = a^{n-n} = a^0$, $a^0 = 1$. 2. Because $a^{\frac{1}{2}} \times a^{\frac{1}{2}} = a^1 = a$ and $\sqrt{a} \times \sqrt{a} = a$, we find that $a^{\frac{1}{2}} = \sqrt{a}$. 3. This is $2^2 2^{0.5} = 2 \times 2 \times \sqrt{2} = 4 \times 1.414 = 5.657$. 4. Because $2^{-4} = \dfrac{1}{2^4} = \dfrac{1}{16}$.

TIME TO TRY

1. What are $9^{\frac{1}{2}}$ and 9^0?

2. Show that $a^{-n} = \dfrac{1}{a^n}$. (Law of Exponents III)

3. Prove $(a^n)^p = a^{p \times n}$. (Law of Exponents IV)

4. Prove: When $a^r = p$, then $a = \sqrt[r]{p} = p^{\frac{1}{r}}$. (Law of Exponents V)

Answers: 1. 3 and $\pm$. 2. If $p < q$, then

$$\dfrac{\overbrace{(a \times a \times a...a)}^{p \text{ times}}}{\underbrace{(a \times a \times a...a)}_{q \text{ times}}} = \dfrac{1}{\overbrace{(a \times a \times a...a)}^{p-q \text{ times}}}.$$

If $p = 0$, then

$$\dfrac{\overbrace{(a \times a \times a...a)}^{0 \text{ times}}}{\underbrace{(a \times a \times a...a)}_{n \text{ times}}} = a^{0-n} = a^{-n}.$$

But $\dfrac{1}{a^n}$. Therefore,

$$\dfrac{1}{a^n} = \dfrac{\overbrace{(a \times a \times a \dots a)}^{0\text{ times}}}{\underbrace{(a \times a \times a \dots a)}_{0\text{ times}}} = \dfrac{\overbrace{(a \times a \times a \dots a)}^{n-0\text{ times}}}{1} = \dfrac{\overbrace{(a \times a \times a \dots a)}^{n\text{ times}}}{1}$$

$a^{-n} = \dfrac{1}{a^n}$. 3. We use our basic definition: $(a^n)^p =$

$$a^{np} = \overbrace{(a \times a \times a \dots a)}^{n\text{ times}} \times \overbrace{(a \times a \times a \dots a)}^{n\text{ times}} \times \overbrace{(a \times a \times a \dots a)}^{n\text{ times}} \times \dots$$

with p times.

4. Given $a^r = p$, then by 3, $(a^r)^{\frac{1}{r}} = a^{\frac{r}{r}} = a^1 = a = p^{\frac{1}{r}}$. Therefore,

$$\overbrace{(a \times a \times a \dots a)}^{r\text{ times}} = p.$$ But the quantity that equals p when multiplied by itself r times is $\sqrt[r]{p}$. Thus, $a = \sqrt[r]{p} = p^{\frac{1}{r}}$.

ADDITIONAL RULES FOR EXPONENTS A few additional rules follow directly from the preceding rules:

Law of Exponents VI. $\sqrt[n]{a} \times \sqrt[n]{b} = \sqrt[n]{ab}$.

Law of Exponents VII. $\dfrac{\sqrt[n]{a}}{\sqrt[n]{b}} = \sqrt[n]{\dfrac{a}{b}}$.

Law of Exponents VIII. $\sqrt[m]{\sqrt[n]{a}} = \sqrt[m \times n]{a}$.

✔ **QUICK CHECK**

1. Find $\sqrt[6]{64}$ without the use of a calculator.

2. Simplify $\sqrt[5]{\dfrac{32}{x^3}}$.

Answers: 1. $\sqrt[6]{64} = \sqrt[3 \times 2]{64} = \sqrt[3]{\sqrt[2]{64}} = \sqrt[3]{8} = 2$.
2. $2 \times x^{-\frac{3}{5}}$.

EXPONENTIALS

We frequently encounter situations where something doubles or decreases by half in a given time interval. Examples are bacterial growth in a medium, or nuclear decay. Although human population growth is also exponential, its rate of increase decreases as a country becomes more prosperous.

A standard example of an exponential change is given in the story of the philosopher who specified his reward as follows. He was to receive one grain of rice the first day, two grains the second day, four the third day, eight the fourth day, and so on through thirty days. The number $1 + 2 + 4 + 8 + 16 + 32 + 64 + 128 + 256 + ...$ seems fairly innocuous, but on the thirtieth day the number $2^{29} = 536,870,000$ would involve major transport problems.

As you can see, this doubling or halving involves 2^n. For some purposes it is more convenient to use 10^n because 10 is the basis of our number system and also is larger than 2. The standard way of writing numbers in scientific notation is as 2.738×10^4 rather than as 27,380, where 4 represents the number of places that the decimal is moved to the right when the number is written without scientific notation. We dealt with why we want to avoid that last zero in an earlier section.

The other base used frequently in physics is e. Expressions of the form e^{at} or e^{-at} occur often. Your calculator has an e^x key. Usually, you enter a number, press the second function key and then the e^x.

✔ **QUICK CHECK**

Use your calculator to find the values of $e^{-2.1}$ and $e^{+2.1}$.

Answer: $e^{-2.1} = 0.122$ and $e^{+2.1} = 8.17$.

EXPONENTIAL DECAY AND GROWTH We can look at exponential growth and decay in several different ways. If you start with N_0 pairs of rabbits, and the rabbits double n times, you end up with $N = N_0(2)^n$ rabbits. But if the rabbits increase by a fraction b, for example 0.4, in a month, then n equals b multiplied by the number of months. Thus we can write $N = N_0(2)^{bt}$. We can also look at the amount $\Delta N = N - N_0$ by which the number of rabbits changes in a given time. Because the increase in the number of pairs of rabbits must depend on the number of pairs we started with—this is an example of ratio and proportion—we must also have $\Delta N = cN_0$, where c is a constant. This equation can be shown to have a solution $N = N_0 e^{at}$. Setting our two solutions equal we see that we can use any base. Here $2^{bt} = e^{at}$ and $at \ln e = bt \ln 2$, so $b = a\dfrac{\ln e}{\ln 2}$. It is most common to use the base e, and we'll do that from now on. See the following section on logarithms for more about e.

When a quantity doubles or halves in equal time intervals, that is the same as exponential growth or decay. To find the value of N at time t, multiply N_0 by 2 or $\dfrac{1}{2}$ n times, that is, the number $n = bt$ times, where n does not have to be an integer, because t can be any time; or multiply N_0 by e^{at} where a is a positive or negative constant. Both a and b, which have units $\dfrac{1}{\text{time unit}}$, are called time constants. ◾

✔ **QUICK CHECK**

1. If $a = \dfrac{3.5}{y}$, how long does it take for N to double?

2. If $a = -\dfrac{3.5}{y}$, how long does it take for n to decrease by one-half?

Answers: 1. $\frac{N}{N_0} = e^{at} = 2$. Therefore, $\ln (e^{at}) = at = \ln 2$. (Remember that the logarithm is the exponent to which the base is raised.) Thus, $t = \dfrac{\ln 2}{a} = \dfrac{0.693}{\dfrac{3.5}{y}} = 0.198\ y$. 2. $\dfrac{N}{N_0} = \dfrac{1}{2} = e^{-at}$. Therefore, $\ln (e^{-at}) = -at = \ln\left(\dfrac{1}{2}\right) = \ln 1 - \ln 2 = -\ln 2$ and $t = \dfrac{0.693}{\dfrac{3.5}{y}} = 0.198\ y$.

The decay products may themselves decay. Then, given the value of a for the decay product, you repeat the same type of calculation. Only a few topics in the introductory physics course use exponentials or logarithms—intensity levels, eye and ear responses, nuclear decay, complex representations of alternating currents, and other uses of phasors—but you need to understand exponentials and logarithms thoroughly when those topics arise. (Phasors are a type of exponential.)

LOGARITHMS

A logarithm is an exponent. If $a^x = N$, then the logarithm to the base a of N is x. This is written as $\log_a N = x$. That's all there is to it: The logarithm is the power to which the base is raised to give the number.

Let's start with the base 10.

If $10^3 = 1000$, what is the log of 1,000 to the base 10?

Answer: 3

What is the log of 595 to the base 10?

Answer: It is a number x such that $10^x = 595$. Before calculators were available, people used tables to find these logarithms. Now we enter 595 in our calculators, press the "2nd function" and "log" keys, and find that the answer is 2.7745. Thus, $\log_{10}(595) = 2.7745$.

✔ **QUICK CHECK**

Find the log to the base 10 of 0.25.

Answer: $\log_{10}(0.25) = -0.602$, so $10^{-0.602} = 0.25$

One special number occurs frequently not only in math, but also in physical processes such as exponential growth and decay. It is called "e," where $e = 2.7187818$ to eight figures. When logarithms have the base e, they are called natural logarithms. The base e occurs in calculus where it occurs as an important limit and crops up frequently. Note that your calculator has an "ln" key as well as a "log" key; the ln key represents natural logs. Find it now, and use it to solve the following example.

What is $\ln_e(1000)$?

Enter 1,000 in your calculator, press the second function key, and then press the ln key. You should find that $\ln_e(1000) = 6.9078$ to five figures.

RULES OF LOGARITHMS Because logs to the base 10 or lns to the base e or logs to any base are exponents, the rules of logarithms follow from the rules of exponents.

Rule of Logarithms I. $\log(MN) = \log M + \log N$

$\ln(ab) = \ln a + \ln b$

Rule of Logarithms II. $\log\left(\dfrac{M}{N}\right) = \log M - \log N$

$\ln\left(\dfrac{a}{b}\right) = \ln a - \ln b$

Rule of Logarithms III. $\log(M^n) = n \log M \quad \ln(a^n) = n \ln a$

Rule of Logarithms IV. $\log \sqrt[r]{M} = \dfrac{\log M}{r} \quad \ln \sqrt[r]{a} = \dfrac{\ln a}{r}$

PRACTICE

1. Find log and ln of a) 18.0; b) 0.0018.

2. Find log and ln of a) 5^9; b) $\sqrt{15}$.

3. Find log and ln of a) x^2y^3z; b) $\sqrt[3]{u}\ \sqrt{w}$.

Answers: 1. a) 1.255 and 2.890; b) −2.745 and −6.320. 2. a) 9 × log 5 = 6.290

and 9 × ln 5 = 1.448; b) log $(15^{\frac{1}{2}}) = \dfrac{1}{2}$ log 15 = 0.392 and 0.903.

3. a) 2 log x + 3 log y + log z and 2 ln x + 3 ln y + ln z

b) log $(u^3w^{\frac{1}{2}}) = \dfrac{1}{3}$ log u + $\dfrac{1}{2}$ log w and ln $(u^3w^{\frac{1}{2}}) = \dfrac{1}{3}$ ln u + $\dfrac{1}{2}$ ln w.

Many physical systems are logarithmic. It takes 10 violinists to sound twice as loud as one violinist because the sense of loudness is logarithmic. Thus the standard unit of loudness, the decibel, is proportional to the logarithm to the base 10 of the intensity of a sound.

INVERSE LOGARITHMS

Just as you can find an angle when given its sine or cosine, you can find a number when given its log or ln. It's much easier than finding inverse trig functions because logarithms are single-valued: There is only one number that corresponds to a given value of a log or ln.

WORKED EXAMPLE 2.10

Given that $\log_{10} N = 3.20$ and that $\ln_e M = 3.20$, find $N + M$. It should be clear that this problem asks us to find two separate quantities, N and M, and add them.

To find N, enter 3.20 in your calculator. Then press the second function and the 10^x key for the anti log.

WHY?

Because the logarithm is the exponent to which the base is raised to give the number, the logarithm is the exponent that goes with the base 10. Pick the correct base and you have the number.

To find M, enter 3.20 in your calculator, then press the second function key and the e^x key. The result is M.

Thus, $10^{3.2} = 1585$ and $e^{3.20} = 24.5$, so $N + M = 1610$, where we have rounded the result to four significant figures. (Check these calculations on your calculator.)

PRACTICE

1. Given $\log_{10} N = -2.22$, find N.

2. Given $\ln_e M = 6.666$, find M.

Answers: 1. 1.603×10^{-3}; 2. 785.2

Transferring Knowledge to New Contexts

If you live in a city with more than one bus line, you know that you can reach your destination by asking for a transfer when you pay your fare. The transfer is a piece of paper that lists the bus line you are on, the bus lines to which you can transfer, and the date and time when you paid your fare. You can then exit the bus and transfer to the connecting bus without paying a second fare.

It would be great if we could take what we learned in math courses and apply it all directly to physics courses, transferring the knowledge as we transfer buses. Unfortunately, a large body of research shows that what we learned in math is tied to the symbols that were used in math, and is even associated with the locations where we used that information. Cues from our surroundings, teachers, and fellow students, and from our activities at the time, make it easier to access knowledge that was learned in the same surroundings with the same teachers, students, class exercises, and homework.

For that reason, some Quick Check and Time to Try problems in this chapter have used symbols for physical quantities rather than just the x and y symbols used in math classes. In this section, we will practice solving math we have already used, but with different symbols or with physical units attached. Rather than simply 3, it will be 3 m for 3 meters or 3 μF for 3 microfarads.

Keep in mind that we learn math at three levels. The first level is numbers. Numbers give us a concrete realization of groups of objects. The number 5 is common to five birds, five fingers, five trees, etc. In the next step we use a symbol for a number: x or N or I or whatever symbol we choose can stand for any number that gives it a value for a particular system or object or problem. At the third level, a symbol can stand for another symbol.

An example of symbols standing for symbols, as mentioned earlier, is the equation for a straight line: $y = mx + b$. If we know how to work with this equation we also know how to solve $v = v_0 + at$, where velocity depends on the initial velocity, the acceleration, and the time. We know how to solve $V = V_0 - Ex$ for the potential at a point x when the potential at the origin is V_0 and an electric field E points in the positive x-axis direction. If you start to realize consciously that what you learned in math is a summary in symbols of what you need to use in physics, it will become easier to apply that knowledge to physics. But only practice will accomplish the goal.

Here are some practice exercises applying math that you know—common denominators and complex fractions—to typical physics measures:

TIME TO TRY

1. Given $\dfrac{1}{4\ \mu F} - \dfrac{1}{5\ \mu F} = \dfrac{1}{C}$, find the capacitance C in μF (microfarads).

2. Given $\dfrac{4\ \Omega}{\dfrac{1}{2\ \mu F} + \dfrac{1}{3\ \mu F}}$ = _____ s, find the missing time constant.

(Here the Greek capital letter omega, Ω, stands for ohm, the unit of electrical resistance. A formula like this may arise when two capacitors and a resistor are in a series circuit.)

3. Simplify the left side of this equation for the time constant τ:

$\dfrac{R}{\dfrac{1}{C_1} + \dfrac{1}{C_2} + \dfrac{1}{C_3}}$ = τ. Here we have used the symbols for three

different capacitances and one resistance.

Answers: 1. We find a common denominator: $\dfrac{5}{20\ \mu F} - \dfrac{4}{20\ \mu F} = \dfrac{1}{20\ \mu F}$, so C = 20 μF. 2. We first find a common denominator, and then use the rule for complex fractions:

$$\dfrac{4\ \Omega}{\dfrac{1}{2\ \mu F} + \dfrac{1}{3\ \mu F}} = \dfrac{4\ \Omega}{\dfrac{3}{6\ \mu F} + \dfrac{2}{6\ \mu F}} = \dfrac{4\ \Omega}{\dfrac{5}{6\ \mu F}} = 4\ \Omega \times \dfrac{6\ \mu F}{5} = \dfrac{24}{5}\ \mu F.$$

3. You should be able to show that

$$\tau = \dfrac{R}{\left[\dfrac{C_2C_3 + C_1C_3 + C_1C_2}{C_1C_2C_3}\right]} = R \cdot \dfrac{C_1C_2C_3}{C_2C_3 + C_1C_3 + C_1C_2}. \text{ You have solved for}$$

the time constant for three capacitors in series with a resistor.

When a mathematical step appears to be difficult or unknown, try substituting symbols you used in math in the equation. That will often remind you of the technique you used for the identical problem in your math courses. Then you can find a common denominator, solve a quadratic equation, remember the formula for an area or a volume, or even determine how to graph data and find slopes. The more you practice, the easier it will become to recognize that the math part of a physics problem is something you have already seen. ▩

The examples in the Time to Try section have also illustrated the need for combining skills. In (2) and (3), you first had to find a common denominator and then simplify a complex fraction. The next chapter will show you that we first analyze observations through pictures and diagrams and reasoning before we come up with mathematical representations of the phenomena. Math is the last step in physics, not the first.

Final Stretch!

Now that you have finished reading this chapter it is time to stretch your brain and check how much you have learned.

WHAT DID YOU LEARN?

- How to estimate the results of calculations
- Rounding, significant figures, scientific notation, and standard prefixes
- Use of calculators for numerical and trigonometric operations
- The solution of simultaneous linear equations and of quadratic equations
- How to work with common denominators and complex fractions
- Use of proportional reasoning in direct, continued, and inverse proportions
- Graphing, including finding slopes of and areas under graphs
- Graphs of nonlinear relationships
- Trigonometric functions and identities
- The representation of physical quantities by vectors
- How to calculate vector components
- How to work with exponents, logarithms, and exponentials
- The need for conscious application to be able to transfer math knowledge to physics

WEB RESOURCES

For additional sources online, type in boldface section headings such as rounding, scientific notation, simultaneous equations, proportions, etc. into a search engine. If you use Google, a very general article at a high level will be listed first, but if you continue checking entries you will find one at a level just right for you. Sites like the Math League and Purplemath tend to offer easy examples.

> *A site that you might not immediately think of, but that offers help with simultaneous equations is*
>
> **http://www.allaboutcircuits.com/vol_5/chpt_4/11.html**

Websites will provide many extra practice exercises. Note that sites at grade school, middle school, high school, and college level will all be listed in no particular order. You will probably want mostly high school level math reviews.

3 Physics Concepts, Part I

When you complete this chapter, you should be able to:

- Explain how to define and calculate the following:
  - Position
  - Displacement
  - Speed
  - Velocity
  - Change in velocity
  - Acceleration
  - Weight
  - Work
  - Kinetic energy
  - Gravitational potential energy
- State Newton's First, Second, and Third laws
- Draw work-energy bar charts

Introductions to the material of courses like biology or chemistry might start with terminology. In biology, you can learn the names of the different types of leaves and their different possible arrangements on a stem, such as opposite or alternating. Because physics started out describing everyday phenomena (things we see around us), it kept the same terminology used by people every day while changing the meanings in line with experimental discoveries. Although the technical meanings of the words as scientific terms changed, the words kept the same meanings in everyday speech. This means that anyone who studies physics has to learn a whole new set of meanings for words he or she already knows well. Trying to change our deep-set beliefs about what words mean is just as hard as trying to change political or religious beliefs when challenged by someone holding different views. In this chapter we won't need to discuss politics or religion, but we will emphasize concepts—as opposed to mere terminology—in everything we do.

Your Starting Point

Let's look at some terms and beliefs that can give you trouble. Although we have not yet provided exact definitions, see if you can decide whether the following sentences are true or false.

1. If you break out in a sweat when pushing on an immovable boulder, you are doing work.   T F

2. You may travel a distance of two miles but have a zero displacement.   T F

3. For an acceleration to occur, your car must increase in speed.   T F

4. A car stuck on railroad tracks gets demolished by the locomotive because the locomotive exerts a bigger force on the car than the car does on the locomotive.   T F

5. If John pushes on a car, it acquires an acceleration of $0.5 \frac{m}{s^2}$. If John's identical twin Edgar joins in and also pushes on that same car with a force of equal magnitude it may have an acceleration of $0 \frac{m}{s^2}$.   T F

6. Heat is energy stored at a high temperature.   T F

7. A ball stops rolling because it uses up the force that started it moving.   T F

8. You move forward when walking because your feet push you forward.   T F

9. Friction always slows objects down.   T F

10. An impulse is a large force.   T F

Answers: 1. False. The physics definition of work on an object combines a force on that object with a change of position of that object. If there is no change in position there is no work *on* the object. Weird? We'll see why this definition makes sense later on. 2. True. Displacement is the difference between the position at the end of a motion and the position at the beginning. If you drive to a friend's house and then return home, you are back where you started. There is no displacement, even if you traveled a distance of several miles each way. 3. False. A velocity has a direction and a magnitude in physics. Any change in a velocity is called an acceleration. Even if the magnitude, the speed, stays constant, a change in direction means that there is an acceleration. And a decrease as well as an increase in magnitude in velocity is also an acceleration. 4. False. Think about the following: a. You step on an ant. Which exerts the bigger force: your foot on the ant or the ant on your foot? b. Is it possible that your foot and the ant exert forces of equal magnitude on one another? We'll return to these questions later. 5. True. This involves scientific reasoning as well as internalized knowledge. How should Edgar push so that the force he exerts cancels the force John exerts? 6. False. Physicists themselves can be careless about the term "heat," but properly used, it refers only to thermal energy moving from one body to another because the two bodies have different temperatures. The thermal energy content of a body depends on the size and temperature of the body and that particular material's ability to store thermal energy. A ton of iron can store a lot more energy than the head of a pin. 7. False. Try rolling the same ball at the same initial speed on a very rough level surface, on a moderately rough level surface, and on a very smooth, possibly oiled level surface. What might the ball do on a surface with no roughness whatsoever? "Friction" is the word we use to describe "roughness"; you can feel friction by rubbing your hand lightly on a piece of sandpaper. 8. False. Suppose someone gave you a quick shove forward while you were standing at the edge of a cliff. What would you do in this life-and-death situation? Stand with your toes at the edge of a sheet of paper you have placed on the floor. Then have someone give you a moderate push when you are not expecting it. What do you do in order not to step on the paper, that is, not to go over the edge of the cliff? We'll discuss this answer later.

9. False. What makes objects move when they are dropped onto a conveyor belt? The conveyor belt exerts a force that is perpendicular to the surface of the object to stop its fall, but the conveyor belt also has to drag the object along. Otherwise the object would slip and stay in the same place. The conveyor belt has to exert a friction force parallel to the surface of the object to accelerate it so that it eventually moves at the same speed as the conveyor belt. What would happen if the conveyor belt were made of Teflon®, a slippery substance?

10. False. This is an example of a technical term having a very different meaning from the same word used in everyday language. An irresistible desire to purchase something you can't afford may be an impulse brought about by modern advertising. In physics, an impulse is the product of the force acting on an object times the length of time that the force acts on that object.

These questions and answers should have made clear to you that what you have to look out for in physics is clarity of ideas, not just math. You must know what each term means. In particular, you must know how to *measure* position, displacement, velocity, acceleration, force, momentum, work, energy, and anything else you want to use in calculations. The mental connection you make between the definition and the measurement procedure will help keep you from reverting to only that knowledge you possess before studying physics.

The part of physics that includes motion, both linear and rotational; forces and torques; energy and work; and momentum, linear and angular, is called mechanics. The study of motion, called *kinematics*, is the first topic we will address.

Kinematics

POSITION AND DISPLACEMENT

The ancient Greeks were pretty smart. They took geometric reasoning to a high level, knew the Earth was a sphere, and had advanced theories of drama and poetry, but they never got very far with the study of motion. They were able to do calculations with angular motion of the sun, moon, and known planets, but they never did the same thing for linear motions. A long time passed before these omissions were corrected. We are fortunate that these studies of motion have been carried out, and we can use the results.

Start with position. Your position is where you are right now: sitting at a desk or lying on a couch or on the floor. But how would you describe your position to me? And how would you assign a numerical value to it?

Describe in writing your position to me so that I can find you while you remain in that position. (Note that the ambiguous second "position" in the last sentence could also refer to how your limbs are arranged.)

You might have written, "Milky Way Galaxy, Planet Earth, Columbus, Ohio, USA, Tower Dorm, Room 1525, seated at my desk." Another student might have written the same thing but specified Room 1532.

I certainly could find both of you. But suppose I now ask you how far apart the two of you are. You have to get a measuring tape, a ruler, or a yardstick.

In physics we are always interested in how far apart two objects are, or how far one object has moved. In the dorm, the architect's plans specify the distances between the two rooms, whether or not the contractor followed the plans exactly. Because we'll look at motion in a straight line first, we need to specify positions along a line, which the mathematicians have already described for us.

WORKED EXAMPLE 3.1

How do we specify positions along a straight line in a math problem?

Answer: We use a coordinate axis. We draw a line that represents the actual physical space graphically. Let's say that we want to look at the motion of cars on a road. Highways usually have mile markers every tenth of a mile.

This is the actual physical situation we have in mind when we idealize the situation to a single line, the coordinate axis, and the cars to points.

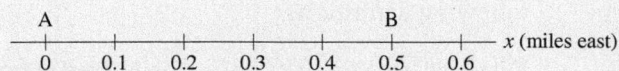

FIGURE 3.1 An idealized pictorial representation of a car at two different positions, A and B, on a highway with distances indicated in tenths of a mile.

Figure 3.1 represents the physical situation in an idealized form so that we can read the positions directly from the diagram. In physics, we'll always start with pictures and words, progress to diagrams, and then go on to graphs and equations. Now let's answer some questions based on Figure 3.1.

Suppose it takes the car 30 s ("s" is the standard abbreviation for second) to go from A to B while moving at constant speed. (Use your instinct about the concept of speed: We'll define it shortly.) How long did it take the car to go 0.1 mi? ("mi" is the standard symbol for mile.)

If it takes 30 s to travel 0.5 mi, the distance between A and B, then it takes 6 s to travel 0.1 mi. (Note that this is proportional reasoning.)

Suppose it takes 30 s for the car to go back from B to A. How long did it take the car to go 0.1 mi, 0.2 mi?

The return trip takes the same amount of time as the initial trip, so it covers 0.1 mi and 0.2 mi in 6 s and 12 s, respectively.

How do we distinguish between going from A to B and returning from B to A?

Answer: There is more than one way to specify this. We can state that we are heading east in going from A to B and west in heading from B to A. We can say that we first go 0.5 mi in the positive x-axis direction and then 0.5 mi in the negative x-axis direction. Either of these works, but we have to state the time as an additional piece of information.

Instinctively we know that longer distances take longer times to cover, which suggests that in distance problems we need to know a ratio of how far to how long an object has traveled. Therefore, we have the following definitions:

Distance. Imagine a roll of string is fixed at point A and the other end is tied to your car so that string unrolls as you drive, until you reach point B. Stretch the string out straight and measure its length: That result is the total distance you have traveled. (If you head back, imagine that the string goes around a stake at point B so it has to keep unwinding as you return.) Distance is always positive. Distance is the length measured by a ruler, yardstick, tape measure, laser, or any equivalent device when the string is straightened out.

Displacement. Displacement is the difference between a body's position at two different locations, as noted by coordinates. If the displacement is from one point to another on a coordinate axis, such as posts at two different mile markers, it can refer to the same time. If the displacement is of a body as it moves from the initial to the final position, such as a car moving from one mile marker to another, it represents the change in position over the time required for the movement. For motion on a straight line, displacement is what you read on the coordinate axis, still the x-axis, at the later time, x_f, minus what you read at the earlier time, x_i: $x_f - x_i$. We indicate relative changes by using Δ, the capital Greek letter delta, so $\Delta x = x_f - x_i$. When studying motion, Δ always refers to a value at a later time minus a value at an earlier time, but not necessarily to a greater value minus a lesser value.

There are instances where x_f has a smaller value than x_i. For example, let's say you started on the road at mile marker 5.6 mi and moved in the direction of decreasing mile marker distances, to post 2.3 mi. In this case, $x_i = 5.6$ mi and $x_f = 2.3$ mi.

TIME TO TRY

Jennie needs a new pair of jeans. She leaves home—point A in Figure 3.2—at time t_{A1} and drives due east to store B, arriving at time t_{B1} and leaving at time t_{B2}. She then drives to store C, arriving at time t_{C1}. She finds that store B has a lower price, so she leaves store C at time t_{C2} and arrives at store B at time t_{B3}. She leaves store B at time t_{B4} and arrives home at time t_{A2}.

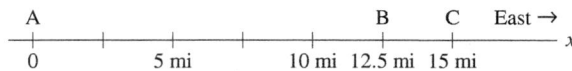

FIGURE 3.2 Jennie's trip to the stores and back.

1. What is the distance in miles to store B from home, point A?

2. What is the displacement of store B from home, point A?

3. What is the distance from store B to store C?

4. What is the displacement of store C from store B?

5. What is the distance to home from store B?

6. What is the displacement of home, point A, from store B?

Answers: 1. 12.5 mi. 2. +12.5 mi. (We either have to say 12.5 miles to the right, or 12.5 mi east, or use the plus sign to give the direction of the displacement relative to the coordinate axis, directed east.) 3. 2.5 mi. 4. +2.5 mi (or 2.5 mi east). 5. 12.5 mi. 6. −12.5 mi (or 12.5 mi west).

SPEED AND VELOCITY

In any motion in life we are as much interested in how long it takes us to get there as in the distance we cover. If Jennie leaves home at 2:00 PM and wants to wear her new jeans when meeting her friend at 3:30 PM, she has to keep an eye on her wristwatch or cell phone. Let's assume she lives on a country road where there are no stoplights, so there are no extra time-consuming stops. Let's assume the times are t_{A1} = 2:00 PM; t_{B1} = 2:15 PM; t_{B2} = 2:23 PM; t_{C1} = 2:30 PM; t_{C2} = 2:38 PM; t_{B3} = 2:45 PM; t_{B4} = 2:55 PM; and t_{A2} = 3:08 PM.

We'll check out time intervals first. A time interval is a "length" of time, the later clock reading minus the earlier clock reading, again indicated by the capital Greek letter delta Δ: $\Delta t = t_f - t_i$.

✔ **QUICK CHECK**

What are the time intervals required for Jennie to go from

1. home to store B?

2. store B to store C?

3. store C back to store B?

4. store B back home?

Answer: 1. 15 min. 2. 7 min. 3. 7 min. 4. 13 min.

Now we can calculate average speeds and average velocities. The **average speed** is the ratio of the distance traveled to the time taken, the time interval. The **average velocity** is the ratio of the displacement to the time taken, the time interval.

TIME TO TRY

1. What is Jennie's average speed when going from home to store B?

2. What is her average velocity when going from home to store B?

3. What is her average speed when going from store B to store C?

4. What is her average velocity when going from store B to store C?

5. What is her average speed when going from store C back to store B?

6. What is her average velocity when going from store C back to store B?

7. What is her average speed when going back home from store B?

8. What is her average velocity when going back home from store B?

Answers: 1. Jennie's average speed is the ratio of distance to time: $\frac{12.5 \text{ mi}}{15 \text{ min}} = 0.83 \frac{\text{mi}}{\text{min}}$. Note that this has no direction; it's just a number, a magnitude with units. 2. Jennie's average velocity is the ratio of displacement to time: $\frac{+12.5 \text{ mi}}{15 \text{ min}} = +0.83 \frac{\text{mi}}{\text{min}} = 0.83 \frac{\text{mi}}{\text{min}}$, east. Note that this has a direction.

For motion in a straight line, a + or – sign relative to the coordinate axis we have introduced is sufficient to indicate direction along that line, although we can provide the same information by stating the direction, such as east or west.

3. Her average speed is the ratio of distance to time: $\frac{2.5 \text{ mi}}{7.0 \text{ min}} = 0.36 \frac{\text{mi}}{\text{min}}$. 4. Her average velocity is the ratio of displacement to time: $\frac{+2.5 \text{ mi}}{7.0 \text{ min}} = +0.36 \frac{\text{mi}}{\text{min}} = 0.36 \frac{\text{mi}}{\text{min}}$, east. 5. Her average speed is the ratio of distance to time: $\frac{2.5 \text{ mi}}{7.0 \text{ min}} = 0.36 \frac{\text{mi}}{\text{min}}$. 6. Her average velocity is the ratio of distance to time: $\frac{-2.5 \text{ mi}}{7.0 \text{ min}} = -0.36 \frac{\text{mi}}{\text{min}} = (+)0.36 \frac{\text{mi}}{\text{min}}$, west. 7. Her average speed is the ratio of distance to time: $\frac{12.5 \text{ mi}}{13 \text{ min}} = 0.96 \frac{\text{mi}}{\text{min}}$. 8. Her average velocity is the ratio of displacement to time: $\frac{-12.5 \text{ mi}}{13 \text{ min}} = -0.96 \frac{\text{mi}}{\text{min}} = (+)0.96 \frac{\text{mi}}{\text{min}}$, west.

If you understand the sign conventions in the preceding eight answers, you are in good shape to deal with graphical representations of motion as presented in Chapter 5.

CHANGE IN VELOCITY AND ACCELERATION

Travel on a highway would not be as dangerous as it is now if everyone drove at the same speed, and cars entered the highway only after having reached that speed. Even so, velocities, which have direction, would change every time there was a curve in the road. On a real highway, people travel at different speeds and different velocities. They veer out of their lanes while on cell phones or text-messaging. Because entering cars are moving at lower velocities than cars already on the road, their velocities clearly change as soon as they are on the highway. We'll look at changes in velocity first, and then at accelerations, the rates of change of velocities.

✔ **QUICK CHECK**

(Note our switch to metric units.)

1. At 2:19 AM, Cherie is driving west at $60 \frac{m}{s}$. At 2:20 AM she is driving west at $40 \frac{m}{s}$. What is Δv, the change in her velocity?

2. At 2:19 AM Joey is driving west at $60 \frac{m}{s}$. At. 2:23 AM he is driving east at $40 \frac{m}{s}$. What is Δv, the change in his velocity?

Answers: 1. Here $\Delta v = v_f - v_i = 40 \frac{m}{s}$, west $- 60 \frac{m}{s}$, west $= -20 \frac{m}{s}$, west $= +20 \frac{m}{s}$, east. 2. Here $\Delta v = v_f - v_i = 40 \frac{m}{s}$, east $- 60 \frac{m}{s}$, west $= 40 \frac{m}{s}$, east $+ 60 \frac{m}{s}$, east $= +100 \frac{m}{s}$, east.

(Note that velocities are written as $\frac{m}{s}$, rather than m/s. When you place units or numbers that should be in the denominator in the same line as the numerator, there is always a chance of mixing up the numbers on a test.)

We often use coordinate axes to give directions to velocities, changes in velocities, and accelerations.

TIME TO TRY

Let west be the positive direction of the coordinate axis. Answer questions 1 and 2 from the previous Quick Check with + for west and – for east.

Answers: 1. $\Delta v = v_f - v_i = +40 \dfrac{m}{s} - \left(+60 \dfrac{m}{s} \right) = -20 \dfrac{m}{s}.$

2. $\Delta v = v_f - v_i = -40 \dfrac{m}{s} - \left(+60 \dfrac{m}{s} \right) = -100 \dfrac{m}{s}.$

Acceleration is the ratio of the change in velocity to the time interval over which the velocity changed. For example, $a = \dfrac{+40 \dfrac{m}{s}}{20\ s} = +2 \dfrac{m}{s^2}.$

✔ QUICK CHECK

Find the accelerations in questions 1 and 2 from the previous Quick Check. (All necessary information is already given.)

Answers: 1. $a = \dfrac{\Delta v}{\Delta t} = \dfrac{-20 \dfrac{m}{s}}{60\ s} = -\dfrac{1}{3} \dfrac{m}{s^2},$ or $a = +\dfrac{1}{3} \dfrac{m}{s^2},$ east.

2. $a = \dfrac{\Delta v}{\Delta t} = \dfrac{-100 \dfrac{m}{s}}{240\ s} = -0.42 \dfrac{m}{s^2},$ or $a = +0.42 \dfrac{m}{s^2},$ east.

Why didn't we need to state that the direction was west in each initial answer, but needed to include east in the second version? Also, Joey could have changed direction in two different ways. Can you figure out what they are?

In your physics course, you will study accelerations that occur when the direction of the velocity changes. For now, you've gotten the basic ideas and definitions here.

PRACTICE

Here are a number of problems for practice in working with displacements, velocities, and accelerations.

1. The positions of a car on a test track at the beginning and end of a 5 s time interval follow. The track is in an east-west direction with distances increasing to the west. Here the symbol "y" is used to represent displacement. Calculate the average velocity for each of the following examples:

   a) $y_1 = 20$ m; $y_2 = 20$ m   b) $y_1 = 20$ m; $y_2 = 40$ m

   c) $y_2 = 40$ m; $y_1 = 40$ m   d) $y_1 = 40$ m; $y_2 = 20$ m

2. The average velocities of a car on a test track are given at the beginning and end of a 5 s time interval. Calculate the average acceleration in each of the following cases:

   a) $v_1 = 10\frac{m}{s}$, E; $v_2 = 40\frac{m}{s}$, E.   b) $v_1 = 40\frac{m}{s}$, E; $v_2 = 10\frac{m}{s}$, E.

   c) $v_1 = 10\frac{m}{s}$, W; $v_2 = 40\frac{m}{s}$, W.   d) $v_1 = 40\frac{m}{s}$, W; $v_2 = 10\frac{m}{s}$, W.

   e) $v_1 = 10\frac{m}{s}$, E; $v_2 = 40\frac{m}{s}$, W.   f) $v_1 = 40\frac{m}{s}$, E; $v_2 = 10\frac{m}{s}$, W.

   g) $v_1 = 10\frac{m}{s}$, W; $v_2 = 40\frac{m}{s}$, E.   h) $v_1 = 40\frac{m}{s}$, W; $v_2 = 10\frac{m}{s}$, E.

   i) $v_1 = 10\frac{m}{s}$, E; $v_2 = 10\frac{m}{s}$, W.   j) $v_1 = 40\frac{m}{s}$, W; $v_2 = 40\frac{m}{s}$, E.

3. A car is headed to the right on a road as you stand alongside the road. Call the direction to the right positive and the direction to the left negative. Explain what will happen to the car in each of the following circumstances:

   a) velocity positive; acceleration positive

   b) velocity positive; acceleration negative

   c) velocity negative; acceleration positive

   d) velocity negative; acceleration negative

Answers: 1. a) $\Delta y = 0$; $v_{avg} = 0$. b) $\Delta y = 20$ m; $v_{avg} = +4 \frac{m}{s}$. c) $\Delta y = 0$; $v_{avg} = 0$. d) $\Delta y = -20$ m; $v_{avg} = -4 \frac{m}{s}$. 2. a) $\Delta v = 30 \frac{m}{s}$, E; $a_{avg} = 6 \frac{m}{s^2}$, E. b) $\Delta v = -30 \frac{m}{s}$, E; $a_{avg} = 6 \frac{m}{s^2}$, W. c) $\Delta v = 30 \frac{m}{s}$, W; $a_{avg} = 6 \frac{m}{s^2}$, W. d) $\Delta v = -30 \frac{m}{s}$, W; $a_{avg} = 6 \frac{m}{s^2}$, E.

3. In two of these the velocity is increasing in magnitude and in two it is decreasing in magnitude. Hint: It is not decreasing in magnitude in (d) because the
change in velocity is in the same direction as the velocity.

i) $\Delta v = 20 \frac{m}{s}, a_{avg} = 4 \frac{m}{s^2}$ W; j) $\Delta v = 80 \frac{m}{s}, a_{avg} = 16 \frac{m}{s^2}$ E.

g) $\Delta v = 50 \frac{m}{s}, a_{avg} = 10 \frac{m}{s^2}$ E; h) $\Delta v = 50 \frac{m}{s}, a_{avg} = 10 \frac{m}{s^2}$ E.

f) $\Delta v = 10 \frac{m}{s}$ W $- \left(-40 \frac{m}{s}\right) = 50 \frac{m}{s}, a_{avg} = 10 \frac{m}{s^2}$ W.

e) $\Delta v = 40 \frac{m}{s}$ W $- \left(-10 \frac{m}{s}\right) = 50 \frac{m}{s}, a_{avg} = 10 \frac{m}{s^2}$ W.

Forces

We know that forces may cause change. A push or a pull is an example
of a **force**, but gravitational attractions, which occur without direct
contact, are also forces. We've experienced pushes, shoves, punches in
the arm, and the difficulty in pushing a stalled car off the road. In
August 2008, 30 bystanders in the Bronx, New York, lifted a bus off a
woman. The difficulty in pushing a car or lifting a bus shows that there
is a built-in resistance to change in motion. Our name for the built-in
resistance—we can use a fancy word and call it "innate resistance"—is
inertial mass, though we usually just call it "mass." Instinct also tells us
that a force acting on a mass that is free to move results in a change of
motion, an acceleration of that mass. Weight is the name for the attractive force that the Earth exerts on another body when that force is
measured with a scale. We'll start with mass, and then define force by
connecting acceleration with force and mass.

MASS

You are buying lemons in the supermarket. You want a juicy lemon. How
would you compare two lemons in order to decide which one to buy?

You could find a scale, but many supermarkets have removed scales
from their produce sections. Or you could hold one lemon in each
hand and see which feels the heaviest. That's a very primitive kind of
balance procedure. A knife-edge balance, such as that shown in
Figure 3.3, lets us compare an unknown mass with a known mass.

FIGURE 3.3   A knife-edge balance.

Although balances actually compare weights, mass is proportional to weight at the Earth's surface. A mass of 1 kg corresponds to a weight of 2.2 pounds at sea level.

We've already noticed that acceleration is proportional to force. When more than one force acts on a body, its acceleration is proportional to the net or resultant force that sums up the action of all the external forces acting on that body or system. We've also noticed that the greater the mass of a body, the more resistance there is to change of motion of that body. This means that the acceleration is *inversely proportional* to the mass. Write an equation that states that acceleration, a, is proportional to external force, F^{ext}, and inversely proportional to mass, m.

Answer: You should have written $a = \dfrac{F^{ext}}{m}$. You may have seen this written as $F^{ext} = ma$, but the version $a = \dfrac{F^{ext}}{m}$ helps remind us of the physical reasoning behind the law. In either form, this equation is known as **Newton's Second law**.

We get the unit of force, the **Newton**, N, by multiplying the units of mass and acceleration: $1\,\text{N} = 1\,\text{kg} \times 1\,\dfrac{\text{m}}{\text{s}^2} = 1\,\dfrac{\text{kg} \cdot \text{m}}{\text{s}^2}$. Like the kilogram, the second (s) is a basic unit by definition, but the meter (m) is found from the definition of the velocity of light. Nonetheless, we can think of the kilogram, meter, and second as our three basic units. We won't need additional basic units until we deal with topics such as electricity or thermodynamics.

WEIGHT

You probably have a good idea of what weight is. Define weight for yourself and then check the following definition.

Weight is another one of those words, like gravity, that has been taken into physics from everyday speech. It has turned out to be a dangerous crossover. We know that the Earth interacts with bodies on its surface because the mysterious force "gravity" is said to pull objects toward the Earth. (It's not at all obvious that the objects also pull on the Earth, but they do.) This gravitational interaction gives rise to the force that we call weight. A small part of this force is used to keep an object at the surface from flying off into space by following its natural tendency to move in a straight line, but most of this force gives rise to what a scale measures. We may think of the weight of an object as this downward force that the Earth exerts on an object. When the object and scale are at rest, the scale exerts a force of the same magnitude back on the object. This force is proportional to the mass of the object, so we write $W = mg$, where g is the acceleration the downward gravitational force W gives to a body of mass m at the surface of the Earth.

Weight is the net downward force that the Earth exerts on an object as measured by a scale.

NEWTON'S LAWS OF MOTION

Isaac Newton developed three important laws that describe force and mass.

NEWTON'S THIRD LAW See what you might already understand about Newton's Third law:

Andrew shoves Jim and Jim falls. Which statement correctly describes the situation while Andrew is shoving Jim?

a) Andrew's hand exerts a force on Jim, but Jim's body does not exert a force back on Andrew's hand.

b) Jim's body exerts a force back on Andrew's hand, but it is not as big as the force Andrew's hand exerts on Jim.

c) Jim's body exerts exactly as large a force on Andrew's hand as Andrew's hand exerts on Jim's body.

d) Jim's body exerts a larger a force on Andrew's hand than the force Andrew's hand exerts on Jim's body.

Answer: (c). This may seem absurd, but forces of the same magnitude have very different results on different objects. Andrew used a frictional force of the Earth on his feet to avoid falling, while Jim, caught unawares, didn't have time to resist.

As Newton's Third law states, *In any interaction between two bodies, each one exerts a force of the same magnitude on the other.* If the force is a pull, each pulls on the other. If the force is a push, each pushes the other away. Another way of stating this is to say that the two forces, one on each body, have opposite directions.

NEWTON'S FIRST LAW If you place a book and a ball on a level, smooth table, what do you expect them to do? Why?

Answer: If we assume that we do not have a trick ball or a hollowed-out book with a mechanism built into it, then we expect the ball and book to sit there. We know that we have to do something to make them move.

If you have a friend who is on a trip place a ball and book on a table in the dining car of a railroad train, what would you see if you could look through the window into the train? Why?

Answer: With the same assumptions as in the previous setting, and the additional assumption that the train moves very smoothly, that is, at constant velocity, we expect to see the book and ball at rest on the table. The person in the train would need to do something to the ball and book to make them move.

Roughly stated, if a system, such as ourselves and our surroundings, is not moving, the system starts to move only when an outside (external) force is exerted on it. This also holds true for changes in velocity in a system that is initially moving at constant velocity relative to us when we are at rest. (Note: An object cannot move itself, but a person in the room can produce the external force on an object.) As Newton's First law explains, *An object remains in a state of rest or a state of motion at constant velocity unless made to change that state by a net force.*

PICTURE THIS

You are standing in the aisle of a bus or subway train at rest. Then it starts moving with the greatest possible acceleration. What happens to your body? Why?

Answer: If you don't dig your feet into the floor quickly and hard, you will probably fall over. Your body wants to stay where it is. (We concluded previously that it takes an outside force to make a body change its position.) If the frictional force the floor exerts on your feet is not large enough to give you the same acceleration as the bus or train, your body won't be able to move with it.

An object remains at rest when its surroundings remain at rest. An object moves at constant velocity when it is part of a system moving at constant velocity. It takes a net external force on an object to make it accelerate. That force may come from bodies inside or outside the system, but not from the object itself.

Let's work through some examples applying Newton's laws of motion:

WORKED EXAMPLE 3.2

1. You place a marble on a kitchen counter. What will happen to it? Why? Are there any external forces on the marble? If so, what are they?

The marble will sit there if the counter is level. Newton's First law tells us that any external forces on the marble must add up to zero. We know that the interaction between the Earth and the marble results in a downward force on the marble. For the sum of forces to be zero, a force of equal magnitude in the opposite direction must be exerted on the marble by the countertop. This is shown in Figure 3.4. Whenever an object is at rest despite the presence of a known force, Newton's First law lets us deduce that at least one other external force is acting on the object. Remember that Newton's First law is particularly useful when objects are at rest or moving at constant velocity.

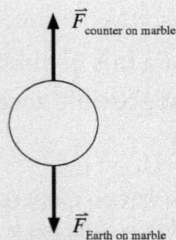

$\vec{F}_{\text{counter on marble}}$

$\vec{F}_{\text{Earth on marble}}$

FIGURE 3.4 Forces acting on a marble that rests on a countertop.

2. You place the same marble on a ramp for handicapped access to a building. What will happen to the marble? Why? Are there any external forces on the marble? If so, what are they?

This is a no-brainer: The marble will roll down the ramp. Because the marble interacts with the Earth, a portion of the force of the Earth on the marble acts parallel to the ramp. The rest of the force that the Earth exerts on the marble is balanced by a force the ramp exerts on the marble. This is shown in Figures 3.5a and 3.5b.

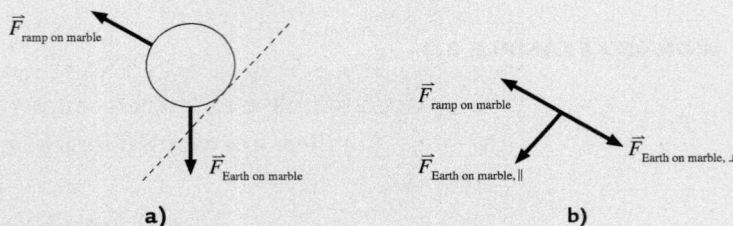

$\vec{F}_{\text{ramp on marble}}$

$\vec{F}_{\text{Earth on marble}}$

$\vec{F}_{\text{ramp on marble}}$

$\vec{F}_{\text{Earth on marble, }\parallel}$

$\vec{F}_{\text{Earth on marble, }\perp}$

a)

b)

FIGURE 3.5 **a)** Forces acting on a marble on a ramp. **b)** Components of the force that the Earth exerts on the marble.

Figure 3.5a shows that the two forces do not sum to zero. Figure 3.5b shows the force of the Earth on the marble broken up into two components, one parallel to the ramp and the other perpendicular to the ramp. We can see that $\vec{F}_{\text{ramp on marble}}$ is equal and opposite to $\vec{F}_{\text{Earth on marble, }\perp}$, while $\vec{F}_{\text{Earth on marble, }\parallel}$ is a net external force on the marble. Figure 3.5a is a force diagram. Figure 3.5b is a free body diagram. In a free body diagram, we show the forces, but the body has been reduced to the point where the tails of the vector arrows representing the forces meet.

3. You hold the marble in your hand and open your hand so the marble is released. What will happen to the marble? Why? Are there any external forces on the marble? If so, what are they?

The marble will fall because of the pull of the Earth on the marble. It goes from a state in which it is not moving to a state in which it is moving at constantly increasing velocity. (This is not obvious because it falls so fast, but you can see the increase in the velocity when you let the marble roll down a ramp with a gentle slope.) The external force on the marble is the force of gravity, the pull that the Earth exerts on the marble. There also is a tiny buoyant force from the air and a force of resistance from the air, but in introductory courses we ignore those most of the time.

Work and Energy

PICTURE THIS

Suppose you had to spend the day working at a plant nursery in a job where you had to put 50-pound bags of topsoil in cars and pickups all day. You would probably say that you had done a full day's work. Let's look at this situation:

Use what we just learned about Newton's First and Third laws to describe the forces on your hands by a bag of topsoil and on the bag of topsoil by your hands.

The Earth pulls down on the topsoil with a force that we call the force of gravity on the bag of topsoil.

1. If the topsoil is to move up at constant velocity, your hands must be exerting an equal and opposite force on the topsoil.

   Which of Newtons' laws are we using here?

2. If your hands exert a force on the topsoil, then the topsoil is exerting an equal and opposite force on your hands.

   Which of Newton's laws are we using here?

Answers: 1. The first law 2. The third law

Is it easier to lift the bag a shorter distance onto the back of a pickup or a greater distance over the side of the pickup truck?

It's always harder to lift the bag a greater distance. Some of that has to do with how high we have to reach and the structure of our bodies, but when lifting with our arms in front it is harder to lift a heavy weight a greater distance.

We define the **work** done when the force and displacement are in the same direction as $W = Fd$, where W is work, F is force, and d is displacement. When the force and displacement are in opposite directions we take the work to be negative. We will later learn that we have to modify this definition to take into account any angle between the force and the displacement, but this equation will be enough to "work" with for now.

The unit of work, the **Joule**, is the product of the units of force and displacement, so $1\,J = 1\,N \cdot m = 1\,\dfrac{kg \cdot m^2}{s^2}$. This same unit is used for all types of energy.

✔ QUICK CHECK

1. Is the work you do in lifting a 50-pound bag 2 feet positive or negative?

2. Is the work the bag does on your hands positive or negative?

Answers: 1. The force you exert on the bag and its displacement are parallel and in the same direction, which means the work is positive. Therefore you do 100 foot-pounds of work on the bag. 2. The force the bag exerts on your hands and the displacement of your hands are in opposite directions, which means the work is negative. Therefore the bag does minus 100 foot-pounds of work on your hands. We say that you have supplied 100 foot-pounds of energy to the bag.

In order to get a 50-pound bag moving as you lift it, you have to accelerate it by applying a force opposite to and greater than the force of gravity to the bag. You could let the bag slow down when it reaches the highest point by letting gravity pull on it. But until you do that, the bag has the energy you gave it to start it moving. That energy it has while moving is called kinetic energy. It turns out that a consistent definition of **kinetic energy** is $K = \dfrac{1}{2}mv^2$, where K is kinetic energy, m is mass, and v is the magnitude of the velocity.

Now suppose you were lifting a large bag of gravel and let it drop on your toe. Ouch! That bag could break a toe or two. It could do work on your toes as a result of where it had been: lifted up so that it could pick up speed while falling. What makes the bag pick up speed? The interaction of the bag with the Earth. We say that the bag has **gravitational potential energy**, because the force of gravity pulling it toward the surface of the Earth can do work on the bag during its displacement.

A compressed spring can exert a force on an object and do work on that object. A person with a pocket knife is in great danger if he or she gets too close to a powerful magnet. A person who gets too close to the edge of a cliff may die of the fall. Whenever the configuration of objects is such that they will attract or repel one another unless restrained, begin to move and pick up kinetic energy because of work the forces do, we say the system of objects has potential energy. Our three examples have elastic (spring) potential energy, magnetic potential energy, and gravitational potential energy.

Now we are ready to introduce the relation between work and energy:

The sum of all types of energy at the beginning time plus work done by a force external to the system over the time interval is equal to the sum of all types of energy at the end of the time interval.

This is known as the **law of conservation of energy**.

Remember that work can be negative as well as positive, so the total energy at the end can be less than the total energy at the beginning. That result can occur when the object doing the work is not part of the system.

✔ **QUICK CHECK**

A bag of topsoil is lying on the ground. Set gravitational potential energy to zero at ground level. (Only changes in gravitational potential energy are meaningful, because no motion occurs unless the relative positions change. When h is the height above ground level, the usual convention is to set gravitational potential energy equal to mgh). State whether the kinetic energy K of the bag, the gravitational potential energy U of the bag-Earth system, and the work that has been done on the bag by the force of gravity are positive, negative, or zero at the following times:

1. At $t = 0$ s the bag is lying on the ground.

2. At $t = 1$ s the bag is 1 ft above the ground and is moving upward at 1 ft per s.

3. At $t = 2$ s the bag is 2 ft above the ground; you are holding it in your arms but have not yet moved to put it in the pickup truck.

4. At $t = 4$ s the bag is lying in the pickup truck.

Answers: 1. $K = U_g = W = 0$. 2. K is positive—the bag is moving, U_g is positive—the bag is above ground level. W is positive—you have done work on the bag to start it moving and to lift it at constant velocity. 3. $K = 0$—the bag is not moving, $U_g > 0$—the bag has been raised above ground level. $W > 0$—the work was done over the whole time interval while you were raising the bag. 4. $K = 0$—the bag is not moving, $U_g > 0$—the bag is above ground level. $W > 0$—the work was done over the whole time interval while you were raising the bag.

Subtle point: When we start to write equations we can include either the work done by the force of gravity on the bag or the gravitational potential energy of the bag-Earth system. If we include both we will be counting gravity twice. Another way of saying this is that we either use the force model or the energy model, but have to be careful not to use the two together for the same interaction. The following section will help to make this clear. ▪

WORK-ENERGY BAR CHARTS A work-energy bar chart is a visual mnemonic (for memorization) device that lets you keep track of the different forms of energy that belong to a system of objects. Once you have drawn a correct work-energy bar chart, the writing of the equivalent equation is trivial. (When we discuss problem-solving in Chapter 5, we will pay much more attention to defining our system.)

Say you are pulling a sled with a child on board. Define the sled and child as the system. Draw a dashed outline to mark out the system (Figure 3.6). In this case the rope is exerting an external force on the system. The rope is doing work on the system either to get the sled moving initially, or against friction while the sled moves at a constant speed. If

FIGURE 3.6   Forces acting on a pulled sled.

we do not include the surface of the snow in the system, friction is an external force that does negative work.

On a work-energy bar chart there is a location for each type of energy at the initial time and for each type of energy at the final time of the situation depicted. Bars representing work are shown between the initial and final forms of energy because work occurs over a period of time. Figure 3.7 shows what the work-energy bar chart for this example should look like.

The first bar in Figure 3.7 represents any kinetic energy the sled has at the time we pick as the initial time. The second bar represents the work done on the sled by the external force exerted by the rope tied to the sled. Because this work is done over a period of time before the final time, the bar is placed to the left of the equal sign. The third bar, representing the work done by friction, is also placed to the left of the equal sign because this work too occurs before the final time. By summing the positive and negative heights of the bars to the left of the equal sign, we arrive at the bar for the kinetic energy at the final time. Even when a problem has not yet been solved numerically, the heights of the bars should be your best estimate of the size of each type of energy and work.

Work-Energy Bar Chart

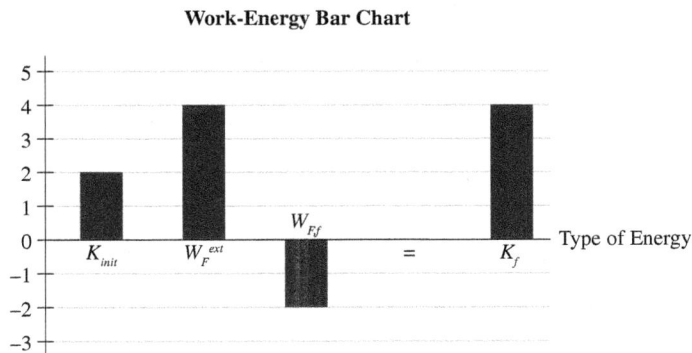

FIGURE 3.7   Work-energy bar chart for sled being pulled.

WORKED EXAMPLE 3.3

A 2.00 kg mass is thrown downward with a 5.00 $\frac{m}{s}$ initial speed from the 3 m high roof of a house and hits the ground. Use $g = 10 \frac{m}{s^2}$ for simplicity. The initial time is when the mass leaves the hand. The final time is the instant when it has stopped moving. Consider the Earth as part of the system, and take the force of friction as being internal to the system. That means that any energy that ends up as thermal energy at the end of the process must have its own bar in the final state. Call that bar $\Delta U_{\text{int. thermal}}$. Because the Earth is part of the system, the relative positions of the mass and the Earth are accounted for in the gravitational potential energy. Construct two work-energy bar charts for this system. First construct a qualitative bar chart without showing any energy values. Then construct bars proportional to the magnitudes of the various types of energy. Use the bars shown in Figure 3.8.

$$\overline{K_i} \qquad \overline{U_{g,i}} \quad \overline{W} \quad = \quad \overline{K_f} \qquad \overline{U_{g,f}} \quad \overline{\Delta U_{\text{int. thermal}}}$$

FIGURE 3.8 Bars represented in a typical work-energy bar chart for a falling mass.

Answer: Only the second bar chart, with actual quantities, is shown. Your first bar chart should have been similar to this. Because K_i is 25 J, and mgh is 60 J, the internal thermal energy at the end is 85 J. Figure 3.9 shows what the correct bar chart looks like. It must be emphasized that you often will just draw bars of relative sizes and use the types of energy you have to determine what to calculate.

FIGURE 3.9 The correct bar chart for Worked Example 3.3.

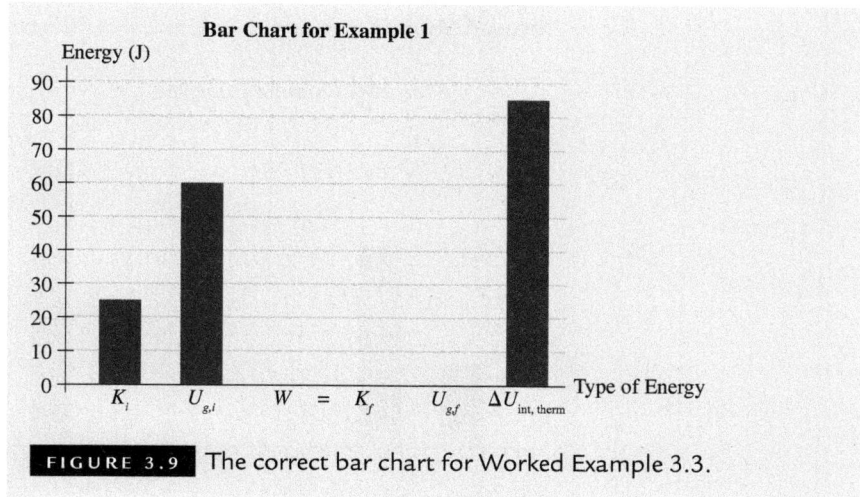

WORKED EXAMPLE 3.4

A 2.00 kg mass is placed at the top of a 15.0° incline, then given a quick shove so that it starts down the incline at 5.00 $\frac{m}{s}$. The mass moves a vertical distance of 3.00 m before coming to a stop. Consider the Earth as part of the system, and take the force of friction as being internal to the system as in Worked Example 3.3. Construct a work-energy bar chart for this system. Use the bars shown in Figure 3.10.

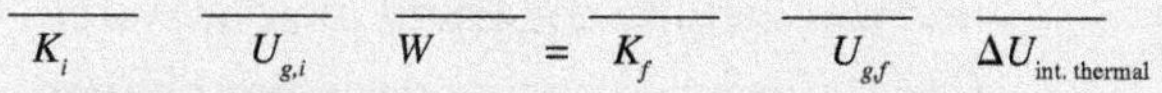

FIGURE 3.10 Bars represented in a work-energy bar chart for mass on incline.

Answer: Your work-energy bar chart should have looked like Figure 3.11:

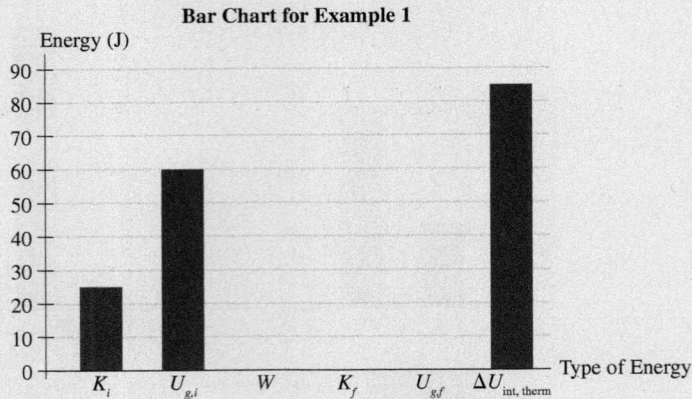

Bar Chart for Example 1

FIGURE 3.11 Work–energy bar chart for mass moving on incline.

There is no kinetic energy in the final state—we could say at the final time—because the mass has stopped moving.

TIME TO TRY

1. A 65 kg skater, originally moving at 20 $\frac{m}{s}$, comes to a stop after gliding a distance of 100 m on a rough sidewalk. Draw a work-energy bar chart showing her energies at the beginning and end of the glide. Note: This bar chart will look the same whether or not you include the Earth in your system because the gravitational potential energy does not change.

2. A 60 kg skater, originally moving at 30 $\frac{m}{s}$, glides up a 50 m long 30° incline. (Can you use trigonometry to show that her vertical ascent is 25 m?) Draw a work-energy bar chart showing her energies at the beginning and end of the glide. Do not include the Earth in your system.

3. Draw a second bar chart for the skater in question 2, but this time include the Earth in your system.

Answers: 1. Here is the work-energy bar chart for question 1.

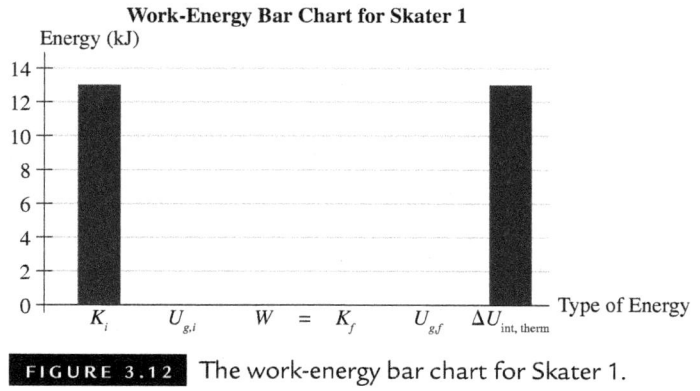

Work-Energy Bar Chart for Skater 1

FIGURE 3.12   The work-energy bar chart for Skater 1.

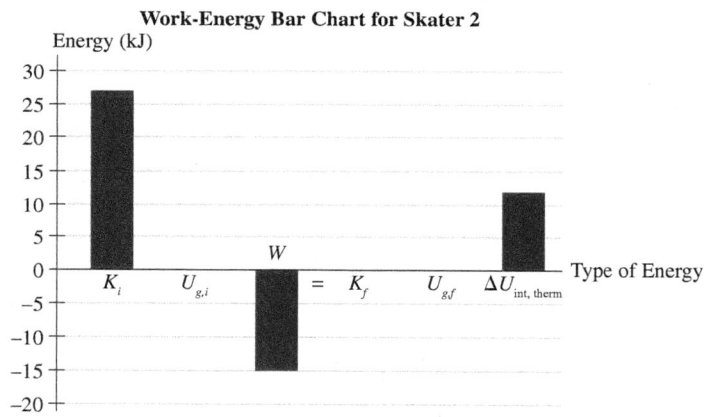

Work-Energy Bar Chart for Skater 2

FIGURE 3.13   The work-energy bar chart for Skater 2.

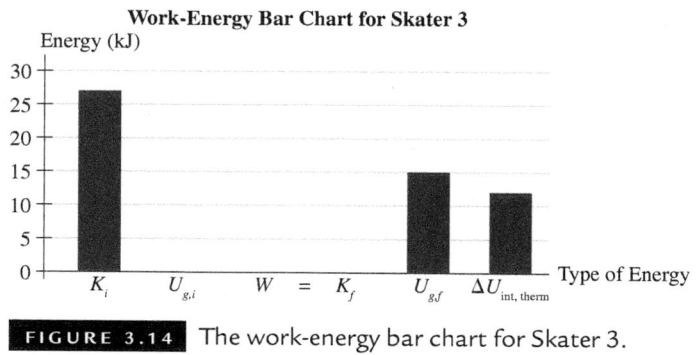

Work-Energy Bar Chart for Skater 3

FIGURE 3.14   The work-energy bar chart for Skater 3.

PRACTICE

1. A friend drops a ball from a dorm window. The ball falls from a height of 21.0 m and is caught by your hand at a height of 1.00 m. Use $g = 10 \frac{m}{s^2}$. The initial time is the instant when the ball is released and the final time is when the ball stops moving. Draw a work-energy bar chart for the ball. (Hint: What is the initial velocity of a ball that is "dropped"?)

2. You throw a ball straight up. It leaves your hand with an initial velocity of $40 \frac{m}{s}$. The final time is when the ball is at the highest point it reaches. Use $g = 10 \frac{m}{s^2}$. Draw a work-energy bar chart for the ball. (Hint: What is the velocity of the ball at the highest point?)

3. You throw a ball straight up. It leaves your hand with an initial velocity of $40 \frac{m}{s}$. The final time is when the ball has fallen back into your hand. Use $g = 10 \frac{m}{s^2}$. Draw a work-energy bar chart for the ball. (Hint: What has happened to the kinetic energy your hand gave to the ball after it has fallen back into your hand?)

Final Stretch!

Now that you have finished reading this chapter it is time to stretch your brain and check how much you have learned.

RUNNING WORDS

Here are the terms introduced in this chapter. Write them in a notebook and define them in your own words. Then go back through the chapter to check on their meanings, and on any formulas associated with them. Make corrections as needed and try to list examples of the use of each term.

Position
Change of position
Distance
Displacement
Speed
Velocity
Change in velocity
Delta
Acceleration
Force
Newton's First law

Newton Second law
Newton's Third law
Kinetic energy
Work
Gravitational potential energy
Energy conservation
Work-energy bar chart
Newton
Joule
Weight

WEB RESOURCES

For additional help, enter any of the topics listed under "What did you learn?" or any bold-face section title in a Web search engine. Check through a number of sites to find one at the right level.

■ *One site with a simulation applicable to this chapter is*

http://phet.colorado.edu/simulations/sims.php?sim=The_Moving_Man

The Phet site was designed by a group working under Nobel prize winner Carl Wieman at the University of Colorado, and will be of help to you when taking your physics courses.

4 Physics Concepts, Part II

When you complete this chapter you should be able to:

Explain how to define and/or calculate the following:

- Forces between like and unlike charges
- Conductors and insulators
- Charge polarization and induction
- Coulomb's law
- Electric field
- Electric potential energy and electric potential
- Ohm's law
- North and south magnetic poles
- Temperature and thermal energy
- Thermometers and temperature scales
- Zeroth and First laws of thermodynamics
- Oscillation, period, frequency, and amplitude
- Light ray and shadow
- Diffraction
- Structure of an atom and atomic nucleus

Electricity

Humans have been giving names to things for a very long time. Our ancestors named plants, trees, animals, themselves, and processes such as eating, running, or hunting. They named lightning and attributed it to the gods of their tribes: Zeus, Thor, and Jehovah. For all we know, some scientific observations may have occurred over and over but were not recorded until writing was invented. What we do know is that someone noticed that a piece of amber rubbed with fur could attract and lift up bits of pith that came from a reed. What is so significant about this attraction is that it is the exact opposite of gravity. Here was a contradictory phenomenon, and it was named for amber, *elektron* in Greek.

Electricity is a property of amber, and, as we now know, of the protons and electrons contained in all atoms. It is a name for a property we observe, not an explanation of how it occurs. All we can do is describe how "electrical"—we now say electrically charged—particles behave. Just as inertial mass is a property that describes how a force is needed to change the velocity of a mass, electric charge is a property that lets particles and the objects that contain those particles exhibit electrical attraction and repulsion. Any two electrically charged particles exert long-range forces on one another—repulsive when the particles have charges of the same sign, attractive when the particles have charges of the opposite sign. Just as masses do not need to be in contact with the Earth to be attracted by it, the objects exhibiting electrical attraction and repulsion do not need to make contact with each other.

In addition, because all bodies are made up of positively and negatively charged particles, a neutral body—one in which the charges sum to zero—can be attracted by a body with a net charge because the particles in the neutral body shift so that there is a net opposite charge closer to the charged particle. This property, called charge polarization, is similar to the shift of mass by gravity, a shift known as the tides. See the further discussion of induction starting on page 147.

Your Starting Point

You have probably studied the structure of atoms in a high school chemistry course or in general science. Some of you may have some experience with physics as well. Try the following questions:

1. What is the structure of a single atom?

2. What particles can be found inside an atomic nucleus?

Answers: 1. Every atom contains a very highly compact nucleus that contains most of the mass of the atom. Outside the nucleus there are electrons that can be thought of as moving around the nucleus in orbits of varying shapes and sizes, mostly very far out compared to the diameter of the nucleus. (When you study quantum mechanics you will learn that this is a simplistic model.) 2. The nucleus contains protons, positively-charged particles, and neutrons, particles with no net electrical charge.

PICTURE THIS

You can check out the properties of static electricity at home.

Experiment 1: Take about 8 inches of cellophane tape, the cheap stuff that sticks, not the more expensive tape. Fold over a bit at an end so you can hold on to it without it sticking to you, and place the tape on a wooden or plastic desk or table. Press it down firmly and prepare a second piece of tape the same way. Then pull them up fairly quickly and bring them close together. What do the two pieces of tape do? (Note: This may not work properly if there is too much humidity in the air, because water molecules can pick the charges off the tape.)

Answer: _____

Experiment 2: Prepare two strips of tape, but now place one piece on top of the other. Pull the two pieces of tape off the tabletop together, then pull them apart. When you now bring them close together, what do you observe?

Answer: _____

You should have observed the two pieces of tape repelling one another in the first experiment and attracting one another in the second experiment. The friction generated in the act of pulling causes some separation of charge. We now have to explain why we see both attraction and repulsion. Other ways of preparing charged bodies include rubbing a glass rod with silk or a rubber rod with fur. After rubbing, one glass rod can repel another glass rod, silk repels silk, rubber repels rubber, and fur repels fur. However, glass attracts rubber and silk attracts fur.

CONDUCTORS AND INSULATORS

After many experiments, scientists in the past found that all charged bodies either attracted or repelled one another. Later experiments measured the strengths of these forces. The results show that there are two kinds of the electrical property called **charge**: one called **positive charge** and the other called **negative charge**. Benjamin Franklin assigned the name positive to the charge of the glass rod, and that name has stuck ever since.

If you can estimate the weight of one of your pieces of tape and the angle it makes with the vertical when near another piece of tape, you can compare the electrical force to the force of gravity. A very rough estimate would be that the electrical force is of the same order of magnitude as the force of gravity. What you will learn in class is that the amount of charge causing that force is very small in comparison to the mass needed for the gravitational force.

Rough experiments show that more vigorous rubbing produces bodies that repel or attract more strongly. But the discovery that made precise experiments possible was that of **insulators** and **conductors**. Metals are examples of conductors: They not only conduct electricity well, they also conduct heat well. Wood and glass are examples of insulators: They do a good job of resisting the motion of charge through them. When a charged body is placed in contact with a conductor, it transfers some of its charge to the conductor. This charge spreads out all over the surface of the conductor.

✔ **QUICK CHECK**

Why does the charge spread out all over the conductor?

spread out as far as possible from one another.
positive or negative. Because charges of the same type repel one another, they
individual charged particles on the conductor all have the same type of charge,
Answer: Because a charged body has one sign (one kind) of excess charge, the

We now know that the positively charged nuclei of atoms hardly move at all. It is a portion of the negatively charged electrons that is free to move in a conductor, toward a positively charged object, and away from a negatively charged object.

INDUCTION

We've seen how you can put electric charge on a body by friction, but there are other ways to charge a conductor.

CHARGE POLARIZATION Before we can explain induction, we must look at how charges in a neutral body redistribute themselves when an object with a net electrical charge is brought close.

Suppose a conducting sphere is hanging by an insulating thread, as in Figure 4.1a, and that a positively charged rod is brought close as in Figure 4.1b.

We can show the distribution of positive and negative charges on the sphere in Figure 4.1a by indicating that positive and negative charges in equal quantities are distributed throughout the sphere as in Figure 4.2.

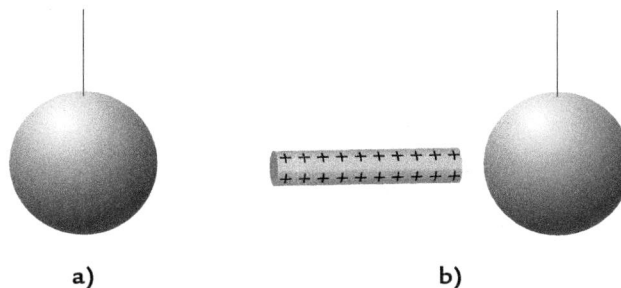

a)   b)

FIGURE 4.1 **a)** A neutral conducting sphere. **b)** A positively charged rod is brought close to the sphere.

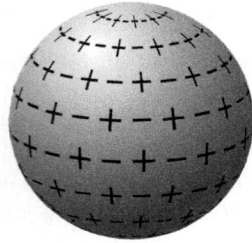

FIGURE 4.2 The charge distribution in a neutral conducting sphere.

In the sphere in Figure 4.1b, the negative charges must have shifted toward the positively charged rod.

PICTURE THIS

Use the sphere in Figure 4.3 to sketch the charge distribution you expect to find in the sphere in Figure 4.1b.

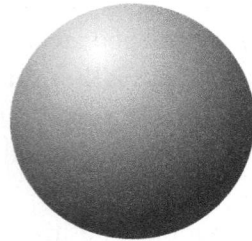

FIGURE 4.3 Sketch the charge distribution in a sphere having a positively-charged rod at its left.

FIGURE 4.4 The charge distribution in a conducting sphere in the presence of a positive charge at its left.

Answer: You should have sketched something like this:

Something similar happens in insulators where the charges are fixed in place. There, however, the negative charges move only a little bit to the left and positive charges very, very slightly to the right, so that each atom remains electrically neutral individually. The shifts, however, still make the left side of the insulating sphere slightly negative and the right side slightly positive.

The shift of charge in a neutral conductor or insulator when in the presence of a charged body is known as charge polarization.

✔ **QUICK CHECK**

If the sphere is free to move when the charged rod is brought close to it, will the sphere remain hanging straight down or will it move. If it moves, in what direction will it move?

Answer: Because the charge on the side of the sphere closest to the rod is opposite to the charge on the rod, the sphere will move toward the rod until the horizontal electrical force is balanced by the horizontal component of the tension in the string.

Next we'll look at how charge polarization can be used to charge bodies without placing charges on them directly.

MORE ON INDUCTION

PICTURE THIS

You have two metal spheres hung by insulating threads. Bring positively charged metal sphere A up to metal sphere B so that they are close, but not touching, as in Figure 4.5a. As explained previously, B, even though uncharged, is attracted to A because of charge polarization. Then touch B with your finger as shown in Figure 4.5b. Predict what the state of B will be after you take your finger away and then remove Sphere A.

Answer: The Earth acts as a big conductor of electricity. The positive charge on A attracts the negative charge in B so the side of B near A becomes negatively charged, and the side of B opposite from A becomes positively charged, as in Figure 4.4. Because charge can move in a conductor—it's generally the electrons that are free to move—a neutral conductor can be attracted by a charged body as shown in Figure 4.5a.

When you touch B, electrons from the Earth can reach sphere B through your finger. When you remove your finger, the electrons remain on B because of the net positive charge on the right side of B that attracted them in the first place. This gives B an excess of negative charge that still remains when A is removed. We have charged B by **induction**, the charging of one object without touching it to a second charged object. Figure 4.6 shows how charge is distributed on Sphere B after the finger is removed.

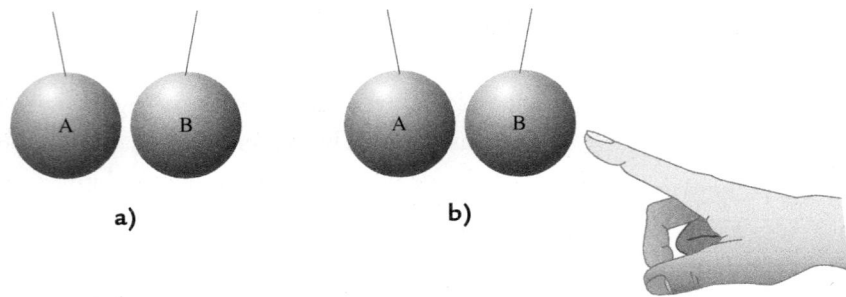

FIGURE 4.6   The charge distribution on Sphere B after the finger has been removed.

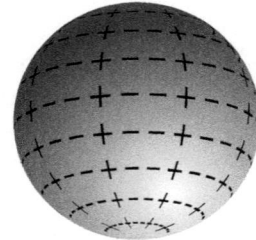

FIGURE 4.5   Charging by induction.

TIME TO TRY

1. Two metal spheres hung by insulating threads repel one another. What can we say about any electric charge on the spheres?

2. Two rubber spheres hung by insulating threads repel one another. What can we say about any electric charge on the spheres?

3. Sphere A attracts sphere B and sphere C, but B and C neither attract nor repel one another. What can we say about any electric charge on the spheres?

Answers: 1. They are both charged and show the same type of charge, but we do not know what the sign of the charge is. 2. They are both charged and show the same type of charge, but we do not know what the sign of the charge is. (Insulators can hold charges on their surfaces or within their volume. They differ from conductors in two ways: The charges on an insulator cannot move around, only shift slightly like a person fidgeting in a chair, and charge can be present inside an insulator, not just on its surface. 3. Sphere A is charged, but spheres B and C are both neutral (uncharged).

QUANTITATIVE CONSIDERATIONS

If we place charge on a metal sphere, and touch that to an identical metal sphere, how much charge does each sphere now hold?

Answer: Our instinct tells us that like charges repel, and the only way that the charges can get as far from one another as possible is to spread out equally on the two spheres. That is correct. The distribution is not spherically symmetrical while the two spheres are touching, but there are equal amounts of charge on the two spheres. When they are separated by a large distance, each has a symmetrical distribution of one-half of the original charge.

How do we obtain two spheres with one-quarter of the original charge?

Answer: Touch one of the spheres with half the original charge to an identical sphere that is uncharged.

What has been described in these two questions is a physical equivalent to the mathematical operations by which a meter or an inch is halved, quartered, etc., so that we can construct rulers and meter sticks.

In principle, this allows us to experiment with charges of different magnitudes. In practice, such experiments are very difficult to carry out because charge leaks off charged bodies into the air.

WORKED EXAMPLE 4.1: DEDUCE A BASIC LAW FROM DATA

Table 4.1 gives the charges on two metal spheres and shows the forces they exert on one another at several distances. Use this table to deduce how the force depends on the charges on the bodies and on their center-to-center distances. The coulomb, symbol C, is the basic unit of charge. You are seeking a formula that relates charge q_1, charge q_2, the center-to-center distance of the charges, r, and a constant k. For instance, line 1 of Table 4.1 tells you that the magnitude of the constant is 9. (The formula you come up with will give you the units of the constant.) Ask yourself how you can get the numbers in the right hand column with 9 as the constant.

TABLE 4.1 Charges on spheres and forces the charges exert on one another.

Charge on Sphere 1 (μC)	Charge on Sphere 2 (μC)	Center-to-center distance (m)	Force each charge exerts on the other (mN)
1	1	1	9
2	2	1	36
3	3	1	81
1	2	1	18
1	3	1	27
2	3	1	54
1	1	2	2.25
1	1	3	1.00

Answer: Two 1-μC charges 1 m apart exert a 9×10^{-3} N force on one another. But a combination of a 1-μC and a 2-μC charge yields an 18×10^{-3} N force, while two 2-μC charges yield a 36×10^{-3} N force. Because $1 \times 1 \Rightarrow 9$, $1 \times 2 \Rightarrow 18$, $2 \times 2 \Rightarrow 36$, and $3 \times 3 \Rightarrow 81$, we conclude that the force in milliNewtons (mN) is equal to the product of the two charges times a constant 9, as long as the distance is itself held constant at 1 m. We can write $F \propto q_1 q_2$ by using the "proportional to" sign $\propto$. But we have $\frac{9}{4} = 2.25$ when the distance is doubled and $\frac{9}{9} = 1$ when the distance is tripled. The force is inversely proportional to the square of the distance r: $F \propto \frac{1}{r^2}$. If we put the two proportions together and add a constant of proportionality, k, we have **Coulomb's law:**

$$F \text{ (each charge on the other)} = \frac{kq_1 q_2}{r^2}$$

where $k = 9 \times 10^9 \, \frac{Nm^2}{C^2}$.

ANOTHER PICTURE: THE ELECTRIC FIELD

We will now find a way to find the force that a charged body fixed in place can exert on any other charge. When we complete these exercises we will be able to define a new concept, the **electric field**.

Figure 4.7 shows a 3-nC charge $(1 \text{ nC} = 1 \times 10^{-9} \text{ C})$ fixed in place. It also shows four other points where we could locate another known charge, a "test charge." When we measure the force on the test charge, we determine how big a force the fixed charge can exert on it. Because we know Coulomb's law, we can predict the strength of the force. Assume that the fixed charge and the test charge are both positive charges. In that case the arrow at each point in Figure 4.7 shows the force on the test charge at that point. Note that each arrow points in the direction of the force on the test charge at that point. Its length is proportional to the magnitude (the strength) of the force. The tail of the arrow is located at the position of the test charge.

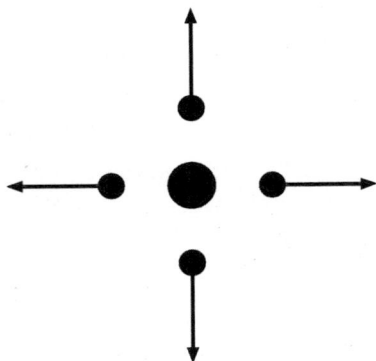

FIGURE 4.7 Fixed charge and test charges.

DEFINING THE ELECTRIC FIELD Next imagine that we take the ratio of the force to the magnitude of the test charge at each point. Because the test charge is small, the force is small. But when we divide the force by the test charge, a small number, the ratio is a larger number. We want to draw arrows representing this *vector* ratio, $\dfrac{\overrightarrow{\mathbf{F}}_{\text{on test charge}}}{q_{\text{test charge}}}$, in the same way we drew arrows for the forces in Figure 4.7. Do this below on the points where the test charge is located in Figure 4.8.

If you have sketched this correctly, your drawing should resemble, but not necessarily be exactly the same as, Figure 4.9.

The quantity that we represented symbolically in Figure 4.9, $\dfrac{\overrightarrow{\mathbf{F}}_{\text{on test charge}}}{q_{\text{test charge}}}$, is known as the electric field, $\overrightarrow{\mathbf{E}}$. We write that

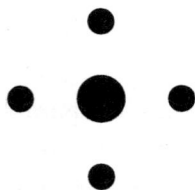

FIGURE 4.8 A central charge with four points where a test charge may be located.

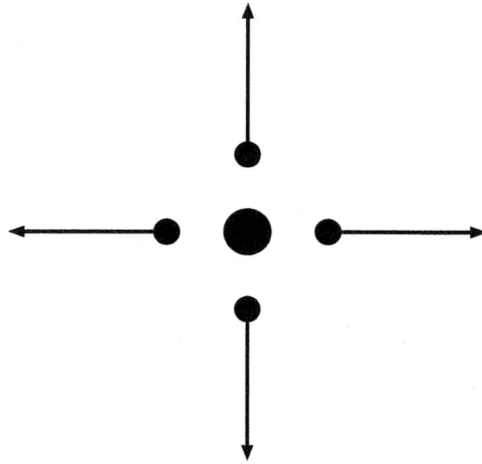

FIGURE 4.9 Arrows showing the ratio of force to test charge.

$\overrightarrow{E} = \dfrac{\overrightarrow{F}_{\text{on test charge}}}{q_{\text{test charge}}}$. Because a test charge will experience a force at any point at any distance from another charge, we say that there is an electric field in the space surrounding the fixed charge.

For any fixed charge, the arrows representing the electric field are larger when the test charge is closer and smaller when the test charge is farther out. All arrows point radially outward when we have a positive point fixed charge and a positive test charge, because like charges repel one another.

✔ **QUICK CHECK**

1. What happens to the size of the arrows representing the electric field when the points are closer to the fixed charge? Farther from the fixed charge?

2. What happens to the size of the arrows representing the electric field if the magnitude of the fixed charge is increased? Decreased?

3. What happens to the arrows representing the electric field if the sign of the fixed charge changes from positive to negative?

4. What happens to the size of the arrows representing the electric field if the magnitude of the test charge is increased? Decreased?

Answers: 1. The arrows are larger when the test charge is closer to the fixed charge, and smaller when the test charge is farther from the fixed charge, because the arrows represent the magnitude of the field as well as its direction. 2. All the arrows are proportionally larger when it increases and proportionally smaller when it decreases. 3. All the arrows point in the opposite direction because a negative fixed charge attracts positive test charges. 4. All the arrows stay the same. This will be explained next.

We are getting a picture of the forces that can be exerted on a fixed charge, but it would be great if we didn't have to draw a new diagram every time the source charge changed in magnitude. To avoid having to draw more than one diagram for a given source charge, we have taken the ratio of the force on the test charge at a point to the magnitude of the test charge: $\dfrac{\vec{F}_{\text{on test charge at point p}}}{q_{\text{test charge}}}$, and called that ratio the electric field at that point: $\vec{E}_{\text{at point p}} = \dfrac{\vec{F}_{\text{on test charge at point p}}}{q_{\text{test charge}}}$.

(To avoid sign confusion, we always use a positive test charge.)

✔ **QUICK CHECK**

Use Coulomb's law to calculate the electric field of a point charge.

1. Write Coulomb's law for the magnitude of the force, $F_{\text{fixed charge on test charge at point p}}$, that a fixed source charge, q_{fixed}, at the origin of coordinates exerts on a test charge, $q_{\text{test charge at point p}}$, at a distance, r, from the origin.

2. Find the ratio of that force to the fixed charge.

Answers: 1. $F_{\text{fixed charge on test charge at point p}} = \dfrac{kq_{\text{fixed}} \cdot q_{\text{test charge a point p}}}{r^2}$.

2. $\dfrac{F_{\text{fixed charge on test charge at point p}}}{q_{\text{test charge a point p}}} = \dfrac{\dfrac{kq_{\text{fixed}} \cdot q_{\text{test charge a point p}}}{r^2}}{q_{\text{test charge a point p}}} = \dfrac{kq_{\text{fixed}}}{r^2} = E$.

●

FIGURE 4.10 A fixed source charge.

The magnitude $E = |\vec{E}|$ of the electric field $\vec{E}$ at a point depends only on the fixed source charge. That's why we wanted to define it. For any test charge at a point where the electric field has magnitude E we get the magnitude of the force back by using $F_{\text{on test charge}} = q_{\text{test charge}}E_{\text{at point p}}$. If we want to include the directions of the force and the electric field we can use the vector equation $\vec{F}_{\text{on test charge}} = q_{\text{test charge}}\vec{E}_{\text{at point p}}$.

We only showed a small number of points in Figures 4.7 and 4.9. Imagine that there is one fixed positive source charge in Figure 4.10. Imagine placing a (positive) test charge anywhere. In what direction will the force on the test charge point? Draw some arrows representing the forces on test charges at different points.

Did you use your knowledge that two positive charges repel one another to draw arrows pointing radially outward? An example is shown in Figure 4.11, where we have drawn arrows from arbitrary points in place of the symmetric figures shown earlier.

✔ **QUICK CHECK**

Wherever there is a force, or a force would exist if a charge were there, there is an electric field present. We represent the electric field at a point with an arrow in the same way we represent a force with an arrow. However, if we note that there is an electric field pointing outward at every point along any radial line from the center, we can use a directed line to represent all these electric field vectors in a single direction. Try drawing such lines in Figure 4.12.

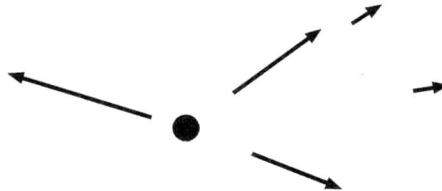

FIGURE 4.11 Force arrows pointing radially outward, greater for points closer to the source and smaller for points farther away.

FIGURE 4.12 A charge from which lines representing electric fields are to be drawn.

Did you draw lines radially outward from the source? Each such line is tangent to an infinite number of electric field vectors and represents all those vectors that start on points along the line. We call any line that is tangent to electric field vectors an **electric field line**. We indicate the directions of the electric field vectors by little arrows on the line, as in Figure 4.13.

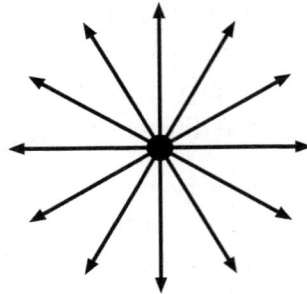

FIGURE 4.13 Electric field lines from a positive charge.

PRACTICE

1. Draw the electric field lines of a negative source charge. Use the charge shown in Figure 4.14.

2. Use what you now know about the electric field lines of positive and negative charges to draw the field lines of an equal positive and negative charge as shown in Figure 4.15.

FIGURE 4.14 The electric field lines of a negative charge.

FIGURE 4.15 The electric field lines of a dipole, a positive and a negative charge of equal magnitude.

Answers. Figure 4.14 should show all the electric field lines drawn radially toward the center with the directions shown pointing inward, as shown in Figure 4.16. Figure 4.15 should show the electric field lines starting on the positive charge and ending on the negative charge, as shown in Figure 4.17. We say that a positive charge is a source for field lines and a negative charge is a sink for field lines.

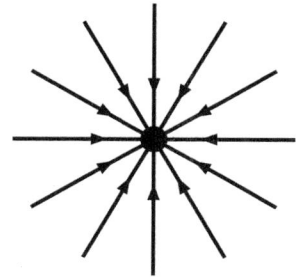

FIGURE 4.16 The electric field lines of a negative source charge.

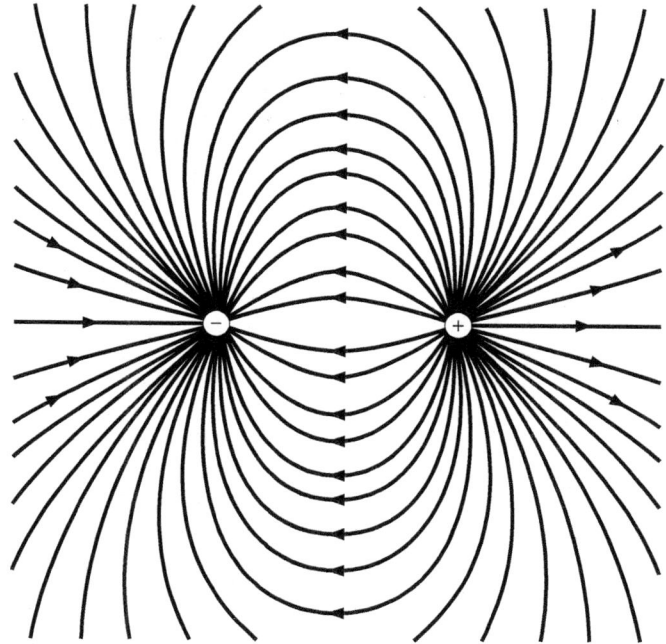

FIGURE 4.17 The electric field lines of a dipole.

TIME TO TRY

1. The Earth, shown as a sphere in Figure 4.18, has an excess of negative charge on it. Think about what we know about field lines for positive and negative point charges, and draw electric field lines for the Earth.

2. The field lines end at the surface of the Earth, a conductor. Why can't there be any charge inside a conductor; that is, why is all the charge on its surface?

Answer: 1. The field lines are exactly the same as those of a point negative charge, except that they end at the surface of the Earth rather than at its center. They point toward the Earth because the charge on the Earth is negative. 2. Like charges repel. Therefore, each individual charged particle placed on a conductor tries to get as far away from every other charged particle as possible. The only way for this to happen is for all the charge to be on the surface. Another way to look at this is to think about electric fields. If there were charges inside a conductor, there would be an electric field inside a conductor. Each charge's electric field would cause a repulsive force on every other particle of the same charge. If we place electrons on a metal, they repel the electrons that are already in the metal. The electrons that are in the metal repel the electrons we just placed on it. Each has an electric field. They move to positions where their electric fields are paired up to be equal and opposite. (More correct, the vector sum of the electric fields inside the metal is zero.) In class, you will learn how to prove mathematically that there can be no electric field inside a conductor in an electrostatic situation.

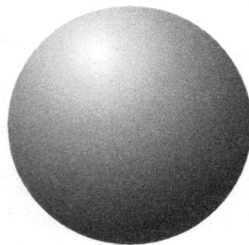

FIGURE 4.18 Earth, a sphere with negative charge on its surface.

Summary:

1. Any two charged particles or bodies exert forces on one another. Particles of the same charge repel one another. Particles of opposite charge attract one another. For point particles the force that each particle exerts on the other is proportional to the product of the charges and inversely proportional to the square of the distance from each particle to the other (**Coulomb's law**).

2. We can picture this by drawing lines tangent to force directions on test charges brought near fixed charges. These **electric field lines**, a diagrammatic representation of force on each unit of charge (the fancy way of saying force per unit charge), point out from positive charges and in toward negative charges.

3. A body can become charged by friction, by receiving charge from another body that already has a charge on it, or by induction. We can charge a conductor by **induction**, because the presence nearby of a charged body induces a shift in the charges in a conductor. When grounded (placed in contact with a source of charge, usually a larger body), the conductor attracts charge opposite to that of the polarizing body from the ground.

ELECTRICAL ENERGY

Positive charges repel positive charges; negative charges repel negative charges; and positive and negative charges attract one another. If we allow two charged bodies to move freely, they will either move toward or away from one another. Either we have to do work on the charged bodies to separate them or force them together, or they can do work for us as they move toward or away from one another. We say that the **electrical potential energy** of the bodies increases when we have to do work on them because they will move back to their original positions while acquiring kinetic energy when released. We say that the bodies use up their electrical potential energy when their kinetic energy is increasing.

✔ **QUICK CHECK**

In each of the following examples, the charges either do work for us or we do work on them. For each example state whether work is done on or by the charges:

1. Two positive charges move toward one another. _____

2. Two positive charges move away from one another. _____

3. Two negative charges move toward one another. _____

4. Two negative charges move away from one another. _____

5. A negative and a positive charge move toward one another. _____

6. A negative and a positive charge move away from one another. _____

Answer: We do work on the charges in 1, 3, and 6. The charges can do work for us in 2, 4 and 5.

ELECTRICAL POTENTIAL

Electrical potential is the ratio of work done on one unit of positive charge to that positive charge when we move it closer to another positive charge. Because the unit of work is the joule and the unit of charge is the coulomb, the unit of electrical potential is the joule per coulomb, in magnitude the joules for each coulomb. Therefore the unit of potential, the **volt**, is given by $1 \text{ V} = \dfrac{1 \text{ J}}{1 \text{ C}}$.

That is not work per unit charge at a point, but work per unit charge over a distance when charge moves between two points. Likewise we can determine the amount of work done if we know the difference of potential between the two points. Formally, that **potential difference** is written as ΔV, but in sloppy yet common notation is often indicated as V and is called a "voltage." If the potential difference is positive, it means that the potential is increasing and we are approaching a positive charge or receding from a negative one. Because a potential difference is the work for each unit of charge that is moved, we only need to multiply the potential difference by the amount of charge to find out how much work has been done or has to be done: $W = q \times \Delta V$.

✔ **QUICK CHECK**

If +3.5 C is moved through a potential difference of +20 V, how much work is done on or by the charge?

Answer: To move +3.5 C toward a positive charge we must do work,
$W = q \times \Delta V = 3.5 \text{ C} \times 20 \text{ V} = 70 \text{ V}.$

OHM'S LAW Because the work done in each unit of time is power, the charge moving through a potential difference in a given time, a current, uses or supplies power. This relationship is explained by Ohm's Law.

Divide both sides of the equation for work in terms of charge and potential difference by the time interval. Define power (work done in each unit of time) and current (charge moved in each unit of time) and make appropriate replacements: that will give you a relationship between power, current, and potential difference.

To show these steps, we write $\dfrac{W}{\Delta t} = \dfrac{q}{\Delta t} \times \Delta V$, which can then be expressed as $P = I\Delta V$, where P and I represent **power** and **current**, respectively. The unit of current, the ampere, abbreviated A, is 1 C/s (one coulomb per second).

In space empty of everything except electric charges and their electric fields, particles will be accelerated by electric forces. Inside a wire, even when the wire is a conductor, particles cannot keep on accelerating because they bump into other charged particles. Table 3.2 gives some data that might have been recorded by a scientist in the early days of experiments on electricity. Use this data to determine the relationship between current, voltage, and resistance.

TABLE 4.2 Experimental data for *V, R,* and *I.*

Potential difference in V	Resistance (R) in ohms (Ω)	Current in amperes (A)
24	2	12
24	4	6
24	6	4
12	2	6
12	4	3

Experimentally, we find that the current, the charge moving through a uniform wire per second, is proportional to the potential difference we apply to the ends of the wire by a device such as a battery. Current is inversely proportional to the resistance. It has become customary to write the constant of proportion as $\frac{1}{R}$ so that the rule is $I = \frac{V}{R}$. This is Ohm's law.

We can combine our equation for power with Ohm's law to obtain an equation for **power** in terms of current and resistance:

$$P = IV = I(IR) = I^2R.$$

Note that the equation $P = I^2R$ describes the power that is used to make a current go through a wire or other resistive device. The equation $P = IV$ is more general and can describe situations where some of the power is used to run a motor.

WORKED EXAMPLE 4.2

An air conditioner is hooked up to a 240 V power supply. (Ignore for now the fact that this is alternating current rather than direct current.) It uses a 0.7 A current. The air conditioner cools the air but the motor heats up and has to be air cooled. Don't worry about the numbers for now. Use the bar chart in Figure 4.19 to draw a work-energy bar chart for this process:

Initial energy + Energy supplied = Energy for cooling   + $\Delta U_{\text{int. thermal}}$

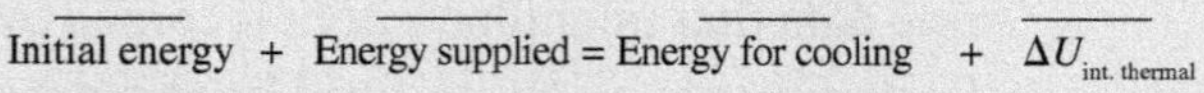

FIGURE 4.19   Work-energy bar chart for an air conditioner.

Answer: Here is a possible work-energy bar chart for this process:

Initial energy + Energy supplied = Energy for cooling   + $\Delta U_{\text{int. thermal}}$
                        IV $IV - I^2R$ I^2R

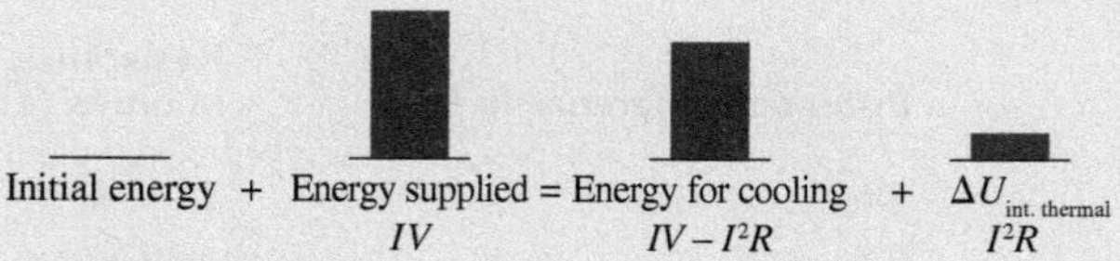

FIGURE 4.20   Work-energy bar chart for air conditioning.

This figure also illustrates how the energy supplied electrically cannot all be used for work when there is any kind of dissipative aspect to a system—in this system, some of the energy supplied is lost to thermal energy. You will learn later that the second law of thermodynamics tells us that this must always occur.

Magnetism

Most of the forces we encounter day to day are contact forces. When we push or pull or lift an object, we are in contact with it. With electrical forces we saw that a charged body could attract another charged body and would always attract an uncharged body even though the two bodies were not in contact. Most of you have probably had a chance to play with magnets and have seen that their ends also attract and repel at a distance. Like electricity, magnetism is a long-range force.

How do we know that magnetism is not static electricity? (This is not an easy question, but consider all you know about static electricity from our discussion of that, and think about magnets you have played with. Scientists had to answer this question when research on electricity and magnetism took off seriously in the nineteenth century.)

We can answer this question by describing four observations:

1. If a bar magnet is suspended so that it is free to turn, it rotates and settles down into a position where one end points toward a spot near the geographical north pole and the other end points in the opposite direction. Unmagnetized bodies do not have a preferred orientation even if they have an electric charge on them. The end of the bar that points toward the north is called the "north-seeking" pole of the magnet, or **north pole** for short. The other end is called the "south-seeking" or **south pole**.

2. When two north poles are made to approach one another, they repel. You have felt this if you have ever played with magnets. Two south poles also repel one another, but a north pole of one magnet and a south pole of another magnet attract one another, and "click"

together unless you forcibly hold them apart. If you have any magnets around your house or dorm room, check out the repulsion and attraction for yourself.

3. If you place charges of equal magnitude but opposite sign—one positive, one negative—on two conducting spheres, and then let the spheres touch, the two spheres are then uncharged and neutral. If you pull the north and south poles of two magnets apart after contact, they are still magnetic. That's different from the behavior of electric charges.

4. If you break a magnet in half, each half has a north pole and a south pole. No one has succeeded in producing an isolated north pole or an isolated south pole. If such things existed they would be magnetic charges, but they do not seem to exist.

PICTURE THIS

1. You stack a batch of bar magnets so all the north poles are at one side and all the south poles are at the other side. Is the magnetic field weaker or stronger than the field produced by one bar magnet? Why? (Hint: Think of magnetic field lines going out of the north poles and into the south poles of the magnets.) See Figure 4.21.

2. You place a batch of bar magnets end to end, south pole to north pole as in Figure 4.22, so that there is one south pole at one end and one north pole at the other end. Is the combined magnetic field weaker or stronger than the field produced by one bar magnet? Why?

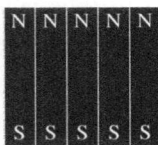

FIGURE 4.21 Magnets stacked side by side.

FIGURE 4.22 Magnets arranged end to end.

the field is the same as that of one magnet.
magnets end to end, there is just one free north pole and one free south pole, so
duce field lines, so the total field has a greater magnitude. When we connect the
magnet. When we stack magnets side by side, there are more north poles to pro-
each magnet has both a north and a south pole, fields start on and at each
lines. By convention, field lines leave north poles and enter south poles. Because
field magnetic of sources as poles magnetic the of think can We .2 and 1 :Answer

Thermal Physics

If you put something you have just rinsed into a bit of hot oil in a frying pan, you may get spattered by a few drops of hot oil. If you accidentally tip over a pan filled with hot oil onto yourself, you will have to get to a hospital's emergency room. There clearly is a quantitative aspect to thermal physics.

On the other hand, you can pour as much oil from the bottle in the kitchen into your hand as you wish without getting burned. The same substance that can burn can also cool us. Boiling water and ice are examples. There clearly are both qualitative and quantitative aspects to thermal physics.

We call the qualitative aspect **temperature**. We call the quantitative aspect **thermal energy**.

✔ **QUICK CHECK**

Let's see what your current impressions are of temperature and thermal energy:

1. The higher the temperature of a solid body, the more thermal energy it contains.   T F

2. The more of a given substance we have, the more thermal energy it contains at a given temperature.   T F

3. Given equal amounts of the same material, the one at a higher temperature contains more thermal energy than the one at a lower temperature.   T F

4. Equal amounts of different substances at the same temperature may contain different amounts of thermal energy.   T F

5. The greater the difference in temperature between two bodies, the more rapidly thermal energy is transferred from the hotter to the cooler body.   T F

Answers: These statements are all true.

Temperature is a rough measure of the amount of thermal energy in a given body, but a better definition is that temperature indicates the ability of a body to transfer thermal energy to another body. The more "matter" we have at a given temperature, the more thermal energy it contains. One reason why temperature is not a direct measure of thermal energy in a given body is that the body may be in different states, such as ice and water, but at the same temperature. Water contains more thermal energy than ice at the same temperature.

Now we can look at experiments that demonstrate what we know instinctively.

TEMPERATURE

Every material substance changes in some way when its temperature changes, but those that undergo large enough but continuous enough changes may be used to measure temperature. Because mercury, which is liquid at room temperature, expands significantly as its temperature rises, for quite some time it was used in **thermometers**, devices that measure temperature. Unfortunately, mercury also has a high rate of vaporization and is poisonous, so colored alcohol solutions or substances that change color when the temperature changes are now used for household thermometers. Labs use substances with electrical properties that change when the temperature changes.

Thermometers need to be calibrated. Calibration is accomplished by placing a thermometer in substances that maintain constant temperature and marking the thermometer to indicate its reading at each such temperature. The two main **temperature scales** are those devised by Fahrenheit and Celsius. Temperatures are read in "degrees Fahrenheit" or "degrees Celsius," symbolized by °F or °C, respectively.

✔ QUICK CHECK

You may have heard of how these two temperature scales are set. Let's check:

1. What substance is used to mark 32°F or 0°C on a thermometer?

2. What substance is used to mark 212°F or 100°C on a thermometer?

Answers: 1. A mixture of ice and water in equilibrium is at 32°F or 0°C. At that temperature water starts to freeze if thermal energy is removed or ice to melt if thermal energy is added. 2. Water boils at sea level at 212°F or 100°C.

THE KELVIN SCALE Thermal energy can be extracted from any body as long as a body of lower temperature is available. When an object reaches a temperature at which no thermal energy can be transferred from it, it's at the lowest possible temperature. This temperature is called absolute zero or zero Kelvin, written as 0 K. We speak of these units as kelvins, not degrees Kelvin.

TEMPERATURE CONVERSIONS You probably already know something about temperature conversions. Let's check it out:

✔ QUICK CHECK

1. How many degrees Fahrenheit are there between the ice point and the boiling point of water?

2. How many degrees Celcius are there between the ice point and the boiling point of water?

3. What is the ratio of those degrees Fahrenheit to those degrees Celsius?

Answers: 1. We find that 212°F − 32°F = 180 Fahrenheit degrees. (NOT 180°F, because a temperature difference is not a temperature.) 2. We find that 100°C − 0°C = 100 Celsius degrees, (NOT 100°C.) 3. The ratio of Fahrenheit to Celsius degrees of the temperature differences between boiling water and freezing water is $\dfrac{180 \text{ Fahrenheit degrees}}{100 \text{ Celsius degrees}} = \dfrac{9 \text{ F degree}}{5 \text{ C degree}}$.

We can convert from one temperature scale to another using the 9/5 ratio of Fahrenheit to Celsius:

1. Degrees C to degrees F: $T_F = \dfrac{9°F}{5°C} \cdot T_C + 32°F$.

2. Degrees F to degrees C: $T_C = \dfrac{5°C}{9°F} \cdot (T_F - 32 \text{ Fahrenheit degrees})$.

3. Degrees C to degrees K: The Kelvin scale uses degrees of the same size as the Celsius scale, but it sets the lowest possible temperature at 0 K. We then find that 0°C = 273.3 K. Therefore,

$$T_C = T_K + 273.3 \text{ Celsius degrees.}$$
$$T_K = T_C - 273.3 \text{ kelvins.}$$

THERMAL ENERGY

In our current atomic model of matter, we believe that all atoms and molecules in solids, liquids, and gases move randomly, at greater speeds at higher temperatures, and at lower speeds at lower temperatures. The molecules vibrate around fixed positions in solids, move more freely but are still connected to their neighbors in liquids, and move completely freely in gases. In all three, the motions are restricted by bonds to or collisions with neighboring molecules or atoms. That is why the motion is random.

Thus, **thermal energy** is a form of energy where individual parts of a body—molecules within a substance—move differently; the energy is not connected with motion of the body as a whole. When a body with more random energy in its molecules is placed in contact with another body with less random energy in its molecules, the more energetic molecules transfer energy to the less energetic ones and the temperature of the body with more energy decreases while the temperature of the body with less energetic molecules increases. While thermal energy is moving from one body to another we call the *process* **heat transfer**. When you touch a hot dish that has just been removed from the oven, there is a transfer of thermal energy from the pot to your finger. While the energy is moving to your finger there is a heat transfer. We always speak of thermal energy, never of heat as energy, in a body at a constant temperature to emphasize this difference.

Now we can check what you might suspect instinctively:

✔ QUICK CHECK

1. Into which of these other forms of energy can thermal energy be converted?

    a. Kinetic energy

    b. Chemical energy

    c. Gravitational potential energy

2. Which of these forms of energy can be converted into thermal energy?

    a. Kinetic energy

    b. Chemical energy

    c. Gravitational potential energy

Answers: 1, 2, a, b, and c.

Thermal energy can be converted into organized energy of motion (kinetic energy), energy stored in chemical bonds (chemical energy), and energy a body has because of its tendency to approach another body while picking up speed in the process (gravitational or electrical potential energy). The steam engine is an example of the first kind, an endothermic chemical reaction illustrates the second, and any process in which an expanding object lifts another object illustrates the third.

THERMODYNAMICS

Thermodynamics studies the interactions between thermal energy, other types of energy, and work done by forces. These interactions are described by the laws of thermodynamics. We'll look at three of them very briefly.

Can a body A at temperature T transfer thermal energy to body B when body B is also at temperature T?

Answer: No. This leads to the **zeroth law of thermodynamics**: When two bodies are in equilibrium—neither one is able to transfer energy to the other—they are at the same temperature. This law was assumed in the discussion of temperature and temperature scales.

Is it possible to create thermal energy out of nothing?

Answer: Your instincts were undoubtedly correct about this. If it were possible to create any kind of energy out of nothing there would not be an energy shortage. (Anyone who advertises a perpetual motion machine is a fraud.) This leads to the **first law of thermodynamics**: The sum of all types of energy within an isolated system remains the same over time; the sum of all types of energy within a system that is not isolated remains the same over time unless energy is provided from or taken away by a body external to the system.

What is a system in thermodynamics? It is similar to a system in mechanics: one or more bodies interacting with one another or being acted upon together by external sources of force and energy over some time period. Part of the art of physics is in selecting one's systems. Good choices—relevant situations to represent a topic of study—make problem solving easier. We will look at that in Chapter 5.

Another statement of the first law of thermodynamics is that energy can neither be created nor destroyed. We can paraphrase that by saying that there is no free lunch.

The **second law of thermodynamics** says that energy can be converted completely from thermal energy to another form only if a body at 0 K is available to act as the body of lower thermal energy. In that case, all the thermal energy can be extracted from a body at a higher temperature in order to do work. Because such a body (at 0 K) is not available in this universe, thermal energy cannot be converted completely into another form of energy, but some must end up in a body at lower temperature, where it is less useful. This says that even if you receive a free lunch, you can't eat it all.

Oscillations

Almost everyone reading this has a yo-yo or something else that can be attached to a string. All you need is something of much greater mass than the string. Hold on to the string and let the mass swing back and forth while your hand remains almost still. Time 10 complete swings back and forth, both for a short length of string and a long length of string.

A body swings back and forth in less time when the string is

a) long.   b) short.

Answer: b) short.

The time for one complete swing back and forth is called the period. If you have tried the experiment you have found that the period is less for a short string and greater for a long string. How can this result be used to create a clock?

Any back-and-forth motion that repeats in time is called a **periodic motion**. We say that the moving object oscillates and call it an **oscillator**. A massive object at the end of a light string is a type of oscillator called a **pendulum**. An ideal pendulum—a point mass at the end of a massless string—has a special type of motion called **simple harmonic motion**. If you can find an old-fashioned phonograph that has a turntable that rotates at a constant rate, and can place a small object on the turntable, the shadow of the object on the wall behind it also executes simple harmonic motion, as in Figure 4.23.

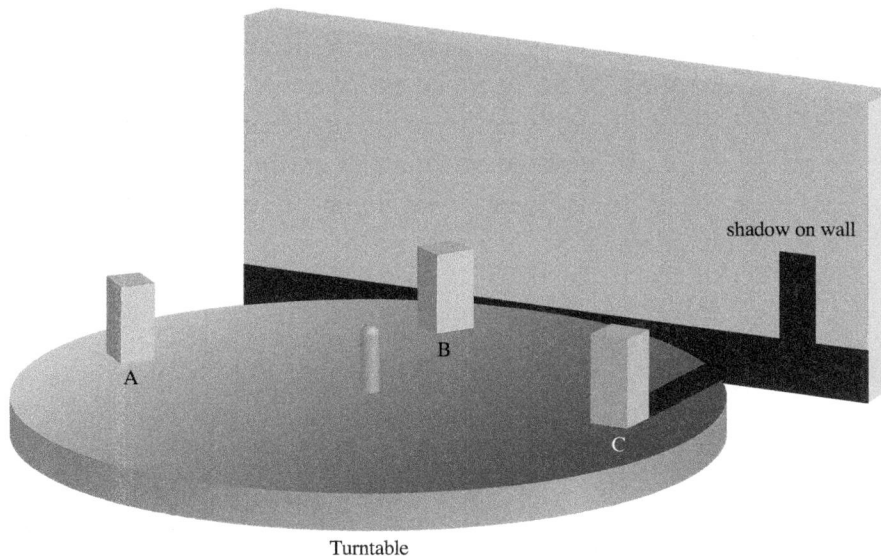

FIGURE 4.23   Shadow in simple harmonic motion of an object in circular motion.

WORKED EXAMPLE 4.3

Describe the movement of the shadow on the wall in Figure 4.23 when the object is at

a) position A.   b) position B.   c) position C.

Answers: a) and c) At the ends, A and C, the object is turning through an arc that is roughly perpendicular to the wall, so its shadow moves slowly. Those are the arcs in Figure 4.24a. b) At position B the arc is now roughly parallel to the wall whether the object is at the front or the back of the turntable, so the shadow moves quickly. Those are the arcs in Figure 4.24b.

a)

b)

FIGURE 4.24 Movement of an object on a turntable at the ends (a) and at the center (b).

You can see that the sort of motion described for the object on the turntable also holds for the pendulum you experimented with. The motion is slow at the ends of the swing and fast at the center.

Look at the motion of your pendulum again. The **period** is the time for one complete back-and-forth motion, but you can get a more accurate value for the period by timing 10 such oscillations and dividing the total time by 10. If you divide the number of complete oscillations by the time, you get the **frequency**—the number of complete oscillations for each unit of time.

PRACTICE

1. Catherine's pendulum goes back and forth in 10 complete oscillations in 4.8 s.
   a) What is its period?
   b) What is its frequency?

2. An object on Marie's turntable goes around in 10 complete circles in 18.0 s.
   a) What is its period?
   b) What is its frequency?

Answers: 1. a) Because the period is the time for one back-and-forth motion of the pendulum, we divide the time for 10 oscillations by 10. The period is 0.48 s. b) The number of oscillations divided by the total time gives the frequency. We can show this as a proportion: $\dfrac{10}{t_{10}} = \dfrac{n_1}{1\ \text{s}} = f$, where t_{10} is the time for 10 oscillations, n_1 is the number of oscillations in one second, and f is the frequency. Thus, $f = 2.08\ \dfrac{\text{oscillations}}{\text{s}} = 2.08\ \text{Hz}$, where 1 Hz (Hertz) equals 1 oscillation per second. 2. a) The period, T, is 1.80 s. b) The frequency is 0.555 Hz.

Finally, draw a graph that shows the oscillation of a pendulum with the vertical axis showing position and the horizontal axis showing time. Remember that the weight, the bob, must stay in about the same place for a longer time at the ends of the motion and change position more quickly when at the center of its motion. Now let's test your instincts again.

WORKED EXAMPLES 4.4

1. How is the frequency related to the period? Use your pendulum and the two previous examples to help you think about this.

   The period T is measured by timing n complete oscillations and dividing the time t by n. The frequency, f, is measured by timing n oscillations and dividing n by t. This gives us $f = \dfrac{1}{T}$.

2. Does the **amplitude**—half of the distance the pendulum moves in going from one side to the other—depend on the frequency or the period? Again, use your pendulum to help you think about this. What is it that you do that determines the amplitude?

If the frequency and the period are determined by the length of the string, they are not affected by the amplitude. (This is true as long as the angle of swing from the vertical stays below about 20°.) You can't change the frequency or period by how you move your hand, only the amplitude. A tiny motion produces a small amplitude and a bigger motion produces a bigger amplitude. The amplitude depends on how much energy you provide to the pendulum. This applies to all oscillators.

3. What general shape does your graph have? What have you seen in math that looks like that graph?

The graph you draw should have a wavelike appearance. It should look like Figure 4.25. The highest points on the graph are the points where the pendulum has the maximum positive displacement from the center. The lowest points are where the pendulum has the maximum negative displacement from the center. (You have to decide which direction of displacement is positive and which is negative.) The horizontal distance between two such high points represents the difference in time between two maximum displacements. The horizontal distance between two such low points also represents the period.

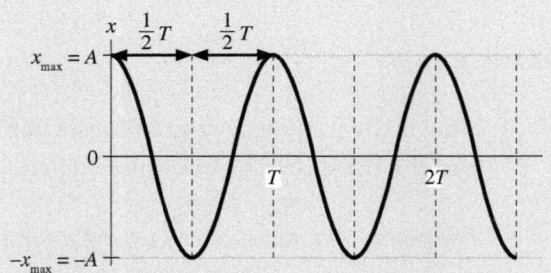

FIGURE 4.25   Graph of the oscillation of a pendulum.

Note that the bob is staying in about the same place when at a crest or a trough, but that position is changing rapidly in time when halfway between a crest or a trough. When we have true simple harmonic motion, the wave shape that results is a **sine wave**. Let's call the displacement of the bob from its center position y and the time t. Then $y = A \cos(\omega t)$ if $x = A$ when $t = 0$, where A is the amplitude and ω is called the **angular frequency**. When you study the mathematical details of this sort of motion in the exercise below you will find that $\omega = 2\pi f$.

TIME TO TRY

Use the fact that $y = A$ both at $t = 0$ and one period later to show that $\omega = 2\pi f$. (You need to know some trigonometry to be able to do this.)

Answer: After one period, we have $A = A \cos(\omega T)$. This can hold only if $\omega T = 2\pi$ radians, so $\omega = \dfrac{2\pi}{T} = 2\pi f$. You will find that radian measure is much more useful than degrees when studying waves and oscillations. Remember, 2π radians $= 360$ degrees.

PICTURE THIS

Run some water in a bathtub, and slosh a sponge up and down at the end of the bathtub. This too is a periodic motion. When you find the correct period the water will slosh up and down in a regular way. The height of these waves varies with the time but the wave crests go up and down in the same places. The number of times per second that the sponge goes up and down or the crests go up and down is the frequency. Half of the vertical distance from a trough, a lowest point, to a crest, a highest point, is the amplitude.

If you take a snapshot of this wave at one instant in time, it is like a graph of vertical position of the water on the vertical axis versus horizontal position in the bathtub on the horizontal axis. This is shown in Figure 4.26. The graph in Figure 4.25 showed the change in displacement from a single central position with time. We can draw such a graph for any point of a wave. Make sure you distinguish it from the picture of the wave in space.

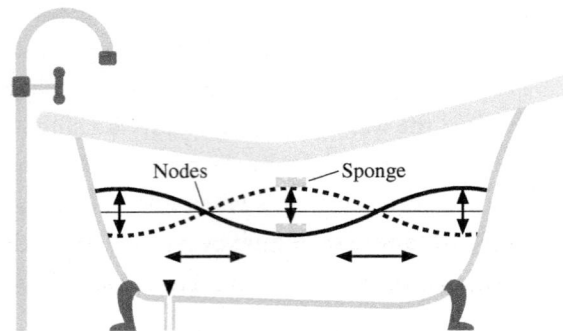

FIGURE 4.26 A seiche, a standing wave in water, may be demonstrated in a bathtub.

We've been looking at objects that move back and forth around one point. When many points are able to move back and forth, such as air molecules bumping into one another, water molecules in the bathtub, or points on a string pulling adjacent points along with them, we get wave shapes. The equation for waves modifies that for oscillations by also including a term that describes a wave shape in space as well as time. Think about how we might modify $y = A \cos (\omega t)$ so that the part that includes time could also include position along a string.

The motion of an oscillator may be described by giving its period or frequency and its amplitude. Because periodic motion occurs in many bodies and systems, along with mechanics it is one of our basic descriptions of nature. ■

Optics

When you stop to think about light and what it might be, you might realize that, with its many different effects, light is very mysterious. Natural philosophers—what scientists were called in ancient and medieval times—could not decide whether an object emitted light or whether light was something emitted by the eye that then returned to the eye. We now know that heating materials so they are very hot produces light. Even in ancient times, people realized that fire and lamps produced light. However, we now also know how to produce light without heating the material. In this section, we'll only be able to look at some of the most obvious, basic observations and their current interpretation.

SHADOWS

WORKED EXAMPLES 4.5

Everyone has seen his or her own shadow. Suppose you turn on a single light bulb and try to stand so that you cast a shadow on a wall.

1. If light is traveling in all directions when it leaves the light bulb, why is there a shadow?

   When light leaves the light bulb, it travels in straight lines. These lines are called **rays**. The rays that your body blocks do not reach the wall and that's why you see a shadow.

2. Why are shadows sometimes very dark and sometimes much less dark?

   When the object is far from the light source, so that the rays are traveling almost parallel to one another, rays traveling toward the position of the shadow are blocked except at the edges of the shadow. When the light source is extended and some rays can reach the shadow because they are not blocked by your body, the shadow is not as clear. Figure 4.27a shows the absence of light at the right when parallel rays strike an arrow-shaped object. Figure 4.27b shows what happens when light rays can reach into the shadow area.

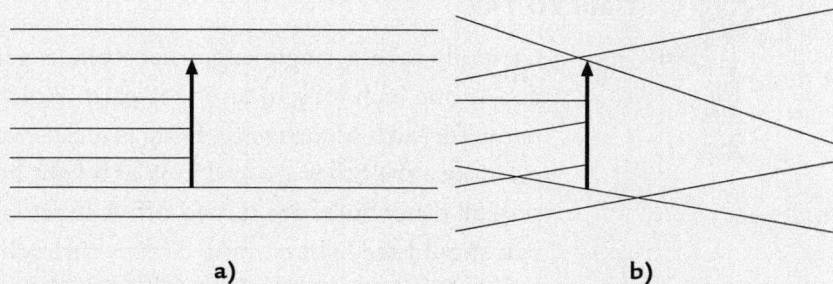

a)   b)

FIGURE 4.27 **a)** Dark shadow produced by absence of light. **b)** Faint shadow produced when some light passes into the region of the shadow.

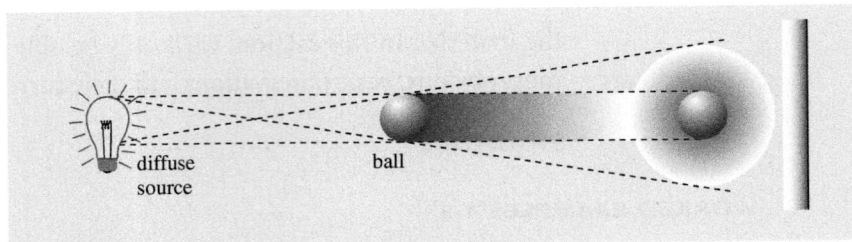

Everyday observations indicate that light travels in straight lines. The sun is very far from the Earth and the rays reaching us are almost, though not perfectly, parallel. Because of this we can use the sun's rays in many experiments where we need parallel rays. An example of this occurs during eclipses of the sun, when the moon obstructs rays from all but a crescent shape of the sun. When the sun's rays go through a small opening the figure seen is a crescent. If the rays traveled in all directions we would just see a blur.

What does travel in straight lines tell us about the nature of light? Keep this question in mind as you read the following sections.

DIFFRACTION

Let's talk about sound waves for a minute. Do you have to be in a direct line with a person who is talking to hear that person's voice? The answer is no, because sound waves bend around obstacles the way that water waves bend around pilings at a pier. Waves in a liquid or solid medium can change direction at openings and obstacles.

TIME TO TRY

Carefully take a single-edge razor blade and make a straight cut about one inch long in an index card. Hold the cut—our technical name for such a narrow opening is a slit— vertically in front of one eye. Close the other eye and look at a light bulb from a distance. Be sure all other bulbs are turned off. A street lamp works well for this. You should see light coming directly through the slit, but also see a band of light on either side of the slit. There will be a pattern there with some vertical dark lines intersecting the bright areas. A schematic drawing of the pattern should look something like Figure 4.28. A picture of an actual pattern is shown in Figure 4.29.

FIGURE 4.28 Pattern seen in diffraction of light through a single slit.

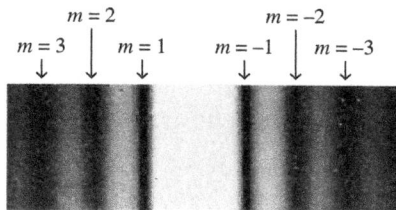

FIGURE 4.29 A diffraction pattern produced by a single wavelength of light.

The darkest band in Figure 4.28 shows where your eye sees the most light and the lightest band shows where your eye sees the least light in the single-slit **diffraction pattern**. What do these diffraction patterns tell you about light?

Answer: The patterns show that light has bent when going through the slit in the same way that sound waves bend when going through a door. This indicates that light has wave properties. The pattern will be clearest if you look at a sodium lamp street light, because there is one predominant color in the light. If you look at an incandescent bulb you will have the same pattern in many different colors but spread out to differing extents. In class, you will learn how to represent this same information with a graph of intensity versus horizontal position for such a picture on a screen.

COLOR

When you listen to music you hear many different pitches. Pitch describes how low or high a particular tone sounds. It turns out that pitch is the brain's subjective interpretation of frequency, and volume is its subjective interpretation of amplitude (technically, amplitude squared). Color is the brain's subjective interpretation of frequency, and brightness is its subjective interpretation of amplitude. You see many different overlapping patterns when you look at a white light, because white contains all frequencies of visible light. The different frequencies bend through different angles when going through a slit.

WHAT IS LIGHT?

How can you interpret the existence of shadows and diffraction? Can you reconcile the different ideas?

Answer: Water waves bend around pilings, but when you look at waves in the ocean or in a large lake, you see that they pretty much travel in straight lines. Although Newton used a particle model for light, physicists had to change their ideas after early-nineteenth-century experiments showed diffraction and also indicated that light from two different slits could interfere to make different patterns from those produced by diffraction from one slit alone. When we can ignore the bending and look at rays of light, we say that we are dealing with geometrical optics. We only have to look at the straight lines along which the light waves travel. When we have to consider bending and recombining of light waves, we say that we are using the physical optics model of light.

You may have heard of photons. When light is absorbed by certain metals, and electrons are ejected, there is a minimum amount of light energy that must be absorbed for this to occur. This quantum of light energy is called a **photon**. A photon acts like a particle of light. Quantum mechanics has now shown that light can act both as a particle and as a wave, but not simultaneously. If you take up quantum mechanics in your physics course, your instructor will have time to go into this.

Atomic and Nuclear Physics

Even as late as the nineteenth century, a scientist as good as Ernst Mach, whose musings on the origin of mass contributed to Einstein's work, could claim that there was no evidence for the existence of atoms. By 1900, however, radioactivity, the electron, and quantum physics had been discovered.

Pure gold is soft and can be beaten down to incredible thinness to form gold foil. Cut the foil in half, and then cut that in half, and keep on going. How many such cuts can you make and still have gold? We now know that each gold atom has a diameter of about 3×10^{-10} cm, but it took a combination of theory and experiment to show that the atomic hypothesis was correct.

You probably have absorbed some ideas about atoms. Let's check:

✔ **QUICK CHECK**

(True or False)

1. An atom is the basic unit of matter and cannot be subdivided further.   T F

2. An atom is composed of a massive positively charged nucleus and very low-mass electrons.   T F

3. The size of an atom is determined by the size of the nucleus.   T F

4. The size of an atom is determined by the range of its electrons.   T F

5. The nucleus of an atom is made up of positively charged protons and negatively charged electrons.   T F

6. The nucleus of an atom is made up of positively charged protons and neutral particles called neutrons.   T F

7. The electrons in an atom are organized into shells with those of lowest energy closest to the nucleus.   T F

8. It's easy to remove electrons from completely filled shells, as is the case in the noble gases helium, neon, argon, and krypton.   T F

9. All nuclei are always stable and never change.   T F

10. Radioactive nuclei can emit electrons, gamma rays, and helium nuclei (alpha particles).   T F

Answers: 1. False. By providing energy we can eject electrons from atoms. The existence of radioactivity shows that nuclei are not all stable. 2. True. 3. False. Electrons are distributed outside the nucleus in what is sometimes described as an "electron cloud." This electron cloud is of the order of 100,000 or 10^5 times larger than the nucleus. 4. True. (See answer 3.) 5. False. This is a subtle quantum effect, but electrons confined to a region the size of the nucleus would have to have preposterously high velocities and kinetic energies. 6. True. This has been verified by many experiments. 7. True. On average, this is true, although the angular momentum of the electrons also determines their distribution. 8. False. The ionization energy, the energy needed to remove an electron from a filled shell, is very high. That's partly why the noble gases don't react chemically. 9. False. If that were so, there would be no radioactivity. 10. True.

Your physics course will introduce atomic theory after covering older topics such as mechanics, thermodynamics, electromagnetism, waves and optics, and a brief introduction to quantum physics. If there is time it will also cover the properties of atomic nuclei and the basics of radioactivity. Rarely will your course have time to cover some of the most fascinating topics: the smallest particles known—those which make up the proton and the neutron and other newly discovered particles—and cosmology, what is known about the universe as a whole.

Final Stretch!

Now that you have finished reading this chapter it is time to stretch your brain and check how much you have learned.

RUNNING WORDS

Here are the terms introduced in this chapter. Write them in a notebook and define them in your own words. Then go back through the chapter to check on their meanings, and on any formulas associated with them. Make corrections as needed and try to list examples of the use of each term.

Electric charge, positive charge, negative charge
Coulomb's law
Charge polarization and induction
Electric field and electric field lines
Electric potential energy, electric potential and potential difference
Insulators and Conductors
Ohm's law and electric power, current and resistance
Magnetic poles

Temperature, thermometers, and temperature scales
Temperature conversions
Thermal energy
The laws of thermodynamics
Periodic motion
Oscillation, period, frequency, and amplitude
Light rays and shadows
Diffraction, photons
Structure of an atom and its nucleus

WEB RESOURCES

For additional help, enter any of the topics listed in "What Did You Learn?" or boldface section titles in Google or another search engine. Again, Wikipedia will give you a very high level overview, so you should look for sites at an appropriate level.

> *Several of the Phet simulations—Balloons and Static Electricity, John Travoltage, and Electric Field Hockey—will help illustrate electric field concepts. Try some other topics on that site as well.*
> **http://phet.colorado.edu/get_phet/index.php**

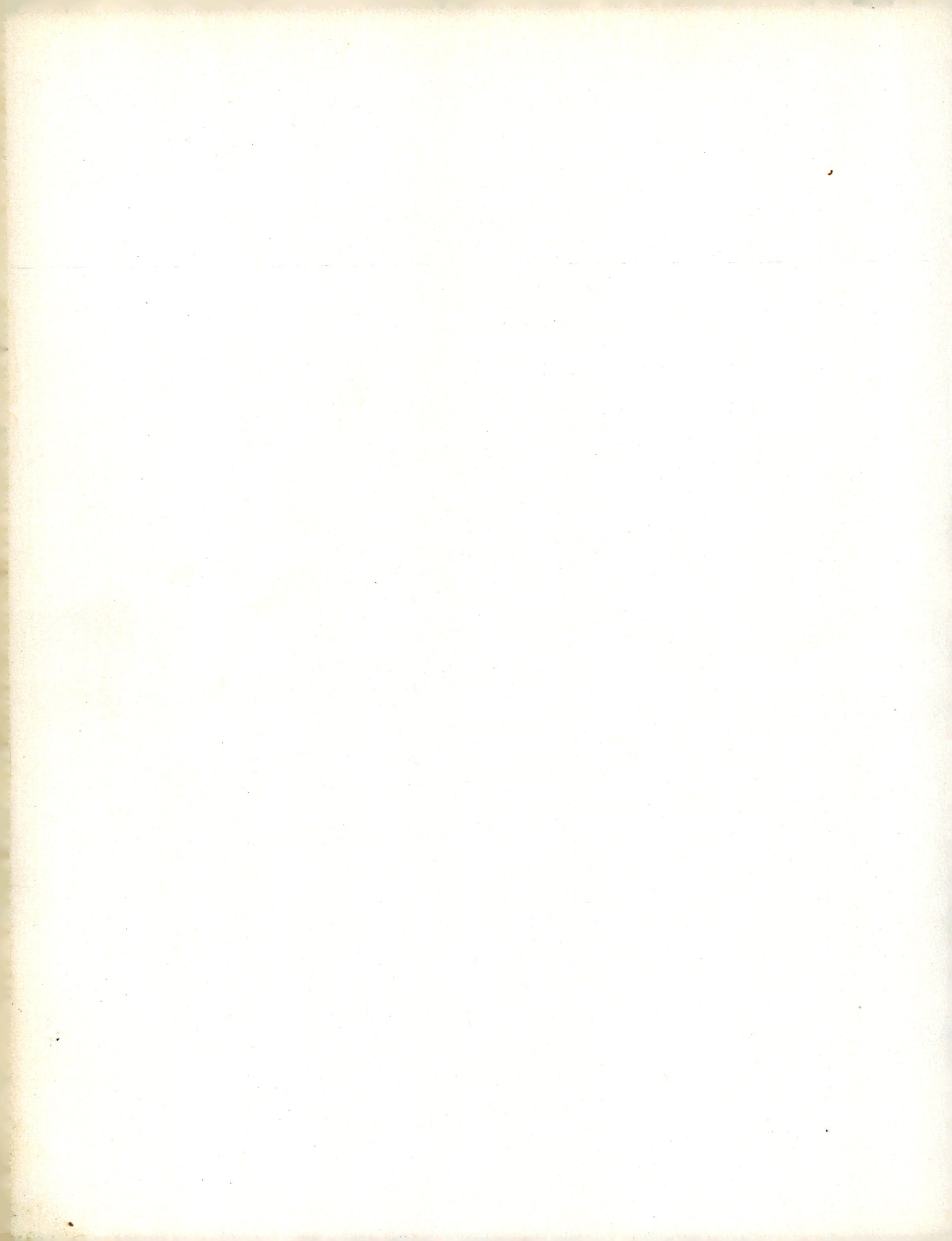